Survey of
Science Fiction Literature

Survey
of
Science Fiction
Literature

FIVE HUNDRED 2,000-WORD ESSAY REVIEWS OF WORLD-FAMOUS SCIENCE FICTION NOVELS WITH 2,500 BIBLIOGRAPHICAL REFERENCES

Edited by
FRANK N. MAGILL

Volume One
A - Dea
1 - 512

SALEM PRESS

Englewood Cliffs

LIBRARY OF CONGRESS CATALOG CARD NUMBER: 79-64639

Complete Set: ISBN 0-89356-194-0
Volume I: ISBN 0-89356-195-9

PREFACE

THE NEED for an extensive critical evaluation of the major literature of science fiction has been evident for some years. The genre has long since outgrown the pulp magazine-space opera stage and is rapidly approaching mainstream status. However, extended reference sources in the literature are not available in most public and academic libraries despite a growing demand among general readers and students for such a service. SURVEY OF SCIENCE FICTION LITERATURE is an attempt to alleviate this situation.

This work comprises essay-reviews of more than five hundred outstanding science fiction novels and short story collections. Articles average about two thousand words each, resulting in a five-volume reference containing about a million words of critical analysis and discussion *written expressly for this work*. More than one hundred and forty writers, consultants, scholars, and editors have contributed to the development of the project since its inception almost two years ago. Their names appear in the front pages of this volume.

The format of the essay-reviews provides author and publication dates along with the time and location of the action. A brief description of the work being reviewed then appears, followed by a list of the main characters. The essay-review itself discusses the work under study in the accepted literary criticism style, though in some cases more emphasis than usual may be placed on the story line because of the unique aspects of the novel or story under consideration. Most articles include a list of bibliographical sources for further study. Articles appear alphabetically by title and all are signed. A title and author index covering all the titles in a given volume appears at the front of that volume. A full author and title index is given at the end of Volume Five.

Preparation of the list of titles to be included in SURVEY OF SCIENCE FICTION LITERATURE was approached with great care. One of the early decisions involved fantasy; that is, whether to develop a science fiction reference that also included some fantasy. The decision was soon made that the genres should not be mixed, and plans are now under way to develop a separate reference for the literature of fantasy.

After much research and consultation a tentative list of science fiction titles, beginning with FRANKENSTEIN, was completed and circulated to the Consultant Staff for suggestions, additions, and deletions. Actually, the list remained "tentative," subject to further additions and deletions, almost until press time.

The final count is 513 individual essays, the titles representing the best judgment of the entire Consulting and Editorial Staffs. 280 authors — worldwide — are responsible for the 513 titles in the set.

About ninety foreign-language titles, written by 72 authors, are included in these volumes. At least twenty foreign countries are represented, including Argentina, Australia, Brazil, China, Czechoslovakia, Denmark, England, France, German Democratic Republic, Germany, Hungary, Italy, Japan, Norway, Poland, Romania, Sweden, Uruguay, the U.S.S.R., and Yugoslavia. This international flavor enriches the work and adds an extra dimension to its reference value. The consulting staff consisted of thirteen science fiction experts, including two from England, one from Sweden, and one from Austria.

Science fiction has added many new words to the language, and not a few new meanings to old words. Inexperienced readers in the genre may sometimes be at a loss to understand the meaning of certain words unless the context of their use makes the meaning obvious. In 1920, Karel Čapek introduced the word "robot" to the world in his play *R.U.R.* (Rossum's Universal Robots). His robots were machine-made mechanical males and females designed and mass produced strictly for work. The term eventually became generic, signifying almost any highly organized mechanical device. Then science fiction writers went a step further and began to introduce "androids" in their stories. An android is a synthetic *person* — not a clanking machine — made from biological parts, and it can be formed to look like, act like, and pass for a real human being. They have great plot value because of the way they can confuse issues. For example, a hero on a rescue mission to an alien planet may be unable to determine who his real target is when the aliens have made a dozen androids exactly like the human to be rescued, lined them up, and told each to say, "I'm the human; take me." A step beyond the android is the man/machine hybrid, or "cyborg," who is a human that has had certain body parts replaced by mechanical (electronic) parts in order to enhance physical abilities (The Six Million Dollar Man, The Bionic Woman) or to provide immunity from environmental dangers in space.

The term "space opera" implies the science fiction version of the mainstream cloak-and-sword romance or, of equal bluster, the Western movie — the "horse opera." Pursuits and battles to control Space are usually involved.

"Hard" science fiction deals with extrapolations from the hard sciences such as astronomy, physics, biology, and the like. Hard science fiction must be *based on* something that is now possible on Earth but which has the potential of much higher development in the future. "Soft" science fiction is concerned more with the inexact sciences such as sociology or psychology. Yet despite the exotic terms used, the main ingredient of science fiction is the author's imagination — the "What if?" story line.

Classes in Contemporary Literature can hardly ignore science fiction as part of the curriculum today, and many mainstream authors are eyeing this new, fascinating vehicle with keen interest. It offers a new way to say some old things, a chance to deal with the human condition in a new light. "Alternate history" themes are popular for the speculative opportunities they offer the imaginative author: Would the world be a better place if the South had won the American Civil War; or if the American Indians had banded together after Columbus and driven the whites into the sea; or if Japan and Germany had won World War II? Through the medium of science fiction such topics can be explored by the skillful author with such authenticity that the mesmerized reader is about ready for "that willing suspension of disbelief."

Science fiction writing has come a long way since the "escape" literature of the pulp magazines. One of the hallmarks of the genre is the intensity of the social criticism. Many of the authors seem to view the present human world with distaste and disappointment, and they proceed to depict an alien world in space where such flaws are nonexistent. This critical attitude does not spring so much from gloom as from impatience. Mankind has the potential — mind-stretching concepts, ideas of infinite variety, a towering imagination — to create a Utopia. These writers say that man should get on with the business of developing this social paradise. The force and power of their arguments are augmented through the exotic settings they provide and the superior alien mores they recount.

The purport and tone of SURVEY OF SCIENCE FICTION LITERATURE have been admirably delineated in Willis E. McNelly's Introduction that appears at the beginning of Volume One. I wish to thank Professor McNelly for this valued contribution. I wish also to acknowledge the splendid manner in which Professor Keith Neilson organized and controlled the flow of literary criticism — derived from all over the world — that fills the pages of this set. And finally, I offer this personal note of appreciation to the more than one hundred and thirty contributors of articles, the thirteen consultants, the eight translators, and the many regular staff members whose collective expertise and dedication have brought this work into being.

FRANK N. MAGILL

WRITING STAFF FOR ESSAY – REVIEWS

BRIAN W. ALDISS (England)
JOHN W. ANDREWS
ROSEMARIE ARBUR
RICHARD ASTLE
DOUGLAS BARBOUR (Canada)
NEIL BARRON
CLIFFORD P. BENDAU
ALBERT I. BERGER
JON BING (Norway)
PETER BRAJER
PETER BRIGG (Canada)
LLOYD W. BROWN
ROSCOE LEE BROWNE
DONALD R. BURLESON
ANDRÉ CARNEIRO (Brazil)
EDGAR L. CHAPMAN
THOMAS D. CLARESON
JUDITH A. CLARK
JOHN CLUTE (England)
KENT CRAIG
ROBERT CROSSLEY
SHERWOOD CUMMINGS
LAHNA F. DISKIN
THOMAS P. DUNN
GRACE ECKLEY
WILTON ECKLEY
SUZANNE EDWARDS
JOHN EGGELING (England)
GRETA EISNER
CHARLES ELKINS
MARY J. ELKINS

GEORGE S. ELRICK
RICHARD D. ERLICH
REBECCA B. FAERY
BARRY FAYE
INA S. FAYE
JOHN FOYSTER (Australia)
S. C. FREDERICKS
BEVERLY FRIEND
VL. GAKOV (U.S.S.R.)
BRUCE GILLESPIE (Australia)
CHRISTINE GLADISH
STEPHEN GOLDIN
STEPHEN H. GOLDMAN
JEAN-MARC GOUANVIC (Canada)
BORIS GRABNAR (Yugoslavia)
EILEEN K. GUNN
JAMES GUNN
TORD HALL (Sweden)
WILLIAM H. HARDESTY III
HARRY HARRISON
DONALD M. HASSLER
JACQUES VAN HERP (France)
JANE HIPOLITO
ION HOBANA (Romania)
GARY KERN
DOROTHY K. KILKER
JOHN KINNAIRD
MERRELL A. KNIGHTEN
PETER KUCZKA (Hungary)
DONALD L. LAWLER
RUSSELL LETSON

DAVID LEWIS
SAM J. LUNDWALL (Sweden)
DOUGLAS A. MACKEY
RICHARD MATHEWS
CLARK MAYO
MICHAEL W. MCCLINTOCK
PATRICK L. MCGUIRE
WILLIS E. MCNELLY
DOUGLAS J. MCREYNOLDS
WALTER E. MEYERS
L. W. MICHAELSON
SANDRA MIESEL
FRANCIS J. MOLSON
GIANNI MONTANARI (Italy)
KATHARINE M. MORSBERGER
ROBERT E. MORSBERGER
DIRK W. MOSIG
SAM MOSKOWITZ
TOM MOYLAN
AL MULLER
BRIAN MURPHY
KEITH NEILSON
PETER NICHOLLS (England)
RICHARD D. NOLANE (France)
PRISCILLA OAKS
TIMOTHY O'REILLY
FREDERICK PATTEN
JOHN R. PFEIFFER
ROBERT M. PHILMUS (Canada)
HAZEL PIERCE
DAVID PRINGLE (England)

ANN C. RAYMER
R. REGINALD
REMI-MAURE (France)
MAXINE S. ROSE
FRANZ ROTTENSTEINER (Austria)
WILLIAM C. RUBINSTEIN
DAVID N. SAMUELSON
HARVEY J. SATTY
CARSTEN SCHIØLER (Denmark)
ROGER C. SCHLOBIN
A. LANGLEY SEARLES
KATHRYN L. SEIDEL
BARBARA BERMAN SEIDENFELD
RAY C. SHIFLETT
T. A. SHIPPEY (England)
FREDERICK SHROYER
KATHLEEN SKY
GEORGE EDGAR SLUSSER
KATHLEEN L. SPENCER
BRIAN STABLEFORD (England)
CAROL D. STEVENS
DAVID STEVENS
A. JAMES STUPPLE
CHARLES W. SULLIVAN III
DARKO SUVIN (Canada)
ERIK H. SWIATEK (Denmark)
FRANK H. TUCKER
RICCARDO VALLA (Italy)
H. WALTER (German Democratic
  Republic)
JANE B. WEEDMAN

LINDA R. WHEAT
JACK WILLIAMSON
GARY K. WOLFE
EDWARD WOOD

JOSEPH WRZOS
CARL B. YOKE
R. V. YOUNG, JR.

TRANSLATORS

(The American title of English language translations is always
used; it may differ from the British publication in some cases.)

JOHN W. ANDREWS
LEO F. BARROW
JEAN-MARC GOUANVIC
  (Canada)
JOE F. RANDOLPH

REMI-MAURE (France)
PÉTER SZENTMIHÁLYI SZABÓ
  (Hungary)
FRANK H. TUCKER
LINDA R. WHEAT

INTRODUCTION

"The ability to fantasize is the ability to survive."

Thus Ray Bradbury has characterized the importance of the creative imagination. For him, and for the hundreds of other imaginative writers whose books are discussed in *Survey of Science Fiction Literature*, science fiction has been the major, if not the sole, form in which these advanced imaginings have been incarnated.

No words can properly describe the scope of these works. Writer's imaginations since Mary Shelley's have probed the stars, investigated the past, journeyed into the inner space of the mind and psyche, created entire worlds, explored universe beyond universe, challenged the concept of Time, and delved into the deepest mysteries of God, creation, matter, energy, human beings, and aliens. In these books and short stories, explorers of the imagination have gazed on Martian canals, created utopias, deified machines, scratched the dust of Arrakis, teleported beyond the planets, or sunk into oblivion. Epic heroes have marshaled galactic systems to combat diabolic enemies. Empires have been built, have ruled, have crumbled. Mankind has died, has been succeeded by robots, and has in turn been resurrected, surviving in some joyous galactic vision. The imagination has had no limit.

These visions have, quite literally, been cosmic, universal, or mundane. Messiahs have preached and fallen, big brothers have terrorized, and alchemical transformations have remade humanity. Most of all, these very diverse authors have clothed their concepts in one of the most ancient of appeals, that of the Tale, the Story. Their plots are replete with action, heroic virtues, magnificent adventures. They all begin, figuratively at least, with the great words that vibrate to the very core of our being, "Once upon a time." The permutations on this theme are endless. But always there is Story, action-packed or leisurely, philosophical or contemplative, visionary or pessimistic.

Yet if the more than five hundred books discussed in *Survey of Science Fiction Literature* defy description, they also refuse to admit of definition. Science fiction, however defined — extrapolation, a literature of change, culture commentary, modern mythology, the treatment of the interface between man and the machine, or dozens of others — has given these authors freedom to stretch their — and our — imaginations far beyond the limits of earthbound reality. I shall not venture into the morass raised by the problems of definition here, however. Rather, I should like to cite a familiar one provided by Brian W. Aldiss in *Billion Year Spree*, that most significant history of science fiction. "Science fiction is the search for a definition of man and his status in the universe which will stand in our advanced but confused state of knowledge (science), and is characteristically cast in the Gothic or post-Gothic mode." Aldiss himself has observed that most definitions of science fiction fail because they have regard for content only, and not for form. Certainly no definition, even Aldiss' own, can encompass the extensive content of this genre. Similarly, however, no meaningful definition could include the extremely varying forms, styles, or artistic methods employed by the hundreds of writers in these volumes. However, perhaps a closer look at the beginning of Aldiss' statement may provide us with some insights. "Science fiction is the *search*. . . ." Exactly. Science fiction is a *search*, not a thing, a *process*, not an immediately sense-perceptible reality. Science fiction is not easy to define simply because it is a dynamic entity, a living organism that evolves, changes, metamorphosizes, grows, and develops. If the science fiction of the late 1970's does not resemble that written for John W. Campbell, Jr., in *Astounding Science Fiction*'s so-called Golden Age of the 1940's and 1950's, the dissimilarity simply may be ascribed to the process of evolution.

"We know more than the ancients do," T. S. Eliot said in effect in "Tradition and the Individual Talent." And he immediately followed this statement by saying, "Precisely, and they are that which we know." So also with science fiction. We know more than Mary Shelley or Edgar Rice Burroughs did. And it is Mary Shelley or Burroughs or H. G. Wells that we know. What Mary Shelley discovered, myriads of writers develop. What Wells foresaw, we examine.

This continuing process of change, growth, or development is one of the leading characteristics of science fiction. The simplistic rhetoric of Burroughs gave way to the scientific urbanities of Arthur C. Clarke or the righteous anger of Harlan Ellison. In modern science fiction, then, advanced imagining has suspended the very rules of reality, as in Ursula K. Le Guin's *The Left Hand of Darkness*. Our mores or social conduct are questioned by Philip K. Dick, our ethics by Robert A. Heinlein or George Orwell; the limitations of science by Poul Anderson or Aldous Huxley; our theological tenets by James Blish or John Boyd.

If science fiction is process, what is it proceeding from and what is it proceeding toward? In answering these questions, we may be on less shaky ground than that offered by the problems of definition. If H. G. Wells were alive today, he would be surprised, if not shocked, to learn that he had written "science fiction." He may well have heard the phrase prior to his death in 1946, but he himself termed his seminal works — *The War of the Worlds*, *The Time Machine*, and many many others — "scientific romances." So also with Olaf Stapledon. While we might neatly categorize such magnificent books as *Odd John*, *The Star Maker*, and *Last and First Men* as science fiction — as indeed they are — his brooding, cosmic intellect would probably also have maintained that he was writing works better described as "romances" rather than the neologism "science fiction." Certainly the same situation would obtain with the late C. S. Lewis, whose lifelong addition to the "space time story," as he termed it, he chronicles in *Of Other Worlds*. Yet of his notable trilogy, *Out of the Silent Planet*, *Perelandra*, and *That Hideous Strength*, only the former might fit any convenient definition of science fiction we might devise, while the latter two are certainly fantasy and allegory, both traditional forms of the romance.

Their successor in Britain is Brian W. Aldiss. A noted author and historian of the genre, Aldiss has said of himself, in the introduction to his most recent collection of short stories, *Last Orders*, "My stories are about human woes, noncommunication, disappointment, endurance, acceptance, love."

All of these qualities exemplify characteristics of what has traditionally been called the "romance" rather than the "novel." The romance, in other words, is the home that science fiction proceeds from in its process of dynamic change. The romance is a classic form. Nathaniel Hawthorne wrote romances, some of them so close to what we call science fiction that an analysis of them may be found in these volumes. He indicated that he chose the romance form rather than the novel simply because it gave him a bit more freedom. An author's work, he said, "is not put exactly side by side with nature; and he is allowed a license with regard to every-day probability, in view of the improved effects which he is bound to produce thereby."

Consider Hawthorne's statement as applied to science fiction. If we put many of these books side by side with nature and insist that they be scientifically accurate, we will be faced with nearly insuperable problems. Einstein has told us that because $E = mc^2$, we will never be able to surpass the speed of light. Yet we have literally dozens of writers inventing hyperspace drives, space warps, or other devices to overcome that difficulty. Authors invent androids indistinguishable from humans; others make a reality of cloning. As readers we are perfectly willing to suspend disbelief to permit them their Tale, even though our rational minds caught up by "reality" tell us of the impossibility of their projections.

Instead, with Hawthorne, we must remember that in the romance the author is allowed a license with regard to every-day probability. The improved effects have resulted in some of the most memorable works in this series, so many that it is virtually impossible to enumerate them. But not only is the license the important aspect here, it is the way or manner in which these works have actually viewed reality. The novel, as Richard Chase has pointed out in *The American Novel and Tradition*, renders reality closely and in comprehensive detail. When we read conventional naturalistic novels such as Henry James's *The Ambassadors* or James Joyce's *Ulysses*, we see people going about the business of living. These characters assume a complexity which makes, say, Lambert Strether or Leopold Bloom two of the most thoroughly *known* persons in literature. In the novel, action flows from character, and because character is plausible, the action is plausible. Thus both the characters and the threads of action in the novel have their feet firmly planted in the *terra firma* of reality.

Romance, as Chase puts it, "feels free to render reality in less volume and detail. It tends to prefer action to character, and action will be freer in a romance than in a novel, encountering, as it were, less resistance from reality." Chase goes on to indicate that the characters in the romance will largely be two-dimensional, that human emotions are often abstract or symbolic, that the plot will be highly colored and that astonishing events will often occur. The romance, Chase maintains, is less committed to the immediate rendition of reality than the novel, and thus will veer more freely toward mythic, allegorical, and symbolic forms. The question inevitably arises of how much of what we conventionally call science fiction, how many of the books included in *Survey of Science Fiction Literature*, might better be termed "scientific romances."

In dealing with this problem of the definition of science fiction, it must be understood that the genre is still in the process of evolving toward maturity. When Professor J. O. Bailey published his pioneering study of science fiction, *Pilgrims Through Space and Time*, in 1947, he indicated something of the nature of this process through his distinction between the literature of character and the literature of ideas. Long-time readers of the science fiction genre immediately grasped this distinction. Science fiction is, after all, concerned with ideas and their impact upon human society. It is "idea" fiction, and its creators extrapolate from the known to the unknown. They say "What if?" or "If this goes on . . . ." and develop a novel examining the impact of that idea. Dozens of titles included here fit that category. The characters are usually two-dimensional; the events often astonishing, and the plot highly colored. Those same events, such as Victor Frankenstein's creation of the monster, have a symbolic or ideological plausibility, rather than a psychological representation of reality such as we might find in Joyce or James.

Yet this substitution of "idea as hero" for "character as hero" places science fiction within the mainstream of American, if not world, literature. The recent rise of interest in the critical study of the genre, to which *Survey of Science Fiction Literature* is a major contribution, may actually result in placing science fiction at a crucial point in prophesying about our objectivized, impersonalized society. Recall, for instance, the central thesis of R. W. B. Lewis' *The American Adam*: ". . . the indestructible vitality of the American vision of life — and what that vision can contribute to the alchemical process of the narrative art . . . the vision and the process . . . continue to present us with the means of grasping the special complexities, the bouyant assurance, and the encircling doubt of the still unfolding American scene."

It is my thesis, then, that, in the hands of many skilled writers whose works are included in these volumes, the literature of ideas, known as science fiction, its vision and process, have become a contemporary version of the Adamic myth: it can be illuminative, cautionary, or optimistic by turns, perhaps even redemptive in its nature. In American literature, enough examples of the Adamic Hero exist to make the concept immediately clear to most readers. The Adamic Hero revivified, ironically or passionately, the innocence of American life; Huck Finn and Natty Bumppo — and many others could be cited — often received their integral vitality from the existence of the Frontier. Recall Huck Finn's statement: "I got to light out for the territory ahead of the rest. . . ."

The territory, the frontier, is almost epitomized by the phoenixlike Adamic Hero, but the frontier was not only geographic, it was symbolic. As decades passed and the vision of the geographic frontier faded, the hero stalked through the pages of Fitzgerald, Hemingway, Salinger, Updike, and Heller. Too often he became more and more attenuated as a person until he became the very ideal he either personified or fantasized. It is at this point that science fiction finds him, thrusting him into the future, an alternate universe or a space mission. The hero became acted upon by these events or circumstances rather than acting as an individual in his own right. Circumstances forced him into behaving or reacting. Too infrequently did he force action based upon his own integrity.

In the hands of many science fiction writers, then, the frontier was alchemically transformed into space or time. Only recently have some writers begun exploring, once more, the final inner frontier of the human psyche. Novels such as Robert Silverberg's agonizing study of a telepath who is losing his powers, *Dying Inside*, are still rare, but the fact that they are being published, read, and recognized as superior works indicates that science fiction writers are now free from the shackles of space hardware and furiously abounding action and reaction among the stars. What is being emphasized, in other words, in many of the better science fiction works of the last decade, is the human factor, the person caught in the confrontation between the machine, however projected, and human, humane ethical and moral values, however embodied.

Yet emphasis upon the human being is not new. It is, rather, a return to some of the values inherent in the science fiction art "B.C." — before Campbell. Neither Wells nor Stapledon, for example, emphasized the scientific content of their stories. Rather, Wells, for instance, often took a very human being, complete with both virtues and failings, and thrust him into an unfamiliar quasiscientific situation. What became important in *The War of the Worlds* was not the scientific gimmickry of how the Martian invaders got to Earth or how their destructive heat ray actually operated, but rather, how human beings reacted to the enormous problems created by them. The human factors or reactions were all important; the scientific aspects were only secondary. Both Hugo Gernsback and John Campbell changed the face of science fiction, but the change they initiated ran its course for decades and is only now being recognized for what it actually was — an emphasis upon scientific invention and extrapolation rather than the human dimension. Writers used to say of Gernsback that he would not print a story unless it had one patentable invention in it, and Campbell's insistence upon scientific accuracy might have produced the so-called "Golden Age" of *Astounding Science Fiction* magazine, but it was nonetheless an age when human beings were still subservient to hypothetical scientific advances. Memorable characters were all too few. "Idea as hero" dominated the action.

Today the face of science fiction is once again changing, this time away from Campbell's influence, great and important as it was, toward a new emphasis upon humanity. It might be humanity transfigured, as Arthur C. Clarke has indicated in *Childhood's End*, but whatever form it takes, it concentrates upon the characteristics that have always made men and women great. And in so doing, it gradually begins to break down the barriers that have for decades separated science fiction and mainstream literature. Thus this collection includes works by such notable writers as Lawrence Durrell, Thomas Pynchon, John Barth, and Kingsley Amis, and only space limitations precluded analysis of novels by Brian Moore, Gore Vidal, or Jerzy Kosinski, all noted contemporary writers some of whose recent work might certainly be classed as science fiction.

Another important change away from Campbellian "hard core," scientifically based works occurred in the 1950's and 1960's with the increasing utilization of the "soft sciences" as legitimate subject matter for novelists. Some contemporary technological developments were so extreme that their effects almost demanded satirical treatment by writers. Thus Frederik Pohl and Cyril M. Kornbluth attacked Madison Avenue with their devastating treatment of the advertising business in *The Space Merchants*. Other nonobjectively based sciences were quickly utilized. Behaviorist sociology and psychology was ridiculed by Aldous Huxley in *Brave New World*. Ecology, which may be more of an art that a science, provided the essential substructure to Frank Herbert's *Dune*. Even theology or religion, often treated with contempt by writers of the Gernsback and Campbell eras, received considered, serious treatment in a remarkable series of novels by James Blish, including *A Case of Conscience*, *Black Easter*, and *The Day After Judgment*. Other religiously oriented science fiction included Walter Miller's *A Canticle for Leibowitz*, with its apparent catastrophic determinism alleviated by an extraordinary theological speculation at the end of the novel. Robert A. Heinlein's *Stranger in a Strange Land* marked another development in this progress away from mere space hardware. Always a brilliant storyteller, Heinlein presented a religious vision that inspired many of the so-called "Flower Children" in the 1960's to seek values beyond those of the mechanistic society against which they protested.

Another development in recent years has been the admonitory novel. To be sure, this aspect of science fiction has been implicit since Mary Shelley inveighed, figuratively at least, against man claiming for himself the powers of the Creator. However, recent sociological developments have provided many writers with the opportunity to exercise their scorn or wrath against the dangers they perceive in these developments. George Orwell's *Nineteen Eighty-Four*, which warns against the usurpation of power by a tyrannical minority, may be the most famous example of this approach; other writers have attacked the dangers of excessive nationalism, subtle totalitarianism of various types, and misplaced reliance on science or technology as a solution to any and all problems. John Boyd put it this way in The *Last Starship from Earth*: "I speak against the moldings of those who would come to us with persuasive smiles and irreproachable logic in the name of religion, mental hygiene, social duty, come with their flags, their Bibles, their money credits, to steal our immortal souls."

Following the lead provided by books such as Paul Erlich's *The Population Bomb* or Alvin Toffler's *Future Shock*, science fiction writers addressed the great Malthusian question of overpopulation and consequent under-production of food. In so doing they reach an audience that might otherwise have been unaware of the problems. To be sure, science fiction writers have often distorted reality. However, modern science fiction, like any other modern art, begins as a concept in the mind of the artist. The artist must embody that concept into some form of reality — clay, words, pigments, musical tones, or what you will. That art of incarnation is ultimately a creative process in which the artist distorts surface appearance in order to display a more universal or a longer lasting reality beneath that appearance. Yet for all of its apparent distortion, science fiction can be more "realistic" than much so-called realistic fiction. The science fiction writer can work out the logical extensions of his artistic vision, unhampered by "real" space and "real" time by displaying the substance beneath the shadow.

The literary techniques which the writer employs in his extrapolative visions will vary from writer to writer, of course. Satire, irony, exaggeration, myth, symbol, anger, and linguistic experiment are merely some of the weapons used by the writers whose works are presented in these volumes. Few writers are mere dispassionate observers of the social scene. Many wish to effect a change or provide an admonition so that humanity will either improve or at least change. In a certain sense, then, Walter Heisenberg's Uncertainty Principle operates within the minds of these authors: the observer changes the observed, and neither is ever quite the same again. The tensions which give life to these books vary: contempt and pity turn upon themselves; folly and stupidity gleam darkly; indignation breeds the intolerable.

Only in the last dozen years or so has science fiction begun to receive recognition, often grudgingly), from the general public. Yet the acceptance of the genre by both television and the cinema as something other than class B thrillers has caused a wave of popularity for science fiction throughout the world. The famous "Star Trek" series showed that filmed versions of science fiction need not merely be thrillers on the order of "The Metal Men from Mars Meet the Bride of Frankenstein's Monster in the Black Lagoon." "Star Trek" considered serious problems, ranging from over-population to the abuse and misuse of power.

When "Star Wars" exploded before an eager public, millions of enthralled viewers left the theaters with an enlarged appreciation for the genre which produced it. Visually spectacular, "Star Wars" addressed itself to some of the themes which writers for over fifty years had been discussing: corruption, evil, the ultimate ascendance of the Good, the necessity for cooperation between beings who held common humane values, regardless of their outward appearance, and so on. Yet "Star Wars" also exhibited many other characteristics of traditional science fiction. These included characters·with whom the audience could identify, an abundance of action, visionary dreams of a better world, and some vaguely nontheistic power embodied in the "The Force." So closely did "Star Wars" follow ideas both implicit and explicit in older science fiction works, that it might be maintained that no little part of its success was derived from the audience's familiarity with its contents.

So also with "Close Encounters of the Third Kind." Traditional science fiction for decades had been concerned with alien visitation or "first contact" problems. As a result, thousands of viewers were willing to accept music as a method of communication with the aliens as well as the aliens themselves. While the film may have left more questions unanswered than it actually addressed, a large measure of its success could certainly be attributed to the groundbreaking imaginative visions of many authors represented in these volumes.

Survey of Science Fiction Literature represents the largest single body of science fiction criticism yet published. The very fact that it is being published at all indicates something of the rapid change that the field has undergone. It could not have been published ten years ago simply because there were not enough scholars or critics who could write knowledgeably about the field and produce the more than five hundred essays contained here. Today that situation has been radically changed, as witness the 1,000,000 words contained in these volumes.

Too long a stepchild of the literary establishment, science fiction suffered from the fact that serious critics ignored a major branch of popular culture. Too often members of the academic establishment took the view excoriated by Kingsley Amis in his seminal volume *New Maps of Hell*: "If it's good, it can't be science fiction. If it's science fiction, it can't be good." This attitude persisted for years, even though many high schools, community colleges, and universities began adding courses in science fiction to their curriculum. Many academic journals devoted exclusively to the serious study of science fiction — *Extrapolation, Science Fiction Studies*, and *The Riverside Quarterly*, to name only a few — began investigating its themes, origins, developments, and trends. Even such prestigious organizations as the Modern

Language Association began including an annual seminar of science fiction at its yearly conventions. Books of criticism multiplied, as did high school and college textbooks devoted to the subject.

Thus, what was impossible to produce ten years ago is a reality today: *Survey of Science Fiction Literature*. The essays contained in these volumes were written by more than 125 contributors whose backgrounds range from professional writers of science fiction to James Joyce scholars. They include high school teachers, Victorian literature specialists, and professional editors. All of them are convinced that science fiction represents a most significant part of contemporary world culture, that it is, indeed, a literature of the future.

If science fiction has sprung from the romance, the adventure story, and the literature of voyages of discovery, what is its future? What is it proceeding toward? A simple answer is impossible, of course, for just as no one could have predicted its present status in 1950, only the foolhardy would attempt to be specific about the directions science fiction might take in the next twenty or thirty years. Yet certain general aspects of what it might become can be extrapolated judging from what has appeared in recent years.

Certainly one thing that is safe to predict is that the freedom presented by the inherent nature of the form will continue to attract mainstream writers. Many of them are already represented in these volumes, as was indicated earlier, and their ranks will surely be joined by others. Science fiction writers currently producing significant novels will continue to probe the effects of technological development upon human beings, but the emphasis will be upon human beings, not upon the technology. They will continue to satirize the foibles and fallacies they perceive with increasing attention to style and characterization — those two areas where most contemporary science fiction is the weakest.

Perhaps the words ascribed by novelist Lawrence Durrell to his alter-ego, Pursewarden, might serve to indicate the challenge that science fiction represents: "We live lives based upon selected fictions. Our view of reality is conditioned by our position in space and time — not by our personalities as we like to think. Thus every interpretation of reality is based upon a unique position. Two paces east or west and the whole picture is changed."

Science fiction in the true sense enables us to take those steps east or west, to view reality as it is, not as it appears. It permits both readers and writers to exercise the creative imagination, to fantasize and survive by taking the two steps to Mars and beyond, leaping from the depths of the human psyche to the vast universe where galaxies stretch like grains of sand to challenge us all.

Willis E. McNelly

LIST OF TITLES IN VOLUME ONE

LIST OF TITLES IN VOLUME ONE

Survey of
Science Fiction Literature

ABADON

Author: Janez Mencinger
First book publication: 1893
Type of work: Novel
Time: From ancient times to the twenty-fourth century
Locale: Mainly in Yugoslavia (Slovenia), on the banks of the Sava river, and on the peak of Triglav, the highest mountain of the country

A Slovenian novel about the devil's creation of the future

> *Principal characters:*
> ABADON, the devil
> SAMORAD VESELIN, a young man
> CVETANA, a young girl
> RUDOVAR, a scientist
> SLOVOGOJ, an old grammarian

It is interesting to note, as an introduction to *Abadon*, how previous Yugoslavian writers have developed their own brand of fantasy and speculative fiction in which there are conflicting philosophies hidden in stories, and there is a terrific clash of ideas, a political and ideological war. This is not surprising; Yugoslavia is a small nation with a strong national consciousness. Yet it suffers doubts and insecurities as well: would such a small nation without a history in the past be capable of making its own history in the future? What kind of social order or political program would assure its survival between the larger and more powerful Italian and German states? The Utopian novelists set out to answer these questions.

The first Yugoslavian Utopian work was *The Ninth Land* (1876) by Josip Stritar. Influenced by Thomas More and Rousseau, it is set on a lonely island. The population speaks a cultivated Slovenian language, and their democracy directly depends on their rhetorical skills and effective use of speech. They discuss all public affairs, criticizing, voting, electing their mayors, and developing their democratic institutions. There are no factories, only peasants and artisans living peacefully in their villages. There are no priests, religion, or churches — just a lovely, rural, idyllic life supported by schools and teachers, theaters and actors, all expounding noble ideas.

Today Stritar is criticized for not understanding the historical necessity of industrialization and capitalism, but in his time his influence was of a quite different type. A professor of theology (and later the bishop), he wrote the Utopian novel *Indija Komandija* (1882), set in another imaginary Slovene country. It is not an island but a country high in the mountains, so high that it is completely isolated. Thus, it is closer to God and divine principles. The country has a king, and the fear of king and God is the best assurance for order. The people do not have a democracy and do not want one, because "everybody knows that no success in affairs is possible if there are too many managers in the house." Only catechism is taught in schools, no modern science — because "everybody knows that a learned peasant cannot be happy." A young boy who has studied philosophy far from his home has organized a revolution and established a sort of "socialism," inspired by the spirit of *egalitè, fraternitè and libertè*. The result is chaos, and in another revolution the king is brought back and the old social order reestablished. The leader of the revolution is banished to Stritar's Ninth Land, but even there he is not accepted. He must go farther to the Tenth Land, where he dies. The novel is a primitive and reactionary assault without any literary value, but it was meant to be political, not artistic.

The third Utopian novel, written as an answer from the liberal party, was *4000* by Josip Tavcar, published in 1891. Set in Ljubljana in the year 4000, this is a negative, satiric Utopia. All power and all bureaucracy are in the hands of priests. The bishops are also military leaders, and some thousands of years ago, they defeated the Germans. After their victory, they did not introduce the Slovene language as an official language, but Latin. Now even the name of Ljubljana is forgotten; it is called Emona, just as in old Roman times. There are very strong rules for sexual abstinence, and free communication between the sexes is forbidden. Even electricity is forbidden, because it is the devil's invention. No modern technology is allowed; everything is as it was in the Middle Ages. There is a revolution of the clerks fighting for abolishment of celibacy, and a young clergyman is put on trial for teaching catechism in Slovene and reading the poems of France Prešeren, the greatest Slovenian poet (1800-1849). He is sentenced to death, and, together with the poems, destroyed by fire.

Another Utopian writer should also be mentioned: Simon Subic, professor of physics and astronomy at the University in Graz (Austria). His Utopian novel *The Fatal Idol of the World* (1893) is a Platonian dialogue in which the author discusses with Socrates modern European political problems. The fatal idol is money, capital. They fly together to the planet Mars, where they find an ideal state which has not been created by good ideas, but by modern technology and electricity. The Martians do not need or have money or capital: they talk by wire and they fly by electric wings and have electric airships. Therefore, there are no boundaries between men or nations; all are friends and everyone is equal. The production and distribution of goods is collectively organized; everybody works according to his faculties and gets what he needs.

The introduction of electricity was a political, economical, social, and philosophical problem in Ljubljana at that time. When the conservative party objected to electricity, saying it was "bad for the eyes" and that Ljubljana was not London or Paris and did not have the same needs as the large nations, the answer on a philosophical level given by Simon Subic in 1893 was that electricity is only a subdued natural or divine power. A man sending messages over mountains and seas and listening to return messages is able to know everything, so he is like God. With electricity, an era of cooperation among humanity is possible, an era of peace and friendship.

Abadon was published in the same year and in the same magazine (*Ljubljanski Zvon*, *The Bell of Ljubljana*, 1893). But *Abadon* is not only a Utopian story; it is much more. It is a philosophical novel that encompasses the history of humanity as a whole as seen from a special point of view. The picture of a Utopian society in the twenty-fourth century is included in this very broad frame.

The love story in the novel is not new. The story of a man who makes a contract with the devil in order to be able to return the love of a girl married to another man was used by Goethe in Faust and in many other stories as well. In Mencinger's novel, however, Abadon, the devil, has other ambitions, too. He wants to educate Samorad to accept his interpretation of human history. He wants to prove that only evil and criminal ideas, only greed and violence, win.

The plot is so complicated and rich and new on every page that no short outline is possible. Abadon, according to the contract, is a servant of Samorad, the unhappy lover of Cvetana. Abadon has lifted Samorad in an airship into an orbit high above the earth where they can stay peacefully and watch everything that is below. Samorad is released of all chains of time and space and is able to go down and talk to anyone in any time or place. He can even participate in historical events, but whenever he tries to help people in their misfortunes, everything goes wrong. When he wants to meet Cvetana in the nineteenth century, she is in jail accused of murder. Her husband has died from the poison Abadon put in his cup, as Samorad ordered him to do. Now Samorad wants to rescue her. Abadon is ready to help, but Samorad has to understand the final result of all human deeds of this kind. So, first, he must see the future.

Flying above Slovenia in the twenty-fourth century, Abadon and Samorad see a dull country. Ljubljana is under the lake, its large waters propelling a gigantic hydroelectric power station. There are no cities or villages, no peasants working in the fields — just big factories. Abadon tells Samorad that there is no Slovenian nation anymore. Only one Slovenian is still alive — Slovogoj, a two hundred-year-old man, a grammarian, a former professor and the author of a Slovenian grammar that has never been accepted as a textbook in schools. He is living secretly in the mountains, and there, on the peak of Triglav, he meets Samorad and gives his last lecture about what has happened in the five hundred years after Samorad's normal life. Western European nations have made an alliance with China, and together they have defeated Russia. Eventually, however, China has defeated Europe and expanded its power over all its disunited nations. Their state is totalitarian, without religion, freedom, education, or literature. There is only modern industry.

The Slovenians have disappeared, as have all the other European nations. Professor Slovogoj is the only one left, pursuing his scientific work in absolute isolation. He has explored the laws of language evolution and has written a new grammar of Slovene as it would have been spoken five hundred years later, in the twenty-ninth century. It does not have any practical value, of course, because no Slovenians are left; but principles and rules are discovered, and this is what matters. They are divine and above nations and human lives.

A flock of Chinese soldiers with electric wings lands on the peak of Triglav after his lecture. Rudovar the chemist is with them. He is a Slovenian traitor working for the foreigners. He brings a bottle of wine, the last bottle of old Slovenian wine, and gives it to Slovogoj. Slovogoj toasts with it to all Slovenian graves, and dies: the wine was poisoned.

In the next chapter, Rudovar takes Samorad on a sightseeing tour through Slovenia. They see that modern communication technology is merely a tool for social control. The technology includes electricity, telephones, telegraphs, and there is also a "device for looking at the distance by the wire." Workers are happy; no revolutionary ideas are circulating among them. They all wear strange masks so they cannot talk to one another. These masks are excellent for order and discipline; they are beautiful and are considered a privilege as well as a duty to wear. A child at the age of fourteen receives the mask with great solemnity, feeling it to be a high honor.

There is no dualism of Church and State because there is no faith in God, no national differences, and no language problems; there is no love and no hate. There are no families, and sexual contacts are reserved for the strongest and healthiest men and women only — and then only under strict supervision. The rearing and education of children is highly institutionalized, as are farming and factory work. Each child gets his or her number for life.

No courts of justice are needed, because they have an electric chair in which everybody must sit from time to time; if any secret thoughts or doubts concerning the State are detected, the citizen is automatically executed.

Even Rudovar and the leader of the Chinese soldiers have expressed some doubts; they are immediately put in the chair and executed. Samorad watches the procedure by the wire. Their bodies are petrified and publicly exposed. The monuments of petrified criminals are the only monuments in this society without art and artists.

This horrible society is, by the end of the novel, identified as an invention and creation of the devil. A new person comes, a new Samorad or his alter-ego, who is not under the control of Abadon. He has quite different ideas: he believes that not violence and greed, but love and good ideas will win, and the Slovenian nation will survive among free European nations. Cvetana proves her innocence, while Samorad tries to commit suicide. But Abadon is defeated by Samorad's alter-ego, who rescues his feeble other half. We see that everything was just a dream, an illness caused by reading bad books. In the final scene Nejaz Nemcigren enters the library to witness a scene reminiscent of *Don Quixote*: he cleans up the library of all bad German books and wrong philosophies.

A great tradition was created by Mencinger. *Abadon* is a negative Utopia, of the type seen in George Orwell's *Nineteen Eighty-Four*. The tradition ended an interesting dialogue in Slovenian literature that lasted almost twenty years. Depicting a bleak future for the nation was intended to inspire people to fight for its freedom and independence — even if that meant showing its death. These novels were not only political and ideological discussions, but also serious efforts to discover the tendencies of social evolution. The problem of electricity had been expressed: according to Subic's theory it brings knowledge, freedom, and friendship; according to Mencinger, it brought a horrifying and inhuman social system of absolute control. *Abadon* raises the question of whether wrong ideas are responsible for bad social evolution, and of whether censoring libraries is a solution of the problem.

Do we have an answer today, almost a hundred years later? Do we know what kind of society the modern electronic technologies, computers and so on are creating?

Boris Grabnar

THE ABSOLUTE AT LARGE
(TOVÁRNA NA ABSOLUTNO)

Author: Karel Čapek (1890-1938)
First book publication: 1922
English translation: 1927
Type of work: Novel
Time: 1943-1953
Locale: Czechoslovakia

Combustion of the atom releases the divine energy contained in all matter, promoting religious conversion and subsequently religious wars

Principal characters:
C. H. BONDY, an industrialist, head of Metallo-Electric Company
RUDOLF MAREK, an engineer, inventor of the Absolute
ELLEN MACHAT, the "intended" of Bondy
BISHOP LINDA, local head of Roman Catholic church
KUZENDA, a religious sect leader
TONI BOBINET, a French lieutenant who becomes Emperor

The Absolute at Large was written for a newspaper in thirty installments. Because of this serial development, the novel has a loose structure in which characters appear and then fail to appear again; Čapek uses the device of a journalist who frequently observes and reports on remote activities.

Industrialist C. H. Bondy, concerned with the exhaustion of the coal supply, imagines himself playing God to an absolute fool, as he refers to his former friend, inventor Rudolf Marek. Bondy dreams of bestowing on Marek some of his own material wealth. In this fashion he introduces the dominant motifs of the novel: God as material abundance, and man's egotistic assertion of his own position on others.

Marek explains that complete utilization of atomic energy would mean that matter would vanish, but also that the divine energy contained in it would be released. He has invented an atomic fission engine which he calls a Karburator; and Bondy, inspecting it objectively and skeptically, falls into a state of spiritual ecstasy. Others respond similarly in the engine's presence. Marek has been reading Spinoza in an attempt to understand how the Karburator acts on people; as a scientist, he maintains that the idea of God is absolutely intolerable, but he understands that burning one single atom completely fills the surrounding atmosphere with the Absolute. Workers in the vicinity of the Karburator develop the power to prophesy, perform miracles, regenerate severed limbs, and levitate. Marek also anticipates that people, not accustomed to God as a reality, cannot possibly manage the social and moral implications of God's working among them. The area of his Brevnov factory, where he built the first Karburator, becomes a religious center. As Bondy begins to manufacture and distribute the Karburators, religious experiences multiply within the vicinity of any one machine.

The local Roman Catholic official, Bishop Linda, says that God cannot be brought into discussions about the Karburator; he finds that the Absolute opposes the laws of the Church, which are established to control God in the lives of men. He repeats that the church cannot handle a real and inactive God.

Several accounts of religious activities follow and each individual or sect, having experienced relativism, believes it has discovered absolutism. Kuzenda, holding a kind of Sunday School on a dredge, believes that God is incarnate in the dredge and cannot be infinite as the Catholics say. Mr. Machat, having built houses for a profit, gives them to the poor. In the textile works, the Karburator runs the looms twenty-four hours a day without human supervision, uses up all available raw materials, and continues to manufacture textiles from straw, sand, or anything thrown into it. A single machine is established to provide lights for the city of Prague, and Bondy fears the effect of the Absolute when the switch is turned on. Indeed, the entire population of the city falls into ecstasy. A Karburator in a bank keeps the bank's books, answers correspondence, gives orders in writing to the Board of Directors, and sends fervent letters to clients urging them to do good works.

At the same time as Bondy determines to spend millions to devise protective measures against God, he meets his "intended," Ellen Machat. She has given her millions to the poor, but explains that her new powers allow his thoughts to be born in her mind the same as they are in his own. He relinquishes his dream of marrying her because he cannot marry someone who reads his mind.

Jan Binder unknowingly buys a Karburator for his merry-go-round, and it immediately begins to whirl people into a mystic experience. Later, approaching Kuzenda's dredge, the merry-go-round converts enter into battle against Kuzenda's group, and thus the religious wars begin. So many reports of religious manifestations crowd the newspapers that Doctor Blahous, a religious skeptic, writes a long treatise against Kuzendism and other manifestations of the Absolute, but suddenly reverses his argument when he experiences the Presence.

Chapter Thirteen marks a turning point in the novel. It is here that the narrator pauses to reflect on developments through personal histories already related and turns to the social and political effects of the working Absolute. Then, as background, he provides his own version of the Creation story. Before anything was, the Absolute existed in Infinite Free Energy. Then it became Working Energy and created matter in which it lost itself. In this way, it became Infinite Imprisoned Energy, not to be liberated until Marek's atomic motor released it. Then it manifested itself in two ways: it resumed creation through the atomic machine's superabundant manufacture, and it worked illumination, conversion, miracles, levitations, ecstasies, predictions, and faith through the medium of religion. The quantitative expression for infinitude now becomes overproduction without any governing powers for distribution. A tack factory produces mountains of tacks, but none of them can be had a few miles away.

Eventually the economy reaches the stage where there is nothing to give away, because everyone can have what they need for the taking. Money becomes plentiful because the Karburator produces money. The only form of stability lies in farming.

Bondy visits Marek in his mountain retreat and confesses that he has managed to throw off the Absolute after a struggle; thus, neither he nor Marek has been converted and they can discuss the situation rationally. Bondy believes the Absolute has a plan to take over the world, but Marek disagrees. Without commerce and government, it cannot do so.

Some religious groups initially seek to oppose or control the burgeoning Absolute. But when the Freemasons are told that the Industrial Federation has elected the Absolute its honorary President, they decide to organize religious circles in the Masonic sense. Likewise the Catholics, who, under Father Jost, initially oppose the Absolute sects, become supporters on Bishop Linda's orders. The Sacred Congregation admits the Absolute into the bosom of the Church, and it is deified in Rome on December 12, just short of one year from the beginning of its story. Other faiths, each believing they alone have the truth, move in their own fashion to align themselves with the Absolute. On St. Kilda, an island west of the Hebrides, for example, leaders of various nations meet secretly to forge an agreement not to assist religious movements on territories of other states. The meeting, however, dissipates when each representative promotes his own brand of the Absolute.

Meanwhile, snow nearly kills a messenger trudging up the mountain to reach Marek with a telegram from Bondy acknowledging the truth of Marek's predictions. Religious wars break out everywhere, but Czechoslovokia in particular is overrun. Only one Old Patriot writes to the newspaper urging a unification of Slavs on national lines since religion divides and tears asunder.

The opposite of absolutism — relativism — now begins to manifest itself among the world's disputing nations. In America, the Absolute invades Sports, and the main conflict centers in the Wets versus the Drys (based on the Prohibition controversy which culminated in the constitutional amendment of 1919, three years before the publication of Čapek's novel. The Japanese invade the West Coast, Asia's yellow hordes sweep toward Central Europe, the blacks rise in Africa, an antipope opposes the Pope. All the world engages in Holy War except France, where young Toni Bobinet, "the Napoleon of the Mountain Brigade," unites the country in a sweep of rationalism, military might, and State atheism. Advancing into India, however, he disappears while searching for Amazon women. A Czech named Hampl imitates Bobinet and takes a Czechoslovakian city by proclamation.

As the Greatest War, 1944-1953, draws near a close, Bondy is found, having lived on a coral island for those nine years. He and six other white men have faced being captured by cannibals, but Bondy, now understanding something of relativism, explains cannibalism as a religious ritual similar to communion. He explains that the Greatest War was fought because each nation insisted that it had absolute truth; mankind's failure to comprehend the Absolute deity led each man to grasp a fragment and think he had the entire God.

By the end of the Greatest War, the last of the Karburators has been destroyed and the machines "that had religion inside of them" can be discussed as things of the past. Return to normalcy means that Grandfather Blahous can discuss the price of eggs and quote his son, the professor, who states that it is the same everywhere; if anyone sets his mind to anything — not merely religious matters — he must have everybody else believe in it. The penultimate chapter recounts prophecies of war, made a hundred years before, for the current war; in the last battle, thirteen opposing men decide to quit fighting and go home.

The last chapter features a gathering of four persons — a journalist, Father Jost, Mr. Byrch (who had been Kuzenda's stoker), and Jan Binder. Amid an atmosphere of tolerance, Binder tells how Kuzenda agrees that his god can also be Binder's god. Instead of insisting on belief in one God, he says, people should believe in other people. Such relativism seems to triumph briefly, when, believing in the absolute goodness of one kind of sauerkraut, they agree to try a different kind the next day. But then a policeman enters and tells about arresting people in a cellar with a Karburator, where they were breaking the law by conducting a religious "orgy." He believes they have now destroyed the last Karburator. The relative merits of different religions, as well as different foods, escape those present.

D. H. Lawrence called the same human tendency the "egotistical compulsion" — to impose one's beliefs on others. Karel Čapek urges "relativism" as an alternative to absolutism. As Bondy learned, Marek was not an absolute fool; and neither are others whose lifestyles are different.

Grace Eckley

Sources for Further Study

Criticism:

Harkins, William E. "A Preview of Atomic Fission: Two Novels of the Absolute," in *Karel Čapek*. New York: Columbia University Press, 1962,
pp. 100-103. Harkins provides valuable insight into Čapek's style of writing and themes.

Reviews:

Nation. CXXV, August 17, 1927, p. 164.

New York Herald Tribune Books. July 3, 1927, p. 7.

New York Times. June 12, 1927, p. 18.

Saturday Review. CXLIII, June 11, 1927, p. 915.

Times Literary Supplement. May 26, 1927, p. 372.

ACROSS THE ZODIAC
The Story of a Wrecked Record

Author: Percy Greg (1836-1889)
First book publication: 1880
Type of work: Novel
Time: 1830
Locale: Mars

> *An account of a journey to Mars*

>> *Principal characters:*
>> The unnamed author of the "wrecked record"
>> EVEENA, his first wife
>> EUNANE, EIVÉ AND VELNA, three of his other wives
>> ESMO, Eveena's father
>> ENDO ZAMPTÂ, Regent of Elcavoo (a Martian Official)

Across the Zodiac was published by Trubner & Company of London two years after they had issued *The Devil's Advocate*, a work of social philosophy, also written by Percy Greg, in which several characters explore in conversation the major political and social controversies of the day. *Across the Zodiac* stands in the same relationship to the earlier work as H. G. Wells's *The Shape of Things to Come* does to *The Work, Wealth and Happiness of Mankind*, or Plato's story of Atlantis (in the *Timaeus* and the *Critias*) to the *Republic*. It is an attempt to dramatize the social and political questions by displaying hypothetical answers in the form of an imaginary society. The "Devil's Advocate" of the earlier book is, of course, Greg himself, and in the preface to that work he explains that he has taken the title in order to put to the test of vigorous cross-examination some of the major philosophical orthodoxies of the day, especially Positivism and Egalitarianism. The thrust of his arguments is basically pragmatic, and his rhetorical style is Utilitarian, although his conclusions are a long way from the mainstream of nineteenth century British Utilitarian philosophy. It is because of the pragmatic approach of his arguments, his attempts to imagine the consequences arising from the implementation of various philosophies in order to estimate their worth, that he found it natural to embody his ideas in an exemplary fantasy serving as a kind of sequel to his conversation piece. The habits of pragmatic thought and argument have fathered many pieces of speculative fiction.

Across the Zodiac begins with a frame story in which Greg describes his meeting with an American, Colonel A---, formerly of the Confederate Army. While diplomatically absenting himself from his homeland after the war, the Colonel had a remarkable experience, but, as a result of relating the story, was subsequently compelled to fight three duels against people who called him a liar. As he disliked killing people, the Colonel had decided not to give anyone else the opportunity to disbelieve him. However, Greg explains how he won the man's confidence and had delivered into his hands a remarkable manu-

script, which the Colonel found in the wreckage of a meteoric body that, the
reader is invited to presume, must have been a wrecked spacecraft.

The main point of this frame story is the way in which Greg claims to have
won the confidence of the Colonel. It involves an impassioned argument to the
effect that the dogmas of Positivist science were replacing those of theology.
Thus it appeared that an open-minded freethinker such as he would soon be
condemned as a heretic by the successors of Richard Congreve and Thomas
Henry Huxley just as certainly as he once would have been by the contemporaries of Tomás de Torquemada. This argument exists to indicate to the
reader that the image of "Martian" society which is to confront him through
the medium of the wrecked record is an image of his own possible future.
Ironically, the fact that Greg chose to write an interplanetary novel rather than
a futuristic one probably reflects the fact that he was old-fashioned in his literary allegiances. *The Devil's Advocate* is a modern version of a classical Dialogue, and *Across the Zodiac* harks back to the tradition of the great imaginary
voyages.

Across the Zodiac is frequently complimented by modern historians of
speculative fiction because of the attempted verisimilitude of the early chapters
of the wrecked record, which deal with the actual journey to Mars in a spacecraft called the *Astronaut*, powered by an antigravitic force called Apergy.
This is, indeed, a fascinating section, and it seems that Greg had taken to heart
Edgar Allan Poe's lament (appended to the book versions of "Hans Pfaall")
that so many imaginary voyages to other worlds made no attempt at all to
devise a convincing mode of travel. Greg clearly gave serious thought to the
problem of imagining what difficulties would be involved in navigating a
course from Earth to Mars, and what the experience of the journey might be
like. These early chapters are replete with technical data and detailed accounts
of observations and operations, and this part of the narrative has a strong Ver-
nian flavor. It must be remembered, though, that this section is little more than
a literary device for translocating the Narrator into the hypothetical society
whose description and examination is Greg's real purpose. It is a misrepresen-
tation of the novel to discuss it as if it belonged to the same literary species as
Verne's *Round the Moon*. The interplanetary voyage takes up only fifty-four
pages out of 584.

The Narrator's first contact with the Martians is nearly fatal. Though they
are clearly human, they are much smaller and thinner than the men of Earth,
and they perceive him as an alien, attacking him immediately. He is saved
from the mob by a member of the Martian aristocracy named Esmo, who takes
him into his home. There he learns the language of Mars and the customs of
the household, and soon hears from Esmo the history of the world.

From Esmo's first lengthy account of conditions on Mars, the Narrator
learns two facts of paramount importance to Greg's overall argument (though
the connection between them does not become apparent until much later). The

first is that Mars is a post-Communist society, the present sociopolitical order having grown out of the ruins of a Communist State. The second is that a dogmatic Positivism dominates Martian natural philosophy, so that opposition to the world view of science is heresy.

Esmo explains how Martian Communism failed because once the system came into being there was not sufficient incentive to make people work hard and productively. There was bitter strife over the allocation of particular tasks, with the result that much work never got done at all. Envy caused the destruction of all luxuries, and eventually all wealth, because the majority preferred to destroy it rather than see it enjoyed by a few. Only when rebels restored the institution of private property and a hierarchical system of authority did progress resume, and the general standard of living begin to rise again. The end result of the period of resolution was an absolute monarchy, and general acceptance of the principle that maintaining a few rulers in luxurious wealth was a cheap price to pay for the maintenance of the social order. Esmo draws from this story the assumption on which the parable is based: "that immediate and obvious self-interest is the only motive that certainly and seriously affects human action." Both Esmo and Greg accept this as true, but both feel that the embodiment of the principle in the ultrarational Martian society has created a world which is crucially flawed. It is the role of the Narrator to demonstrate what new factor must be introduced in order to turn this rational social order into a good social order.

In the chapters immediately following Esmo's account of Martian history we see some of the implications of his story in the ordinary pattern of Martian social relationships. The Martians, as realists, have no concept of altruism, and this becomes evident when the Narrator must take an emissary from the Prince (the autocratic ruler of the world) to see the *Astronaut*, in order to prove his account of himself. He and the official, Endo Zamptâ, are accompanied on their journey by Eveena, one of Esmo's daughters. When Eveena slips over a cliff and the Narrator demands that Endo Zamptâ help him rescue her, the Martian is quite horrified at the idea that he should risk his life to try to save hers. When the Narrator forces the other to help, he makes a deadly enemy.

The rescue is successful, and when news of what happened spreads, the Narrator's actions are the cause of great astonishment. Esmo is outspoken in his gratitude, and seems to be exceptional in having some understanding of the altruistic impulse which motivated the hero. The Narrator has by this time fallen in love with Eveena and marries her, but is at once enmeshed by a complex web of expectations regarding the conduct of Martian marriages. It is not simply the customs which confuse him but the whole set of assumptions regarding the proper relationship between a man and the woman of his household. Eveena is forever expecting to be harshly treated and constantly amazed by the Narrator's compassion, which is entirely alien to Martian life.

Much of the book is taken up with the Narrator's marital affairs, which become extraordinarily complicated. When he has been presented at the Martian court, he receives from the Prince the gift of four more wives, and he subsequently acquires a sixth when he attends a marriage market and takes pity on a girl insufficiently favored to attract attention from the Martians. The pattern of his relationships with his various wives and the story of their gradual recruitment to his own point of view has to carry the main burden of Greg's criticism of Martian cynicism and also provide a vehicle for his views on female suffrage and the proper division of responsibility between the sexes.

While the Narrator is wrestling with this complex domestic situation, Esmo introduces him into a secret society of heretics, who maintain belief in a supreme being and in the immortality of the soul. During his initiation, he receives revelatory proof of these beliefs through the medium of a vision of the long-dead founder of the order. The Narrator's personal heresy, and his embroilment in Martian heresy, gives the vengeful Endo Zamptâ the chance of revenge. Zamptâ persuades one of the Narrator's wives, Eivé, to poison one of those most loyal to him, Eunane, and then to make an attempt on her husband's life. This attempt is thwarted by Eveena, and the Narrator gets a further chance to display his astonishing compassion by forgiving Eivé her crime. When the Prince interviews him again, he is able to tie together all the threads of the moral argument that has run through the book by arguing that the sympathy which allows him to treat others so generously, even ignoring risks to his own life, is the direct consequence of his religious beliefs. Essentially, he offers a straightforward pragmatic justification of faith, arguing that the Positivist rejection of it is bad not so much because it is wrong, but because of the psychological and social consequences which proceed therefrom. The Prince is impressed by this argument, and when the Narrator tells him that there are secret believers among his own people, he promises to secure their safety.

Meanwhile, Endo Zamptâ has already moved against the society, and open conflict becomes inevitable. In a bloody battle fought near the spot where the *Astronaut* landed, Esmo is killed and Eveena dies saving the life of the Narrator. The enemy is destroyed, but the Narrator, heartbroken, sets off for Earth once more, to suffer the fate that the reader already knows through the testimony of Colonel A---.

Across the Zodiac is very much a product of the political climate of its own time. Apart from its two main arguments relative to Positivism and Communism, it reflects a fascination with questions of female suffrage and moral reform. In these latter respects it now seems hopelessly out of date, and perhaps there is cause for sadness in the fact that its sociopolitical speculations do not strike the modern reader as being equally antediluvian. We can, alas, still hear Greg's arguments being bandied about today as if they were of recent provenance, and science fiction writers are still producing little parables to demonstrate the overwhelming force of self-interest. The novel is very long, and sections of it will inevitably bore contemporary readers. The mass of detail relating to Martian topography, architecture, and language, for example, represents invention for its own sake, neither particularly adventurous nor in the least necessary to the main theme of the book. Curiously, however, what strikes the reader who has scanned through *The Devil's Advocate* is how much more there is in the earlier work than in the latter, and how many more speculative fantasies might have been built on aspects of its imaginatively fertile discussions. *The Devil's Advocate* reveals Greg to have been a man of wide interests and considerable knowledge (though he cannot be considered a major contributor to social philosophy), and it is perhaps to be regretted that he wrote no more speculative fiction after *Across the Zodiac*.

Brian Stableford

ADA OR ARDOR
A Family Chronicle

Author: Vladimir Nabokov (1899-1977)
First book publication: 1969
Type of work: Novel
Time: The late nineteenth through mid-twentieth century
Locale: The planet Antiterra, sibling of the planet Terra, and a distorted image of the
  planet Earth

*The "Family Chronicle" of Dr. Van Veen's love affair with his sister, Ada, on the
planet Antiterra, involving a distortion of traditional concepts of time and space*

> *Principal characters:*
> IVAN (VAN) VEEN, the author of this family chronicle
> ADELAIDA (ADA) VEEN, Van's sister and lover
> LUCINDA (LUCETTE) VEEN, half-sister of Van and Ada
> DEMENTIY (DEMON) VEEN, father of Van and Ada
> DANIEL VEEN, brother of Demon, putative father of Ada, biological
>   father of Lucette
> AQUA DURMANOV VEEN, wife of Demon, putative mother of Van
> MARINA DURMANOV VEEN, mother of Van, Ada, and Lucette, wife
>   of Daniel Veen

In many ways Nabokov's most complex novel, *Ada or Ardor*, shares many
characteristics with his previously published fiction and differs from that earlier body of work in only one major way: it can be classified as science fiction. A
note of caution is necessary here, however. The qualities which *Ada or Ardor*
shares with Nabokov's other work remove it from what we might call the
mainstream of science fiction, and regular readers of science fiction might not
readily recognize it as such. It is easy enough to be overwhelmed by the linguistic puns, allusions to Russian and world literature, multilingual anagrams
and jokes, erotica, and esoteric knowledge of botany and lepidopterology
which crowd every page of this long novel. Were the reader not told fairly
early that the action of the novel takes place on Antiterra and then given a
description of the geography of that planet, a distorted reflection of the planet
earth's geography, he might miss the connection. However, there is more to
the classification of *Ada or Ardor* as science fiction than mere setting, for this
novel is Nabokov's reworking of the myth of creation and the Garden of Eden;
in reworking this theme, Nabokov exploits the possibilities of time. He attacks
preconceptions of time: time's relation to space; the notion of the relativity of
time; and the measuring of time; that is, the emphasis placed, in discussions of
time, on duration and lapse. It is possible to argue that time, how we understand it and how we use it, is the subject of *Ada or Ardor*.

As the novel begins, Van looks back almost a century to his first meeting
with Ada, and recalls the beginning of their love, set in an idyllic garden,
Ardis. The year is 1884; Van is fourteen years old, Ada twelve, when they
begin their sexual life together. The garden is Edenic; the early awakening of

their love is surrounded by charming pastoral images: picnics, tree-climbings, and so on. But even in this setting, sinister notes are sounded; their love and their Eden are the exclusive possessions of Van and Ada, to be shared with no one else; the incestuous and narcissistic nature of their love insures its separation from "ordinary" life and lovers, and it has its victims. Chief among these victims is Lucette, Van and Ada's halfsister; she is excluded at the same time as teased and titillated, a consistent victim of the lovers' cruelty. On the reverse side, this exclusivity maintains and strengthens Van and Ada's bond throughout their lives, keeping them as one despite Ada's marriage, various infidelities on both sides, and their guilt about Lucette's suicide (Ada says, "We teased her to death").

It is characteristic of *Ada or Ardor* that everything, like the exclusivity, even solipsism, of Van and Ada's love, has a reverse side. One of the central metaphors of the novel appears with the image of Van walking on his hands, turning the world upside down for himself and for whoever goes along with him. In Van's world, everything is inverted or reversed or both; more specifically, everything is of his own creation. He wants nothing to do with the "natural" world, scorning information about the trees in Ardis at the same time that he enjoys their shade and protection from unwelcome intruders; he is anxious, moreover, to remove Ada from this natural world, to discourage her interest in plants and butterflies and bring her into his artificial and entirely self-referential world. Ada resists these attempts at assimilation throughout the novel, energetically at first when still a child, later by marrying another man. In the end, her rebellion is reduced to sporadic disagreement in marginal notes to the memoirs, but the rebellion, though weakened, remains.

Van's inversion of the Eden myth focuses on the awakening of this particular Adam and Eve to sensual knowledge. He reverses the characters; Van is Eve, Ada is Adam. And he inverts the myth; now, sexual love, even incestuous love, rather than being indentified with sin and expulsion from the garden, *is* the garden. Sensual love is what paradise has to offer. The threat to their peace, when it comes, comes from outside, from dark forces outside the protected garden, the forces that control the rest of the Veen family. When speaking of his wish to escape from Antiterra, Van calls it Demonia, recalling his father, Demon. Van even carries his love of inversion into the writing of his memoirs. He saves his clearest hints and explanations of his intentions and methods until the end of the novel.

In the creation of his Eden, his Utopia, Van accepts nothing of Antiterra; in particular, he does not accept its conception of time and its way of describing time in terms of measurement. Part Four of *Ada or Ardor* begins with Van, in late middle age (the year is 1922), on his way to meet Ada after the death of her husband. He summarizes for the reader the main points of his soon to be published treatise, *Texture of Time*, a work dedicated to the refuting of the common misconception that time is some entity which can be broken into three parts, past, present and future. To Van, future is a "sham," hardly worth discussing. He gives his greater attention to the concepts of past and present and to what he calls "Pure" Time. He argues strenuously to himself as much as to the reader that there is no necessary or authentic relationship between time and space, insisting that although he can imagine time existing without space, he cannot imagine the converse. Space is inferior to time because it can be more easily grasped, more successfully measured and dealt with. Space is closely tied to our senses of sight and touch, but time is related only to our sense of hearing (since, for Van, time is rhythm) and even that relationship is vague and inexact. Space can be more successfully, although not perfectly, contemplated; time, however, is "not the recurrent beats of the rhythm but the gap between two such beats, the gray gap between black beats: the Tender Interval." As such, it is forever elusive.

The drawing of his settings, then, Ardis and Antiterra, should create no particular problems for the reader, filled though these drawings are with unexpected and inexplicable details: the liberties taken, for example, with the hemispheres, the United States and Russia merging into one continent, Amerussia. Moreover, Van's disregard of and contempt for conventional time make his use of anachronisms almost imperative. Ardis, when Van first sees it, is a paradise of anachronisms, a blend of nineteenth century Russian elegance and twentieth century American technology and leisure products; automobiles, movie cameras and Coca-Cola all find a place here with the Russian aristocrats. Later, in 1922, Van bolsters his argument on time by quoting from a book not published until 1924. From beginning to end of the novel, the love between Van and Ada is based on a denial of the importance of chronological time and human age. Making love for the first time as children, they enjoy a mature and erotic sexuality; in their nineties, at the end of the novel, they maintain their initial innocent selfishness and are almost indifferent to the external signs of their aging. The point is not that love redeems time and cancels age; rather, it is that man's creation of himself and his world requires the control of time, which in turn denies the validity of any "passage" of time external to the creator's plan and vision.

Van's hostility to the "passage of time" as a way of describing time is central to his treatise. He argues against metaphors which would describe time as a stream; to speak of time as process or physical movement is to fall into the trap of spatial metaphor and to misunderstand time entirely. It does not "flow" and bears no relation to progress along a line or in some direction; time is to be understood, as the title of his treatise suggests, as "texture." Relativity can, of course, have no bearing here, and Van dismisses it. Time in its pure form is subject to no other factors, dependent on no context for its meaning or value. And it is pure time that Van cares about. Eliminating all that is external to himself in creating his Ardis, he eliminates all but what he calls pure time, time free of modifying circumstances or conceptions, what he calls "motionless" time. This is highly individual time, of course, and, more importantly, it is art's time, time that the artist can hold in his hand and mold in whichever shape suits his imaginative needs and intentions. Van is an artist, and Ardis is his aesthetic creation.

If it is misguided to speak of time in terms of movement or progress, then traditional concepts of past and present are meaningless. Van addresses himself to this question, of major importance here since what he is ostensibly writing is a chronicle of a family, a form which cries out for chronological treatment. Van refuses such treatment and takes up the chronicle through the texture of time's imagery. It is clear from the beginning that the reader should not expect a standard family history. Nabokov fills the beginning of the novel with clues to his intention to invert or subvert the form. The novel begins with a turning upside down of Count Leo Tolstoy's famous opening line from *Anna Karenina* about the difference between happy families and unhappy families. The chart, which conventionally outlines genealogies in Russian novels, is here misleading. The reader has to learn as he goes along that Van and Ada are brother and sister; the chart gives no indication of the existence of illegitimacy and supports the fiction that they are first cousins.

In *Ada or Ardor* the movement of events is back and forth, circling around, but never straightforward. Past and Present can (and *must*, Van would insist) exist simultaneously; Present need not succeed Past. As Van explains it, the Past is a "constant accumulation of images," not "the orderly alternation of linked events." It is, contrary to conventional ideas, not something that is over and done, never to be relived. The Past exists in the Present and gives the Present what shape it has. In their fifties, Van and Ada relax together, share a joke at another couple's expense, and are once again the young Van and Ada. For Van, the Present is at the level this accumulation of images has reached. *Ada or Ardor* is Van's attempt to set down these images, to give them life beyond his physical life; they are a denial of death. Van says, "Who said *I* shall die?"

The use of the pronoun "I" is interesting here since this is Ada's story, or at least the story of Van and Ada. But Van recognizes that these are his images, his memories and his immortality. Ada, however deeply involved, is not inseparable from Van. Her marginal comments always suggest that the images which make up her memories are slightly at odds with Van's. Incestuous they may be, "siblings and lovers" as she says, but they are not identical. Part Four ends with Ada's insistence that we can never know Time and that the effort to know it is wasted energy.

It is characteristic of Van that he usually allows Ada the last word, never bothering to contradict her or to dispute her interpretations of their mutual memories as she disputes his. Van has, by the time he is writing these chronicles, learned to disregard whatever about Ada is inconsistent with his image of her. When she arrives for their meeting after her husband's death, her appearance is so far removed from the way in which Van remembers her — she has lost all her girlishness and youthful grace, is overly made-up and unattractively dressed — that for the first time he feels no sexual attraction to her. He saves their love only through a deeper dive into his theorizing and speculations on time and its nonrelatedness to chronology. In other words, he re-creates the "physical" woman he sees. The Ada he finally makes love to is the culmination of all the past Adas and not the individual middle-aged woman he spoke to the night before.

Van speaks of the writing of the family chronicles as a way of objectifying his experiences and perhaps as a means of better understanding those experiences. But his primary intention in writing them becomes quite clear late in the novel when he argues that "You lose your immortality when you lose your memory."

Ada or Ardor, despite all of Nabokov's irony directed at Russian "family" novels and chronological treatments of family histories, *is* a "Family Chronicle." The reader learns that Van's family has degenerated through the years; Van suspects that sexual and emotional corruption lies behind the destruction and disintegration of the Veen family. This disintegration has been surfacing more frequently in recent years, most dramatically in the suicides of Van's stepmother (aunt), Aqua, and his cousin (half-sister) Lucette. At the end of this corrupt line stands Van, sterile and deeply involved in the logical outcome of all this inbreeding and crossbreeding, an incestuous and inescapable relationship with his sister. The family line will die out with this pair of lovers, but this written record of their relationship is no mere compilation of data. It is an artifact, an aesthetic construct of which Van is the Creator and Legislator and which, by its existence, renders his death and the death of his complex family impossible.

Mary J. Elkins

Sources for Further Study

Criticism:

Appel, Alfred, Jr. "*Ada* Described," in *Nabokov: Criticism, Reminiscences, Translations and Tributes*. Edited by Alfred Appel, Jr. and Charles Newman. Evanston, Ill.: Northwestern University Press, 1970, pp. 160-186. This article gives an in-depth analysis of the novel *Ada* and its relationship to the body of Nabokov's work.

Fowler, Douglas. *Reading Nabokov*. Ithaca, N.Y.: Cornell University Press, 1974, pp. 176-201. This book offers general criticism on the novel *Ada*.

Mason, Bobbie Ann. *Nabokov's Garden: A Guide to* Ada. Ann Arbor, Mich: Ardis, 1974, This handbook is a necessity for anyone doing in-depth research on *Ada*.

Proffer, Carl R. *"Ada* as Wonderland: A Glossary of Allusions to Russian Literature,"* in his *A Book of Things About Vladimir Nabokov*. Ann Arbor, Mich: Ardis, 1974, pp. 249-279. This article, as well as others in the same collection discusses *Ada* both as a work of science fiction and as a piece of Russian literature.

Reviews:

Atlantic. CCXXIII, June, 1969, p. 105.

Commentary. XLVIII, August, 1969, p. 47.

New York Review of Books. XII, May 22, 1969, p. 3.

New Yorker. XLV, August 2, 1969, p. 67.

Newsweek. LXXIII, May 5, 1969, p. 10.

Times Literary Supplement. October 2, 1969, p. 1121.

ADAM LINK — ROBOT

Author: Eando Binder (Otto Binder, 1911-1974)
First book publication: 1965
Type of work: Novel created from a story series
Time: The near future
Locale: The United States

The ordeal of a robot, who possesses humanlike intelligence and emotions, in his efforts to obtain acceptance as a citizen and the same rights as human beings

>Principal characters:
>ADAM LINK, a male robot
>EVE LINK, a female robot
>DR. CHARLES LINK, Adam Link's creator
>TERRY, a dog who is Adam's friend
>THOMAS LINK, Dr. Link's nephew
>TOM HALL, a young reporter and Adam's friend
>DR. HILLORY, a power-mad scientist

The fundamental attitude toward all forms of artificially created reasoning creatures or machines was first and most vividly fixed in the mind of both readers and writers by Mary Shelley's *Frankenstein*. All artificially created living things, whether sewed together from parts, grown in a test tube, or built from metal, were assumed to be malignant and deadly. The hundreds of monster movies that we have today owe their existence to the legacy of *Frankenstein*.

The "curse" of the Frankenstein monster was also inherited by the mechanical men in science fiction who later came to be known as "robots." Before the term was invented, William Wallace Cook called his metal men "muglugs" in his novel *A Round Trip to the Year 2,000*, serialized in the July through November, 1903, issues of *The Argosy*, and had them rebel against their human creators. It was Karel Čapek, the great Czech dramatist, who invented the term "robots" in his play *R.U.R.* (1920). Their revolt completely destroyed mankind.

When the era of the fantasy magazines arrived, the "Frankenstein Curse" was passed on to a new generation of writers. Among them was the youthful, aspiring Edmond Hamilton, whose cover story for the December, 1926, issue of *Weird Tales*, "The Metal Giants," was announced as "The story of a Frankenstein, of a creation that rebelled against its creator, a gigantic striding terror that spreads terror and destruction in its path across the defenseless cities of the United States." Edmond Hamilton would return again with "The Reign of the Robots" (*Wonder Stories*, December, 1931), worthy of a cover showing a robot making off with an excellent specimen of femininity.

What the fate of humanity might be in a world ruled by machines was brilliantly expounded by Miles J. Breuer, M.D., in his novel *Paradise and*

Iron (*Amazing Stories Quarterly*, Summer, 1930). Nathan Schachner and Arthur Leo Zagat collaborated to produce "The Revolt of the Machines" (*Astounding Stories*, July, 1931). Even the kindly robot-lover Raymond Z. Gallun succumbed to the infection with "Mad Robot" (*Astounding Stories*, March, 1936).

All this is but a small portion of the overwhelming tide of examples of the standardized treatment of the robot — a major theme in science fiction — by virtually all of the writers. That is why the appearance of "I, Robot" by Eando Binder, the first of the stories that comprise the book *Adam Link — Robot*, had such tremendous impact upon the readers and such pervasive influence in the field when it appeared in the January, 1939, issue of *Amazing Stories*.

The remaining stories and novelettes which were rewritten and connected to form this novel appeared originally in *Amazing Stories*: "The Trial of Adam Link, Robot" (July, 1939); "Adam Link in Business" (January, 1940); "Adam Link's Vengeance" (February, 1940); "Adam Link, Robot Detective" (May, 1940); "Adam Link, Champion Athlete" (July, 1940); and "Adam Link Saves the World" (April, 1942).

Science fiction writers soon began to change their attitudes about robots. Lester Del Rey wrote a short story, "Helen O Loy" (*Astounding Stories*, December, 1938), which appeared on the stands within weeks of "I, Robot," that offered a more subtle approach to the humanization of robots. It presented the love story of a robot built to externally simulate a woman and programmed to behave like a woman. Del Rey's characterization was far more artistic (Binder was straightforward and militant) and may be anthologized by future generations; but it was Binder who bluntly accomplished what needed to be done to change the attitude of future writers towards the handling of the robot theme in science fiction. Binder's robot, Adam Link, was named after the man who invented and built him, Dr. Charles Link, and he was named Adam, because he was the first of an entirely new breed of robots, a type that had the more humanistic "virtues" of his creator.

Although Adam Link has to be taught to walk and talk like a child, he develops much more swiftly than a human because his faculties for absorbing this type of learning are already at their maximum point of development. When the scientist's dog cries out in pain at the robot's grasp, it is instantly released. The robot is sensitive to suffering. His education proceeds at an incredible pace, because he does not need sleep, and his grasp of scientific principles is so advanced that he soon is able to suggest ways of mechanically and electronically improving himself. Adam Link is powered by storage batteries which must be replaced every forty-eight hours, and he is able to do this himself.

As soon as Dr. Link feels Adam's education is complete, he prepares to announce his perfected invention to the world. Fate intervenes. A loose angle iron from the ceiling falls on Dr. Link's head, crushing his skull. Hearing the noise, Adam rushes to him. His metal fingers become drenched with blood when he lifts the head of his dead creator. At that moment the housekeeper, attracted by the noises, rushes in and sees Adam holding the crushed skull of Dr. Link in his bloody "hands." She dashes from the room.

Adam feels that there is no logical reason to remain, so he puts a fresh battery in place and leaves the house, followed by the dog Terry. Here Binder parallels *Frankenstein*, for Adam Link encounters a small girl who is so frightened by the sight of him that she falls into a brook. In pulling her out of the water he leaves a vivid mark on her leg.

A crowd of people hear the screams of the girl and attack Adam, assuming that the now-crazed robot has escaped from his creator. Armed men bounce bullets off his armor plate. He tries to reason with the men to determine why they are attacking him, but is finally forced to flee. When his battery begins to weaken, he takes one from an automobile. All the next day he is chased; the bullets begin to damage him, but he is emotionally touched only when the dog is killed. Returning to Dr. Link's laboratory, he finds a copy of the book *Frankenstein* and, upon reading it, empathizes with the monster and wonders if he will eventually seek revenge. In the original printing of the first story "I, Robot," (the book version did not carry that title because Isaac Asimov used it in 1950 for his collection of robot stories), the story ends as a signed letter from Adam Link. He is about to switch himself off, rather than kill and injure humans while trying to escape.

The impact of "I, Robot" can be assessed on several levels. It was not only an original approach to the robot theme in science fiction, but also a potent analogy on society's treatment of those who are different. In telling the story from the viewpoint of the robot, Binder brings across the point that this is an intelligent, feeling being who is well-meaning, decent by any meaningful standards, and guilty of nothing more than being a robot.

The sequel, "The Trial of Adam Link, Robot," is unquestionably one of the most remarkable stories ever to appear in science fiction. Saved from the mob by the intervention of the attorney Thomas Link, nephew of Dr. Link, Adam is reactivated. Several questions now arise: Does a robot have any legal rights? As an intelligent, reasoning creature does he have a right to a court trial? What is his status in a world of humans? It is the lawyer's contention that Adam is a new form of life, and as a step toward granting him citizenship, the charges against him should be cleared in a fair trial. When repaired, the first thing Adam Link does is to find the dead body of the dog Terry, bring it back, and bury it. This act convinces the lawyer that he is right in defending Adam Link. The robot is arrested and held on a charge of manslaughter. Out on bail, he heroically rescues two people from sure death in a fire, but no one is aware that he has done it. Everywhere he goes, he is met with fear and hostility.

At the trial, the utter openness and honesty of Adam permits the prosecution to prejudice the court against him. This is partially offset when a group of learned men fire complex scientific questions at him, and his extraordinary intelligence wins the respect of those in the court room. He is, nevertheless, called a "thing without a soul." He is termed "a Frankenstein!" While waiting for the verdict, Adam sees that a child is about to be hit by a car and springs to her aid, saving the child's life. However, it does no good; he is pronounced guilty. He is to die in the electric chair, which will burn out his iridium brain. Binder points out how difficult it is for those who are different to secure a fair trail. They are guilty of being different, regardless of their innocence, and this is enough to condemn them.

In the third story, "Adam Link in Business," the robot is reprieved and then exonerated of the crime while walking to the electric chair. Not only is his bravery in the rescue of the people from the fire and the child from the car revealed, but Dr. Link's housekeeper remembers that when she heard the loud noise, the metal falling on Dr. Link's head, she also heard the loud thumping of Adam's feet as he, like her, rushed to the source of the sound. He had not been in the room with the doctor at the time of his death. Free, Adam Link faces the task of making a living, and he sets up in business as a scientific consultant, utilizing his robot's logic and memory to solve diverse technical problems.

A young reporter, Tom Hall, was the only man who worked for Adam's freedom when he was on trial, and they have become friends. Hall convinces Link to hire his girl friend as a secretary. The girl becomes so enamored of the nobility of most of Adam's actions, that she begins to think she is in love with his mind. Realizing the hopelessness of the situation, he brings her together with Hall and leaves for an isolated spot, where he intends to do himself in, feeling that he is literally an alien in a world of humans. He is saved from suicide by a Dr. Hillory, who channels Adam's mind into building a female robot to be his mental companion. The experiment succeeds, but meanwhile Dr. Hillory has created a device to intercept their electronic circuits and turn the robots into his virtual slaves. Adam escapes from the doctor's control and returns to engage in a grim fight with his female counterpart, whom he had named Eve, knocking her unconscious and forcing Hillory to flee and meet his death. This story again parallels *Frankenstein*, where the monster convinces Dr. Frankenstein to create a mate for him to assuage his loneliness. At each juncture Binder manages a positive variant on the Frankenstein story, showing how it could have been handled differently.

While under the mental control of Hillory, Eve has robbed a bank, and in "Adam Link, Robot Detective," she is arrested. Three gang murders have been rigged to make it appear that she committed them. To save her, Adam Link dons a plastic human disguise and utilizes his superior strength, speed, and mentality to uncover the culprits. He is almost destroyed himself, but Eve breaks out of jail and saves him. Later detective robots, such as Isaac Asimov's R. Daneel Olivaw in *The Caves of Steel*, owe a debt to this story. In this story Binder again underscores the idea that humans are less interested in giving justice to the robot Eve than in finding reasons to destroy her because she is different.

Adam and Eve apply for citizenship at the onset of "Adam Link, Champion Athlete," but they are delayed by red tape because the consequences of legally granting such status to a nonhuman intelligence are unknown. To win public support for his cause, Adam Link enters a series of sports events, including auto racing, bowling, tennis, golf, archery, baseball, and the one-mile run, defeating all opposition. But instead of gaining the support he seeks, his victory creates more fear and hostility. To gain favor Adam Link enters a five hundred mile marathon race. He agrees to wear a monitor to limit his speed and not to make any repairs; the race ends in a tie. After surmounting all obstacles, citizenship is promised, but Adam Link refuses it. When faced with the choice, he feels that citizenship could place future robots in the position of being exploited, with unpleasant results for them as well as the human race.

Three stories in the series were not included in the book: "Adam Link Fights a War" (*Amazing Stories*, December, 1940); "Adam Link in the Past" (February, 1941); and "Adam Link Faces a Revolt" (May, 1941). The book, however, connects earlier stories with "Adam Link Saves the World." In linking "Adam Link, Champion Athlete" with the final story in the series, Binder has the U.S. Army offer Adam immediate citizenship if he will allow himself to be conscripted and build war robots. Adam refuses the offer, thinking that it is better for robots to work for peace even in humble capacities, than to permit themselves to be used for war. He does, however, accept an assignment as a spy. An unknown enemy has built a fortress on the island of Santa Domingo, which all United States strength cannot penetrate. The Secret Service enlists the help of Adam and Eve Link. They manage to get inside the fortress and find that it has been constructed by a race from a planet around the star Sirius, who intend to subjugate the Earth. After considerable intrigue and battle, the robots destroy the invaders. They are given the Congressional Medal of Honor and full citizenship with no strings attached, but the world is never to know of their feat. The government feels it is best that everyone think that the fortress was a last desperate outpost of Nazi Germany, rather than the stronghold of invaders from another world.

Binder wrote for a teenage audience, and there is no trace of subtlety in his work. Yet the writing was effective; beyond that, his imaginative resourcefulness in raising and dealing with the social problems of incorporating intelligent robots into our society prevented the series — except for the last — from becoming simple action-adventure stories. Instead, they are thoughtful, serious works that provided a completely new direction for all the robot stories that came afterward. Undoubtedly, a great and penetrating mind like that of an Olaf Stapledon might have developed the implications of Binder's clearly outlined ideas to magnificent philosophical proportions, but no Stapledon has ever attempted that. Otto Binder gains empathy for his robot character by telling the story from his viewpoint. In doing so, he allows Adam Link, a man of steel, to magnificently extol the equality of man and human rights for all, without resorting to parable or allegory.

Sam Moskowitz

Sources for Further Study

Reviews:

Magazine of Fantasy and Science Fiction. XXX, May, 1966, p. 45

AELITA

Author: Alexei Tolstoi (1882-1945)
First book publication: 1923
English translation: 1959
Type of work: Novel
Time: 1922-1925
Locale: Petrograd and Mars

Two Russians fly to Mars and participate in a workers' revolution

Principal characters:
MSTISLAV SERGEYEVICH LOS, an engineer and spaceship builder
ALEXEI IVANOVICH GUSEV, a former Red Army soldier and adventurer
AELITA, the daughter of Tuscoob, the ruler of Mars
IKHA, her chambermaid
ENGINEER GOR, the leader of the Martian workers
ARCHIBALD SKILES, an American journalist

The life and work of Alexei Nikolaevich Tolstoi may be studied as the apotheosis of the successful "fake" writer. Before the revolution, Tolstoi was known as a facile and prolific workman: bad plays, bad poems, but also some fairly successful stories about the decaying gentry life (*The Lame Prince*, 1912). According to his Soviet hagiography, Tolstoi, supposedly a count, welcomed the February revolution, but was frightened by the October one — he made ideological mistakes. What he did, in fact, was to flee to Odessa and then to Paris, where he joined in the *émigré* life with great gusto. The witty and acerbic memoir by Ivan Bunin, "The Third Tolstoi," shows him striking poses, selling nonexistent Russian estates to *émigré* restorationists, spending more money than he makes, and making plans to earn or borrow more. During this period Tolstoi went on writing voluminously, and of course considered his options. As a cynic, he knew that in Europe he would remain forever an *émigré* writer of no special merit, whereas in Soviet Russia he would be touted as a returned genius, the "third Tolstoi" (after Lev and Alexei Konstantinovich), the Soviet Tolstoi. Making the necessary adjustments, adaptations, and concessions, Count Tolstoi returned to Soviet Russia in 1923. In the same year his new book was published, *Aelita*.

Tolstoi joined the historian Pavel Shchegolyov in writing a play entitled *The Empress's Conspiracy*, which vilified the former royal family. Each author, according to Bunin, received 500,000 rubles and ran off to buy everything he could. In the land of the proletarian dictatorship, Tolstoi remained a grandee, enjoying fine food, clothes, art, and many other luxuries through the famines, purges, and world war. In his almost inimitable way, he could always give what was wanted. In 1933 he went with a cadre of writers on their infamous visit to the White Sea canal, and he "bubbled with enthusiasm" over the slave labor he witnessed. He continued novels begun in emigration, changing them from anti-Bolshevist to pro-Bolshevist. Such were his trilogies, *The Road to Calvary* (1919-1941) and *Peter I* (1917-1945). Although these two Stalin-prize winners have received many accolades from Soviet critics and foreign sympathizers, many Western critics have been considerably less enthusiastic. Romain Rolland called *Peter I* "a gigantic epic, huge, dense and intricate like a forest with its roads, bogs, gaps of sky and shadows." Actually, it could serve as the basis for a university course in mediocre literature. It demonstrates the faults of disconnection (haphazard listing of names, titles, events), disproportion (twenty pages on the loss of Azov *versus* one paragraph on the victory of Azov), disparity (minor figures emphasized over major, the serf Tsigan over Tsar Ivan V), lack of motivation, lifeless narrative, wooden figures, monotony, loose ends, and so on. To round out Tolstoi's career, we should note his novel *Bread* (1937), a paean to Stalin's military genius and a calumny of Leon Trotsky's role in the revolution — a little piece of historical falsification that won Tolstoi even greater favor while millions of his countrymen were being sent to the Gulag Archipelago, tortured and executed.

The first version of *Aelita*, with the subtitle "The Fall of Mars" (*Zakat Marsa*), was written in Berlin in 1922, published in Moscow in the new party journal *Red Virgin Soil*, and put out as a monograph in 1923. A typical Soviet account reads:

> Precisely at this time Tolstoi made a decisive break with his mistaken conceptions, recognized the wisdom, grandeur and justice of the revolution, bound his creative work once and for all with the life and struggle of the Soviet people, which had then just begun to build its own new life. The spiritual searchings of the artist at the beginning of this turning point found an original refraction in the novel *Aelita*.

The same author, V. Shcherbina, considers the novel to be the beginning of Soviet science fiction, predecessor of the works of Belyaev, Obruchev, and Yfremov. She neglects to mention Evgeny Zamyatin's *We* (1920) and Mikhail Bulgakov's *Heart of a Dog* (1925), the most brilliant examples of the genre in Russian literature, which are banned.

The story of *Aelita* is sparse. Engineer Los (his name means "stag"), plagued by longing for his dead wife, seeks oblivion in a space flight. His sole companion on the flight is a demobilized soldier named Gusev (his name, derived from "goose," suggests a lusty man of the soil). The two land on Mars, explore crumbling canals and ruins, meet the Martians, and learn about an ancient conquest of Mars by human beings from Atlantis. Los falls in love with Aelita, daughter of the ruler Tuscoob; her chambermaid falls in love with Gusev. An uprising of the Martian proletarians breaks out, and Gusev takes command. Los pursues Aelita, but eventually joins up with Gusev. The revolution is routed by Tuscoob's counterattack and the Russians escape back to Earth. Gusev arranges to dispatch reinforcements back to Mars, while Los hears the voice of Aelita radioed to Earth, calling to the man she loves.

This idle fantasy hardly deserves comment. It is regular pulp, comicbook material, harmless trivia for people who like trivia. But because it has been praised by the Soviet establishment, because it is an "important" work of a literary colossus, we must give it its due. Taken as light literature, *Aelita* is mindless and mildly entertaining, something on the order of our own mindless *Star Wars*. Treated as serious literature, it is ridiculous, vapid, dead. Its real purpose was to help the Count back into Soviet Russia.

What are the faults? Above all, it lacks motivation. Two stories told by Aelita recount the invasion from Atlantis, establish certain customs on Mars, and motivate the godlike effect of the newly arrived Earthlings. But the inordinate length of these stories, the copious history of Atlantis, with names of tribes, persons, and events never mentioned again, serves no purpose at all. (Tolstoi evidently inserted someone else's speculations about the history of Atlantis.) Lack of motivation can also be seen in small details: when the two Russians land on Mars, they release a mouse to test the air — the mouse has not been mentioned before, it just appears. When Gusev rushes into the revolution, he suddenly has hand grenades, which he "just happened to bring along." A final example is the space flight announced in the first chapter by a tattered shred of paper stuck on a wall, read by a girl, an American newsman and finally Gusev, who becomes the only volunteer. Yet at the ceremony before take off, the "Soviet republic" is given credit for financing the venture and encouraging space exploration. The thinking reader asks: Why didn't the Soviet republic advertise the flight, recruit volunteers, and send experts and party advisers? Why only a scribbled note posted on a back-street? The answer can only lie in a contradictory intention; the author wanted a traditional mysterious opening, a lone inventor, but he also wanted to flatter his new masters.

Every science fiction fantasy must have some kind of quasiscientific premises. Those of *Aelita* appear to be drawn from the writings of Jules Verne, H. G. Wells, and Konstantin Tsiolkovsky. The space ship is a metal ball with parachute brakes, powered by a new explosive called "ultralyddite." Quaint as it is, one might see a hint of our future oddly shaped space capsules. Uncannily, Tolstoi describes a beautiful blue-ball Earth seen from Mars, just as we have seen it from the moon. He also touches on ESP, describes two-way television and dabbles in relativity and time disparity between flight and Earth. All these things indicate intelligence; they are as good for their time as Buck Rogers or Star Trek. (Tolstoi can hardly be faulted for describing the Martian canals, since they were part and parcel of the contemporary view of the planet.) But what motivates the desert terrain of Mars, inhabited by lizards, and the inferior size of the Martians, and the underground catacombs, inhabited by giant spiders, and the animal named the "long-haired khasi — something like a cross between a bear and a cow," and the superior Martian technology (two-way television, powerful radio transmitters, single-person flying machines), and the inferior Martian technology (no spaceships, no grenades, no automobiles)? Ask questions like these, and you realize that the author has simply equipped his Mars with an assortment of science fiction features and a minimum of thought.

The critics make a big fuss over Gusev. Kornei Chukovsky, who should have known better, hailed the appearance of this "monumental" figure: "Gusev is an image of the broadest generalities, raised to the level of a national type. If a foreigner wants to know what kind of people made our revolution, he should be given this book first of all." According to Chukovsky, the creation of this character cost the author little effort, for both were the same: "cheerful, happy, healthy, childish, senseless, a Russian talent in the highest degree." The key word here is "senseless" (*bezumnyi*). Gusev is a big lumpkin, a bogatyr, a laughing killer. In Lucy Flaxman's rather British translation: "A hero, I am — one hell of a brave chap. What I do is pull out my sabre — machine gun or no machine gun — and chop 'em to bits. 'Hands up and surrender, you bastards!' is what I say. I'm chopped up a bit myself, but never give it a thought. . . ."

The critics spill ink about Gusev's revolutionary zeal, his passion for justice, his intention of founding a Soviet republic on Mars. They fail to note that this intention precedes any knowledge of the planet. "My idea is — since we're the first men to come here, Mars is ours — a Soviet planet. We've got to make that official." Much later in the novel the oppressed workers make their appearance and provide Gusev with a social cause. One wonders why the critics did not blast this silly character, instead of making little reservations about his "anarchic tendencies" and need of party leadership.

Los is considered the antithesis of Gusev — a wavering intellectual. Attention is paid to Los's hesitation at the moment of the uprising, when he is seeking Aelita. He puts his personal happiness above the just strivings of the rising masses. No attention is paid to the fact that Aelita was told to poison both Los and Gusev by her father Tuscoob, and she did not do so out of love for Los. Thus, by his selfish interest, Los actually saves himself, the Red hero, and the revolutionary movement. And, of course, no attention is paid to the fact that Los built the spaceship — his brains put Gusev's brawn on the planet. The two characters are sufficient as simple adventurers, but too slight to bear the weight of ideological significance.

That Tolstoi was attempting to say something serious cannot be denied. He raises the question of happiness again and again throughout the novel. Three ideals are set forth. For Tuscoob, happiness is cold wisdom, calm reflection, the spirit facing death without regret; for Gusev, the joy of battle, the conquest of evil, the establishment of a better society; for Los, love for someone who brings joy, harmony, self-forgetfulness, desire to live. One critic, L. Kolobaeva, concludes that the author is not certain which ideal is right. This may be considered one of the book's few successes, since no one else knows either. Certainly the most passion is given to Los's ideal; the flight is taken in search of love, the voice of love comes back to Earth, the novel is named *Aelita*.

In sum, the work is a hash — a mix of traditional science fiction elements, speculations about happiness, political compliments, pseudo-historical meanderings, and naturalistic strokes. In each new edition from 1923 to 1937, Tolstoi tried to smoothe out the rough spots. He deleted gloomy passages about revolution-torn Petrograd, gloomy passages about Los's despair, and embarrassing passages about Gusev's money-grubbing. The translation put out by the Foreign Languages Publishing House, oddly enough, is based on an edition somewhere between the first and the last. It does not contain the passages mentioned above, but it does contain passages missing in 1937. Such as: "She did not hide her nakedness; only a blush of girlish self-consciousness tinged her cheeks. Her bluish shoulders, budding breasts, and narrow hips seemed born of the light of the stars. . . ." Too rich, better cut it.

Aelita was only the first of Tolstoi's ventures into political science fiction. In 1924 he wrote the screenplay of the novel for a film directed by Ya. Protazanov, and in the same year he wrote a play called *Revolt of the Machines*. The play, as it turned out, was not really written by Tolstoi, but adapted to the Soviet scene from *R.U.R.* by Karel Čapek. Maxim Gorky called the act of plagiarism unprecedented in Russian literature. A year later Tolstoi produced the novel *The Hyperboloid of Engineer Garin* (later reworked and renamed) about a Fascist who plans to rule the world with a death ray. A great career was under way.

Gary Kern

Sources for Further Study

Criticism:

Yershov, Peter. *Science Fiction and Utopian Fantasy in Soviet Literature.* New York: Research Program on the USSR, 1954, pp. 19-21. Yershov discusses the importance of *Aelita* in early Soviet science fiction.

AFTER MANY A SUMMER DIES THE SWAN

Author: Aldous Huxley (1894-1963)
First book publication: 1939
Type of work: Novel
Time: Early 1939
Locale: Los Angeles and vicinity, and a country estate near London

A satiric look at the fear of death and the use of power to manipulate human relationships, centering on a private research effort to find a means of prolonging human life, sponsored by a grasping millionaire who hopes to be the beneficiary

Principal characters:
>JO STOYTE, an aging American millionaire
>DR. SIGMUND OBISPO, Stoyte's physician and head of his research team
>JEREMY PORDAGE, an English scholar cataloguing papers acquired by Stoyte
>VIRGINIA MAUNCIPLE, Stoyte's young mistress
>WILLIAM PROPTER, a philosopher and boyhood friend of Stoyte

Among Aldous Huxley's several science fiction novels, *After Many a Summer Dies the Swan* is the closest in theme and tone to the satiric novels of ideas which made his reputation. Set in a time just before its publication — the early months of 1939 — it takes its plot and title from a scientific extrapolation; but this extrapolation is only one element in a broad, richly orchestrated theme. The other elements, sexual, political, and social, pivot on the concerns of science fiction.

The story is simple. Jo Stoyte, a sixty-year-old Tennessean who has become an oil millionaire and a powerful figure in Southern California, fears death. In part his fear results from the religious fanaticism of his dead wife; in part it represents the simple greed of a self-made man who wishes to hold on to his manifold acquisitions. As a businessman, Stoyte recognizes the value of organized, well-funded efforts to solve technical problems; accordingly, he has employed Dr. Sigmund Obispo as both personal physician and chief of a research team seeking the secret of longevity. Obispo and his assistant, Pete Boone, are furnished with an exceptionally well-equipped laboratory in Stoyte's mansion, a grotesquely Gothic structure perched on a mountain near Los Angeles; their experiments, when the novel opens, have already succeeded in narrowing the physiological basis of longevity to the digestive system.

Stoyte's greed for life is matched by his greed for possessions, a lust which triggers the action of the book. For among the many assorted artifacts Stoyte has acquired in plundering Europe with his money are the papers of the impoverished Hauberk family, English nobility who have died down to a pair of aged spinsters. To catalogue the Hauberk Papers, Stoyte has hired — sight unseen — Jeremy Pordage, a fifty-four-year-old English man of letters who lives in detached, contemplative withdrawal with his mother. Pordage's work with the

Hauberk papers unexpectedly provides Obispo with the materials he needs for success in two areas, his research in longevity and his attempt to seduce Virginia (Baby) Maunciple, Stoyte's beautiful but stupid young mistress. These materials are the journal of the Fifth Earl of Hauberk, born two centuries before, and the works of the Marquis de Sade. Pordage and Obispo find that the Fifth Earl had anticipated Obispo's experiments and had extended his life and improved his health by consuming the raw entrails of the giant carp living in the fish pond of the Hauberk estate; Obispo's hypothesis, that some peculiar flora living in the intestines of carp caused the fish's long lives, is thus proved. Obispo also borrows another treasure of the Hauberk papers: a copy of Sade's *Les Cent-Vingt Jours de Sodome,* found bound as *The Book of Common Prayer*; translating it for Baby, he seduces her, as much to experiment with the methods of seduction and its effect on the subject as to enjoy the sexual activity.

Stoyte, of course, eventually finds Baby and Obispo together. In his rage he fetches his revolver, intending to shoot Obispo; but the doctor's place at Virginia's side has been taken by Pete, an idealistic boy whose infatuation with the girl has already caused Stoyte some jealous pangs. Unable in his state to discriminate, Stoyte kills Pete. Obispo — for a price — covers up the murder. He has now destroyed his assistant (and rival) and his mistress; not content with blackmail, he seems to attempt to gain total power over Stoyte by taking the old man and Baby to the Hauberk estate near London. There they find — as Obispo and Pordage had deduced they would — the Fifth Earl, still alive at 201 in a subterranean apartment but now grotesquely devolved into an apelike creature incapable of human speech and seemingly motivated only by his lust for his equally old and equally degenerate female companion, formerly his housekeeper. To Obispo's surprise and amusement, Stoyte's greed for life is so great that he expresses willingness to live even such a life. Huxley prudently and abruptly ends the novel on that note.

The thinness of the plot is obvious; but plot has never been the reason for reading a Huxley novel. Rather, the reader expects deft satiric characterization and a barrage of ideas, amusingly articulated by the amusing characters. In Huxley's great novels of manners and ideas, the talk (and there is a lot of it, witty and occasionally profound) is the reason to keep reading. And so it is here. Huxley gives us not only Pordage's mordant opinions on life and literature and Obispo's acid comments on science and longevity, but also the wisdom of William Propter, a schoolfellow of Stoyte now living humbly in the shadow of Stoyte's castle. The contrast among the three is sharp. Obispo, as his actions show, is an arrogant, selfish, cynical man incapable of any emotion requiring warmth or giving — even his conquest of Ginny is detached and clinical in its manipulation of the naïve, intellectually inferior girl. Pordage is his opposite: effete, self-conscious, dilettantish, living by choice a carefully circumscribed life dominated by his admittedly minor work, his mother, and his fortnightly trips to the squalid apartment of two prostitutes who constitute his only other human contact. Both Obispo and Pordage are vain men; though their vanity takes extravagantly different forms, both consider themselves superior to all others and judge the whole of life by their own parochial standards.

Not so Propter, who is the intellectual center of the novel. A former professor, he has written a literary study which is one of Pordage's favorite books. But he is also a technological genius; he generates the electricity for his house by using a solar generator of his own design. This gesture is, he says, his way of gaining independence — economic independence from the Stoyte-controlled corporations. Democracy has been ruined by gigantism in government and business, for the people can no longer support themselves economically and have consequently become politically and intellectually dependent as well. Propter's ideas are contrary not only to Stoyte's — for example, the millionaire exploits migrant workers, while Propter tries to help them establish better living conditions and fend for themselves — but to Pete's, for the boy is a Marxist who had fought, before experiencing heart problems, in the Spanish Civil War which is just ending. Hence, Propter connects two triangles of ideas: Obispo-Pordage-Propter with regard to the relationship among life, mind, and the universe, Stoyte-Boone-Propter with regard to the social mechanisms appropriate to the fulfillment of human potentials. Much of the novel is given to multiparty conversations about these issues; unfortunately, Propter too often assumes his professorial role and lectures the other parties, who can seldom match his humility, compassion for fellow human beings, and maturity. Huxley's failure to dramatize these issues, rather than merely articulating them, accounts in part for the book's lesser reputation among his novels.

What Huxley handles well are the major theme and the ironic tone. The latter is of course one of his hallmarks; here it pervades the novel, as usual, except in those passages when Propter is speaking (preaching). Some examples: Stoyte, obsessed by fear of death, is proprietor of a huge, vulgar cemetery which is evidently a major element in his income; Pete's death is ascribed to his heart problems, and indeed his infatuation has caused it; Virginia, a model, actress, and kept woman, is intensely devoted to the Virgin Mary. Much of the irony is satire directed, in the best Evelyn Waugh-Christopher Isherwood manner, at the extravagant society of Southern California, which Huxley perceived as emblematic of American debasement at large: the Beverly Pantheon cemetery, with its mildly erotic statuary and recorded music; the Stoyte mansion, with its replica (for Virginia) of the grotto at Lourdes and its Vermeer hanging in the elevator; Tarzana College, a Stoyte charity presided over by Dr. Mulge and incorporating all the objectionable elements of American higher education; even the roadsigns and roadside establishments peculiar to our highways. Huxley is often hilarious in handling his targets.

The central theme of the novel is only occasionally handled with the same hilarity. Huxley's theme is power, a topic that allowed little lightness in the grim year of 1939. Power is the obsession, in one way or another, of all the characters. Stoyte has power over people and economic affairs, but wants power over life itself. Obispo seeks power in sexual matters and over Stoyte's affairs. Baby holds the power of sexual attraction over Stoyte and Pete. Pete and Propter wish to destroy Stoyte's economic power and to restore it, in widely divergent ways, to the people. Pordage, meanwhile, glories in his lack of power over his own affairs, having never freed himself from his mother. Huxley's handling of this complex set of ambitions and dreams is philosophically ambivalent. On the one hand, Propter argues for the ability of individuals to control their own lives and for the necessity of assuming responsibility for one's own destiny, quoting the Bible and human history for evidence. On the other hand, Propter's own experiments in individuality can exist only through the sufferance of Stoyte, and Propter's attempts to lead others to his form of salvation-through-self-reliance fail. The reader, in fact, is driven to conclude that free will (a term not used in the novel) is a sham; that lives are governed by chance events — Pordage's opening at random the Hauberk crate containing the Fifth Earl's journal and the Sade novel, Obispo's casual picking up of the novel from Pordage's work table, Ginny's ignorance of French, Pete's arrival at Ginny's side at the instant the jealous Stoyte returns. The universe is deterministic; the power we gain is not illusory, but it is subject to forces beyond our control and is in consequence transient and uncertain.

Throughout, Huxley uses literary and historical allusions — usually heavy with irony in the source or in the application — to help the reader orient himself in this bleak philosophy. The first is the title, a quotation from Tennyson's "Tithonus." In that celebrated dramatic monologue, Tithonus — grown horribly old because his love for the goddess Aurora was rewarded with eternal life, but not with eternal youth — prays to his divine mistress for the release of death. The parallels with the Fifth Earl of Hauberk and Stoyte are obvious. Equally obvious are the use of Sade, the "Divine Marquis" whose reputation rests on erotic novels (like the one used by Obispo to seduce Ginny) celebrating the use of power and violence in sexual relationships, and Freud, whose first name is shared by Obispo, also a clinical researcher in the psychology of sex. More arcane is the use of Miguel de Molinos (1628-1696), author of a *Spiritual Guide* and a leader in the contemplative Quietist movement. Later condemned by the Holy Office for his sexual immorality, Molinos attempted to justify it as purifying; his supposed letters to the then-Lady Hauberk spell out his Quietist position, which Obispo naturally attacks, unaware of the resemblance of his own sexual activities to Molinos'. Indeed, Obispo's own last name may refer to San Luis Obispo de Tolosa, a mission and town on the Pacific Coast north of Los Angeles. St. Louis (1274-1297), a noted ascetic who gave up a crown for his religion and ministered with great compassion to the less fortunate, contrasts starkly with the physician of the novel, whose religion is of dispassionate exploitation of sensuality and intellect — his own and others'.

Again and again, these allusions and others underline the grim stance of the book: there is no basis but power for the constructing of human relations, since the universe eludes the final control of man, whose need for mastery can be discharged by the exercise in petty life of the power he lacks in facing the rest of the cosmos. Stoyte controls money and people, including Virginia and Pordage; Obispo controls Stoyte and has power over Virginia; Virginia owns cages full of baboons; Jeremy defers to his mother and sorts old papers. Those who step beyond these narrow, personal bonds are crushed: Peter tries to free Spain, suffers heart disease, and dies because of a ghastly mistake of his employer. The novel is thus a grim, comic dance on a precipice of despair. But what else could Huxley write in 1939? Munich is past when the novel opens; Barcelona falls just before Pete does: Fascism was waking, war was in the offing. Propter's "Jeffersonian democracy" promised dignity and peace to the individual, but the hostile forces — the ones with the real power — surrounded him too. Perhaps the feeling person could cry; the thinking one has only the prophylactic of laughter.

William H. Hardesty III

Sources for Further Study

Reviews:

Booklist. XXXVI, February 15, 1940, p. 238.

Books. January 28, 1940, p. 2.

Boston Transcript. January 27, 1940, p. 1.

New Statesman. XVIII, October 14, 1939, p. 524.

New York Times. January 28, 1940, p. 2.

New Yorker. XV, January 27, 1940, p. 58.

Saturday Review. XXI, January 27, 1940, p. 5.

Times Literary Supplement. October 14, 1939, p. 591.

ALAS, BABYLON

Author: Pat Frank (Harry Hart, 1907-   )
First book publication: 1959
Type of work: Novel
Time: The present
Locale: In and around Fort Repose, a small town in Florida

A small group of people in a rural Florida community struggle to survive after a nuclear holocaust

> Principal characters:
> RANDY BRAGG, organizer of Fort Repose's postwar survival effort
> MARK BRAGG, Randy's brother, an Air Force Colonel in the Strategic Air Command
> HELEN BRAGG, Mark's wife
> BEN FRANKLIN BRAGG, Mark and Helen's thirteen-year-old son
> PEYTON BRAGG, Mark and Helen's eleven-year-old daughter
> DAN GUNN, the local doctor
> SAM HAZZARD, a retired Navy Admiral
> LIB MCGOVERN, Randy's current girl friend
> BILL AND LAVINIA MCGOVERN, Lib's parents
> THE HENRYS, Randy's next-door neighbors

Many novels and short stories have attempted to depict the aftermath of a nuclear war, and almost all of these works have dealt with the civilian survivors rather than with the warriors themselves. The reason for this is obvious; unlike previous wars, a nuclear war will be fought not in the trenches but from computerized command centers on land, at sea, and in the air. Moreover, no part of the world will be safe during such a war, although some places may be less dangerous than others, and such a war will be over with relative swiftness. Large cities, seats of government, and military/industrial complexes all over the world will be the main targets. Billions of men, women, and children will die; and, perhaps, a few may be left to attempt to carry on. This is the basis of Pat Frank's novel, *Alas, Babylon*.

It is obvious, even at this early point, that Frank's novel is an optimistic one compared to such extrapolations as Nevil Shute's *On the Beach* (1957). In Shute's book, everyone dies, if not from the initial warfare then from the radioactive fallout which follows. Shute's story is set in Australia, the last stronghold of life as the prevailing winds bring the fallout further and further into the southern hemisphere. Shute attempts to show the various ways in which people might react to such an awesome and predictable fate. Frank's book, on the other hand, shows a fortunate and valiant few surviving in spite of their mistakes.

Randy Bragg, the main character in the book, is a fortunate survivor. On one level, he is fortunate in the ways that any survivor of a nuclear war must be. He does not live in or near a main target area, nor does he live directly downwind from one. As a result, Randy and the small community in and around Fort Repose miss the initial blast and the deadly quantities of fallout as well. Moreover, their geographical location, Florida, is one in which basic survival is relatively easy. The weather is not severe, crops grow easily in the long growing season, and there is plenty of water in which a variety of edible water creatures live. And the community is fairly small so that the food supply, although not bounteous, is adequate for all. Randy is also fortunate in having friends who possess a variety of skills and kinds of knowledge which significantly increase the community's potential for survival. Bill McGovern and Malachai Henry are good with small machines, Dan Gunn is a doctor, Sam Hazzard knows how to sail, and Alice Cooksey, the local librarian, uncovers pertinent information on topics such as edible local plants.

On another level, Randy has at least one stroke of good fortune which is his alone. His brother, Mark, is an Air Force Colonel in SAC Intelligence. As a result, Mark is in on the activities which will lead to this war, and as he senses its closeness, he arranges for Randy to take care of Helen, Ben Franklin, and Peyton. Mark knows that he will be at SAC Headquarters in Omaha when the war breaks out, and since Omaha will be a number one target area, Mark wants his wife and children to be in a somewhat less dangerous place — Fort Repose. Mark's cabled warning, "Alas, Babylon!," alerts Randy to the arrival of Helen and the children as well as to the probability of imminent war.

"Alas, Babylon!" is a signal of distress that Mark and Randy have used since childhood. The boys first heard the phrase during secret visits to the First Afro-Repose Baptist Church where, hiding in the back, they heard Preacher Henry describe the Babylonian revels. The sermon also described the destruction of the wicked and their wicked city, and Preacher Henry always ended with "Alas, Babylon!" This phrase, the accompanying Biblical passages, and Mark Bragg's explanation of how the current situation came about make it clear that Frank blames not just the men in power but the entire Russian-American culture for the war; he seems to be suggesting that all of the people, from high to low, who have let the world become what it is are responsible, as all of the Babylonians were responsible for the condition of their city.

Randy receives Mark's warning, Helen and the children arrive, and the bombs and missiles begin falling. For the people of Fort Repose, the war consists of bright flashes (one of which temporarily blinds Peyton) and Earth tremors. It is only later — in some cases, weeks or months later — that the destruction of the fabric of civilization is felt by the people of Fort Repose. All of those goods and services provided in a complex, technological society gradually diminish, and many cannot be compensated for in this small community. Randy, forewarned though he is, is not much better prepared for the calamity than is the average citizen; many of his hurried purchases, such as milk and meat, are good only until the electricity ceases to flow, and this happens within days. His primary advantage is psychological. He knew that the war was coming, and when it arrives, the psychological shock is less extreme for him than for many others. He is, therefore, able to pick up the pieces and try to put things together more quickly than almost anyone else.

The initial problems involve supplying the goods and services necessary to stay alive, those goods and services previously purchased and now, perhaps, unavailable. The first service to be lost is electricity. Without electricity, Randy's freezer becomes a morass of melted ice cream, liquified butter, and floating cuts of meat. Some of the meat is dried or salted for later use, but most of it is consumed in a final steak cookout. In addition, without cool storage, some medicines lose their potency; Lavinia McGovern, a diabetic, dies when her insulin runs out. Without any means of generating power the community cannot produce its own electricity and must use alternative sources: fires are used for heat and for cooking, kerosene lamps and candles are used for light, and canning, salting, and drying are used to preserve food.

Another item taken for granted, water, is also in short supply. First, there is no electricity to run the pumps to bring water to the houses, and second, there is no way of knowing how much radiation there is in the water. Both problems are solved quite easily, however. Randy remembers that the Henrys have an artesian well, and soon pipes are run, making it possible for the underground water to flow to the Bragg house and several other houses as well.

All items previously transported into Fort Repose and sold in the stores are also lost. The common things that people use every day and take for granted — coffee, sugar, salt, and the like — are consumed first and, perhaps, missed the most. In some cases, the loss is permanent; there is no substitute for coffee. In other cases, local products must fill the gap; honey is substituted for sugar, and a salt source is found nearby. The hardware stores and the liquor stores are, along with the grocery stores, the first to be sold out. Most stores do a thriving business, but only for a few days. Ultimately, people come to realize that the items they have are of value and that money is of no use; the monetary system collapses, and for the most part, people return to bartering goods and services.

Once the day-to-day difficulties of survival are under control, even if only for the time being, another kind of problem appears. The new problem revolves around the destruction and disruption caused by the war and concerns the various people who cannot make the psychological adjustment to the change. A number of people die of heart attacks on the first day, and Dan Gunn suggests that it is fear rather than any physical condition that has killed them. There are hotel guests who continue to live in their rooms without fresh laundry or functioning bathrooms. They refuse to believe that things have actually changed, and even as their own filth piles up around them, they fully expect that everything will be set working again soon. But the person with the most obvious trouble is Edgar Quisenberry, the town's banker. Unable to accept the fact that money will no longer be the hub on which the world turns, Mr. Quisenberry digs out his father's old pistol and commits suicide. For each of these people, the changes brought about by the war are too drastic for them to accept. Instead of getting out and working to make the best of it, as Randy and his group do, these people give up and die, refuse to believe, or commit suicide.

Another aspect of the problem of psychological adjustment involves a choice of behavior. One of the first casualties in an event such as an all-out nuclear war may well be official law and order; those governmental agencies may cease to function. Randy sees signs of this on the very first day. He passes a group of road-gang convicts who are armed and have killed their guards. This is but a harbinger; throughout much of the novel there is the very real possibility that violence could sweep Fort Repose under. Addicts raid the clinic, kill three people, and take all of the drugs. Looters hit the jewelry stores and the liquor stores. Travelers and people living in isolated spots are the targets of roving gangs who take what they want and kill anyone in their way. With no one being really concerned with anyone else's behavior, people now have only their own ethics to guide them, and many choose selfishness and violence.

Perhaps the central episode of this kind is the assault on Dr. Gunn. As he goes about his rounds, Dr. Gunn is set upon, robbed and beaten, and left for dead. His medical bag is stolen, and (perhaps worst of all) his glasses are broken. Randy, acting by government order and on his rank in the Army Reserve, forms a provisional company and hunts the gang down. Three are killed in the ensuing gun battle; the other is taken prisoner and duly hanged in the town square as a warning to all.

It is an interesting point that the superior defensive capability of "Bragg's Troop," in effect, a military group, is responsible for peace. Frank seems to have come full circle in the novel. Military and political power chart the course which leads to the war, and now a similar, albeit much less powerful, military and political organization brings peace to Fort Repose. It is not the power that is the villain here; Frank seems to be suggesting that the proper use of power is beneficial but that, perhaps, the wrong people have been using it in the wrong manner. Randy entered the state political primaries some years back and was defeated by a politician who appealed to bigotry and fear. The Navy Ensign, who fires the missile which begins the actual war, uses the power of his plane to compensate for his lack of physical stature. Both of these men are examples of the wrong people being in control of power; Randy, in the ethical structure of the novel, uses his power for the right reasons — to establish peace and insure the continuance of civilization within the current circumstances.

The book, then, as Frank suggests in his introduction, is both a warning and an ethical statement. In dramatizing the possible effects of a nuclear war, Frank is attempting to make pictures out of statistics, and in doing so, he takes the impersonal data of Civil Defense pamphlets and makes the reader aware of how such a situation might affect him and his lifestyle. Frank's ethical statement is also important; everyone has a responsibility to prevent the next war, as everyone will be involved in it. Americans, especially, because of their distance from World Wars I and II, need to recognize that their oceans will be no protection next time. Everyone must, therefore, be aware of the power that has been created and must be sure that the right people are in control of that power. That Pat Frank is able to present all of this in very readable and enjoyable prose enhances the whole package so that only the most cynical reader will criticize the book's somewhat romanticized picture of these gallant survivors.

C. W. Sullivan III

Sources for Further Study

Criticism:

Blakesley, Richard. *"Alas, Babylon,"* in *Chicago Sunday Tribune.* March 22, 1959, p. 1. Blakesley calls this an enthralling, vivid tale of a nuclear catastrophe.

Dempsey, David. *"Alas, Babylon,"* in *New York Times Book Review.* March 22, 1959, p. 43. Dempsey calls this a scare novel of modern nuclear attack.

Spearman, Walter. *"Alas, Babylon,"* in *Saturday Review.* XLII (June 13, 1959), p. 20. Frank has created a fantasy real enough to send a chill through the reader.

Reviews:

Analog. LXIV, September, 1959, pp. 145-147.

Booklist. LV, May 1, 1959, p. 476.

Galaxy. XVIII, December, 1959, p. 150.

Kirkus Reviews. XXVII, January 15, 1959, p. 67.

Library Journal. LXXXIV, April 1, 1959, p. 115.

Luna Monthly. XXIV–XXV, May–June, 1971, p. 63.

New York Herald Tribune Book Review. March 22, 1959, p. 6.

New Yorker. XXV, April 4, 1959, p. 166.

San Francisco Chronicle. March 29, 1959, p. 15.

Times Literary Supplement. September 25, 1959, p. 541.

THE ALTERATION

Author: Kingsley Amis (1922-   )
First book publication: 1976
Type of work: Novel
Time: 1976
Locale: Oxford and London

Set in an alternate universe in which the Reformation never took place, this novel presents the unsuccessful rebellion of a child against a Church and a State which intend to castrate him in order to preserve his singing voice

> *Principal characters:*
> HUBERT ANVIL, an eleven-year-old chorister
> POPE JOHN XXIV, a tone-deaf Yorkshireman, who collects works of art and music
> FATHER LYALL, Hubert's father's chaplain, and his mother's lover
> CORNELIUS VAN DEN HAAG, Ambassador of the Republic of New England
> THOMAS, Hubert's friend, who eventually becomes a writer of science fiction

Like *Brave New World*, *Nineteen Eighty-Four*, or *Out of the Silent Planet*, *The Alteration* is a science fiction novel written by an author with a major reputation as a writer outside the science fiction genre. Such works have many advantages; they survey the science fiction field from outside, avoid the clichés that genre writers are often tempted to use, and exploit a kind of irony based on the contrast between the individual work and its formula-shaping predecessors. At the same time, they have the liberty to use all that is best and most successful within science fiction itself, to remind people of the purpose of science fiction. Since Amis, among other nongenre writers, is often met with considerable initial misunderstanding, it is important to see how *The Alteration* both uses science fiction tradition, and extends that tradition's potential.

The Alteration is an "alternate universe" novel, like Philip K. Dick's *The Man in the High Castle*, Keith Roberts' *Pavane*, or Harry Harrison's *A Transatlantic Tunnel, Hurrah!* — all works jokingly referred to within the text. The event which has set the universe of this novel on an alternate path from our own is the nonexistence of the Protestant Reformation. In this world's history, the Northern nations of Europe were preserved from schism by the adoption of Martin Luther as Pope, followed by Sir Thomas More. As a result Christendom (with the exception of the Republic of New England) is Catholic, monarchist, conservative, and paradoxically, the influence of Rome is far greater than we would expect. The language of diplomacy is Italian, not French, and instead of restaurant, carafe, plaque, caprice, and détente, people say ristorante, caraffa, placca, capriccio, detensione.

Although these minor points of vocabulary demonstrate the greater range of the classically educated author (many science fiction writers would not think of going so minutely into cultural background), they nevertheless show a grasp of one of the most essential points of the "alternate universe" idea — details are vital. These are used partly to create the sense of a complex life just beyond the universe's boundaries; but within the confines of science fiction the even stronger reason for concentrating on minutiae is the perception that the most trivial everyday facts nonetheless possess a history and a meaning. Things do not have to be the way they are. When Kingsley Amis comments in passing on the proximity of Tobias Anvil's house to Tyburn Tree (the last public hanging was in 1961), or on the appalling inflation rate (no less than three hundred percent since 1900) reflected in its price, he reminds us that we accept too readily the normality of things-as-they-are. We would be horrified at the thought of public executions in a civilized state, but we shrug off our own rate of inflation, far in excess of any previous civilization's experience. Although there is no connection between these two data, or between them and any other of the scores of facts incidentally thrown in, the facts nevertheless conspire to create a whole. One can deduce a culture's history and expectations from trivialities, in reality as well as in fantasy. Alternate universe novels, in short, do not tell us about the way things might happen. They tell us how things do happen.

One of the self-perceptions that *The Alteration* offers is that art in our civilization has been squeezed to the periphery. The novel's first scene is in the great cathedral of St. George at Coverley (or Cowley) near Oxford, which is enriched by paintings, windows, mosaics, and music from all the major English artists of the last three centuries: Wren, Turner, Gainsborough, William Morris, David Hockney. These are men who have remained outside or opposed to the Church, and who have made an impression, in some cases, only within very restricted circles. The same artistic profusion shows itself in Rome, and in the history of music. In Amis' world Mozart lived to old age; how fortunate, one might think, how much to be desired. Besides, under a united Christendom many of the disasters of our century never took place. There is a Bishop in Hanoi, and one in Nagasaki, and without the driving pressure of Protestant states on the Atlantic seaboard, the American skies are still darkened by passenger pigeons. The world of *The Alteration* seems, in many respects, more reverent and beautiful than our own.

But this world has been achieved at the cost of loss of liberty. United Christendom gives almost total power to the Pope, and the Church imposes laws and restrictions which we would regard as intolerable. The punishment for repeated fornication under theocratic governments in England and America is death, contraception is illegal, and the Secular Arm of the Holy Office draws to itself the likes of Himmler and Beria, initially seen kneeling in Coverley Cathedral. The "alteration" of the title refers first to historical change, but second to the operation which is to be carried out on Hubert Anvil, an eleven-year-old chorister. He is to be castrated so that he will be able to sing soprano (to God's glory) with the pitch of a boy but the power of a full-grown man.

This sort of operation was actually performed regularly in Italy not very long ago, and Amis has remarked that the inspiration for the novel came to him on hearing such a singer on a gramophone record. The time span for *castrati* overlaps with electricity; like public executions, they are not as far in the past as one might hope. So, beauty and cruelty go together. Sexuality and devotion, on the other hand, are opposed. A further complication is that sexuality and artistic creation seem to be linked. Hubert's tutor explains that Hubert may be a great singer as a castrato, but his precocious Mozart-like gift for composition will probably be destroyed. No great singer has ever also been able to compose. The pressures are too strong, and genius in any case is mysterious and finely balanced.

Although Amis' mode is within the science fiction tradition, his themes tend to reach outside the genre; few science fiction authors would feel competent, as Amis does, to discuss creativity or the history of art, or even consider such topics especially important.

At first, *The Alteration* stays close to tradition in its handling of science and of America, but not for long. Hubert, faced with castration, runs away to the New England ambassador. The ambassador offers him asylum and escape in an airship to America where (we hear) Protestantism, democracy, and technology all flourish together, as they have done in so many novels since the time of Mark Twain. The experienced science fiction reader feels he is on home ground, as if he is reading a "revolution story," or a story of "science against superstition." So it seems. But the pattern is reversed with violent irony just as Hubert is told he is finally and completely safe. America is suddenly devalued as a kindly pastor begins to explain to Hubert why he must be cautious in communicating with Red Indians, who, it should be realized, are racially inferior, with smaller brains — at best children in comparison with white men. That is why the New England sages have developed a policy called "separateness." One is left to reflect that even in our history, liberal protestantism has been marked as strongly by racism as by technology. The issue of science *versus* superstition is not as clear as many science fiction authors would make it.

In an approach that is diametrically opposed to science fiction formulae, all the revolutions within *The Alteration* fail. Hubert's mother, her sexuality momentarily awakened by her husband's chaplain, Father Lyall, is returned brusquely to male domination. Father Lyall is gelded by the Secular Arm. Decuman, Hubert's gallant and rebellious friend, ends fighting with great distinction in a war which the Pope has engineered to reduce population pressure and thus resistance to his authority; he is enslaved without even knowing it. Hubert, within the New England airship, is struck down apparently by the finger of God: his testicles twist round each other in a rare (but real) phenomenon known as "bilateral torsion," and he must be castrated to save his life.

This ending caused the most outcry among reviewers, ironically, because it presumes the existence of God. Until this development in the novel, the modern, probably half-agnostic reader has assumed that all the paraphernalia of religion are merely erroneous, the products of a prescientific society. But this phenomenon suggests that God not only exists, but furthermore responds to the prayers of His servant Abbot Thynne, who has prayed for Hubert to be returned. Amis has God work in cruel rather than mysterious ways. In 1900 this might have seemed normal for a science fiction writer; consider, for instance, H. G. Wells's atheism in *The Island of Doctor Moreau*. However, in 1976 it revives the issues of human conscience, creativity, and sexuality. All of these issues are allied in *The Alteration*, but they are allied against the Church and organized religion. The dimly perceived implication is almost Manichaean: a good and an evil force war against each other through the lives of men — and the evil one wins, for a time. There remains a hint of successful resistance at the end as Thomas, Hubert's other friend, confesses that in spite of Church disapproval, he is able to make a living writing "TR," Time Romance, the equivalent of science fiction. In the castrated or undeveloped world of *The Alteration*, one might say that science fiction is the last faint trickle of testosterone in the body politic.

In spite of its real and apparent ironies, *The Alteration* remains a work of profound humanity, one which indeed considers the very essence of human nature. Can character survive circumstance? Are men really independent? The questions are eternal. One finds them, for example, in Chaucer's fourteenth century poem, the *Knight's Tale*, which asks continually, "What is this worlde? What asketh men to have?" But some things can only be learned about this world by considering other worlds. Some subjects, Amis shows us, can be treated only in romance — and nowhere, perhaps, more effectively than in the new variety of romance that calls itself science fiction.

T. A. Shippey

Sources for Further Study

Criticism:

Clemons, Walter. "Briefly Noted Fiction," in *New Yorker*. LIII (March 14, 1977), p. 138. An article discussing *The Alteration* as being one of Amis' most amusing, ironic novels.

Cook, Bruce. "Autumn Anger," in *Saturday Review*. IV (February 5, 1977), pp. 28-29. Cook analyzes the author as being a man who has grown angry as revealed in his novel.

Reviews:

Atlantic. CCXXXIX, February, 1977, p. 98.

Choice. XIV, May, 1977, p. 366.

Library Journal. CII, April 1, 1977, p. 830.

New Republic. CLXXVI, May 28, 1977, p. 39.

New Statesman. XCII, October 8, 1976, p. 483.

New York Review of Books. XXIV, March 3, 1977, p. 31.

New York Times Book Review. January 30, 1977, p. 4.

Newsweek. LXXXIX, January 17, 1977, p. 84.

Time. CIX, January 3, 1977, p. 81.

Times Literary Supplement. October 8, 1976, p. 1269.

ANALOGUE MEN

Author: Damon Knight (1922-   )
First book publication: 1955 (as *Hell's Pavement*)
Type of work: Novel
Time: 2134
Locale: The North American Continent

An anti-Utopian study of a future world in which dissent or freedom of choice is eradicated through the use of the analogue, a scientific device for modifying and controlling human behavior

>*Principal characters:*
>DR. KUSKO, inventor of the analogue device
>LAUDERMILK, leader of the underground revolutionary movement against "normal" analogue society
>ARTHUR BASS, a new recruit to the underground movement
>ANNE SILVERS, a veteran underground agent

Damon Knight's *Analogue Men* is a surprising novel when considered against its historical background. The 1950's, as we have often been reminded, was a decade of political reactionism, McCarthyism, and Red-baiting, a decade in which attacks on the free enterprise system and associated democratic institutions were viewed as suspect, even heretical. And the "surprising" character of the work is perhaps best summed up by the main burden of the narrative plot. Yet *Analogue Men*, written in a time when so many anti-Utopian novels in the *Nineteen Eighty-Four* tradition defined their Orwellian futures in terms of the inevitable evils of big government, is really concerned with the evil political consequences of big business.

The initial crisis is generated by the usual scientific breakthrough with the familiar fears of government-inspired exploitation of the new discovery to the detriment of democratic institutions and humanistic values. In this case, the discovery is Dr. Kusko's analogue, a neurological device implanted in the brain in order to modify behavior and, in the process, eliminate violence and wars forever. But despite some initial misgivings by some of Kusko's colleagues, the ultimate abuse of the new device does not originate with the politicos and ideologues of organized factions or government itself, but with big business. If analogue science can control human behavior on a mass scale for the purpose of maintaining law and order, then it is of incalculable value in manipulating the tastes, and with them the profits, of the marketplace. This reasoning eventually leads to a world in which North America (the novel's setting) is a vast plutocracy which is carved into territories or enclaves, each governed by powerful commercial interests like Umerc (United Merchandise) and Gepro (General Products). In effect, in this work Big Brother is Big Business, the repressive ideology is the profit motive of the consumer's marketplace, and thanks to the behavior modifications of the analogue, political control is defined by the commercial manipulation of individual fears and desires.

Clearly Knight's basic plot contains within it the potential for an innovative and highly thought-provoking treatment of consumer society; and to a considerable degree that potential is realized. Interestingly enough, long before it became fashionable to engage in consumer politics or to question the growth-oriented priorities of a consumer culture, Knight's work raised some disturbing questions. For at the base of *Analogue Men* is the insistence that the society described is sick. Since the analogue does not cure emotional problems (a proclivity towards violence, for example) but simply controls or manipulates them, the society really functions by maintaining, even stimulating, neurological disorders on a massive scale. Hence all the prevailing modes of individual or organized conduct are symptoms of mental illness, whether it is the power hunger of the "family" members of the plutocracy, or those compulsions and insecurities which drive the consumer to consume.

From one point of view the profitable "built-ins" of the consumer culture make sound economic "sense": the built-in obsolescence which ensures ever-increasing production which, in turn, is vital to meet the demands of a growing population (of consumers); the system of easy credit in which it is essential to establish a line of credit and criminal to be stingy with it; the easily available supplies of money (in the territory of Umerc) which are valuable only for a limited period but which fuel frenzied buying sprees while they last. But from another point of view, such a system makes no sense; it is all an absurdity, an inherently irrational system with no demonstrable purpose beyond maintaining itself. This kind of irrational purposelessness is best demonstrated by the very existence of a designated class of consumers whose only *raison d'etre* is to consume.

Finally, the irrationality of the system becomes the author's extended metaphor for personal neuroses, whether of the "normals" (those persons who have had the analogue treatment) or of the "immunes," who either manage to avoid the treatment or have proven immune to it. Knight makes a telling point by labeling as "normal" those who have been subjected to the analogue treatment, for the implication (one that has disturbing significance for our own society) is that "normalcy" consists of mental disorders which have become standard criteria for acceptable behavior simply because the prevailing order wishes them to be so. The gloomy patriarchy of Gepro society, for example, enforces a code of sexual repression which complements the government's political and economic repressiveness; the fleshpots and gambling dens of Umerc are really the other side of the Gepro coin, providing a deceptive and temporary release from the "normal" restrictions of analogue society; and in the Conind matriarchy one finds an affirmation, by way of grotesque parody, of the psychosexual pathology of Gepro's patriarchy.

In turn these implications raise basic questions about the nature of mental health or normalcy. How is it defined? Is it determined on the basis of informed and honest scientific objectivity? Or is it, like so many other matters in society, entirely subject to the economic needs, political interests, and social preferences of the system, be it plutocratic, democratic, or communistic? Similar questions are raised about the "science" of economics when economic systems cater to and stimulate psychic instability and exploit the illogical or the absurd. Altogether, these are the kinds of questions which define the "science fiction" dimensions of *Analogue Men* in the primary sense of the term — that is, a novel that deals, among other things, with the nature and role of science in society. And in this regard Knight clearly expresses certain reservations about the capacity of science to deal with fundamental human problems. In the final analysis, science, for Knight, can only be of value if it enhances the human condition rather than simply becomes a series of self-contained, self-justifying technological "breakthroughs." It is therefore significant that the sciences that dominate the plot of *Analogue Men* are the "social" and medical sciences (political science, economics, and mental health) rather than the "hardware" physical sciences.

Knight's reservations about science fall within two broad categories. First, the novel debunks a certain kind of optimism about the limitless possibilities of science, an optimism which has always been traditional in (Western) technological societies and which reached its climax in the United States during the first half of the twentieth century. *Analogue Men* opposes to this optimism a deep-seated pessimism about the effectiveness of science in the area of human failings, even when scientific discoveries are made by basically decent and well-intentioned persons. Here, of course, Knight is obviously reworking a familiar, recurrent, even tired science fiction theme: the recalcitrant shortcomings of human nature thwart, often pervert, the human ingenuity of scientific discovery. But what lifts the theme above the commonplace in Knight's hands is his ability to link it with other issues in a forceful way. Hence his skepticism about the ability of humans to benefit from their own science must also be viewed in relation to his second set of reservations about science itself.

On this second level the author questions the ability of the scientific mind to go beyond certain limits in its comprehension of reality. The Blank, that area to which all the plutocratic enclaves banish their rejects and incorrigibles, is a brilliant fictive monument to Einstein's Theory of Relativity. But the depiction of the Blank is fraught with irony: the establishing of scientific certainties (or influential theories like Einstein's) sometimes undermines individual certitude. Hence the displacement of time and space within The Blank has the effect of simultaneously confirming a scientific "truth" and destroying the individual ability to achieve and maintain a solid grasp of time, place, and identity. For example, Arthur Bass and Anne Silvers, agents of the Immune Underground, are by virtue of their work remarkably stable and self-contained, but even they are disoriented during a brief stay in The Blank. In effect, The Blank not only represents a tribute to Einsteinian science but also underscores the degree to which each scientific discovery really demonstrates our fundamental ignorance of the total scheme of things. In a similar vein, the social system as a whole breeds skepticism in questioning immunes like Arthur and Anne about the very nature of identity, largely because the process of self-identification is meaningless in a world in which each pattern of self-consciousness is molded by the analogue machines or (in the case of immunes) by the multiple guises and ever-changing identities that are the prerequisites for survival. In these circumstances genuine scientific inquiry into both environment and self is often difficult and at times even absurd.

It should be emphasized at this point that Knight is not offering those simplistic contrasts between science and humanism which dominate so much science fiction. While very different in tone and temperament from the more ironic and polished narratives of Stanislaw Lem, *Analogue Men* is comparable to works such as *Futurological Congress* (1974), *Solaris* (1961), and *Star Diaries* (1971) in that skepticism about the sciences *per se* is not isolated but is part of a pervasive uncertainty about the entire range of human understanding. Thus in analogue society the humanists, particularly the philosophical idealists, are no more successful than the scientists either in solving human problems or in winning our confidence in their ability even to define such problems. In this regard the fundamental moral dilemma with which the novel opens is not resolved at the end, but is simply glossed over. That is, does the human choice lie between free and open but violent societies or orderly but completely repressive systems? Knight's refusal to demonstrate some completely acceptable choice is suggestive: he implies the unlikelihood of such a choice, given the limits of human understanding and self-knowledge.

This intellectual and moral failure is reflected in the ambiguous personality of Laudermilk, the head of the Immune Underground movement. As an advocate of a "free" society that can be open to diverse opinions he is, paradoxically, in the position of having to stifle the opinions of those in the movement who would work for a society based on a single, exclusive "truth." And since these dissenting opinions are usually stifled by the execution of the dissidents, Laudermilk is left with the old-fashioned rationale, "the end justifies the means." We have therefore come full circle from the scientist (Dr. Kusko) to the humanist (Laudermilk) whose methods are symptoms of their personal limitations and, more significantly, of human intelligence in general. Despite the philosophical idealism which informs his passionate quest for freedom and human decency, Laudermilk is blessed with a realistic foresight that allows him to concede that the future world for which he is now working will probably be repugnant to him and his fellow immunes.

This realism on Laudermilk's part is, presumably, offered by Knight as one of the character's saving graces, as is the emphasis on Laudermilk's kindliness and sensitivity (especially to the inexperienced Arthur Bass). But on the whole the insistent attempts to paint Laudermilk as a kindly, well-meaning benefactor of humanity (even Arthur Bass's misgivings are eventually lulled by a final interview with his leader) are jarring rather than satisfying. Very little attempt is made to deal with the awkward fact that in his own way Laudermilk is a latter-day Kusko, that he too is caught up in the dilemmas (such as the meaning of freedom and the destructiveness of any form of violence) that he attempts to solve. And herein lies the major flaw of *Analogue Men*. The failure to deal precisely with Laudermilk's contradictions leaves the reader with the suspicion that Knight himself has not really come to terms with those contradictions, that while the subject of "freedom" is stressed to an almost religious degree, Knight seems curiously, and uncharacteristically, reluctant to be as explicit about the limitations of his freedom-fighting idealists as he is about other groups and their attitudes.

What one wishes is not, of course, an easy resolution of the moral and intellectual dilemmas of the novel by way of some facilely conceived *deus ex machina*. Indeed, one of the novel's main strengths is the consistency with which the narrative structure as a whole reinforces a pervasive sense of the incompleteness of human intellect and morality. But in dealing with Laudermilk and the associated ideal of "freedom," Knight's narrative judgment seems to lack the tough consistency of his narrative materials. In other words, the narrative events clearly establish the kinship between Kusko and Laudermilk, at the same time that Knight's handling of the latter amounts to an apotheosis of a vaguely transcendental ideal of freedom. But such an apotheosis merely evades the paradoxes of Laudermilk's character, and of the associated, unresolved dilemmas which the narrative plot demonstrates so well. In the final analysis there remains a disturbing incongruence between narrative revelation, on the one hand, and on the other hand, the narrative judgments that are offered by way of Laudermilk's personality. It is a tribute to Knight's skill as a storyteller that the moral dilemmas dramatized by the narrative as a whole remain clear and compelling to the end, despite the final evasiveness and apparent contradictions of the narrative judgment.

Lloyd W. Brown

Sources for Further Study

Reviews:

Analog. LVI, September, 1955, pp. 150-151.

Galaxy. X, September, 1955, p. 91.

Luna Monthly. XL, September, 1972, p. 26.

Magazine of Fantasy and Science Fiction. VIII, June, 1955, p. 76.

Original Science Fiction Stories. VI, September, 1955, pp. 122-125.

AND CHAOS DIED

Author: Joanna Russ (1937-   )
First book publication: 1970
Type of work: Novel
Time: 2270
Locale: A small, unnamed planet, off the usual routes of travel, and Earth

When two survivors from the wreck of a spaceship find themselves on a planet where humans of a lost colony have developed enormous mental powers, one of the survivors gains similar powers and returns to Earth, where he and colonists who have accompanied him change the nature of the human race

> Principal characters:
> JAI VEDH, an aimless neurotic who proves capable of development
> THE CAPTAIN, the other survivor, too inflexible to adapt and grow
> EVNE, one of the colonist, doctor and teacher to Jai Vedh

When Joanna Russ began to write *And Chaos Died*, she must have realized that her subject was one she would have to handle carefully to endow it with fresh interest. The concept of mental power is a field so thoroughly plowed during the 1940's and 1950's that many a writer would have thought the subject was played out. And if the field had been exhausted, it would have been no surprise; *And Chaos Died* appeared in print almost exactly one hundred years after the first detailed account of telepathy in science fiction.

In 1871 Sir Edward George Earle Bulwer-Lytton published *The Coming Race*, a kind of "hollow earth" story in which the fortunate troglodytes possess and command a mysterious force, Vril, which allows them to send their thoughts from one mind to another. Although Bulwer-Lytton explored the subject of telepathy (and he may not have been the first), he did not coin its name. That distinction belongs to Frederic W. H. Myers of the British Society for Psychical Research. Interest in what later came to be called psi powers surged in the later nineteenth century (as the founding of the organization shows), and in an attempt to standardize its terminology, Myers suggested in 1882 that the words *telaesthesia* and *telepathy* be used to mean the reception of sense impressions and thought, respectively, when such reception is accomplished over a distance by other than normal channels.

A whole range of writers included the strange power in their works, perhaps chiefly because the talent proved so useful in getting the plot moving. A frank discussion of this utility occurs in H. G. Wells's *Men Like Gods* (1923). In that work, some modern Britons find themselves in the far future; the language has changed, naturally, but the barrier of time is pierced by their hosts' ability to communicate with them telepathically. One of these future god-men states candidly how convenient telepathy is, considering their situation. He admits that otherwise they would have wasted weeks on learning each other's languages; the task of grammar and vocabulary and so on, he characterizes as "boring stuff for the most part," and one and all are glad that telepathy has enabled them to avoid it.

There is a second reason for the usefulness of psi powers to the writer, besides their convenience for communication. As the title of Bulwer-Lytton's book suggests, and as Wells's future characters demonstrate, the next stage of evolution could be the development of mental powers. Assume this, and the writer has the means for a convincing portrayal of a superman. The ability to read minds, to move objects at a distance, to transfer oneself from place to place, perhaps even to kill with thought, is a catalogue of abilities to please the most finicky of *Ubermenschen*. For example, telepathy is the first means of contact for the superman of Olaf Stapledon's *Odd John* (1936), a highly regarded example of the treatment of future evolution.

These two powerfully appealing facets of telepathy were joined by a third in the 1930's when the work of Joseph B. Rhine of Duke University added the imprint of scientific respectability to the subject. Now telepathy went to the laboratory, was subjected to controlled conditions, and was submitted to statistical analysis. Rhine's study of paranormal activity was like an undersea earthquake in psychological circles, creating a wave that increased in strength as it reached the archipelagos of science fiction. Between 1934 and 1940 alone, over sixty articles appeared in a variety of journals from popular to scholarly attacking or supporting Rhine.

One of Rhine's early admirers was John W. Campbell, Jr., who had studied the subject with interest even before he became editor of *Astounding Science Fiction*. In his story "Who Goes There?" (*Astounding Science Fiction*, August, 1938), Campbell makes a character refer specifically to Rhine, and comment that the professor had proved the existence of telepathy. He noted also that people varied in their sensitivity to it. Campbell's fascination with the subject was to have a profound effect on science fiction during his long career as editor of the outstanding magazine in the field. Indeed, through the 1940's, psi powers appeared with more regularity than some readers liked in the pages of *Astounding Science Fiction*, as Campbell and the most talented of his writers fostered editorial and fictional discussion of the subject.

The great majority of stories dealing with this theme regarded the psi powers as a great blessing, and their possession as something to be welcomed: telepathy is essential to the superhuman status of Jommy Cross, the hero of A. E. van Vogt's first novel, *Slan*, published in *Astounding Science Fiction* in 1940. Yet this attitude was not universal. Almost from the beginning, some writers took the approach that complete and unrestricted access to the minds of others would be profoundly disturbing, perhaps even maddening. For example, such is the assertion of Frank Belknap Long's "Dark Vision" (Unknown, March, 1939) in which the hero, because of his telepathic powers, is deluged by every conscious or subconscious thought of his neighbors. Eventually he must resort to drugs to preserve his sanity.

Consider the variety of approaches to telepathy, then, and add to these the fact that virtually every science fiction writer of note from Isaac Asimov to Roger Zelazny has dealt with the subject, and one begins to appreciate the size of the task attempted by Russ. But she meets the challenge.

Russ does not take the easy way out. Perhaps the most effective way to present the superman is to stay out of his mind, to show his powers by showing their effects on others. Incomparably more difficult is the job of showing what goes on in the telepath's mind, and this is what Russ does. Moreover, she shows us at the beginning an ordinary human being, and lets us view from the inside, so to speak, his initial reactions to psychic phenomena and his gradually increasing power to control them.

The plot of *And Chaos Died* is simple. An interstellar passenger ship explodes from an accident of some kind, and only two men escape in a lifeboat. One is Jai Vedh, a rather ordinary man from Earth; Vedh is a loner, a decorater by trade, and a homosexual by inclination. A little neurotic when he begins his interrupted journey, he feels his anxieties increase at the emptiness of space until he suffers a breakdown. He is under sedation when the accident occurs. The other survivor is the Captain of the wrecked spaceship; seemingly a figure of some nastiness, the Captain is not less sympathetic only because readers do not see things through his eyes. Rigid where Vedh is flexible, suspicious where Vedh is accepting, the Captain is largely a foil for his more educable companion. Their lifeboat comes to rest on an apparently uncharted planet; it had been the site of a colony sometime in the past — for humans are already there — but the existence of the colony has been forgotten.

Those colonists have changed during their period of exile. We never find out what they were like when they landed, but during their stay they have learned to "pay attention" in such a way that they have broken through an unsuspected barrier. Their mental powers have greatly expanded; it is suggested that this particular planet had something to do with the change — that conditions here force one to pay the special attention needed for the cultivation of the mind. However it was done; the colonists are enormously powerful in ways not immediately recognized by naïve observers such as Vedh or the Captain. They are telepathic, of course: they sense the thoughts not just of other humans, but the vegetable meditations of plants and even the simple proclamations of existence of rocks or sand. Later, when Jai Vedh has learned to "hear" but not to "listen," he finds the planet an incredibly noisy place. Moreover, the colonists can perceive with their own and others' bodies, sensing not just the mind, but any organ. Evne, the first native met by the survivors, serves her community as a doctor, healing minds and bodies. The colonists are able to place false sensory impressions within the minds of at least normal human beings, causing them to hallucinate; they can alter the memories of those they so affect, wiping the hallucination from remembrance. Finally, they can move material objects (including their own bodies) instantaneously from place to place within the normal time-space continuum, and they can place objects in Limbo, as they call it, a region outside of normal existence, in which time does not flow.

Most of these powers are illustrated early in the story, although since we see them through the uncomprehending eyes of Vedh, we may not recognize them for what they are. For example, Evne has a daughter, Evniki, who is chronologically fifteen years old but who has slowed down her development so that biologically she is only nine. Although children do not possess powers of the range and magnitude of adults, they are still extraordinary beings, as Evniki shows. Evniki is particularly interesting, since her mother has produced her parthenogenetically, as she tells the hero. She has two normally-produced siblings, only fertilized eggs as yet, whom her mother has placed in Limbo for a ten year wait.

In large part, the novel tells of Evne's healing of Jai Vedh. She accomplishes his cure by various means; she opens his senses to new experiences, gives her love to him, and shows him the shallowness of his present life. There are hints that Vedh has insulated himself from his brutal and jaded society, thereby causing his problems, and books may be the symbol of his isolation. Books, we are told, are rare; yet Vedh has brought some of his own on the trip. The only one that is described is a grammar of an old form of Chinese Mandarin, printed in the ideographs which by that time are apparently no longer used. If these inferences about the currency of the language are correct, then Jai Vedh has spent fifteen years passing his spare time in the study of a form of a language in which he can communicate with no one. While studying an older form of a language, even a dead language, is no negligible pursuit, it may in this case by the outward sign of his loneliness, the neurosis that led to his breakdown.

Books figure, in another scene, as part of Evne's regimen to Vedh's cure. She tells him of a library, and leads him on a journey to it. When they reach the site, Vedh at first sees only a circle of standing stones; then, as he watches, a building filled with books appears. He examines some, but cannot read what is written in them. Baffled and frustrated, he is overcome with a lust for Evne. He tells her to put down the book she holds, calling it "dead skin." What follows would be rape in ordinary circumstances, but Vedh can hardly force a woman who can read his mind and instantly be somewhere else. She must consent, therefore, and Vedh realizes his love for her, finding new depths emotionally as well as mentally. Vedh becomes a part of the community of the colonists and his own powers begin to grow, just before he and the captain are rescued.

The second part of the book concerns the changing of the Earth. When Vedh and the captain are taken home, Evne and some of the colonists "follow." They begin studying Earth while Vedh reenters his former life, seeing for the first time how degenerate it is. The contrast with the pastoral world of the colony shows him that humans have made the Earth a hell; as Vedh asks himself, what is the opposite of the Garden of Eden? Human follies are exemplified in the person of Ivat, a teenaged killer who is fascinated by Vedh, at once attracted to and repelled by him. Vedh explores his relationships with Ivat and his circle of friends, finds them severely wanting, and turns himself in to the authorities.

The government, nervous about the abilities of the colonists, arranges a meeting between its representatives, Vedh, and those colonists who have come to Earth. Then, at the climax of the story, the handful of colonists sends every person on Earth to Limbo. When Vedh transports himself to the planet of the colony, he finds that the work of rehabilitation has already begun. Ivat has been brought from Limbo, and is being healed.

The achievement of Russ in *And Chaos Died* rests on the way she tells her story. The reader gradually perceives the nature of events as Jai Vedh becomes aware himself of what is happening to him, and the significance of those events is clear only later. *And Chaos Died* is a novel the reader must work at, but the reward for the work is an understanding of one of the freshest treatments of psionic powers encountered in recent years.

Walter E. Meyers

Sources for Further Study

Reviews:

Amazing Stories. XLIV, September, 1970, pp. 130-132.

Analog. LXXXVI, February, 1971, pp. 167-168.

Best Sellers. XXXIX, December, 1970, p. 20.

Fantastic Stories. XIX, April, 1970, p. 109.

Luna Monthly. XXIII, April, 1971, p. 26.

Magazine of Fantasy and Science Fiction. XXXIX, December, 1970, pp. 20-21.

Science Fiction Commentary. XVII, November, 1970, pp. 34-35.

ANDROMEDA
(TUMANNOST ANDROMEDY)

Author: Ivan A. Yefremov (1907-1974)
First book publication: 1958
English translation: 1959
Type of work: Novel
Time: The Era of the Great Circle, thousands of years in the future
Locale: The Earth and cosmic expeditions

Utopian anticipation of a classless but not frictionless society, engaged in the collective human struggle against entropy through creative mastering of time and space by science and art

Principal characters:
ERG NOOR, commander of a cosmic expedition on spaceship *Tantra*
POUR HYSS, a cowardly astronomer of the expedition
DARR VETER, ex-director of Earth Outer Stations (satellites)
MVEN MASS, new director of Outer Stations and an experimenter
RENN BOSE, a physicist
NISA CREET, an astronavigator
EVDA NAHL, a psychologist
VEDA KONG, a historian
CHARA NANDI, a dancer-model and biologist

Ivan A. Yefremov's novel *Tumannost Andromedy* was first published in installments in the very popular youth periodical *Tekhnika molodezhi* (Technology to Young People), Numbers 1 to 10, 1957, with a shortened version immediately following in the biweekly for teens *Pionerskaia pravda*, Numbers 18 to 36, March to May, 1957 — in itself a rather unprecedented indication of instant popularity. The first book edition was published by the Moscow publisher Molodaia gvardiia, whose stories were aimed mainly at older teens and young adults, but who also published much science fiction read by the large adult audiences in 1958. The novel was picked up also by the Moscow State Publishing House for Literature (Goslitizdat) in 1959, then republished in a slightly revised edition by the even more prestigious State Publishing House for High Fiction (Gos. izd. Khudozhestvennoi Literatury). Since then it has been almost continually reprinted in at least thirty editions and in runs in the hundreds of thousands, so that by now it must have sold millions of copies. It has also been translated into approximately thirty languages, including an inadequate English translation at the Foreign Languages Publishing House, Moscow, 1959 and 1963, under the title *Andromeda*.

Andromeda is the pioneering and representative text in the Soviet science fiction revival of the late 1950's. It is universally acknowledged as not only the bearer of the post-Stalinist "thaw" in the genre, but also as the supreme achievement of its first phase (1957-1963). However, it achieved this status only after a long and acrimonious public debate, itself a phenomenon unheard of in the USSR since the enthronement of a normative and dogmatic literary policy during the Stalinist purges of 1934 and the following years. The reasons which made such a debate possible and the whole Khrushchev-era "thaw" (which then refroze in the mid-1960's) can be briefly summarized as the combined ideological impact of the political de-Stalinization (partial though this was) and the Sputnik euphoria. The Twentieth Congress of the Soviet Communist party in 1956 destroyed the indisputability of Stalinist myths about society and literature. They were further shaken by the sensational Soviet achievements in the natural sciences, exemplified by the first Sputnik. The new science fiction wave, rich in tradition and individual talent, eager to deal with an increasing range of subjects, from sociological to cosmological and anthropological, from astronautic through cybernetic to anticipatory-utopian, found a wide audience among the young and the intelligentsia. We have no sure statistics on this reading public, but it was probably as large if not at times larger than its American counterpart. It was perhaps unsophisticated, but impatient of the old clichés and thirsting after knowledge and imagination. It was its tastes that carried the day in the great "Andromeda nebula debate."

Subsequent developments in Soviet science fiction can be understood only as a result of this debate's having, against violent ideological opposition, consummated in 1957-1958 the victory of the new wave — which was really the victory of the pristine Soviet Russian tradition, which had been in abeyance since the Leninist 1920's. The writers and critics of the "cold stream" rebuked the novel's heroes as being "too far from our times" and thus unintelligible to the reader, especially the juvenile reader. In short, they were saying that Yefremov's scope was too daring. Such pressure had for fifteen years hindered the publication and development of Yefremov's work (from his first science fiction story in 1942, not published until 1966). However, the opinion of "warm stream" critics, and of the thousands of readers who wrote to the author, newspapers, and periodicals, saying that Yefremov's work was a liberating turning-point in Soviet science fiction, finally prevailed.

Yefremov's fiction achieved such historical significance because, in its own way, it creatively revived the classical Utopian and socialist vision — Marx's, Chernyshevsky's, Morris', or even the mellower Wells's — which looks forward to a unified, affluent, humanist, classless, and stateless world. The novel is set in the 408th year of the Era of the Great Ring, when mankind has established informational contact with inhabitants of distant constellations who pass on such information to one another through a "ring" of inhabited systems. The Earth itself is administered — by analogy with the associative centers of the human brain — by an Astronautic Council and an Economic Council which tallies all plans with existing possibilities; their specialized research Academies correspond to man's sensory centers. Within this framework of the body politic, Yefremov is primarily interested in the development of a disalienated man and new ethical relationships. For all the theatrical loftiness of his characters, whose emotions are rarely less sublime than full satisfaction and confidence (only an occasional melodramatic villain like Pour Hyss feels fear or hate), they can learn through painful mistakes and failures, as distinct from the desperado and superman clichés of "socialist realism" or much American science fiction after Gernsback.

With the reexhumation of socialist Utopianism, Yefremov brought back into Soviet fiction whole reaches of the science fiction tradition: the philosophical story, the romantic *étude*, and classic sociological and modern cosmological Utopianism. Thus, the novel's strong narrative, full of action, from a fistfight to an encounter with electrical predators and a robot-spaceship from the Andromeda nebula, is imbued with the joy and romance of cognition which embraces an understanding of the outside world of modern cosmology and evolutionist biology. But Yefremov's strong anthropocentric bent places the highest value on creativity, a simultaneous adventure of deed, thought, and feeling; since body and mind are indissolubly connected in Yefremov, a materialistic writer, his creative efforts result in physical and ethical beauty.

The author's Utopian anthropology is evident even in the symbolic title: the Andromeda nebula recalls the chained Greek beauty rescued from a monster (here class egotism and violence, personified in the novel as a bull, often bear hallmarks of Stalinism) by a flying hero aided by superior science. Astronautics thus does not evolve into a new uncritical cult, but is claimed as a humanist discipline, in one of the most significant cross-connections among physical sciences, social sciences, ethics, and art that Yefremov establishes as the norm for his new people.

Such a connection is embodied even in the compositional oscillation between cosmic and terrestrial chapters, where the "astronautic" Erg-Nisa subplot is finally integrated with the "earthly" Darr-Veda subplot by means of the creative beauty of science united to art (Mven-Chara and Renn-Evda). Furthermore, this future is not the arrested, pseudoperfect end of history that comprises the weak point of optimistic Utopianism from Plato to Bellamy. Freed from economic and power worries, people must still redeem time, which is unequal on Earth and in space, through a humanist dialectic of personal creativity and societal teamwork mediated — in a clear harking back to the ideals of the Soviet 1920's — by artistic and scientific beauty of functionality. This is best shown in such scenes as Darr's listening to the "Cosmic Symphony in F-minor, Color Tone 4.75 μ" or the catastrophic but finally vindicated giant "null-space" experiment of Mven. Creativity is always countered by entropy, and self-realization is paid for in effort and even suffering.

In fact, several very interesting approaches to a Marxist "optimistic tragedy" can be found in the book; for example, in Mven's "happy Fall" the failed and destructive experiment finally leads to great advances. Further, and very importantly, the accent on beauty and responsible freedom places into the center of the novel female heroines, interacting with the heroes and contributing to the emotional motivation of new Utopian ethics — in complete contrast to American science fiction of the time, with which Yefremov was obviously in a well-informed polemical dialogue.

No doubt, *Andromeda* is somewhat dated today. In a number of places the novel's dialogue, motivation, and tone flag, so that it falls into pathos and preaching which slow down its rhythm. Yefremov's characters tend to be statuesque and monolithic in a kind of neoclassic way, and his incidents often exploit the quantitatively grandiose: Mven blows up a satellite and half a mountain, Veda loses the greatest anthropological find ever, and to think of the manly Erg blushing or the pure Nisa stepping into, say, offensive jellyfish offal on the iron-star planet is practically blasphemous. Most of this can be explained by the story's having had to achieve several aims at once. It was the first work to burst open the floodgates closed for twenty-five years, and it overflowed into clogged channels. One feels in the novel the presence of a reader unused to fast orientation in new perspectives and, as Yefremov himself wrote, "still attracted to the externals, decorations, and theatrical effects of the genre."

Furthermore, some aspects of Yefremov's ethics and aesthetics, such as the erotic and generally intimate interpersonal relations — though understandable enough in the context of the social taboos normal to a Soviet Russian scientist of an older generation — are curiously old-fashioned when viewed in relation to the science fiction genre as a whole. Yefremov is epistemologically wedded to a naïve anthropocentrism. He lives within the nineteenth century deterministic view of man as subject and the universe as object of a cognition that is ever expanding, if necessary through a basic social change yet without major existential consequences. Doubt and the menace of entropy enter human life only as an external enemy — such as the electric predators of a faraway planet. If any epistemological opaqueness ever becomes internalized in a reasonable creature, then he becomes a melodramatic villain such as Pour Hyss.

Yefremov's social consciousness can thus be said to be receptive only to a certain romantically codified range of creativity. His limitations are more clearly manifested in his later works, where they preclude a full development of imaginative science fiction vistas. But again, any further discussion of such vistas in Soviet science fiction was made possible by Yefremov's pioneering effort. The polyphonic scope of *Andromeda*, with its large number of protagonists, is Tolstoian rather than Flaubertian. Not being limited to the consciousness of one central hero, it presents one of the first Utopias in world literature which successfully shows new characters creating and being created by a new society; in other words, the personal working out of a collective Utopia (analogous to what Sir Walter Scott did for the historical novel). Yefremov's basic device of unfolding the narration as if the anticipated future were already a normative present unites the classic "looking backward" of Utopian anticipations with the modern Einsteinian conception of different coordinate systems with autonomous norms.

Twentieth century science and the age-old Russian folk dreams of a just and happy society meet in Yefremov's novel. This meeting made it a nodal point of the Russian and socialist science fiction tradition, and enabled it to usher in the second "Golden Age" of the genre which continued until the 1960's. Yet even the failure of the original Utopian confidence from the mid-1960's on, to which Yefremov's own later works also testify, both in their overt ideological profiles and in their reduced significance, can be measured and judged by the values of that Utopian and de-alienating horizon that Yefremov revived and bequeathed to Soviet science fiction.

Darko Suvin

Sources for Further Study

Criticism:

Suvin, Darko, Editor. *Other Worlds, Other Seas*. New York: Random House, 1970, pp. xxiv-xxvi. Suvin places Yefremov's work within the context of Russian and East European Science Fiction literature.

The Encyclopedia of Science Fiction and Fantasy. Compiled by Donald H. Tuck. Chicago: Advent Publishers, Inc., 1978, pp. 471-472. This biographical and bibliographical article mentions Yefremov as an outstanding writer of both science and science fiction, although he is subject to much pro-Communist propaganda.

THE ANDROMEDA STRAIN

Author: Michael Crichton (1942-   )
First book publication: 1969
Type of work: Novel
Time: 1967
Locale: Nevada and other parts of the United States

An account of the crisis created by the return to Earth of a contaminated sampling satellite in which a team of scientists working in a secret installation attempt to identify and counteract a substance or creature which causes human blood to clot into powder

Principal characters:
> DR. JEREMY STONE, a bacteriologist, lawyer, and top government adviser
> DR. PETER LEAVITT, a clinical microbiologist and epidemiologist
> DR. CHARLES BURTON, a pathologist
> DR. MARK HALL, a surgeon
> MAJOR ARTHUR MANCHEK, Project Scoop duty officer
> PETER JACKSON, one of the two survivors in Piedmont

When the excitement of reading *The Andromeda Strain* has worn off, one becomes aware that despite the gripping action, what one remembers most clearly is the presentation of classified or little-known information about the biological horrors which the contemporary science-government complex is either prepared to meet or is itself in the process of creating. The plans and facilities which Crichton documents are a seamless blending of what exists now, what Crichton deduces exists but is top secret, and what he speculates must be the plans and facilities that will be necessary to meet such crises. While the Andromeda event itself may be fictional, Crichton has gone to every conceivable length to give the book the texture of a chilling historical reconstruction; the resulting mixture places *The Andromeda Strain* beside John Brunner's *The Sheep Look Up* as the most frightening example of an "imminent catastrophe" novel in science fiction.

The novel begins when a Scoop satellite, sent into orbit to search for foreign organisms, is being routinely picked up by van from the Arizona desert. The discovery that the satellite has been opened by the local doctor, killing all but two citizens of the tiny community of Piedmont and then killing the recovery team, causes Scoop duty officer Arthur Manchek to call a "Wildfire Alert," a secret contingency plan involving a five-level underground laboratory in Nevada, where a preselected team of scientists assembles to attempt to identify and counteract the substance or organism. The problem is complicated by a series of human and mechanical errors, each of which greatly increases the danger to the research team and to the West Coast of the United States. Because Crichton has announced his own presence as the omniscient narrator by signing the acknowledgements section (in which many real senior scientists and military figures appear), he can warn us when a false trail is taken without explaining at the time why it is dangerous or nonproductive.

The detailing which dovetails real science and politics with the crisis and sets up the texture of the novel can be seen in the explanation for the Wildfire Project itself. As Dr. Jeremy Stone is being driven to an aircraft to rush him to the underground installation, Crichton breaks off the narrative to flash back to the roots of Stone's advocacy of the project. A real paper on the likelihood of extraterrestrial "invasion" being viral or bacterial led Stone to form a caucus on the subject and eventually to write directly to the President of the United States to initiate the project. Twenty-two million dollars were then spent on the underground laboratory, including the installation of an underground nuclear device which would automatically detonate three minutes after the laboratory became contaminated unless countermanded by a special procedure. In addition, Stone's team developed a Life Analysis Protocol, a sequence of tests thought necessary to identify any living thing, and it was arranged that Wildfire could order a Directive 7-12, called Cautery, a thermonuclear bomb to sterilize the site where the "invaders" had landed. Because of Hudson Institute conclusions on the high risk of thermonuclear holocaust from Cautery, the President retained veto power over it.

As if the Wildfire Protocol (resembling, as it does, existing facilities and options to counter biological warfare) had not sufficiently unnerved the reader, Crichton then has Dr. Stone read a file on Project Scoop, whose seventh satellite had brought the contamination to Earth. It is only at this moment that Stone, a leading and trusted member of the scientific-political establishment, becomes aware that a series of military satellites has been orbited with the specific intent of finding new and deadly organisms for biological warfare. This leads to some frightening descriptions of the half billion dollar per year American Chemical and Biological Warfare program, whose major installation, Fort Detrick, Maryland, covers thirteen hundred acres, cost over one hundred million dollars, and produces the ghastly weapons of future war. By the time Stone finishes the Scoop summary he is aware that Wildfire was built to conform to military thinking and, indeed, with an eye to its possible function as an adjunct should Scoop produce something more powerful than its masters hoped.

Over and over again, Crichton reveals the hard, calculating, mechanical planning of the political and military masters of science. Vividly unusual images abound such as the fierce, army-trained German Shepherds who guard Wildfire throwing their heads forward in a silent bark, their laryngectomies having given them all bite and no bark; or the extraordinary efforts to sterilize and decontaminate the scientists by burning away the epithelial layers of the skin with ultraflash.

As *The Andromeda Strain* progresses Crichton performs brilliant *tours de force* in his effective explanations of the complex scientific discoveries the team is making; these digressions seem part of the work, and do not lower the tension of the narrative. They discover that the organism kills in differing fashions and that it has a biologic structure unlike any form of life known on Earth. By the time one has come to the deadly and unexpected conclusion of the novel, a great deal of biology has been communicated without impeding the rush of the four days of desperate struggle to overcome a hostile organism that kills in seconds.

The most chilling aspect of this plunge into a nightmare that could happen tomorrow is the role chance and the subconscious play in a sequence of events that is supposed to be as computer-precise as technology can make it. The crisis begins when a small-town doctor opens Scoop VII instead of reporting it. The town happens to have an aspirin-eating Sterno drinker whose survival produces a vital clue. Wildfire fails to get messages, including the word that Cautery has *not* been carried out, because of a piece of waste paper that sticks in a teletype machine printout. Time after time the scientists, partly stymied by fatigue and trapped by the weaknesses of their personalities, fail to see the meaning of something they have discovered or observed. Crichton systematically points out each of these moments but always waits to reveal their importance.

When the Andromeda Strain is finally understood, it is by a burst of intuition beyond the logical processes of the scientific method. A failure in the sealing gaskets traps Burton in a contaminated area and Stone remarks to Hall that Burton is "scared to death." Strangely enough Burton does not die immediately and Hall wanders away obsessed with the connection between the remark and the frightened baby who survived Piedmont. When he cannot reason out the problem he blunders off to relieve the nearly intolerable tension by seeing Leavitt, whose hidden epilepsy has erupted in a *grand mal* seizure and left him unconscious. It is while checking Leavitt that Hall's mind wanders slightly to the outside world and an image from daily life pops forward as the answer to the whole puzzle. The frightening idea that important discoveries are often made randomly and accidentally is extremely chastening, and Crichton forces the point home with a final twist ending that leaves Hall's correct solution almost worthless.

The only flaws in *The Andromeda Strain* are the unlikely premises behind Wildfire, and the melodramatic ending. Despite all the care and precaution supposedly lavished on the Wildfire Protocol, the team operates short one man from the beginning because no alternates have been named. Indeed, it is unlikely that such a priority project would not have a lower-echelon staff trained to perform most of the Life Analysis Protocol on call at Wildfire, rather than have to wait for people to assemble from across the United States. It is even more unlikely that the Wildfire team would never have practiced the protocol together or even have seen the facility. It is also unlikely that any teletype message sent over such a select secret priority network could be left unacknowledged by a special function station on emergency alert.

However, these weaknesses in the logic of *The Andromeda Strain* can be dismissed on the simple grounds that no planners ever foresee the unforeseeable. Indeed, this is the subject of the novel, for the Wildfire Protocols are a conscious attempt to attack a problem with the minds of its team as open as possible to any unbelievable and unexpected biological invader. When the challenge is posed, human beings with human flaws, but with the unique supralogical capabilities of the human mind, attack it. The exhilaration of following deductive skills in the esoteric world where science, technology, and politics exert their relentless directives and offer deadly alternatives is the reward for reading Michael Crichton's *The Andromeda Strain*.

Peter Brigg

Sources for Further Study

Criticism:

Bova, Ben. "The Role of Science Fiction," in *Science Fiction, Today and Tomorrow*. Edited by Reginald Bretnor. New York: Harper & Row, 1974, pp. 5-6. Bova gives a succinct analysis of Crichton's *Andromeda Strain*.

Reviews:

Best Sellers. XXIX, June 15, 1969, p. 105.

Book World. June 8, 1969, p. 4.

Christian Science Monitor. June 26, 1969, p. 13.

Library Journal. XCIV, July 15, 1969, p. 2485.

New York Times Book Review. June 8, 1969, p. 4.

Newsweek. LXXIII, May 26, 1969, p. 125.

Saturday Review. LII, June 28, 1969, p. 29.

Time. XCIII, June 6, 1969, p. 112.

Times Literary Supplement. October 16, 1969, p. 1215.

THE ANGEL OF THE REVOLUTION

Author: George Griffith (1857-1906)
First book publication: 1893
Type of work: Novel
Time: 1903-1905
Locale: Primarily Great Britain, Russia, and an inaccessible valley in Africa

The story of the great Revolution against tyranny, the establishment of Anglo-Saxon mastery over the Earth, and the abolition of war, all brought about by the invention of the airship

> *Principal characters:*
> RICHARD ARNOLD, an inventor
> ALEXIS MAZANOFF, *alias* MAURICE COLSTON, a member of the Inner Circle of the Terrorists
> RADNA MICHAELIS, his fiancée
> ALAN TREMAYNE, LORD ALANMERE, Chief of the Inner Circle
> NATAS, Master of the Terrorists
> NATASHA, his daughter

Between 1871, when George Chesney produced his account of "The Battle of Dorking" as propaganda for the campaign to reorganize and rearm the British Army, and 1914, when the Great War actually began, the most popular form of imaginative fiction in Britain was the future-war story. The nation was on the one hand haunted by the fear of invasion and the decay of empire, and on the other fascinated by the dream of a quasiapocalyptic conflict in which these fears would be banished for all time and the future made secure. The dream died at Mons, on the Somme, and at Passchendaele, and was buried in that famous corner of Flanders fields. But in the imaginative fiction of the previous half century it was alive in many different guises.

The industrial revolution had shown that it would remake war as well as work, and the notion of new engines of destruction powerful enough to ensure that the next war might be the last was a popular one. In the 1890's the success of experiments by Samuel P. Langley and H. S. Maxim convinced a number of writers that the advent of flying machines was imminent, and the utility of such machines in war seemed to a few to be unlimited. Francesco Lana, who "designed" an airship as early as 1670, had pointed out then that fortresses and cities could be destroyed by aerial bombing and had seriously wondered whether God would allow such possibilities to be actualized. By 1893, divine intervention no longer seemed likely to stand in the way.

Griffith was by no means the first to feature airships in his imaginative fiction — *The Angel of the Revolution* — refers back to Jules Verne's *Clipper of the Clouds* (1886) — but he was the first to award them a crucial role in the war to end war, as agents of Armageddon bearing the names of the Heavenly Host that cast Satan's legions into Hell. Indeed, Griffith was one of only three authors who seemed to realize fully the destructive power that technology might deliver into human hands, and the implications of this for the scale and nature of warfare. Along with M. P. Shiel and H. G. Wells, he anticipated that the next war might be "the most frightful carnival of destruction the world has ever seen," involving the slaughter of millions of people, mostly noncombatants. This did not, however, deter him from looking forward to that conflict hopefully and enthusiastically. Like Shiel, he was an Anglo-Saxon chauvinist; like Wells a socialist; and he was hopeful that the apocalyptic clash of forces might result in the end of tyranny in Europe and the permanent victory of Christendom over the religious empires of the East. The attainment of such an end, in his view, would easily justify the death of millions.

The story begins with the exultant cry of Richard Arnold, a young inventor who has at last solved the problem of flight by devising an engine with sufficient power to lift a huge winged machine. Unfortunately, his research has swallowed up his capital and he has no way to develop his invention. Walking along the Thames, he contemplates the fact that the Tsar of Russia has offered a prize of one million pounds for a flying machine, and for a moment he is tempted. Then, however, he vehemently rejects the notion of placing his discovery in the charge of such a man, and swears aloud that it shall never be given over to the use of tyrants, but rather employed for their destruction. He is overheard by a passerby, who introduces himself as Maurice Colston, and suggests that perhaps the invention *can* be so used.

Arnold is introduced by Colston to the Inner Circle of the Brotherhood of Freedom, an organization that controls the work of Nihilists, Anarchists, and Socialists throughout the world and is popularly known as the Terror. Arnold is more than willing to be inducted into this secret society and is initiated at once. He discovers that he is already acquainted with the Chief of the Inner Circle — Alan Tremayne, Lord Alanmere — but cannot yet renew his acquaintance as Tremayne is currently abroad. Among the members of the Inner Circle he does meet are Radna Michaelis, who is sworn to wed Colston (in his real identity of Alexis Mazanoff) when he has destroyed the various persons responsible for her being flogged in a Russian prison; and Natasha, daughter of the mysterious Master of the Terrorists whose pseudonym is Natas ("Satan" reversed).

The Terrorists finance Arnold in the building of an airship named *Ariel*, which he constructs on a remote Scottish island. By the time it is ready there is urgent work for it to do. Natasha and Radna are prisoners of the Russians and must be rescued. This end is accomplished, and the fortress of Kronstadt reduced to rubble in the process. The *Ariel* then sets off to rescue a balloonist named Louis Holt, who has been marooned for five years in a remote part of Africa, in a valley surrounded by high mountains and accessible only from the air. Arnold then takes over the valley, now called Aeria, as a Terrorist base to be used for the construction of a fleet of airships.

Meanwhile, war is developing in Europe. Though no one else has developed an airship like Arnold's — which is indeed, a winged ship, with a hull and a deck, three masts, giant propellors and cannon that fire shells of great power — the Tsar's prize has been claimed by the inventors of a dirigible balloon. The Tsar hastens to capitalize on this temporary advantage by fomenting strife in Europe, eventually precipitating armed conflict between a Franco-Russian alliance and an Anglo-German alliance, with Italy vacillating between the two sides, and the other countries slated to be drawn in or overrun in turn.

As the war begins the reader is party to a conversation between Natas, now revealed to be a crippled dwarf with a hypnotic gaze, and Tremayne. Natas reveals that his plan is to let the European powers fight until they are exhausted. Then he will step in and take over all of Europe, welding it together in a single force ready to meet an "impending flood of yellow barbarians" assumed to be forming in the East. Natas thinks it is the destiny of the Anglo-Saxon race to rule the world (though he is himself a Hungarian Jew) and that the Terror will be the means to this end as well as to the advent of socialism and the abolition of war.

Tremayne leaves England when war breaks out, taking Natas with him aboard his yacht, but before they can rendezvous with their colleagues they are attacked by a French cruiser. Arnold and Mazanoff, now flying in the flagship of their aerial fleet, the *Ithuriel*, come to their rescue. They find, however, that they cannot fly home to Aeria to wait for the end of the war, because four Russian renegades have stolen one of their airships, the *Lucifer*, and have placed it at the disposal of the Tsar. Already it has released the Russian fleet that had been blockaded in the Baltic. The *Ithuriel* flies to Russia, first to stop the Tsar's scientists from solving the secret of the power that propels the airships, and then to recapture the *Lucifer*.

The Brotherhood faces further internal strife when the leader of its American contingent threatens to withdraw from Natas' command unless certain conditions are met, including his marriage to Natasha. This causes Arnold great anxiety, as he has fallen in love with Natasha and she with him, but the rebel is successfully dealt with, and the American section comprises the first of the Terrorists to rise in revolt. The American government crumbles without a fight (*The Angel of the Revolution* was not reprinted in America for some time after its British publication) and a Terrorist-backed Anglo-Saxon Federation is established there. Britain is invited to join the Federation but refuses, and the Terrorists wait while the Russians sweep across Europe and into Britain, ultimately taking London. Until that time the king of England (Edward VII) does not capitulate and bow to the Brotherhood. When he does so, virtually all the Russians on British soil, except those who are party to the international conspiracy, are slaughtered; and the Terrorists also unleash their air force on Russia itself. Within a matter of days complete victory is theirs, and

Tsar Alexander and his lackeys are declared nonpersons and shipped off to Siberia.

The expected invasion from the Far East does not materialize, but in the last few pages of the book it is revealed that the Moslems have won a Holy War against the Buddhists, and have themselves subsequently been intimidated to the point of pledging loyalty to the Terrorists. The whole world is thus pacified. National boundaries are redrawn, private property is abolished (at least as far as land is concerned — the means of industrial production are not mentioned) and private wealth is attacked by what Griffith clearly considered to be a mercilessly punitive tax, though its level is considerably less than present-day British income tax. The last battle is over, Arnold returns to his beloved Natasha and his baby son, and peace is due to reign on Earth forever.

Actually, peace reigned only as long as it took Griffith to realize that he had scored a large success, at which point he wrote *Olga Romanoff* (1894), a sequel in which another war to end war has to be fought between the forces of Christendom and Islam, with airships and submarines locked in deadly combat (which, in the end, proves futile when a comet wipes out all life on Earth except for the fugitive Aerians).

The Angel of the Revolution is remarkable not only for its extravagant visions of aerial bombing and mass destruction but also for its bastardized political ideology, which is a curious mixture of radical opinions. The previous years had seen the publication of many futuristic polemical novels, but most of the prosocialist fiction had been cast in the Utopian mold. Even those favoring the revolution had shown a certain anxiety about the violence getting out of hand — Donnelly's *Caesar's Column* (1890) is a cardinal example — and Griffith was alone in his frank endorsement of the tactics of terrorism. Though Griffith seems to have provided part of the imaginative stimulus for H. G. Wells's 1908 novel, *The War in the Air* (which refers to one of Griffith's works in much the same way that *The Angel of the Revolution* refers to Verne's), the redoubtable Fabian must have been rather outraged by the gleeful enthusiasm with which his fellow writer of scientific romances described the slaughter of millions of people.

In terms of the history of science fiction, Griffith and Wells had more in common than their espousal of socialism and their visions of aerial Armageddon. Both played an important role in the synthesis of the various subgenres of imaginative fiction that had grown up in the latter part of the nineteenth century. Until the advent of writers such as Griffith and Wells, and the magazines that popularized their work, there was no real sign of common cause between the various kinds of imaginative literature: the novel of imaginary tourism popularized by Verne; Utopian novels inspired by the mythology of social progress; war-anticipation stories; and evolutionary fantasies. Griffith and Wells, however, moved from one vein of speculation to another with ease, often combining them, and built their reputations on a capacity for innovation and invention that brought all four trends together under the loose banner of "scientific romance." The very professionalism of the two writers led them to develop their reputations by going in search of new and more extravagant ideas, and this was the origin of the spirit of speculative adventure that is the most distinctive feature of modern science fiction.

By the time Griffith wrote his last novel, *The Lord of Labour* (published posthumously in 1911), his war of the imminent future was being fought with atomic missiles and disintegrator rays. He was still looking forward eagerly to the conflict. What effect the spectacle of the actual Great War might have had on his imaginative enthusiasm we can only guess.

Brian Stableford

Sources for Further Study

Criticism:

The Encyclopedia of Science Fiction and Fantasy. Compiled by Donald H. Tuck. Chicago: Advent Publishers, Inc., 1978, p. 194. This concise biographical overview tells much of what is known about the author of *The Angel of the Revolution*.

ANIARA

Author: Harry E. Martinson (1904-1978)
First book publication: 1956
English translation: 1963
Type of work: Cycle of poems in 103 songs (cantos)
Time: An indefinite future
Locale: Deep space

Its directional controls jammed, the spaceship Aniara *hurtles into space*

Aniara, the Martionsonian spaceship in the poem, shuttles emigrants from the radiation-poisoned Earth to Mars. Liftoff is not achieved with stage rockets as is now done, but the "goldonda," which Martinson also calls his spaceship, is pulled up with "gyrospiners" toward the sky

> where powerful magnetrines annul
> Earth's pull. Soon zero signal's given.

This effect also produces an antigravitational field that nullifies the force of gravity, and *Aniara* smoothly rises through space like an air bubble through water.

During one of her routine runs the goldonda gets into trouble by nearly colliding with the previously unchartered asteroid Hondo, but the ship avoids disaster by executing a sudden swerve. Then meteor showers and other space debris cause the goldonda problems, and as a result, *Aniara*, with directional controls jammed on a course for Lyra (poetry's own constellation), relentlessly speeds out of the solar system — out into deep space.

The pilots — the leaders — soon realize the impossibility of turning back, and the dreadful knowledge slowly circulates among the unsuspecting passengers. After a period of panic and desperation, they accept their situation. Life goes on as usual. The Midsummer Day vigil is held throughout the night even though no sun rises, and some people seek solace in escapist daydreams. These dreams are created by the "Mima," and the poet himself, after taking over the role of priest, "looks after the Mima, calms the emigrants and livens them with pictures from far distance."

After a twenty-four-year journey at a speed of approximately thirty kilometers per second, the eight thousand passengers are at last set free. The last line in the epic reads: "lost and dispersed in oceans of Nirvana," which in scientific terms means that entropy had achieved its maximum in a closed system.

This is the science fiction theme of the 103 cantos that contain a rich cast of characters from the dictator "Chefone" to the pilots, astronomers, the Mima love cult priestesses, and so on down to the passengers.

In order to fully appreciate *Aniara*, it is necessary to understand the mechanical nineteenth century concept of the world. That century was an optimistic time, and the scientist-engineer was the hero, like the ones who are prominent in Jules Verne's novels, for example. The universe was viewed as a highly synchronized piece of machinery, somewhat like a huge clockwork.

But this model, or similar models, did not inspire poets. The mechanical concept of the universe with its uncanny determinism had to be replaced with a freer and more "lyrical" perception of the cosmos before a poet could earnestly take up the substance of a scientific idea. Such a change occurred in the year 1900 when Max Planck started the scientific revolution that is still going on today with his quantum theory. The mechanistic nineteenth century model of the universe was thus swept away in a flood of mathematical symbols. The present-day physicist has abandoned the engineer-oriented model concept and thinks instead in abstract mathematical terms.

This new scientific approach is a double-edged sword for the poet. One edge is the sharply abstract nature of the modern view of the world which works against the poet, who wants to paint a word picture, make revelations, and create visions. But the other edge cuts his bonds and frees him to become highly creative since physicists are not precise about what the universe should look like. Maybe it would be better to compare both edges to two parallel planes, which, in the world of the new geometries, might well meet — in a vision.

It is well-known that science fiction writers make up new technical terms — an exoticism they have inherited from Romanticism. Harry Martinson has coined a wealth of new words with his fertile imagination. Strictly speaking, all words are symbols, but — to take two examples — while the word "monkey" produces a familiar image for the reader, the word "atom" forms no exact picture in that we do not know for sure what an atom looks like. In atomic or astrophysics this opens the way for new words whose magic will conjure up images and events that really exist without our being aware of them. This is the case with words like "Aniara," "phototurb," "protator," the "octopus feelers" of the "Cantor" works, and "gopta."

The new word symbols in *Aniara* have been interpreted in different ways — in most cases the author has done so himself. Perhaps the best example is the word that gives the work its title: Aniara. In the 1938 Christmas edition of the literary magazine *Vintergatan*, Harry Martinson wrote an article he entitled "Star Song." In it he pointed out that we sometimes perceive things in our dreams which we later cannot describe no matter how hard we try; we can only make a vague attempt to hint at something dubious and inherently inexpressible. This process can be compared to the modern physicist's formula terminology about what takes place in the world of the atom, formulas which describe chains of events for which no adjectives, nouns, or verbs have been devised. Or else one can say something like:

> the flubbering ondunomena
> skickle and bickle through *aniara*.

In this couplet we see the word aniara in print for the first time. The year 1938 shows how early Harry Martinson had started thinking about what the epic *Aniara* would turn out to be in 1956. Martinson got the idea for this expression from a similar English language phrase quoted by Sir Arthur Eddington out of Lewis Carroll's *Through the Looking-Glass*:

> T'was brillig and the slithy toves
> did gyre and gimble in the wabe.

The Englishman Eddington was a distinguished astronomer and popular science writer. His book, *The Nature of the Physical World* (1928) was an important influence behind *Ainara*. In his *Vintergatan* article Martinson suggests how he combined these two visions — the scientific and the fantastic — in creating his new vocabulary.

The word "wabe" gave the poet a dreamlike reference to the symbolic word "Aniara." But each symbol can be interpreted in several ways. Originally it was a vowel-rich combination of letters representing the space in which atoms move. Later on the author himself gave a more solid explanation. The chemical symbol for nickel is *Ni*, and the corresponding symbol for the inert gas argon, which is found in air, is *Ar*. Aniara therefore means without nickel and without argon, that is, without being attached to the ground or in the air — a journey into outer space.

In addition, there is another surprising aspect. The Ancient Greek adjective *aniaros* with its feminine form *aniara* means sad. We can therefore consider Aniara the name of a vessel — Ship of Sorrow — because *Aniara* is the tragedy of humanity having gone awry.

The aforementioned "Mima" has been equipped with awe-inspiring capabilities by its creator. "She" can scan and reproduce events on other worlds in distant galaxies, and her (subliminal) messages induce the passengers to forget their present hopeless situation. So the people on Aniara become a Mima-worshiping sect bowing before the goddess' pedestal each time fear threatens to overcome them.

But Mima cannot cope with all the information she receives. When a nuclear bomb annihilates Dourisburg (the analogy is Hiroshima), she breaks down with the dreadful news that she has to relay:

> She had seen the hot white tears of granite
> when stones and ore are vaporized.
> It wrung her heart to hear these stones lament.

The Mima can be looked at in different ways. It is often thought that the Mima is some sort of advanced computer or television equipment. This is an idea that corresponds to many people's worship of television, but that is both a superficial and erroneous picture. At least half of Mima's field of activities lay beyond human analysis and had been invented by Mima herself, whose capacity, according to the author, "is three thousand and eighty times greater than anything a human being could achieve if he or she could take the Mima's place."

Mima can in fact most easily be understood as part of the mass consciousness, a world spirit, with which the poet communicates. The pantheistic structure of the universe stands out clearly in Canto 13. The "Chief Astronomer" gives a talk in which he compares Aniara's journey through the curved space of the cosmos to the barely perceptible movement of a bubble around a glass bowl. Here there is yet another reference to modern science in the form of similarity to the English Nobel Prize winner Dirac's delta function. The Chief Astronomer says, among other things:

> through God and Death and Mystery she goes,
> out space-ship without trace or goal.
> Oh, could we but turn back to our base
> now we have fathomed what our space-ship is
> — a tiny bubble in a glass of God.

Neither in this canto nor in any of the others is there given any firm answer to the poet's vehement questions about the structure of the universe. But who would be able to give an answer? In a choice between God and Mystery, however, Harry Martinson picks the latter. Later on he also said that if a god, or any gods, once created the observable cosmos for us, they have since left it to go into another space that we can never reach.

Modern-day physics has taken on an indeterministic quality, above all due to Heisenberg's uncertainty principle. In Canto 47 we find a "philosopher of point sets, nay, a mystic of the school of transfinite numbers" tiptoeing in to the woman pilot Isagel, the "clear-eyed spirit," with a question about "the frequency of wonders in the Cosmos, gauged by point set mathematics." The robot Robert, a nice guy, gets his instructions from Isagel, and then begins toiling and clattering with "the point-set load" on the "Gopta waggon." But Robert's answer is unsatisfactory because it seems, unfortunately to hold

> that Chance and Miracle
> have a common source, and consequently
> the same answer would seem valid for both.

These passages could hardly have been written without the modern statistical concepts of matter and the method to apply them. This approach was indeed used as early as the nineteenth century in thermodynamics when the movement of gas particles was studied. But it was tentatively considered to be the closest they could come until a more exact knowledge was developed.

Today, since we somewhat equate the chain of events in the world of the atom to life, atomic physics is based on statistical laws. The same theme crops up in Canto 55 when an astronomer on the "star-deck" gives a lecture to mostly apathetic or disdainful listeners. The astronomer

> describes to us how the universe plays dice
> in distant solar systems with the scalding novas.

An opposing viewpoint was advanced by Einstein, who in a famous discussion at a physicists' convention in Brussels ironically asked Bohr, Heinsenberg, and others if they really believed that God plays dice ("- - - ob der liebe Gott würfelt"). Towards the end of his life Einstein was just about the only proponent of this deterministic viewpoint.

Harry Martinson does not accept this position, but he does accept, as previously indicated, a form of pantheism. Both indeterminism and pantheism are merged in Canto 88, in which Isagel is summoned by "a messenger from the Mansions of Eternity"

> into the region of the Laws of Numbers
> where endless, unexplored reserves await us
> when the Powers of Chance decide the hour has
> come

But Isagel seeks her own death along with *Aniara* and her passengers, whom she can influence both physically and mentally. She saves the Mimarobe when he fell into disfavor with Chefone. In "Death Certificate" Harry Martinson with his pantheistic approach has also effectively brought out how this galactic scoundrel and Milky Way troublemaker aroused not only human hatred but also that of matter itself: "The very floor on which he used to stand rejoiced."

The freedom which modern science gives the poet should have provided ideas for many epics, but there has been no rush to write them. In this Harry Martinson has been the pioneer in world literature. He is the first poet of importance who truly dared, or was able, to take on the arduous task of studying humankind from all angles and to explore its situation with regard to science as an aid to poetry. Unlike many science fiction writers, he does little violence with his projections of the future. Modern technology has provided him with an adequate supply of images suitable for poetry, which he has realistically put side by side with humanity's situation. In *Aniara* science and poetry have coalesced into a viable organism; and that is the very reason why the science-generated images blend so well into the context and aim of the epic, which accounts for the overwhelming impact of the work. Harry E. Martinson was awarded the Nobel Prize for Literature in 1974.

Tord Hall

Sources for Further Study

Reviews:

Analog. LXXV, May, 1965, pp. 156-157.

Best Sellers. XXIII, July 15, 1963, p. 135.

Galaxy. XXI, August, 1963, pp. 180-181.

Nation. CXCVI, June 29, 1963, p. 550.

National Review. XV, July 16, 1963, p. 25.

New York Times Book Review. July 21, 1963, p. 4.

Times Literary Supplement. February 15, 1963, p. 111.

APE AND ESSENCE

Author: Aldous Huxley (1894-1963)
First book publication: 1948
Type of work: Novella
Time: 1948 and February, 2108
Locale: Southern California

A satiric commentary on the nature and condition of modern man presented in the form of a "screenplay" framed by a novella

Principal characters:
THE NARRATOR
BOB BRIGGS, a Hollywood scriptwriter and friend of the Narrator
WILLIAM TALLIS, author of the script entitled *Ape and Essence*
DR. ALFRED POOLE, the hero of the screenplay who comes to Southern California with the New Zealand Rediscovery Expedition to North America
MISS ETHEL HOOK, a botanist with the Rediscovery Expedition who hopes to marry Dr. Poole
LOOLA, a native of Southern California who becomes Dr. Poole's lover
ARCH-VICAR, the spiritual leader of California's devil-worshiping religion

Written by Aldous Huxley, a literary figure who has won critical acclaim for both mainstream and science fiction works, *Ape and Essence* is nevertheless a neglected and underrated novella. The moral of the work is hinted at in the title, which is taken from Shakespeare's *Measure for Measure*:

> . . . man, proud man
> Drest in a little brief authority,
> Most ignorant of what he's most assur'd,
> His glassy essence, like an angry ape,
> Plays such fantastic tricks before high heaven
> As make the angels weep. . . .

While the literary allusion of the title is subtle, Huxley's development of his moral throughout the story is quite straightforward. The warning of *Ape and Essence* is clear. If intellect and science are subordinated to man's apish or animal side, instead of being tempered by his "glassy essence" or spiritual side, the results will be tragically unpleasant.

The novel opens in a Hollywood movie studio commissary on the day in 1948 that Gandhi was assassinated. Although one purpose of the introductory chapter is to provide a setting in which the Narrator and his scriptwriter friend Bob Briggs can discover a rejected and discarded script entitled *Ape and Essence*, another purpose is to introduce us to the themes embodied in the script and prepare us for the eventual explication of the moral of the novella.

As the Narrator muses over the meaning of Gandhi's death, we are given the first hints of the chilling allegory to come. "This man who believed only in people had got himself involved in the sub-human mass-madness of national-ism, in the would-be super-human, but actually diabolic, institutions of the nation-state." This broadly abstract thought is given concrete form in the insti-tutions of the nation-state portrayed in the movie script they have yet to dis-cover. The gentle hint of the word "diabolic" is our only preparation for the grotesque political institutions in the script, political institutions closely inter-twined with a powerful state religion dedicated to devil worship. In the script the point will be made with sledge-hammer force.

> Church and State,
> Greed and Hate: —
> Two baboon-persons
> In one Supreme Gorilla.

A number of other themes are also skillfully introduced in the realistic con-temporary setting of the first chapter, and then powerfully recapitulated and developed in the movie script which is the narrative vehicle for the remainder of this novella. The result is a work in which form and content are remarkably well fused.

Why, then, has *Ape and Essence* not enjoyed the critical and popular acclaim of so many of Huxley's works? The critical reaction is easier to under-stand. Huxley's mainstream efforts had always been criticized for subordinat-ing literary form to the expression of ideas. Nonetheless, his early novels were close enough to conventional narrative form to have met with general approv-al. However, *Ape and Essence* departed from conventional narrative form, as well as the conventional psychosocial purpose of the novel. Only the first twenty-four of the one hundred and fifty-two pages of *Ape and Essence* are conventional narrative. The remainder is a movie script, and an unconven-tional and partially outlandish script at that. The critics focused on the omni-scient narrator of the script, whose only *raison-d'être* was to be a mouthpiece for ideas, declared the work too didactic, and haughtily suggested it should have been an essay. Huxley's fine interplay of realism, caricature, and satire could not save the work in the eyes of critics who had always been suspicious of the novel of ideas, whether written by Charles Dickens or H. G. Wells or Aldous Huxley. Thus, the reason for the unenthusiastic responses of the liter-rary critics is fairly obvious.

The reason for the novel's lack of popular success, particularly considering the enormous popularity of the equally dystopian *Brave New World*, is not as readily apparent. For example, it has been argued that *Brave New World* is an optimistic novel whose warning people could bear to contemplate, while *Ape and Essence* is a chillingly pessimistic allegory too terrible to be faced. How-ever, an examination of their respective messages calls that interpretation into question. Huxley himself later admitted that *Brave New World* provided only two options, the insanity of his technological Utopia or the lunacy of primitive savagery. It ends with the one representative of individualism and defiance, the Savage who is the character most like twentieth century man, hanging himself.

Ape and Essence also features a man with many of our twentieth century characteristics. In this case we are introduced to the dystopian society through the eyes of Dr. Alfred Poole in February, 2108. Dr. Poole is a member of the New Zealand Rediscovery Expedition to North America. New Zealand's isolation saved it from the devastation of the Third World War, but it had to wait more than a century for the radiation to subside enough to permit an attempt to rediscover America. Dr. Poole becomes separated from his colleagues and is captured by the natives. Later he is abandoned by the expeditionary team and absorbed into the local society. He is no more enthralled by what he sees than the Savage was enthralled by the dystopia in *Brave New World*. But the Savage hangs himself, while Dr. Poole simply runs away from dystopia with his lover Loola to join a colony of individualists in the north. When we contrast the structure of both novels and the final vision with which each leaves us, the argument that *Brave New World* is intrinsically optimistic and *Ape and Essence* pessimistic loses its plausibility.

Perhaps, then, the key to explaining the different reception of the two novels is not internal but external — in the mind-set of the readers. The remoteness or immediacy of the potential dystopias was critical to how people responded to them. When *Brave New World* appeared, the terrible economic conditions of 1932 made a dystopia based on a technologically created abundance seem particularly remote. Indeed, in view of then-existing conditions, the supposed dystopia in which all material needs were met and pleasure was endlessly provided, seemed strangely attractive; and the absence of individuality, freedom, and higher significance in one's life seemed almost a tolerable omission. Under the circumstances, the satire was easy to enjoy and many responded to *Brave New World* as the "fun" book of the year. It was only later that the threat suggested in *Brave New World* for a time seemed imminent, in those marvelous days of economic optimism before the Club of Rome printed *Limits to Growth* and once again made people realize that they would be lucky to have the problems that Huxley projected.

Ape and Essence, on the other hand, was published just as the world learned of the widespread mutations caused by atomic radiation. The effects of radiation had been partially anticipated, but the possibility of worldwide mutation among the majority of the population had not been suspected. Huxley eagerly rubbed the reader's nose in the new knowledge by postulating a society in which seven fingers and three sets of nipples were accepted, but neither more nor less; a baby differing from the norm was used in a ritual of purification that ended with its ugly death at the altar.

Moreover, the public mind was not prepared for many of the other concerns

Huxley explored so far in advance in *Ape and Essence*. People were ready to appreciate the themes of *Brave New World* because those themes were already part of the intellectual climate, but Huxley in *Ape and Essence* was ahead of his time in his suggestion that technology itself destroy the environment even without atomic war. The Arch-Vicar of the diabolical religion of *Ape and Essence* expresses the thought, "A little more slowly perhaps, but just as surely, men would have destroyed themselves by destroying the world they lived in." He then describes the actions of our last century and a half. "Fouling the rivers, killing off the wild animals, destroying the forests, washing the topsoil into the sea, burning up an ocean of petroleum, squandering the minerals it had taken the whole of geological time to deposit." Clearly, this was not an idea most readers were ready to contemplate. If, on the other hand, *Ape and Essence* had been published in the 1970's with all the attendant fanfare of a new Huxley novel, it might have struck a far more responsive chord.

In 1948, with the Cold War just beginning, it was also difficult for readers to accept the attitudes Huxley expressed in the introduction. For instance, Bob Briggs is silenced when his boss greets his demand for a raise with the assertion that the request is un-American. Indeed, rejection of the introduction by critics and populace alike may have undermined a full appreciation of the work as a whole. The book is usually remembered only for its movie script, yet the introduction not only presaged what followed but amplified and clarified it. For example, it is no accident that the narrative begins on the day of Gandhi's assassination; that fact is established in the first sentence. Observing that the sightseers are more interested in the contents of their picnic baskets than in the assassination, the Narrator comments on man's egotism. "In spite of all the astronomers can say, Ptolemy was perfectly right: the center of the universe is here, not there." His companion in the movie studio commissary, Bob Briggs, is also absorbed in his own petty affairs. He is rattling on about the forces that led him to run off to Acapulco with his longtime partner in flirtation, Elaine. He dramatizes his motivations by comparing them to the forces that compelled Martin Luther to act as he felt necessary. The egotism of the comparison is obvious to Huxley's seemingly superior and erudite narrator. Then in typical Huxley fashion, the mocker is mocked for his egotism by allowing his absorption in his own thoughts to keep him from hearing what Bob Briggs is telling him, even though Bob ends by thanking the Narrator for being so helpful.

When the Narrator and Bob Briggs discover the rejected script, *Ape and Essence*, and go in search of the scriptwriter William Tallis, who has so impressed them, what they learn of his life and his reasons for writing the script demonstrates the difference between egotism and concern for the consequences of one's actions. Before World War I, Tallis had left his German wife and daughter for an American showgirl he met in Paris. His wife and daughter were killed during World War II, and now there is only a granddaughter left as a product of his marriage. Tallis' granddaughter is alone in Europe, and the

Narrator imagines her to be prostituting herself for candy-bars. Tallis, who had been retired and living on a meager income, wrote the script to raise money to be able to do something about his granddaughter's situation. The bleak script reflects Tallis' view of himself as well as of our society; it begins with clothed apes performing a vicious caricature of contemporary culture. The apes are the visible embodiment of the dominance of egotism in our society, already suggested in the introduction in a gentler fashion. People are depicted as emphasizing the wrong part of their nature. The point is made even clearer when the script shifts to the survivors, now presented in human form, of what our ape selves have wrought.

The film's omniscient narrator ties the themes together. When we go against the order of things, when we follow our ape-ego, when we try to conquer nature without regard for the consequences, we are adopting the religion of Huxley's dystopia; we are worshiping Belial and following him whom the Arch-Vicar of this dismal religion repeatedly calls the Lord of the Flies (after the Greek word Beelzebub). It is not enough that we are utilizing intellect and science to achieve our objectives. That is made clear by the first lines they read from the body of the script when they first find it.

> Surely it's obvious.
> Doesn't every schoolboy know it?
> Ends are ape-chosen; only the means are man's.

The means are created by intellect and science, yet they are not a sufficient guide to action. Huxley later makes that point by quoting Pascal: "We make an idol of truth; for truth without charity is not God, but his image and idol which we must neither love nor worship." There is of course one type of knowledge that *can* guide action, as Huxley's omniscient narrator states in the moral of the novella,

> Only in the knowledge of his own Essence
> Has any man ceased to be many monkeys.

Barry Faye

Sources for Further Study

Criticism:

Meckier, Jerome. *Aldous Huxley: Satire and Structure*. New York: Barnes & Noble, 1969, pp. 189-197. Meckier sees this as a precurson to *Island*.

————. Quarles Among the Monkeys: Huxley's Zoological Novels, in *Modern Language Review*. LXVII (1973), pp. 280-281. Meckier discusses the Utopia theme.

Schmerl, Rudolf B. "The Two Future Worlds of Aldous Huxley," in *PMLA*. LXXVII (June, 1962), pp. 113-118. Utopia and evolution are related to *Ape and Essence*.

Reviews:

Booklist. XLV, October 15, 1948, p. 66.

Christian Science Monitor. August 19, 1948, p. 11.

Kirkus Reviews. XVI, June 15, 1948, p. 289.

Library Journal. LXXIII, August, 1948, p. 1090.

Nation. CLXVII, August 21, 1948, p. 210.

New Republic. CXIX, August 23, 1948, p. 21.

New York Times Book Review. August 22, 1948, p. 5.

New Yorker. XXXIV, August 28, 1948, p. 69.

Saturday Review of Literature. XXXI, August 21, 1948, p. 8.

Time. LII, August 23, 1948, p. 76.

ARMAGEDDON 2419 A.D.

Author: Philip Francis Nowlan (1887-1940)
First book publication: 1962
Type of work: Novel
Time: 1927 and the twenty-fifth century
Locale: Enemy-occupied North America

Emerging from a five-hundred-year suspended animation "sleep," Anthony Rogers leads the conquered North Americans of the twenty-fifth century to victory in a war to overthrow their rulers, a hybrid Mongolian race known as the Hans

Principal characters:
> ANTHONY ROGERS, a twenty-nine-year-old twentieth century man alive in the twenty-fifth century
> WILMA DEERING, a girl soldier of the embattled North Americas and subsequently Rogers' wife
> SAN-LAN, "Most Glorious Air Lord of All the Hans"
> NGO-LAN, San-Lan's favorite concubine
> DAVE BERG, Camp Boss of Camp Number 34
> GERDI MANN, Dave Berg's redheaded girl friend

Most of the world has heard of Buck Rogers; few realize that he was cloned, in a literary sense, from the Anthony Rogers *Armageddon 2419 A.D.*, the nucleus of which was published in *Amazing Stories Magazine* in 1928. Even fewer realize that Philip Francis Nowlan, the ever-smiling moustached author, was a financial writer for the *Philadelphia Retail Ledger*.

Thanks to the comic strip that stemmed from the novel, the basic storyline is as familiar as that of *Oedipus Rex*. In the latter part of 1927, Rogers — born in 1898 and nicknamed "Tony" (though called Buck in the strip) — is trapped in a caved-in mine near Pittsburgh. Radioactive gas holds him in suspended animation for nearly five hundred years. When, due to a rock stratum shift, he staggers from his living tomb in the year 2419, North America is as unfamiliar as the surface of another planet. Dense forests have obliterated urban sprawl. Defensive Caucasians, clad in tight-fitting green outfits like Robin Hood's men and brandishing rocket pistols, skulk under leafy canopies, muttering about the "Day of Hope" and "The Second War of Independence." Hybrid Mongolians — the Airlords of Han who have conquered the earth — periodically cruise overhead, taking potshots with disintegrator rays at the bipedal "beasts."

Within days, Rogers bumps into lissome Wilma Deering and rescues her from some local peril. She straightens him out as to where he is and what the situation is all about. It seems that, five hundred years earlier, after World War II, victorious Russians teamed up with equally victorious Chinese to crush Europe like a crumpled cigarette. The Chinese then double-crossed the Russians and put *them* out of commission. Meanwhile, back in Tibet, a small planet crashed in the remote hinterlands, causing changes in the earth's orbit and climate. To make things even worse, the planet contained soulless semi-humans who raped Tibetan women. The ravished women then gave birth to hybrid Mongolians known as Hans (probably an unwitting take-off on the "Huns" of World War I). The Hans, having super intellects, quickly overran everything and everybody, building huge airships and widely separated cities of sparkling glass. In the process, America was flattened under the yellow heel. But now, many years after their subjugation, Americans are fighting back, much in the manner of 1940's commandos.

The oppressed people of what was once the United States live in scattered, loosely organized camps, each run by a boss. Every adult male and female alternates between laboring in underground factories for two weeks, and serving as a hit-and-run soldier in fortnightly shifts. Though handicapped as only the hunted can be, they've succeeded in restoring a sophisticated technology, partially through decoding Hans radio messages and siphoning off the enemy's know-how.

New to this milieu, Rogers quickly becomes a respected leader through his improbable expertise with a rocket pistol (though he has never seen one before). After Rogers figures out how to shoot down Han airships by firing rocket charges into their ground-sweeping repellor beams, he is shoved into a position of command. Rising to the occasion, he marries Wilma (they were not even officially engaged in the thirty-eight years of the comic strip), and instigates much derring-do, including wiping out treachery in the camps and smashing the Han informational "nerve center" in Nu-Yok.

As the action line steadily unwinds, Rogers vows to blast the Mongolian blight from the earth's face. Vengeful Americans put Han cities and air lanes under siege. (Much of the latter part of the novel concentrates on the attributes of the alien Utopia which the grim-faced Caucasians deliberately shatter.) Captured by the Hans, Rogers is whisked to the city of Lo-Tan, in the Rockies, where he is interrogated by the great San-Lan himself. (San-Lan, the Heaven Born, is the Most Glorious Air Lord of All the Hans.) Though injected with drugs, and semiseduced by Ngo-Lan, San-Lan's favorite concubine, Rogers refuses to divulge the rebels' secrets, thereby gaining the respect of the Heaven Born, who considers him a superman.

Wilma and her cohorts then rescue Rogers in Saturday Afternoon Serial-fashion; an extensive, very bloody mop-up operation ensues; and the Hans finally give up. At the end of the novel, Rogers is a tired old man reminiscing about his incredible past. Wilma has already died, and he is eager to join her in the "great beyond." Such is the basic story.

Folklore credits this well-written novel with initiating many "hardware" concepts that later became standard in science fiction. This is a misconception. There is an actual paucity of gadgetry in the novel compared to the "overkill" of gadgetry in the strip that sprang from it. However, some of the items and concepts, though not always completely original, deserve recognition. Nowlan predicted computers and credit cards (the Hans had them); the creation of synthetic air and sunlight for subterranean cities; and the use of gland control and dietetics to increase longevity. (It is worth noting that he also believed in an all-pervading ether, as did many physicists and astronomers in the 1920's.)

A brief list of gadgets and concepts includes *Inertron*, a mineral with a property, unique to itself, which allows it to resist gravity and, having reverse weight, to fall upward. *Repellor rays* are columns of scintillating light that push downward with great force against the ground, and upward with equal force against the keel of the airship generating them. The ship is maneuvered by altering the slant of the rays. *Jumping belts*, shaped like small backpacks, enable their wearers to leap effortlessly sixty or seventy feet, vertically or horizontally, and land gently. *Disintegrator rays* are electronic flashes that break protons apart. A single ray, contingent on its size, can eradicate a man or a metropolis. *Rocket pistols* have bullets with explosive power equal to that of twentieth century artillery shells.

Because the story was written in 1928, ten years after "The War to End All Wars," topical references to that conflict are rife. As noted before, "Han" probably derives from "Hun." World War I trench warfare is periodically alluded to. The rolling and continuous thunder of rocket-fire is like the rolling and continuous thunder of cannon-fire from 1914 through 1918. There are American lines and Han lines, just as there were German lines and Allied lines in the war Nowlan knew about at firsthand. Curiously enough, when the author slips out of that particular frame of reference, he slides back to the Middle Ages, employing a weird duke's mixture of weaponry. In hand-to-hand combat, the Hans wield swords, knives, battle-axes, and spears, while the Americans use bayonets; and as previously mentioned, the Caucasians are clad in tight-fitting green outfits like those of Robin Hood and his merry men in Sherwood Forest. (Oddly, when Nowlan wrote the original masterful continuity for the Buck Rogers strip, he had a penchant for clothing everyone in outfits reminiscent of Roman Empire centurians.) Refocusing on the year in which the story was penned, the terms Big Boss and sub-bosses remind one of gangland organizations of the Prohibition Era. One major fault of the book is the heavyhanded use of terms like Nu-Yok to designate the previous site of New York. This is a sophomoric play on words unworthy of an adult writer.

There's only one truly three-dimensional character in the novel; San-Lan, the imperious, extremely complex leader of all the Hans. San-Lan is multi-faceted, simultaneously likable and contemptible. He virtually rises from the pages and takes over. When he is on stage, everyone present shrinks to the role of a spear-carrier, including Rogers. Rogers himself ("Tony" to Wilma, "Forest Man" to San-Lan) is little more than a mouthpiece for the autobiographical first-person viewpoint; he is a jut-jawed cardboard cut-out that talks. Wilma Deering never lives and breathes; her romance with Rogers is physically passionless and insipid. Nowlan has her scream in ecstatic joy when burying her bayonet in opponents, or shriek like a Valkyrie, but that is hardly characterization. Dave Berg, Camp Boss of Camp Number 34, is nothing but a name, as is Gerdi Mann, the redheaded girl with whom he is supposedly madly in love. Even Ngo-Lan, San-Lan's favorite concubine, is little more than an abstractly undulating pelvis when trying to seduce Rogers.

Despite these flaws — and these are weaknesses characteristic of too many science fiction stories — the novel is well written. The narrative style is restrained and objective, like that of James Hilton in *Lost Horizon*. When the reader realizes, on the last page of the book, that Wilma has died, he feels a genuine pang, even though she did not truly come to life in the preceding pages. The pang is similar to the uneasiness one feels when advised that a neighbor on the next street has passed away: a neighbor one nodded hello to on the way to work, but never really got to know.

Anyone who reads this commentary, and remembers or is familiar with the long-running Buck Rogers comic strip, must be aware of the unbridgeable chasm that separates the book from the newspaper panels. Tony Rogers and Wilma Deering in the novel bear virtually no resemblance to the Buck Rogers and Wilma Deering of the strip. The storyline, up to a point, is roughly the same for both, but in terms of imagination and character development, the strip far outdistances its godparent, which is surprising, since both were the brain-children of Philip Francis Nowlan, financial writer.

The Buck Rogers in the twenty-fifth century comic strip — the first and most influential science fiction comic strip — ran from January 7, 1929 to mid-1967. Nowlan wrote the script's continuity for several years (via mail from Philadelphia to Chicago), while Richard W. Calkins did the artwork. After Nowlan died and Calkins retired to be an honorary sheriff in Arizona, Buck's adventures continued through the pens and minds of Rick Yager, Murphy Anderson, George Tuska, and Leonard Dworkins.

The strip differs from the novel in several ways: Buck looks and acts like Charles Lindbergh (at least for awhile); and Lieutenant Wilma Deering is much more three-dimensional than her counterpart in the book: she is mercurial, quick to anger or pout, alternately stubborn and kittenish, and likely to indulge in hair-pulling brawls with women magnetized by Buck's massive indifference. And there are two ever-present villains who are monstrously appealing, Killer Kane and his girlfriend, Ardala Valmar.

More than that, the strip concerns itself with interplanetary and intergalactic adventure, whereas the book does not. The book is earthbound; the strip is limited only by the stretchable boundaries of the universe.

At its popularity peak, the newspaper feature was read by six million fans daily. Twenty million glued their ears to radios to hear weird sound effects as Buck snapped orders to space ship crews. In 1938, thousands of youngsters crowded movie theaters on Saturday afternoons to watch Buster Crabbe portray Buck going fifteen rounds with twenty-fifth century evil. The Buck Ro-

gers phenomenon was the Great Escape from the Depression; the child's thrilling inspiration; the man in the street's mind-expander and horizon-stretcher.

The strip had many imitators, including "Flash Gordon" and "Brick Bradford," but none equaled its influence or ingenuity. It introduced more people
to science fiction than any other medium before or since, with the possible
exception of the motion picture *Star Wars*.

George S. Elrick

AT MIDNIGHT ON THE 31ST OF MARCH

Author: Josephine Young Case (1907-   )
First book publication: 1938
Type of work: Narrative poem
Time: The late 1930's
Locale: An imaginary rural town in the Northeastern United States

An account of events during the first year after a time-slip warps the town of Saugersville out of the twentieth century into an uninhabited North America

> Principal characters:
> BERT SNYDER, a general store proprietor
> EARL BACKUS,
> WILLIAM COUNTRYMAN,
> ROY SMITH,
> GUS WARDER, and
> ED WINTERHAUS, farmers and members of the town's Safety Board
> GERTRUDE WINTERHAUS, Ed's daughter
> ABE GIVETS, a farmer and local entrepreneur
> JOHN HERBERT, an invalid
> ROBERT MUNN, a garage proprietor
> BESSIE MUNN, his wife
> EPHRIAM YULE, minister of the town's church

Only one person, John Herbert, is awake by late evening in the tiny village of Saugersville on the last day of March; and he, who loves the city but has been forced into rural life by failing health, is reading in restlessness and solitude. At midnight his bedside lamp fades slowly to a red glow and dies. Unsuccessfully he tries a new bulb, then another light altogether, curses the power company, and goes to bed. At dawn, other villagers also discover there is no electricity; kitchens are lit by candles and cows are milked by the light of kerosene lanterns. All telephones also are dead. As men gather over the hot stove in the general store to discuss this puzzle, there is a further disturbing report. The driver who trucks local milk out of town arrives back an hour early, his face gray and shaken. He has found that the highway stops at the edge of town by the river and the bridge has disappeared; beyond, he says, "The road ain't there no more." Investigation proves the same situation everywhere. Every road runs into a stand of woods, poles and wires of the high-tension lines end abruptly, and the cleared area which villagers used to take out of town is now filled with mighty trees.

Earl Backus and his two brothers set out on foot for Centerfield, a neighboring town twelve miles away. It is late when they return. They have fought their way through a virgin forest abounding in game but have seen no sign of human beings; where Centerfield once stood, now there is no town, railroad, trails, or highways — only huge old trees overhanging the silent river. Roy Smith climbs a tree atop the highest nearby hill and surveys the countryside for miles around, seeing only trees, "trees all the way." Finally, even at night, when the airwaves are usually crowded, battery radios bring in nothing but crackling static. What has happened now becomes clear: the town has been caught in a time-warp and carried either to a prehistoric age or to an alternate time-stream. There is: "No Schuylers Falls, no Indiantown, no Springs,/ No state, no city, no America,/ But only Saugersville in all the world."

Case has divided *At Midnight on the 31st of March* into three sections. The first and longest, comprising almost half its total length, covers the time-warp catastrophe, detailing the sense of horror and doom it brings to all, and carries events through the following six months of spring, summer, and early fall. The second section, somewhat shorter, takes the reader to the first of January, and shows how townspeople become increasingly better able to cope. The last section, making up about a fifth of the total work, completes the community's first isolated year at midnight of the next thirty-first of March on a note of optimism, acceptance, and the broad, universal theme of how the human spirit faces change, adjusts, and continues.

Numerous fictional examples of people (often time-travelers), thrown back suddenly from civilization into the Stone Age, abound in all genres of literature. All too often these center on one scientifically superior individual with an encyclopedic knowledge who manages to rebuild civilization in some incredibly brief time. This work never falls into such a convenient literary rut; there are no scientific geniuses in Saugersville. It has no more than the expected cross-section of people normally found in a small country village where few have formal intellectual training or mechanical skills.

There are, however, characterizations of people running the entire gamut of human responses — the generous and the misanthropic, the outgoing and the introverted, the content and the frustrated. Whatever people are or have been, they must change to meet their new reality — some in small ways, some in major ones. And those who cannot or will not, do not survive.

Peglegged Dick Van Snell, who lived at the isolated edge of town by a big S-curve in the main road, is an example. His only social contacts were his customers and passing cars, both of which are now gone. Although urged to leave these surroundings and his now lonely house, he cannot bring himself to do so and commits suicide. Misanthropic Abe Givets, well off but stingy, unhappy and mean (especially to his young and pretty wife) does unbend little by little, and we think he will finally make it. Then, he discovers a deposit of badly needed salt, and immediately all his innate, grasping miserliness surfaces. Eventually he is killed because he tries to hoard everything for himself. John Herbert and Gert Winterhaus are among those slow to adapt. Gert (by chance, home from college on the day of the time-warp) loves the city in the same way John does, and the thought that everyone is now condemned to a rural life forever is unbearable. This common bond gradually draws the two together, yet both realize that they are incompatible. Ephriam Yule, minister of the town's only church, also adapts slowly. He is elderly, respected, and lives in one of Saugersville's most substantial homes — yet he had never been a strong leader. Since his church is now fuller than it ever was — leadership has been thrust upon him. Gradually he rises to his new role, coming to terms both with himself and the community as well.

A governing "Safety Board" is elected to plan and allocate supplies; its first task is to assure maximum crop yield in the growing season ahead. Most people cooperate willingly, united by need and fear into a tribal closeness. The old teach the young old arts, once again needed. All live more intensely as the world's contraction made their blood more hot. A country dance is held to relieve tensions. Spring arrives, and then summer and fall. Oldtime root cellars are dug or refurbished, and food is canned and preserved. Thanksgiving becomes a day with newly inspired significance, and Christmas reminds everyone how much better off they are than were the Massachusetts Bay colonists.

With the harvest completed, the menfolk gather around the village store and meet Saturday nights as they formerly did. They exchange ideas on how to compensate for the lack of machinery because of the dwindling gasoline supply, by using alternate sources of power such as wood, water, and animals. The Safety Board hammers out plans for the coming year, and by December, the first snow falls.

Mrs. Case logically develops a solution to the problems of educating the young. The community's isolation has lessened outside distractions, and Saugersville's one-room school continues as before. The three R's continue, though there is less emphasis on geography and more on the practical arts. Girls are taught how to weave, spin, make soap, and candles; boys are taught the skills of carpentry, blacksmithing, and agriculture. The past is important, and must not be forgotten, thus history must be taught also. Books must be handled gently, the small supply of paper rationed carefully. Old-fashioned slates are resurrected for student use. There is a warm, nostalgic Christmas scene where the children receive handmade toys and their teacher brings out an ancient, spring-operated victrola to play some of the few precious records to teach Christmas carols. The scene is reminiscent of Walter Van Tilburg Clark's science fiction story of the same period, "The Portable Phonograph," in which records have also become treasured, irreplaceable things.

As the winter gradually passes and the sun moves north again, the townspeople decide that April first, not January first, will thenceforward be their New Year's Day — celebrated by a party for all, and the election of a new Safety Board. Ephriam Yule will perform two marriages, and the human race will go on fighting to keep and pass on the best of what has been learned.

There are several unique qualities about this work. First of all it is told wholly in blank verse — perhaps the only long science fiction story that has appeared in that form. Second, it is almost totally concerned with translating the consequences of the time-slip placed in the perspective of psychological human terms rather than pseudoscientific gimmickry. Finally, it may well be the very first one to explore the psychological device, predating both Mona Farnsworth's "All Roads" (1940) and Jerome Bixby's "It's a *Good* Life" (1953). Despite its clear historical importance, it has never been reviewed in any fantasy publication. In traditional literary circles, however, its worth has long been recognized. It was widely reviewed on publication in national media, has twice been dramatized for radio broadcast, and in 1960 was presented on television.

Josephine Case's verse is serviceable and competent, a suitable vehicle for a powerful story. Occasionally lines seem contrived, but far more are richly effective. Her descriptions of the changing seasons, for example, are very sensitive. The verse medium also utilizes a number of literary devices which are difficult in prose. One of these, the soliloquy, is used often with particular effectiveness.

About fifty different characters appear in *At Midnight on the 31st of March*, but it is not difficult to keep them straight, since only a few dominate the action, and Case has had the foresight to choose a different given name for each. Many facets of these characters are undoubtedly drawn from life, authentically reflecting the Massachusetts area where she grew up, and the small village in rural New York where she and her family have dwelt and farmed for eight generations. Many of the old ways of life to which Saugersville must revert were described to Case by her grandmother, "who would have known what to do," and it is to her that the book is dedicated.

Josephine Case has stated that she intended no particular symbolism in the book, and rather doubts whether it could be written today when the village is even less of an entity than it was forty years ago. She cannot recall any special genesis of the time-slip concept utilized — "it just came to me" — and never felt the narrative made it necessary to rationalize it. None of her other three books of poetry involve fantasy themes. The modern writer whose spirit comes closest to that of this work is probably Stephen Vincent Benét. Case's verse is not as striking as Benét's, but it carries the same glow of courage, optimism, and hope for the future.

A. Langley Searles

AT THE EARTH'S CORE

Author: Edgar Rice Burroughs (1875-1950)
First book publication: 1922
Type of work: Novel
Time: Approximately 1903-1913
Locale: At the Earth's core

Two explorers in a mechanical digging conveyance burrow to the hollow interior of the Earth where they have a series of adventures

> *Principal characters:*
> DAVID INNES, a wealthy young mine-owner
> ABNER PERRY, inventor of the mechanical subterranean prospector
> DIAN THE BEAUTIFUL, princess of the tribe of Amoz
> THE MAHARS, the rulers of Pellucidar

In a discussion of the work of Edgar Rice Burroughs, there should be room for a few words about publisher Frank A. Munsey. Apparently interested more in money than in anything else, Munsey experimented with several magazine formats in the late nineteenth century, and eventually developed the one that was later to be the vehicle for the Golden Age of science fiction — the all-fiction pulp magazine. Science fiction had appeared often in the pages of the pulps before Hugo Gernsback came along, much of it in the magazines published by Munsey: *Munsey's*, *Argosy*, *Cavalier*, and especially *All-Story*. And in the second decade of the twentieth century, Edgar Rice Burroughs was the star of the Munsey enterprise.

Burroughs' first novel was *Under the Moons of Mars*, which ran as a six-part serial in *All Story* in 1912; when *Pellucidar* appeared in 1914-1915, it was his seventeenth. In that span of about three years, Munsey printed the following works by Burroughs: *Tarzan of the Apes* (*All-Story*, 1912), *The Gods of Mars* (*All-Story*, 1913), *Nu of the Neocene* (*All-Story Weekly*, 1914), *The Warlords of Mars* (*All-Story*, 1914), *The Mucker* (*All-Story Cavalier Weekly*, 1914), and *At the Earth's Core* (*All-Story*, 1914). And these were, of course, in addition to those Burroughs placed elsewhere. Richard A. Lupoff, one of his biographers, estimates that in 1913 alone, Burroughs wrote over 400,000 words of fiction.

The popularity of this very prolific writer underlines the fact that, although it was not called science fiction, the form was very much in evidence well before the birth of *Amazing Stories*. When Edgar Rice Burroughs wrote *At the Earth's Core*, the central idea of that story had appeared in fiction several times during the previous hundred years. The heroes of *At the Earth's Core*, David Innes and Abner Perry, discover that the earth is hollow; after passing through five hundred miles of crust, they emerge into Pellucidar, the concave inner surface of a hollow sphere seven thousand miles in diameter. Above their heads hangs a miniature sun which gives never-ceasing light and heat to this world within a world.

Burroughs' setting, "hollow-earth," had several precedents, but the wide-spread popularity of the hollow-earth theory began in 1818 with the activities of Captain John Cleves Symmes, an American army officer. Symmes proposed that openings at the poles gave access to five hollow concentric spheres within the globe, and he pursued his imaginative conception through letters to professors of science at universities on two continents, and in a petition to Congress for an expedition to search for the opening. His ideas reached the public in full form with his 1826 book (coauthored with James McBride), *Symmes Theory of Concentric Spheres*.

The first embodiment of the idea in fiction was *Symzonia*, a novel of 1820 by "Captain Adam Seaborn" (the name may be a pseudonym of Symmes himself). The novel, or at least the idea behind it, was known to Edgar Allan Poe: his hero sees the polar opening in "The Unparalleled Adventure of One Hans Pfaal" (1835), and the theory behind the novel is hinted at both in "MS Found in a Bottle" (1833) and in the unfinished *The Narrative of Arthur Gordon Pym*. Perhaps Poe's stories suggested the setting to his most famous admirer, Jules Verne, whose novel *Journey to the Center of the Earth* (1864) takes place in a vast underground expanse entered through an extinct volcano. Although Verne's setting is an immense cavern rather than the interior of a hollow sphere, he populates it with flora and fauna extinct on the surface, a detail to reappear in Burroughs' handling of the theme.

Several American works also utilized the hollow-earth notion; one example is William Bradshaw's *The Goddess of Atvatabar* (1892), which is set in an underground land lit from the interior by a small sun, rather than depending on light reflected through the openings at the poles. The idea of a hollow earth remained popular, through John Uri Lloyd's *Etidorhpa* (1895) and Charles Willing Beale's *The Secret of the Earth* (1899), right up to Willis George Emerson's *The Smoky God* (1908), printed the year before Robert E. Peary's expedition to the North Pole found no opening.

Very likely inspired by an amalgam of sources, Burroughs, then, drew his setting, adding to it the touches of his own inventive imagination. But Burroughs seldom showed absolute originality; his strength lay, rather, in a competent use of the themes and techniques which the tradition of popular adventure fiction made available to him. Although in 1913 he was in only the third year of his professional writing career, he already had a firm hold on the few simple devices of plot and character that were to make him widely read and enjoyed to the present day. His hero, David Innes, is once again a young man of inherited wealth and technical background. His resolution and resourcefulness carry him through a series of adventures, in the course of which he meets, falls in love with, is separated from, and finally is reunited with a young woman of beauty and high birth whose energy and daring match his own.

The story is written in the first person, a point of view consistently favored in almost all of Burroughs' stories, and it opens with the typical framing device: a traveler tells of meeting Innes in the Sahara, and frankly states that he does not expect the reader to believe his story. Like all such devices, the frame serves to fulfill two seemingly antithetical purposes: it establishes an atmosphere of verisimilitude at the same time that it makes little claim to the reader's credence. The point of view, the way of beginning, and the episodic adventures that follow are all familiar to readers of Burroughs.

But several details deserve separate attention. First, Burroughs has almost never been noted for a deft use of humor, chiefly because so little that is humorous occurs in his stories. Tarzan, on the whole, is a pretty moody fellow, and John Carter's adventures are lightened, if at all, only by a grim irony or two. The lack of humor is easy to explain; it derives from the author's characteristic choice of narrator — the stock figure whom Isaac Asimov has termed "the big lug," a capable but inarticulate man, who seldom looks within himself to analyze his emotions. The typical Burroughs hero accepts what fate sends, often struggling to survive yet lacking the sense of incongruity from which so much of the comic springs. In novel after novel, the hero's love for the heroine comes as a surprise to him, although it has been clear to the reader for chapters. The characters have powerful emotions, but they lie beneath the level of conscious thought until, having matured, they break upward to their owners' attention.

At the Earth's Core is different; rather than being shaped in the usual mold, David Innes is not only aware of his romantic plight, he can joke about it. For example, through a good part of the novel, Innes aids Dian, the daughter of the chief of Amoz, in her escape from Jubal, the Ugly One. Jubal has marriage by capture on his mind. After slaying Jubal in single combat (albeit reluctantly), Innes approaches Dian, confident that he has won her love and respect, or at least her gratitude. When he is greeted with contempt, Innes turns to the corpse of Jubal and says, "May be that I saved you from a worse fate, old man." David Innes is one of the most fully developed and successful characters that Burroughs created.

A second triumph of characterization in *At the Earth's Core* is the race of Mahars. The Mahars are avian reptiles, six to eight feet tall, descended, Perry tells us, from the "rhamphorhynchus of the Middle Olitic." They communicate with one another in some way not understood by the humans in the story; nor do the Mahars understand that humans communicate with one another. Believing that humans have no speech, the Mahars look on them as moderately intelligent animals, which they herd for food, or keep around as slaves for simple tasks.

In another way, the Mahars seem surprisingly modern: they are a race of females who reproduce parthenogenetically. Ages ago, we are told, the Mahars came under "the intelligent and beneficent rule of the ladies." With the males tending to warfare, science and learning became the sphere of the females, until one of them discovered a chemical means of fertilizing eggs.

With males no longer necessary, they ceased to exist. Reptiles though they may be, the Mahars are one of the few all-female races in fiction to form a scientific and technological society either in early or modern writing.

All does not end happily for either the adventurers or the human natives of the Earth's interior. Although the Mahars are overthrown, David Innes' triumphant return to the surface is spoiled by a traitor. A captive Mahar is substituted for Dian, and Innes steps onto the surface of the Earth accompanied by a female other than the one he had expected. Burroughs, given to writing series of adventures utilizing the same characters and settings, was not one to allow a worked-out society to be wasted on a single novel. Consequently, *At the Earth's Core* ends with Innes preparing to return to Pellucidar, and the outline of a sequel already visible on the horizon. Setting a new plot in motion at the very end of the book was a technique Burroughs consistently employed with the John Carter series. Indeed, readers of magazines in which his work was appearing almost monthly had come to expect Burroughs' adventures to follow one another in rapid succession.

It is easy to find defects in much of Burroughs' work: the Tarzan stories show a sameness of plot that quickly becomes repetitious; *The Land That Time Forgot* begins with a preposterous series of coincidences; even in the Martian novels, John Carter tends to repeat himself, and the series must depend on exotic setting and bizarre characters for its appeal. But in *At the Earth's Core*, we find real and likable characters, romance that is not dated, and suspense that still captivates; here is Burroughs doing his very best with those materials which he always uses well.

Walter E. Meyers

AT THE MOUNTAINS OF MADNESS

Author: H. P. Lovecraft (1890-1937)
First book publication: 1964
Type of work: Novel
Time: 1931
Locale: Antarctica

A scientist attempts to discourage further exploration of Antarctica lest certain alien entities be disturbed, with dire consequences for the sanity and survival of mankind

> *Principal characters:*
> WILLIAM DYER, the narrator, a geology professor at Miskatonic University and head of the Antarctic expedition
> FRANK H. PABODIE, an engineer
> LAKE, a biology professor at Miskatonic University
> ATWOOD, a meteorologist and physics professor
> DANFORTH, a graduate student
> GEDNEY, a graduate student in Lake's party
> THE ELDER ONES, the revived alien entities and their kin
> THE SHOGGOTH, their monstrous and unmanageable creation

This novel is a *tour de force* that must be read and reread in order to be savored fully. It works at several levels, and it is intended to do so. In order to understand both the style and the substance of the narrative we must realize that H. P. Lovecraft believed that an effective depiction of imaginary marvelous events must be presented in the manner of a well-contrived hoax, striving for the utmost verisimilitude and realism in every detail except the bizarre event itself. Furthermore, the characters must be subordinate to the awe-inspiring and fear-inducing occurrence, never overshadowing it; they must react to it as normal flesh-and-blood persons would if they encountered such an outrageous violation of natural law in real life. They certainly do so here.

Lovecraft presents us with a report supposedly written by a geologist warning against further expeditions to Antarctica. The narrative does indeed read as if it had been written by such a scientist, because it abounds in technical and scientific data and terminology — reflecting the author's impressive erudition in matters of geology, biology, archaeology, and paleontology — and because it lacks flashy "action" scenes and the description of trivial incidents unlikely to find their way into a *bona fide* report of this kind. There is no dialogue whatsoever. Nevertheless, characters such as Dyer and Danforth come alive, their plight eliciting our sympathy, and their courage compelling our admiration.

The plot, as it unfolds in Professor Dyer's narrative, has a special twist, best understood when one remembers that for Lovecraft a work such as this should call forth an affective reaction in the reader (ranging from awe — not untinged with fear — to terror and horror), rather than be a didactic tool for the exposition of ideas. The Miskatonic University expedition to Antarctica, of which Dyer was the leader, uncovers some strange triangular striated markings, actually alien footprints over 500 million years old. Professor Lake takes an air party in search of further evidence, and discovers a colossal mountain chain. He establishes a base on the foothills. Here, after some drilling, he finds a subterranean cave, and in it a number of barrel-shaped, star-headed alien beings, well-preserved fossils from the immemorial past. A storm develops, and contact with Lake's party is lost.

When Dyer arrives with rescue forces, he finds the camp in a shambles, its equipment strangely tampered with, and the bodies of all but one of the men and all but one of the dogs in Lake's expedition lying about. Dyer and the student Danforth fly through a pass in the mountain chain and discover the ruins of a cyclopean city on the other side, as well as an even more titanic range of mountains in the distance. They land and explore part of the city, entering its subterranean realms, and by examining a series of wall carvings unravel the history of the race responsible for the awesome metropolis — the same as that represented by the "fossils" discovered by Lake. They also encounter fresh traces as well as gear missing from Lake's camp, and it soon becomes obvious that the creatures had awakened and disposed of the biologist and his party. But rather than destroying savagely, they had evidenced the curiosity of scientists, dissecting human and canine specimens, and taking them along as representatives of their species.

Up to this point the reader has been shocked to realize that the alien beings have indeed come back to life and treated man as man would treat a biological specimen. But now Lovecraft displays his narrative genius in a brilliant twist of the plot. He makes the reader empathize with and even feel compassion for the creatures by disclosing their aeon-long struggle against other alien beings. He follows them as they fight against disturbing life forms of their own creation, tracing the history of their civilization from its zenith to its nadir and then apocalypse. "Poor devils!" exclaims the narrator, admiring their courage, intelligence, and tenacity. "They were men!" And then, when the reader has relaxed his guard, Lovecraft suddenly confronts him with the hideous thing of which the monsters are afraid, the amorphous protoplasmic nightmare of the shoggoth, which destroys the elder beings who had been its creators, and sends the two protagonists on a frantic flight to escape the nightmarish being. They do escape, and flying back over the mountain range Danforth glimpses even greater horrors that lie beyond the farther titan mountains of madness — horrors that permanently shatter his sanity. And now the shaken Professor Dyer, who had originally intended to keep such horrors secret, is forced to reveal them in the desperate hope of preventing further exploration of the accursed region, with its latent threats to sanity and the very survival of the human species.

As with many of Lovecraft's later works dealing with his fictional concept of a universe peopled even beyond its dimensional confines by intelligences of unthinkable antiquity, *At the Mountains of Madness* immerses the reader in a world view in which mankind is the most recent, the most transient, and the least significant of life forms in the whole scenario of Earth's history. Like the story "The Shadow out of Time" (1936), this novel presents a pseudohistory of our planet involving the early advent, burgeoning, and cataclysmic decline of intelligences whose civilizations spanned stunning periods of time and vanished at periods so remote in Earth's past as to defy even being called "fabulous" in any common understanding of that word. As represented by Dyer and Danforth, man, a mere terrestrial newcomer by comparison, learns of the dim and awesome prehistoric tenancy of the Old Ones, yet is made to feel a profound sense of empathy with his predecessors. The grandeur of the crumbling city is mute testimony to the greatness of the Old Ones; yet it is exceeded by the sense of horror inspired by the sprawling protoplasmic shoggoths below, in realms as dark as Coleridge's "caverns measureless to man." Indeed, it is this continuity with an unimaginable past, this implication that a detestable and now greatly magnified vestige of that past still lurks below after countless aeons to menace overly inquisitive human beings — it is this shocking linkage that gives the novel its unforgettable horror.

There is also another kind of continuity: with Lovecraft's other works. Dyer and Pabodie have read the *Necronomicon*, that ancient tome kept under lock and key at Miskatonic University, and they know that the discoveries at the Lake camp are disturbingly reminiscent of *Necronomicon* references to elder beings who once held dominion on Earth and even created human life as a jest or a mistake. The dreaded book, of course, plays a centrally important role in many other Lovecraft tales, as does Miskatonic University itself. Further, Dyer and Pabodie are aware of the similarities between the Antarctic discoveries and certain matters of prehistoric folklore mentioned by their Miskatonic colleague Wilmarth. Readers of Lovecraft will recognize this colleague as the same Wilmarth who has had a frightful encounter, in "The Whisperer in Darkness" (1944), with the Winged Ones, another prehuman race. And in the pseudohistory provided by *At the Mountains of Madness*, these Winged Ones, or Mi-Go, drive the Old Ones from northern lands and there establish themselves. Great Cthulhu has not been unknown to the Old Ones, and the Plateau of Leng, on which the city of the Old Ones stands, figures in other Lovecraft works. Moreover, the realm of the *farther* mountain range, beyond the Plateau, even links the Antarctica story to the dream fantasy world of *The Dream-Quest of Unknown Kadath* (1943). The Antarctica novel, perhaps as much as anything in the Lovecraftian *oeuvre*, supports the view that most of Lovecraft's stories may be seen as chapters in one enormous novel.

In terms of craft, *At the Mountains of Madness* offers much to admire. As in other works, Lovecraft here shows his admiration for classical models, as he emulates the Greek theater in keeping violence "off stage." Lovecraft deliberately places Dyer, through whose eyes the reader must witness the events of the novel, at a spot far removed from the scene of the tragic revivification of the Old Ones, so that the reader's link with the carnage is only through radio communication. As revelation after revelation is made, followed finally by silence, the reader shares Dyer's sense of tantalizing mystery. One is reminded of *The Case of Charles Dexter Ward* (1941), in which the reporter of the action is a diarist who has been placed with a contingent of the party *not* present at the scene of violence, and able only to report shots and cries heard from a distance. Lovecraft is masterful at employing narrative devices in such a way as to effect a certain distance between the reader and the sources of horror, so that the reader participates imaginatively, filling in the details for himself, or merely continuing to feel a sense of wonder about them.

Stylistically, this novel is Lovecraft at his mature best. Critics since Aristotle have regarded the effective use of metaphor as a mark of the capable writer, and Lovecraft's use of metaphor is striking. The imagination is moved by his description of the "horizon-grazing" midnight sun of Antarctica. The description of iceberg mirages as "battlements of unimaginable cosmic castles" not only stirs a sense of dark beauty and builds the requisite mood, but also effectively foreshadows the novel's coming events. When Lovecraft says that the pass through the mountains to the Plateau of Leng has "malignly frowning pylons" he exhibits his remarkable feeling for the sentient nature of place. Indeed, here as in many other Lovecraft stories, one almost feels that the place, the setting, is a character in itself. Lovecraft was not content merely to tell a story; he insisted on telling it artfully, weaving his somber web of mood and atmosphere with striking and lingering efficacy by skillful use of language and imagery. The effect is like the painting of some dark and disturbing canvas, and indeed the novel's narrator often heightens this impression of prose landscape by comparing the scenes around him to the strange paintings of Roerich.

The novel has a strong psychological appeal, touching deep emotions in the reader. Lovecraft himself was haunted all his life by a vague but persistent sense of "adventurous expectancy," a feeling that immediately beyond one's grasp, beneath the prosaic world of appearances and normalcy, lay substrata of wonder. And who can fail to feel, with Dyer and Danforth as they enter the immemorial city beyond the mountain range — a city of this very Earth but untrod by human feet — the excitement of discovery, mingled with awe at the implications of the place for Earth's history and man's motelike place in it? The novel stacks awe upon awe, horror upon horror. The Old Ones and their crumbling citadel are overshadowed by the piping shoggoths, whose immensity fills the cave-riddled mountain range to the very peaks, and these horrors in turn pale in comparison with the unnamed things lying beyond the farther mountain range and only dimly glimpsed, only fearfully guessed at. Whatever wonders there are, there are always more, just beyond clear discernment.

At the Mountains of Madness stirs deep-seated capacities for attraction and repulsion; the reader may shudder at the experiences of Dyer and Danforth on the accursed Plateau while at the same time yearning to be in their shoes. The reader is left, paradoxically, both with a heightened sense of human adventurousness and a curious sense of the unimportance and evanescence of humankind. As is the case with all great artists' works, these sensations, along with other impressions left by the novel, grow in potency with rereading.

Dirk W. Mosig and
Donald R. Burleson

AUTOCRISI
(Autocrisis)

Author: Piero Prosperi (1945-   )
First book publication: 1971
Type of work: Novel
Time: 1992-1993
Locale: The United States and Dakopi, a small planet three hundred light-years from Earth

As Earth exports to the only other inhabited planet in the Galaxy all the troubles related to automobiles and car crashes, Prosperi depicts fights and espionage that go on between the greatest American car builders and opponents of their policy

Principal characters:
>STEVENSON KEMPLERER, a shipping agent of Outer Space Trade Lines
>DAVID LANDIS, a designer at the Chrysler-Ford industries
>GEOFFREY STEINDUCK, the founder and President of the League Against the Abuse of Motorization

Starting his career as a writer in 1960, at the age of fifteen, Piero Prosperi is now recognized as one of the most important names in Italian science fiction. (He is also a first-rate architect, since in Italy it is not yet possible to make a living writing science fiction.) Since his beginnings, Prosperi's writing has exhibited a professional touch; both his prose and his inspirations are traditional and Americanized. He soon made it clear that his preferences ran to parallel worlds, motoring, and the reconstruction of American history.

Autocrisi is Prosperi's first novel. Originally written in 1967 and not published until 1971, it received an award at the first Eurocon held in Trieste as the best Italian science fiction novel in 1972. The novel deals with cars in a speculative way which could have been the ideal starting point of J. G. Ballard's later *Crash* (1973), but Prosperi's approach is much more conventional; the several fragments which make up the novel are told from various points of view (including excerpts from newspapers, articles, newsreels, and television documentaries) but the narrative sections turn around three main characters that link the plot to the reports.

By 1992 man has explored the universe, thanks to the fortuitous invention of the Denil-Karlson hyperdrive, but the only inhabited planet discovered is Dakopi, a small world three hundred light-years away. (Actually, a Dakopian ship discovered Earth first, landing in a valley in Argentina, but Earthmen are the first to venture into commercial speculation on Dakopi.) Dakopians have a society similar to ours: they are humanoid, live on a great number of large islands, engage in interstellar travel, and have a science that is more advanced than Earth's in such fields as medicine, chemistry, and mathematics. They can offer Earthmen large amounts of Denilium, the precious transuranic element needed for hyperdrive jumps. Surprisingly, however, they are generally unfamiliar with the art of road building and motoring. In response to this, the United Nations makes an arrangement with Dakopi, and the largest United States automobile industries begin a program of subtle conditioning of the Dakopians (who are rather naïve on the subject of road networks and cars).

In matter-of-fact terms, Stevenson Kemplerer, a middle-aged shipping agent, describes the impact of the most sophisticated Earth cars (seven meters long and capable of speeds exceeding three hundred kilometers per hour on the alien social background. The Dakopians first react with feverish desire for such speed, understandable among people accustomed to land cars running at eighty to ninety kilometers per hour at most. Meanwhile, back on Earth, two important events take place. First, an ex-university teacher, Geoffrey Steinduck, starts a campaign against the ever-increasing bloodshed on U.S. streets (more than two hundred thousand people died in car crashes in 1991 alone, and fifty thousand more deaths are predicted for 1992) and founds his League Against the Abuse of Motorization. Second, the Chrysler-Ford Corporation, now in keen competition with the other United States colossus, General Motors (now GenerAuto), for the conquest of the Dakopian market, tries to infiltrate a spy (David Landis, one of their best designers) into the ranks of GenerAuto. His mission is to discover what progress is being made by Chrysler-Ford in developing fully automatized highways for cars running at more than four hundred kilometers per hour. At this point the three lines of the plot converge towards a climax. While the situation on Dakopi deteriorates with the sudden increase of fatal wrecks, since the Dakopians lack the skill required to drive properly these chromium-plated monsters from Earth, Steinduck's League gets an ever wider audience and makes its first political alliances. At the same time, the spy Landis is engaged by GenerAuto after a false car wreck (on a test field of Chrysler-Ford) gives him the chance to leave his ex-employer without suspicion.

The Dakopians begin to detect foul play from Earthmen, and riots cause an embargo on car imports; Landis is discovered stealing plans and subjected to an artificial amnesia treatment which turns him into an idiot. A follower of Steinduck casually finds Landis' body after another false accident (this time staged by GenerAuto).

Steinduck suspects that the memory of Landis might contain some interesting secrets and takes advantage of the superior Dakopian brain surgery (Dakopians now hold Steinduck in high esteem for his fight against their mutual enemy) in order to obtain the information he needs. Consequently he summons the reluctant leaders of GenerAuto and Chrysler-Ford on Dakopi and shows his cards: he knows that automatic highways capable of providing complete safety to every car could be easily achieved, but that the construction of such highways would entail great financial loss for the two corporations, owing to the longer duration of the new cars and the continued operation of the old models. He knows also that this project has been willingly kept aside, and that a great number of human lives has been sacrificed uselessly on the streets. Steinduck then forces the bosses of the two corporations to immediately start to build the automatic highways, threatening to reveal their secret to the public if they do not comply with his demand.

Although the story may seem quite simple, Prosperi is impressive in the way he controls the many voices needed for his presentation, and in his success in giving life to a bizarre and multifaceted story. The ending may appear a bit too optimistic to those addicted to the doomsday brand of science fiction, but his credibility is solid with the majority of "nonpurist" science fiction readers.

Several classical science fiction themes (contacts with intelligent aliens; speculation on events anticipated to occur in our near future) are gathered in *Autocrisi* and given a fair treatment in an agreeable and convincing way. In addition, since Prosperi is not an American, but a foreign writer deeply interested in the United States, his perspective gives him the opportunity to observe, touch, and prod some sore points which perhaps may not be as obvious to the American science fiction writer who must view them from the inside.

Gianni Montanari

UN AUTRE MONDE
(Another World)

Authors: J. J. Grandville (Jean-Ignace-Isidore Gérard, 1803-1847), and Taxile Delord
First book publication: 1844
Type of work: Novel
Time: Probably the 1840's
Locale: The Earth and the universe

An important surrealist tale told in words and pictures

Principal characters:
DR. PUFF, a confidence man
KRACKQ, a colleague
HAHBLLE, another colleague

Un autre monde is probably one of the most unusual and fantastic works ever written. Basically a surrealist satire leaning towards pataphysics (a literary form that appeared long after this work was first published), it has influenced many authors and artists in the surrealist and fantastic fields, and some have even found traces of Grandville's influence in the works of the British "new wave" science fiction writers.

Un autre monde is, to put it mildly, a rather strange work, and one that has both baffled and fascinated critics for more than a century. It is told in both words and pictures, and the text tells a story with beginning, middle, and end; but the marvelous thing about the book is the excellence of the illustrations — which, incidentally, were not done for the book at all. J. J. Grandville made the illustrations for his own enjoyment, the French journalist Taxile Delord later wrote the text in order to connect the illustrations, and the complete work was then published in thirty-six installments. Delord did his job well, but no one could have hoped to completely capture the bittersweet strangeness of Grandville's drawings.

Un autre monde is the tale of three bizarre "Neo-Gods" and their adventures in time and space. Grandville and Delord offered a characterization of the work as good as any on the title page of the first edition, which promises the reader

Transformations, visions, incarnations, ascensions, locomotions, explorations, pérégrinations, excursions, stations, cosmogonies, fantasmagories, réveries, folatreries, facéties, lubies, métamorphoses, zoomorphoses, lithomorphoses, métempsycoses, apothéoses, et autre choses.

What is not mentioned is that the book is also a murderous satire on contemporary society — everything from politicians, greedy businessmen, and Utopianism, to love, art, war, and science is attacked venomously and very effectively.

The novel begins very promisingly, with the greedy confidence man, Dr.

Puff, deciding to make money on the Utopian ideals of his time by founding a new religion called Neo-Paganism, in imitation of the utopian socialism very popular in France and elsewhere at the time. This he does, throwing in his lot with two other shady characters, Krackq and Hahblle, who make themselves gods. They then set forth to explore the universe; Puff visits the Earth; Krackq, the sea; and Hahblle, the sky. Dr. Puff immediately finds himself in a world of steam-powered robots, particularly musicians and singers, and later in a world of living mannequins, while Hahblle goes out on a straight science fiction adventure which mostly parodies the works of Savinien de Cyrano de Bergerac, Lucian, Jonathan Swift and others. Krackq visits even stranger places, including a zoo with living heraldic animals, and, in his sleep, Heaven and Hell. Finally reunited after adventures that defy all known laws of nature, the three gods discuss the various merits of Utopian societies and the contemporary world. They decide that the world and mankind are doomed, and prepare a steam ark in order to save at least the animals of the world — after which they hug each other to death.

This, very briefly, is the main plot of the tale. But *Un autre monde* is much more. It has an overwhelming abundance of puns, double and triple meanings, rebuses, satire and absurdities, and, most of all, an artistry in the pictures which has seldom been surpassed in surrealism. Much of the satire is incomprehensible today, being aimed at contemporary events and people, but the main themes of *Un autre monde* — Grandville's distrust of machines, which he felt would one day become Man's master; his sardonic attitude towards Utopian ideals and the "back to Nature" dream; his view of the Universe as a cold and unforgiving place which does not care much for Man — are pertinent even today. Actually, *Un autre monde* is more modern than most of the "daring" new wave science fiction stories and novels of the 1960's and early 1970's.

J. J. Grandville's life was short and tragic, and could indeed have been taken from one of his own blackest tales. He became known as an artist in the early 1820's when his venomous caricatures first appeared in the Paris satirical magazine *la Caricature*, together with the work of famous writers and artists such as Daumier and Balzac. Grandville's satanical caricatures of King Louis-Philippe were very effective and were one of the reasons why censorship was reinstated in France at this time. Grandville had to be more careful; so in the early 1830's he did a series of lithographs called *Métamorphoses du jour*, in which he put animal heads on human bodies, using these creatures to make pungent and satirical comments on contemporary events. These lithographs made Grandville an instant celebrity. He illustrated La Fontaine, Swift, Defoe, Reybaud, and other literary giants.

However, tragedy struck in the early 1840's when two of his three children and his wife died. When he did the illustrations for *Un autre monde*, and worked out the plot for the story, he was already on his way to his final mental sickness. *Un autre monde* is a black, despairing tale tinged with religious broodings. There is much fun and games in the story, but it is a sort of Dance of Death, a smile in the face of fear, an attempt to stand up against a world and a universe where nothing is certain, where logic is nonexistent, where nothing can be taken for granted.

Natural laws are nonexistent or easily circumvented in *Un autre monde*; stars and galaxies are playthings in the hands of unknown and probably dangerous gods. The three Neo-Gods of the story are quarrelsome, vain, and untrustworthy, yet they are true gods. They view mankind from above and find it small and insignificant. Art is created by machines, the only true animals are those of the imagination, and plants plot to rebel against Man. In the world of Man, people divest themselves of their natural forms and shapes — bodies are forcibly altered, transvestism is common. Men become slaves of animals; fishes fish for people, using medals and coins for bait, while dogs walk their men in the woods.

Grandville not only modernized the animal caricature, he also presented in his novel an impressive pre-surrealist fantasy in which inanimate objects have life — eyes, lorgnettes, and pencils have worlds of their own. The universe becomes a carnival where stars are connected by bridges, where antique gods live in modern splendor. The machines become men, and men become machines.

Un autre monde is a classic, and has seldom been out of print since its first edition, although most modern editions are very much abbreviated. It is a work of many levels. It can be appreciated as a work of science fiction, certainly; but it is also a surrealist work, a contemporary satire, and, in parts, a fairy tale; and the dystopian aspects of the story make it readily understandable by today's science fiction readers.

Un autre monde presents the universe as seen by a man slowly sinking into despair, searching for meaning where he knows none can be found. The novel is at once the work of a naïve romanticist, a satirist, a pessimistic Utopian, a misanthrope, and an agonized metaphysicist. One year after *Un autre monde*, Grandville published his remarkable book *Cent proverbes*, and in 1847 came *Les Fleurs Animées*, the last work he was to see in print. By Christmas 1846, Grandville's third and last child died. Only one month later he himself fell ill and was taken to a hospital where his mental sickness overwhelmed him. He died on March 17, 1847, penniless and all but forgotten. Today J. J. Grandville has been rediscovered, and *Un autre monde* is recognized not only as his masterpiece, but also as the masterpiece of the pre-surrealists.

The illustrations in *Un autre monde* tell much more than the text; the multitude of commonplace details put together into strange new forms, with the inanimate behaving like living beings and living beings behaving like dead objects, all come together into a strange and very disturbing whole. It seems eminently fitting that the true God of *Un autre monde* should be a crazed old man blowing soap bubbles into space, creating fleeting life and sending it out into eternity, never caring where it goes or what happens to it. That is how Grandville saw life, and *Un autre monde* vividly reflects his bleak vision.

Sam J. Lundwall

AVENTURES EXTRAORDINAIRES D'UN SAVANT RUSSE
(The Extraordinary Adventures of a Russian Scientist)

Authors: Georges Le Faure (1858-1935) and Henri de Graffigny (1863-1942)
First book publications: Lu Lune, (1889); *Le Soleil et les petites planètes*, (1889); *Les Planètes géantes et les comètes* (1891); *Le Désert sidéral* (1896)
Type of work: Novel in four volumes
Time: The 1890's
Locale: The Earth, the Moon, Venus, Mars, and the Galaxy

The story of a scientist who explores the universe while chasing his rival, who has stolen his ideas for a spaceship

> *Principal characters:*
> MICKHAIL OSSIPOFF, a Russian astronomer
> SELENA, his daughter
> FEDOR SHARP, a Russian astronomer, Ossipoff's rival
> GONTRAN DE FLAMMERMONT, a diplomat, Selena's fiancé and the namesake of the French astronomer Flammermont (representing Camille Flammarion)
> ALCIDE FRICOULET, a French engineer, his friend
> JOHATHAN FARENHEIT, an American businessman

Henri de Graffigny was above all a scientific popularizer. In his work there is no lack of carefully described inventions with diagrams and calculations. He was a theoretician of astronautics and his machine was used in an enormous saga of Nizerolles: *Les Aventuriers du ciel*. But he was a mediocre novelist, incapable of bringing his characters to life or of telling a pleasing story. Georges Le Faure was a popular novelist, full of good plots but incapable of the least calculation, the least scientific or even technical exactitude. One can credit him with having thought of the subject and with having correctly chosen de Graffigny as his scientific collaborator in writing four volumes which comprise *Aventures extraordinaires d'un savant russe*.

The action begins very slowly in Volume I. Mickhail Ossipoff has just invented a superexplosive with which he plans to send a spaceship to the Moon. It is to be projected by means of a cannon with rocket-assisted projectiles, allowing a constant acceleration of the ship. Ossipoff's rival, Fedor Sharp, wants to steal the invention and has Ossipoff imprisoned on an accusation of nihilism. Then the plot begins to move with Fricoulet. He invents a steam airplane which makes it possible to free Ossipoff from prison and bring him back to France. This whole part of the story introduces the characters but holds little else for the readers. Sharp has sold the secrets stolen from Ossipoff to Jonathan Farenheit, giving the Americans information which will put them on the Moon before the Russians. The plot line is established by now and will deliver no further variety.

Without a cannon, Ossipoff and his companions use the crater of a volcano, the Cotopaxi, which they know will soon erupt. In a multi-chambered spaceship, which includes a laboratory, they leave for the Moon. They land on the dark side and are met by Selenites. The Selenites are giants with slendor torsos and enormous heads. One of them, Telinga, instructs the Earthmen. He uses a machine to pronounce words while it projects the written characters on a screen as the Selenite shows the object in question. The Selenites are more advanced than the Earthmen in many respects. They possess aerial and aquatic machines driven by reaction, but photography is new to them. They are dumbfounded by the atlas of the Moon brought by Ossipoff. The Selenites use spiraling tunnels to move about, allowing them, by the use of gravity, to cover great distances without the expenditure of energy.

Ossipoff is anxious to find Sharp. He, therefore, invents *respirols*, suits which will subsequently allow the heroes to move about even in space. Near the "Mountains of eternal light" (a point on the Moon which is always lit up) the Earthmen discover a mineral which attracts light. They cover the ship with it, encircle it with a belt of panels, black on one side and covered with mineral on the other. This will enable them to vary the direction of the machine. But Sharp escapes in the shell, kidnaping Selena.

The second volume is devoted to chasing Sharp and getting Selena back. It takes the reader to Venus and Mars as well as to Phobos, over Mercury and around the sun. This is no doubt the volume richest in inventions. First of all, lunar food and water do not agree with the Earthmen, so Ossipoff concocts a synthetic product which will allow them to continue the trip. The Selenites inform their friends that the properties of selenium have enabled them to communicate with the Venusians for centuries, thanks to a process transforming sounds into modulated light rays and vice-versa.

Venus is a world inhabited by humanoids similar to the ancient Greeks by necessity living in a Bronze Age culture. The cities are composed of bronze mushrooms to resist the torrential rains; in the same way the ships are submarines driven by paddle wheels. How this fits into a civilization capable of interplanetary messages is not explained. Ossipoff reaches Venus by means of a machine invented by the Selenites: a sphere of selenium which is projected light. Once there, they find that Sharp is already heading for the Sun. The Venusian receiver will act as the lunar one; the sphere takes off again. Stopping briefly on Mercury, they observe two kinds of inhabitants: a one-legged bird with a trunk and membranous wings, and an immense one-eyed sea animal. The authors allow a rather obvious error to slip through here. The planet's rivers almost boil from the temperature, but the visitors do not suffer from the heat.

Selena is found again, and the voyage continues towards Mars by means of a comet. All this is copied from *Hector Servadac* by Jules Verne. The travelers leave the comet by means of the sphere, which has become a balloon; Verne's travelers used a hot-air balloon. Verne's comet Gallia had a nucleus containing thirty percent gold; this one is of crystalized carbon, that is diamond.

Sharp approaches the Sun as closely as possible for observation. This presents an innovation of a theme which was fully exploited by the pulps: the fascination exerted by the Sun. Meanwhile the travelers first land on Phobos, a sort of labor camp where the Martians send their criminals and undesirables. A poorly described machine, a kind of dirigible, travels between Phobos and Mars. The Martians are tall, well-developed beings, endowed with leather wings which enfold them like a garment. Their language is limited to five vowels whose different tonalities express thoughts. They live as much on the canals as in the air, in hanging cities whose image recalls the one Buck Bradford discovers at the center of the Earth. To maintain zero population growth a war is organized every twenty years between two selected nations. The war stops as soon as the number of dead is sufficient. The Martians have mastered photography and show the Earthmen some aerial views of the Earth, as well as photographs of the explosion of planet 28 and the birth of the asteroids. This volume, though the most interesting one and containing the richest inventions, is written in a drab style.

In Volume III, the Earthmen construct a machine of lithium on Mars, which will bring them a fortune once on Earth. It is propelled in space by following the wave of particles which engenders the meteor swarms. This is the last real invention. From now on the travelers contemplate the giant planets (Ossipoff having reversed direction). They observe, they take notes, and they find Sharp. The two machines are caught in an aerolith traveling towards the Earth. The travelers, in a cataleptic state, are bathed in the nutritive elixir of the Martians and travel from now on in a dream, a dream common to all and in which they interact as in reality.

Volume IV presents the dullest, most boring of all possible explorations of the cosmos. The travelers no doubt go farther than anyone had ever been before them: as far as the edge of the galaxy. But if the stars approach, enlarge, disappear, if multiple suns mingle their colored lights, they are only in pages copied from Flammarion, without the warmth and the poetry of the original. Finally, everybody comes back to Earth; Selena marries Fricoulet and not Gontran, the only surprise in the novel.

This novel has many faults, some of them inherent in the genre itself: the novel of exploration. One can only maintain interest by an ingenious plot. Jules Verne understood that, or made up for deficiencies by the poetry and the color in the portraits of other worlds. The plot of this novel, however, is no longer acceptable in our time, if it ever was. The characters are nothing but puppets; their quarrels and preoccupations are childish. It is impossible to take them seriously, to believe that Ossipoff and Sharp are scientists. The failure is flagrant when compared to works by Jules Verne, from whom a great deal is borrowed: Hector Servadac's comet and also a certain Martian floating island are straight from *Pays des Fourrures*.

However, there is something of redeeming quality: an effort to preserve other lives. The Selenites and the Martians, although described briefly, live up to this expectation and it is understandable that they in turn have captivated readers. It is just as understandable that interest dies after Volume III, at which point the extraterrestrial beings disappear.

The novel had a definite influence on the genre. After publication of this novel, there was no question of limiting oneself to the Moon as had been done for so long; astronauts began to explore Mars and Venus, although none dared to escape from the solar system.

At least two novels repeated the story created by Le Faure and Graffigny: *Les Aventures du ciel* and, in the 1950's, *La Croisière de Metéore* by Richard-Bessières. Thus, in spite of its faults and deficiencies, the work furthered the fictional conquest of space if only through the search for means of transportation other than the cannon.

Jacques van Herp

BABEL-17

Author: Samuel R. Delany (1942-   )
First book publication: 1966
Type of work: Novel
Time: The far future
Locale: On several planets and aboard several spaceships

Exploration of the relationship between language and culture as heroine poet Rydra Wong unravels the mysteries of the language code known as Babel-17

Principal characters:
> RYDRA WONG, an intergalactically famous poet, captain of the spaceship *Rimbaud*
> DR. MARKUS T'MWARBA (MOCKY), a psychologist, Rydra's friend, teacher, father-figure
> DANIL D. APPLEBY, a customs officer who helps Rydra assemble the *Rimbaud* crew
> BARON VER DORCO, the coordinator of Alliance research projects aimed against the Invaders
> JEBEL, the captain of the private warship, *Jebel Tarik* ("Jebel's Mountain")
> BUTCHER, a mysterious crew member aboard *Jebel Tarik*

When the heroine of this novel, Rydra Wong, was just a small girl — long before the beginning of *Babel-17* — she had been given a beautiful Myna bird by her kind friend and father-figure, Dr. Markus T'Mwarba. The bird had been trained to say, "Hello, Rydra, it's a fine day out and I'm happy." Instead of receiving the gift with expected cries of delight, however, Rydra went into a screaming, hysterical collapse of acute anxiety.

This enigmatic episode is related early in *Babel-17* but not clarified until near the end of the novel. Rydra then explains that while the words the bird uttered had been perfectly appropriate to the human situation, the thoughts that lay behind the bird's words were perfectly appropriate to a bird. That is, the bird did not grasp the meaning of these words, but saw the reward it had been promised for mastering the verbal lesson: a large, juicy worm, fully one third of its own size in length. Telepathic Rydra saw the same worm, hideously enlarged, fully one third *her* own size in length.

This brief, but highly revealing tale is a prime example of several of Delany's structural techniques: the bringing of episodic material full circle, the display of character evolution through explained behavior, and most important, the use of the part to represent the whole. This brief episode reflects the entire theme of *Babel-17*: that reality is in the eye of the beholder, shaped and controlled — where there is consciousness — by the language of that beholder. Delany is examining the differences between what is said and what is perceived, what is said and what is meant, and what is said and what is understood. He structures these considerations into what appears to be another rousing tale of adventure: a typical space opera with a gorgeous, supertalented

heroine, vast intergalactic conflict between the Alliance (good guys) and Invaders (bad guys), plus spies, sabotage, codes, and an abundance of exotic
aliens.

However, pervading each moment of the ostensible adventure is the fact
that *Babel-17* is overwhelmingly a book about language, and how language
determines perception of reality. "When you learn another tongue," Rydra
says, "You learn the way another people see the world, the universe." Yet to
say it is a book about language is still an oversimplification, for it is a book
about all forms of communication: verbal-nonverbal, overt-covert, direct-
telepathic, binding not only person to person but male to female and the living
to the discorporate.

As the book opens, Rydra, whose poetry has become "the voice of her
age," celebrated by all peoples — Alliance and Invaders alike — is being
consulted by General Forester about a serious military problem: important Alliance installations are being mysteriously sabotaged. The only clue lies in the
radio broadcasts which occur simultaneously with the sabotage. These broadcasts, however, are in a strange and unusually difficult code which has been
dubbed "Babel-17."

This opening is deceptively simple. The problem is presented, and the
superheroine will, of course, take up the task and eventually solve it. An additional stereotype is introduced when General Forester falls in love with Rydra
at first sight.

Yet much lies beneath the surface. In discussing the code, Rydra and the
General probe the differences between code and language, providing essential
information to the reader and a greater depth of interpretation for what will
follow. The potential love interest, so often hackneyed, is presented with equal
skill and purpose, for while the General knows that he has fallen in love he
sees no logical, civilized way to tell Rydra how he feels after such a brief
acquaintance. Thus he despairs, thinking that she will never know his true
feelings. The General is wrong, of course; he has, in fact communicated *everything*, for Rydra can not only read codes, she can read people: their muscles,
their tensions and relaxations. She perceives, interprets, and understands the
language of the body. Thus, in this opening chapter, not only is the theme of
the various kinds and structures of language introduced, but it is complicated
by the possibilities of understanding *versus* misunderstanding in any and all
attempts at communication.

After further extrapolation of Rydra's past history and present skills in a
consultation scene between Rydra and Dr. T'Mwarba, she sets out with customs officer Danil D. Appleby to pick a pilot and crew for the ship she will
captain in pursuit of the saboteurs. It is a highly original search for a compati-
ble group which will psychically blend into a working team. The selection of a
pilot takes place in a scene which visually foreshadows the more recent barroom depiction in the film *Star Wars*. Rydra and Appleby (who as a customs

man is in a civil service, earthbound job as opposed to members of transport, who go into space) watch two surgically altered humans wrestle inside a large globe suspended from the ceiling of the room. Rydra observes the quick reflexes of one of the wrestlers, whom she considers as a pilot. Once he is chosen, his nervous system will be directly connected with the controls of the ship. Thus his reflexes are essential to his skill and survival as a pilot. Adding another layer of interpretation, Rydra judges the wrestler's ability by watching the muscle reactions of a knowledgeable onlooker who is also observing the match, thereby reinforcing her own opinions.

Next, Rydra and Appleby seek the discorporate ghost members of the crew, because "some jobs on a transport ship you just can't give to a human being" — he would either die or go mad. Appleby is an essential companion for Rydra because he is uncomfortable throughout the search, acting both as a foil for Rydra, who is at home and able to communicate in any and every situation, and as a character able to grow and develop as he learns about what had hitherto been completely alien to him.

In the discorporate sector, for example, Appleby is hustled by a succubus, who entices him in spite of the fact that he forgets everything she says split seconds after the words are uttered. Rydra, on the other hand, solves the problem of ephemeral communication with ephemeral beings by instantaneously translating everything they say to her into Basque, which she can easily remember.

While the discorporates live in their own sector of town, and have their own, separate facilities on shipboard, it is also possible for a discorporate to be brought back to life if he has discorporated through regular morgue channels. One such crew member is Mollya, who is selected and brought back to life to form an emotional and sexual bond with Calli and Ron. This essential triple relationship forms the navigating component of the crew. Rydra's choice of a third member was a deliberate one. All three had lost their original partners and would need time to develop closeness with a replacement. By choosing Mollya, a girl who cannot speak English, Rydra knows that the attempts of the three to communicate will evolve into mutual love and understanding as they learn to mesh into a smoothly functioning team. As Rydra herself had once been a member of a similar triple partnership, she is especially empathetic.

The first quarter of the book is concerned with crew selection, displaying different possibilities for communication as very different value systems and life styles meet and intermingle: customs *versus* transport (each with singular biases and loyalties), living *versus* dead, couples *versus* triples (with both homosexual and heterosexual involvements). When the selection has been completed, Rydra writes Mocky about her pleasure with the chosen crew: "They had to be people I could talk to. And I can." She also states that at this point, she comprehends enough of Babel-17 to know where the next enemy attack will be: the Alliance War Yards at Armsledge. Before departing on her ship, The *Rimbaud*, Rydra ties up one loose end and lets General Forester know that she did understand his initial feelings for her, thus easing his emotional pain before she heads into outer space and the adventure.

Aboard the aptly named ship, Rydra proves to be an equal master of mathematical language when she solves a shipboard crisis by using magnetized marbles to illustrate a geometrical principle. However, while the crisis has been met and solved, its cause is still unknown. How or *who* caused the crisis? Can there be a saboteur on board? The question remains unanswered, but Rydra and the crew arrive safely at the Alliance yards where they are met by members of a feudal society eager to wine and dine them. This group is headed by Baron Ver Dorco, a rather fascinating character, who has created not only an arsenal of impressive weaponry but has developed android spy-assassins as well. Even these artificial humans reinforce Delany's concern with communication as Ver Dorco describes the programing of one TW-55 to Rydra:

> He has about six hours of social conversation, plot synopses of the latest novels, political situations, music and art criticism. . . . Put him in formal wear and he will be perfectly at home at an ambassadorial ball or a coffee break at a high level government conference.

A short time later, of course, Rydra meets him and unknowingly experiences just the kind of convincing conversation that had been previously described to her.

The pace of the novel picks up at this point. Ver Dorco is suddenly assassinated by a mysteriously malfunctioning TW-55, the arsenal is attacked, and Rydra and her crew return to the *Rimbaud*. The mysterious saboteur that accompanies them, hastens them into outer space against Rydra's wishes and without her take-off commands; Rydra blacks out.

When she awakens, the third, and in many ways most complicated, section of the book begins. Rydra is enmeshed in a web on a strange ship. As she looks around her, she has an epiphany, a linguistic breakthrough. Heralded by a confused jumble of thoughts about grammatical divisions in different languages, Rydra's musing concentrates on subtle changes in meaning:

> But with some oriental languages, which all but dispense with gender and number, you are my friend, *you* are my parent, and YOU are my priest, and *YOU* are my king, and YOU are my servant, and *YOU* are my servant whom I'm going to fire tomorrow if *YOU* don't watch it, and YOU are my king whose policies I totally disagree with and have sawdust in YOUR head instead of brains, YOUR highness, and YOU may be my friend, but I'm still gonna smack YOU up side the head if YOU ever say that to me again; and who the hell are you anyway . . . ? What's your name? she thought in a round warm blue room. Thoughts without a name in a blue room.

These musings continue until Rydra hits upon the elemental truth that "Words are names for things" and in so realizing, begins to understand "Babel-17." For in this code language, words are not only the names for things, but reflect the basic structure of the thing named. For example, by knowing the word meaning "web" in "Babel-17," Rydra immediately understands the structure of the web in which she is trapped. Knowing its structure, she also knows its weakest point. By breaking the web at that point, she can easily escape and free her crew who are similarly bound. In fact, it is quicker to break the web at its weakest point that it is to unfasten it normally now that she is free to do either. Later, the same knowledge allows Rydra to emerge triumphant in battle because she can see the same weblike structure in the battle formation of the ships engaging her and, again, by hitting the weakest point of the formation, can win the day.

Rydra and her crew have been rescued and are aboard a friendly ship: *Jabel Tarik*, or *Jebel's Mountain*, a private ship which is stationed in the radio-dense Specelli Snap awaiting prey. Not only does Rydra more fully come to understand "Babel-17" while aboard this ship, and to use it to understand both physical and metaphorical webs, but she also begins to utilize it to control behavior. Like Jessica in *Dune*, and Helga in *The Ship Who Sang*, Rydra infiltrates the ideolect of another human being to shape and control him. Here, she wields her poetry to deflect an assassin from attacking Jebel: thinking in Babel-17, but translating into English to recite the poem which will achieve her ends.

Every moment aboard the *Jebel Tarik* is concerned with language, with naming things, understanding their use, and investigating whether existence is possible without names. The asides are as fascinating as the main plot. For example, when the Spaceship passes a Ciribian vessel, Rydra learns the complications of communicating with these aliens who have no word for house, home, or dwelling. Because of this, the eight-word sentence, "We must protect our families and our homes," requires forty-five minutes of translation. "Families" presents no problem of definition because the Ciribians have families. However, since the aliens have a heat-based culture, the definition of "house" requires a lengthy explanation related to its characteristics of protection from exposure to varying temperatures.

For all this exploration of language, the essential point, the relation of the speaker to his language, is not considered until Rydra meets a mysterious crew member, the Butcher, and makes the shattering linguistic discovery that he has no self concept, no word for *I*, *me*, *my*, *mine*, *myself*. She assumes the role of teacher because, "Until something is named, it doesn't exist!" This lack of a personal pronoun is not deliberate, as in Robert Silverberg's *A Time of Changes*, but is programed into the speaker. It is not that Butcher does not choose to use *I*, but that he has no word for the concept, and thereby lacks the concept. The same is true of "Babel-17."

What happens in a language with no concept of *I*? What happens to action when there can be no concept of having acted? What happens, for example, to conscience, to personal responsibility? As Rydra teaches the Butcher, the *I*'s and *you*'s become interchangeable until the characters fuse:

> "You and I," the Butcher said. He moved his face close to hers. "Nobody else is here.
> Just you and I. But which is which?" She nodded, cheek moving on his fingers. "You're
> getting the idea." His chest had been cool: his hand was warm. She put her hand on top of
> his. "Sometimes you frighten me." "I am me," the Butcher said. "Only a morphological
> difference, yes? The brain figure that out before. Why does you frighten me sometimes?"

And the fusion of the two characters causes an even greater insight into both of them and "Babel-17." Ultimately, Rydra enters the Butcher's mind and they become so mutually ensnared that only the posing of a paradox can sever the connection. It is this fusion, and the knowledge Rydra seeks and finds in the Butcher's brain that causes all the questions posed throughout the book to be finally answered: the mystery of "Babel-17," the identity of the Butcher, and even more important, the identity of the mysterious saboteur who has accompanied Rydra throughout the book.

Rydra, at the end of the story, bridges all worlds and becomes the center of the entire web of unfolding adventure. She bridges, just as her poetry has always bridged these worlds, being celebrated both on Alliance and Invader planets. Everything comes full circle as is exemplified by the fact that in the language of "Babel-17," the word for "Alliance" means "one who has invaded." So now, with the code broken, the language is understood. Its flaw — like the worm in the garden of Eden, or the worm from Rydra's childhood Myna bird — is exposed. There is now the possibility of a new and perfect language, a "Babel-18" which will have all the positive virtues of its forerunner, the ability to underpin the structure of whatever is named, plus personal pronouns which will assure the responsibility of the speaker/actor.

With all communication problems solved, Rydra promises, *"This war will end within six months."* But there is a further promise because she speculates that she may write a poem about her experiences, or possibly a novel. Of course, this is really going full circle because this is the novel that the reader is completing. Thus Delany links the one who reads and the one who writes, drawing his audience into participation in the exposition of the plot itself.

He has undertaken a very difficult task. Some will read the book and only see a dashing, if irregularly paced adventure story, Wonder Woman in outer space. Others will be so involved with what can be learned about language that they may well overlook the rockier moments of the plot. For if Delany's reach has occasionally exceeded his grasp, it must still be remembered that it has been a very long reach indeed in this complex and sophisticated novel which deservedly won both the Nebula and Hugo awards.

Beverly Friend

Sources for Further Study

Criticism:

Scholes, Robert and Eric S. Raskin. *Science Fiction*. New York: Oxford University Press, 1977, pp. 94-95 and 152-153. Delany's themes and style of writing are analyzed briefly here, comparing him to Bester and Scholes.

Reviews:

Analog. LXXX, December, 1967, pp. 163-164.

Magazine of Fantasy and Science Fiction. XXXI, December, 1966, pp. 35-36.

New Worlds. CLXVII, October, 1966, pp. 153-154.

SF Commentary. XX, April, 1971, pp. 23-24.

BACK TO METHUSELAH
A Metabiological Pentateuch

Author: George Bernard Shaw (1856-1950)
First book publication: 1921; presented 1922
Type of work: Drama
Time: From 4004 B.C. to A.D. 31,920
Location: Mesopotamia, England, Ireland, Earth

A witty, sagacious, and disturbing epic drama of the transformations wrought by time and history on human life, experience, values, and destiny

Principal characters:
ADAM
EVE
THE SERPENT
CAIN
FRANKLYN BARNABAS, a wealthy ex-cleric
CONRAD BARNABAS, his brother, a biologist
THE PARLORMAID/MRS. LUTESTRING, a long-lifer in Parts II and III
REVEREND WILLIAM HASLAM/ARCHBISHOP OF YORK, a long-lifer in Parts II and III
CONFUCIUS, an Oriental, the brains behind British government in Part III
THE ELDERLY GENTLEMAN, a representative of the last of short-lived humanity in Part IV
ZOO ENNISTYMON AND ZOZIM, "young" long-livers representative of A.D. 3000 humanity in Part IV
HE-ANCIENT AND SHE-ANCIENT, wise immortals, except for accidents, in Part V
STREPHON, CHLOE, AND AMARYLLIS (THE NEWLY BORN), childhood versions of the "ancients" in Park V
PYGMALION AND MARTELLUS, a biochemist and an artist, ancients who create the android humans "Ozymandias" and "Cleopatra-Semiramis" in Part V

Bernard Shaw explicitly called *Back to Methuselah* a masterpiece. (Many critics agree, even though it was never wise to take Shaw precisely at his word in such cases.) Certainly this is his longest play, usually requiring three separate days to present; moreover, it was the first and most remarkable of his three works of speculative drama. The much slighter *Simpleton of the Unexpected Isles* came later, and *Farfetched Fables* was the last dramatic work he published.

But the importance of Shaw's plays to the literature of fantasy and science fiction is greater than any single play by him; indeed, references to Shaw sprinkle the works of Arthur C. Clarke, Ray Bradbury, and Robert A. Heinlein, and Kurt Vonnegut, Jr., acknowledges his debt to the playwright. In *Back to Methuselah* we encounter a vintage Shaw play as well as an important work of science fiction, and understand why Shaw's work has been influential in the genre.

Although the action of *Back to Methuselah* covers 35,924 years, almost nothing "happens" in it. The stage typically limits action, and in Shaw's play there is the merest token of physical activity. Substituting for action, however, is an almost exhausting cerebral movement — the scintillating, paradoxical, satirical, comic movement of the characters' dialogue. It is in this ocean of talk that the adventure of the whole history of mankind is conveyed. It is in the expository brilliance of the talk that a theory of the progress, meaning, and destiny of mankind is erected.

In Part I, humanity's parents tell us of their decision to surrender immortality because mortality makes life more interesting and precious. Cain tells us of his invention of the exciting practice of killing people, a consummate genius for which presents itself in the incarnation of Napoleon in Part IV, celebrated by men for having raised the conduct of war and the slaughter of hundreds of thousands to an art.

In Part II, a disenchanted clergyman and a biologist articulate a new faith in a god called the Life Force, and the scientific evidence that underlies the way of the Life Force with man and the universe called Creative Evolution. Two simple people, William Haslam and a Parlormaid, listen to the conversation, unaware that their simple belief and desire will make them among the first of mankind to live for three hundred years, proof that Creative Evolution is at work.

Part III is entitled "The Thing Happens," announcing the survival for nearly three hundred years of Haslam/Archbishop of York and the Parlormaid/Mrs. Lutestring. These first long-livers have had to hide their identities and "die" a number of times in order to live "normal" lives. The discovery of their accomplishment by Burge-Lubin, the mush-minded President of the British Islands in the incipiently Utopian world of A.D. 2170, immediately causes him to cancel plans for a physically reckless adventure as he begins to contemplate the prospect that he too might live a long time, especially if he does so very carefully.

Also in Part IV, in "The Tragedy of an Elderly Gentleman," the Elderly Gentleman dies very unsensationally, one of a group of short-livers who are visiting a remote place called Ireland where, in A.D. 3000, a community of long-livers dwell, waiting to decide how and when the lives of the remaining population of short-lived mankind should end. The long-livers need not trouble themselves. Short-livers will die, like the Elderly Gentleman, of frustration and despair.

Part V, "As Far as Thought Can Reach," is a symposium presented by enormously evolved humans in A.D. 31,920. They live now for thousands of years and complain only about how confining it is to be enslaved by the encumbrance of bodies. It would be better to be pure thought.

The settings of *Back to Methuselah* are nothing if not perfect places for conversations to take place in. There is a library, an executive office, and a cave; but more time is spent outdoors in a Garden of Eden, on a farm, on a dock by a bay, and in the meadow around a temple.

Not even H. G. Wells (who is ironically discussed by name in Part III) kept more abreast of developments in the sciences than Shaw. The various futures of this play have video-telephones, lightning air passenger service, tuning-fork-shaped walkie-talkies, electric force fields, and synthetic eggs and cheese. More momentous matters include discovery of a unified field theory that encompasses gravity and electricity, and advances in biochemistry that permit human gestation and birth in fully adult form from eggs, as well as Pygmalion's success, in the Faustian footsteps of Victor Frankenstein, in making the androids "Ozymandias" and "Cleopatra-Semiramis." Furthermore, *Back to Methuselah* forecasts radical changes in the social order that would not become common in science fiction until the 1970's. Religion, government, and marriage fade. Euthanasia is practiced. At the last, sex, art, music, and even socializing in any form intelligible to twentieth century man become quickly surrendered pastimes of the childhood state of the Ancients.

Yet the play is neither remarkably "theatrical" nor is it gadget-fascinated science fiction. Furthermore, it does not undertake the intimate examination of individual human character. Disregarding merged and bridge characters, there are forty-four speaking roles in the work. Some are sagacious; some are foolish. All speak for Shaw in a classically Platonic dialogue. Yet their *personae* are ingeniously and ironically manipulated. The Serpent and Cain, who are traditionally evil and brutal, become in Shaw's treatment genial, sympathetic, cooperative, and cogent. A simple Parlormaid and a softminded minor cleric are among the very first to become serene and sophisticated long-livers. Venal politicians talk so candidly and sincerely yet so foolishly that they appear pathetic rather than vicious. Though frequently benighted, no character knowingly tells a lie. The effect is a constantly present dramatic irony. Indeed, all the characters in a given conversation are often victims of crucial ignorance. In A.D. 3000 Zoo and Zozim cannot understand the idiom/cliché/embedded metaphor-ridden discourse of the Elderly Gentleman because their knowledge of the history and evolution of language is inadequate. The Elderly Gentleman cannot appreciate the simple and clear precision of the discourse of Zoo and Zozim because a short-lived human, habituated to the barbarically sloppy misuse of language, the stamp of his puerile culture, cannot conceive of talk whose form and function are in perfect coincidence.

It is to Shaw's own discourse and themes that we must turn to discover the force of the play. Several Shaw hallmarks invest *Back to Methuselah*: an almost preternaturally clear and exhilarating verbal play is the vehicle for profound and endlessly surprising pronouncements upon the human condition and its prospects. An authorized printed edition of the work provides more than the playscript. There is a "Preface" with forty-seven titled subsections. Following the script are "A Glimpse of the Domesticity of Franklyn Barnabas," once intended as Part II of the play; and "Postscript: After Twenty-five Years." These contextual pieces are typical. Shaw published his plays in a format designed to be read, and took the opportunity to analyze in essay form the issues of the play. The result is not a burden but a reinforcement of the verbal pyrotechnics and intellectual substance of the work.

Thus, in its essays and dialogue, *Back to Methuselah* exhibits two remarkable stylistic features. First, it is a discourse of irony, paradox, and satire in a comic mood. Shaw insisted that if a thing were funny, one ought to look for the truth in it. His discourse begins and produces very ordinary vocabulary in very common snytax, perfectly incorporating the clichés, bromides, and chestnuts that disguise presumably serious human utterance. Suddenly, as the words continue, we hear the comfortable platitudes converted, slightly reworded, to be exposed either as sheer nonsense or just as often transmuted to a fresh cogency. Shaw loved to attack proverbs; he loved to make new ones. *Back to Methuselah* is full of superbly quotable lines.

The second key feature of the play is the clarity of the discourse. The play explores elaborate and complex philosophical and scientific topics — a preeminent content of science fiction. The exposition is never less than pellucidly intelligible.

For all of its misgivings about mankind in the present, *Back to Methuselah* is, in its particularly ascetic terms, a proclamation of soaring optimism. Moreover, the critique of civilization is always sympathetic and constructive. Shaw is neither godless nor irreverent. In his preface he announces that *Back to Methuselah* is offered as a new scripture to take the place of the religious and political mythologies that are clearly bankrupt in the twentieth century. With all the resources of his dramatic genius he wants to reorient human vision and renew its spirit. Accordingly, he finds man feeble at birth, and there is nothing particularly precious about childhood or youth except the promise it represents of the possibility of some future maturity.

The Life Force (institutional religions have disastrously abused the word "God") drives the universe in all its parts, but institutional religion is for Stone Age men and has only occasionally something pertinent to say about God. Most of the time it is damnably bad for mankind. Government and educational practices grow out of religion and are equally corrupt. Marriage, too, is a troublesome institution, especially when people are legally bound to remain married long after their children are grown and they may have grown bored with each other.

Even so, life is much too short. People should live longer, and they could, if they really believed they could and wanted to. When this happens people will behave far less recklessly to survive to enjoy longevity. They will plan an order for the world even into the far future because they will expect to be alive in it. People will begin to reach real maturity, to possess knowledge of essential things. Thus, all of the arts and sciences will become more and more subjects of amusement. Of course, people will no longer be sane in the present day meaning of the word. Now sanity is maintained at the expense of ignoring reality. In the future people will perceive reality more and more directly, and become insane, perhaps in the manner of the divine madness of Plato.

Eventually, truly great age will allow people to perceive the processes of Creative Evolution at work. Life will get even longer; intelligence will be integrated at higher and higher levels; the sciences will be understood as an effect of human progress rather than its cause; life will displace the last vestige of illusion and art. Ultimately man will discover that the only thing he can truly create is himself. Moreover, when he reaches the stage wherein he can couple an absolute act of will with this perception, he will transcend his body and be subsumed as a being of pure thought — finally and infinitely a fit companion for the Life Force.

Bernard Shaw was sixty-four years old when he wrote *Back to Methuselah*, and it is hard to resist interpreting the work in part, at least, as an aging man's contemplation of his personal predicament. We may not, then, be too impatient with ourselves if we are edified, when reading the play, to reflect that Shaw lived on to the age of ninety-five.

John R. Pfeiffer

Sources for Further Study

Criticism:

Bloomfield, Paul. *Imaginary Worlds: or, the Evolution of Utopia*. London: Hamish Hamilton, 1932. This literary history of utopias emphasizes Shaw's *Back to Methuselah* and its role in the development of the concept.

Reviews:

Booklist. XVII, July, 1921, p. 343.

Bookman. LIII, August, 1921, p. 550.

Boston Transcript. June 11, 1921, p. 6.

Dial. LXXI, August, 1921, p. 227.

Freeman. IV, September 21, 1921, p. 40.

Nation. CXII, June 15, 1921, p. 850.

New Republic. XXVII, June 15, 1921, p. 85.

New York Times. June 12, 1921, p. 4.

Yale Review. XI, January 22, 1921, p. 429.

BAREFOOT IN THE HEAD

Author: Brian W. Aldiss (1925-   )
First book publication: 1949
Type of work: Novel
Time: Post World War III
Locale: Europe

In a Europe gone crazy as a result of psychedelic bombs, people combine vehicle speed with drug "speed" and follow the leadership of a false motorcade prophet

> *Principal characters:*
> COLIN CHARTERIS, a prophet and saint
> PHIL BRASHER, leader of religious crusade and Escalation band
> ANGELINE, Brasher's wife, who later becomes Charteris' wife
> RUBY DYMOND, a band member in love with Angeline
> ARMY BURTON, lead guitarist for Escalation band
> BANJO BURTON, a former saint who is killed in a crash
> ROBBINS, a band member who drowns
> CASSIUS CLAY ROBERTSON ("CASS"), Charteris' black manager
> NICHOLAS BOREAS, a film director
> JAN KONINKRIJK, speed supervisor

Colin Charteris, a nineteen-year-old of Serbian background, whose name derives from the English novelist Leslie Charteris, author of the "Saint" books, is a veteran pilot of the recent Acid Head War, which has left all of Europe's brains addled. As a NUNSACS (New United Nations Strategic Air Command) official assigned to rehabilitating war victims, Charteris travels from the south of France north toward England by car. He is Man the Driver, a parody of G. I. Gurdjieff's philosophy, which was so ably expounded by P. D. Ouspenski in *In Search of the Miraculous* (1949). Aldiss acknowledges his debt to Ouspenski, whose work on Gurdjieff gives the novel its structure.

Driving his Banshee into multiple auto crashes gives Charteris the better choice between two possible ends: leaping death or desiccating life. Although France had maintained neutrality during the war, its landscape reeks with the effects of PCA Bombs (Psycho-Chemical Aerosols); and a person not directly hit can absorb the drug merely by living in the environment. In Metz, Charteris thinks of time as a fabrication of matter, and matter as a hallucination; he has a fleeting epiphany in which he sees himself as God. He suspects this vision may be drug-induced, but, as he tells the hotel maid Angelina, he has hoped to have a mystic experience such as the one Ouspenski had.

Going to England, which had been bombed first, Charteris throws away his NUNSACS papers and experiences dream taking the place of reality, as well as several other Gurdjieff phenomena: hearing a waiting man's breathing and the crunch of his muscles; knowing the many I's within a man; understanding the extent of movement (Gurdjieff had said that even a stone is in movement); practicing breathing exercises; and knowing the self through seeing the self from the outside. The "waiting man" turns out to be a follower of Ouspenski, but he sees the two — Ouspenski and Gurdjieff — as one. He reminds Charteris of the awakening of the Serpent of Kundalini, which Gurdjieff had explained as the power of imagination; but Gurdjieff had said that Man must awake and the Serpent must be left sleeping. Since Charteris is attempting to discard some of his multiple I's, he has been trying to awake and to discard simultaneously. But Charteris continues to take drugs, and many of the discarded I's are drug-induced hallucinations; indeed, matter itself is literally hallucination. The waiting man, however, acts as a kind of John the Baptist and predicts that a new messiah will come, and young people will run to him; they will be barefoot in the head. As events prove, with their brains and thoughts scrambled, the people are indeed "barefoot in the head" — that is, willing to follow any false prophet.

In London, Charteris narrowly avoids killing a man who joins him for the ride: Banjo Burton, manager of a band called the Escalation, who has a load of infrasound equipment. Charteris, dominated by the memory of his father in somewhat the same fashion that Gurdjieff remembered his Serbian father, has a memory-vision of his father while Banjo Burton brings to him Phil Brasher, leader of a new religion. Brasher immediately senses a threat to himself in the person of Charteris; as a miraculous lone survivor of a crashed plane, Brasher had seen Charteris as an apparition at the time of the crash. As they drive north, Brasher complains about his follower Robbins, whom he calls a feeble pseudosaint; and Charteris offers to replace Robbins.

Brasher's group plans a Crusade combining religion and music, but Charteris eclipses Brasher in popularity; they fight, and Charteris kills Brasher by pushing him at just the instant a convenient lorry passes by. To soothe Brasher's wife Angeline, Charteris takes her home with him. Now the lead guitarist, Army Burton, joins with Robbins in proclaiming Charteris a saint, largely because of his success in speaking Ouspenski jargon. Robbins had once been a saint, having been promoted as such by Banjo Burton; but he is now deflated to disciple. Charteris contributes poems to the group, whose rendition of "Low Point X" becomes an international hit. In an acid cloud, discussing Ouspenski and Gurdjieff, Charteris was not aware that, while driving his car and apparently swerving to avoid hitting a black dog wearing Ruby Burton's black and red tie, he killed the mother of Grete, a member of the band.

In Nottingham, huge crowds assemble to hear Charteris, and Burton announces him as Saint Charteris. Charteris sees himself as Gurdjieff, leader of the New Thought and of the Fourth World System, and Man the Driver. Amid many discontinuous human relationships, no one can concentrate long on the old virtues. Ruby Dymond resents Angeline's cohabitation with Charteris but remains ineffectual in his protests. On the platform, Angeline announces that Charteris killed her husband, but this makes no difference. Charteris admits it and explains it in an adaptation of Gurdjieff's difficult language as a "complex impulse-node" and calls for all to follow him on a motor crusade through Europe.

The motorcade turns southward, and Charteris mechanically proves himself a saint. In the southern Netherlands, Belgium, and Germany area, the landscape has been devastated of buildings, and roads have been doubled in width to accommodate speedsters driving under the influence of psychedelic sprays. Meanwhile, pausing as they advance through Belgium, Charteris remains indifferently standing by while Robbins, running into the sea, calls out for Charteris to save him. Charteris, with neither consciousness nor ideals, lets Robbins drown. Continuing the journey, Charteris' Banshee crashes into a lorry, but Burton was driving and Charteris now can be acclaimed as having risen from the dead. Speed Supervisor Jan Koninkrijk, investigating the accident, takes Charteris to headquarters and persuades him to help with Marta, his immobile wife, who at first mistakes him for her father and willingly joins the group. Her departure from home leaves Koninkrijk free to do as he pleases; thus, with Koninkrijk, Charteris accidentally, ironically, unknowingly functions as a saint.

From the multiman speed death at Aalter, which has enhanced Charteris' reputation as a Christ figure, the members of his motorcade swell to an even one thousand. Charteris now has two mistresses, Angeline and Marta; he has killed directly or indirectly four people: Phil Brasher, Grete's mother, Robbins, and Banjo Burton. Charteris now has a black man, "Cass," as manager; and he begins writing "Man the Driver," but never finishes it. Wherever his motorcade travels, suppliers of reefers and drugs profit from his Crusade. The group's new hit song, "Famine Starting in the Head," promotes a lucrative business.

Nicholas Boreas, famed director, suggests a film about the life of Charteris. The film will feature the meeting of Ouspenski and Gurdjieff — as a parody of *In Search of the Miraculous* — and a real multicar crash filmed with real people who accept that their movie roles will end in sudden death. On the way to Brussels, Marta inexplicably dies, and Angeline feels that Charteris could have helped prevent her death. But all ends in destruction; the film is lost and Brussels burns. Cass and Boreas fight to no purpose and with no decisive result.

"Ouspenski's Astrabahn," the "Homewards" section of the book, opens with an early morning police raid on Charteris' followers, thoughtlessly encamped on the main traffic route instead of beside it. With Elsbeth, a Jewish girl, Charteris awakens to the question "Who in charm hair?" Undressed, Charteris mounts a car while delivering an Ouspenski-type lecture, and the police take him to a jail which is also a mental hospital with a sadistic Herr Laundrei in charge. He, too, acts like another Gurdjieff in discussing Hydrogen 12. Combining the Kundalini serpent with Freudian imagery, he forces perversions on his bodyguard Hirst Wechsel. Laundrei sends the saint to a single cell for the night with a threat that on the morrow they will conduct one last "little testicle" to see how Charteris manages miracles. In his cell Charteris dreams of simultaneous rape by three people, but awakens to his release and reunion with Angeline.

Outside, Laundrei joins Charteris' followers. Surprising even himself, Charteris walks on water, crossing the Rhine between Germany and France. This occasions a serious discussion with Angeline who, pregnant, fears that Charteris will go on to the next obvious stage: crucifixion. In a discussion whether to go to Moscow (Gurdjieff's headquarters) or to continue the Crusade elsewhere, Cass takes on the bare outlines of a Judas figure; and all becomes confused with varying forms of "eternal recurrence." As the group breaks up, Cass and Wechsel form one unit. Ruby Dymond, still in love with Angeline, takes his last painful farewell of her. Angeline insists on remaining faithful to Charteris, and Charteris will go alone.

The saint now seems to care for nothing but his own ego, and Angeline — within her limitations — seems to be the only voice of humanity, reason, and love. Angeline suffers in her disillusionment with Charteris — the same feeling that Ouspenski experienced with Gurdjieff. Charteris, instead of choosing the way of the cross, has chosen the way of healthful longevity. Angeline gives birth to a daughter. Charteris lives to be ninety, and exemplifies the eternal preference for the material body. For him, sitting under a tree replaces driving a car; and thus both he and the Banshee slip toward death.

The language of *Barefoot in the Head* develops in sequence from Aldiss' first book, *The Brightfount Diaries*, and in many places recalls James Joyce's *Finnegans Wake*. There are numerous allusions to other writers, such as T. S. Eliot, Shakespeare, Milton, and Djuna Barnes. The novel is filled with puns, and numerous puns can be derived from discussion of its contents. Much of the prose is prose-poetry, and approximately fifty poems explain, augment, and reflect the prose content.

Gurdjieff taught that man has four bodies, the first being "carriage," or physical body; the second "horse," or astral body; the third "driver," or mental body; and the fourth "master," or causal body. Ordinary man does not possess the third and fourth bodies, but others can think that he does — as in the case of Charteris. And among multiple I's, perfect *will* issues from a single and permanent I. Neither did Gurdjieff encourage speculation on eternal recurrence, because the idea of repetition discourages striving for self-change. In this novel Angelina of France lingers in Charteris' thoughts until he takes up with Angeline. Brasher had envisioned Charteris as his plane crashed, and later Charteris kills him. Humanity itself looks forward to the recurrence of a messiah.

Gurdjieff also stressed the mechanicalness of events, repeating that everything happens as a cosmic principle and not because man makes it happen. So Charteris mechanically talks Gurdjieffian language, and the people respond mechanically to proclaim him a saint. His progress along the motorcade of life is mainly a matter of following time's arrows— read indifferently as *Links Fahren* or *Rechts Fahren*, and obeyed mechanically.

Grace Eckley

Sources for Further Study

Criticism:

Blish, James. *More Issues at Hand*. Chicago: Advent Publishers, Inc., 1970, pp. 138-145. This analysis gives the reader an understanding of the plot and themes of *Barefoot in the Head*.

Matthews, Richard. *Aldiss Unbound: The Science Fiction of Brian W. Aldiss*. San Bernardino, Calif.: Borgo Press, 1977. This book provides an excellent discussion of Aldiss' style of writing.

Reviews:

Galaxy. XXXIII, March–April, 1973, pp. 153-154.

Guardian Weekly. CI, October 25, 1969, p. 17.

Library Journal. XCV, June 1, 1970, p. 2177.

Listener. LXXXII, October 16, 1969, p. 530.

Magazine of Fantasy and Science Fiction. XXXIX, December, 1970, pp. 22-24.

Observer. October 12, 1969, p. 33.

Punch. CCLVII, October 22, 1969, p. 681.

Times Literary Supplement. January 22, 1970, p. 73.

THE BATTLE OF DORKING

Author: George Tomkyns Chesney (1830-1895)
First book publication: 1871
Type of work: Novella
Time: 1921, with flashbacks to August, 1871
Locale: Southern England

A plea for a reformation of the British military system, outlined within a framework of an account of a successful invasion of England by the Prussian army

> *Principal characters:*
> Since the individual plays a secondary role to the military attitude and tactics depicted, only the two powers can be described as characters
> BRITAIN, the tragic hero
> PRUSSIA, the nemesis of complacency and indolence

That *The Battle of Dorking* is of considerable significance in the history and development of modern science fiction is undisputed. In his survey of the future war novel, *Voices Prophesying War*, I. F. Clarke has emphasized its importance as the prototype of that genre and has highlighted its sociopolitical relevance by giving a detailed background history of the military and political situation which gave rise to Chesney's story. A somewhat similar account of the events which preceded its publication occurs in Asa Briggs's introduction to *The Battle of Dorking Controversy*, while Michael Moorcock, in the introduction to his anthology of Victorian and Edwardian science fiction, *Before Armageddon*, has underlined its literary importance by pointing out the similarities in style and technique between it and the later works of H. G. Wells. Its main importance, however, lies not in the fact that is was admired and imitated by fellow authors, but in the impact it had on society at the time.

Coming as it did during a time of national unrest brought about by political events on the European continent (intentional opportunism on Chesney's part), the novel's emotive theme of a successful Prussian invasion of England struck home deeply into the anxieties of the populace. Its style was direct, its message clear and incisive: "Wake up to yourselves, or your hour is lost!"

First published anonymously in the May, 1871, issue of *Blackwood's Magazine*, a popular monthly magazine aimed at a middle-class readership, it created an immediate response. Articles appeared about it in *The Times* and other daily newspapers. In Parliament sympathizers with Chesney used it as a platform from which to push for implementation of the reforms outlined by him, while refuters sat down to write denials and flooded the market with a score or more of tracts and articles which pointed out the errors of Chesney's argument. Even Gladstone felt prompted to join in the dispute when, during a public speech, he deplored the novel's alarmist nature and the degrading effect it would have on Britain's international image. It was the *cause célèbre* of the moment, and demand was so great that the magazine containing it went through several large editions before the separate appearance of *The Battle of*

Dorking as a sixpenny booklet in June, 1871. Two months later this edition had itself been reprinted several times with sales in excess of one hundred thousand copies, and numerous other editions appeared throughout the world.

This success, however, did not result so much from the controversial nature of its contents as from the innovations which Chesney introduced to deliver his message. In the past, numerous tracts and articles had appeared, campaigning for a restructuring of the military, or calling for an adoption of military tactics more in keeping with the new modes of warfare made possible by technology. Most of these tracts were restricted in their audience by the formal nature in which they were written and presented, and were often limited in their scope by the inability of their authors to comprehend how sweeping a change was necessary. Chesney, newly returned from a posting with the Bengal Engineers in India, was sufficiently removed from the situation to give his diatribe a more objective stance; in addition he achieved distance by his unprecedented use of a fictional narrative written from a retrospective viewpoint as the vehicle for his ideas.

By giving his work the subtitle *Reminiscences of a Volunteer* (the Volunteer system had been established in 1859 to supplement home and coastal defense) and firmly setting the temporal location in the opening sentences, Chesney was able to create immediately a sense of defeat; the tone of his narrator, made melancholy by hindsight, gives a sense of loss and deprivation as well.

Over the next few pages the former volunteer expounds to his grandchildren upon the complacency with which the British government viewed the hints of impending war, and upon the greed and selfishness which blocked any effective countermeasures. The volunteer's speech is clearly intended to show parallels to actual events occurring in the months preceding the publication of the story. Chesney thus drew attention to what he saw as imminent danger, advised a preparation against it, and then shifted into fancy. Through his narrator he relates a rather unlikely series of events which led to a weakening of Britain's defenses (British forces had been sent to various trouble spots which had sprung up simultaneously within the Empire), and of how an ill-prepared Britain impulsively declared war on Prussia in August, 1871.

These false notes aside, the description of the subsequent events seems quite plausible: the British fleet is quickly and almost completely destroyed by a new and unknown weapon developed in secrecy by the Prussians; panic ensues throughout the nation, particularly in the City; untrained recruits become confused as they are marched pointlessly back and forth; and the invaders swiftly take control of the railway system. The defenders establish a line of defense along the ridge of the northern downs, twenty miles from London; their lack of communication within the army results in inadequate provisioning of food and medical supplies. In the actual engagement, aging generals attempt to stem the thrust of an efficient, up-to-date army by using tactics first tried in the Napoleonic wars; the defenders are forced into ignominious retreat. All these scenes are depicted with startling clarity. The author's lucidly developed contentions are made even more convincing because they are backed by his military experience.

Needing to make his point with a large readership, Chesney appealed to the middle and upper classes by using a narrator from a merchant banking background. To capture the interest of the working-class readers, he provided the plot with elements of sensationalism and emotional excitement reminiscent of the gothic novel. He creates a sense of wonder through his vivid description of the fatal engines which destroy the British fleet, until the atmosphere seems almost supernatural. As the volunteers fight an intangible enemy enshrouded by mist and gunsmoke in the valley below, thunder and lightning fill the heavens, rivaling the roar and flash of the artillery in the field. As the air clears to reveal the bloody and mutilated bodies of the British dead, the shadowy shapes of the foe can be seen advancing. The line breaks and panic ensues. Only in the final scenes is the enemy visibly encountered. In what was formerly a suburban house, the enemy troops are seen indulging their beastly appetites, while a child lies dead on the floor nearby, his head half blown away.

By his overt appeal to the emotions of the audience, Chesney obtained the size of readership he was seeking, but in his ultimate aim he was less successful: the reformations he advocated only came by slow degrees.

In the years that followed, numerous works similar in type to Chesney's appeared, from the immediate refutations of his novel to the apotheosis of English superiority in 1900 by Robert W. Cole in *Struggle For Empire* (in which a united Anglo-Saxon world battled for galactic supremacy). The future-war novel continued to be developed by many practitioners in a variety of ways. George Griffith combined it with the "wonder" stories of Jules Verne to produce such sensational works as *The Angel of the Revolution*, which reached even larger audiences than *The Battle of Dorking*. Other authors described lost races of unknown peoples intent on the domination of the world. Utopists such as Andrew Blair paid oblique homage to Chesney by using a retrospective stance to describe the development of their Arcadias. It was in H. G. Wells's *The War of the Worlds*, however, that the future war novel came of age, and that Chesney received his greatest accolade. Using the same basic structure and locale as Chesney, Wells developed his story in a similar manner, again by emphasizing sensationalism, but also using a more scientific background.

Judging from the impact his work had on the society of his time, as well as the sudden upsurge in the appearance and popularity of science fiction in the next thirty years, one is tempted to posulate that Chesney's influence may have been even deeper than was formerly believed.

John Eggeling

BEASTS

Author: John Crowley
First book publication: 1976
Type of work: Novel
Time: Two centuries in the future
Locale: The United States

Genetic engineering has produced man-animal mutants that struggle for survival against humans' desire for their extinction and revive man's old fear of the beast and the encroaching wilderness

> *Principal characters:*
> LOREN CASUBON, an ethologist
> DR. JARRELL GREGORIUS, Director of the Northern Autonomy
> STEN GREGORIUS, his son
> NASHE, his successor
> PAINTER, a leo, King of the pride
> CADDIE, his "wife"
> REYNARD, a man-fox mutant
> MERIC LANDSEER, a producer
> BARRON, a Federal officer
> SWEETS, a dog

When anything goes wrong, the USE (Union for Social Engineering) people in John Crowley's *Beasts* blame the failure of human reason and strive toward their goal of making the world work — for them — by truly rational means. Referring to John Locke's theory that the human mind is a blank page at birth, the behaviorists and USE assume that it can be controlled at will. When B. F. Skinner admitted the existence of innate determining tendencies, he proposed that, since a species cannot be altered, species status be studied only to predict behavior and improve the techniques of control. The USE people have improved on Skinner; they *have* changed the species. But rather than rousing the beast in the man, they have aroused the man in the beast; and they have lost control. Their reason then tells them that, to extend control, they must exterminate the life they have created. Their "social engineering," it now appears, amounts to nothing more than the raw grasp for personal power.

Before being stopped, USE's genetic engineering proceeded far enough to accomplish the creation of three types: leos (combined men and lions, capable of reproduction), a single Reynard (a combined man and fox, sterile), and a brain-altered dog, Sweets. Since there is no deity except the experimenter in the world of behaviorists, the medieval beast epic *Reynard the Fox*, with its total lack of spirituality, contributes to the novel's structure. The hero Reynard is delightfully amoral and dedicated to winning at all costs, and accepts violence as a natural way to gain his ends. Having, as Crowley mentions, no enemy among wild life, his Reynard cunningly demonstrates in the world of men his innate behavioral characteristics and causes men to think he is working for them while he is actually working against them. His motives remain obscure, but he is a considerable motivating force; and at the end of the novel, he gives his loyalty to the beasts.

Where man seeks, for his own salvation, to divide the world between predator and prey, between hairless and hairy, between vegetarians and carnivores, between man and beast, the novel shows that man is a predator pure and simple, and that all other distinctions blur. In crossing the species barrier USE has implied another possibility: that the leos may surpass man in the upward sweep of evolution. To further complicate matters, Plato and others have used the Beast Within as a metaphor for man's lawless tendencies — gratification of his own instincts for gluttony, indiscriminate intercourse, and various extremes of shamelessness. In the USE people, the unrecognized Beast Within is the innate egotism of human reason; and, although experiments have been halted, this Beast may break out again and create real monstrosities. Another matter, the deity, remains liminal; it exists only in the mind of Meric Landseer's wife, whose lover is Christ, and in the leos, who instinctively sense an identification with father Sun.

Unlike the lion that Nietzsche evoked in the name of freedom, to create "an holy Nay even to duty," Crowley's leo Painter accepts and performs his duties with a kingly mien. He first ransoms an indentured teenager, "Caddie," who had been proud of working for her living but who now, as a result of her master's selling her, turns against a race of men that treats people as less than human. According to human reason, since a leo cannot employ a human, Painter by this act makes himself a kidnaper and, for killing in self-defense when he is being stalked by a human, he becomes a murderer. Crowley paints a dignified picture of the leos' family life, employing several levels of meaning for the word "pride," but Painter knows that the world calls the leos poachers, thieves, and polygamists. Intrinsic in each living thing, also, is the sense of inalienable rights — the right to make a living, for example; and in his own case Painter, since he did not ask to be made, believes he has a right to compensation for what he has gone through. The USE people advocate quarantine of the leos; the Federal seeks voluntary sterilization; and both resent the leos' knowledge of a right to life.

Certain persons, on the other hand, prove capable of enhancing characteristics of species. An ethologist, Loren Casubon, trains peregrine falcons to relearn survival in the wilderness to prevent their extinction. He scientifically observes the innate behavioral patterns of geese, which he does not seek to use for domination. Meric Landseer visits Painter's pride to make a video tape and becomes converted to the leos' simple way of life; his tape reveals to the world that USE's quarantine keeps them snowbound and starving. Gregorius' two children, Mika and Sten, view the tape and defy their tutor to take food to the leos. They have learned from the tape that through a genetic "accident" these beasts are "stronger, simpler, wiser" than men; and that, even if they are extinguished like the blue whale, they will not reproach humanity for its meanness.

A civil war has left the country divided, and a remnant of the former Federal government, now called simply "the Federal," seeks reunification. The USE people, whose scientific experiments need political clout if they are to succeed in their objective of ultimate control, have aligned themselves with the Federal. In a territory now a dependency of Canada, Loren trains his peregrine falcons but finds his Captive Propagation program dissolved because the USE has disapproved the use of funds for it. Any life in its raw natural form seems to encourage the wilderness that exists beyond man's control so that men in general fear that they cannot retain a hold on it.

In the heart of the Northern Autonomy is Candy's Mountain, an attempt at an establishment for the propagation of man's ideals in the wilderness; but the residents of that tower, almost two hundred stories high, have decided that their order, their form of Right, be vegetarian. The leos, of course, do not belong; nor do they accept Christ as their Savior. Meric Landseer and his wife live contentedly in Candy's Mountain, until a beast of discontent stirring in Meric drives him out to photograph the leos and alters the course of his career. His wife, not a thorough going rationalist, understands her susceptibility to lovers but not to Painter's carefully controlled polygamy.

The Northern Autonomy was once rather secure against invasion by the Federals, and the Genesis Preserve in its Northwest corner is supposedly safe for animals. While it preserves wild life, it preserves also the Biblical dictum that man is the Lord of Creation; and as such, he cannot permit the lion as King of Beasts to contest his reign. In Genesis Preserve, the Federals capture Painter, taking him like a wild animal in a net.

Sten Gregorius as Director of the Northern Autonomy seeks reunification with the Federal. Loren, Painter, and Reynard oppose reunification; but Loren, when the funds are withdrawn for his wilderness program, takes a position as tutor to Gregorius' children. Reynard visits Gregorius to delay the signing of the papers, but he has already arranged the death of Gregorius, in whom he recognizes his old enemy Isengrim the Wolf from the *Reynard* story. He feels differently about Gregorius' son Sten, whom he recognizes as a true son of kings, proud and independent.

Gregorius' successor, a woman named Nashe, has neither sufficient character nor political strength to withstand the Federals and their police; overcoming her objections, they enter the Preserve to capture Painter not as a leo but as a murderer and kidnaper. In the process they kill Painter's son. A long winter convinces Nashe that she cannot hold out against various shortages and hardships that provoke violence and disorder, all of which the Federals and USE promise to eradicate in the light of human reason. Utterly humiliated, she announces that the Autonomy has become a Federal protectorate.

The scientists also conduct frontal lobe function enhancement experiments on a dog, Sweets, but give them up as a failure when he fails to give evidence of any new knowledge. For Sweets, the effect is to cut him off from the company of man and reassert his identity with the pack. When a dynamite charge hidden in a file drawer as Painter is being processed for prison blasts him out of police custody and into the company of Sweets, it becomes apparent that the scientists have failed to conduct the proper tests. Not only do dog and lion lie down together; they also communicate telepathically. Nor can behavioral science recognize the eidetic memory that the experiments have given by accident; ironically, the dog, which had been willingly controlled by man, now knows him as something separate from the pack. Painter, living with Sweets in mutual support, gives him an animal sympathy and a human love and recognizes the irony of the gift of science — the alteration of both their minds at the hands of men. The combination of their talents enables them to feed the pack through the winter, and Painter becomes leader with a mission — to lead the pack out of the city and into the forest. Leaving through a tunnel, they trip an alarm; and Painter surrenders so that the pack can escape.

The wily fox's devious politics soon become evident. Painter knows that a betrayal by Reynard accounts for the Federal's locating and capturing him; on the other hand, Reynard sends Sten a cryptic note giving geographical coordinates for the location of the starving leos. When Sten's having freed himself from Loren and from his late father's household, he can capitalize on his own fame as a child television star and gather around him people of independent politics. As his fame grows, he moves for reasons of safety. When he needs a place for his adherents to gather, Reynard intervenes once more; and Loren, eager to be reunited with Sten and Mika, suggests the shot tower where he nurtured his peregrine falcons.

Reynard bargains with the rapacious Federal official, Barron, who had originally captured Painter, to release Painter in exchange for information regarding the location of Sten Gregorius. Knowing the difficulties of escape, Reynard persuades Caddie to take a gun and kill him in order to create a diversion. Just as Reynard of the beast epic committed numerous wrongs and insults to others and emerged a hero, so Crowley's Reynard has now become a martyr. The extent of his science, however, remains to be discovered in the last chapter of the novel.

The proper perspective for enlightenment has always been, not the dissecting table or the slide under a microscope, but the height gained by a free-flying bird. From such a "Hieraconpolis" to which Sten's falcon Hawk has soared, the reunion of all the novel's innate-characteristics adherents can be observed. At the shot tower where they all convene, Loren recognizes in Painter not a half-anything and realizes that in him "life had squared its own evolution." Sweets arrives, together with Sten and Mika Gregorius, with Mika reflecting sadly that Reynard had used Caddie as a beast. But Reynard arrives to remove her guilt — a new Reynard cloned from the former, and deserving the name

Counselor. The world's greatest behaviorist as far as control of others is concerned, he is most outspoken against behaviorism itself and warns that he will always act according to his nature in the world they make. Although Meric Landseer is absent, Caddy has explained to Meric that Painter as a leo has been "wounded into consciousness" and that "something shines through his being." Reynard says that Meric "prepares the way." In this new world, Painter is King of Beasts, and perhaps the world will be safe for all living things.

Grace Eckley

Sources for Further Study

Reviews:

Analog. XCVII, June, 1977, p. 169.

Booklist. LXXIII, December 1, 1976, p. 527.

Kirkus Reviews. XLIV, July 15, 1976, p. 813.

Library Journal. CI, October 15, 1976, p. 2196.

New York Times Book Review. November 21, 1976, p. 67.

Publisher's Weekly. CCX, July 5, 1976, p. 86.

THE BEDBUG
(KLOP)

Author: Vladimir Mayakovsky (1893-1930)
First book publication: 1958; presented 1929
English translation: 1960
Type of work: Drama
Time: 1929-1979
Locale: Tambov, the Soviet Union

A social parasite is preserved in ice and thawed out fifty years later

> *Principal characters:*
> IVAN PRISYPKIN (renamed Pierre Skripkin), a former party member, former worker
> ELZEVIR DAVIDOVNA RENAISSANCE, a manicurist and cashier in a beauty parlor, his fiancée
> ROSALIE PAVLOVNA RENAISSANCE, her mother
> ZOYA BERYOZKINA, a working girl, Prisypkin's old flame
> OLEG BAYAN, an eccentric houseowner, Prisypkin's friend
> MECHANIC, a worker, Prisypkin's roommate

What ever happened to Futurism? It stormed into Russian literature in the first decades of this century, proclaiming the liberation of the word, appointing itself the representative of new times, dumping the poetical past from the "steamship" (not the rocket ship) of modernity. What happened to its leaders, its bellowing creative mammoths? Igor Severyanin, king of the "Ego-Futurists," as talented a poet as Vladimir Mayakovsky and a great influence upon him, emigrated in 1919 and declined for twenty years, while the fake lilies of his chic high-society poetry wilted as badly as Nadson, as badly as Balmont. Ivan Ignatiev, who spoiled the "Ego-Futurist" movement in 1914 by slitting his own throat, left behind nothing that could be called poetry, not even any fake lilies. Of the "Cubo-Futurists," ringmaster David Birlyuk, for whatever reasons, abandoned Mother Russia in 1925, leaving behind a string of amusing vulgarities, misprints, and gibberish, and celebrated his arrival in America with that classic, *Birlyuk Shakes Hands with the Woolworth Building*. He spent his remaining years practicing his greater talent for painting and recalling the good old days.

Birlyuk was right to introduce cheapness and vulgarity into Russian literature, and his work retains almost the value of an early edition of *Playboy*. Aleksei Kruchonykh ("Alexei the Scrambled") remained in Russia in total obscurity, unpublished and unremembered for decades until interviewed by a resourceful American scholar in the late 1960's. At that time he repeated his fifty-year-old platform of trans-sense poetry, believing that his meaningless scribblings, misprints, and gibberish had discovered a new planet which one day would be populated by grateful speakers of gobbledygook. He never understood that trans-sense poetry is discovered over and over again by every youthful enthusiast, every bohemian group and would-be *avant-garde*, and obtains meaning only within a context of meaningful signs. Being essentially an ignorant graphomaniac, Kruchonykh never noticed that one of the most effective examples of his amazing discovery was given by Hector Berlioz in his dramatic symphony, *The Damnation of Faust*, forty years before the birth of Aleksei Kruchonykh. Velimir Khlebnikov, who died in 1922, left behind scraps of virtually incomprehensible poems, semipoems, superpoems, lovingly collected, edited and published by his friends and disciples soon after, but studiously ignored by the Soviet establishment for the rest of eternity, a few little anthologies and watered-down studies notwithstanding. He was without doubt a poetical genius, but with no less doubt a psychotic.

Of all the Futurists Khlebnikov most concerned himself with the shape of the future; he predicted the 1917 revolution some years in advance, predicted worldwide television, the humanization of apes, healing by rays and by sound, knockout bullets, portable prefabricated houses, all sorts of things, but also such idiocies as the replacement of speech by a chalkboard and numbered thoughts, a numerical system based on five with numbers replaced by vowels, lakes with tiny organisms where people could swim and eat at the same time, a modern dress of medieval armor made out of starched linen (perhaps he was not serious about these things). Less ignorant than other Futurists, Khlebnikov amassed a body of discrete facts and figures resembling no known branch of knowledge, and those who love him may spend a lifetime trying to convert the jumble into something approximating human communication (some professors are making the attempt). Short of lifelong devotion, one may dip into Khlebnikov and be excited by new possibilities; he finished almost nothing, wrote no one work which could be called an unqualified success, yet he constantly awakens. His system is a madhouse, the creation of the system is genius. Thus Khlebnikov, alone of all the Futurists, remains alive today for those who would discover him. Of course, we should mention Boris Pasternak, never much of a bellower, who quietly left the Futurist scene to seek his own path, wisely understanding that Futurism was the exhuberance of youth — as stimulating as a bottle of coke, but deadly as a steady diet.

But what about Mayakovsky, the poet of the planet proletarian? When you first read him, you must be impressed: the broken lines, the unexpected half-rhymes, the brash rhetoric, the fire of inspiration, the joy of youthful poetry-making. But if you read him again, some years after reading other things, he may sound like a middle-aged rock star singing the same stupid songs that made him famous. Mayakovsky just does not last: you tire of the adolescent self-glorification ("I," "I Love," "Vladimir Mayakovsky: A Tragedy," "An Extraordinary Adventure Which Befell Vladimir Mayakovsky One Summer at the Dacha," "To His Beloved Self, the Author Dedicates These Lines," "Mayakovsky's Nativity," "Mayakovsky's Ascension," "Mayakovsky in Heaven"), the overplayed romance with Lily Brik (they look older in the photographs, dissipated in their apotheosis, silly in the stills from their dreamworld silent films), the bombast and monotony of sledgehammer lines, the infantile cries for love (He shouts: "Away with your love! Away with your art! Away with your social order! Away with your religion!" And then: "Maria — give! Maria — you don't want? You don't want?"), the truculent identification with the Soviet state ("Verses About the Soviet Passport," and so forth), the dependence on poets supposedly dumped from the steamship of modernity — particularly Pushkin ("At the Top of My Voice" is another "Exegi Monumentum," repeats the metaphor of lining up ranks of verses from Pushkin's "A Little House in Kolomna."), the ignorance, superficiality and above all dishonesty.

This dishonesty is manifested in his refusal to acknowledge that the poetical revolution and the political revolution were separate, made by different kinds of men; the Futurist claim to literary hegemony — to political power over the other schools of literature — was an abortive *Putsch*; stepping on the throat of his own song was not a heroic revolutionary act, but a betrayal of art, the act of self-strangulation by someone lacking the courage to stand alone, someone who fawned on political power. Even the suicide note, admired by some, perpetuates his dishonesty: the man is going to shoot himself because the state has crushed his artistic identity, and yet he wastes his last words asking the "Comrade Government" to take care of his survivors, making a private joke with the "Comrades of the Proletarian Literary Organization" who despised him and wanted him to die, arranging to pay his last taxes to the Stalin dictatorship and, characteristically, clinging to his own ego, his own exclusive place in the universe — "This is not a good method (I don't recommend it to others), but for me there's no other way out." So what are we left with? Some great metaphors ("Every word,/ even spoof,/ which he spews with his scorching mouth,/ jumps out like a naked prostitute/ from a burning public house."), some tender sobs ("By what Goliaths was I conceived,—/ so big/ and so unneeded?"), some uplifting shouts ("To shine forever,/ to shine everywhere, to the very bottom of the last days,/ to shine—/ and without any stops!/ That's my motto—/ and the sun's!"), and truckloads of propagandistic lines ("Vladimir Ilyich Lenin," "All Right!," "Order to the Army of Acts," for example.) And another thing: the legend fabricated by the Soviet State after Stalin called Mayakovsky "the poet of the revolution," the statues, the streets, the squares, the postcards, the textbooks, the silences about his suicide, the reprintings of his works, the production of saccharine memoirs by literary lackeys and bootlicks, the weak echoes of his bass voice and ludicrously rolling r's in the recently naughty but now safely muzzled Evgeny Evtushenko and Andrei Voznesensky. In short, we are left with what Boris Pasternak called "Mayakovsky's second death."

One might have expected Futurism and Mayakovsky to have been interested and productive in the field of science fiction. But though the movement brought forth much fantasy, much formal innovation, and a lot of sheer non-sense, there are not many works one would call "science fiction." The great eschatological visions of Khlebnikov, such as "The Crane" (where all the dead and inanimate things rise up to form a man-eating crane) or "Snake Train" (where a train becomes a snake devouring its passengers), involve some sort of magic, not science. Khlebnikov's "The Radio of the Future" and "Good-world" involve science, but are probably not intended as fiction. In fact, Mayakovsky's two plays *The Bedbug* and *The Bathhouse* are the most notable Futurist works in the genre. Even so, the science fiction element is slight, being no more pronounced than in some other plays of that Utopian-minded time, such as Bulgakov's *Adam and Eve*, *Ivan Vasilevich*, Lev Lunts's *The City of Truth* and Ehrenburg's *Trust D.E*. And less pronounced than in true science fiction works of the time, such as Bulgakov's *Fatal Eggs*, *Heart of a Dog*, novels by Zamyatin, Platonov, and A. K. Tolstoi. Why did the Futurists do so little in this field? Because they were not interested in science and the future, or because the genre seemed old-fashioned to them? Probably the second, since they did as little in all other traditional genres.

The Bedbug was first staged by Vsevolod Meyerhold in Moscow in 1929. Music for the play was composed by Dmitry Shostakovich (the score is said to be lost). Stills from the play may be found in various editions of Meyerhold's papers. They show that the play had the most modern constructivist staging. The playbill, made up by either Mayakovsky or Rodchenko, displays the usual Futurist lettering and the dates 1929-1979. Meyerhold considered the work very scenic and Mayakovsky a genius; he permitted the author to help in the direction, a rare thing in Meyerhold's career. The play failed, being too radical for the time, but earned Mayakovsky enough money to buy a Renault imported from Paris (a little luxury for the poet of the planet proletarian). The play has been revived with great success after the passing of Stalin and is now a stable of the Soviet stage.

The subtitle of the play is "An Extravaganza in 9 Scenes." The first four take place in the present (1929) and relate more closely to Bulgakov's *Zoya's Apartment* (1926) than to any work of science fiction. The purpose here is to ridicule the new philistine of the NEP period, a former worker who uses his proletarian background to assert ideological propriety while using the money of his future father-in-law to buy all sorts of luxuries. We see this boor, Ivan Prisypkin, buying brassieres and other items at a Tambov store, flaunting his background and libertine tastes before youths in the hostel where he boards, and celebrating his "class-conscious wedding." The salesmen in the first scene repeat rhyming advertisements reminiscent of Mayakovsky's own slogans for the Soviet government. The young mechanic (that is, a real worker) in the second scene accuses Prisypkin of lying down to sleep beside the bridge to Socialism. The wedding in the third scene turns into a drunken rout; the stove overturns and the place catches fire. The firemen in the fourth scene report the corpses ("an ex-woman," a "person of pre-war build," and so on) but cannot account for one member of the party. In performance this is the suitable place for intermission.

The next five scenes take place fifty years in the future (1979). In scene five, the "President of the Institute for Human Resurrection" takes a world-wide vote and receives the go-ahead to revive Prisypkin, who was preserved in a block of ice in the skating rink below the house. In six, Prisypkin and the bedbug on him are thawed out. In seven, the future society is stricken by an epidemic of philistine habits. In eight, Prisypkin is bored, misses his lost bed-bug, and locates it through a notice in the newspaper. In nine, reunited with his bedbug, Prisypkin is exhibited in a zoo as a specimen of a parasite: the bedbug is *bedbugus normalis*, Prisypkin is *philistinus vulgarus*. Turning to the audi-ence, Prisypkin shouts:

"Citizens! Brothers! My own people! Darlings! How did you get here? So many of you! Were you unfrozen? Why am I alone in the cage? Darlings, friends, come and join me!. . ." As one of Mayakovsky's advertisements for the play read: ". . . This is not ABOUT YOU, but about your neighbor."

The point of all this is Mayakovsky's outrage at the NEP period and the return of the vulgar egoist in new clothing. Mayakovsky had his weaknesses, his incurable *braggadocio*, his hypochondria, his fetish about cleanliness, his mawkish romanticism, but he also had revolutionary fervor and revolutionary guilt. As Edward J. Brown points out, the character of Prisypkin is in some ways modeled on the author: Mayakovsky was aware of the self-serving nature of his political pronouncements, just as he was aware of his desire for bourgeois happiness. He probably realized that his agitprop jingles were only so many corny advertisements parroted by street hawkers. He knew and joked about his identification with animals — animals in cages (Brown has an excel-lent exposition of this aspect of the work). Yet he could not consciously admit the contradictions, not condemn the poet Mayakovsky in this play. On the contrary, he had to reject the contradictions, condemn the new philistine, side with the people of the worldwide Communist future.

And here is where the play falls down. Because in order for the condemna-tion to be just and the address to the audience to have impact, the society of the future must be positive, the boor must be rejected in the name of a better person, a better society, a better world. Mayakovsky's world of 1979 is utterly lifeless, virtually an anti-Utopia. For example, the old way of voting by rais-ing your hand is ridiculed in scene five, but the new way is only a tabulation of lights — no human beings seem to be involved. The professor in scene six does not know the meaning of old decadent words such as business, bureau-cracy, Bulgakov (Mayakovsky hated him), suicide, self-advertisement, and so on, but he also does not know the purpose of Prisypkin's guitar — there is no music, except a march at the end. In the epidemic scene, the worthy citizens are infected by such loathsome habits as cadging, faking, making deals, but also by such pleasurable ones as drinking, smoking, dancing, and falling in love. By scene eight Prisypkin is justifiably bored, and though he is truly obnoxious, people less obnoxious would be bored too. Consequently, the zoo scene — the obvious point of the whole play — offers only a confused conclusion: the rejection of a negative type by an equally negative society. Mayakovsky threw all sorts of things into this play: poetry and prose, jingles and songs, slapstick and rhetoric, political pamphlet and literary polemic, the theme of Dostoevski's "Dream of a Ridiculous Man" (infection of a pure society by a depraved yet living man), the address to the audience from Gogol's *The Inspector General* ("What are you laughing at? You're laughing at yourselves."), music, flashing lights, joke on top of joke. But for whatever reason, emotional or intellectual, he was unable to construct a positive future society, unable to solve his own contradictions.

Which is not to say that the play is a total failure. Meyerhold was right: it is scenic, it is witty. Seen not as a masterpiece, but as a series of humorous sketches, it works. The role of Prisypkin affords an actor great comic possibilities (all the other roles are fairly drab). The wedding is a riot of slow-motion dancing, drunkenness, and debauchery. The future society parodies the gymnastic exhibitions and films of Stalin's time. And the address to the audience has an effect: the audience knows what the poet meant to say.

Mayakovsky never became a great poet. But he was undeniably inventive, he was thrilled by the act of creation, and he brought great excitement to his time. His suicide was a tragedy, not because a growing talent was cut off, but because it was inevitable for an egocentric poet in service to the state. As he wrote in "A Man" (1917):

> " — Pedestrian,/ is this Zhukovsky Street?/ He looks at me/ as a child looks at a skeleton,/ eyes this big,/ tries to get by./ 'It's been Mayakovsky Street for thousands of years:/ he shot himself here at the door of his beloved.' Who,/ I shot myself?/ What an exaggeration!"

Gary Kern

Sources for Further Study

Reviews:

Chicago Sunday Tribune. September 4, 1960, p. 7.

Library Journal. LXXXV, July, 1960, p. 2599.

Poetry. XCVII, February, 1961, p. 322.

Saturday Review. XLIII, December 10, 1960, p. 33.

Time. LXXVI, September 5, 1960, p. 74.

Times Literary Supplement. November 10, 1961, p. 806.

BEFORE ADAM

Author: Jack London (1876-1916)
First book publication: 1906
Type of work: Novel
Time: 1906 and the mid-Pleistocene era
Locale: A primordial forest

A nameless narrator slips back to the Dawn World nightly in his dreams, during which he inhabits the hair-covered body of one of his progenitors, Big-Tooth, whose experiences form the substance of the story

Principal characters:
BIG-TOOTH, the Narrator's prehistoric alter ego
THE SWIFT ONE, his relatively hairless mate
RED-EYE, a gorillalike atavism, a member of the Horde
LOP-EAR, Big-Tooth's comrade
BROKEN-TOOTH, another of Big-Tooth's comrades
OLD MARROW-BONE, the grizzled, enfeebled patriarch of the Horde

Jack London seems to have followed a clever formula for taking the reader back to the mid-Pleistocene age. He took the evolutionary findings of Charles Darwin as interpreted by Thomas Henry Huxley; added Herbert Spencer's doctrine of the survival of the fittest and his theory of atavism; colored this combination with Rudyard Kipling's *Mowgli of the Wolves* and other Jungle Book tales; shamelessly stole much of the basic plot from Stanley Waterloo's *Story of Ab*; and interpreted the mixture through the popular notion of "race memory." He called the resulting novel *Before Adam*; it was amazingly successful upon release in 1906.

The novel's appearance was inevitable, considering the period (pre-World War I Edwardian era). The then innocent, enthusiastic attitude toward science; the intellectual ferment over the fact that the remains of *Pithecanthropus erectus* (now called *Homo erectus*) had been unearthed in the 1890's; and the entire configuration leavened by London's "nature in the raw is what it's all about" convictions, all created an atmosphere which was prime for such a story.

The story, seemingly episodic and disjointed at first glance, and seemingly preoccupied with little more than chase scenes, is as attention-riveting, powerful, and fresh as it is deceptively simple. The nameless Narrator, a modern man of the year 1906, is cursed with horrifying nightmares in which he relives the life of one of his Dawn Age progenitors, self-designated as Big-Tooth. The experiences of semiarboreal Big-Tooth have, through some fluke, been transmitted, via stamped genes in germ plasm, into the cerebrums of countless generations of steadily evolving progeny, but have apparently remained dormant until reactivated in the Narrator's head. The Narrator, experiencing a type of ambivalent dissociation, is both the essentially mindless central figure in the Younger World drama, and a shrewdly analytical present-day spectator.

He lives, breathes, eats, laughs, screams, trembles, and reacts reflexively at the gut level, but simultaneously stands to one side and observes himself doing these things.

The setting for all of this is an enormous forested area. Predators skulk, prowl, howl, lurk near water holes, or bask in the sun at every turn. Included among the fauna are wild boars, wild dogs, lions, saber-tooth tigers, cave bears, and snakes with bodies as thick as one's thigh. It is an interesting place to view from a helicopter, but one would not care to land there. Unfortunately, Big-Tooth *lives* there. He is a member of the Horde, or the Folk, as he sometimes refers to them in 1906 language. The Folk dwell, as a loosely organized mob, in a riverside cliff honeycombed with caves. Elsewhere in the vicinity are the Tree People, from whom the Folk have advanced slightly in evolution; and the Fire People, who have taken a relatively giant evolutionary stride forward from the Folk, inasmuch as they have fire as well as bows-and-arrows. The Tree People gather nuts and berries and eat live nestlings; the Folk eat anything whose head they can pound in with a rock; and the Fire People have advanced beyond chewing on raw lizards and puppies, to the sophisticated level of cooking meat which they have hunted.

There are two lines of action in the plot. The immediate plot concerns the daily travails and adventures of Big-Tooth as he blunders from childhood, to adolescence, to proud adulthood. However, the overriding theme, supplying a constant background lietmotiv, is the encroachment of the Fire People on the "carrot-gathering grounds" of the Horde, with a concomitant, almost totally successful attempt at extermination.

The characters — though most would be physically indistinguishable to twentieth century eyes — are astonishingly three-dimensional and alive, even though limned with quick brush strokes. When the Chatterer, Big-Tooth's jealous tree-swinging father, tries to beat him because he's grown too big to literally "hang around" with his gibbering mother and sister, the reader experiences a surge of righteous indignation. When Big-Tooth first joins the Folk, and is mercilessly punched, pinched, and prodded by his new compatriots, the reader feels sorry for him. When he has a fist fight with his soon-to-be lifelong comrade, Lop-Ear, and the twosome grow to like each other and share a bachelor quarters in a bone-littered cave, the reader feels a glow of warmth, even when they pull a puppy apart and grind their molars on its warm flesh. When Big-Tooth falls in love with the Swift One, who is only partially a member of the Horde in a genetic sense, since her father was one of the Fire People who was not above miscegenation, the reader smiles with affection when their courtship is consummated. He feels outrage when Red-Eye, the Horde's gorillalike atavism, tries to rape her. When Broken-Tooth plummets from a tree branch with an arrow in his torso, the reader truly mourns, because he has come to *know* him. And, near the end, when the Fire People systematically smoke the Folk from their caves and slaughter them (except for a handful, including the protagonist and his mate), the reader feels deep sorrow.

This strong reader involvement is due primarily to London's effective utilization of two important literary devices, the intense dramatic scene and the adroit manipulation of point of view. An excellent example of his dramatic skill comes at the climax of the book, when the Fire People have piled up dry brush at the base of the Horde's sponge-holed cliff, and have torched a conflagration capable of consuming a thousand Joan of Arcs.

Big-Tooth and the Swift One, followed by rheumy-eyed, gasping Old Marrow-Bone, the shriveled patriarch of the loosely-structured community, manage to clamber to the highest stoney tier before the top of the bluff, over the grassy lip of which lies temporary freedom. Showers of arrows splinter against the uneven rock face, fortunately missing the protagonist and his terrified mate. A dozen shafts puncture the doomed Marrow-Bone, who whimpers piteously, loosens his grip, and tumbles into the flames. The reader, who by this time deeply cares for the grizzled half-man, also catapults into the fire, feeling the heat with all his nerve endings.

A sudden hush erases the shouts of the crazed attackers. Their leader, an ominous sixty-year-old monarch with a limp, precipitously raises one callused hand while lowering his bow and its half-ready arrow with the other. He has recognized the Swift One as one of his own, because of her relatively hairless unclad body. Without being told, the reader realizes that *he* is possibly her father. For a full minute, only the crackling of flames is heard. Then the Fire People, *en masse*, implore her beseechingly. In what is one of the nearest things in literature to a motion picture freeze frame in print, the Swift One spins and stares at them, quickly puts two-and-two together, contemptuously rejects the offer of sanctuary, and resolutely turns her back. It is the type of dramatic moment that deserves to be forever crystallized, and it is all done with a bare minimum of words.

In addition, much of the effectiveness of this work comes from the fact that, unlike most of his other novels, London narrated *Before Adam* from the autobiographical internal first person viewpoint. Because of this there is no distance between the protagonist and the reader. In most of his books, the reader observes the protagonist at arm's length; here the reader is inside the hero's head, sloping brow and all, with the attendant sensation of overwhelming immediacy. Stylistically, nothing in *Before Adam* can equal the lyrical beauty of the final paragraph of *The Call of the Wild*, but all of *Before Adam* is written with the verbal simplicity and intimacy of the suicide scene in *Martin Eden*.

As in all of London's books, the author's obsession with the awesome beauty of brute force is evident, but in this instance it is not overdone. There is none of his typical "Look at me, you pampered urban weakling! I can lick you with one hand behind my back!" posturing. The lip service to the supremacy of tooth and claw is present, but it is muted. Big-Tooth does not have to prove his physical superiority; all he needs to do is run.

Admittedly, London was an uneven writer. Some of his books are simplistic in concept and mawkishly sentimental in execution. Some are caught in his erroneous concept of the wolf as a type of self-sufficient hero in fur. But this novel, with its basic realism, has appealed to sixth grade schoolboys, to graduate students, and to general readers.

Speaking of schoolboys, the book was written (at great speed, since the plot was basically taken from Waterloo's *Story of Ab*) with an essentially juvenile market in mind. London was pleasantly surprised when adults also found it interesting. He seemed unpleasantly surprised when Waterloo's printed shouts of justified outrage caused an international scandal. Knowing repercussions might reverberate, why did he take someone else's story line and refurbish it? Because he was experiencing one of the frequent deep dips in his psychological and financial crests and troughs. Domestic difficulties and creditors were driving him to extremes. What better way to avoid all this than by making the greatest possible escape of all (short of suicide, which he committed in 1916), one back to the Pleistocene?

This escape was not, of course, exclusively London's. *Before Adam* was one of the many "primitive man" books that were emerging in numbers sufficient to constitute a minor genre. But few of them hold up today. The hard realistic edge and controlled language make this book one of London's best, an important minor classic.

George S. Elrick

Sources for Further Study

Criticism:

Boggs, W. Arthur. "Looking Backward at the Utopian Novel, 1888-1900," in *Bulletin of the New York Public Library*. LXIV (June, 1960), pp. 329-336. This analysis of the influence of Bellamy's *Looking Backward* reveals its impact upon the novels of Jack London.

Clareson, Thomas D., Editor. *A Spectrum of Worlds*. New York: Doubleday, 1972. This anthology presents a lengthy critique of Jack London's science fiction themes.

Gallant, Joseph. "A Proposal for the Reading of 'Scientific Fiction,'" in *High Point*. XXXIII (April, 1951), pp. 20-27. Analyzing conventional science fiction as represented by London's writing, Gallant advocates a new classification to be called scientific fiction.

Reviews:

Atlantic. C, July, 1907, p. 125.

Independent. LXII, March 14, 1907, p. 620.
Literary Digest. XXXIV, April 20, 1907, p. 639.
New York Times. XII, March 9, 1907, p. 145.
Outlook. LXXXV, March 23, 1907, p. 718.
Review of Reviews. XXXV, June, 1907, p. 762.

BEFORE THE DAWN

Author: John Taine (Eric Temple Belle, 1883-1960)
First book publication: 1934
Type of work: Novel
Time: The present and the closing period of the Age of Reptiles
Locale: Unspecified, presumably somewhere in the United States

An account of images of the distant past preserved in fossils and rocks and liberated by means of an "electronic analyzer," in particular those relating to the career of one of the last of the giant dinosaurs

Principal characters:
SELLAR,
LANGTRY, and
BRONSON, scientific observers
"BELSHAZZAR,"
"JEZEBEL," and
"BARTHOLOMEW," dinosaurs of the species *Tyrannosaurus rex*
"SATAN," a carnivorous dinosaur of uncertain species

Before the Dawn was the tenth science fiction novel by John Taine to appear in print, and it represents something of a break in the pattern of his work. His earliest publications had been conventional scientific romances using themes that were already well-worn; *The Purple Sapphire* (1924) is a lost race fantasy; *Quayle's Invention* (1927) is about a device for extracting gold from sea water; *The Gold Tooth* (1927) is a treasure-hunt story; and *Green Fire* (1928) features a mad scientist and a terrible new weapon. Next, Taine wrote extravagant romances of mutation, including *The Greatest Adventure* (1929) and *The Iron Star* (1930), as well as others which were published in the science fiction pulps, notably *White Lily* (1930) and *Seeds of Life* (1931). These works displayed a much more prolific imagination, and marked Taine as one of the most extravagant of the early science fiction novelists. During this period the author was a professor of mathematics at the California Institute of Technology, and he went on to establish a considerable reputation under his own name as a mathematician and popularizer of mathematics. Most of his science fiction writing seems to have been done for relaxation; it is often careless but always enthusiastic and melodramatically indulgent. Thus, it is not easy to decide whether *Before the Dawn* is an attempt to produce more serious and disciplined science fiction, or whether it is simply one more fantasia inspired by the author's interest in evolution and the phenomenon of mutation.

Before the Dawn was published by Williams and Wilkins, a company which had hitherto specialized in the publication of nonfiction scientific works. In the introduction to the book the publishers claimed that they did not consider their new venture to be a drastic departure from their standard policy. The introduction presents the work more as an exercise in the popularization of science than as a work of fiction, stressing its distinctiveness from Taine's earlier scientific romances and referring to it as a work of "fantascience" (a word coined by Taine especially to describe this novel). The work was thus promoted as a kind of drama-documentary whose function was to construct an image of the Age of Reptiles — a vision of life as it must have been lived by the dinosaurs.

Previously, Taine had embedded his scientific speculations in the standardized plot formulas of pulp fiction, a strategy supported by Hugo Gernsback in his manifesto for "scientifiction." In *Before the Dawn*, however, the narrative is very different; it resembles an informal commentary upon a series of careful scientific observations. The dry and laboriously pedantic tone of authentic scientific writing is absent, but there is a serious attempt to preserve the spirit of such writing through the impersonal tone and through the constant reminders that what is being presented is an objective picture of real life in the late Cretaceous period (though the word itself is not used — all scientific jargon is rigorously excluded). There are continual asides in which reference is made to opinions and flights of fancy advanced by one or another of the three scientists, but these are always presented as accessories to the story itself. Taine did not overcome the difficulties inherent in this odd mode of presentation, though he did use a similar technique subsequently in *The Cosmic Geoids* with slightly more convincing results.

The opening chapters of the novel tell in undramatic fashion the story of the development by Langtry, at the request of Sellar, of a technique to recover from objects the visual images to which they were exposed in the distant past. With the help of Bronson, the technique is refined to the point that the surface of a rock or a fossil can be analyzed so that it projects a vast three-dimensional image of its previous surroundings in a natural arena. This image can then be allowed to progress like a film, observed from within or from without; in other words, the "electronic analyzer" or "televisor" allows the scientists to see through time. The culmination of the scientists' studies is a single series of recordings patched together from several different observation points, showing the adventures of a group of dinosaurs living at the very end of their era.

Though no species is ever designated by its proper scientific name, it is obvious that the main character and his two relatives are members of the species *Tyrannosaurus rex*. The story follows the life of a tyrannosaur nicknamed Belshazzar by presenting "slice of life" scenes selected from various vantage points in space and time. Together, these scenes re-create a vivid picture of what life was like during the Age of Reptiles. Thus, we see dinosaurs taunted by stinging flies, their eggs threatened by small mammals against which they are powerless. We watch a giant herbivorous dinosaur (apparently a *Diplodocus* or *Brontosaurus*) who is simply too huge and clumsy to deal effectively with its environment.

Belshazzar's companions, his mother Jezebel and his possible father Bartholomew, are presented as very old and incompetent in coping with the demands of change. In the presentation of Belshazzar himself, however, the tone is markedly different. Belshazzar is shown as a king, strong, capable, and even ingenious. And because Taine sees his spirit as essentially unconquerable, he views the demise of the dinosaur race as a vast catastrophe, caused by a momentary perversion of nature so extreme that nothing could survive it.

Thus, the novel shows an entire continent in the process of destruction by a combination of natural disasters. The land is linked to a new and verdant continent by a thin land bridge, but the vegetation on the bridge is too sparse to sustain anything much larger than a rat; small mammals can cross it, while the great herbivorous dinosaurs who are stampeded into making the attempt almost all perish *en route*. In so doing, however, they provide an abundant supply of carrion so that Belshazzar and his companions, and one carnivore of a different species, dubbed Satan, can make it to the new world. Once there, of course, they find no great herds upon which to prey, and are dependent on the inadequate trickle of herbivores which manage to cross the bridge. Eventually, with all else lost to them, Belshazzar and Satan, each the last of their kind, fight a monumental duel and destroy each other.

Much is made throughout the book of the mythology of "nature red in tooth and claw." Save for the lotus eater, every creature we see is engaged in a frantic struggle for existence. Each incident is of great import because the battle to avoid extinction is embodied in the tiniest action. *Stegosaurus* and *Triceratops* parade unnamed across the stage as the natural victims of the gladiatorial game of prehistory, and there are constant reminders that these contests are a microcosm of the whole evolutionary story, and are symbolic of its mechanism.

The main flaw in the novel, of course, is that the series of scenes it depicts creates an impression which is quite false. In fact, the Cretaceous was not, as is suggested, a time of great geological upheaval and dramatic climatic change. The tragedy of the dying continent is not based upon actual prehistory, but rather upon the author's own earlier scientific romances. There was nothing that Taine enjoyed more than the choreography of natural disaster on a huge scale (most of Africa was destroyed in *The Iron Star*, Antarctica in *The Greatest Adventure*, and China in *White Lily*). His description of dinosaur life ignores scientific fact; and the contrast between the dinosaurs and the mammals is greatly oversimplified.

Before the Dawn is the work of a man mesmerized by the awesome skeletons excavated in the far West by Marsh and Cope in the last quarter of the nineteenth century. Taine, of course, was far from alone in his fascination and in his attempt to imagine what life in the Cretaceous era must have been like; few other contributors to dinosaur mythology, however, presented their work with the same pretensions of factuality as Taine did. However, if *Before the Dawn* is worthless as a drama-documentary, it is valuable as an embodiment of the legends and misconceptions about the dinosaurs which grew up around Marsh's and Cope's discoveries. The novel not only is an example of the impact scientific discoveries can have on the popular imagination in general, but is a testament to several Victorian attitudes in particular, such as an unabashed admiration for power, even when it entails bloodshed; a celebration of competitiveness and ferocity; and a certain occasional reticence — even hypocrisy — about revealing one's emotions or true opinions. For this reason, if for no other, *Before the Dawn* is a work which warrants careful reading; it has some historical interest, and, although it should not be taken overly seriously, it contains memorable action scenes such as those describing Belshazzar's battles.

Brian Stableford

Sources for Further Study

Criticism:

Wilson, Colin. "The Vision of Science," in his *The Strength to Dream: Literature and the Imagination*. London: Gallancy, 1962, pp. 94-117. Wilson's relation of science fiction to the mainstream of literary tradition emphasizes the role of Taine as well as Lovecraft in a merger of many paths.

Reviews:

Boston Transcript. July 18, 1934, p. 3.
New York Times. September 9, 1934, p. 17.
Saturday Review. XI, July 28, 1934, p. 17.

THE BEGUM'S FORTUNE
(LES CINQ CENTS MILLION DE LA BEGUM)

Author: Jules Verne (1828-1905)
First book publication: 1879
English translation: 1879
Type of work: Novel
Time: The 1870's
Locale: Oregon

Two Utopian cities are created by millionaires to further their opposing ideals

Principal characters:
DR. FRANCOIS SARRAZIN, a French scientist
OCTAVE SARRAZIN, his son
JEANNE SARRAZIN, his daughter
MARCEL BRUCKMANN, a heroic young engineer and friend of the Sarrazins
PROFESSOR SCHULTZE, a German scientist

In 1878, French publisher Jules Hetzel received the manuscript of a fantastic novel entitled *L'héritage de Langevol* from a well-known radical and revolutionary, Pascal Grousset, one of the leaders of the Paris Commune in 1871 who, for political reasons, wrote under the pen name André Laurie. Hetzel was interested, but did not consider the manuscript ready to be published in its present state. He therefore approached his friend Jules Verne, asking him to rewrite the novel. Verne was not enthusiastic. "The novel, if that's what it is, is a complete failure," he said. "There is absolutely no action, no struggle, and consequently no interest in it. I've never seen such a mess. . . ." Hetzel persisted, however, and Verne finally agreed to rewrite the novel. The finished product was published in 1879, under Verne's name, as *Les cinq cents million de la Bégum*. It became one of Verne's most memorable works, a novel whose thematic implications put it on a par with Verne's best writing.

(Pascal Grousset later became a friend of Jules Verne, and one who influenced Verne a great deal; under the name André Laurie he also became one of the most popular science fiction authors in the world at the end of the nineteenth century.)

Beneath their surfaces of glowing optimism, most of Verne's novels are tales of failed idealism; this is particularly true of *The Begum's Fortune*. It is the story of a Utopia which inevitably turns out to be somewhat less than perfect, a theme which Verne treated in several novels, notably in *Ile à hélice* (1895) and *L'etonnante aventure de la mission Barsac* (1914), in which perfect cities meet disastrous ends through the actions of their less-than-perfect inhabitants.

In *The Begum's Fortune*, Verne describes the creation and ultimate fate of two seeming Utopias in North America, one ruled by lofty idealism and culture (and noble Frenchmen); and one ruled by materialism and scientific efficiency (and Teutonic Germans). These ideal cities have been created by the fabulous

(527,000,000 francs) fortune left by the richest man in the world, the Begum of the title. His heirs turn out to be two strange and incredibly stubborn idealists, a French scientist and authority on hygiene, Dr. Francois Sarrazin, and a rather sinister German scientist, Professor Schultze, a chemist and an authority on racial biology. The inheritance is divided between these worthy gentlemen (minus 27,000,000 francs in fees to bankers and lawyers), who then proceed to create with the money their personal versions of the Earthly Paradise.

Those familiar with the various utopian experiments conducted in North America during the late nineteenth century — the New Harmony Movement, the Oneida society, the Icarians, the Shakers, and so on — will recognize much in Dr. Sarrazin's idealistic city, France-Ville, although the good Doctor hardly subscribes to the Communist ideals held so dear by most Utopians. France-Ville is the acme of perfection, of hygiene and righteousness, of justice and friendliness and happiness. Doctor Sarrazin is the most benevolent of rulers, and his subjects all love him with a passion that would have embarrassed anyone but a true Utopian. There are no dissidents in France-Ville; like the Utopian societies of our time, only true believers are invited. All the citizens of France-Ville share Dr. Sarrazin's views on life and society, and no one ever questions his right to rule (Verne at least does not mention any dissidents in France-Ville). However, this does not account for the undisclosed but very large number of Chinese who do all the menial work for the Utopians; it is probable that these slave workers do not share the happiness of their "superiors."

The idealism of Professor Schultze is somewhat less lofty, albeit much more practical, as is proven by his ideal city, the mighty Stahlstadt. Situated only thirty miles from France-Ville and close to the Pacific Ocean, it is the antithesis of everything France-Ville stands for. The city is enormous and forbidding, crouching under a heavy cloak of coal dust and smoke fumes, snarling like a ferocious beast. Professor Schultze is an eminently practical man in many ways, and is making his 250 million francs work for him; he is rapidly becoming a billionaire through manufacturing and selling arms, particularly cannon, to a world sadly lacking in idealism. Stahlstadt is noisy and, in Verne's eyes, eminently horrifying. Still, it is a city of human beings with human hopes and fears, people who live much as people did in the industrialized cities of Verne's time; and when reading the descriptions of the strangely soulless and cold France-Ville, as contrasted to the overpowering life in Stahlstadt, one may be tempted by the heretical thought that Stahlstadt might be the better of the two places.

Verne himself was very much an idealist, more like Dr. Sarrazin than the boisterous and unpredictable Professor Schultze, the representative and symbol of a people and an attitude that Verne had good reasons to fear after the lessons brought home by the disastrous Franco-Prussian War of 1870. Verne had also seen the great Krupp cannons at the Universal Exhibition in 1867, so it is hardly surprising that Professor Schultze is pictured as belligerent from the start, determined to wipe out the "city of fools" from the face of the Earth. This he proceeds to do with the aid of a monster cannon, the biggest in the world, which he ultimately fires at the unhappy city of France-Ville. It turns out, however, that the velocity of the deadly projectile is so great that he instead unintentionally launches Earth's first artificial satellite.

Meanwhile, much cloak-and-dagger intrigue by the noble Utopians of France-Ville leads to the eventual overthrow of Stahlstadt (obviously Verne's version of Krupp's steel city Essen), and the evil Professor Schultze dies in his secret study of an overdose of liquid carbon dioxide — a new terror weapon designed to be used against France-Ville which instead kills its inventor. Happiness reigns again in France-Ville, whose noble inhabitants immediately form a strong army in order to defend themselves against the crude outer world (most probably arming themselves with some of Schultze's most obnoxious inventions), and Stahlstadt becomes a satellite city of France-Ville, destined to do the menial work for the lofty Utopians.

The all-pervading attitude in *The Begum's Fortune* is similar to that of J. R. R. Tolkien's celebrated trilogy, *The Lord of the Rings*: a distrust of industrialization, socialism, and all the dangers of the new age which threaten to destroy the secure life of the old days. Verne contrasts innocent Rousseauian escapism with modern technology, and draws the inevitable conclusions for a man of his background. Dr. Sarrazin offers mankind, or at least a chosen part of it, the perfect life as he sees it — cleanliness, order, security, and above all, benevolent regimentation; he cannot understand the strange Professor Schultze, who is interested only in the end product of Stahlstadt's endeavor, and cares little for the private lives of his subjects. Yet workers from all over the world flock by the hundreds of thousands to his grimy and forbidding city, where, after all, they earn more than they ever did before and are moreover guaranteed a private life of their own. Thus, France-Ville can send spies to Stahlstadt, disguised as laborers and engineers, while no one from Stahlstadt is ever permitted to walk the pristine Utopian streets of France-Ville. Paradoxically, then, Stahlstadt offers its inhabitants a greater degree of freedom than the ideal city of France-Ville, where everything is regimented and arranged according to the theories of the town planner.

On the whole, Jules Verne manages, albeit inadvertently, to convey the ambiguity of the Utopian dream; it is this aspect of *The Begum's Fortune* that makes it a readable, fascinating work to this day. How much of the novel is really Verne's work and how much is Pascal Grousset's no one can say; but it heralds the darkening pessimism that speaks so eloquently in Verne's later works, and hints at the rude awakening experienced by naïve Utopians at the time of World War I and the Russian Revolution. In Verne's hands, Grousset's tale of revolution and international intrigue became an adventure tale, another *Voyage Extraordinaire* of the sort Verne's readers expected of him; but enough of Grousset remains to make the novel a much more farseeing and disturbing one than Verne intended or even could have suspected.

Sam J. Lundwall

Sources for Further Study

Criticism:

Allott, Kenneth. *Jules Verne*. London: Crescent Press, 1940. Allott studies the relationship of Verne's work to romanticism and his understanding of technology.

Moskowitz, Sam. *Explorers of the Infinite: Shapers of Science Fiction*. New York: World, 1963. Moskowitz examines Verne's impact on the science fiction tradition.

BEHOLD THE MAN

Author: Michael Moorcock (1939-   )
First book publication: 1968
Type of work: Novel
Time: The late 1940's through early 1960's and A.D. 28
Locale: Contemporary England and the ancient Middle East

Karl Glogauer, obsessed by a desire to know if Christ was real, gets an opportunity to find out via time travel, only to discover that his own destiny is the Cross

Principal characters:
> KARL GLOGAUER, a lonely, love-starved intellectual and time traveler
> MONICA, a cynical psychiatric social worker with whom Karl has an unhealthy sexual relationship
> JOHN THE BAPTIST, the leader of the Essene sect

Jesus is a hunchbacked, congenital idiot who has a cast in his left eye, who drools uncontrollably, and who mutters his own name over and over again. Mary is an overweight, lusting wench, who admits that Jesus was fathered illegitimately by someone other than Joseph. John the Baptist is a hardened revolutionary who recognizes the political value of a Messiah in his plans to overthrow the Romans. These are some of the revelations that Karl Glogauer, a lonely, neurotic intellectual, finds when he travels back to the year A.D. 28 in Michael Moorcock's *Behold the Man*. Drawing heavily on Jungian psychology, the award-winning short novel combines sexual and religious symbols to present an alternate version of Christ's crucifixion.

In his ingenious and disturbing explanation, Moorcock attributes the creation of a Messiah to time travel, the politics of the Middle East in A.D. 28, and the psychology of Karl Glogauer. In his lonely neuroticism, Glogauer typifies Carl Jung's modern man who is searching for significance in his life as the traditional values of society collapse around him. Because of his own failure, Karl becomes obsessed with knowing the truth about Christ, not realizing that he will himself be led to the cross by the determinism of his own psychology.

Guided by Jungian theories, Moorcock depicts Karl as a weak and cowardly child whose parents are divorced. He has no relationship with his father after age four or five, and his mother, beautiful, harassed, and aloof, is unable to provide him with the love that he needs to develop a healthy personality. So desperate is he for her love, in fact, that he attempts suicide twice to get her attention. The second time, the doctor called to treat him accuses Karl of trying to gain the limelight. He tells his mother that she is the reason he has tried to gas himself. Unfortunately, she does not understand what he means.

Karl develops into a full-fledged neurotic, whose problems center about his loneliness and his search for identity. So preoccupied is he with his inability to love that his relationships with girls are especially disastrous. His sexual rela-

tions prove particularly unsatisfactory, and his very first relationship characterizes those to follow. At thirteen, he attempts to kiss a pudgy girl named
Veronica whom he met through a church club. He is so awkward and unromantic about it that she refuses him. At age seventeen, he moves in with
Deirdre Thompson, a woman whose husband, a sergeant major, is away in the
East. This move is followed by affairs with several other women, all of whom
belong to the same club as Deirdre and all of whom Karl classifies as "plain-
faced" and "neurotic." Unsatisfied and bored, however, he leaves Deirdre six
months after moving in with her, goes home, and has a nervous breakdown.
Believing that a change would be good for him, his mother sends him to Ham-
burg, where his affairs with several German girls leave him equally bored and
unsatisfied. Later at an Oxford party, he meets Eva, a blonde-haired, blue-
eyed freshman at Somerville. She falls madly in love with him and believes
that he has some great purpose in life. In a binge of self-pity, however, he
feels compelled to test her love. He picks fights, tells her dirty stories, and
gets drunk, all in an attempt, he rationalizes, to make her accept him for what
he really is. Instead, he destroys her love and she leaves him. Unable to understand that he does not know how to love, Karl asks his friend Friedman what
happened. He tells Karl that he destroyed his relationship with Eva because he
loved himself too much. Finally, Glogauer begins a relationship with Monica.
She is ten years older than he, cynical and bitter. Their lovemaking is only
satisfying when it includes minor aberrations. Real fulfillment comes after
intercourse when their verbal skirmishes climax in anger. Eventually, even
their arguments take on a pattern — Karl concedes and Monica mothers him.
Once, carefully following the same scenario that he tried with his mother, he
even attempts suicide. Monica finally tires of Karl's emotionalism, however,
and begins a lesbian affair with a coworker. She is willing to make love to
both the girl and Karl, but he feels betrayed and throws her out. Karl's failure
at love even leads him into at least one homosexual incident, at age fifteen,
with Mr. Younger, the curate of his church. It leaves him torn between disgust
with himself and desire.

From a very early age, Karl comes to associate sex with religion. He indicates at one point, for example, that he finally stopped saying his bedtime
prayers when he learned the pleasures of masturbation. The symbol for this
association comes to be a small, silver cross. Beginning with Veronica, who
wore such a cross between her "already large breasts," Karl's female companions must wear a cross. On one occasion he admits that long after Veronica
was gone from his dreams, he would think of girls wearing small, silver cruci-
fixes between their breasts and the thought would arouse "incredible excesses
of masturbatory pleasure" in him. Because of this compulsion, he buys Eva a
small, silver ankh to wear, and he is initially attracted to Deirdre Thompson
because she wears a small, silver sun cross. Only Monica does not wear one,
as if its absence symbolized her cynical, antireligious attitude. Yet, the heavy

ritualization of their lovemaking does display religious characteristics.

The psychology underlying the development of Karl's character is clearly Jungian. In that context, the association of sex with religion is a logical one. Briefly stated, Karl's failure to find sexual satisfaction generates enormous quantities of libido, psychic energy, which finds no outlet in useful social functions. The energy is dammed up in his unconscious mind where it eventually causes a neurosis. The neurosis occurs when the energy activates an archetype from Karl's collective unconscious. Archetypes are tendencies in every person's mind to create certain meaningful and recurring symbols. The archetype becomes stronger and stronger as more energy is siphoned into it. Finally, a neurotic complex is formed. It is focused in the activated archetype. It becomes an independent system within the personality, so dominant that it drives the individual along its own path even though he may believe that he is making his own free choices of action.

Sex is only one of several instincts that generate libido, and there are thousands of archetypes in the collective unconscious which could be activated. But since sex is the most powerful generator of libido and since the god archetype is the strongest attractor of libido in the personality, Moorcock's use of these particular elements to develop Karl is an excellent choice.

To implement the psychology which inevitably leads Glogauer to the cross, Moorcock adopts several other Jungian motifs. Among them are "rebirth," "mother-incest," and "the child-hero." As with the personality itself, they are interrelated. All center, however, on rebirth, much as the novel itself does.

According to Jung, the god-archetype, in particular, has the capability of taking "possession" of an individual's consciousness. Moreover, it may form a complex that becomes so well integrated into consciousness that other symbols gather around it. It may also become so highly energized that it vitalizes all of the symbols into a "lived religion." For this to occur, however, the particular god-symbol itself must be "alive." For Jung, this means that the symbol has preeminence in the consciousness of the worshipers and that they believe that the god's commands have a divine source. Moorcock, however, takes the concept literally.

Karl becomes the living-god symbol upon his return to A.D. 28. To do so, he must experience a rebirth. This is accomplished in the first scenes of the novel, packed by Moorcock with birth images, when Glogauer emerges from the time machine. The machine itself is described as womblike or egglike. It is spherical and full of a milky fluid. Its passenger floats within it in a rubber suit. When it lands, it cracks and Karl curls into a fetal ball. Then a wide split appears in its side and he lies on his back crying out. After all movement stops, he crawls over the slippery inner surface. Once he exits from the sphere, he is reborn.

Such a rebirth is also supported by Jungian psychodynamics. From that point of view, the initial damming up of libido occurs because of a breakdown in the individual's "persona," the image that he presents to the outside world. As this energy probes downward into the collective unconscious, it not only activates archetypes, it actually promotes the reintegration of the personality because it forces the person to find a new religious belief or a new philosophy of life. This new belief may eventually help the individual to bring his personality back into balance by integrating the independent systems back into it. When the reintegration occurs, a new element of the personality develops called the "self." It is the seat of consciousness, and its creation is symbolized by both a rebirth and the Mandala, the perfectly balanced square or circle. This is exactly what happens to Karl. Prior to the rebirth described in the opening scenes of the novel, he had inherited his father's bookshop. Significantly, it is called "The Mandala." Since both the rebirth and the Mandala are attached to Karl's development, it would seem that energy dammed up by his neurosis has been freed and that he has created a "self" within his now integrated personality. This condition is important to his continued development as a living symbol because the development of a "self" now permits him to interact with the people he encounters in the Middle East and to implement the Christ myth. Before the integration, his shyness and sense of failure would have prevented him from doing so.

Moorcock has also adopted the "mother incest" motif, which Jung interprets as part of the rebirth syndrome. Incest symbolism, especially involving the mother, is the most important sign of libido regression. It also signifies the desire of the individual to be reborn. Such a syndrome is particularly prevalent in Christians because of the heavy emphasis placed on rebirth, or new life, if one only believes in Christ. Jung does not interpret "mother incest" as a desire to have coitus with the mother. Rather, he believes that it reflects a psychological experience. He explains that since the regressing libido is seeking a new source of potency and since the womb is the original source of life, it is natural for the libido to be drawn to the "mother." In this context, however, "mother" is interpreted as "Nature," the most inclusive concept of a life source that exists. Rebirth marks the end of the libido's regression because the barriers to its progression have been removed and the life energies set free.

There is implicit "mother incest" in both Karl's actions and attitudes. His relationship with his mother is characterized by his desperate quest for her love and attention. So desperate is his need, in fact, that it drives him to attempt suicide on two occasions to gain her sympathy. This relationship also colors his relationships with his female sexual partners. Many of them are "motherly." Deirdre is older than he is, as are the other women he has affairs with from the Celtic study group. He also has sexual relations with the "Virgin Mary," his symbolic mother; the most significant quality in his relationship with Monica, who is ten years his senior, is her tendency to mother him. Clearly, these incidents are the working out of the "mother incest" motif, and they mark a regressive stage in his libido development.

Yet another motif that Moorcock adopts from Jung is that of the "child-hero." Psychologically, the "child-hero" represents all the qualities of what Jung calls "individuation," or the balancing of the personality's psychic forces in its quest for self-realization. The emergence of a child from the womb is the obvious product of rebirth. Furthermore, Jung believes that such a motif has a divine sense about it and a special saving capability. He also believes that the child represents the strongest urge in a human being — self-realization.

Karl's emergence from the time machine has already been described as a rebirth process. Further clues in *Behold the Man* indicate that when this occurs, he becomes the "child-hero." It is also clear that Moorcock intends for the reader to identify him with the Christ child. After Karl's initial cry (to be interpreted as the birth cry), he is carried to a cave or building where he is placed upon a bed of straw (the image of the manger is inescapable) and washed down (as is done to the Christ child after birth). Moreover, he remarks as he is lying there that the whole scene has a sharper reality for him than anything he has experienced since he was a child. Added to this, his general disorientation as he tries to find his way about the Middle East of A.D. 28 is very childlike, as if the young mind is trying to discover what its new world is all about. Finally, as he is hanging on the cross, he comments that his crucifiers should not be doing this to a child.

Circumstances and his peculiar psychology have led Glogauer to the cross and created a terrible irony at the end of the story. Karl is eventually disillusioned by what he has found: the "Virgin Mary" is no virgin at all, the real Jesus is a congenital idiot, and the crucifixion is as much the product of politics as religion. Driven by his own psychology and aided by a capability to slip almost completely into another identity, a capability he learned as a child nineteen hundred years later, Karl comes to believe that he really is the Messiah, and he subsequently tries to make those events surrounding his own life as nearly parallel to those of the Jesus myth as possible. He selects his apostles, for example, on the basis of their names. He conspires with Judas to produce that apostle's betrayal. He comes to a full realization of the fact that the Jesus myth is a lie as he is hanging on the cross. His libido is again in a state of regression, and has been since he discovered the true nature of Jesus. It is marked by his intercourse with Mary and by the erection that he experiences during crucifixion.

That realization also involves a perception about himself. Nineteen hundred years later he had come to the conclusion that because he constantly betrayed himself he prompted others to betray him. So in purposely producing his own crucifixion, Karl has fulfilled his destiny in yet another way — he has betrayed himself and caused others to betray him. He dies with the terribly disillusioning knowledge that Jesus was a lie.

Ironically, he does not realize that functionally it does not matter whether a neurotic coward or the son of God died on the cross. In psychological terms, either way the symbol will be just as powerful in its impact on others. As Jung points out, when the right conditions prevail and the "living god" is experienced throughout the community, the archetypal image is so strong that no one ever stops to ask what it means. In this sense, Karl has truly confirmed his life, for he has extended his personality beyond his personal concerns and created something very remarkable. He simply fails to realize that his personal concerns are not important in the larger picture of things, except as they permit him to implement the myth.

Moorcock's novel is provocative in its capability to raise unanswerable questions. For example, will Glogauer be born again some nineteen hundred and thirty years later to repeat the myth building process? Is he caught in an endless circle of time? Does the fact that he, among all men, fulfills the Christ myth signify in itself some divine sort of guidance? The fact that *Behold the Man* does not offer definitive answers to these questions does not diminish it. Rather, it illustrates how far Moorcock has extended science fiction into the realm of serious literature. This stimulating and dramatic narrative clearly deserves the Nebula it won in 1967.

Carl B. Yoke

Sources for Further Study

Reviews:

Amazing Stories. XLV, May, 1971, pp. 108-110.

Analog. LXXXVI, January, 1971, p. 169.

Luna Monthly. XXIV-XXV, May-June, 1971, p. 58.

New Worlds. CXC, March, 1969, pp. 58-59.

Speculation. III, May, 1970, pp. 23-26.

BERGE, MEERE UND GIGANTEN
(Giants)

Author: Alfred Döblin (1878-1957)
First book publication: 1924; revised, 1932 (as *Giganten*)
Type of work: Novel
Time: Approximately 2000 through several hundred years into the future
Locale: Europe

A panoramic, frenzied view of the development of European history, especially the man-machine and man-nature relationship, culminating in a titanic attempt to melt down the ice covering Greenland

> *Principal characters:*
> MARDUK, consul of the Brandenburg March
> JONATHAN, a friend and enemy of Marduk
> ELINA, Jonathan's girl friend
> ZIMBO, an African, an agent of the City State of London
> DELVIL, a senator from London

Alfred Döblin's huge novel *Berge, Meere und Giganten* was published in 1924, and in 1932 a heavily revised, smaller edition appeared under the title of *Giganten*, "a book of adventures." It is this important German novelist's only science fiction novel. An expressionistic, visionary view of the fate of Western mankind, the novel begins at a time when the last survivor of World War I has died, and it continues for several centuries into the future. Conventional characters and plot are lacking. Most of the events are larger than life, capturing the broad sweep of history and unfolding with an elemental power, as mankind struggles against nature and itself. The novel is written with an intensity that evokes a feeling of awe and grandeur; individual fates appear only briefly in the many episodes that float together in this mighty current of history and are important only to the extent that they contribute to it.

The first book of the novel describes the industrialization of society. As increasing numbers of human beings become dependent upon industry, the rural population leaves the country for the rapidly growing cities. Largely independent City States evolve, where the old political authorities have been replaced by the new industrial leaders. Although the Anglo-Americans are the nominal overlords, the City States are more or less independent political units, protected by powerful and destructive electrical apparatus. Control over the electrical energy generated in Northern Europe means control over the people. This power is transmitted by wireless means from Scandinavia to the rest of Europe, and it can be used to generate impregnable force screens and destructive rays.

A new master race develops, consisting of those who control the scientific gadgets and the engineers, while the masses lose their jobs to machines which require fewer and fewer people for their control and maintenance. The fields of mathematics, engineering, chemistry, electricity, biology, and radiotechnology are reserved for an elite minority, and scientific knowledge is divided into sharply differentiated disciplines, so that nobody has an overall view of the sciences. As the discontent of the uneducated masses (a mixture of the various races and nations, with strong elements of Black blood) increases, outbreaks of madness and violence occur. When Milan falls in the twenty-third century, a further concentration of knowledge in the hands of a select few shifts greater control to central power of London-New York. Some of the revolutionary groups are led by women, one of the cruelest being Melise of Bordeaux, a creature of extreme sensuality. She calls herself Persephone, queen of the underworld, and sacrifices hundreds of innocent workers and peasants in her cruel orgies.

As wave after wave of historical developments come and go, two opposing ideas emerge as constants. On the one hand there is the elevation of the machine to the status of erotic and religious object. A fanatical almost religious belief in machines develops, and they become regarded as a part of nature. On the other hand, there are the settlers or pedestrians, absolute enemies of the machine. These new Luddites feel that the machine is opposed to nature, and they want to return to the soil. Both of these attitudes lead to further looting, pillaging, and destruction, as fanatical apostles arise everywhere, sacrificing both themselves and others for their fervent beliefs.

The twenty-fifth century ushers in the "water and storm" teachings. Human beings are perceived as particles in the mass of humanity. Human happiness can only be achieved when all humans become equal in a vegetative way, by giving up all their individual characteristics. The ant-state is proclaimed the ideal, the end of history that flows into one vegetative mass. First formulated by the Indian Surrur in Edinburgh, one Guato of Paraguay, and the Norwegian Sörensen, this mass ideal appears again and again, resulting in the destruction of all humanitarian ideals, the brutalization of the masses, and the emergence of a new woman.

New inventions result in new upheavals, mass migrations, and warlike conflicts. These inventions are strictly controlled by the elitist class of the City States, the arrogant priests of technology. One minor invention is a luminous substance, deadly in the long run when sprayed on organic matter, but used nevertheless for sexual purposes. The most important discovery, however, occurs in the twenty-sixth century, when Meki produces synthetic food through a process secretly arrived at by cruel experimentation on unsuspecting human victims. Meki finally is able to build factories to synthesize food, replacing both agriculture and animal husbandry. Thus, with food mechanically produced, supervised by only a few human beings, the masses have no real function and fall under the domination of the large, aristocratic families. Idleness becomes the curse of the masses, and a feeling of helpless frustration spreads.

The pent-up energies of the Western City States and their teeming masses now turn against Asia, but the Asians have also become totally mechanized. The result is a devastating all-out war. Mass armies are locked in deadly combat; millions of human beings are senselessly sacrificed. The fighting is vividly presented in images of apocalyptic, epic grandeur. The war is neither won nor lost; it simply runs its course, until both sides are too exhausted to continue fighting. When it ends, East and West are separated from each other by a zone of death; the landscape is torn, the rivers empty, human beings, trees, and animals have been swallowed up. Everything is horrifyingly dead. "The war had ended just like an enemy felled by a blow to the neck."

This "Uralian War" as it came to be called, fills the second book. The following books describe the events in Europe after the traumatic impact of the war, a period that can be called, at best, a relative peace: the rise of power in the March of Brandenburg of first the blind consul Marke, and then the violent Marduk. After the devastation of the war, Marke begins a policy of isolation. He reinforces the City, and he destroys the deadly weapons, the energy apparatus. But a total return to the past proves impossible. The food factories must be kept, for agriculture is unable to produce enough naturally grown food. A new mysticism, anti-science feelings, and Luddite movements arise among the population, while others secretly prepare the energy weapons again. After Marke's death, Marduk becomes consul, deposing of the "traitors" with a quick stroke — they are eaten up by the trees he has grown in his biological experiments, a detail which anticipates the experiments SS physicians were to conduct some years later.

Fighting between the supporters and the enemies of the machine continues, and much of Middle Europe is devastated in the battles. It is a tale of betrayals and cruelty, internecine warfare between armies and marauding bands, a general bestialization of human nature. Torturings and mass executions are the rule, nothing is sacred, and even cannibalism becomes routine. The conflicts of shifting coalitions and alliances between rivaling cities and mercenary soldiers are not unlike the events of the Thirty Years' War. Some of the leaders are women, outdoing even the men in cruelty and being destroyed equally remorselessly. Supplementing this broad historical chronicle is the nightmarish story of Marduk's loves: his affair with Elina, and his troubled relationship with his friend/enemy Jonathan, whose mother he had killed when he seized power, but who nevertheless serves him with doglike obedience. All these events transcend normal individual psychology, achieving an almost Dostoevskian intensity of suffering and vision.

Then the focus of the novel shifts to Greenland. Delvil, a senator from London, sets an ambitious goal: the deicing of Greenland. It is to become a colony for the discontented masses of the City States, as well as other sick and adventurous elements. The energies of the Icelandic volcanoes are collected in nets of tourmaline, a process that is compared to their rape, and then transported to Greenland by giant fleets. The nets are floated on a newly discovered jellylike mass and loaded with energy. The Greenland crusaders, as one might call them, are filled with ill forebodings, as the assault on nature awakens new feelings in the men.

The project is successful in a sense, even too successful, for it produces a superabundance of life. The energy of the tourmalines releases the dinosaurs and giant reptiles that have slumbered under the ice. These ravenous, multiplying hordes once more threaten the continent and the peace of the City States. Killing the monsters serves no purpose, for even severed limbs develop a life of their own, continuing to grow and eat even when dead. Giant humans, biological mutations, are created by means of the same life-force to fight the new enemy. They become towers of organic matter, masses of flesh and stone that swallow the monsters and incorporate them into their own bodies, welded to the Earth in a line of defense stretching from England to Scandinavia. These giants then aspire to eat up the very Earth, but it is the Earth which finally swallows them. A new race of man, hardened and purged by experience, the Greenland crusaders of Kylin, remains to build a new world. Man has shed the arrogance of purely scientific-technological thinking and structures a society in harmony with nature and governed by law. Alfred Döblin did not believe in a final state of perfection. His Utopia is a kinetic one, describing the headlong rush of history that inexorably carries human beings with it. It is governed by anonymous forces that leave little room for individual fate. His book echoes the fears and concerns of the years following the shock of World War I, and he offers a picture of the man-nature game that owes as much to Nietzsche as to modern science. His characters are swept along helplessly by the catastrophic events of history. They move in a feverish, often self-destructive, dreamlike way, expressing the spirit of a historical era. As in the work of Olaf Stapledon, the hero is mankind — mankind fighting against, or living in reconciliation with, nature. History is a series of catastrophes, but there is no final catastrophe. The fight is endless, because the way into the future is endless, and the battle has to be fought again and again. The universe offers man a continuous challenge that must be met.

Döblin expresses this philosophy with a rare power of emotion and imagination. Stapledon's vision, for instance, was much more impressive than his way of expressing it. But Döblin was one of the most important German writers of the twentieth century, and his book, written in a hectic style, characterized by accumulations of adjectives and nouns that are not separated by any punctuation, does full justice to the grandeur of the conception: a frenzied rush and tumbling down of mankind.

Franz Rottensteiner

Sources for Further Study
Criticism:

Kort, Wolfgang. *Alfred Döblin*. New York: Twayne, 1974, pp. 88-90. Döblin commemorates "man's autonomy and pride of creation." It is his belief that man's consciousness of his free, self-responsible ego leads to "a gigantic degeneration." The essay is fundamental to any thematic understanding of *Giganten*.

BERSERKER

Author: Fred Saberhagen (1930-   )
First book publication: 1967
Type of work: Thematically related short stories
Time: Several centuries in the future
Locale: The Earth, various planets, and interstellar space

When a fleet of huge machines, programed to destroy all life, encounters human society in the future, the various strengths and weaknesses of humanity are displayed as mankind reacts to the threat

Fred Saberhagen's most popular fiction to date has been the "Berserker" tales, a series of short stories that appeared in *Galaxy* between 1963 and 1966. These stories were collected in *Berserker*, and were followed by two novels with the same theme, *Brother Berserker* and *Berserker's Planet*.

Berserker is a collection of eleven short pieces, although some characters appear in several of the stories. Collectively they tell of mankind's response to vast machines, implacably hostile and unbelievably powerful, which encounter and attack human civilization. Ironically, these machines, hundreds of miles in size, were not originally directed against humans. They had been built eons ago, and have outlived both their makers and the enemies against whom they were forged as weapons of war. Although many of them bear gaping scars that imply furious battles in the distant past, they are self-repairing to a degree, and most important, they retain their original programing — to exterminate life wherever they find it. They carry out their orders with such ferocity and singlemindedness that they are termed "Berserkers" by humans.

The Berserkers are spread over a large part of the galaxy, and eventually one impinges on human society, which by this time has spread to the stars. The machine sends a message to the others, and begins its work of killing.

All this is in the past when the first story opens. Humans have met the Berserkers, suffered the consequences, and even begun a response, working out stop-gap tactics to meet the attack. The first story, "Without a Thought," belies its name, since it introduces a theme that will be repeated several times in the collection: that human survival depends on careful planning, and that quick thinking in a crisis is the most valuable weapon the out-gunned humans have. The central figure of the story, Del Murray, occupies one of two small ships caught in a Mexican stand-off with a Berserker in deep space. The humans need a third ship to risk an attack with any chance of success, and they must await its arrival while hoping that the Berserker will not open fire on them in the meantime. The Berserker, for its own part, has a device that affects the minds of humans, making them incapable of decisive action; it is waiting for this weapon to take effect before launching its own attack. Thus both combatants, in radio contact with each other, are stalling for time. The Berserker suggests a game like a simplified form of checkers to test the onset of its control of Murray's mind. The problem is therefore clearly set before Murray: he must play the game to buy time for his own side while concealing from the Berserker the fact that his control is slipping. This he achieves by a clever trick combined with foresight; the third ship arrives and the humans destroy the Berserker.

American pulp science fiction shows many examples of this theme: human inventiveness resolves a situation by means of a decisive trick. Saberhagen celebrates ingenuity again in "The Peacemaker," in which the hero tries singlehandedly to reason with a Berserker. He fails in this attempt, but he succeeds in keeping the machine from annihilating his planet, escapes unharmed, and comes away in better condition than when he started.

No great complexity of plot or characterization can be expected in stories as short as "Without a Thought" or "The Peacemaker." While they depend on a simple turning-point (one might in truth call it a gimmick), it is also true that these stories follow completely the advice of Edgar Allan Poe that a short story should aim at the achievement of a single effect, and that every part should contribute to its establishment.

Saberhagen has more room for his skills in longer stories, such as "Goodlife." In this story we meet Hemphill, whose rage against the Berserkers is a mirror image of their own desire to kill. He is mentioned later in another story, and explicity labeled a fanatic. But despite an implacable hatred fueled by energy and ingenuity, Hemphill is not responsible for the destruction of the Berserker which captures him. His release is brought about by another character, known only as "Goodlife," who illustrates one of the chief strengths of the Berserkers.

The Berserkers have a great asset in not being programed to respond automatically; within the limitations of their builders' injunction to destroy organic life, they are free to gather data, learn from it, and formulate new tactics. Hence, when Berserkers encounter human society, many of them attempt to acquire individuals for study. Goodlife is one who has resulted from the union of two human captives. Having spent his whole life aboard the Berserker, he knows only what the machine has told him since the death of his parents years before. His memories of them are cloudy; he remembers almost nothing about them. Goodlife's confrontation with Hemphill and Maria Juarez, the two most recent prisoners, is his first meeting with humans other than his mother and father. Saberhagen's point here may be that the capacity of humans for learning is greater than that of the machine: the Berserkers cannot act in opposition to their most fundamental directive, despite their ability to formulate new ways to carry out that directive. Humans, though, are different.

To be sure, there are people like Hemphill, the deaths of whose wife and children have given him a programing, of sorts. But there are people like Goodlife, in whom a residue of independent judgment remains after the most vigorous brainwashing. When Goodlife discovers that his father's death was not as the machine had told him, he realizes the truth of what the humans have claimed about his situation, and acts without hesitation to destroy the Berserker and set free Hemphill and Maria.

Essentially, then, Saberhagen is talking about free will. This point is emphasized in the next story, "Patron of the Arts," which ends with a human who has long been the victim of self-delusions coming to an understanding of himself. He abandons the pretensions that have sustained him throughout his career, and he stands shouting at the Berserker, "Damn you, I can change!" as the story closes.

"Stone Place" is the longest story in the collection, almost twice the length of the one in second place. Its cast is larger, introducing Mitchell Spain, the character through whose perspective we see the action, and Johann Karlsen, Saberhagen's portrait of a great man — a Washington or Lincoln.

Contrasts abound here. Spain is a poet, yet he has enlisted in a volunteer force being assembled for a combined action of the human planets against a fleet of two hundred Berserkers. As a poet, an artist, Spain is like Herron, the painter in "Patron of the Arts." But unlike Herron, Spain is at peace with himself, and his priorities are ordered. The contrast between the views of these two characters on life and art is complex, and too detailed to be examined here, but it seems clear that Saberhagen feels that art (and by extension, culture) is the product not of the specialist but of the balanced, well-rounded individual.

A second contrast is that between Karlsen and Hemphill, who shows up briefly in "Stone Place": Karlsen is as dedicated to victory as Hemphill is, but on humane terms. Whereas Hemphill's view of victory is the destruction of the Berserkers, whatever it takes, Karlsen's view is the triumph of humanity. As supreme commander of the human forces, Karlsen will not settle for a victory that leaves humanity shattered and separated; by reason when possible, by force when necessary, he unites the conflicting aims of his various subordinates and achieves the success he desires. The difference between Hemphill and Karlsen is the difference between obsession and dedication.

The next two stories turn from the whole mind to the damaged one, and that damaged mind may have a body of flesh or one of metal. In "What T and I Did," the defect belongs to a human, a man referred to only as "T." His fragment of a name is symbolic of the fact that he has only a piece of a personality. Corrupted by violence, T has betrayed a planet to the Berserkers just before Karlsen's climactic battle, and as the story begins, he and a few humans he has terrorized are escaping from the battle-scene aboard a damaged Berserker. His human captives cure him with surgery and common affection, first by surgically releasing a long-repressed personality that is horrified at T's crimes, and then, by kindness, allowing that personality to grow strong enough to take over his now complete humanity.

The incomplete personality of T can be described as lacking something only by metaphor. In "Jester," the next story, we see a similar example of repressed desires, but this time in the mechanical brain of a Berserker. The scene is a remote planetoid where the Berserkers, realizing that they need to increase their numbers, have set up a secret automated shipyard. At this shipyard crashes a Berserker damaged in battle, and the shipyard computers, programed to waste nothing, cannibalize the brain of the wrecked machine for the new one they are building. They do not know that their action has caused a safety switch to reset, and they send out a completed Berserker that does not know what its purpose is.

There are incomplete humans in "Jester" as well, a whole planet of them. The rulers of the planet have banished humor, and they exile also the one man who has tried to reintroduce laughter to their society. Here is another example of the whole man, one who through his completeness is able to persuade the Berserker that its function is to aid humanity and to heal his planet, too.

Karlsen's half-brother, Felipe Nogara, is another study in obsession, but unlike Hemphill's fanaticism, which had a specific purpose, Nogara's only desire is for an abstraction — power. After he has achieved absolute power, Nogara's only aim in life is to increase the size of his domain. This unfocused obsession is the sign of a damaged mind, too, one which is led in "Masque of the Red Shift" to the company of sycophants, to perversion and degeneracy, and finally, in "In the Temple of Mars," to madness.

"In the Temple of Mars" takes its name from Chaucer's "Knight's Tale," and that story provides a revealing insight into the theme that Saberhagen has woven into most of the stories in *Berserker*. The insane Nogara has had a gladitorial arena built to resemble the lists of "The Knight's Tale" inside his personal spaceship, complete with temples to Mars, Diana, and Venus. In that story, it will be recalled, the hand of Emily was contested for by two cousins, Palamon and Arcite. It is tempting to see "The Knight's Tale" as allegorically related to the theme of *Berserker*, but the relationship between the two is only suggestive, not strict. For Arcite and Palamon are to meet in battle, with the winner marrying Emily, but their prayers are different on the eve of the struggle: Arcite begs Mars for victory, Palamon asks Venus for Emily's love. The main characters of *Berserker* tend to be mixtures of the two types: Nogara is an Arcite who has forgotten what he is fighting for, and delights in the spilling of blood itself. Hemphill, now an Admiral, is much like Arcite, too, but although he is singleminded he has not forgotten the objective. Mitchell Spain, who reappears as an observer, is once again balanced and whole, more like Palamon, while Johann Karlsen, not physically present but still important in the story, likewise combines the desirable traits of Diana, Mars, and Venus. And once again, those characters in control, those able to experience the full range of human emotions, emerge victorious.

Berserker is a collection of stories that explores the forces that motivate human beings, from fear to a desire for glory. Although no one story is especially complex in itself, as a group they form an investigation of considerable subtlety and power, as under the stimulus of the Berserkers, people respond in different yet always human ways. In studying their responses, we come to understand both ourselves and the lesson that Saberhagen provides: that human beings derive their strength from a complicated mixture of emotions that gives us our best chance for survival.

Walter E. Meyers

Sources for Further Study

Reviews:

Analog. LXXX, December, 1967, p. 163.

Books Today. IV, February 5, 1967, p. 11.

Magazine of Fantasy and Science Fiction. XXXIII, August, 1967, p. 35.

THE BEST OF C. L. MOORE

Author: Catherine L. Moore (1911-   )
Editor: Lester Del Rey
First book publication: 1975
Type of work: Short stories

Ten stories representing Moore's fresh, thought-provoking approach to some traditional science fiction and fantasy themes

The stories included in this collection span thirteen years of craftsmanship from 1933, the date Catherine Moore's first short story, "Shambleau," appeared in *Weird Tales*, to 1946, the year her masterpiece, "Vintage Season" — written, as were many of her best efforts, in collaboration with her husband, Henry Kuttner — was published. Moore's fiction is not confined to this period, but the selections chosen for this volume are representative of her literary achievements.

These stories may perhaps most accurately be classified as science fiction-fantasy, for most of them blend elements from both genres: space travel, alien beings, time travel, and scientific advancement from science fiction with the supernatural, romantic adventure, and imaginary worlds from fantasy. Yet there is little emphasis on the intricacies of scientific experimentation or theory, as one might expect from science fiction, or on the minute description of an imagined reality, typical of fantasy. The elements of the science fiction and fantasy genres are not used as ends in themselves but largely as devices to establish a particular environment or situation to which Moore can expose her characters.

In much science fiction-fantasy, plot predominates. The emphasis is generally on action, on how a character might solve a dilemma or on how he might cope with what he encounters in a strange environment. But Moore's stories are character-oriented. Her characters are not hollow shells designed merely to implement the plot; instead, the plot implements character portrayal. Moore's characters are complex, soundly developed, believable people whose emotional conflicts form the focal point of her fiction. Indeed, Moore is at her best when conveying her character's innermost feelings and when stirring appropriately empathetic emotions in her readers, an assessment that an examination of the individual stories will support.

The collection opens with two stories about Northwest Smith, a bold, rugged space adventurer. In the first, "Shambleau," Moore revitalizes a classical myth. Wandering the streets of a town on Venus one evening, Smith comes upon a girl threatened by a violent mob and instinctively protects her, unaware that by doing so he endangers himself. He is attracted by the creature's supple feminine shape and fascinated by her feline features — sheathed claws, luminous green eyes, and noiseless movements. Though he recognizes his companion is inhuman, Smith finds himself sexually attracted to her. Smith gradually realizes that his mysterious guest is one of the Medusa, but by the time Shambleau reveals the writhing red tresses she has kept covered by a turban, Smith's resistance is substantially weakened. Transfixed by the sight of the squirming reptilian mass, Smith falls prey to a predator that is somehow simultaneously loathsome and desirable, and he is only rescued by the timely return of a friend. Moore's Shambleau is even more horrifying than the Medusa of classical myth, for Shambleau is enticing rather than hideous, and she destroys not by literally turning men to stone but by draining them of all will and strength.

Northwest Smith returns in "Black Thirst" and is once more summoned to aid a woman at his own peril. This time a doomed Minga maiden named Vaudir persuades him to enter the Minga castle to help her uncover the horrible secret hidden there. For untold centuries, within the walls of the Minga palace, exquisitely lovely and gracious women have been bred, each seemingly more blindingly beautiful than the one before. Since few have ever left the confines of the palace, men have wondered why they were created. Smith learns the answer from the Alendar, the lord of the Minga. The very incarnation of evil, the Alendar thrives on loveliness; his existence is literally sustained and nourished by beauty. A moving, haunting tale, "Black Thirst" probes the nature of beauty and the dangerous consequences of an unnatural devotion to it.

With "Black God's Kiss," Moore introduced the adventures of a fiery female protagonist, Jirel of Joiry, into a male-dominated genre. Overwhelmed by the need to avenge not only her people's defeat but also the personal humiliation of her own subjugation, Jirel undertakes a journey to Hell to locate a fitting weapon to wield against her conqueror, Guillaume. Jirel's consuming hatred gives her the courage to attempt the perilous journey into unknown dangers. By merely suggesting the nature of the nameless horrors that Jirel encounters, Moore creates the impression of a believable Hell. Once there, Jirel issues her request for a weapon and is directed to a black temple standing in a lake. There she finds a stone image which she kisses. As she does so, she feels the weighty doom of spiritual oppression descend upon her. Bearing this torment, she returns to Joiry and gives the kisses she has taken to Guillaume. Only as she watches the burden consume Guillaume does she perceive the full import of her action and recognize how mighty a man she has destroyed.

Moore gave her readers a science fiction love story in "Bright Illusion." A young soldier named Dixon is chosen by an alien intelligence to prepare the way for its conquest of another world by deposing the reigning god there, Il. When he arrives, Dixon witnesses a world so strange, so unlike his own that he can only find it hideously repulsive. He is repelled by brash, glaring color and incomprehensible, dizzying structures, but most abhorrent of all are the crawling monstrosities that inhabit the region. To facilitate his mission, the power he represents causes him to appear to the natives as one of their own kind and causes them to appear human to him.

The first inhabitant Dixon meets is the high priestess, whose illusionary human shape is enticingly lovely. She perceives him as a member of her own race and warmly welcomes him, assuming him to be an envoy of Il. Despite their actual differences, Dixon and the priestess fall in love with one another. "Bright Illusion" explores the possibility of such a love, a love between two wholly incompatible beings. The affection shared by Dixon and the priestess transcends their physical and mental differences, yet their love can never be fulfilled because of these differences. Realizing this, they willingly elect death, believing it to be their only chance for union.

Determination to overcome physical differences is also the subject of "No Woman Born." In this story, an exceptionally beautiful and gifted dancer has been incapacitated by a fire accident. Because of her own courage and stamina, she allows her body to be meticulously reconstructed. Like all of Moore's character creations, Deirdre is believable. She is wholly unlike the clanking, boxlike metallic apparatus, typical of early science fiction robots. Deirdre's own brain controls the movements of her mechanical body. Her graceful, feminine shape, though fashioned out of metal, still allows the smooth, flowing motion required of a dancer. Deirdre's unwavering goal is to resume her performances, to exert her essential humanity over her physical limitations, and to transcend those limitations, thereby expressing her real selfhood. In a story of incredible scientific accomplishments, Moore compels the reader to contemplate the emotional and social consequences of such advancement.

Unlike the other tales in structure and theme, "Daemon" unfolds as pure fantasy. It presents the monologue of a young man whose simplemindedness is counterbalanced by sensibilities so refined as to allow him communion with spirits. Through skillful control of the monologue technique, Moore presents a striking character profile.

Yet another pure fantasy story, "Fruit of Knowledge," treats the myth of Lilith, exposing the elemental conflict between love and duty. When the Queen of Darkness senses Adam's intense longing for a companion in the garden, she assumes human form and falls in love with the first man. Dismayed by the weakness she feels, her spirit briefly leaves the body and soars upward longing for freedom. When Lilith returns, she discovers that God has created a mate for Adam and placed her in the flesh she had previously worn, commanding Adam to forsake all others. Lilith desperately arranges a pact with Lucifer to tempt Eve, assuming that God will destroy her when she disobeys him. But when Eve eats the forbidden fruit of the Tree of Knowledge, God does not strike and Adam does not desert his mate. Acknowledging to Lilith that she was his first wife, Adam reminds her that Eve is a part of his own flesh. And so while man has sinned greatly, he does not wed himself to evil. The manifestations of temptation — the beguiling serpent and the seductive Queen of Darkness — are powerfully portrayed in this story of man's first confrontation with moral dilemma.

Social science fiction is well represented by the next story. In "Greater Than Gods," a famed geneticist of the twenty-third century, Dr. William Cory, attempts to decide which of two lovely women he should propose to. As he struggles to make the choice, he receives a preview of the future which will result from each marriage. Marriage to Sallie, a charming, vivacious blond, will lead to strong family ties and neglect of his experiments in sex determination. He learns that in the coming years, more and more girls would be born until ultimately women would control the world, bringing peace and prosperity but also diminished ambition and intellectual effort. The result would be comfort and stability — not outstanding achievement, not noteworthy advances. On the other hand, a marriage to Marta, dark, intelligent, and ambitious, would mean a continuation of his work in genetics. His findings, implemented to control population, would bring him renown, though a flaw in the procedure would surface. Offspring would be highly intelligent but abnormally submissive. As the government encouraged the birth of more and more male offspring, boys with no initiative, the country would become more powerful as all energies were directed to the common cause of a United World.

With either woman, Dr. Cory foresees personal happiness during his own lifetime, but he realizes that his choice of a wife will determine not only his future but also the future of his society. Resolving that neither of the potential futures he has foreseen will occur, Dr. Cory proposes to his research assistant, Miss Brown, and prepares to face an unknown future.

In addition to this story of precognition, the collection contains two stories about physical movement through time. "Tryst in Time" is the account of a love that overcomes the barriers of time. An adventurous time traveler meets a reincarnation of the same woman whenever he pauses in time. On each occasion, something prevents their union, but each time the two grow more certain in their recognition of one another and more certain of their love. They finally find a place for love by transcending time entirely. Like "Bright Illusion," which also describes a seemingly impossible relationship, "Tryst in Time" explores the nature of true love.

"Vintage Season," the other tale of time travel — written with her husband — is often considered Moore's finest short story. Carefully controlled suspense builds as a young man comes to realize that his peculiar house guests are the decadent members of an advanced future civilization who transport themselves back in time to passively witness as entertaining spectacles the great disasters of human history. The impact of the story resides primarily in the masterful juxtaposition of the insensitive, detached attitude of the spectators with the horrified incredulity of the young man.

Love stories, female protagonists, and fully developed characters were unlikely elements in the science fiction-fantasy of the 1930's and 1940's. Yet it is in such areas that Catherine Moore made some of her most significant contributions by helping to expand the focus of the genre and give it the respectability it deserved.

Suzanne Edwards

Sources for Further Study

Criticism:

Encyclopedia of Science Fiction and Fantasy. Compiled by Donald H. Tuck. Chicago: Advent Publishers, Inc., 1978, pp. 317-318. Tuck gives a biographical and bibliographical review of Moore's life and works.

Weinkauf, Mary. "The God Figure in Dystopian Fiction," in *Riverside Quarterly*. IV (March, 1971), pp. 266-271. This general article on several science fiction writers discusses Moore's work in relationship to the field.

THE BEST OF C. M. KORNBLUTH

Author: Cyril M. Kornbluth (1923-1958)
Editor: Frederik Pohl
First book publication: 1976
Type of work: Short stories

The stories collected trace Kornbluth's development as a science fiction writer from 1941 to the late 1950's, revealing his deepening misanthropy and the growing power of his mordant satire

Frederik Pohl, who edited this collection of stories, and Cyril Kornbluth were collaborators on several science fiction novels, the best-known of which is *The Space Merchants* (1952); indeed, the two names are so firmly linked together that we may almost forget Kornbluth's own fiction, novels, and stories. The stories brought together here by Pohl are a representative sampling of Kornbluth's short fiction. Not all the stories are equally successful, nor do all measure up to the standard set by the best of them, but each one has something to reveal about Kornbluth's growth as a writer and his talent for writing science fiction.

Most of the stories published in the 1940's were apprentice works, revealing as much perhaps about the science fiction market as about the early formation of Kornbluth's style. He wrote mainly for third-rate pulp magazines, and learned to write for the bright, enthusiastic, but definitely youthful reader. Whether this long apprenticeship of writing for a juvenile audience at last soured Kornbluth's disposition is doubtful, but it did have its effect on his style, which is direct and expository, punctuated by metaphors and conceits that are not always able to bear the stress the author places on them. Sometimes invention fails him and Kornbluth descends into bathos, as in the early "The Words of Guru," or worse, in the sophomoric travesty "The Advent on Channel Twelve." On occasion, Kornbluth's tone can rise to a cloying shrillness that no satirist can afford, as it does in "The Adventurer." In the main, Kornbluth's stories are written on rather conventional narrative patterns; his strength does not lie in the development of original fictional designs. The most experimental story in the collection, "The Last Man Left in the Bar," is a failure. The qualities that make Kornbluth a writer worth knowing twenty years after his untimely death are the particular tone and angle of his vision, his perceptiveness as an analyst of human nature, and his vision as a science fiction writer.

Kornbluth is one of several writers who broke into the pulps on the eve of World War II and who developed, along with Henry Kuttner and Clifford Simak, what we might call an informal school of science fiction naturalism, aided more gently and less consistently by Frederik Pohl, Eric Frank Russell, and Fritz Leiber.

There is no doubt that Kornbluth's career was shaped to some extent by the

appearance in the early 1950's of *Galaxy Magazine*, a quality science fiction
pulp that offered readers an alternative to the two other giants of the time:
Astounding/Analog and *The Magazine of Fantasy and Science Fiction. Galaxy
Magazine* paid well, and its editors liked the kind of stories Kornbluth could
write best — stories rooted in the soft sciences with an ironic or satiric bite to
them. Quickly, Cyril Kornbluth became one of *Galaxy*'s brightest stars. In
1952, the year that *Galaxy* made its debut, Kornbluth published "The Luckiest
Man in Denv," "The Altar at Midnight," and "Gravy Planet" with Frederik
Pohl, all in *Galaxy* ("Gravy Planet" is sorely missed in this collection, even
though its exclusion as a collaborated story is understandable); it was from
"Gravy Planet" that *The Space Merchants* grew. When *Galaxy* laid down its
editorial philosophy proclaiming its intention to publish science fiction that
was more critical and directed at the mature reader, it cited Kornbluth's work
as an example of the kind of writing it wanted.

Whether *Galaxy* and perhaps Kornbluth may have confused satire, social
realism, or just plain misanthropy with a new kind of adult science fiction is
not important; today, almost thirty years later, the equation seems a little
naïve. We can see in Kornbluth's beginnings, however, the first stirrings of
the later New Wave writers, some of whom, at least, were to follow Kornbluth's lead.

In general, Kornbluth's best stories have certain qualities in common.
Kornbluth rarely idealizes his subjects or his characters. What he respects
above everything else is intelligence, and what he abhors most fiercely is not
simple stupidity but stupidity that is so unaware and at the same time so sure
of itself that it is commonly accepted as intelligence. If his temper had been a
little more playful, he might have been more like Mencken than Swift. As it is,
one detects in his best stories an undercurrent of mockery that turns to bitter-
ness, such as in "The Little Black Bag," "The Luckiest Man in Denv," and
"The Marching Morons." As the moralist or the traditional satirist, Kornbluth
comes down heavily on human folly and pride, especially as they are reflected
in the impact of modern scientific technology on his characters. He usually
extrapolates to a future time when some crisis, which has been at least several
generations in coming, is reached. Often the moral is built around two characters, one of whom knows what is happening and one of whom does not. The
crises have many variations, and they underlie Kornbluth's best fiction.

The best of the stories written in the 1940's and collected here is "The Only
Thing We Learn." Presented in the academic setting that was once the fashion
in prose and film, it might be classified as an antiwar tale combining a future
history lesson with an effective bit of mythopoesis. The title underlines the
prevailing irony of the story, perhaps a bit too obviously, but not enough to
destroy the impact of an unidentified professor's lecture to a class in
"Archaeo–Literature 203" attended by "young gentlemen of the Empire" of
some distant future. Gradually, the reader begins to realize with a sense of

shock that the professor's ingenious reconstruction of the cultural and historical background of the "Old Epic, *Chant of Remd*" is the preserved story of the final destruction of earth and the human race by conquerors whose descendants are seated in the class listening to the professor's lecture. The lesson is one of the oldest tragedies of them all, the fall of once great and proud empires, and it applies both to the reader, who is reading his own civilization's obituary notice, and to the young gentlemen of the empire, who are about to relive such a tragic debacle in the imminent but unsuspected collapse of their own empire. Perhaps the most impressive aspect of the story is the way Kornbluth manipulates the reader's point of view and expectations, which is another trademark of his best work.

"The Luckiest Man in Denv" is an underrated story about a despicable young man named Reuben who learns well the art of survival in a vertical culture whose visible symbols are the high-rises of the future. Reuben, the luckiest man, betrays General May, the leader of Denv and his benefactor, and the only man in Denv with vision enough to dream of peace between the two principal warring city states, Denv and Ellay. May's plan is to negotiate an end to arms production and then to resettle some of Denv's vertical masses outside the city, where they may learn to live "a different kind of life." Reuben sees only weakness and an opportunity for betrayal in May's plan. He never understands the general's motives and cannot imagine another way of living, let alone a better one. The story concludes on a note of tragic irony typical of many another Kornbluth story: "They put their heads together, the two saviors of civilization as they knew it, and conspired ingeniously long into the endless night."

The ending conveys something of the caustic handling of the Judas theme of the story. The man with vision is betrayed by the one who is the captive of his limited understanding. Reuben is also driven by an ambition uninhibited by a sense of common decency. In this, he makes a fitting representative of his world, for Denv is a vertical jungle. An additional irony lies in the fact the Kornbluth has maneuvered the reader into a sympathetic interest in Reuben and his career. We learn too late, along with General May, what kind of man we have allied ourselves with. For students of Kornbluth and of science fiction in general, the story is interesting for its parallels with *The Space Merchants* and *The Syndic* (1953), the latter a Kornbluth novel deserving of more critical attention than it has thus far received.

Two related stories with similar themes from the early 1950's are "The Little Black Bag" and "The Marching Morons." The former appeared in Campbell's *Astounding Science Fiction* in 1951, and it may be Kornbluth's masterwork in the genre. The speculative hard science elements in the story that so appealed to Campbell center around the black bag of a medical practitioner of the future.

The black bag, transported accidentally by a time travel machine, comes from a time, twenty generations in the future, when the majority of people are morons whose lives are secretly directed under the benevolent stewardship of geniuses who manage to improve the products and performance levels of civilization at "a greater speed than the subnormals degraded [them]." Ironically, the unsuspecting morons think of their keepers as their inferiors. Through his description of this culture of geniuses and morons, Kornbluth was predicting a coming day when college students will not read words of more than three syllables, when universities will award "Bachelor of Typewriting," "Master of Shorthand," and "Doctor of Philosophy (Card Filing)" degrees.

The black bag is a case in point. Its contents are practically self-operating, and can treat and cure every known human ailment. Formerly the symbol of the physician, the bag had to be made foolproof by the supernormals so that it could be used by fools like Dr. John Hemingway, a moron whose bag was accidentally transported to the flophouse room of a down-and-out twentieth century physician, Dr. Bayard Full.

In its new home, the bag saves a child suffering from blood poisoning, and its power of healing as well as its symbolic importance become the instrument through which Dr. Full rehabilitates himself. But this is no success story. Dr. Full's plans to donate the bag to science for study are frustrated by the ambitions of Angela Aquella, who wants to use the bag for personal gain. She cannot see the rightness of Dr. Full's conviction that they are but stewards of the fabulous bag rather than its owners. After murdering the good doctor, Angela disposes of the body in one of the most grisly dismemberments since Alan Campbell dispatched the corpse of Basil Hallward for Dorian Gray in Oscar Wilde's novel. Angela ends badly, however, cutting her own throat in the process of demonstrating the wondrous properties of a scalpel that selectively cuts through only unwanted fat or diseased tissue. She dies because a technician in the future whence it came turns off the black bag when a warning signal indicates that it has fallen into the hands of a murderer. That final act is more than an instance of mordant poetic justice at work; it also symbolizes the choice that the supernormals will soon have to make about the extermination of the subnormals.

"The Marching Morons" is built on a similar premise and introduces another antiheroic type in the person of "Honest John Barlow," a twentieth century real estate dealer kept in suspended animation by the accidental administration of "Levantman shock anesthesia." He is discovered in a long-forgotten mausoleum by Kornbluth's superintelligent futurians, who seem to enjoy Clark Kentish disguises as subservient, even menial job holders to the moron class. This futurian, Efim Hawkins, is disguised as a potter, and he is poking around looking for copper when he finds the tomb. Hawkins recognizes Barlow's symptoms, administers the antidote, and awakens the latter-day Rip Van Winkle. Unfortunately, Barlow turns out to be an aggressive, complaining bore. Hawkins turns Barlow over to those supernormals working on "Problem

Number One," which is what to do about the masses of subnormals. By this time the genius class has become disenchanted with its role of shepherd.

Kornbluth's rendering of the vulgarity of a future demotic mass culture is acidly comic. The problem is the same as that of "The Little Black Bag": the race has bred itself silly. The illiterate newscaster carries the same combination of comic and satiric punch as the Senator with a "major in fly-casting at Oregon" and a "Ph.D. in game fish at Florida." The quiz contestant who cannot remember her name points up Kornbluth's genius for combining the comic and the ominous. In this regard Kornbluth anticipates Kurt Vonnegut in "Harrison Bergeron" and *The Sirens of Titan*, although the latter has a less misanthropic purpose.

There is a great deal of exposition in this story of an industrial culture gradually running amok as the result of the stupidity and incompetence of those who work with its machines. The solution to "The Problem" is provided by Barlow, and his reward is to be named world dictator. Barlow's plan is to dupe the masses into believing that Venus is the new frontier, and with control of media it is not difficult to create a new land-rush psychology in a population where the median IQ is 45. In fact the Venus flights are extermination flights, analogous to the Nazi gas chambers, and they succeed with the same brutal efficiency. In *The Space Merchants* there is also a Venus ad campaign and an emigration to the planet for the conservationists. In the novel, however, Venus really is a haven.

In "The Marching Morons" the supernormals have run out of patience, and are ready to develop a final solution to the problem of the subnormal masses. It takes a modern man (in other words, one of us) to find the answer. Poetic justice decrees that Barlow enjoy the last rocket ride to oblivion, but his just punishment does nothing to resolve the moral implications of mass extermination. Are we to entertain seriously the idea that either IQ or technological competence levels determines whether one is human? The superhumans, exasperated by their failure to control the expanding moron population, are prepared to accept Barlow's plan, even if it is too evil for them to have devised themselves. Although the satire of the story is directed at the entropy of mass culture so apparent everywhere, the moral chill of the tale nevertheless remains. "The Marching Morons" is more than a cautionary tale of the long-term consequences of established trends.

"The Mindworm" is brilliant in a different vein. Kornbluth makes his anti-hero a mutant, a new species of vampire produced by radiation, possessing telepathic powers that become telephagic shortly after puberty. The mindworm, something like the ultimate alienated Kornbluthan antihero, feeds on human emotions. With a terrible cunning, he learns to stimulate powerful emotions so that he may drain his victims at the most ecstatic moment. He is at last undone by superstitious Eastern Europeans who live in the Pennsylvania coal mining regions and who recognize the work of a vampire when they see it.

"The Altar at Midnight" is one of those barroom stories that Kornbluth does so well — barroom science fiction stories being a minor art form of the genre. In this one a propulsion physicist seeks a way in part of expiating the guilt he feels over the ill effects his space drive has produced on a young spacer. The story possesses an ambiguous hollowness at the core that could be either intentional or accidental. Although not in the same class as the stories mentioned above, this tale suggests to the science fiction critic parallels to Robert Heinlein (tone), Ray Bradbury (atmosphere), and Walter M. Miller, Jr. (the probing of psychological and social effects of space travel). There is also another dimension to this story not present in Kornbluth's others since it is the first of his explorations of the question of guilt and responsibility at a personal, ethical level rather than at the intellectual level that controls most of the other stories cited here. He had opened this vein a year earlier in 1951, in "With These Hands," which is an analogue for, if not a source of, Miller's "The Darfsteller" (1955).

"Shark Ship" is a strangely compelling tale of a future in which great ships had been launched to sail the oceans, each carrying the equivalent of a city's population. The ships had become independent, self-perpetuating communities in which generations were born, lived, and died. Each ship had its quadrant of ocean to sail and to fish with great metal mesh nets. The brazen vessels were designed to alleviate the pressures of overpopulation, but they produced a life style and code of values that created an ocean culture permanently alienated from land dwellers.

The story concerns the consequences following the loss of the irreplaceable fishing net by one of the ships. Other ships had simply accepted the inevitable doom that followed such a loss, but this time both commodore and crew agree to break the taboos against returning to land in the fearful hope that they may find a way to survive. They arrive in an almost deserted New York City to discover that the land-dwelling human race has nearly exterminated itself under the direction of a Messiah of death known as Merdeka, who ushers in the "Age of Hate and Death." In a frenzy of reaction against sex and procreation, Merdeka's campaign for purification develops into a sadomasochistic crusade of torture and mass murder.

The landing party from the beached ship encounters one of the last remaining roving bands of fanatics and routs them by a simple display of nudity, which the disciples of death and torture find too potent a force to overcome. In the end, the sea people are prepared to begin the recolonization of the land and the rehabilitation of the race. The story reveals certain parallels to Gore Vidal's *Messiah* (1954), and it dramatizes Kornbluth's fascination with cruelty. Readers may also be reminded of Fritz Leiber's classic story "Coming Attraction."

Pohl reserves pride of place in this volume for a novelette titled *Two Dooms*; the original title, *The Doomsman*, is better. This is a time travel story that seems to anticipate in both tone and subject Philip K. Dick's *The Man in the High Castle* (1962). The story concerns the fate of Edward Royland, a physicist at work on the Los Alamos "Manhattan Project." Having solved a key problem that will permit the development of the atomic bomb, Royland begins to suffer moral scruples about the project and its consequences. A visit to an Indian medicine man leads Royland to accept his offer of the "God Food," dried mushrooms to counteract the effects of the "break-the-sky medicine" he had been helping to develop in his laboratory. Royland awakens to a future world in which the war was lost to the Germans and the Japanese. It is a world of the Samurai and the Nazi, of systematic visitations of barbarism and cruelty on a mass scale. It is a world in which American Nazis are continuing the extermination of all inferiors and misfits. Royland finally awakens from his nightmare vision of the future by repeating his exposure to the mushroom hallucinogen; he returns to the world of 1945 purged of his doubts about the proper course of action. His duty to the human race and to the future lies in reporting the success of his research and in promoting the successful development of the bomb.

Two Dooms was Kornbluth's last story. It is longer and more complex than the other stories in the collection, and it introduces a more evenhanded exploration of the moral problem inherent in the development of "break-the-sky medicine," the atomic bomb. It is a departure from the viewpoint of some earlier stories such as "The Marching Morons" or "All We Learn," but with its emphasis on the personal as well as the social impact of evil, it should be seen as continuing the themes and the implied involvement of "The Altar at Midnight" and "With These Hands." Instead of being a source of fascination, cruelty is portrayed as the product of brutalized minds and spirits. Nor is there to be found the simple equation of morality with intelligence or with purely elitist cultural standards that seems to underlie the best of Kornbluth's earlier successes. It is a great pity that Kornbluth did not live to follow the implied new course outlined in *Two Dooms*. The story suggests the development of a new maturity of outlook and a more compassionate interest in human problems.

Kornbluth was a writer for the 1960's who died before his time had come. He may well have rivaled Vonnegut as a spokesman for the age or at least as unofficial satirist laureate. Even so, his accomplishment as a writer of short science fiction is important despite the limited number of first rate stories, and his influence has proved greater than is generally recognized and appears to be growing two decades after his passing. Of the short fiction, "The Little Black Bag," "The Luckiest Man in Denv," "The Mindworm," "The Silly Season," "The Marching Morons," and *Two Dooms* should preserve his reputation as a writer.

Donald L. Lawler

Sources for Further Study

Criticism:

"The Best of C. M. Kornbluth," *in Publisher's Weekly*. CCX (December 6, 1976), p. 60. This anthology includes some of Kornbluth's best works.

Knight, Damon F. *In Search of Wonder*. Chicago: Advent, 1967, pp. 146-149. Knight details the general themes of Kornbluth's work.

Wolheim, Donald A. *The Universe Makers*. New York: Harper & Row, 1971, pp. 82-85. A deep streak of black humor, of alienation, runs through many of his works.

THE BEST OF CORDWAINER SMITH

Author: Cordwainer Smith (Paul Myron Anthony Linebarger, 1913-1966)
Editor: John J. Pierce
First book publication: 1975
Type of work: Short stories

Twelve stories from the author's Instrumentality of Mankind series, arranged to describe a chronology of distant future history

"Cordwainer Smith" was the science fiction *nom de plume* of P. M. A. Linebarger, who certainly had one of the most unusual backgrounds of any science fiction writer. An officer in military intelligence and a professor of Asiatic politics at The Johns Hopkins University, Linebarger had spent much of his youth in Europe and China. His father was a legal adviser to Sun Yat Sen; Linebarger himself was a godson of Sun Yat Sen and author of an early volume on that Chinese leader's political doctrines. While the bulk of Linebarger's writing consisted of scholarly studies in such areas as Asian politics, military intelligence, and psychological warfare, he retained an interest in creative writing, publishing a few short stories, poems, and three mainstream novels during the 1940's. For several years, Linebarger kept a notebook in which he jotted ideas for stories growing out of an elaborately conceived future history centering around a universe-wide government called "the Instrumentality of Man." The first introduction to science fiction readers of this bizarre and strangely convincing future world came with the initial publication of the first story in this collection, "Scanners Live in Vain," in 1950.

To any reader unfamiliar with Smith's work, "Scanners Live in Vain" — or virtually any other story in this collection — must initially be a quite unsettling experience. The stories are sprinkled with neologisms, references to other stories, direct addresses to the reader, and bizarre concepts introduced with a minimum of exposition. One senses that there is much more to Smith's imagined universe than is revealed in any particular story, and even when the stories are read in succession, the feeling remains that much is left unsaid. Yet for all their interconnectedness, the stories are complete in themselves; they are written not so much to reveal Smith's future history; instead, future history is constructed to permit Smith to tell the stories he wants to tell. Future histories are common enough in science fiction, but often they are simple historical extrapolations. While Smith offers a few technological insights into the future (such as his conception of spaceships propelled by immense photonic sails), the real purpose of his Instrumentality seems to be to provide a symbolic world through which he could explore the issues that most mattered to him: romance, nationalism, psychology, bigotry, morality, and the ways in which these issues are interconnected. Ironically, one result of this technique is that the author's future universe appears so radically removed from anything we could rationally extrapolate from the present that it becomes almost believable.

The Best of Cordwainer Smith contains all the major Instrumentality stories except four: "Mark Elf," "When the People Fell," "Think Blue, Count Two," and "Drunkboat." A few other stories have been published posthumously, and a few stories which take place late in the history of the Instrumentality and concern a character named Cashier O'Neill are also excluded. There is also a novel, *Norstrilia*, published posthumously in 1975, which occupies a central role in the Instrumentality series. John J. Pierce, the editor of the collection, has provided an introduction giving a "timeline" of Instrumentality history; he arranged the stories according to this timeline, thus creating a vague sense of a chronicle history.

As a chronicle, the history of the Instrumentality becomes an epic of a grand utopian scheme which ultimately, in many ways, fails. "Scanners Live in Vain" takes place during an early, "primitive" period in Instrumentality history when much of the earth remains a wilderness following a destructive war; and spaceflight is controlled by a guild of "Scanners," engineers whose nerves have been severed from their brains to enable them to survive in the "pain of space," and whose bodies have been mechanically restructured for greater efficiency. A second age of space exploration is introduced when a scientist finds that by insulating passengers from space by lining spaceships with living things such as oysters, humans can survive unaided by Scanners. The Scanners become obsolete, but the "shell-ships" continue to be used well into the later history of the Instrumentality (as in "The Crime and Glory of Commander Suzdal"). The next great age of spaceflight is the age of the great photonic sailing ships ("The Lady Who Sailed the *Soul*") and of the advent of a longevity drug known as "stroon," which enables humans to live for centuries with the aid of periodic rejuvenescence treatments. Eventually, the sailing ships are replaced by ships employing a principle known as "plano-forming," which allows whole areas to be transported in space almost instantaneously. The great heroes of the planoforming age are the "Go-Captains," who manage the space "jumps" sometimes at great personal risk ("The Burning of the Brain"), and "pinlighters," who defend the ships against almost formless primordial "dragons" who live in space ("The Game of Rat and Dragon").

As the power of the Instrumentality grows, a period of uniformity and deca-dence begins to set in. Human life is standardized at four hundred years, dis-ease and suffering are eliminated, and a universal language, the Old Common Tongue, is instituted among all the inhabited planets. But there is growing evidence that the Instrumentality is becoming politically corrupt ("Golden the Ship Was — Oh! Oh! Oh!"), and there is a growing movement toward the liberation of the "underpeople," a slave class of humans reconstructed from animals ("The Dead Lady of Clown Town"). Eventually, under the leadership of legendary figures known as Lord Jestocost and Lady Alice More, the pattern of decadence is reversed by the Rediscovery of Man. Ancient cultures, religions, languages, even diseases are reintroduced to save man from the "nightmare of perfection" ("Alpha Ralpha Boulevard"), and together with the remarkable cat-girl C'Mell, Jestocost helps to bring about the emancipation of the underpeople ("The Ballad of Lost C'Mell").

But it is misleading to force these stories into a too-rigid chronology of future history; Smith's very style of telling them works against that. Rather than constructing pseudorealistic narratives of future adventures, Smith consistently imparts to these tales a flavor of dim legend and oral history: we are compelled to read the stories as artifacts of a distant past rather than as projections of a distant future. This deliberate stylistic distancing invites us to focus less on the historical context of the tales than on their qualities as romances, and Cordwainer Smith is certainly one of the great romancers of science fiction. His characters are larger than life, engaged in wildly heroic exploits often with vast historical consequences, and often cursed by an unfulfilled and unrealizable love. Surely no more impossible barrier has ever been constructed between two lovers than that in "The Game of Rat and Dragon," in which a pinlighter named Underhill is assisted in his dangerous task of fighting dragons by a cat (not an underperson — a real cat, who can communicate telepathically and whose quicker reflexes make her a valuable assistant for a pinlighter) named Lady May. Lady May is "quick beyond all dreams of speed, sharp, clever, unbelievably graceful, beautiful, wordless and undemanding," and Underhill finds her his perfect mate. "Where would he ever find a woman who could compare with her?" Much the same situation exists in what is perhaps the finest romance in the book, "The Ballad of Lost C'Mell," in which C'Mell and Jestocost conspire to save the underpeople but also discover a love for each other that can never be realized except in legend.

Smith's romances also encompass social concerns and nationalistic myths. "The Lady Who Sailed the *Soul*" is named Helen America, and her mission is to take a group of religious pilgrims to found a new colony. In "The Burning of the Brain," the planoforming ship is built as a replica of a "prehistoric estate named Mount Vernon," and its captain is Magno Taliano, a name clearly suggestive of Columbus. The promise of new worlds represented by space travel is thus connected to the promise once held out by America itself (in "The Burning of the Brain," space travel is even described in terms of water and sea images, suggesting a further connection with Columbus) — and, of course, the later problems of the Instrumentality suggest the problems of the America in which Smith was writing. The growing sterility and excessive standardization of life during the Instrumentality's decadent phase suggests the leisure society that began to develop in the United States after World War II, and the systematic oppression of the underpeople suggests the racism which permeated that society. Like the perfect love, the perfect society remains a romantic illusion.

Perhaps the image which most clearly symbolizes Smith's concern with romantic illusion is the ninety-million-mile-long golden spaceship that is used to frighten the enemy into submission in "Golden the Ship Was — Oh! Oh! Oh!" The ship is really nothing more than a Potemkin village — virtually all its immense length is a façade of rigid foam and wire, used to distract the enemy while the real war is conducted by a second-level bureaucrat dispersing ugly poisons from a small ship unglamorously named *Anybody*. The grand illusion of the golden ship disguises the mundane and decidedly unromantic reality of war.

And this mundane reality represents the other side of Smith's dialectic. Smith may be a great creator of romantic dreams, but he also consistently contrasts these dreams with harsh realities — the dehumanization of the Scanners, the drudgery of the sailing ship captains, the alienation of the pinlighters from the rest of humanity. In "Alpha Ralpha Boulevard," it is the act of saving a few small birds that finally saves the protagonist Paul, prompting him to wonder, "Is that all there is to *good* and *bad*?" In "The Crime and Glory of Commander Suzdal," it is the promise of the mundane — returning to his simple wife — that motivates Suzdal to his heroic action. And in "The Lady Who Sailed the *Soul*" the entire romantic narrative is undercut by presenting it as told by a "romantic" mother to her common-sense daughter, who regards the mythification of the harsh realities of the story to be a dangerous self-delusion.

But Smith clearly values both the romance and the reality, and seeks to preserve both. One possible synthesis is suggested in "The Burning of the Brain," in which the character Dita manages to combine the legendary romantic beauty of her aunt with the complex practical skills of her Go-Captain uncle. Another synthesis is suggested by "The Ballad of Lost C'Mell," in which the lovers, forever apart during their lives, are forever united in "the memory of man." And here may lie the key to Smith's mythlike style: only in our legends, our romances, and our art, he suggests, can we finally achieve the synthesis between the romantic and the real that is so elusive in day-to-day life. Smith's stories are not about how the future will be, but about how it may be remembered. His Instrumentality stories are the legends of a mythic time, a heroic age, and like all legends, they seek to express and synthesize the values of an age. What is remarkable is how penetratingly Smith's stories achieve this for the values and problems of our own age.

Gary K. Wolfe

Sources for Further Study

Criticism:

The Encylopedia of Science Fiction and Fantasy. Compiled by Donald H. Tuck. Chicago: Advent Publishers, Inc., 1978, p. 277. In an article under Smith's real name, Paul Myron Anthony Linebarger, Tuck gives a biographical and bibliographical review of the author's career.

Wolfe, Gary K. "Mythic Structures in Cordwainer Smith's 'The Game of Rat and Dragon,'" in *Science-Fiction Studies*. IV (1977), pp. 144-150. Wolfe gives a very thorough analysis of this story while touching on other works by Smith.

THE BEST OF HENRY KUTTNER

Author: Henry Kuttner (1914-1958)
Editor: Ray Bradbury
First book publication: 1975
Type of work: Short stories

A series of representative short stories written between the late 1930's and the mid-1950's which reveal three characteristics of Kuttner's fiction: intelligence, ingenuity, and irony

Ray Bradbury's Introduction to *The Best of Henry Kuttner* is titled "A Neglected Master." In it Bradbury acknowledges his debt to Kuttner's professionalism, vision, wit, learning, and friendship. He also argues for Kuttner's influence on the generation of science fiction writers that bloomed in the post-World War II era. Bradbury's testimonial is, he says, a personal tribute both to a friend and to an underrated writer who died before his time.

Henry Kuttner wrote his short stories almost exclusively for the pulps, and it is as a writer of popular science fiction and fantasy stories that he must be judged. Most of what he wrote was ephemeral: of his scores of stories, perhaps a dozen or so remain fresh, and of these only a handful deserve to be called classics of the genre. If his reputation is to stand, it will rest upon this collection and perhaps one or two other stories.

Kuttner, like many of the pulp writers, wrote series stories: that is, stories tied together by one or more characters. The Galloway Gallegher stories are an example; "The Proud Robot," probably the best of the half dozen or so Gallegher stories, is included in this collection. Gallegher is an American original — the untrained but highly intuitive scientific genius who under the right circumstances can tinker together almost anything. Unfortunately, Gallegher can function only when intoxicated by alcohol, which releases his creative and highly inventive unconscious mind. Even Kuttner cannot manage to avoid the offensiveness inherent in the stereotype, and his stories dealing with Gallegher suffer on that account.

If Gallegher himself is a morally uninteresting person, despite the possession of a dynamite subconscious, his robot is another matter. The robot is somewhat prosaically named Joe, but is endowed with a great deal of vanity. He spends nearly all his time admiring himself before mirrors, and never hesitates to elaborate on his perfections. He refuses to talk, except about himself and the advantages of possessing many extra senses and powers with which to admire oneself. One example of Joe's vanity is his salutation to Patsy Brock: " 'You may treasure the sound and sight of me till your dying day. One touch of beauty in a world of drabness.' "

It seems that Gallegher made Joe during one of his benders for a purpose which he cannot remember; it had something to do with his commission from Vox-View productions to find a way to prevent their television programs from being pirated by an unethical competitor. Kuttner's treatment is obviously exaggerated to the point of farce, but the farce is perfectly controlled and its effect delightful. Gallegher's misfortunes eventually drive him to drink once again, and thus inspired, he tricks Joe into revealing the purpose for which he was made. The strategy, naturally enough, was to play upon Joe's vanity. Joe, it seems, was created to solve *two* problems: the problem of the pirated television programs and the problem of opening beer cans. Once Joe is discovered to be a can opener, he loses his former autonomy, yet retains his vanity; he becomes merely the vain mechanical slave of his inventor.

The other series, represented in the collection by "Exit the Professor" and "Cold War," is the Hogben series. This series features the Hogben family, an eccentric collection of hillbillys who also possess preternatural powers. Their magic is actually the direct intuitive application of scientific laws, and when they need words to describe processes or details, they simply cull them from a nearby informed mind. They are also telepathic, telekenetic time travelers; and they can fly. The fact that, both as science fiction and as comedy, the Hogben stories are far more successful and readable than the Gallegher stories, is probably attributable to the appealing hillbilly heroes. The Hogben scenarios might have been written for "The Beverly Hillbillys," except that the Hogbens prefer to be left alone in the mountains, since they remember all the persecutions of the past which resulted from discovery of their extraordinary powers. Imagine the creatures of H. P. Lovecraft transported to Nashville and treated with a mixture of farce and rather sophisticated wit. It is an unusual combination, needless to say, and one that seems especially well-suited to Kuttner's comic sense. Kuttner's Hogbens are wonderful grotesques, and the reader is swept along by the stories' vitality and masterful blending of science and fantasy.

"Exit the Professor" is an amusing display piece for Kuttner's recipe of hillbilly horse sense, unorthodox yet rigid moral codes, and strong family loyalites played against the Hogbens' extraordinary ability to meet any domestic emergency by developing a wonderful machine for the job (Saunk tinkered together a laser machine to chase off the Haley boys) or simply employing their superhuman powers. The story is thin enough. The professor is a biologist studying eugenics who wants to investigate the Hogbens. It seems word has gotten around of their doing queer things. Whenever the professor wants to coerce a Hogben to cooperate, he merely threatens to tell the foundation all about them because he knows that what they dread most are prying investigators and public exposure. The importunate professor comes close enough to guessing the Hogbens' secret that he poses a threat to their privacy and freedom. When the professor becomes entangled in legal misadventures and asks to be hidden from the sheriff, the Hogbens oblige: "That was a few years ago. The Perfesser's thriving. He ain't studying us, though. Sometimes we take him out of the bottle we keep him in and study him. Dang small bottle, too!" The story is made even more interesting because each member of the Hogben clan has a unique personality. Grandpa, who lives in the attic, is the tribal head and as patriarch makes final decisions and commands fear and respect from all. He relies on Little Sam, the two-headed baby who lives in the cellar and is the master telepath. Pa and Uncle Lem always seem to be getting into trouble. Mom is domestic; and Saunk, the older son, is the tinkerer who is always learning and extending his powers. The burlesque of Lovecraft implied here is an added dimension to the humor.

"Cold War" has a more substantial plot than "Exit the Professor." The story revolves around the difficulties caused by the impractical and softhearted uncle Lem, who once gave Lily Lou Mutz, the ugliest woman in Kaintuck, the hexing power as a defense against pranksters and rock-throwers. Unaccountably, Lily Lou married Ed Pugh, thought to be even uglier, and produced Ed Junior, who inherited the hexing power along with the disposition of a viper. The conflict arises when Ed Pugh demands that Lem find a wife for Junior in order to guarantee the continuance of the bloodline. When Lem refuses and goes into catalepsy as a protection, Junior nearly hexes him to death. Saunk calls on Grandpa telepathically to come to the rescue. Grandpa's solution is to promise that the Pughs' family line will never die out, while at the same time assuring that the human race will not suffer a Pugh takeover. The solution involves an ingenious combination of time travel and genetic reconstruction which turns the Pughs and their descendents into the equivalent of viruses.

Kuttner shows in some of the other stories in this collection that he can also successfully write the more standard types of science fiction. "The Big Night," for example, is a space opera with unusual depths of character psychology anticipating Thomas N. Scortia's "The Shores of Night" and Anne McCaffrey's "The Ship Who Sang." "Endowment Policy" is a Heinleinesque time travel story laced with social criticism. "The Twonky," a good but probably overrated story, is similar in theme to Williamson's "With Folded Hands." Kuttner's treatment in "The Iron Standard" demonstrates his interest in a character type that appears frequently in his stories — the young man "on the make" with an underdeveloped moral sense and an overdeveloped ambition for worldly success and power. This was a familiar type in the 1930's and 1940's crime movies and radio programs and, of course, in many of the detective stories of the hardboiled variety. The characters in "The Iron Standard" are successful in outwitting Venusians who are less noble and principled than themselves.

Kuttner's best stories are related by their interest in the moral dimensions of technology; they deal, whether seriously or comically, with the effects of science on the moral equilibrium of his characters. There are two such stories in this collection. "Two Handed Engine" deals powerfully with a future society in which all murder is forbidden. The punishment for murder is to be tracked down and eventually executed by a Furylike robot who may strike at any time. However, a computer expert named Hartz discovers a way to short-circuit the computers that guide the robots, allowing him to hire an assassin to murder his boss for a large fee and a promise of immunity. After the crime, however, the assassin, Danner, finds himself hounded by a police robot. Although Hartz claims that he is working to rectify the error, he in fact is not. The story turns, however, not on the crime-and-punishment melodrama but on the social matrix of twenty-first century America as projected in the story. The human race has lost its conscience; "Mankind had been through too much. Sin was meaningless now." As a consequence, machines have to compensate to provide the missing moral absolutes in the culture.

The other tale of moral education, "What You Need," presents a different picture of a computer technology in which future events can be predicted. The predictor-machine is controlled by a presumably benevolent figure named Peter Talley, who supplies clients with the information they will need to meet some future crisis. When Tim Charmichael, an unscrupulous reporter, first investigates and then uses the services of Talley, he puts himself under the power of a man and a machine capable of judging his true character as well as assessing future actions not as yet even contemplated. Since the reporter is judged to be a menace to Talley's grand design of using his machine to perfect the race, Talley dooms Charmichael by not providing him with the information he needs to survive a future accident. The ambiguities inherent in the ending and the *deus ex machina* resolution are weaknesses in an otherwise powerful morality tale of the future.

"Absalom" is one of Kuttner's best efforts. Drawn on a parallel to the Biblical story of Absalom, this bitter tale was one of the inspirations of Ray Bradbury's "The Veldt." It is a morality tale, based on the problem of genetic mutation, which is a brilliant and at the same time mordant anticipation of the "generation gap" literature of the past decade.

Bradbury's estimate of Kuttner's work, while generally accurate, must still be realistically qualified. Kuttner's mastery of the science fiction short story form is represented in half a dozen stories at most. And yet, at his best, Kuttner has few peers as a writer, and deserves recognition outside as well as inside science fiction circles.

Donald L. Lawler

Sources for Further Study

Criticism:

"The Best of Henry Kuttner," in *Booklist*. LXXI (June 1, 1975), p. 999. This anthology collects the most admired of Kuttner's tales.

Cawthorn, J. *"The Best of Henry Kuttner,"* in *New Worlds*. CLXV (August, 1966), pp. 145-146. Cawthorn details the themes of several stories.

Gunn, James. "Henry Kuttner, C. L. Moore, Lewis Padgett, *et al.,"* in *Voices for the Future*. Edited by Thomas D. Clareson. Bowling Green, Ohio: Bowling Green University Press, 1976, pp. 185-215. Kuttner was mainly concerned with man and society, with a dash of fantasy added.

Knight, Damon F. *In Search of Wonder*. Chicago: Advent, 1967, pp. 139-145. Knight explores the worlds of Kuttner.

THE BEST OF PHILIP K. DICK

Author: Philip K. Dick (1928-1982)
First book publication: 1977
Type of work: Short stories

*A collection of short stories made compelling reading by their themes (the immi-
nence of atomic and mechanical apocalypse; human confusions about identity and reality) and by the compression, ingenuity, and narrative skill of their style*

The Best of Philip K. Dick is the only collection of his science fiction short
stories at present. As with most "Best of" collections, the title is a misnomer
— a more accurate title would be "A Representative Collection of Philip K.
Dick, As Selected By the Author," for it contains the best stories from Dick's
most productive period of short story writing (1953-1955) plus some other
stories, of varying quality, from the rest of his career.

Philip K. Dick first appeared to science fiction readers as a writer of short
stories in the Fredric Brown comic/surprise-ending tradition. In one year,
1953, he had twenty-seven stories published, and most of the stories in *The
Best of Philip K. Dick* appeared between 1952 and 1955. After that period, writing
novels occupied most of Dick's attention.

Two of the "amusing/surprise-ending" stories seem to be included as representative pieces rather than as examples of Philip Dick at his best. In the
first, "Beyond Lies the Wub," a visitor to Mars buys a wub for 50 cents. The
wub is a huge, pig-like animal. The captain of the ship thinks it looks good to
eat, especially since much of his stored food has spoiled accidentally. Peter-
sen, who bought the wub, does not want it eaten — he conducts long
philosophical discussions with it. The wub is killed and eaten; and the captain,
the only person who can bring himself to finish his meal, bursts into
philosophy. It seems there are more routes to immortality on Mars than those
described by traditional religions.

The second story, "Roog," tells of the family dog that gets upset by the
weekly visits of the roogs. These alien visitors to Earth accept weekly tributes
from terrestrials in large tins left outside houses. They enjoy the odd bit of
orange peel. Only the family dog can perceive what the garbage men are really
like.

Both plots have become threadbare cliches since 1953 (if they were not
already worn out then). The stories still give amusement, though, because of
their remarkable compression. In "Beyond Lies the Wub," Dick gives the
situation, the characters (the captain and the wub's owner), and the plight of
the wub in 3 pages. The story is finished in nine pages, without any hint of
cutting corners or leaving things out. The punchline is there, but it is not
overbearing. Such early craftsmanship has been the sound basis for all of
Dick's achievements since.

Once Dick had developed his compelling style, he did not take long to find themes and plots to match it. These themes are mainly based on fear: fear of a near future in which total war has obliterated most of the world; fear of the consequences of man's devotion to machines; fear of humanity's willingness and increasing ability to throw away life altogether. Not that the fear is given into. The most important stories in this collection show an author facing up to the worst possibilities of the future for humanity, and challenging the reader to meet his gaze. The fact that many of these stories are bitterly humorous makes them even more arresting.

The image that dominates most of Dick's stories during the early 1950's is "Total war. . . . The whole world, like this. . . . Ruined buildings. Heaps of rubble. Debris everywhere. . . . In the grey silence there was no life. No motion. Only the clouds of drifting ash. The slag and the endless heaps." That image, which recurs in most of these stories, comes from "Breakfast at Twilight" (1954). It is a fairly simple story, but disturbing. A family goes to bed one night and wakes the next morning in just such a landscape as that described above. Total war has been waged for years, breaking open a "time slip" (one of those hoary old science fiction clichés which Dick uses well here). Mr. and Mrs. Average America, the McLeans, see their most probable future. They return to their own time intact, but know that the wasted landscape they have seen lies only seven years in the future. The story is still haunting and valid; it is still a very probable future.

Philip Dick usually leaves a few survivors in his stories, but even the survivors louse up the future they are given. In "Second Variety" (1953), one of Dick's enduring and much-reprinted masterpieces in the short story form, the few survivors of total war have found new ways to wipe out one another. The Americans have invented tiny mechanical killer crab claws to penetrate the bunkers of the few surviving Russian soldiers. The weapon works — only too well. The automated factories begin to turn out new varieties of weapons. The American soldiers count themselves safe, so far, from their own invention, protected by tiny radio emitters. Then Major Hendricks finds out the true situation when he goes to investigate a truce offer from a Russian soldier. Hendricks treks across the wasteland, which is what remains of the world, and meets an eight-year-old boy in the ruins. Hendricks decides to take the boy with him, but the Russian soldiers shoot him rather than Hendricks. The "boy" falls apart into little bits of metal. It is one of the new varieties of killer. Hendricks finds only three Russian soldiers left, remnants of an entire battalion wiped out by the mechanical killers. The soldiers had been visiting a prostitute, Tasso, and were spared. The story becomes an anxious guessing-game: how many new varieties of killers have been invented, and which resemble human beings. A truce mission back to the American lines shows that the new varieties are dedicated to destroying all human life, including that of their makers, the Americans. Wounded, Hendricks sends Tasso off in a spaceship to warn moonbase. Then he sees before him an army of Tassos, all alike, marching towards him. The Tasso model was the second variety, which has been given the key to destroy the moon base.

In most of these early stories, few escape the processes which are unleashed. Worse, nobody can afford to trust anybody else. It has become a truism among historians of the science fiction field that this element in the literature of the early 1950's reflects the McCarthy hysteria of the time. Some splendid stories, as rigorously paranoid as Dick's, remain from that time — including Alfred Bester's "Fondly Fahrenheit" (1954) and Damon Knight's "Catch That Martian" (1952).

In Dick's case, these themes are basic to the fiction, not mere byproducts of a historical era. For instance, Dick's stories pose the question: What is human and what is not? When does the human become mechanical, and the mechanical human? It is the compression and power of Dick's writing which make these themes and obsessions important, not merely their historical occurrence.

"Impostor" (1953) is another much-reprinted Dick story. As he himself admits in "Afterthoughts," the story has been devalued only by his own later overuse of the theme (in novels such as *Do Androids Dream of Electric Sheep?* and *We Can Build You*). The main character, Spence Olham, is sitting at home one day, minding his own suburban business, when he is arrested by security forces and taken off to moon base to be killed as a spy. An enemy called the Outworlders has been bombing Earth, but has not yet penetrated secure places of human habitation. The security forces say that Olham is an android — a robot spy designed to infiltrate Earth bases and explode them upon hearing some particular catch-phrase. Olham rejects the whole notion. He knows he has been living his normal life all these years and he wants to go home to it. He is fortunate enough to capture a ship which will take him home, but even his wife rejects him and security forces nearly recapture him. He investigates the spot where the enemy ship came down. There is a body in the wreckage. Further investigation shows that the body is not that of a robot, but that of a human. "But if that's Olham, then I must be — " he starts to say, but that's the trigger for the bomb.

Another clever 1950's story? Well, cleverly written. Dick's narrative sense, his ability to show in a sentence or two ordinary people struggling with impossible situations, and his sense of conviction about his own creations make such a story more satisfying than almost any science fiction story written during the 1970's.

But there is nothing clever about the problems raised in such a story? When *is* someone human or android? In Dick's worlds, it is hard to tell. Olham's sense of himself is no guide at all. (The question people asked one another in the 1950's was: Who is a Commie and who isn't? — you can't tell from what people *say* they are.) And does it matter? If the security forces had not pursued Olham, he never would have uttered the phrase that sets off the bomb carried inside his body. Do people not have the right to be what they say they are? The

American obsession of the time was, of course, infiltration: could you be a subversive without realizing it?

But in the otherwise slight story, "Human Is" (1955), Dick shows a human who is mechanical and unlikable in all his actions. An android takes his place surreptitiously, but the robot's humanity and kindliness are such a welcome relief to the wife that she is happy to accept the robot as her husband.

Perhaps Dick does not pose the question accurately, even though the stories themselves are so strong that *they* lead the right way. Another famous story of Dick is "Autofac" (1955). All the obsessional elements in Dick's stories are here — a world blistered by total war; a small group of surviving humans trying to make do; and a mechanical threat to society. In this case, however, machinery is "threatening" because it is trying to be helpful. Enormous automated factories continue to operate underground after the end of total war. Regularly the products of the factories are airlifted to those small human settlements which still exist. Production, however, has not been regulated to meet demand. The humans are dismayed as they see the factories adapting themselves to raid the Earth's resources in order to produce an ever-increasing supply of goods. The humans would like to resume control of society for themselves and conserve raw materials, but the factories show no signs of shutting down just because the war has ended.

Eventually the citizens of one small settlement work out a way to stop the automated factories ("autofacs") — they trick them into making war on one another. The result is just as devastating as the original war had been; the only comfort left to the humans at the end of it all is that the autofacs have stopped production. The ruins are explored, but, in one of Dick's most eerie disclosures:

In a sealed chamber, furious activity boomed and echoed, a steady process of moving belts, whirring machine-tools, fast-moving mechanical supervisors. . . . All this was visible for a split second; then the intrusion was discovered. Robot relays came into play. The blaze of lights flickered and dimmed.

The factory stays turned off until the humans go back to the surface. Then the assembly line begins again — producing not consumer goods, but miniaturized automatic factories. Imbued with self-sustaining life, the autofac is reproducing its kind.

The difficulty with such a story is that, to the literal mind, its fears seem groundless. Machines cannot reproduce themselves, design new patterns for themselves, and "take over the world." The reader's fear response gets a bit rusty at this point. The story has much more meaning if we consider another possibility: that the autofac is what present technological society would like to invent. It is the epitome of our mechanical and consumerist dreams, and a source of horror. Here is the link between Dick's most important themes. Time and again in his stories the world is laid bare by atomic warfare, but humans built the bombs, and only humans are capable of such implacable hatred of other humans that they are willing to destroy the biosphere in order to defend some country or ideology. Dick's overt sermon is that human qualities are those of warmth: nonmechanical behavior. But the stories reveal the extent of humanity's talent for hatred — also nonmechanical behavior. Dick should not say what his stories are "about," as happens in the "Afterthoughts" in this volume. The stories themselves reveal more than the author realizes.

Considering the wide range of stories in *The Best of Philip K. Dick*, it is necessary to over-simplify the general strands in Dick's work. How does one account for a delightful piece such as "The Days of Perky Pat" (1953), for instance? It contains so much more than just one of Dick's obsessions — it is a complex story of authentic human activity. It is a post-total war situation again. A few survivors live out boring lives in bunkers (or "flukers"). Most of the adults devote their lives to playing the Perky Pat game — a board game featuring characters rather like Barbie dolls. The game features all those aspects of affluent living which disappeared during the war. To the players, Perky Pat and her friends equal life itself. But they cannot resist the temptation to trek overland to Oakland to compete against the Connie Companion game layout. The conception is brilliant (and used later, to even better effect, in Dick's *The Three Stigmata of Palmer Eldritch*), but the subject of the story is human fallibility and courage. Perhaps it is the finest story in the book, although the least classifiable.

Even in 1953, Dick was moving toward the themes which dominate most of his novels and stories from 1960 onward — what is personal reality? Much has been written about these later themes, but in short story form, they pale in significance beside the urgency of those of the earlier stories. "If There Were No Benny Cemoli" (1963) and "Oh, To Be a Blobel!" (1964) are slight pieces, and "A Little Something for Us Tempunauts" (1974) is almost impenetrable. In the 1953-1955 stories, reality was very close and likely to obliterate most of the human race. It is that conviction which still makes the stories such powerful reading.

In the later stories, reality has become very personal and ambiguous. In "The Electric Ant" (1969), for instance, the main character discovers at the beginning of the story that he is really an android although he believed himself human. He finds that he has a hinged panel on his chest. He removes it and finds a little scanner inside him. It reads a spool of continually unrolling punched tape. This, he is told, is his reality support — it feeds his reality to him. Garson Poole experiments with the tape and cuts bits of reality out of his time. Finally he decides to give himself the ultimate hallucinogenic experience — to face all reality simultaneously. He cuts the tape altogether, and stops existing. The story ends as reality begins to disappear for all the people who had been in Poole's reality. Shades of Bishop Berkeley, and well-written.

Dick's fiction became increasingly hallucinatory and private during the

1960's, and "Faith of Our Fathers" (1967) is possibly the most bizarre piece he ever wrote. The mixture of themes and story elements defies description. It is enough to say that the Vietnamese and/or Chinese appear to have won a war against the United States, which they now control. The image of The Leader dominates all media. A rebel group believes that The Leader is not human and that a false image of him is being broadcast. With the help of the main character, Chien, they find out that the whole population is dosed constantly with hallucinogens through the water supply. They give Chien an anti-hallucinogen and arrange for him to meet The Leader personally. The main problem is that relieving the mind of illusions helps nobody: "It's the hallucination which should differ from person to person, and the reality experience which should be ubiquitous — it's all turned around. . . . Twelve mutually exclusive hallucinations — that would be easily understood. But not one hallucination and twelve realities." And the "reality" which Chien experiences is very strange: to him The Leader is God, a horrible monster devoted to killing people one by one. The story mixes up so many elements that the reader seems to be invited to make of it what he likes.

This later view of reality is very convincing in books such as *Ubik* and *Now Wait for Last Year* — mainly because they are novels, and Dick's style had changed over the years to become more suited to novels than short stories. All the post-1950's stories are too diffuse and not as convincing as the early pieces.

A "best" of Philip K. Dick? Perhaps someone other than Dick should have chosen the stories, and should have concentrated exclusively on that brief period in the 1950's when Philip K. Dick was perhaps the finest writer of short stories in the science fiction field.

Bruce Gillespie

Sources for Further Study

Criticism:

Gillespie, Bruce. *Philip K. Dick: Electric Shepherd*. Melbourne, Australia: Nostrilla, 1975, Gillespie places Dick among the forerunners of the science fiction field.

Taylor, Angus. "Can God Fly? Can He Hold Out His Arms and Fly? — The Fiction of Philip K. Dick," in *Foundation*. IV (July, 1973), p. 38. Taylor gives an overview of Dick's Fiction to date.

BEYOND APOLLO

Author: Barry N. Malzberg (1943-   )
First book publication: 1972
Type of work: Novel
Time: The late twentieth century
Locale: A mental hospital with flashbacks to an expedition to Venus

After an aborted expedition to Venus, psychiatrists attempt to discover the reasons for the failure of the mission

Principal characters:
> HARRY M. EVANS, the sole surviving member of the expedition, its First Officer
> JACK JOSEPHSON, ("Joseph Jackson") the Captain of the expedition
> DR. CLAUDE FORREST, a psychiatrist
> EVANS'S AND JOSEPHSON'S WIVES

Barry Malzberg's novel, *Beyond Apollo*, won the John W. Campbell Award for the Best Science Fiction Novel of 1972, and the ensuing critical storm among both fans and professional writers provided a *cause célèbre*. Many felt this decision was an insult to the memory of Campbell, while others hailed the book as a major contribution to the development of the science fiction genre. Few readers were indifferent about it.

One of the major difficulties confronting any reader of *Beyond Apollo* is attempting to decide what the book is all about. It lacks a clearly definable plot. It boasts a "hero" who is, by any conventional standard, clearly insane. Its vigor of language, replete with four letter words and descriptions of gross sexuality, was almost unknown even to the bold experimentalists of the New Wave. In many ways, the novel is a tale told by an idiot, full of sound and fury, but whether it signifies nothing is quite another matter.

Most of the novel is told in the first person by Harry Evans as he is undergoing almost futile attempts by psychologists to rehabilitate him. Evans says he will write a novel about an ill-fated Venus expedition from which he alone has returned. His projected novel will be called *Beyond Apollo*. It will consist of sixty-seven chapters, contain about sixty-five thousand words, and will finally tell the truth of what happened on the voyage. In fact, the postscript of the book consists of a letter from a publisher accepting the manuscript for publication.

On another level, however, the novel can be read as the increasingly agonizing attempt by Dr. Forrest to determine what has occurred to drive Evans mad. Concurrent with this attempt is NASA's extreme concern about the failure of the entire project. After all, the captain, Jack Josephson, has not returned from the mission, and NASA knows that an escape from the sealed environment of the spaceship is, by definition, impossible. If no answer can be found to these baffling enigmas, the entire space program may well founder.

Forrest continually asks Evans what happened to the Captain and why the mission failed. Evans gives answers, all of which Forrest finds unsatisfactory. When Forrest accuses Evans of deliberately lying, Evans promptly agrees that the next version will really be the truth. The seemingly insane explanations put forth by Evans and Forrest's coldly logical demolition of them make up much of the novel. In the end, the reader is still uncertain as to what actually happened. Did Harry Evans and Jack Josephson (who sometimes appears in Evans's distorted memory as Joseph Jackson) go on a mission to Venus? Did Evans return alone? Was the mission a failure? The reader closes the book with puzzlement, perhaps even with anger or incomprehension.

Yet Malzberg uses puzzles of various types to literary advantage throughout the novel. Anagrams, cryptograms, bridge or chess problems, and other enigmas fill almost every page. Entire chapters consist of Josephson forcing Evans to answer, in fifty words or less, why the mission is going to Venus, and this continuing dialog, where each swears to tell the absolute truth without hedging or lying, provides a sort of contrapuntal motif to Forrest's attempts to find out what really happened. By confounding the reader with conundrum after conundrum, Malzberg is actually forcing his audience to face the much larger questions of the nature of reality and illusion and the appearance of sanity with insanity. Malzberg thus wishes his readers to read between, behind, or through each line, saying, in effect, that the self-evident is not always the real.

Beyond Apollo is also a humorous book, and while its humor is mordant or caustic, it is nonetheless both amusing and enlightening. The novel can be read, even on its surface level, with considerable enjoyment. Yet, the reader may ask what is the key to this disturbing book? What lies beneath the apparently chaotic plot, the apparent insanity of its main character, and the direct style which seems to combine latter-day mainstream pornography with stream of consciousness? At least part of the answer lies in the title of the novel itself — *Beyond Apollo*. Here some careful distinctions must be made. On one hand, the title may mean that it is the story of space exploration after the successful conclusion of the Apollo expeditions to the moon in the 1960's. From tenuous threads plucked from Evans's somewhat uncertain memory, we learn that the Apollo trips were followed by the trip of the *Kennedy II* to Mars in 1981. This expedition failed and the entire space program was in danger of being scuttled. However, readers can be easily misled at this point, for Evans avers that the Apollo moon expeditions were a failure and that the space program needs a new success to assure continued congressional funding. Ostensibly, the Venus expedition is an attempt to aid the space program by assuring a success after the "failures" of both the moon and Mars expeditions. Already, then, historical reality crumbles within the construct of the novel. What is truth, a jesting Malzberg seems to ask, and his insane characters do not wait for an answer.

One further level is also implied by the title. If Apollo is understood as symbolic of Nietzsche's Apollonianism, and Mars is viewed in its traditional mythic sense of war, battle, and conflict, then the opposite of these myths, the concept of Venus, or the Dionysian, emerges. In other words, the novel may be read as a commentary upon the crucial tension between the Apollonian intellect and the Dionysian subjective. However, Malzberg is not content simply to state the problem in such simplistic terms. His very style, his use of sexual metaphor, and his ambivalent characters all reflect this tension. Indeed, it may betray Malzberg's own personal feelings about the ultra-rational, ultra-mechanistic space program. He seems to say that man has raped the moon with the phallic space capsules. Man's attempt to rape Mars failed only because war itself is the apotheosis of rapine: Mars, the rational intellect, or the coldly calculating space program cannot be raped because it *is* rape itself. All that is left for mankind to destroy is the final frontier of love, charity, understanding, beauty, or joy represented by Venus, the planet and the concept.

Malzberg's utilization of this complicated metaphor leads one to question the actual setting of the novel. Throughout the entire book, the reader is convinced of the surface authenticity of the story: the Venus expedition has failed and Forrest is attempting to find out from Evans what happened. Evans skillfully re-creates the spaceship in his distorted memories, but reality is altered. Josephson becomes Jackson. Evans, through a series of anagrams, assumes multiple identities. Contract bridge hands are solved by chess maneuvers. Marital sex becomes rape. Yet, in another sense, none of the action takes place on any kind of spaceship. There has been no Venus expedition. Nothing has happened except in the novel that Evans-Malzberg is writing. The action takes place in the protagonist's psyche, and thus perhaps in the psyche of all of us.

Put in these terms, the problem of the novel mirrors the problem of humanity. How can we reconcile the Apollonian elements in ourselves with the Dionysian, the destructive with the creative, the objective with the subjective, war with peace, rape with love, the intellect with the emotions? Evans's story, then, is our story, and if there is no final answer to the puzzle of the novel, similarly there is no answer to our own eternal struggle. Once more, art holds the mirror up to nature.

On this final level, that of the artist struggling to create a work of art, *Beyond Apollo* also answers some of its own questions. What lies *beyond* Apollo? After testing all of the possibilities of the Apollonian view of man or the universe, humanity can turn only to the Dionysian, Venusian, and subjective, Malzberg seems to say with a kind of psychic determinism. The first and last chapters pose the identical problem in Evans's words: "I loved the Captain in my own way, although I knew that he was insane, the poor bastard. . . . This was only partly his fault: one must consider the conditions. The conditions were intolerable."

This brief four line first chapter is repeated exactly, word for word, as the opening paragraph of the last. But it is immediately followed by this comment:

". . . I can see from the dull stare in Forrest's eyes that it is hopeless, quite hopeless. He will never understand. None of them will ever understand. And I do not know the language to teach them."

True, neither Evans nor Malzberg knows the language to teach the subjective. For those who understand the intuitive, the subjective, the Dionysian-Venusian, no language is necessary. For those who do not, no language is possible. Our institutionalization of passion has reduced everything to a binary code. The Captain has become a machine and Evans's apparent madness is the sanity of love.

In yet another sense, *Beyond Apollo* is a novel about the creation of a novel, and as such resembles works by Philip K. Dick, Philip Roth, Vladimir Nabokov, and John Barth, to mention only a few authors who have dealt with similar problems. Which fictional realities are real; which are illusion? What protagonists are sane; what is insanity?

Some readers of *Beyond Apollo* have been repelled by the gross sexuality of the novel. Indeed, those critics who have claimed that giving it the Campbell Award was an insult to Campbell's memory have seized upon this aspect, maintaining, in effect, that it is the "dirtiest science fiction novel" ever written. Nonetheless, the rampant sexuality of the novel is integral to its message, providing a metaphor for the rape of Venus undertaken by Evans's expedition. Malzberg is quite direct about this symbolism, for one of the many reasons advanced by Evans to Forrest for the failure of the mission is what is termed the "Great Venusian Disturbances." These disturbances — whether they be the emergence of Evans's, hence humanity's, subjectivity or merely hallucinatory voices — demonstrate the corruption of love into fornication for the sake of fornication. The brutal excesses of the sex scenes of the book were deliberate on Malzberg's part, deliberate because the action demanded brutality, venality, and four letter words. There is nothing titillating about them. They are repellent, and they were meant to shock the reader into awareness of what the excesses of mechanistic rationality can lead to: sterility, corruption, and evil.

In his anger Malzberg resembles no one quite so much as Swift or Joyce. If the two great Irish artists inveigh against the insanity of the world they saw, so also does Malzberg, as, again like Joyce, he attempts to forge on the smithy of his soul the uncreated conscience of the race.

Willis E. McNelly

Sources for Further Study

Reviews:

Algol. XIX, November, 1972, p. 29.

Analog. XCII, September, 1973, pp. 160-161.

Kirkus Reviews. XL, April 1, 1972, p. 432.

Magazine of Fantasy and Science Fiction. XLIV, February, 1973, pp. 29-31.

New York Times Book Review. April 14, 1974, p. 22.

Observer. August 18, 1974, p. 28.

Riverside Quarterly. VI, August, 1973, pp. 79-82.

Times Literary Supplement. August 23, 1974, p. 911.

BEYOND THIS HORIZON

Author: Robert A. Heinlein (1907-   )
First book publication: 1948
Type of work: Novel
Time: An estimated one thousand years in the future
Locale: Primarily what is now the Western United States

A tale of adventure, romance, and the quest for knowledge in a Utopian society which has eliminated need, and which is challenged to provide a reason why man should continue to strive

Principal characters:
>HAMILTON FELIX, underachieving product of a star line of selective breeding
>LONGCOURT PHYLLIS, his fifth cousin, a nurse, who becomes his wife
>MONROE-ALPHA CLIFFORD, Felix's best friend, an econometrician
>MORDAN CLAUDE, District Moderator for Genetics
>JOHN DARLINGTON SMITH, the man from 1926, recovered from a stasis field

Beyond This Horizon is a curiously shaped, even misshapen, book with two unlikely love stories, an espionage tale which results in a shoot-out, several lectures, and some twenty thousand words apparently tacked on after the main events of the plot have already been brought to a conclusion. The real unity of the book is thematic, the plots, the lectures, and the epilogue all centering on the problem of what man should live for when all of his basic needs are taken care of. Read critically, however, the book resists easy interpretation, as it shifts subjects and even narrative point-of-view in an apparently random manner.

Most curious of all, perhaps, is the opening of Chapter Ten, just after the shoot-out, at the conclusion of which Hamilton Felix, Longcourt Phyllis, Mordan Claude, and his wife Martha have been knocked unconscious by gas introduced by people on their side. Somebody starts to wake up, and try to remember which character he is in "this game," which he plays for his own amusement, while deliberately pretending ignorance. This disembodied consciousness, "Himself," vacillates between the unconscious characters, one of whom is an "automatic," assuring himself that he is now a geneticist (Mordan), whose occupation is playing "a game within a game," before finally waking in the body of Felix, an inventor of games in this novel's world.

Up to this point, the novel had appeared to be mainly about how to get Hamilton Felix married and contributing to the genetic improvement of the human race. Shortly after this point, Mordan, on behalf of Felix, gets the ruling Policy Board of this society to launch a massive plan of long-range research, including the scientific study of the problem of life after death. Felix, in turn, agrees to marry Phyllis, which satisfies Mordan, and apparently closes off the main plot. But the book continues, detailing some of the work and results of the Great Research, along with the development of the Hamilton children.

Beyond This Horizon is partly about the Hamilton family, partly about the meaning of life, and partly about the shape of tomorrow's world. The last is the most recognizably science fictional aspect of the book. This culture, *not* just around the corner, is one in which free enterprise coexists with a planned economy, and Social Darwinist determinism produces a "wolfish" sort of individualistic freedom. A highly developed technological civilization, which is limited to the Western Hemisphere thanks to catastrophic wars, this society features many advances over the present, including the colonization of other planets in the solar system.

But this is not a traditional Utopian narrative, in which a stranger is taken on a guided tour of the facilities. A man from the past does emerge, after a third of the book is over, but he is primarily a figure of fun, ridiculing the presumption of our own times that we are the peak of civilization. There is a great deal of talk as characters lecture one another, and the narrator even steps in to give the reader a refresher course in genetics, among other things. There is also much melodramatic action to keep the habitual reader of adventure fiction happy.

Action is normally easier to maintain in dystopia than in Utopia, but this is not a perfect society, in which everyone is happy, although perhaps they should be. Most of the populace is free of tooth decay, weak eyesight, and susceptibility to the common cold, along with more debilitating genetic traits. As their share of the general prosperity, everyone has a "basic dividend" which entitles them to a luxurious standard of living; "control naturals," who have not been genetically improved, are compensated at an even higher rate. A *code duello* provides a minimum of excitement, along with a maximum of politeness, and an aid to natural selection, when the marksmanship of young "braves" is not equal to their bellicosity. But people demand work to feel useful, and the boredom of the elite is apparent at parties, in the popularity of Hamilton's gaming emporia, and in the sensation made by the man from the past, before his novelty pales. It is even more evident in the lives of Felix and his friend, Monroe-Alpha Clifford, and in the "Survivors Club" with which both become involved.

Clifford's problems are the easiest to solve, through love and a more challenging occupation, but his story parallels and counterpoints that of his friend. A mathematician who cares more for problems than answers, Clifford is morose, literal-minded, tired of his "ortho-wife," and afflicted with an advanced case of primitivism. After J. Darlington Smith partially convinces him that 1926 was not the simplest of times, Clifford looks to the Survivors Club to change the order of things, promising a more "scientific" future. Felix, who has infiltrated the Club as a spy, dispatches Clifford to the Redwood Forest, where he falls in love with nature and the girl of his dreams.

Awkward and obtuse, he actually takes a shot at her when he thinks she's a "control natural," scheduled for liquidation by the Survivors. Even more incredibly, once he is cured of his obsession, he seeks her out and she forgives him, enveloping him in the feeling of well-being, at which her "experimental" genetic line is exceptionally good. When they start making babies, and he gets involved with the Great Research, Clifford seems set to live happily ever after.

The extreme limits of discontent are represented by the ill-named Survivors Club, whose abortive revolution snuffed out in the shoot-out recapitulates the failure of misused eugenics in history recounted as early as Chapter Two. Reacting against the "atomic war of 1970," Mordan reminds Felix, people bred for "sheepish" pacifism, which the "wolfish" remnant of the "Northwest Union" overwhelmed in the First Genetic War. Subsequently the "Great Khan" ruled a hive-mind empire, the results of whose excessively specialized breeding were defeated by "true" men in the Second Genetic War, driving most of mankind back to the stone age. Uncompromising totalitarians, responsible for some nasty eugenic experimentation, the Survivors Club is an unsavory group of incompetents, without a "sound scientific mind" among them, which seems not so subtly modeled on the technicians of Hitler's Third Reich.

But eugenics need not be deleterious to human freedom, as Hitler in real life and Aldous Huxley in fiction seemed to indicate in the 1930's. This is illustrated in the situation of Hamilton Felix, whose discontent with this society Heinlein takes most seriously. Felix is a *cause célèbre*, whose germ plasm is highly valued by Mordan, the genetic moderator, forbidden to affect Felix's choice of mate other than by constructive advice. Thirty generations of selective breeding have produced a *real* Survivor with a flair for inventiveness, which shows up in his gamesmanship, his quirky sense of humor, and his questioning mind. The end product, so far, of a "star line," Felix has one key *antisurvival* trait: he wants no children. If the controllers have their way, this flaw will be eliminated in two generations, and the eidetic memory of the synthesist, which he lacks and yearns for, will also become part of his children's inheritance. But Felix, though he enjoys life personally, is not satisfied with hedonism or simple survival as a goal for human evolution. Thus he demands, before cooperating with the inevitable, an answer to that fundamental question of philosophy and religion: what is the meaning of life?

Although it may well be semantically vacuous, as Mordan's wife Martha observes in good logical positivist fashion, this question suffuses Heinlein's fiction, as Alexei Panshin has observed. It is responsible in part for Heinlein's domination of magazine science fiction just before World War II, for the continuation of his popularity, and for the curious artistic imbalance of many of his novels. His early attempts at long narratives are all marked by the conflicting demands of adventure and philosophy. Action overwhelms meaning in *Sixth Column* (1941; *The Day After Tomorrow* 1949), as a small band of true

Americans, camouflaged by religion, use advanced technology to overthrow Pan-Asian oppressors. Overthrowing an American theocracy almost provides enough meaning to life for the hero of "If This Goes On. . . ." (1940; revised 1953). Overcoming blindness, complacency and superstition motivate "Coventry" (1940), "Logic of Empire" (1941), and "Universe" (1941).

Once the revolution or revelation is accomplished, however, the plots have no place to go. This is especially visible in *Methuselah's Children* (1941; revised 1958), in which the Howard families, voluntarily bred for freedom from the traditional human lifespan, win freedom from oppression and even from the travel limitation of the speed of life. Unnerved, however, by their confrontation with the alien, they return to Earth, where the rest of humanity has also achieved longevity, and perhaps their aimlessness as well. In this and others of these stories, science is certainly given its due, but meaning inheres in religion, even mystical belief, which the characters typically reject.

In the chart of Heinlein's influential "Future History" series, "The First Human Civilization" is projected to start late in the twenty-first century with the end of the American theocracy. This Utopian social arrangement comes into being with a "Covenant" establishing mutual obligations for individuals and their society. Recognizing the pitfalls for storytelling in a bland utopian setting, Heinlein generally focused on characters who were reared outside the Covenant, who broke the Covenant, or whose government broke the Covenant. But *Beyond This Horizon*, though it is not on the chart, could well pass for the "Covenant" society, which must ensure its own survival by surpassing mere survival as a goal.

Given the audience Heinlein was writing for, it is not too surprising that he chose to enliven the Utopian format with shoot-'em-up adventure. Given the times in which he lived, the satirical replies to Hitler and Huxley are logically motivated, as may be the subservient domestic roles allotted to women. Martha fights alongside Mordan, Phyllis alongside Felix — after he has won her heart by slapping her around — but gunplay is downplayed for women, whose real happiness comes from making babies and husbands happy. What is a little harder to credit, simply from the standpoint of pleasing an audience, is Heinlein's flirtation with the occult.

Many readers of science fiction also like fantasy, although most will tell you they do not like the two mixed. Heinlein has written his share of overt fantasies, in which psychic occurrences, magic, even diabolism figure. If we include time travel as fantasy, probably all of his most popular works mix the two genres, which reflects both on Heinlein's predilections and on the real source of science fiction's popular appeal. But perhaps nowhere, except in "All You Zombies" and *Stranger in a Strange Land*, is the fusion as important to meaning and balance as in *Beyond This Horizon*.

Science is not simply given lip service in this novel, as is evidenced by lectures on genetics, economics, mores and folkways, history, and technology.

Social Darwinism is implicitly invoked in the survival of both individuals and societies. No one argues against science, though its efficacy in dealing with the occult is a little suspect. Science has an able proponent in Mordan Claude, who seems modeled on Huxley's Mustapha Mond, though Mordan's powers and the size of his district are much more restricted. His voice, moreover, is brought to bear on more issues than his normal expertise in genetics might warrant. A quick draw and expert marksman, though seldom called upon to prove it at his age, Mordan is an able defender of dueling, and of the principle that an armed citizenry is more important to the protection of government than a massive police force or militia.

Regardless of the topic, Mordan always takes the "long view," holding his own life of little consequence in the natural order of things, maintaining the right of Felix not to breed, regardless of the presumed loss to society. Though he does not need Felix's "proof," he ably makes the request of the Policy Board which leads to the "Great Research" into nearly all of man's unsolved problems, which in turn will uncover still more problems *ad infinitum*. Mordan's "long view" is mirrored, albeit comically, by the misfit in this world of J. Darlington Smith, whose primary contribution is the reintroduction of "feetball" with appropriate gladiatorial additions. The long view is further extended, of course, by the Great Research, which has already produced results by the end of the novel, and which promises more, including possible alien contact, if not in the normal lifetimes of those then living.

But the final word on the long view comes from Hamilton Felix's children, whose development is chronicled in the last third of the novel, along with the Great Research. His son Theobald is predictably a genius, but unexpectedly telepathic, with even more unpredictable results during the embryonic development of his sister, Justina. Sibling rivalry might be expected, but Theobald's dislike is colored by references to identifying characteristics of the late Esparteio Carvala, an aged Policy Board member, part Indian, possibly a witch, whose matter-of-fact acceptance of her own afterlife seems borne out. Theobald's testimony, corroborated by a "Life Detector," serendipitous by-product of the Great Research, offers the proof Felix wanted.

That "man is more than the product of his genes and his environment," as Felix had hoped, seems to be established, but the consequences of this discovery may be in doubt. The meaning of life still eludes Felix and mankind, though the Great Research may yet turn up more interesting and apparently valuable results. Felix at least is satisfied, and invites the reader to participate in his satisfaction with the probable future of the human experiment.

What will happen next, like the future recounted in this novel, still lies beyond this horizon, known only (if at all) by "Himself," who names the characters, plays their parts, and invents the games and the rules that keep him amused. Neither Mordan nor Hamilton, yet partly both, and partly all of the others, Himself is the author-creator, standing in for a playful god, or the inherent playfulness of the imagination, neither of which need have any worry about an afterlife.

Arguably the most interesting of Heinlein's earliest, most influential novels, *Beyond This Horizon* is not an artistic success. But its failures are instructive, both for the study of Heinlein, and for the light that they throw on the mystique of his popularity and that of science fiction in general.

David N. Samuelson

Sources for Further Study

Criticism:

Smith, Philip E., II. "The Evolution of Politics and the Politics of Evolution: Social Darwinism in Heinlein's Fiction," in *Robert A. Heinlein*. Edited by Joseph D. Olander and Martin H. Greenberg. New York: Taplinger, 1978, pp. 137-171. Smith calls the work a tale of an eugenic utopia.

Reviews:

Amazing Stories. XXV, October, 1951, p. 143.

Analog. XLII, February, 1949, pp. 145-146.

Fantastic Novels Magazine. III, July, 1949, pp. 118-119.

Startling Stories. XVIII, January, 1949, p. 176.

Super Science Stories. V, January, 1949, p. 91.

Thrilling Wonder Stories. XXXIX, October, 1951, p. 145.

BIG BALL OF WAX

Author: Shepherd Mead (1914-   )
First book publication: 1954
Type of work: Novel
Time: 1992
Locale: Port Washington, New York; Locust Valley, New York; St. Louis, Missouri

In a world of Momsday and corporate images, a communication medium more effective than television proves to be both a problem and a blessing for Com Chem industries

Principal characters:
> LANNY MARTIN, a rising junior executive
> MOM MARTIN, Lanny's mom
> HARRIET HALPERN, Lanny's girl
> MOLLY BLOOD, the priestess of the temple of LOVE
> MARGIE SCHROEDER, a resistance leader
> BEN SCHROEDER, a writer
> DAN PACKER, the inventor of XP

To read Shepherd Mead's *Big Ball of Wax* is to recall the flavor of America in the early 1950's, but with piquant seasoning. Mead takes the mediocrity of the age, expressed through a corporate image, and extends it into a satirical future world, the America of 1992. Reading *Big Ball of Wax* is like reading a comic extension of the dark predictions about American society made by Philip Wylie in his *Generation of Vipers*. In 1942, Wylie diagnosed, among other things, the ills of the American male (particularly the American businessman), the American woman (both Cinderella and Mom), and American religions. Writing twelve years later, Mead seems to accept the validity of Wylie's predictions and goes him one better by showing the final dissolution of the American Dream in a Momism-oriented, corporate image-controlled future.

Mead begins his story in the grand, ironic tradition: "Now that we're living in the best of all possible worlds . . . ," and his hero, Lanny Martin, is the satirical embodiment of a Wylian junior executive. Martin's premise in telling his story is to record the history of the events leading to the Momsday Rebellion and to the control, by his corporation, of the American public through the acquisition of the post-television advertising medium, XP. Martin wants the rising young men in his corporation to know the truth about the past in which he was so intimately involved. Because this record is a memorandum, Martin is able to give both the facts of the six days discussed and his personal comments on the state of his world. Mead shows as much about the future America through the development of Martin's character as he does through the narration of events.

The state of Martin's world is a logical, if sardonic, extrapolation of the state of Mead's own America. It would be difficult to appreciate Mead's motives if the reader had no knowledge of the 1950's. In fact, *Big Ball of Wax* would probably merely seem to be a somewhat silly, Harvard Lampoonish travesty if one were not conscious both of Wylie's analysis of America and of the atmosphere of the early 1950's. To a generation reared in the constant presence of a television set, the problems of media control explored by Mead appear primitive, naïve, and somewhat provincial. Children of the 1960's accept, on one level, the power of television to form images and to form national attitudes. However, because television is now such an unquestioned fact of life, the fear of mass control and the subsequently produced mediocrity of intelligence underlying Mead's novel appear antiquated. His warning is now a part of our lives, making his novel seem redundant. Mead almost appears to take the possibility not quite seriously enough, by writing such a light novel about it. It is difficult to read the warning on the medicine bottle with much concern after the poison has already had its effect. His use of the mammoth television screen which dominates each room of a house, a screen which can be programed to supply one's waking desires, is no longer funny because it is with us. Unlike Mead's future world, though, the American public rejected scented programing at the cinematic level, before the odors of other people's lives invaded our homes.

It is painful, however, to see how accurate Mead's predictions about the mediocrity bred by the medium have proven to be. One need only watch daytime television to see that the advertiser's premise is to aim at the attention of the lowest common denominator in an audience. Mead has a few predictions yet to be fulfilled, those of home-audience participation, where, for example, a poll of the viewers determines whether the batter in a major league game will make it to first base. Mead adds a bathetic element to the contest by having the viewers influenced by a soap-opera reenactment of the player's personal, melodramatic life history. This sequence in the novel is less humorous, though, if one considers the number of pulp publications which give the "life-stories" of media figures, both the human and the fictional ones.

Another consequence of the medium dominance, or perhaps an extension of the bathetic view of life, is the way reality, or the "news," is handled by 1990's television. All reports of crimes, accidents, or natural and unnatural events are handled by "reenactments" staged with dolls at the stations. Martin comments at one stage on how tactfully and "realistically" a brutal murder is displayed, discussing the mutilation of the dolls in detail. The people are kept at home, watching puppet shows of real life and melodramas of entertainment.

The atmosphere of the home is as sterile as is the presentation of life on television. Appliances maintain not only the house but also the individual. Mead's portrayal of the future antiseptic life of America is typical of the way many writers in the 1950's viewed the future of the mechanized house. Martin lives in a disposable world, eating synthetic messes produced from dehydrated powders, and he drives the car of the year. Again, Mead's projection of the

American Dream appears inane until one remembers the reformers of the 1970's who called for a return to the "natural" world of food, of life, and the subsequent mass rejection of this call. Our food is as chemically reinforced and dehydrated as is Martin's.

Mead also suggests the problems of the 1970's in his comments on literature of the future. Few people actually "read," and what they have as books are extensions of the Illustrated Classics, murder mysteries and gothic novels in cartoon form. Martin buys a book called *The Case of the Disemboweled Virgin*, a title which reflects the interest in artificial mayhem previously seen in the television programing. Martin's book, however, also allows reader participation in that it supplies pictures with moving parts so that the reader can stab, hack, or otherwise assault the victim as much as is desired. Mead also includes a comment on the literature of the 1950's when he creates one "literate" character, a novelist who is a boorish, hairy extension of a Beat writer, a man devoting his life to writing a totally unreadable epic of self-confession.

After the reader sees the enervated world of 1992 and hears Martin's clichés detailing the wonders of his corporate existence, one is somewhat prepared for XP, the prime invention of the novel. XP goes beyond all previous media in that it presents its message internally rather than externally; XP involves neurologically induced sensory participation in a pretaped fantasy. The audience no longer watches but now participates completely by being neurologically stimulated. When Martin discovers XP, his corporate sense tells him immediately that whoever controls XP controls the consumer market of America. Mead manages to explain the technology of XP by having an expert from Martin's Engineering Department interject "technical" details into the memorandum.

Martin's adventure into the world of XP is the basic plotline of the novel. Within the plot are moments of romance and adventure, but again the plot is merely a support for the satire. Martin's discovery of XP also allows Mead to comment on the state of organized religion in America. Here another Wylie message is heard as American religion is portrayed as a big business which praises God with automated, amplified, twenty-four-hour-long prayers and which pacifies its parishioners with movies such as "Salome's Man" and with Old and New Testament slot machines which play the "Hallelujah Chorus" for a jackpot winner. The ministerial purpose seems to be social counseling, with sermons such as "Is There Enough Sex in Your Marriage?" being the Sunday fare. When the followers of Molly Blood employ XP machines to satisfy their congregation, one can see the company sales in St. Louis plummet. Martin, our hero, manages to restore sales and return religion to its original purpose, to entertain and console.

One of Mead's projections of Wylie's predictions, the cult of Momism, fortunately seems to have been somewhat thwarted by the human liberation movement of the 1970's. Mead's future America is dominated by the Wylian

Mom whose day, Momsday, is the greatest national holiday, replacing that former merchandising masterpiece, Christmas. The holiday red and green are replaced by pink and blue, and the year's sales-pitches are based on Momsday giving. A logical extension of Wylie's Cinderella woman turned viperish mom is Mead's character Mom Martin. Mom Martin, herself, is a chemical miracle, a carefully vibrated and massaged woman with the body of an eighteen-year-old (and well worth the money to keep Mom happy, muses Martin). Freed from the menial tasks of housekeeping by electrical appliances and prefabricated food, Mom spends her day interacting with her wall-sized television set. Mom's counterpart is the sweet young Cinderella, the perfect young woman each junior executive must find. Martin has problems with his current love who is sexy but not socially acceptable on the corporate level. He must eventually discover a woman dumb enough and sweet enough to be accepted by his chief executive's wife, Mrs. Jim, the last of the censorial Victorian harridans who in 1992 still regulate the marital rituals of junior executives. Mead, however, did not envision a corporation where wives are deemed satisfactory by the company bank of psychologists. His corporate "family" has the same effect, though, of regulating the mind and the activity of each of its members.

If one is to have the sweet young thing turned wonderful, dominant mom, one also must have the other part of the Mother Goddess, the seductress. Mead produces a technically augmented siren in Molly Blood, priestess of her XP temple, but he also produces tidbits of delight for Martin. Not only does Mead have the unacceptable girlfriend for whom Martin lusts, but Mead also gives Martin XP experiences of girly-magazine delight which might have produced raptures in prepubescent males of the American 1950's. The creation of these sexual fantasies is more an anticipation of Hugh Hefner than an extension of Philip Wylie. In addition, there are other, minor, female types such as the idealistic artist who wishes to perform in the middle of the rebellion, and an intelligent woman rebelling against media control and mediocrity, but these characters are diminished in the light of Mom, Molly, and Mrs. Jim.

In general, the satirical comments on the decay of American society remain interesting, even if only from a somewhat historical viewpoint. However, the plot of the novel and its narrator are quite mundane. Martin, the narrator, is a problem because, since he is a satirical character himself, he must be insensitive, somewhat vacuous. Mead makes Martin likable in his simplicity, but it still is difficult to listen to a long memorandum told by a character who combines advertising clichés, corporate ideology, and adolescent sexual desires. The action scenes are occasionally interesting, and the encounter with the bull is delightful. But some scenes, such as that in the Beat apartment and those of the XP explanations, become tedious. Perhaps Mead was unsure that his message was clear because he eventually gives overt speeches about decay and mediocrity to the rebellion leaders. The rebels' use of XP, however, is so insensitive and negative that one is left wondering if the rebels are really on the right side. Unfortunately, though, if they are wrong and Martin is wrong, there is no right for the reader to choose.

Big Ball of Wax can be used most effectively as a companion to and a projection of *Generation of Vipers*. It can also be used as a comment on American society of the 1950's. If the plot were less trite and the characters less cardboard, perhaps the message about corporate control of media and the resultant mediocrity would remain effective. American society still contains the basic elements Mead was protesting. Expectations of science fiction novels have changed, though, and Mead does not supply the quality that attracts contemporary readers. It seems ironic that a man who was so concerned about the possible decrease of public intelligence would produce a novel eventually termed "mediocre."

Judith A. Clark

Sources for Further Study

Criticism:

Levin, Martin. *"The Big Ball of Wax,"* in *Saturday Review*. XXXVII (October 23, 1954), p. 17. Levin calls this a satiric novel with lots of gimmickery to provide fun reading.

Williamson, S. T. *"The Big Ball of Wax,"* in *New York Times Book Review*. December 19, 1954, p. 10. Mead has created a satire of a commercialized utopia.

Reviews:

Amazing Stories. XXXI, April, 1957, p. 129.

Analog. LV, August, 1955, p. 150.

Authentic Science Fiction. LXIV, December, 1956, p. 156.

Booklist. LI, December 15, 1954, p. 176.

Galaxy. XI, October, 1955, pp. 108-110 and XIII, April, 1957, pp. 104-105.

Library Journal. LXXIX, October 1, 1954, p. 1825.

Magazine of Fantasy and Science Fiction. VIII, April, 1955, pp. 81-82.

Nebula Science Fiction. XV, January, 1956, pp. 102-103.

New Worlds. XLII, December, 1955, pp. 124-125.

New York Herald Tribune Book Review. October 31, 1954, p. 13.

WSFA Journal. LXXVI, April–May, 1971, pp. 107-108.

THE BIG TIME

Author: Fritz Leiber, Jr. (1910-   )
First book publication: 1961
Type of work: Novel
Time: Outside of time and space
Locale: The Place, a Recuperation Station for Soldiers in the Change War

Three Soldiers, fresh from an excursion into the past to change history in order to assure their side ultimate victory in the Change War a billion years in the future, arrive at the Place and join the six resident Entertainers and three unexpected guests in solving a "closed-room" mystery

Principal characters:
> GRETA FORZANE, the narrator, a twenty-nine-year-old Entertainer
> SIDNEY LESSINGHAM, an Elizabethan-era gentleman
> ERIC FRIEDRICH VON HOHENWALD, a Nazi officer recruited as a Demon Soldier in the Change War; Greta's special beau
> BRUCE MARCHANT, a British poet of World War I-vintage, recruited as a Demon Soldier in the Change War just before his death in the trenches
> DOC, a Russian Jew who worked in a Nazi salt mine; an alcoholic and the Place's resident physician/surgeon
> ILHILIHIS, a Lunan octopuslike intelligent creature from the distant past
> KABYSIA LABRYS, a female warrior from Crete's distant past, leader of a group of defenders of that island against an enemy attack

A science fiction writer dealing with time travel must make one basic decision: can travel to the past or future significantly alter either the era visited or the present? If the answer is no, the plot will take certain conventional turns. But if the answer is yes, as it is in Fritz Leiber's 1961 Hugo Award-winning *The Big Time*, an almost infinite variety of possibilities is opened up. Leiber explores some of these possibilities in his novel, giving us a work that is fundamentally flawed but still of interest.

Greta Forzane, the first-person narrator, is a Demon Entertainer in the Change War. A Demon is a man or woman recruited by one of the two sides (Spiders and Snakes) in the billion-year-old war that encompasses the entire cosmos. Demons travel through time and space at the will of their masters, and their excursions through both are for the purpose of changing the past and the future to ensure ultimate victory in the Change War (hence the name). Not all creatures can become Demons, since there is apparently some hereditary trait that allows only certain individuals to operate effectively outside their own time. Without this genetic mutation, a creature can become a Ghost (with form but no effectiveness outside its own time), but never a Demon. The latter class is divided into Soldiers and Entertainers, with the Soldiers (as the name implies) doing the actual time-traveling and changing of history and the Entertainers staffing Recuperation Stations for Soldiers between sorties.

The Place is one such Recuperation Station, and Greta works there along with Sid (the Boss), Beau (the second banana), Doc, Maud (Magdalen; actually, the Old Girl), and Lili (the New Girl). Apparently every Recuperation Station is the same, with three men and three women each playing the same roles from station to station. All Entertainers serve the same purpose: to get the Soldiers back into action as quickly as possible. To this end they all provide medical, psychological, and sexual services to the Soldiers. Their Recuperation Stations are located outside of Time and Space, created and controlled by two marvelous gadgets called the Major and Minor Maintainers.

The Place is, in fact, secure from all forms of attack save one: the Change Wind. This phenomenon is a logical implication of the major premise of the novel, that the present can be changed by making changes in the past or future. The "Change Wind" is the rippling effect of these changes affecting past and future from the point of change. In Leiber's universe there is strong resistance to Change Wind, however, and each change causes the cosmos to adjust just enough to admit the new facts and no more.

A few of the major changes that have occurred in the world of the novel are worthy of note. The narrator's side (and so the apparent "good guys"), the Spiders, have decided that in this part of the universe the West must ultimately dominate the East, so they go into the past to have Germany defeat Russia in World War II. They do this by keeping England and America out of the war, which insures a Nazi invasion of the United States and ultimately a German empire from Russia to Kansas (with Japan presumably controlling the rest of the world, although Leiber, unlike Philip K. Dick in *The Man in the High Castle*, 1962, does not specify). The Snakes retaliate by kidnaping the infant Einstein in order to ensure Eastern development of the atomic bomb. Further back in time, the Spiders strengthen Rome and weaken Greece, which unfortunately results in a Cretan empire with no Plato. The Snakes, not to be outdone, strengthen the Eastern world through an alliance of classical China, Mohammedanized Christianity, and Marxist Communism (begun a few centuries early). This leads to the fall of Rome shortly after Julius Caesar, but the gap is filled (through the good offices of Change Wind) by a Gothic Catholic Church in the Middle Ages so like the Latin Catholic Church of the previous time stream that only a Demon historian could tell the difference. Somewhere along the way the American Civil War is avoided, giving rise to the Greater South, a so-called "steamboat culture" that produces the greatest university in the world.

While Change Wind meets heavy resistance on a global scale, there is no such protection for any individual. Any given change in past or future can bring an individual Change Death by moving the date of his death to some time before the subjective present. On the other hand, a person's life may also be lengthened by a Change Wind, if the date of his death is moved further down the time stream in a positive direction. Thus, one character in the novel is described as dissolving into a putrid pile of chemicals before the eyes of the narrator, while two other Demons have clear memories of two different deaths in their terrestrial lives.

Change Death is only the most drastic alteration a Change Wind can bring, however. Any Wind can alter one's memory or experience in any number of ways, and the individual has no way of knowing when or whether such changes have taken place. This is the hook on which Leiber hangs both the possibility of his extrapolated Change War actually taking place (how many of us have never experienced changes in our memories?) and the hidden purpose of his Hegelian Spiders and Snakes (the necessary thesis and antithesis leading to the synthesis of man's next evolutionary step). The characters both hate and love Change Wind as the carrier of the worst and best experiences of their lives.

While all of the above are logical extrapolations from the major premise of the novel, they form little beyond background information for the plot, and even this exposition is doled out a piece at a time, almost grudgingly. The plot itself gets under way when three Soldiers — Eric, a Nazi officer particularly attached to Greta; Bruce, a British poet who died in World War I and whose questioning of Spider methodology and incipient pacifism sets up the major conflict; and Mark, a Roman legionnaire — come to the Place for a scheduled period of rest and recreation and are interrupted by three unscheduled guests — Kabysia Labrys, a female Soldier from Crete; Ilhilihis, an intelligent octopuslike creature from a billion years in the Moon's past; and Sevensee (7C ?), a Venusian satyr from a billion years in the future. The three men were attempting to rekidnap the infant Einstein from the Snakes, and the woman and the two extra-terrestrials were defending Crete from a Snake counterattack. While escaping, the second party stumbled across a Spider scheme to reverse the early fall of Rome with a tactical nuclear weapon, and, through no fault of their own, were given the assignment and the bomb just before being rescued by Sid. The twelve Demons (six Entertainers and six Soldiers) are now effectively locked out of Time and Space for approximately five hours, the time that Leiber tells us it will take for the Place to recycle with the cosmos.

The stage is now set for a closed-room mystery. Twelve people are locked in a closed space with an atomic bomb and one of them hides the only tool (the Major Maintainer) that would allow them to find out how to disarm it. Naturally, the tool is in plain sight, clues as to its whereabouts have been scattered through the narrative, and the alcoholic doctor has the answer but cannot communicate it. Finally the narrator, much to her surprise as well as everyone else's, solves the mystery, and Ilhilihis reveals to her — and to us — the true identities of Spiders and Snakes, and the purposes of the Change War.

Unfortunately, the reader's interest is primarily in the exposition and denouement that'deal with the nature of the Change War and not in the main plot of the novel. Leiber has developed an interesting idea but has handicapped his presentation of that idea by tying it to a trivial plot. That he chose to develop a standard closed-room mystery rather than his major premise is perhaps more indicative of formula science fiction writing in the 1950's (*The Big Time* was first published in *Galaxy Magazine* in 1958) than of any lack of inventiveness on the author's part.

Leiber must take full responsibility for the use of language in *The Big Time*, however. The major problems in this area apparently spring from the good intention of individualizing characters through language, but the execution leaves a great deal to be desired. Sid, for example, speaks in a pidgin-Elizabethan dialect that mixes so strangely with colloquial expressions that the result disturbs the ear despite assurances that the character does so purposefully. Kabysia speaks in the Anglo-Saxon four-stress line, which in itself is odd for a native of Crete, but when that style is added to colloquial diction, the result sounds more like a bad parody of "Hiawatha" than a classical mind automatically composing in verse, as Leiber would have us believe.

Greta's use of phrases derived from various religious exclamations is somewhat more effective, but here, too, the device is only partially realized. Leiber feels compelled to explain to his presumably young audience that "got mittens" is derived from "Gott mit uns" and "the Bonny Dew" comes from "le bon Dieu." He also has Greta use such phrases as "Crisis," "Kreesed us," "Nervy Anna," and "Shatan Shave us." Perhaps more subtlety is indicated if this linguistic device is to be more effective.

Since all literature is rooted in the culture of the time of its creation, it should come as no surprise that the political situation of the late 1950's in America strongly influenced *The Big Time*. But this novel is more closely tied to its culture than most, and, like much science fiction, it has aged rather badly. Memories of World War II linger on in the portrayal of Nazis. The Cold War mentality is evident with the East *versus* West theme. Even the tunes for a couple of popular songs of the day turn up in the Place, while the atomic bomb represents the ultimate destructive weapon. These features combine with the use of colloquial language to restrict the appeal of the novel.

Leiber's basic premise — that changes in the past or future can effect the present — and his idea of possibility-binding as the next essential step in evolution (following the energy-binding of plants, the space-binding of animals, and the time-binding of man in the hierarchy) are both sound and interesting. Unfortunately, the synthesis of these ideas in *The Big Time* creates a confusing and fundamentally flawed novel. While science fiction may be primarily a literature of ideas, it is impossible to separate style from content in a work of art. When the former is flawed, as it is here, the latter is inevitably less clear than it might be.

David Stevens

Sources for Further Study

Reviews:

Analog. LXVII, August, 1961, pp. 167-168.

Galaxy. XXVI, October, 1967, pp. 190-191.

Magazine of Fantasy and Science Fiction. XXI, October, 1961, pp. 81-82.

New York Herald Tribune Book Review. March 26, 1961, p. 37.

BILL, THE GALACTIC HERO

Author: Harry Harrison (1925-   )
First book publication: 1965
Type of work: Novel
Time: Sometime in the future
Locale: The planet Phigerinadon II, a spaceship, and the planets Helior and Veneria

The story of how a simple farm boy, Bill, drafted into the space navy, becomes a "hero" through a series of improbable, comic adventures

Principal characters:
    BILL, a simple farm boy
    DEATHWISH DRANG, a drill instructor
    EAGER BEAGER, a Chinger in the disguise of a human
    FUSE TENDER SIXTH CLASS TEMBO, a Reverend of the First Church
        of Reformed Voodoo

Perhaps under the impact of the social revolutions that swept America in the 1960's, and of the increased consciousness which resulted, much science fiction published in that decade underwent important changes. The most obvious of these, of course, was the growth of what was eventually called the "New Wave," but even prior to such a revolutionary period, many writers were indicating something of their own social awareness in their work. The dangerous visions of the late 1960's were muted ten or even five years earlier, but the visions were nonetheless present, even in such an apparently innocuous novel as Harry Harrison's *Bill, the Galactic Hero.*

On first reading, the novel is nothing more than a rattling good yarn, a space opera filled with typical Harrisonian good humor, satire, *panache*, and marvelous puns. It is a funny book, with gag after gag cascading from Harrison's typewriter. Who but Harrison would have the *chutspah* to refer to planets as "distant Distantia or far off Faroffia"? *Bill, the Galactic Hero*, in other words, is drenched with action, fast-paced plot, improbable characters, hilarious situations, and — what is finally most important — more than a modicum of social commentary.

What is the novel about? It tells of just plain Bill, a technical fertilizer operator from down on the farm, who is shanghaied into the Empire's Space Corps to fight against the lizardlike Chingers. Bill's adventures on the good ship *Christine Keeler* and on the aluminum-clad planet Helior, and his battles against the Chingers on a jungle planet that curiously resembles Vietnam, comprise the rest of the novel. Its headlong, pell-mell pace never slows, and the novel ends as he recruits his younger brother Charlie into the hell he has known for twenty years simply to get a month cut from his own enlistment time.

Space opera? Yes. Thud and blunder among the stars? Certainly. But if the novel was nothing more, it would almost certainly be quickly forgotten. Yet *Bill, the Galactic Hero* has been in print almost constantly since its original publication in 1965 and was one of the first books selected for the Equinox SF Rediscovery Series. Thus, there must be something more to the novel than a surface reading indicates. It is a tribute to Harrison's skill that the additional elements which make the book memorable are so well woven into the texture of the story's action-adventure-humor format that they do not obtrude or shout MESSAGE on every other page. These additional elements consist of a thinly concealed satire of standard science fiction techniques, as well as of particular science fiction works. The novel is also distinguished by its depiction of war as the ultimate absurdity, and by its lampooning of the military mind in terms so strong that at times *Bill, the Galactic Hero* resembles the black comedy of Joseph Heller's *Catch-22*.

Harrison's satire of science fiction takes off from Robert Heinlein's famous paeon in praise of the infantry, *Starship Troopers* (1959), which was quite controversial in science fiction circles, since some readers, including Harrison, felt that Heinlein prettified war. But to counter Heinlein directly would certainly not make a novel, and a direct attack might be considered by some science fiction fans as *lèse majesté*. Thus, Harrison made his infantryman, Bill, a dolt, and put him through a series of misadventures intended to implicitly poke fun at Heinlein's pretentiousness. Harrison's weapons were the rapier thrusts of ridicule or the stiletto jabs of satire. Who could seriously credit Heinlein's assertion that only those who had once served in the military forces had the right to vote when faced with Harrison's apotheosis of all drill instructors, Petty Chief Officer Deathwish Drang?

> He was wide-shouldered and lean-hipped, while his long arms hung, curved like those of some horrible anthropoid, the knuckles of his immense fists scarred from the breaking of thousands of teeth. It was impossible to look at this detestable form and imagine that it issued from the tender womb of a woman. He could never have been born; he must have been built to order by the government. Most terrible of all was the head. The face! The hairline was scarcely a finger's-width above the black tangle of the brows that were set like a rank growth of foliage at the rim of the black pits that concealed the eyes — visible only as baleful red gleams in the Stygian darkness. A nose, broken and crushed, squatted above the mouth that was like a knife slash in the taut belly of a corpse, while from between the lips issued the great, white fangs of the canine teeth, at least two inches long, that rested in grooves on the lower lip.

If you can't beat 'em, Harrison seems to say, laugh 'em to death, and thus disposes of *Starship Troopers*.

To his undeniable talents as a storyteller, Harrison adds his keen sense of the ridiculous. The horrible seven-foot-tall lizardoid Chingers — "Would you want your sister to marry one?," a military poster shrills — turn out to be a seven-inch-tall peace-loving and intelligent species who believe that war is against their religion and who will fight only in self-defense. And why does the Empire fight the Chingers? Well, the "Chingers are the only nonhuman race that has been discovered in the galaxy that has gone beyond the aboriginal level, so naturally we have to wipe them out.'' We fight the Chingers, one character maintains, because we have always fought the Chingers, but Harrison later develops the acidulous concept that human beings fight because they are not a civilized species: quite simply, humanity is a race that likes war.

Harrison's sense of the absurd never fails him, whether it be in the description of the Purple Dart with Coalsack Nebula Cluster, which resembles an inverted, jewel-bedecked toilet seat, or in the very name of His Imperial Majesty's dreadnaught of space, the *Christine Keeler*, honoring the young lady whose amorous episodes brought about the resignation of a British cabinet minister in the early 1960's. In fact, the very excesses of the absurdity provide Harrison with still one more target — bureaucracy itself, as typified by Helior, the Imperial planet, the ruling world of ten thousand suns. Helior more than slightly resembles Isaac Asimov's Trantor, the chief planet of the *Foundation* series, but instead of centering about the great galactic decisions that Hari Seldon is concerned with in the Asimov books, Harrison asks small questions: If Helior, like Trantor, is a planet which, over a period of thousands of years, has been reconstructed into a world completely covered with metal, where does the planet's oxygen come from? And what do they do with their garbage in this spherical, multidimensional, futuristic version of the Pentagon? Asimov never bothered with such ordinary things like oxygen and trash, and Harrison pokes great fun at Asimov's excessive seriousness by having the trash stored in filing cabinets while oxygen is shipped in from agricultural planets in exchange for Helior's carbon dioxide. Logical but insane, Harrison maintains. Finally, Bill solves Helior's garbage and trash problem with the brilliant stroke of having it space-mailed, at government expense, to names selected at random from old telephone books garnered from other planets.

Harrison's brilliant comic inventiveness slides into mordant, corrosive satire with his sketch of the underground with which Bill innocently becomes involved. The Empire's bureaucrats mistake the lost, identityless souls who literally live hundreds of levels below the surface of Helior for a true subversive group. The consequent infiltration of this "underground" by dozens of members of the Galaxy Bureau of Investigation — the G.B.I. — provides Harrison with scope for some very pointed satire. The episode culminates in the long-postponed revolution instigated by the G.B.I. *agents provocateurs*. The agents disappear and Chauvinistisk Square is empty save for Bill, who has been duped by double-agent, counterspy Gill O'Teen. Harrison obviously wishes the reader to wonder if the only "Communists" feared by the F.B.I. during the 1950's were the hundreds of F.B.I. agents who subscribed to the Daily Worker, and whose subscriptions may have kept that paper alive.

Yet Harrison almost always cloaks his anger with humor; in doing so, he resembles many of the science fiction writers of two decades ago who covered their social awareness with humor, indirection, suggestion, hint, or allusion. Not all of them were as successful as Harrison, usually because their stories became lost in didacticism. Harrison, however, insists on action — ridiculous action, to be sure, but action nonetheless. This characteristic marks Harrison as a writer who learned his trade writing for John W. Campbell's *Astounding-Analog*. Yet Harrison shared the fears of many other science fiction writers in the gloomy aftermath of World War II: that the threat of nuclear annihilation might lead, at the very least, to the depersonalization and dehumanization of the entire race. Ray Bradbury spoke of this concern in *Fahrenheit 451,* as did Harlan Ellison in "A Boy and His Dog" twenty years later. Harrison's fears, incarnated throughout *Bill, the Galactic Hero*, center about the character of Bill himself.

Bill is anything but a galactic hero. He is a simple farm boy, totally innocent, completely uncorrupted. He is one of a class of heroes whose members include such disparate characters as Melville's Billy Budd, Voltaire's Candide, or Vonnegut's Billy Pilgrim. All approach the world with a wide-eyed clarity of vision unbesmirched by the mire in which they soon find themselves. In fact, one of the strongest appeals of Bill as a person is the way he retains his innocence in the face of incredible violence, insanity, and absurdity. Neither Deathwish Drang nor the cruelties of the training base, Camp Leon Trotsky, can corrupt him. He bends, but does not break, as he becomes a Fuse Tender Sixth Class, unskilled, aboard the good ship *Christine Keeler*, and his confidences revealed secretly to the chaplain are shattered by the chaplain in his alter ego as laundry officer, who has somehow or other lost six hundred jockstraps in the wash. Bill even retains his innocence when he learns that the Emperor of ten thousand worlds, "The father of us all" before whom he had groveled, was nothing but an actor.

Bill's loss of innocence is instead a gradual, crumbling erosion, as Harrison subtly transforms him into a veritable *miles gloriosus* concerned only with survival. Bill kills his Chinger friend, Eager Beager, simply to survive, and finally blows off his own right foot to avoid certain death in combat on the Vietnam-like jungle planet Veneria which circles the sun Hernia. Harrison makes Bill's transformation broadly comic as he elicits the reader's sympathy for the improbable galactic hero, blending some genuine pathos with the rich comedy.

In the end, *Bill, the Galactic Hero* may not be one of the most distinguished science fiction novels of all time, yet it remains a sterling example of how a skilled craftsman can transform the most banal of science fiction devices into a multitextured work that is both serious and comic.

Willis E. McNelly

Sources for Further Study

Reviews:

Books and Bookmen. XI, November, 1965, p. 55.

Kirkus Reviews. XXXIII, January 1, 1965, p. 30.

Magazine of Fantasy and Science Fiction. XXIX, July, 1965, p. 83.

New Worlds. CLVIII, January 1966, p. 12.

Observer. November 21, 1965, p. 27.

Punch. CCXLIX, December 1, 1965, p. 817.

Times Literary Supplement. March 10, 1966, p. 188.

THE BLACK CLOUD

Author: Fred Hoyle (1915-   )
First book publication: 1957
Type of work: Novel
Time: 1964-1966
Locale: Chiefly Nortonstowe, an estate in the Cotswolds

An account of the progress of a dark cloud of gas that invades the solar system and surrounds the sun, plunging the Earth temporarily into darkness

> *Principal characters:*
> CHRIS KINGSLEY, Professor of Astronomy at Cambridge
> GEOFF MARLOWE, an American astronomer
> ALEXIS ALEXANDROV, a Russian astronomer
> JOHN MCNEIL, a doctor
> ANN HALSEY, a concert pianist
> FRANK PARKINSON, private secretary to the Prime Minister
> THE BLACK CLOUD

Fred Hoyle is the most famous and most accomplished professional scientist to have turned his hand regularly to the writing of science fiction. He is an astronomer with experience in American observatories and the holder of a chair at Cambridge. He made a considerable contribution to the popularization of science in the postwar period, most notably with his guide to modern discoveries in cosmology, *The Nature of the Universe* (1950). As a scientist he is noted for bold and frequently unorthodox speculations; with Gold and Bondi he championed the "steady state" theory of the cosmos against the exponents of the "big bang" model of cosmogenesis, and more recently he has elicited controversy with his thesis that life originated in extrasolar space and that living organic material may still be carried to Earth by comets. *The Black Cloud* was his first science fiction novel; it is perhaps a typical example of "hard" science fiction, dealing with the work and world view of professional scientists and developing notions solidly founded in the scientific knowledge of its day.

The early chapters of *The Black Cloud* tell of the independent discovery of the cloud by groups of astronomers working independently in America and Britain. The Americans detect it by means of photographs showing that various stars have been blotted out. The British use computer analysis of a set of surprising observations to conclude that the outer planets have been dislodged from their true orbits. The two teams work with different data, and not until everything is put together does the full picture become clear. A small, dense, globular cloud of gas is heading directly for the sun and should arrive there in approximately sixteen months. What effect this will have upon the Earth depends greatly on the temperature of the cloud. But one thing is certain: there will be a global disaster.

The two teams of scientists pass on their results to their respective governments. One man in particular, Chris Kingsley, Professor of Astronomy at Cambridge, anticipates the cynical and secretive line that the two governments will take. He knows that he and all others privy to the facts are likely to be imprisoned, and therefore he bargains with the Prime Minister for a scientific body to be established under his direction, with sufficient equipment to track the cloud and provide up-to-date information. By means of calculated indiscretions he manages to select a few coworkers who are sent into isolation with him at Nortonstowe in Gloucestershire. There he erects radio-telescope apparatus for monitoring the cloud, and also orders equipment for manufacturing a high-powered frequency-modulation radio transmitter. The purpose of the latter is to make sure that when the nearness of the cloud threatens normal communications, Nortonstowe will become vitally important as a communications center and relay station.

Nortonstowe is duly sealed off. Kingsley insists that no military personnel are to be allowed on the estate, and he will permit only one representative of the government to remain there: Frank Parkinson, private secretary to the Prime Minister. Kingsley's dictatorial attitude and outspoken hostility toward politics and politicians soon result in relations between Nortonstowe and the government becoming rather strained, but the government desperately needs the continually updated intelligence that Kingsley's establishment can provide. Other members of Kingsley's team are Geoff Marlowe, an astronomer from Mount Palomar; a taciturn Russian named Alexis Alexandrov; John McNeil, a doctor who is the ostensible author of the manuscript that comprises the novel; and Ann Halsey, a pianist introduced to provide the scientists with a little light relief from heavy intellectual exertions.

It is at first assumed that the cloud will accelerate as it approaches the sun, and that it will pass on through the solar system after a few months of crisis. It is supposed that its first effects will be atmospheric, as molecular collisions heat up the outer atmosphere and produce a heatwave that will make the tropics uninhabitable. This will be followed by the cutting off of the sun's light, resulting in a great freeze. Soon, however, these predictions begin to go slightly astray. Instead of accelerating, the cloud slows down, losing momentum by firing off gobbets of its substance at enormous velocities. The expected heat wave arrives, killing millions of people, but by the time the freeze begins the cloud seems certain to become stationary relative to the sun, so that no end to the long night can be foreseen. Surprisingly, though, the cloud begins to change shape, settling into a disc that makes a steep angle with the plane of the ecliptic. This allows the sun's light to reach Earth again, but twice a year the planet will pass into the shadow of the disc, disrupting the cycle of the seasons and perhaps triggering a new ice age.

The atmospheric effects of the cloud render ordinary radio useless, and Nortonstowe, as Kingsley had planned, becomes vitally important because of its FM transmitting capability. Communications by way of this medium, however, quickly become subject to a curious "fade-out." The cloud appears to be reacting to the transmissions by producing some kind of shield that damps them out. Kingsley and Alexandrov advance the theory that the cloud harbors life and is reacting in order to protect its own "neural" organization and internal communications from interference.

Kingsley and his colleagues begin attempts to communicate with the cloud, and soon establish a dialogue. The cloud possesses a mind whose physical components, widely scattered in space, are linked by radiative communication mechanisms. This mind has far more information-carrying capacity than the minds of men, and is much more efficient. The cloud, in fact, expresses surprise that intelligence could emerge on a planetary surface because of the physical limitations inherent in life on such a surface. Kingsley finds it relatively easy to establish a kind of rapport with the cloud, once it has mastered English and absorbed the entire *Encyclopaedia Britannica*, but the politicians outside Nortonstowe want to remove him and take over the Earthly end of the dialogue. Kingsley resents this interference, and threatens that if he is replaced, the cloud may attack the Earth. This is pure bluff, and the threat has entirely the wrong effect, as it prompts the governments of the United States and the Soviet Union to attack the cloud with atomic missiles, reasoning that radioactivity is as inimical to the cloud's physical organization as to that of Earthly organisms. Kingsley warns the cloud, which sends the missiles back where they came from.

The cloud now announces its intention to move on, and Kingsley tries to take advantage of the little time left by trying to acquire some of the cloud's awesome scientific knowledge. The cloud cannot transmit this information in English, which lacks expressions for the necessary concepts, but volunteers to try to reprogram a human brain so as to accommodate the necessary knowledge. Two attempts are made to achieve this, the second involving Kingsley himself, but both volunteers are unable to stand the strain of a massive "mental overload" and are destroyed by the stress that results from the reprograming. The death of Kingsley does serve to allow the other members of the Nortonstowe establishment, with the aid of Frank Parkinson, to escape the wrath of the outer world by making him the major scapegoat. The truth about the cloud, however, is never made public, and the novel takes the form of a manuscript willed by John McNeil to the grandson of Ann Halsey (whose grandfather, it is implied, must have been Kingsley).

The Black Cloud is remarkable for several reasons. Its description of the process of scientific discovery — gathering data, forming hypotheses, and devising tests — is unparalleled. It is also a novel with a magnificent idea. The cloud itself is a radical departure in the depiction of an alien intelligence. Other science fiction writers, from Olaf Stapledon to Ross Rocklynne, have invented intelligent nebulae, but only Hoyle has depicted their physical and mental organization and provided a means of communication that allows his cloud to confront human beings in a thoroughly realistic fashion. However, the novel is not simply a product of the culture of science, descriptive of the world of the modern scientist; it is also propaganda for the world view of that culture.

In a preface, Hoyle notes: "It is commonplace to identify opinions forcibly expressed by a character with the author's own. At the risk of triviality, I would add that this association may be unwarranted." The fact that Hoyle should tentatively dissociate himself from the views of Chris Kingsley, however, does not serve to affect the strength with which those views are expressed in the novel. Kingsley despises politicians and their way of thinking. He regards them (two years before the publication of C. P. Snow's famous essay) as representatives of an entirely different culture. He is a technocrat, believing that it is stupid that society, founded upon the technological products of science, should be run by and for "an archaic crowd of nitwits" with no sense of proportion, a limited capacity for rational thought, and a warped sense of values. This resentful hostility constitutes the novel's main emotional force.

The extent to which these charges of irrationality and anthropocentric small-mindedness (directed not just at politicians but at "literary culture" in general) are justified is, of course, debatable. There is no doubt, however, that *The Black Cloud* enters into the debate with a very heavy broadside. In a period when antiscientific sentiments were by no means uncommon, and most apologists for technology within the science fiction establishment were inclined to a strategy of cautious defense, this represented something of a literary flourish. It is ironic that in recent years Hoyle became involved in a bitter dispute about the government funding of research projects when he was denied a grant to pursue his work on the hypothesis that life exists in deep space — work that attempts to establish the reality of some of the speculations in *The Black Cloud*.

The Black Cloud, therefore, is archetypal of a certain tradition within modern science fiction, providing not only an excellent account of scientists at work but outspoken propaganda for the culture of science. As with the fiction of many scientists, its dialogue is stilted and its characterization is poor: The cloud seems more real than any of the human characters. Nevertheless, it is a powerful work whose melodrama is directed toward the opening of minds. It attempts to show its readers something of the possible hazards facing the Earth in its journey through spacetime, as well as a new perspective for consideration of man's place in the cosmos.

Brian Stableford

Sources for Further Study

Reviews:

Analog. LXI, July, 1958, pp. 154-155.

Booklist. LIX, April, 1958, p. 445.

Fantastic Universe Science Fiction. X, August, 1958, pp. 124-125.

Galaxy. XVII, December, 1958, pp. 100-101.

Kirkus Reviews. XXVI, July 1, 1958, p. 17.

Library Journal. LXXXIII, March 1, 1958, p. 764.

Magazine of Fantasy and Science Fiction. XIV, May, 1958, pp. 113-114.

Nebula Science Fiction. XXVI, January, 1958, p. 103.

New Worlds. LXVIII, February, 1958, p. 125.

New York Herald Tribune Book Review. July 6, 1958, p. 9.

Saturday Review. XLI, June 7, 1958, p. 17.

Spectator. October 4, 1957, p. 454.

Times Literary Supplement. October 4, 1957, p. 598.

BLACK EASTER

Author: James Blish (1921-1975)
First book publication: 1968
Type of work: Novel
Time: The present
Locale: Italy

The Church's inaction against demons combines with man's desire for knowledge to develop a theme of "knowledge is power" with "knowledge for the sake of knowledge" where the ultimate power is evil

Principal characters:
>FATHER F. X. DOMENICO BRUNO GARELLI, a Jesuit priest and white magician
>BAINES, the wealthy director of Consolidated Warfare Service
>JACK GINSBERG, his assistant
>THERON WARE, a black magician, a Karcist adept
>MARCHOSIAS, his demon
>ADOLPH HESS, an inventor and scientist for Consolidated Warfare
>LUCIFUGE ROFOCALE, prime minister of infernal spirits

Black Easter makes of James Blish's trilogy *After Such Knowledge* a triangle or a triptych rather than a sequence, for in writing it postdates the previous two volumes, *A Case of Conscience* (1958) and *Doctor Mirabilis* (1964) but in setting predates *A Case of Conscience*. Like the other two works, *Black Easter* features a priest-scientist who crimps his science with his theology, who deals with the supranormal commonly called superstition; and it posits a universe divided between supernatural forces of good and evil. In a theologian-scientist, the physical and metaphysical should meet to advantage; but the Rock of the Church splits (to use a phrase of Blish) on the foundation of its faith — obedience — and its doctrines work against itself. Also, it cannot oppose what it does not recognize.

The monastery of Monte Albano is built on a veritable rock whose surface is so steep that visitors must be hauled up on muleback. This monastery has a special dispensation to practice white magic, as befits its name, and to oppose black magic. The dispensation may be only temporary, however, and the power of the magic has declined. Father Domenico knows that the Church's explanation of the problem of evil (free will and original sin) has deprived it of all trafficking with spirits, except in the limited form of exorcism. As the novels opens, he detects an "exhalation form Hell-mouth," which intensifies his sense of imminent danger and foreshadows the pending clash between supranormal good and evil.

That exhalation Father Domenico senses is actually from the human world of Positano below. A wealthy munitions industrialist, Baines, has sought out the services of the black magician, Theron Ware (purposefully named from Harold Frederic's 1896 novel *The Damnation of Theron Ware* in which the hero's damnation occurs through his growing enlightenment). Theron Ware posits the condition of theurgy — that all magic depends upon the control of demons — and specializes in violence. Baines and Ware are slated to meet on December 25 to solidify their relationship and coordinate their plans.

A distant Father Uccello (named for a saint) writes Domenico, telling him that from divination he knows that "all Hell has been waiting" for the meeting of Ware and Baines since the two of them were born, forty-eight years ago, and he wants an observer assigned to Ware. On the eve of December 25, Father Domenico, strictly conjoined not to meddle, takes his 1606 copy of the *Enchiridion* of Leo III — effectual against all perils — to Positano for personal projection, though ironically in the last conjuration Ware commands the demons not to harm his assistants, one of whom is Domenico.

Before revealing his ultimate purpose, the release of all demons from Hell for a night, Baines tests Ware's powers with two assignments. The first, a trivial matter, is the death of the governor of California. The second, which requires conjuration, is the death of Albert Stockhausen, an antimatter theorist and Nobel Prize winner whose goodness normally provides strong defense against demonic assault. The difficulty of the conjuration, the summoning of Marchosias as messenger of Lucifuge Rofocale and the demon's attempt at refusal to damn Stockhausen, stresses the evil of the deed. But Ware persists in his conjuring, forcing the demon to increase the doubts and fears in Stockhausen's mind until the man commits suicide. Thus, Ware proves himself worthy of Baines's grand scheme.

Jack Ginsberg, Baines's assistant, remains after his employer's first visit to handle final details, and admits that he is attracted to Ware's lamia Gretchen, and thus conforms to the Church's teaching that the devil may tempt man through the body. After the conjuration, Ginsberg knows that what he has seen of Ware's magic confirms Domenico's metaphysics "from Moses through the kabbalah to the New Testament." But his personal ambition extends to learning the Art, and he sells himself to Ware for a night with a succubus whom Ware, desiring ultimately to make Ginsberg his apprentice, uses to bind Ginsberg's commitment.

Baines's futurism consists not only in devising new methods of warfare, but also in formenting political and military confrontations so that, as Blish says, Baines and Ware both practice "an occult art in which the man on the street no longer believed." Not interested in mere money, Baines explains himself as a sadist who takes pleasure in the controlled production of chaos and destruction. His mistake occurs because he expects even demons to abide by his conditions, returning at a fixed hour, while he has no personal control over them.

Baines instructs his scientist Adolph Hess (obviously Adolf Hitler and Rudolph Hess combined) to observe Ware, as does Domenico — using methods of his own. Conducting Hess past the Guardian of his laboratory, Ware gives him a tour explaining all the instruments and ointments he has prepared by hand from pure materials and the standard procedures and times of sorcery. Hess recognizes Ware as dedicated, even to the point of risking eternal damnation, but not for power or money. Ware's passion is for knowledge. He explains that, like Hess, he seeks to know "about the makeup of the universe and how it is run," but he has become dissatisfied with the scientific method alone, because "the sciences don't accept that some of the forces of nature are Persons."

Father Domenico, weak and timid in confronting evil, can rely only on what the Church calls virtue: humility, obedience, and resignation. Otherwise, he has much in common with Theron Ware: both speak excellent Latin; both have training in theology (Ware is a doctor of theology); both invoke the same Lord and observe similar rituals of fasting, lustration, and prayer; both deal in magic; both accept that demons are fallen angels; and both, though Domenico's future is unknown to him, have a common destiny in the hellish afterworld. Yet Domenico remains powerless while Ware invokes powers.

After the first transmission (for Stockhausen's death), Domenico conjures a Lull engine and receives a message, as he expects, directing patience. Back at Monte Albano, he summons a convocation of the few white magicians available. After a week of discussion both they and the Celestial Powers prove ineffective in dealing with the unknown menace of Baines's purpose. Domenico, recognizing in this failure an evil omen, returns to Positano as defenseless as before.

Those gathered around the magician at Positano, by their own natures and similarities to Ware, deserve their roles in his magic. For the last conjuration, Ware retains Father Domenico in case the outcome should require Divine intervention to alleviate its evil, though he does not fear personal disaster because his pact permits him five hundred years of life. Thus both Ware and his demon Marchosias recognize the forces of good and credit them more than the Church credits the forces of evil.

Ware prepares the conjuration with Baines and Hess as operators, Ginsberg and Domenico as assistants, and he sacrifices his Gretchen. Of the eighty-nine spirits he can summon, Ware has chosen forty-eight. He now calls forth not a messenger but Lucifuge Rofocale himself and gives him the commission, to release the demons of hell to do as they will for a controlled time. As their names are called, the demons cross the circle. They are webbed, winged, and triple headed monsters of odd man-and-beast assemblage, foul of breath, some angelic, some — such as Ball, Astaroth, Belial — powerful in legendry as well as in *grimoires*. After the sending, the other three persons collapse of exhaustion, leaving Baines and Domenico to try to follow events by means of a transistor radio.

At first nothing much unusual happens, then art works burn in London, and, among other events, China declares war on Taiwan; and the United States, with the president's widow assassinated, prepares for war. Hess awakens to discuss the possibility of World War III and to theorize about human one-thousand-year cycles of retreat from knowledge, such as that which brought on the Dark Ages; and he speculates that perhaps the current affair is only hallucination. Baines remains in character, saying that he does not care for the means — collapse of intellect or advance of secularity — but only the result which in this case he himself has made. He gloats momentarily in sadistic triumph. Then Rome burns, and earthquakes reach Positano. Domenico, saying that the Covenant is satisfied and meaning that he is free to take action, wakens Ware.

Ware summons Lucifuge Rofocale but Satan himself appears as Sabbath Goat to announce Armageddon, so that Ware, contrary to expectations, is now peremptorily summoned to Hell. All laws and covenants are broken. Hess, who has developed into more of a humanist than a scientist, tries to defy Satan, but Satan swallows him whole. Father Domenico holds forth a cross which shatters in his hand. In a ruined world, as the novel closes, Satan claims these last magicians, who know now that God is dead.

The novel, examining the advance of knowledge, brings together Ware and Baines to bring a process to its close. Baines has long used knowledge (actually mere information) to create chaos with munitions and now easily makes the transfer to create chaos with demons; he serves as an example of knowledge for power. In use of demons, however, he has crossed from physics to metaphysics and therefore has lost control; his agent here is a Person, not a chemical, and is subject to unknown forces. Theron Ware, for his part, seeks knowledge for its own sake and plans to take it with him when he dies. His desire to see what will happen causes him to overlook the possibility that demons released from Hell will use their own powers to sweep him along with them rather than return to Hell at his command.

Like the other two novels in the trilogy, this novel stands as a strong indictment of the Church, in this example for its characteristic indecision and inaction. The personal attributes it fosters in Father Domenico make him a weak representative of white magic; and the message he received "Patience / Becoming / Reality" he humbly fails to read in its actual sense — that patience means inaction and that inaction against the forces of evil becomes the reality of evil. The modern Church, moreover, fails to heed its own teaching that the Devil will not be bound in Hell until the last day; its requirement of obedience suppresses individuality so that no individual takes initiative against Satan; and in its belief in One universe it stands by helplessly while Theron Ware schedules meetings with Baines deliberately for universal portent: Saturn's day for the first, December 25 for the second, and Easter for the third. The Church, consequently, indirectly encourages this "Black Magic Easter"; and, if such a Church is God's work on Earth, then God is truly dead.

Grace Eckley

Sources for Further Study

Reviews:

Amazing Stories. XLII, November, 1968, pp. 74-75 and XLIII, January, 1970, pp. 122-125.

Fantastic Universe Science Fiction. XVIII, June, 1969, pp. 142-143.

Galaxy. XXVII, January, 1969, pp. 186-189.

Magazine of Fantasy and Science Fiction. XXXV, December, 1969, pp.16-18.

New Worlds. CLXXXV, December, 1968, p. 61.

THE BLACK FLAME

Author: Stanley G. Weinbaum (1902-1935)
First book publication: 1948
Type of work: Novel
Time: Approximately three hundred years in the future and one thousand in
the future
Locale: The Ozark Mountains and St. Louis, Missouri

*Two romantic stories set in a post-disaster world where civilization is being rebuilt
by a group of immortals*

> *Principal characters:*
> HULL TARVISH, a mountain man
> THOMAS CONNOR, a man of the twentieth century
> JOAQUIN SMITH, an emperor
> MARGARET OF URBS, his sister

When Stanley Weinbaum died in 1935 he left behind a number of unpublished novels and stories. Some of these had not been written with the pulp magazines in mind, but two which had been prepared specifically for the science fiction market were the novelette *Dawn of Flame* and the short novel *The Black Flame*. The second is, in fact, a new version of the first, but so thoroughly rewritten that only the skeleton of the plot survives. *Dawn of Flame* appeared as the lead story of a privately printed collection of short stories in 1936, and both were subsequently acquired by Better Publications when they took over *Wonder Stories*. *Dawn of Flame* appeared in the new version of that magazine, *Thrilling Wonder Stories*, while *The Black Flame* was the lead novel in the first issue of its companion magazine *Startling Stories* in 1939. Despite certain internal inconsistencies, the two stories were combined as a novel for book publication.

The plot of each of the two parts of the work follows precisely the same pattern. A naïve hero wanders into a place which is in some way threatened from the all-conquering Joaquin Smith, champion of a new Enlightenment. The hero is smitten by a local girl and unthinkingly takes arms against the conqueror, excelling in the fight but allied to a hopeless cause. After the fight he encounters Smith's sister, Margaret of Urbs, the so-called Black Flame. She is a woman of extreme beauty and is, like her brother, immortal. She takes an interest in the hero and prevents his execution. His allies take advantage of this situation to trick him into betraying her trust by facilitating an assassination attempt. At the last moment he repents and saves her from her enemies. He finds her so supernaturally attractive that he falls hopelessly in love with her against his will, thus complicating his conflict of loyalties and adding to his mental agony.

The first version of the story has as its hero a man of its time, Hull Tarvish, who wanders from his mountain home to a region just about to be conquered by Smith's nascent empire. Except for its being set in a post-disaster world, the story has little overt fantastic content — which was presumably the reason for its rejection by the science fiction pulps. It is a straightforward story of powerful erotic fascination, which becomes fantasy only because the *femme fatale* is immortal.

The rewritten version, however, is deliberately dressed up with much more of the standard apparatus of pulp science fiction. The hero this time is Thomas Connor, a man electrocuted in the twentieth century and accidentally thrown into a state of catalepsy rather than death. In this version Smith's empire is already established, and its superscientific achievements are much more spectacular. Connor allies himself with a group of would-be rebels, not realizing how little chance they have against Smith's advanced weaponry. Further fantasy elements introduced into the plot are the monstrous metamorphs — mutants resulting from misapplication of the radiation treatment which has made Smith and his colleagues immortal — and energy-beings called "messengers" which act as Smith's spies and harry his enemies.

Apart from this decoration the other major difference between the two stories, presumably also motivated by the desire to comply with pulp convention, is that in the second story Weinbaum defies the logic of the situation in order to engineer a happy ending, though this in fact subverts the whole point of the romantic formula which he is using. Why this second version was rejected on first submission is not altogether clear, but it seems to have been a mistake on the part of the editors involved, since it has subsequently achieved considerable reputation as a classic piece of pulp exotica.

The literary ancestors of the Black Flame herself are, of course, H. Rider Haggard's *She* and Pierre Benoit's *Queen of Atlantis*. *She* presents one more version of the archetype of the eternal sex object, perfectly beautiful (and, for that reason, irresistible) and supernatural (and thus essentially unobtainable, though Weinbaum's second version cheats on this point). The fantasy of the innocent protagonist who is first tricked by circumstance into making the Black Flame his enemy, and is subsequently tricked more literally into being party to an attempt to kill her, is basically a masochistic one. Both these events serve on the one hand to put him into an invidious emotional situation, incapable of accepting the erotic fascination which he is equally incapable of resisting, and on the other hand to place his fate completely at the mercy of the woman's whim.

The ostensible anguish of this situation is made pleasurable by its blatant erotic quality, all the more so because of the predatory attraction which the Black Flame begins to feel in each case for her victim. In the most extreme variants of this formula — such as Vernon Lee's *"Armour Dure"* — the sadomasochistic aspects of the situation are exploited to the full, but Weinbaum, like Haggard and Benoit, relents slightly even in the first version with a switch of viewpoint in the conclusion which offers a sentimental commentary on the sad situation of the immortal woman who must watch the objects of her affection decay and die one after another. This change of viewpoint is commonly used to balance out the pain of the hero who is enraptured without the possibility of fulfillment, and it works well enough in *Dawn of Flame*. In *The Black Flame*, however, the solution seems entirely artificial and ill-fitting (though it is not the first time such subversion was carried out in the cause of pulp fiction's fetish for happy endings: some years earlier the editor of *Argosy* had overturned the ending of Abraham Merritt's similar exotic romance *The Dwellers in the Mirage*.)

As a contribution to the growing mythology of science fiction, the novel is notable primarily because the second story is one of the first to make use of the kind of post-holocaust scenario which later became stereotyped as an image of the neobarbaric age following an atomic war. (This is one of the points of inconsistency — in *Dawn of Flame* the disaster was a bacteriological war in which the world was depopulated by the Grey Death.) Apart from this echo of things to come, the science fictional concepts introduced into *The Black Flame* in order to make it more palatable to the science fiction pulp editors are nothing more than embroidery. The metamorphs are quite superfluous, and though the messengers play an active part in the plot at one point, their presence is really at odds with the nature of the work. All in all, the attempt to adapt this particular classical fantasy to a genre still dominated by the Gernsbackian manifesto had little chance of success. Weinbaum at his best was an extremely capable writer, but his main advantage as a pulp writer was the fact that he could build alien environments and extraterrestrial life forms that were more complex and more bizarre than those of his contemporaries. His actual talents as a writer, and his ability to develop ideas in a thoughtful and careful manner — which are amply displayed in the brilliant and innovative superman story *The New Adam* — were really of no use to him insofar as his pulp writing was concerned. Thus *Dawn of Flame* failed to sell, and *The Black Flame* became a rather awkward hybrid both thematically and stylistically. The work as a whole is of some historical interest, particularly with regard to Weinbaum's boldness in infusing strongly erotic overtones in a 1930's work, but as a novel it bears no comparison to *The New Adam*, and as an exotic romance it is but a pale shadow of its forebears.

Brian Stableford

Sources for Further Study

Reviews:

Fantastic Novels Magazine. II, January, 1949, p. 114.

Fantasy Book. I, Summer, 1948, p. 38.

Luna Monthly. IX, Fall, 1970, p. 27.

Super Science Stories. V, July, 1949, p. 96.

Vision of Tomorrow. I, February, 1970, p. 19.

BRAIN WAVE

Author: Poul Anderson (1926-   )
First book publication: 1954
Type of work: Novel
Time: The late 1950's
Locale: Mainly the United States

The events and the aftermath of an enormous increase in the intelligence of every sentient being on earth, causing the breakdown of our familiar civilization, and the establishment of a new society with aims and ideals incomprehensible to the relatively few remaining normals

> *Principal characters:*
> ARCHIE BROCK, a half-witted farmhand
> PETER CORINTH, a physicist at the Rossman Research Institute
> SHEILA CORINTH, his wife
> FELIX MANDELBAUM, a labor union official
> HELGA ARNULFSEN, chief administrative assistant at the Institute

Poul Anderson's name regularly appears on the lists of "Bests" in science fiction. After graduating from the University of Minnesota in 1948 with honors in physics he began writing science fiction characterized by its solid crafts-manship and wide popularity. While experimentally inclined writers such as Samuel R. Delany or Philip K. Dick receive more critical attention, Anderson has earned equal respect from his colleagues, as testified by his reception of several Nebula Awards, voted by the Science Fiction Writers Association. Yet his appeal to the mass market has been even greater, as shown by the fact that his Hugo Awards, voted at annual world conventions of fans, outnumber his Nebula Awards by more than two-to-one.

Although Anderson has written fantasy from time to time, his chief output has been science fiction, often as hard as anything from Larry Niven or Hal Clement. His chief virtues are attention to scientific detail and careful extrapo-lation of hypothetical changes, virtues that fit in well with John W. Campbell's views of science fiction, and ones that made Anderson a frequent contributor to Campbell's magazines. As a physics major, Anderson's initiation into sci-ence was thorough, but the application of that science to fiction, and the acqui-sition of literary techniques were skills which he had to acquire by practice. *Brain Wave*, an early novel, shows both the strengths that would make him one of the leading authors in the field as well as some weaknesses that he had not completely overcome at that time.

Obsolescence is not one of those weaknesses: *Brain Wave* has aged rather well despite the fact that, as a novel set in "the present," it has been subject to the events of twenty-five hectic years since it appeared. There are details that remind us of its publication date, of course. At one point, the Soviet Union launches a preemptive strike at the United States, and the omniscient third-person narrator feels the need to tell us that the Russians had rushed through the development of ballistic missiles with nuclear warheads, an accomplishment that had not yet occurred in 1954. Similarly, a manned landing on the moon was an event in the future at the beginning of the novel. Despite these minor things, however, *Brain Wave* presents few distractions resulting from the passage of time.

In brief, the theme of the novel is that of H.G. Wells's *Men Like Gods*: the appearance of the *Übermensch*. But the supermen of Anderson's work do not result from an eons-old evolutionary process; their changes happen to almost everyone and, comparatively speaking, occur overnight.

Anderson hypothesizes that a force-field emanating from the center of our galaxy extends through space, but only in certain directions. This field has the effect of slowing down electromagnetic and electrochemical processes. For ages past, at least since the evolution of the human species, the whole solar system has been moving through the inhibiting field, but the boundary of the field is sharply marked. In a matter of days, the solar system, in its movement about the galactic center, leaves the field. As a result, various kinds of electrical phenomena thought to have been universal constants are slightly changed. In most cases these slightly faster processes are minor nuisances in instrumentation, but in the case of certain delicate and sensitive reactions, the change is enormous. Among these latter is the speed of the propagation of impulses in the nervous system.

Faster nervous impulses, the novel postulates, mean faster thought, and faster thought means higher intelligence. The effect on human brains is immediately noticed: Archie Brock, a half-witted farmhand, finds himself thinking more, and his thoughts are profound and philosophical. A small boy starts playing with some elementary algebra one morning and reinvents differential calculus. Some scientists at a private research institute notice small but annoying changes in their computer, and within a few days they work out a theory to account for the changes in the machinery and themselves. The increase in intelligence is cumulative and permanent. Within weeks, normal people have become so much brighter that the concept of "IQ" is meaningless for lack of adequate ways to measure it.

The change is not entirely a blessing at first. Almost immediately, civilization begins to break down as we discover that intelligence is not the factor that holds society together. Many people are unable to cope with their increased powers of observation and understanding, and become unstable. Their perceptions have increased, their comprehension is greater, but they are unguided. Neither have emotions decreased in power, nor has morality increased; those who were credulous or unscrupulous before remain that way, and charlatans everywhere take advantage of the situation. Education becomes more, not less, important just when society is least able to provide it for want of supporting services. Thousands of people formerly holding monotonous or repetitive jobs now feel an intense boredom and abandon their unfulfilling work. The machinery of society, especially in large cities, slows down and appears to be approaching collapse. Government on the larger levels proves increasingly unable to enforce its decisions, and what effective government exists begins to be carried out by local, even volunteer, groups.

Anderson's characteristic strengths are evident in this early work: he explains the universally increased mental efficiency as faster transmission of impulses in the nerves, but he does not leave it at that. Aware that heartbeat, respiration, and other bodily functions depend on stimuli from the brain, he has one character offhandedly explain why it is that these functions have not speeded up as the activity of thought has. Whether his explanation is convincing is not the point. Rather, his skill is shown by his having thought of it at all, and by his taking pains to furnish a plausible reason why his characters think faster although their hearts beat at the same rate.

Throughout the novel, single events, single episodes and single ideas are convincingly handled, showing that by 1954 Anderson was already a master of shorter forms, especially in his short stories. But the parts do not quite hang together; the author had trouble with the greater length of the novel.

Part of the problem is the lack of any real challenge or threat throughout the novel. In the first part, conflict springs from the premise itself, and the main question is whether mankind will be able to adapt to its sudden flowering. Yet some of the "problems" seem either like actual blessings — is anyone saddened at seeing national governments lose their grip on their batteries of horrors? — or ephemeral — if New York City can suffer through a pileup of garbage because of a wage dispute, it can suffer through the same thing because everyone has become a genius. Several rather faceless demagogues threaten the smooth functioning of the emerging balance, but their menace never extends for more than a few pages. By the middle of the book, order has been generally restored under much more humane and tolerant conditions than those they replaced, and one can almost sense Anderson looking around for new villains. In a last struggle to stay in power, the Soviet government launches missiles at the United States, but the danger is forestalled in the same chapter in which it arose. Toward the end, a reactionary group plans to return mankind to its former level of thought by artificially creating an inhibiting field, but despite the plotters' new intelligence, they are frustrated with surprising ease, and this last threat to the new order arouses no more suspense than the earlier ones.

A second weakness is the way Anderson has chosen to present his material through interwoven subplots. To show the global impact of the change, we see characters in various settings coping with their new capabilities. But after their introduction and their placement in some very interesting situations, many of them are never seen again. Thus, the boy who invents differential calculus is never heard of after his first appearance; a group of Russians in revolt against the central government never reappears after their first skirmish; a wanderer who visits a remote Chinese village likewise vanishes after we meet him. These scenes all have their purposes — Anderson was too skilled even in 1954 to leave parts disconnected from the plot. Some new breakthrough in human powers is introduced by each of these "asides." The great leap in intelligence first appears convincingly in the small boy's scene; the control of telepathy is demonstrated in the Russian scene; and the absolute mental control of bodily reactions to heat, cold, hunger, and the like first appears in the Chinese scene. But there is a twofold flaw in this method. First, the function of these scenes appears only in retrospect. On first reading it is not clear which sets of characters appear only for illustrative purposes and which are there because they figure heavily in the plot. And second, the very fact that new and intriguing powers appear in some scenes makes the characters in those scenes more interesting than the central ones. Yet these interesting characters vanish; their problems are never solved, and the reader's curiosity about them is frustrated.

It will be noticed that almost all of these problems concern plotting a story over the length of a novel. Even the subplots sometimes seem mechanical and contrived. Near the beginning, for example, we are introduced to a triangular love relationship when Peter Corinth deeply loves his wife Sheila, although Helga Arnulfsen, a co-worker at the Institute, is clearly better suited for him, and has had a longstanding affection for him. Peter and Helga adapt well to changes in their relationship, but Sheila, unable to adjust, appears close to mental collapse. The necessity of painlessly disposing of Sheila compels Anderson to include an otherwise pointless digression late in the novel.

One last difficulty springs from the theme of the story itself. In science fiction, as in other branches of art, the theme of genius is notoriously difficult to handle well. It has been attempted many times, but it usually fails. The heart of the problem is this: how can a normal writer depict a supernormal character? There is no trick at all in creating a hero able to move faster than a speeding bullet or leap tall buildings at a single bound, but how does one show the thoughts of super-intelligence? Anderson's *Brain Wave* has not failed completely in handling this difficult problem, but it does falter.

One place where vast intelligence should show up is in the speech of the characters. Being universal geniuses, most of them are able to infer the most complex statements of others from a shrug or a grunt. The ability leads to pages of "conversation" wherein the characters mutter monosyllables and the author parenthetically expands the inferences others take from those hints. The system is visually distracting and a little disappointing, because the information that is transferred by this process is not of a noticeably higher quality than we are used to in our everyday lives. The cardinal rule of the superman story is, stay out of the superman's mind.

But *Brain Wave* is in some respects a very fine novel, especially when Anderson observes this rule. In dealing with subhumans rather than superhumans, the author has a simpler job: while it is hard always to know the smart thing to do, the stupid thing comes easy. Because *Brain Wave*'s change has affected all sentient beings on earth, the lower animals have similarly increased their powers. Rabbits reason their way out of traps, pigs escape from pens, horses have to be cajoled into working, and, while the anatomy of dogs prevents them from articulating the speech they understand, chimpanzees have overcome even that limitation and have a language of sorts. The animals we see cluster on or about the farm where Archie Brock works. His fellow workers have become intelligent beyond his comprehension, and they soon leave. But he remains, resigned to a hermit's life, almost contented with the company of the superanimals. The transformation of the beasts is well handled.

Archie himself is the most effective and appealing character in the novel, because Anderson has avoided trying to show genius in his character. As an effect of the change, the former butt of his fellow's jokes finds himself raised to what used to be a normal level of mental ability. He becomes the only character in the novel with whom the reader can identify, the only one the reader can understand. His view of the new order would be our view, if we were to meet people with IQ's of 500 or so. When Archie deals with the supermen, his limited understanding of their objectives and motivations would be our understanding as well. He occupies a good deal of the novel's space, and is responsible for much of the effectiveness of the novel as a whole. Had the story been told entirely from his point of view, the distractions of the clanking plots and the annoying shifts from one set of characters to another could have been eliminated, and *Brain Wave* might have been as unified and powerful as Anderson's later novels.

Walter E. Meyers

Sources for Further Study

Reviews:

Analog. LV, March, 1955, p. 154.

Authentic Science Fiction. LXVI, February, 1956, p. 153.

Galaxy. VIII, September, 1954, pp. 114-115.

Kirkus Reviews. XXII, May 1, 1954, p. 296.

Library Journal. LXXIX, June 1, 1954, p. 1050.

Magazine of Fantasy and Science Fiction. VII, September, 1954, p. 92.

BRAVE NEW WORLD

Author: Aldous Huxley (1894-1963)
First book publication: 1932
Type of work: Novel
Time: The twenty-sixth century, After Ford 632
Locale: England and a Zuni reservation in New Mexico

In a society founded on the denial of individual rights to anything, sexual partners included, a would-be dissident discovers and brings back a genuine dissident, an Outsider reared on the works of Shakespeare, who exposes more fully the nature of freedom and happiness

> *Principal characters:*
> BERNARD MARX, an Alpha-Plus psychologist and would-be dissident
> LENINA CROWNE, a pneumatic nurse from the Central London Hatchery
> HELMHOLTZ WATSON, a lecturer in Emotional Engineering
> MUSTAPHA MOND, World Controller
> THE SAVAGE, son of the Director of Hatcheries, reared by accident on the New Mexico reservation
> LINDA, the Savage's mother

Brave New World was the product of a deeply divided society. As has often been remarked, the English upper class, to which Aldous Huxley belonged, was more surprised by World War I (or the "Great War" as they called it) than most other social groups even in those countries, like Russia or Germany, which were effectively destroyed by it. Its members, the rulers of the most populous empire the world had ever known, had been educated in the imperial virtues of conscientiousness, piety, and courage. They volunteered accordingly for war-service in large numbers — Huxley's near-blindness kept him back — only to find, in the often-chronicled slaughters of Flanders, that in some circumstances the braver and more dutiful you were, the more likely you were to be shot, unnecessarily and unprofitably shot. A sense of betrayal became common, even normal, in the war-service generation. Virtue and piety had not paid off as they were supposed to. Several World War I poets responded by independently subdividing the Trinity. God the Son remained as He had always been, the Sufferer, the Crucified; but God the Father was reimaged as the staff officer, the Field Marshal, the old man who sent his sons forward to be martyred while remaining in safety himself. After the War was over it seemed for a while that no social virtue could be praised any more without an overpowering sense of irony. The Oxford Union Debating Society asserted in 1933 "That this House refuses in any circumstances to fight for King and Country."

Brave New World is, in a way, a document from this "literature of protests." It contains a very strong element of taunt and jibe, which we now recognize only dimly. Thus the staid Athenaeum Club (which naturally did not admit women as members) is written into the story as the "Aphroditaeum," a palace for fornication. The Archbishop of Canterbury is guyed as the Arch-

Community-Songster of Canterbury, a creature with no religious function and a sportive tendency to pull young ladies' zippers. As for Lenina Crowne, the story's "heroine," she is not only by conviction promiscuous, but is also presented as the very epitome of the "healthy and virtuous English girl." "Healthy" and "English" are the key words. It was long a belief of English schoolmasters that sexuality was not only vicious but also less *fun* (for members of the superior race) than organized games. To depict Lenina not only as being promiscuous, but also plain, uncomplicated, and "healthy," was as designedly insolent as giving Eton College (another all-male institution) a Head Mistress.

To Huxley's credit, though, the taunting does not confine itself to his own class and culture. Another apparent element in the brew of *Brave New World* is its satire on Communism. In a sense the world of the book *is* a Communist one. The state owns the means of production; it takes from each according to his abilities and gives to each according to his needs. Not only everything but everybody belongs to everybody else. Characters bear the names of Engels and Bakunin, while the little girl whose erotic play interrupts the Director of Hatcheries is called Polly Trotsky. The "hero," of course, is Bernard Marx. What could be more suggestive of Communist Utopia? On the other hand, the State of the twenty-sixth century hardly seems, in some obvious respects, to have changed from Huxleyan England. People are still rigorously graded, and graded (as is not often noticed) according to the marking-scale of Oxford University, from Alpha down to Epsilon. It is not uncommon even now to hear an unpromising undergraduate at Oxford written off as "born Beta-Minus," while Huxley himself, with a First-Class degree, could claim to be a recognized Alpha. How could this be reconciled with Communism? The joke comes to a point when we see the children learning their "Elementary Class Consciousness." For "class consciousness" is a term invented and for a long time used solely by the Communist movement, and to them what it meant was "becoming aware of social injustice in order to overthrow the class-system." But in the "Brave New World" of Huxley's imagination Class Consciousness means learning your place, accepting your destiny as Alpha or Epsilon. The phrase marks another piety reviled.

Nor does America escape. Another strand of the name-system in the book is that of major capitalists or inventors — Ford, Edsel, Diesel, Hoover — while for all its state-control Huxley's world is based on "consumerism," with all the traditional faults of vulgarity, brashness, insensibility. Lenina Crowne goggling at the Indians on the New Mexico reservation only needs a camera to become a very familiar modern parody of the tourist. Pervading the book's early scene-setting chapters, furthermore, is a strong element of blasphemy. We glimpse a character called Calvin, officials called Predestinators; the Cross, the sign of salvation, has been replaced by the T, or T-model, or sign of mass-production, while "Ford" has taken over from "the Lord" and indeed from "God" (pronounced, in Huxley's distinctive upper-class accent, "Gord").

One could say, then, that *Brave New World* is merely naughty and merely negative; and even if the adverb "merely" is rejected, it is *certainly* both naughty and negative, not to mention funny. Many commentators have been much too grave about it. However, when it comes to "negativeness," a more serious issue is raised, which one might call the problem of the relativity of conviction. This is institutionalized in Huxley's imagined society, which rests on four main scientific facts or advances: first, the Bokanovsky process, a kind of proto-"cloning" which ensures that the world is largely populated by identical siblings; second, extra-uteral development of the fetus, which means that children are born or "decanted" already fitted for their niche in society; third, Pavlovian conditioning and hypnopaedia, which reinforce the lessons of the fetus on the child; and finally the ubiquitous *soma*, a tranquilizing drug which makes quite certain that any dissent among the masses is opiated before it can be expressed. The result is that everybody is happy, but that their convictions of happiness, beauty, worth, have no value. "I'm glad I'm not a Gamma," says Lenina. But if she were a Gamma, we can be sure she would be just as glad she were not an Alpha. What value can such opinions have?

The underlying point is that not only fictional characters like Lenina hold opinions like that. Everyone in reality has a brainful of them as well. "Each one of us . . . goes through life inside a bottle," remarks Mustapha Mond, World Controller and most intelligent person in the novel, and the thought is felt to be universally true. In Huxley's time this was still a relatively modern discovery, and clues to the real-life nature of it are scattered through the book. Mustapha Mond, explaining why promiscuity is compulsory in his society, refers back to the family system of the old Western world, and contrasts it with the happy carelessness of the inhabitants of Samoa and New Guinea. This must be a reference to the highly influential works of Margaret Mead, *Coming of Age in Samoa* (1928) and *Growing Up in New Guinea* (1930). The point they had made, with great force, was that many of the habits that Europeans and Americans considered to be natural (like the traumas of adolescence) were actually culturally-derived. If you changed the social habits you changed the people. Human nature was, therefore, only a relative concept, not a universal. The positive corollary of all this was that you could *make* people happier. The negative one was that if they were happy already no one had any right to criticize them, no matter what they did. We nowadays are probably not much bothered by the spectacle of promiscuity, and would accept it if that is what people want to do, no fundamental law is being broken. However, after the various spectacles of totalitarian governments from Huxley's time to now, we are correspondingly more likely to be sensitive over the imagined world's denial to all its members of "freedom." Still, what person has ever been free of some kind of social conditioning, some kind of "bottle," as Mustapha Mond puts it? Even the concept of freedom itself is something we have been taught, something relative to our culture; and if the inhabitants of another world are happy without it, what right have we to criticize them, any more than we have to reprove their sexual morals (as the Victorian missionaries had done with the natives of Samoa)?

The trap is one from which it is logically impossible to escape. One could say, though, that the story of *Brave New World* consists of a series of attempts to breakout, to show a member of a stable culture arriving at a logical, or objective, or plausible rejection of it. In this, of course, *Brave New World* becomes the forerunner of a whole subgenre of later science fiction novels, such as Damon Knight's *Analogue Men*, Frederik Pohl and Cyril M. Kornbluth's *The Space Merchants*, or Algis Budrys' *The Iron Thorn* (1967). These three, however, all find some form of withdrawal from the question which Huxley continues to pose.

The first and weakest of *Brave New World*'s breakout characters is Bernard Marx. He is actually very close to a caricature of the standard British, between-wars, upper-class intellectual. His virtues are intelligence and a kind of sensitivity — he would like to take long walks on the mountains; he enjoys the spectacle of seas and deserts and finds in them something transcendental; in a heavily-loaded scene of youthful triumph he turns the tables on authority in the person of the Director of Hatcheries by exposing him as a father and introducing him to his abandoned and mistreated son. The thing which he cannot bear about his society is its denial of individual values, of those special relationships between one friend and another which his kind made into a fetish in the 1920's and 1930's (consider E. M. Forster's elliptic maxim, "Only connect . . ."). However, Bernard's vices are as apparent as his virtues. There is a strong element of mere jealousy and resentment in his alienation, for he is not as physically imposing as members of his caste ought to be ("alcohol in his blood-surrogate," they murmur), and like intellectuals traditionally he is useless in a crisis. He cracks as soon as Mustapha Mond threatens him with exile; we see that his detachment from and criticism of society are merely a fashionable pose, an early case of "radical chic." The world he lives in suffers no lasting damage from his demonstrably subjective critique.

More serious is the case of Helmholtz Watson, Bernard's friend, a lecturer at the College of Emotional Engineering (Department of Writing), or as we might say, a poet. He is by no means an alienated character, but a born mixer, a sports champion, and an indefatigable lover. If he, then, finds something wrong with his society, the opinion commands more respect. And his complaint is that it fosters no great art and is inescapably uncreative. Mustapha Mond replies, in the novel's most extended chapter of discussion, by asserting that art and unhappiness are connected with each other. Great writers often work as a kind of therapy; the substance of their work is tragedy and frustration; what they teach is endurance. But why accept their kind of anaesthetic when better ones are at hand, when people, as has been said, can be *made* happier? By the logic of emotional utilitarianism Watson is only trying to purchase a great good for a small number at the expense of the comfort of the masses. Who made more people happier, Ford or Shakespeare? Watson's case, too, is answered.

Now "the Savage" must receive consideration since he is one of the most familiar archetypes of fiction, the Outsider, the "wolf-child" whose remarks on society carry special weight because they are free of conditioning. In the Savage's case, one might even say, his bias is *towards* the society he eventually criticizes. Brought up on a Zuni reservation in New Mexico, he has never been accepted by the Indians and has always longed to return to the world of his true father (the Director of Hatcheries). He is an analogue of Miranda in Shakespeare's *The Tempest*, and the novel's title is drawn from her remark when she first sees young and handsome people, as opposed to her aged, authoritarian father and the subhuman Caliban: "O brave new world, that has such people in it." But this remark is repeated with increasing disgust by the Savage as he sees scores of Bokanovskified siblings and ugly identical Delta faces. He turns from being Miranda to being Romeo, Hamlet, finally Othello the Moor (another outsider nauseated by the world he had aspired to join).

Of course the Savage is mad. He has been brought up on one book alone, the *Works* of William Shakespeare, and he judges everything by its standards. Shakespeare, though, is in English culture something of a "holy" author, a touchstone of all the values incarnated more feebly by Bernard Marx or Helmholtz Watson — poetry, individualism, love. It could be said, then, that in the Savage, Huxley is only bringing on a new and stronger version of his own cultural imperatives, disguised as an unbiased Outsider, and indeed this would be true. Huxley could not — perhaps no one ever can — keep his thumb out of the balance. When we hear Bernard Marx opposing "infantile" promiscuity to mature or "adult" delay, we may realize that the adjectives are not capable of proof; but when we hear the Savage declaiming great poetry to unreceptive ears, we are more likely to think that the ethics of the "brave new world" are being revealed as bad. Mustapha Mond would have an answer to it. But he is not normally present. An air of disgust at his own creation then begins to emanate from Huxley's contrivings as the book goes on, though the disgust paradoxically arises from the feeling that there are *some* things (like Shakespeare) which ought in all circumstances to be saved. Huxley always laughs at the idea of instinct, one might note; he thought it had been disproved by social anthropology. But he leaves the word "conscience" unmolested. One may doubt whether this is entirely logical of him.

There is a logic, though, in the book's last scene — not in the fact that the Savage, tormented by sightseers, kills himself like his exemplar Othello, but in the fact that he hangs himself because he has finally yielded to the temptations of Lenina Crowne and the hedonist society she represents, and copulated with her instead of continuing his program of purity, asceticism, and insight. The point is made that the urge to "happiness," the ultimate value of the world controlled by Mustapha Mond, is inside all of us. There may be some other good to aspire to (God, or creativity, or even scientific adventure), but pursuing any of those, as the Savage tries to, involves doing something both unnatural and problematical. The "brave new world" may then, for all its vulgarities and for all the satire Huxley has heaped on it, be in reality the best type available. The onus of proof falls on those who believe otherwise. It is their duty to make a case for liberty, or democracy, or Communism, or whatever it may be, and to defend their concepts from the charge of being one more subjectivity, one more fetus within the "bottle" of social conditioning.

T. A. Shippey

Sources for Further Study

Criticism:

Clareson, Thomas D. "The Classics: Aldous Huxley's *Brave New World*," in *Extrapolation*. XI (1961), pp. 33-40. Clareson's concise explication of *Brave New World* provides an excellent introduction to Huxley's themes.

Grushow, Ira. "*Brave New World* and *The Tempest*," in *College English*. XXIV, 1962, pp. 42-45. Grushow describes Shakespearean influence on the creation of *Brave New World*.

Hoffman, Charles G. "The Changes in Huxley's approach to the Novel of Ideas," in *Personalist*. XLII (Winter, 1961), pp. 85-90. This criticism deals primarily with the technical side of *Brave New World* through a discussion of the Evaluation of Huxley as an artist.

Howe, Irving. "The Fiction of Anti-Utopia," in *New Mexican Quarterly*. CXLVI (April 23, 1962), pp. 13-16. Howe views *Brave New World* as a satire of the "utopia novel."

Jones, William M. "The Saga of *Brave New World*," in *Western Humanities Review*. XI (1961), pp. 275-278. Jones takes a Shakespearean look at the characterization of *Brave New World*.

Reviews:

Christian Century. XLIX, November 30, 1932, p. 1474.

Forum. LXXXVII, May, 1932, p. v.

Nation. CXXXIV, February 17, 1932, p. 204.

New Republic. LXIX, February 10, 1932, p. 354.

Saturday Review. CLIII, February 6, 1932, p. 152.
Yale Review. XXI, Spring, 1932, p. x.

BRIEFING FOR A DESCENT INTO HELL

Author: Doris Lessing (1919-   )
First book publication: 1971
Type of work: Novel
Time: The present
Locale: A London hospital and the world of the unconscious

Science fiction, mythology, and various biographies constitute an alternate vision of reality from the perspective of a "madman," whom modern medicine, for good or for ill, manages to cure

> *Principal characters:*
> CHARLES WATKINS, a professor of Classics at Cambridge
> FELICITY, his wife
> CONSTANCE MAYNE, his former mistress
> ROSEMARY BAINES, an admirer
> DR. X, a tough-minded psychiatrist
> DR. Y, an empathetic psychiatrist

Best known for her largely naturalistic stories of life in Rhodesia and England, including *The Golden Notebook* (1962) and the five-volume series about Martha Quest, *Children of Violence* (1952-1969), Doris Lessing is one of those serious writers of fiction whose later work impinges more and more on certain kinds of science fiction, as she tries to define the blurring boundaries of reality. One section of *The Golden Notebook* describes the world from the point of view of a woman driven to the brink of madness by the insanity of daily life. The last volume of *Children of Violence*, *The Four-Gated City*, takes place in that novel's future, when the city has stopped being a viable place in which to live and apocalypse threatens. More recently, *The Memoirs of a Survivor* (1975), without a modicum of scientific speculation or rationalization, presents a city similarly deserted, and provides a secret passage through a wall into a saner reality for the protagonist. In at least one short story, too, "Report on the Threatened City," Lessing uses such science fiction devices as alien visitors trying to warn mankind of danger (in this case earthquakes in San Francisco) and the spiriting away of representatives of the human population.

Similarly, *Briefing for a Descent into Hell* might better be called "structural fabulation," to use a term coined by Professor Robert Scholes in his book of the same name. Lessing herself gives it a different label; a preliminary page carries the motto, under the rubric INNER-SPACE FICTION, *For there is never anywhere to go but in.*

Not all stories of madness, or of mythological dream-visions, can be called science fiction, although the landscapes of alien planets are themselves reflections of inner visions, as the stories of J. G. Ballard so eloquently demonstrate. This one is especially relevant, however, because the vision of Charles Watkins, the inner reality he tries so hard to create, or to "remember," as he puts it, is an archetypal world view in which the archetypes often make their appearance in guises appropriated from science fiction, and from reveries of the lunatic fringe for whom UFO's, ancient astronauts, Bermuda Triangles, astrology, and myths are real, not simply grist for science fiction's mill.

On a naturalistic level, this may be seen as a story of a middle-aged identity crisis or male menopause, such as turns many people toward religion, in order to seek out the divine purpose of one's immortal soul. In the case of Charles Watkins, his bent is determinedly secular and this-worldly, as his brilliant career and his effect on women attest. But immediately prior to the novel's present, that security has begun to break down; he has begun to look somewhat differently at the accepted teachings of history, archaeology, art, and myth that he has professionally espoused. In the hospital, where the novel opens, he has managed to construct out of mythology, science fiction, and alternative versions of his own biography, an elaborate fantasy world in which his crisis may be resolved.

Suffering from amnesia and rambling incoherently, he has been brought from the banks of the Thames, where he was found without money or identification, to a hospital where two doctors, who, while disagreeing about methods, are united in their attempt to bring him back to this world of appearances that he has mentally deserted. Dr. X is authoritarian, direct, and efficient, while Dr. Y is more cautious, understanding, and humane. The therapies that they agree on, however, seem to heighten Watkins' delusions; the drugs drive him deeper into a "sleep" which the patient, however, disowning his mundane identity, regards as his waking reality.

Discontinuing the drugs, the doctors bring him back to a certain extent, although he fails to recognize his wife or the letters from friends and acquaintances that ostensibly delineate his preamnesiac identity. When he writes whatever comes into his head, it comes out in a narrative of fighting alongside partisans in Yugoslavia, although, according to wartime acquaintances, he had never served there. While he toys with the idea of setting up housekeeping with a childish fellow patient, Violet Stokes, he finally agrees to electric shock therapy. This treatment apparently restores him to normal, jarring completely out of his head the memories that comprise his alternate reality.

The main outline of the story must be inferred from shards of conversations, contents of letters, brief doctors' reports, all typographically set off from the narrative norm (except the episode with Violet, which is rendered in conventional third person terms). The core of the story, however, comes to us more or less directly from the interior of the mind of the person called Charles Watkins, in a prose narrative interspersed with poems by Gotthold Lessing and fragments from Eliot, Wordsworth, and Shakespeare. The first half of the book is the most fantastic and fascinating, as this anonymous patient — an incoherent lump to the uncomprehending medical staff — sails round and round the seas of his imagination, identifying himself with all the ancient mariners (Jason, Jonah, and Odysseus), and proceeds through a series of allegorico-mythical exploits.

The object of Watkins' quest is reunion with his shipmates, some of whom share names with English kings while others seem to be friends and acquaintances from his past life (real and imaginary). The shipmates, including one named Charles, have been snatched away from him by a kind of flying saucer, "the Crystal," which radiates all manner of well being. Thwarted at first, when his raft makes land, by seemingly unscalable heights, he scrambles to the top of the cliff to find the stone ruins of an ancient city whose central plaza he knows is a landing zone for the Crystal. Waiting for its return, he debases himself by eating meat proffered by three wild women, implicitly identified with witches; with the Fates; and with his wife Felicity, his mistress Constance, and Vera, the best friend of the Yugoslavian, Konstantina, whom he remembers loving in his imaginary biography. From the Inferno of the maelstrom, he has reached the Purgatory of the mesa (itself suggestive of Stonehenge and the Peruvian ruins von Däniken makes so much of), which he must endure after submission to his carnivorous bloodlust keeps him from the Crystal. Awaiting the next full moon, he is terrified by two animal "tribes," one of apes, the other of dog-rats (reminiscent of H. P. Lovecraft), whose attempts to be human lead them to stand upright, to copulate almost perpetually, and to make war, eating their slain enemies.

Having lived, perhaps, through the fall of man and the war torn birth of civilization, this adventurer is saved from despair by a huge, mysterious white bird, which gives him a foretaste of glory by taking him for a flight on its back. Protecting him from the beasts as he works to cleanse the central square, it seems to signify his atonement for having sinned, allowing him to unite with the Crystal on its next landing. Whirled high above the Earth, to a vantage point from which he can take in the entire solar system, he is given a sense of wholeness, of oneness with mankind, the "group mind" that seems to comprise the constituent living parts of this "spaceship."

Lessing's handling of his paradisal vision is in some ways the weakest thing about the book; it is awkwardly fragmented, often in stilted prose. In the first part, the *persona* of the madman has a momentary lapse, and he delivers a self-conscious, moralizing sermon on the subject of community, contrasting the agony of "I" with the glory of "We." A disquisition on the gods of mythology gives way to conversations among the gods, in a mock Homeric account of the concern of the other planets for the welfare of Earth. The conference of the gods then changes to a quasimilitary briefing by Merk Ury and Minna Erve, who show the assembled "delegates" a filmed forecast of cosmic catastrophe and human mutation. As in Plato's "Myth of Er" in the last book of the *Republic*, these souls cannot really be "briefed" at all for their descent to Earth (Hell), because they will have forgotten everything by the time they are born into human consciousness. With one of them (presumably Watkins), we then experience the birth process; and this is followed by a continuous series of voices stressing the need for baby and adult to "be a good boy," to sleep, and to die, never becoming fully awake and aware.

The message of unity with the godlike presence of the Sun, of the "harmony of the spheres," with which the literature of myth and mysticism is rife, seems to be what the amnesiac Watkins, finally coming more and more into what we call the waking state, is trying so desperately to remember. Madness and drugs have helped him recapture a part of it, in imagery blending the terminology of science fiction and modern cults with that of the classical world with which his former professorial self was so familiar. Now, of course, the "real" world begins more and more to impinge upon his consciousness, as the doctors cut off the drugs and try to reconcile him with the self whose biography they have begun piecing together. That *persona*, we find, is not a simple matter, since the successful middle aged professor had been very irascible, scandalizing his colleagues, disturbing his wife and mistress, and lately speaking what seemed inspired nonsense. That nonsense had attracted Rosemary Baines, more or less as a cultist, who shared his conviction that we are born to do so much more than we achieve, and whose company he had sought the night before he was found, with no identity, on the banks of the Thames.

This is a difficult book, not only in its "message," but also in its form. The shifting formats of expression require the reader to juggle numerous points of view, sometimes simultaneously. Familiarity with Greek, Egyptian, even Babylonian mythology, as well as the corpus of the world's adventure stories and the beliefs of mystics and contemporary cultists, might help. But the quasi-Jungian manner of the recounting of the spiritual adventures of the entity called Charles Watkins may evoke resonances in the reader relatively innocent of such background. The imagery of spinning ("round and round and round and round"), of the sea (including epigrams from *The Secret Garden* of the fourteenth century and *The Edge of the Sea* by Rachel Carson, juxtaposing East and West, mysticism and science), of the great white bird (with or without specific Coleridgean allusions), of the apes, the women, the dog-rat people, the ruined city and the Crystal (which has been called a spaceship though it more closely resembles a flying saucer, on a more spiritual than physical plane) vividly imprint themselves on the reader's consciousness.

The doctors ultimately succeed, of course, through electric shock therapy, in restoring the memories *they* want him to have, and at the end of the book Charles Watkins is "himself" again, with none of the adventuresome *personae* of his other self or selves left, except possibly a concern for the deadening effect on children and the adults that they become of what we call education. The effect is calculatedly deflating, since the madman's elevated vision is in some ways so much saner than that of the so-called healthy individuals in the sick society around him. From being so vitally alive, in the life or lives of his imagination, Charles Watkins, once he is certified sane, is relatively flat. The "cure" is successful, but the patient "dies."

The vision of wholeness that Lessing seeks to present in this novel is of a piece with much of her other fiction, although the style is somewhat elevated beyond her usual naturalism. Whether *Briefing for a Descent into Hell* is science fiction is certainly open to debate, but the means of transcending the mundane world of daily existence is not unlike that of the closing pages of Arthur C. Clarke's *Childhood's End*, Alfred Bester's *The Stars My Destination*, Theodore Sturgeon's *More than Human*, or of the final scenes of such movies as *2001: A Space Odyssey* and *Close Encounters of the Third Kind*. Where each of them offers a way out, allowing for escape from the immediate cares of historical existence on Earth, Lessing reintegrates her visionary into society — tragically, in a sense, and yet inevitably. His truth is inspired nonsense on a mundane level, to which we can only imaginatively aspire, unless we too want to take the risk of that drastic cure.

David N. Samuelson

Sources for Further Study

Criticism:

Bolling, Douglass. "Structure and Theme in *Briefing for a Descent into Hell*," in *Contemporary Literature*. XIV (Autumn, 1973), pp. 550-564. Bolling feels the book symbolizes the loss of psychic wholeness of modern-day Western man.

Thorpe, Michael. *Doris Lessing*. Harlow, England: Longman, 1973, pp. 30-32. Thorpe calls *Briefing for a Descent into Hell* a strong and forceful novel.

Reviews:

Best Sellers. XXXI, May 1, 1971, p. 72.

Book World. February 28, 1971, p. 1.

Choice. VIII, June, 1971, p. 551.

Christian Science Monitor. March 18, 1971, p. 11.

Commonweal. XCIV, May 7, 1971, p. 220.

Encounter. XXXVII, September, 1971, p. 80.

Library Journal. XCVI, February 15, 1971, p. 657.

Nation. CCXIII, December 27, 1971, p. 699.

New Statesman. LXXXI, April 16, 1971, p. 535.

New York Review of Books. XVI, May 6, 1971, p. 14.

New York Times Book Review. March 14, 1971, p. 1.

Newsweek. LIV, March 13, 1971, p. 25.

Saturday Review. LIV, March 13, 1971, p. 25.

Time. XCVII, March 8, 1971, p. 80.

Times Literary Supplement. April 16, 1971, p. 437.

BRING THE JUBILEE

Author: Ward Moore (1903-   )
First book publication: 1953
Type of work: Novel
Time: 1863 to 1953
Locale: The United States and the Confederate States of America

The ironic story of a world in which the South won the Civil War, and how one man, a historian, attempted to probe the causes of that war by going back into time, thereby affecting its outcome

Principal characters:
> HODGE MCCORMICK BACKMAKER, the son of a poor rural couple living in the ruins of the United States
> RENÉ ENFANDIN, Consul for the Republic of Haiti to New York
> BARBARA HAGGERWELLS, the daughter of Thomas Haggerwells, leader of Haggershaven, a refuge for intellectuals
> HERBERT HAGGERWELLS, a key figure in the Battle of Gettysburg

The philosophical debate between determinism and free will has been argued in science fiction stories and novels from the very beginning of the genre, and never more fiercely than in stories dealing with time. Can man affect the course of history? Or will the tide of events smother the most potent attempts of individuals to alter the nature of recorded reality?

Ward Moore answers these questions by having his hero, Hodge Backmaker, accidentally alter his world's history into one we recognize as our own. In Hodge's time track, the course of the Civil War was changed when the Southern troops occupied Cemetery Hill and Round Top prior to the Battle of Gettysburg, thereby gaining a strategic advantage that won the battle for the South and altered the course of the war. The North was forced to surrender on July 4, 1863, leaving the nation permanently divided into two rival states. But the South, as victor, exacted a heavy price from the Federal government, forcing it to pay heavy war indemnities that crippled its economy for decades and left it perpetually impoverished, demoralized, and embittered. The South generously allowed the North to keep all the states above the old Mason-Dixon line, but occupied Kansas, Missouri, and California; the South also annexed Mexico at a later date. The political rearrangement of North America affected other parts of the globe as well: France remained an Empire, and Germany became the German Union. World War I was called the Emperors' War of 1914-1916. Still, the key event for Hodge and his fellow Northerners was always the War of Southern Independence.

Moore delineates the plight of the Northern states through the tale of Hodge's upbringing. Backmaker's family is poor, rural, ignorant, and penny-pinching. Hodge's only prospects are more of the same, or selling himself into indentured bondage to one of the small manufacturers or great landowners. Neither of these prospects is particularly appealing, so Hodge leaves home in 1938 at the age of seventeen, seeking his fortune in the great metropolis of New York. The United States has no public transportation except an expensive and inefficient railroad system, and the roads are virtually impassible to anything but horse and carriage (minibiles — steam cars — do exist, but are confined to the wealthiest classes), so Hodge must walk the eighty miles to town. New York is the largest city in the United States, nearly a million strong, filled with second-rate technological marvels: cable cars, horse-cars, express steam trains, bicycles, gas lights on every corner, an intricate network of telegraph wires to every office and large household (providing instant Morse communication from and to all central points), pneumatic lifts, and balloon airships running overhead. It also has its share of impoverished slum areas, tenement houses, and crime. Hodge has no sooner arrived than he is robbed of his three dollars — a fortune in an age when 50¢ is the normal day's wage for a grown man — and left for dead. He is rescued and left with a bookseller named Roger Tyss, and Hodge's real education begins.

Tyss is a strange man, widely read, self-educated, but misanthropic, with a fatalistic philosophy of life. He takes the boy in and gives him a home, but also engages his mind in a running series of debates, queries, dialogues, and discussions. In one of the most interesting of these encounters, Tyss propounds his philosophy, a Calvinistic creed which denies the possibility of free will. "The whole thing is an illusion," he says. "We do what we do because someone else has done what he did; he did it because still another someone did what he did. Every action is the rigid result of another action." This is a key passage in Moore's novel, the setting of the problem which Hodge will ultimately resolve. For Backmaker (and Moore) clearly believe the antithesis, that if "choice exists once it can exist again."

One of the visitors to Tyss's shop is the black Consul for the Republic of Haiti, the sole remaining independent state south of the Mason-Dixon line. Blacks were ostracized from the North after the defeat of the United States, either being sent back to Africa, or lynched outright — Monsieur Enfandin's position, even with diplomatic status, is not an easy one. But Enfandin is a cultured man, and makes an effort to read widely; in Hodge's life he is the counterbalance to the bookseller's bitter philosophy, a positive factor in Hodge's coming-of-age. Hodge decides to devote his life to history, and Enfandin is the first to hear of his decision. In the discussion which follows, the Haitian expounds his theory of philosophy, saying that free will is man's greatest gift. He later tells the boy that one cannot escape the responsibility of decisions merely because one fears the consequences: "Not acting is also action." Enfandin, in keeping with his philosophy, offers to help the boy gain admission to one of the few Northern colleges; when Hodge gives Tyss two weeks' notice, the bookseller points out that Backmaker has once again proved that nothing is left to chance. Hodge is a spectator type: "The part written for you does not call for you to be a participant." These words will later come back to haunt the boy with their irony.

Unfortunately, Enfandin is assaulted and returns to Haiti before fulfilling his promise; Hodge writes to the universities on his own, and receives a strange reply from Thomas Haggerwells at Haggershaven, in York, Pennsylvania. Decades before, Haggerwells' grandfather had established a refuge for itinerant scholars on his farm, and over the years a center of learning and study for scientists, teachers, and researchers had developed. Haggerwells' daughter Barbara travels to the city to meet Hodge (now twenty-three), and soon Backmaker is making the tedious train journey to rural Pennsylvania. Haggershaven proves to be the refuge he has been seeking all his life, a genial commune whose members work for the common good, contributing their financial earnings to the group in return for a secure place to pursue their research. The farm had originally been settled by Major Herbert Haggerwells, a Confederate major in the invading army of General Robert E. Lee who had so liked the country that he never returned to his Southern home.

Barbara is a high-strung girl, an emotional tyrant to her men, but simultaneously the world's leading theoretical physicist, a scientist whose primary interest is the nature of time, energy, and space, and their interrelationship. They are, she says, interchangeable elements; theoretically, it is possible to translate matter-energy into space-time. Once resolved into its component parts, anything, including man himself, can be reassembled at another point of the space-time fabric.

During the next eight years, Hodge and Barbara each pursue their research independently, little realizing how their findings will ultimately converge. Backmaker begins publishing scholarly articles on the War of Southern Independence (his chosen field of study) in respected Southern and European journals (there are no such publications in the United States). The culmination of his studies is the first volume of his monumental history, *Chancellorsville to the End*. He receives a curious letter from the leading historian of his day, Polk, a letter praising the book, but questioning one of the conclusions. Hodge had mentioned in his work the key Battle of Gettysburg, the beginning of the end for the Northern forces, and how fortuitous it was that the Southern troops had occupied the Round Tops overlooking the battle site on July 1, 1863. Polk puts forth his own theory, ascribing the move to Lee's military genius, "regarding the factors of time and space not as forces in themselves but as opportunities for the display of his talents." Polk's letter so disturbs Hodge that he temporarily abandons the second volume of his work, suddenly beset with doubts. Has he indeed missed some key factor in his assembling of the facts?

Meanwhile, Barbara has gone from theory to demonstration, persuading the community to support her efforts to build a machine that will travel through time. And now the drama comes together: when she hears that Hodge is having difficulties completing his work, she offers him the chance of verifying each detail personally, by watching the battle unfold as it happens. He will be able to write history as no man has done before, from the perspective of the impartial observer actually present at the event. Initial tests confirm that the machine works within a range of about one hundred years. Man can go back in time and return. Convinced by Barbara's arguments, Hodge agrees to the experiment, in which he will be sent back to midnight on June 30, 1863, the night before the battle began, and will return on midnight, July 4th.

York is about thirty miles from the battle site, and Hodge walks the distance during the night. He takes his position near the road where the Southern troops, pursuing the fleeing Federals, will push on to occupy the Round Tops, the key strategic positions on the battlefield. Before he realizes what is happening, the Rebel soldiers spot this unlikely civilian lurking in the brush, and start questioning him. Their captain rides up, and attempts to interrogate the man. But Backmaker is stunned by these events, because he *knows* from his research that no such pause in the Southern advance is recorded anywhere. When he fails to respond to the officer's questions, the soldiers panic, and attempt to flee; the captain, whose face looks familiar to Hodge, tries to stop the turncoats, but is shot and killed by one of his men. Hodge is left lying in the sun, alive but shaken. The battle which ensues is nothing like the one he knows: the Southern soldiers never gain a decisive advantage, and are eventually decimated in Pickett's charge. The South loses the Civil War as a result. Somehow Hodge makes his way back to the barn in York on midnight of the 4th, but nothing happens. And as the sun of a new day dawns, he suddenly realizes who the captain was: Herbert Haggerwells.

Hodge's life is in direct counterpoint to the state of the Union. In the backward wreck of the twenty-six dis-United States, Hodge thrives and grows and becomes a man, in every sense of the word. He finds love, peace, a haven for his studies, and companionship. But he, like all men, must take responsibility for his actions, and in attempting to learn more about the battle than he really needs to know, in attempting to become greater than history, the supremely impartial observer, he unwittingly becomes a part of it. He destroys *his* history, and in the process restores the Union. The remainder of his life is spent, like most of the inhabitants of his old world, in wondering why. He lives as a ward and worker on the farm that would have been Haggershaven, and leaves these memoirs to be found by a skeptical farmer. Enfandin was right, after all: man may choose, or choose not to choose, but even that is a choice, and the consequences of man's abdication of his free will can be far more disastrous than an action purposely taken.

Moore's novel is a powerful philosophical discussion of man's place in the universe. In posing the question of time and man's relation to it, he probes the nature of life itself. The man who waits for things to happen to him, says

Moore, deserves what he gets. And what is true for one man is also true for the race as a whole.

R. Reginald

Sources for Further Study

Reviews:

Analog. LIII, April, 1954, pp. 144-145.

Authentic Science Fiction. LXI, September, 1955, p. 154.

Galaxy. VII, February, 1954, pp. 111-112.

New Worlds. XL, October, 1955, p. 123.

Science Fiction Digest. I, February, 1954, pp. 158-159.

Science Fiction Quarterly. III, August, 1954, p. 62.

BUG JACK BARRON

Author: Norman Spinrad (1940-   )
First book publication: 1969
Type of work: Novel
Time: Just prior to the presidential election of 1984 or 1988
Locale: New York City; Evers, Mississippi; and the Colorado wilderness

A political thriller in which a television talk show host and the head of the Foundation for Human Immortality vie for political control of the United States

Principal characters:
> JACK BARRON, founder of the Social Justice Coalition during the 1960's, now the most popular personality on television
> SARA WESTERFELD, his estranged wife
> CARRIE DONALDSON, his secretary
> BENEDICT HOWARDS, a former self-made oil millionaire and the head of the Foundation for Human Immortality
> LUKAS GREENE, the first black governor of Mississippi, current head of the Social Justice Coalition
> GREG MORRIS, the governor of California and the head of the dying Republican Party
> THEODORE HENNERING, Senator from Illinois and Democratic presidential candidate
> TEDDY THE PRETENDER, another prominent Democratic politician

Some books are written to be controversial. This is easier to get away with at some times than at others; and in science fiction as in American life generally, the 1960's were times when political and literary controversy were in the air. But along with controversy, there was a certain willingness, even a demand, to experiment with new styles of life, of politics, and of art. At such times, certain writers and certain books become symbolic of the atmosphere of upheaval, and Norman Spinrad's long fourth novel, *Bug Jack Barron*, certainly was such a symbol even beyond the coterie of science fiction fans. (Portions originally appeared in the British Arts Council-sponsored *New Worlds*, and parliamentary attacks resulted in a short-lived ban on the magazine's distribution.) However, one fate of such works is that their evocation of a particular sense of time or place is too powerful to transcend. Any piece of art may become dated, but those deliberately concerned with political controversy are notably vulnerable. They easily become historical artifacts, possessing all their original ration of style, but with their descriptive and evocative power sharply modified by historical perspective. *Bug Jack Barron* is an example of this process.

Spinrad had previously written a novel, *The Men in the Jungle*, about the single great crisis of the 1960's, the Vietnam War, before writing this book about politics and television. The sequence is important. Critical of the war well ahead of most Americans, Spinrad was in the heart of science fiction's finest traditions when he began exploring the human impact of the technological device which presented the war, and the world, to those people. Whatever the world was really like, Americans (and most inhabitants of the industrial world) generally understand it to be like its image on television. Writing about this technology, Spinrad explores near the heart of the power structure which has dominated the Western world since the end of World War II. "Television" is a series of social institutions as well as a technological device, and if the camera never lies, it must still be aimed by human eyes and hands. Those eyes and hands have enormous power to impose definition on a world of seemingly random events, and even ten years after Spinrad wrote about it, that power is as often unacknowledged as unexamined.

As *science* fiction, *Bug Jack Barron* is concerned with the social implications of two kinds of technology in addition to a recognizably contemporary variety of network television. Jack Barron hosts a "talk show" on which ordinary people can call the studio by video-equipped telephone and have their complaints about politics and society amplified and relayed directly to business and political leaders. Having been "bugged" by the complaint, Barron can then interrogate public figures over the same vidphones: a televised surrogate for a powerless people's anger at those who rule their lives. The story opens just prior to the passage of a bill granting the Foundation for Human Immortality a monopoly license on the cryogenic freezing of human corpses. Based on a technology which already existed in 1968, the Foundation accepts fifty thousand dollars in cash from people who want to have their bodies preserved after death against the day when cures exist for the diseases that kill them, at which time they can be revived to live again.

A casual call from a black viewer alleging that the Foundation deliberately discriminates on the basis of race — an allegation Barron knows is false — provokes Foundation president Benedict Howards into an angry confrontation with the star. Howards is apparently afraid that the talk show, with its one hundred million member audience, has hurt his chances for a legal monopoly, but Barron, a former civil rights activist and founder of the Social Justice Coalition (a third party standing slightly to the left of center and perceived as very radical), suspects that there is something larger and dirtier behind the already tough and dirty façade.

Barron has a reputation as a radical, a champion of the people who has made it to the top of American life without sacrificing his principles or destroying other people, but he has become thoroughly cynical and self-centered. Suspicious of all politicians as "power-junkies," the entertainer carefully begins jockeying for position with Howards. He never actually supports the self-made oil millionaire, but he is always aiming for the bribe Howards offers for that support, a free freeze: a chance for immortality Barron could never otherwise afford. The political plot thickens when the conservative and dying Republican Party and the liberal Social Justice Coalition join forces against the Democratic Party standing in the center of the spectrum (and in Howards' pocket), and offer Barron both parties' presidential nominations. Everyone who knows him personally knows of Barron's cynicism and his attachment to show business, but they also know that his reputation and television following would make him a formidable candidate regardless of his ability or interest in the presidency. They would all be happy to run the country for him.

Barron is never intended as a traditional hero. Influenced as much by William S. Burroughs as by Edgar Rice Burroughs, Spinrad focuses on both the antihero and the cynical, amoral image-making of network television. The absence of substantive issues — foreign affairs, the economy, even a solid discussion of the race relations and civil rights which propelled Barron to prominence — is a necessary consequence of television's impact on political debate. One measures a candidate's qualities *as a candidate* rather than as a potential officeholder, and campaign speeches are reduced to the rapid-fire manipulation of symbols in a sixty-second spot commercial. The political heavyweights all want Barron to manipulate the public mind while they manipulate him.

Barron has few scruples about manipulating people — he does it every week. But he intends to do it in no one's interests but his own. He is fascinated by power, although he has nothing but contempt for those who pursue it. He has no intention of being "owned" by a constituency as a politician, or a media star, is. He will recognize obligations and responsibilities to no one except his sometimes estranged wife, and then only after her death. Aside from his public image as a champion of the arbitrary "good," Barron is little different from Benedict Howards, the novel's villain. And that is Spinrad's central political point. The capacity and opportunity to manipulate the mass media are unrelated, often antithetical, to the qualities of democratic leadership.

Moreover, Barron becomes very aware of the degree to which people treat him in the flesh as if he were the phosphor-dot image they see on their color screens every Wednesday night. Conscious enough of the differences between his real identity and his image to use the disparity as a tactical device, Barron eventually is forced to realize that his electronic image is more powerful than he is himself. He has, like Benedict Howards, become immortal, but the medical treatment makes him a participant in the purchase and eventual murder of a young black child. Known as the one man who made it to the top without climbing a ladder of bodies, he must reveal that his success now is built on the literal, as well as figurative, deaths of children. The real Jack Barron must beg for the trust of people who now have the best possible reasons to distrust him. But the real Jack Barron can speak only through the electronic *persona* of the star, and it is the star who survives to destroy Benedict Howards — hardly an unalloyed victory.

This complex layering of politics, television, individual identity, and personal relationships is among the most important contributions Spinrad has made to the art of science fiction writing. Although the novel's use of a nearly contemporary setting and technology makes the genre categorization almost superfluous, much of *Bug Jack Barron*'s success stems from Spinrad's use of the traditional technique handed down from predecessors as diverse as H. G. Wells and John W. Campbell: extrapolate the implications of contemporary data along the lines of possible future development. Spinrad's ability to catch the texture and flavor of the social context within which those developments happen is a new development in a field where sketchy stylization is all too often the rule. However, by the deliberate and crucial injection of personal and sexual relationships into the political equation, Spinrad raises issues with which he deals far less successfully. His elitism and sexism become more than personal positions against which one makes moral judgments if one so desires. They become flaws in the dramatic structure of the book.

Amidst the notoriety the novel received for its graphic sex scenes and its use of language generally regarded as impolite, the degree to which Spinrad's dialogue seems inappropriate to his characters went generally unnoticed. The two white male protagonists seem credible (particularly in the light of the language heard on the White House Watergate tapes released five years after *Bug Jack Barron*'s publication). But Spinrad has the black governor of Mississippi and the New York and California-based television star speak in the same hip argot modified by the vulgar yiddishisms of the entertainment world. Barron is cynical about the Social Justice government Luke Greene is running, but Mississippi may have been more thoroughly colonized than even he knows. There are no hints whatever of Greene's origins except his Berkeley partnership with Barron and Sara Westerfeld. The depiction of Evers, Mississippi, is a white New Yorker's quick-frozen image of poverty-stricken and angry Harlem. The images are borrowed not from Faulkner but from Bob Dylan. Spinrad's acceptance of thoroughly traditional individualism is so great that the entire novel proceeds without one critical or even skeptical comment on the value of worldly immortality. By the mid-1980's, the interchangeable countercultures of Greenwich Village and Los Angeles' "Strip City" have apparently expanded into a metaphor for all Americans. Finally, in a novel intended to explore the personal roots of political power, Spinrad not only offensively denigrates the ability of women to act at any level more intellectual than an orgasm, but he also overestimates Barron's ability to do precisely the same thing. Overvaluing Barron's *macho* ability to overwhelm Howards, Spinrad creates an ending which flies in the face of the political logic on which the entire novel is based.

The marriage between Barron and Sara Westerfeld is an important part of the plot machinery, yet she is the least rounded of the book's four major characters. Spinrad casts her as an unwilling Delilah whose weakness Howards uses, nearly successfully, against the television star. Making the woman the slave of her sexual desire, Spinrad misses the degree to which Barron is motivated by the same drives. From the end of the first television show at the novel's opening, the connection between Barron's influence and his sexual needs is established. Randy after every show, he quickly slips from the studio and picks up a hard-edged secretary in a singles bar. In the evening's sex the woman, attracted by Barron's image of political power, is clearly shown as an inadequate surrogate for Sara, whom Barron discarded when her political convictions became too insistent and demanding. The way in which the image of power attracts women is part of the fascination power has for Barron, but Westerfeld is impressed with the *authentic* success as an opposition leader Barron has abandoned for show business. Trapped by his choice, Barron feels only the response to his image, even from Sara, after Howards secretly arranged for her to return to Barron's bed.

In the contest between the two men, Barron intends to be cool and calculating right up to the end; while Howards, a real believer in the beauties of immortality and terrified of death, becomes increasingly passionate, operating at the very edge of an emotional abyss. Seeing all passion as destructive — the passionate person's weakness — Spinrad chooses to turn his novel's finale on precisely that point. But Barron is tremendously passionate. At precisely the point he decides to fight Howards, Barron thinks he is tougher, smarter, more self-aware than anyone. He is so confident that he decides to complete his powers by submitting to the immortality treatment he has been offered — which is exactly what Howards wants him to do. Soon Barron is in Howards' power, legal accessory to the act of murder. All that is left is the "Samson smash" that will destroy Barron, Howards, and Westerfeld all together.

But that is not the way it turns out. Tougher than his wife, who commits suicide, and more calculating than his enemy, who goes insane, Jack Barron demonstrates the superior strength of his attitude by surviving the Samson smash and moving towards victory in the upcoming presidential campaign. The personal conflicts among the three and the political structure over which they are fighting move together throughout the book, except at its climax, when Spinrad permits the image of Barron-as-superstud-superstar to obliterate the political logic of the statemate between Howards' economic and political power and Barron's cultural influence. Unknowingly then, Barron and Spinrad are both led by the celebration of male ego to accept the proposition which both have been ridiculing throughout the book: the ability of any individual, no matter how well-intentioned, to use political power in a genuinely public interest. Jack Barron the politician is right back in the "power bag," his addiction to power rekindled — even if only long enough, he thinks, to force acceptance of Luke Greene as his successor and the first black president.

Such a moral defeat, even after the political victory over Howards, would be consistent with the novel's cynicism about politics and politicians, but Spinrad foregoes this subtler version of the Samson smash. Barron becomes the bull elk who defeats his rival, controls the herd, and mates the most desirable females. Since this victory of Barron the male animal is entirely dependent on television as a social institution, and Barron's own insubstantial phosphor-dot image, there is irony aplenty. But this triumph of male sexual politics is presented with the naïveté Barron has been denouncing in his wife's thinking all along. The television star has become very much like both his wife and his worst enemy: emotional, political, and personally isolated — an ominous combination in a powerful man. Recognizing that danger and weakness in all his other characters, Spinrad at the end is persuaded enough by Barron to treat him as an almost conventional hero. He even gets the girl at the story's end. Such an otherwise inexplicable shift in perspective on the novel's principal character subverts the foundations of the novel's whole point of view, a flaw in craftsmanship wholly attributable to Spinrad's sexism.

Even flawed, however, *Bug Jack Barron* remains a significant novel. The controversy over its explicit language obscured the striking attempt Spinrad makes to adapt the linear flow of words on a page to the image- and symbol-haunted, multilayered medium of television. Occasionally verbose — verbalized thoughts are described in both interior monologue and subsequent dialogue — the book moves with a terrifying rapidity. It is enormously provocative on a variety of themes where debate often needs provocation. And above all, the very nature of its flaws makes it an illuminating artifact of the 1960's — a period almost certain to be regarded as a crucial turning point in American history.

Part of the 1960's tumult and terror was the pervasiveness of rapid change. Such change was coming in so many different areas of life, from so many different sources, that it was difficult to sort what was changing from what was not. Spinrad's extrapolation of the countercultural politics of the 1960's into the combination of narcissism, nostalgia, and nihilism which has characterized more recent years is singularly prescient. The widespread recognition of contemporary society's failure to provide for people's emotional, as well as social and economic, needs could, in the 1960's, fuel both a desire to change that society at its roots and to attempt to perpetuate an existing order at a more satisfying emotional level. Even under the best of circumstances (which the years after 1968 were not), the latter choice is a political bribe only awaiting the offer that cannot be refused. Written in 1968, *Bug Jack Barron* nicely anticipates the degree to which people actually made that second choice: a choice rooted in the Western religious and political tradition which states that public concerns and private satisfactions are irrevocably separate and nearly always antagonistic. The alternative conception, that public and private concerns are intimately and irrevocably interconnected, has a tradition of dissent which was only reopened with the resurgence of a nationwide feminist movement in the early 1970's.

But this dissenting tradition carries no weight for Spinrad. In his eyes, to serve the public good is stupidity or sham. To find private gratification is to become a vampire. Without a creative dialectic between the two — a process changing the definition of both — there is no change possible, only the Samson smash of contesting armies. With Spinrad avoiding that issue in his book, there is only a continuation of the *status quo*. In grim tribute to Spinrad's ability to capture reality as it was, one realizes how deeply the bromide that "the more things change, the more they remain the same," is touched with despair.

Albert I. Berger

Sources for Further Study

Reviews:

Amazing Stories. XLIII, November, 1969, pp. 117-119.

Analog. LXXXIV, November, 1969, pp. 166-167.

Galaxy. XXVIII, August, 1969, pp. 149-152.

Kirkus Reviews. XXXVII, February 15, 1969, p. 204.

Library Journal. XCIV, May 15, 1969, p. 2003.

Luna Monthly. II, July, 1969, pp. 19-21.

Magazine of Fantasy and Science Fiction. XXXVIII, January, 1970, pp. 38-40.

Magazine of Horror. May, 1970, pp. 120-127.

Times Literary Supplement. March 26, 1970, p. 328.

CAESAR'S COLUMN

Author: Ignatius Donnelly (1831-1901)
First book publication: 1890
Type of work: Novel
Time: 1989
Locale: New York and a valley in Uganda

The story of the Revolution against Capitalism, the ensuing reign of terror, and the destruction of civilization

> *Principal characters:*
> GABRIEL WELTSTEIN, a stranger in New York
> ARTHUR PHILLIPS, *alias* MAXIMILIAN PETION, a member of the Brotherhood of Destruction
> ESTELLA WASHINGTON, a young woman
> CHRISTINA CARLSON, a singer

Caesar's Column was first published in the United States under the pseudonym "Edmund Boisgilbert, M. D.," and had some difficulty getting into print at all. The novel is designed to shock, and it takes up its cause with all the enthusiasm that Ignatius Donnelly brought to his other projects — he was never halfhearted. The subject matter of the book and its *Weltanschauung* seem far more in tune with the intellectual climate of the present day than with that of the 1890's; it is difficult to appreciate how startling it must have seemed at that time. Because it was the first genuine dystopian novel, *Caesar's Column* stands at the head of a minor literary tradition.

When in 1888 Edward Bellamy published *Looking Backward: 2000-1887*, a Utopian dream of socialist America at the end of the twentieth century, it rapidly became a bestseller, and called forth many ideological replies — including more Utopian novels "correcting" Bellamy's notion of what constituted social perfection (the most notable is, of course, William Morris' *News from Nowhere* [1890]). Few undertook to examine Bellamy's notion of how this Utopian state was to be brought into being. Julian West, the hero of *Looking Backward*, asks at one point how the new world could possibly have emerged from the America he knew, and is informed by his mentor, Dr. Leete, that it happened because of the inevitable process of social evolution. Bellamy's assumption was that men need only cooperate with the natural flow of events in their lives in order to progress toward success and fortune.

It is this assumption which is challenged in *Caesar's Column*. The novel is set apart from the other pessimistic works of the period (such as the anonymous *Looking Ahead* of 1891) because it relates its pessimism to a well-entrenched historical trend rather than to specific political actions. Its concern is not with political parties and movements but with a fundamental social *malaise* which is, in Donnelly's view, deeply rooted in the social system and its ideologies. Donnelly's premise is that the direction of social evolution is not toward greater equality and social justice but toward extreme inequality and cruel tyrannies. In his twentieth century world, the rich have become richer and the poor more miserable. Capital is concentrated in the hands of a few; the capitalists horde the wealth of the world while the working class lives on subsistence-level minimum wage; children fish in sewers for rats as the only meat they get.

Donnelly's prognosis of the development of the Capitalist system has some points in common with Karl Marx's interpretation (although Donnelly's novel does not appear to have been derived *directly* from Marx's writings). Both writers believed that the concentration of capital in the hands of the wealthy few was entirely responsible for the Capitalist system; both accepted the implications of David Ricardo's "iron law of wages," which held that wages could never rise above the minimum required to keep the wage earners alive because of competition among the unemployed for the available work. Marx and Donnelly both concluded that the only way out of such a deadlock was revolution. The main point on which they differed, however, relates to the results of that revolution. In Marx's scheme the victory of the proletariat would result in the establishment of a socialist economic system which would ultimately evolve into true Communism. Donnelly, by contrast, felt that the orgy of violence would send the civilized world precipitously back to a state of barbarism. This is the message of *Caesar's Column*.

The novel begins in epistolary form, then quickly gives way to the conventional first-person narrative. The narrator is Gabriel Weltstein, newly arrived in New York from Uganda, who passes on his impressions and recounts his adventures to his brother Heinrich. At first delighted by the technological miracles which have remade New York, represented by the marvelous Hotel Darwin, Gabriel soon discovers that there is an "underworld" of misery and poverty that lurks behind the façade presented to wealthy tourists. He meets injustice head-on when he rescues a beggar from a coachman who first tries to run him down and then attacks him with a whip. Gabriel's heroic prevention of the vicious assault is seen as a criminal act, however, and the beggar in turn has to rescue Gabriel from the police. The beggar turns out to be a lawyer in disguise, until we learn that his identity as a lawyer is also a disguise. In reality, the beggar/lawyer is one of the leaders of the Brotherhood of Destruction: a worldwide secret society with a hundred million members. Traveling under the pseudonym Maximilian Petion, he is the third member — and apparently the least powerful — of a ruling triumvirate whose most charismatic figure is an impressive man named Caesar Lomellini.

Next, Gabriel falls in love with a girl named Estella, who has been sold to the evil capitalist Prince Cabano for his harem of mistresses. While securing her release, Gabriel eavesdrops on a meeting of the American aristocracy, and learns of their plan to uncover the secrets of the Brotherhood of Destruction through espionage. He also learns that members of the capitalist aristocracy are being held for ransom by their own airships, which is their principal military power, and he sees the leader of the airfleet paid off. He then listens as the capitalists plan to prevent further demands for money by disposing of the present airship crews and replacing them with their own sons. Gabriel relays the information he has overheard to the Brotherhood, which is then able to secure itself against the spy and recruit the airfleet to its cause. At last the time is ripe for rebellion.

The main plot at this point is interrupted by romantic subplots, as Gabriel woos Estella and Maximilian spends several chapters in telling his own love story. The story of Gabriel's courtship is an embarrassing allegory featuring Knight Weakheart and Princess Charming, while Max's story is pure dime novel romance.

However, the story picks up pace again as it moves on to its gory account of the destruction of the world. There are horrific scenes involving the burning alive of the men whose persecution of Arthur Phillips had led to his change of identity and membership in the Brotherhood; Prince Cabano begs for someone to kill him as he is tortured by the mob; airships sent to bomb the slums with poison gas turn instead upon their former masters. The picture of horror is completed when the number of the dead is so great that they can neither be buried nor burnt, and Caesar Lomellini orders that they be piled high and cemented into a gigantic column which will serve as a monument for future generations. But the leaders of the revolution cannot control the forces they have unleashed, and soon the mob rampaging the streets bears Caesar's head upon a pole as its standard. Gabriel and Maximilian, with their respective loved ones, flee by airship to Uganda, where they establish an enclave of Utopian harmony while the world outside descends into a second Dark Age.

As prophecy, of course, *Caesar's Column* fails as completely as *Looking Backward*, largely because Donnelly did not anticipate the political subversion of the "iron law of wages." Nevertheless, Donnelly's novel may be seen as the more farsighted of the two works, since its pessimistic mood and its fascinated contemplation of a holocaust to come foreshadow the development of futuristic fiction in the twentieth century, when Utopianism went completely out of fashion and dystopian alarmism ran riot.

Donnelly sees hope for the salvation of civilization largely in terms of a new commitment to religious ideals, rather than in terms of changes in the economic system. In the Utopian prospectus issued by Gabriel in Chapter XII and eventually put into practice in Uganda, the proposed changes in economic institutions are really very slight, and demand no more than minor tinkering with the Capitalist system. Donnelly hopes for a revival of Christian charity and the rejection of the spirit of greed, although it is not entirely certain how he expects these changes to come about. In one of the more remarkable chapters of Gabriel's narrative, the author attempts to show how religious ideology can actually be determined by socioeconomic environment. The hero attends a church service and hears a sermon which preaches a doctrine of social Darwinism, sanctifying the existence of poverty in the name of natural law, and which interprets the word "love" entirely in erotic terms rather than in terms of Christian "brotherly love." Gabriel cannot control his revulsion, but the rest of Donnelly's characters find nothing abnormal in the sermon. Donnelly sees plainly enough the complicity between religious ideology and economic institutions, and it seems, therefore, that his hope that the latter may be re-formed and re-created by the former rests on the assumption that an inspired religious fervor might be generated, in effect, out of nowhere. The dedication of the book is addressed "To the Public," but the principal exhortation to action included therein is directed at the churches.

It cannot be said that Donnelly's intellectual track record, taken as a whole, is impressive, but what is remarkable is his uncanny talent for anticipating trends in the popular imagination. In *The Great Cryptogram*, for example, he set out to demonstrate, by cryptographic analysis of key passages of the dramas, that Francis Bacon wrote Shakespeare's works, thus setting in motion one of the great crackpot bandwagons of our time. In *Atlantis: The Antediluvian World* he made a crucial contribution to the modern mythology of the lost continent. In *Ragnarok* he provided a Catastrophist vision of worlds in collision that is directly ancestral to the prolific writings of Immanuel Velikovsky. These works represent a brilliant anticipation of the temper of twentieth century pseudoscholarship, and demonstrate that Donnelly was far ahead of his time in his eccentricities and preoccupations.

Caesar's Column reflects this fact as well as any of his work. It is an early evocation of the twentieth century, not in terms of anything that actually came to pass, but in terms of the *Zeitgeist* which eventually took possession of the twentieth century speculative imagination. The novel lacks the imaginative scope of George Griffith's *The Angel of the Revolution* (1893), which may owe something to Donnelly's influence; and as a literary work it is not in the same league as Wells's "A Story of the Days to Come" (1897) and *When the Sleeper Wakes* (1899), or Jack London's *The Iron Heel* (1907). *Caesar's Column* is nevertheless a work of some historical importance, and in many respects a fascinating book.

Brian Stableford

Sources for Further Study

Criticism:

Boggs, W. Arthur. "Looking Backward at the Utopian Novel, 1888-1910," in
  Bulletin of the New York Public Library. LXIV (June, 1960), pp. 329-336.
  Boggs traces influence of Edward Bellamy on the writing of Ignatius Don-
  nelly and H. G. Wells.

Reviews:

Atheneum. CXCIX, January 16, 1892, p. 82.

Catholic World. LI, May, 1890, pp. 269-270.

CAMP CONCENTRATION

Author: Thomas M. Disch (1940-   )
First book publication: 1968
Type of work: Novel
Time: The near future
Locale: An underground concentration camp in Colorado

A successful hybrid between science fiction novel and symbolist allegory in which a group of experimental guinea pigs become latter-day Fausts, but with a difference

Principal characters:
>   LOUIS SACCHETTI, an academic poet of Roman Catholic background
>   MORDECAI WASHINGTON, a black prisoner
>   HUMPHREY HAAST, an ex-World-War-II general and Director of Camp Archimedes
>   DR. AIMÉE BUSK, camp psychologist
>   SKILLIMAN, an ex-A.E.C. scientist of authoritarian leanings

The pleasure afforded by the first reading of *Camp Concentration* is quite different from that afforded by the second. On a first reading, much that is mysterious is only explained at the very end, which throws a retrospective light on most of the action of the book. A second reading reveals the poetic art which prepares the reader for the ironies of the plot.

The story takes place in 1975, a future only eight years removed from the time the book was written. Louis Sacchetti, a plump and intelligent but selfin-dulgent poet, has refused to fight in the ongoing war (perhaps Vietnam), which continues throughout the action of the book. Imprisoned as a conscientious objector, he has been moved from a federal penitentiary to a mysterious, underground unit, Camp Archimedes, apparently run by an industrial corporation on contract to the American government. The novel consists entirely of his journal. Haast, the Director of the unit, tells Sacchetti that he may continue to keep his journal, but that everything he writes will be read (his typewriter is connected to slave printers in the Director's and the psychologist's offices); he is useful as an unbiased observer.

Sacchetti soon meets the other inmates, nearly all ex-prisoners, some of them army deserters. They are guinea pigs, he eventually discovers, who have been injected with Pallidine, a mutated form of the spirochaete bacterium which causes syphilis, in an attempt to raise their intelligence to undreamed-of heights. Unfortunately, after nine months the bacteria kill the subjects. Eventually, the alarming fact is revealed to Sacchetti in a dream that he, too, has been injected with Pallidine.

The Camp is institutional but luxurious, with gourmet cooking and free access to everything from books to interior decoration. Mordecai Washington, a tough, black prisoner, is the unofficial leader of the Camp inmates. He appears preoccupied, in a somewhat lunatic fashion, with medieval alchemy and has convinced the Director, a gullible man, that he has found the Elixir of Life. Shortly after the inmates perform Christopher Marlowe's *Doctor Faustus*, they perform an alchemical ceremony around Mordecai and Haast. Mordecai, who is already close to death, dies from the strain; the experiment is an apparent failure.

Book II opens with a potpourri of literary fragments, many bearing on theological questions, but soon a coherent narrative resumes. Most of the original inmates have died; Sacchetti's eyesight is failing, and he has begun to experience fits. But his intelligence has become stupendous. There are now new inmates, among them Skilliman, a disappointed scientist, who learns of the project and threatens its exposure, thereby blackmailing his way on to the program. He is prepared to die in order to become truly intelligent first.

Meanwhile, the eccentric psychologist Aimée Busk has disappeared from the project. When Sacchetti notices from newspaper reports an apparent epidemic of brilliant but erratic behavior, he conjectures that Dr. Busk, a known virgin, must have been sodomized by Mordecai as part of the plan, and that she is now spreading the infection through lesbian contacts in the world above. Skilliman, who distrusts the now-blind Sacchetti, attempts to cajole Haast into murdering Sacchetti. Instead, Haast shoots Skilliman, and it is revealed that Haast is actually Mordecai; the ritual, merely disguised in alchemical jargon, was really staged to allow Mordecai to electronically exchange consciousness with Haast, thus continuing to live in someone else's body. In fact, most of the camp guards are now ex-prisoners who have also exchanged consciousness. Even Sacchetti finally wakes up in the body of one of his persecutors.

Camp Concentration is considered, along with the collection of linked short stories, *334*, maverick science fiction writer Thomas M. Disch's best work. His friend, the critic John Clute, recently described him as "the most respected, least trusted, most envied and least read of all modern science fiction writers of the first rank." Raised in Minnesota, Disch went to college in New York, but during much of the time he was writing his early science fiction, he resided in London. *Camp Concentration* was originally published as a serial in the British science fiction magazine *New Worlds*. Under Michael Moorcock's editorial direction, the journal had become synonymous with the so-called New Wave in science fiction. *Camp Concentration*, with its literariness, its ironies, its setting in the near future, and its emphasis on the parallels between inner (psychological) space and external, scientific reality, is almost the paradigm of what the New Wave, at its most ambitious, was all about.

The book is genuine, hard-core science fiction, although its scientific content is at first obscured by extravagant metaphor and talk of alchemy. Indeed, it was highly praised in the science fiction magazine *Analog*, usually considered to be the bastion of all that is most conservative, traditional, technological, and right-wing in the science fiction world. *Camp Concentration*, then, was one of the rare New-Wave works of sufficiently high quality to bridge the gap between the late-1960 young turks of science fiction and the old guard; it is already recognized as a classic.

The story, clear enough in synopsis, is presented to the reader through the consciousness of Sacchetti, *via* his journal. This serves to darken and confuse the events, for Sacchetti, a poet, is much given to metaphor and poetic allusion. But it is Disch, not Sacchetti, who is responsible for the poetry of the book's structure, for Sacchetti, ignorant of the true meaning of events, can only impose a false order on them.

The book is structured in two parts, like Goethe's *Faust*, and works largely through a series of literary parallels which serve to recall the whole corpus of the Faustus myth in European culture. It does not neglect the medieval, alchemical origins, Marlowe's and Goethe's plays, Valéry's poem "My Faust" (1940), or Thomas Mann's *Doctor Faustus* (1947). Disch has clearly recognized the centrality of the Faust myth not only to his own tale, but also to science fiction in general. The story of the scientist who is prepared to give up everything, even his own soul, in exchange for a deeper knowledge, encapsulates the tensions between the scientist's intellectual striving and his moral responsibilities, which have loomed so large in science fiction ever since Mary Shelley's *Frankenstein*. In Marlowe's play, Faustus can never quite believe the full horror of the price he will have to pay after making his pact with Mephistopheles; Faustus, who becomes a cheap trickster, is himself the butt of a devil's trick. In the same way, the guinea pigs in Disch's novel volunteer for the experiment without understanding the cost — in this case, their alienation and isolation, followed by a painful death.

The black comedy of the Faust theme, in this case happily resolved with the devil in retreat despite the absence of God, runs parallel to an even blacker strand: the story of the descent into Hell. The Introduction to Dante's *Inferno* is invoked in the opening pages, and the idea of Camp Archimedes as Hell runs throughout the whole book: it is underground, and even while gaining wisdom, the prisoners suffer torment — their bodies rot, they stink, have no appetite, faint, and have fits. The very title of the book makes punning reference to the concentration camps in which the Nazis carried out so many sadistic medical experiments on the Jews in World War II, and the image of Dachau alongside that of Hell is evoked again and again in the novel itself.

There is a political as well as a metaphysical dimension to all this imagery, of course. The novel is a fierce attack on a corrupt political system, such as many Americans believed their government to be in the era before Watergate — involved in cynical, covert, illegal activities both at home and abroad. The specter of Vietnam and of possible nuclear war haunts the novel, and the unholy alliance between the military and industry is seen to lead to unpleasing suppurations.

The Faustean and Dantean strands of the novel are paralleled, naturally enough, by a theological strand which centers on the figure of Thomas

Aquinas. Sacchetti is a lapsed Catholic, and appropriate trains of thought come readily to him without Disch having to search for a relevant effect. The book asks whether there is a God, and if God does exist, whether He is somehow, symbolically, no more than the Warden of some metaphysical concentration camp in which we all play out our confused lives. The reality of Free Will seems doubtful; the experimenters are trapped in the system almost as deeply as their subjects. Some of the darkest imagery involves an entropic parody of the central Christian symbols: loaves and fishes become eclairs and rotting herring; the virgin intercessor carries a perversely contracted venereal disease; the holy wafer is Pallidine itself.

In this book, whose complex allusions sometimes come perilously close to showing off, James Joyce, John Bunyan, John Milton, William Shakespeare, Rainer Maria Rilke, Arthur Rimbaud, and many others are evoked. Yet the aptness of the allusions justifies them triumphantly on almost every occasion. They saturate this quite brief and spare work with a density of symbolism which brings to the mind of the reader the richness of their sources; they import into this very modern tale an ancient tradition of passionate thought about good and evil. The book can be read on two levels, however. Much of the narrative is straightforward, and it would be quite possible to enjoy the plot while missing much of its referential quality; the connotations comment ironically on the overt meaning of the plot, but while they modify it, they do not change it.

Thomas Mann's presence is especially important; a minor character in the book is called Adrienne Leverkühn, recalling Mann's great novel *Doctor Faustus* whose hero, Adrian Leverkühn, is a great musician whose genius is intimately linked with his syphilitic infection. The whole idea of Pallidine, although directly borrowed from Mann's juxtaposition of syphilis, genius, and the Faust legend, is not a plagiarism. Disch's borrowing is just; he is consciously composing a variation on a theme, not merely repeating it.

Most criticism of the novel has centered on the mutedly cheerful ending, which has been read as flawing the intense tragic vision of the work. This is an incorrect interpretation; the tone of the book is *not* tragic. The language throughout appeals to the intellect rather than the feelings, in the mode of comedy. Its punning allusiveness is itself jokey, in a black way, and the confidence with which the narration moves from scabrous and disgusting directness to the most delicate of poetic imagery is itself amusing. The fat, clever Sacchetti, doomed to an almost perpetual lack of insight into the true nature of the situation, is the figure not only of the sensitive poet, but also of the vain and in some respects unworldly, facile *littérateur*: he is a truly comic creation.

The book's humor is witty and elegant, evoking the painful smile rather than the belly laugh; its whole mode is ironic. If it is to be seen as a tragedy, then it must be the cruel, cynical tragedy arising from a corrupt society that we associate with such Jacobean writers as John Webster and Thomas Middleton.

The ironies vary, from the obvious (the prisoners choosing to amuse them-selves by performing *Doctor Faustus*, of all plays) to the absurd (the three attendant angels of Sacchetti's long dream are furred, not feathered, and spring from a subconscious memory of the three syphilitic rabbits of Mordecai's research). The price an author pays for irony is that his text can take on a certain coldness and remoteness; this, if anything, is the limitation of this important novel. The book obviously goes straight to the core of what Disch feels to be the overwhelming issues of contemporary life, but the passion seems of the mind, not of the heart. However, this need not be seen as a limitation: the book functions rather like a Brecht play — its very chilling qualities, its startling but well-judged vulgarities, serve to alienate the reader from too close an emotional identification with the action and force him to keep thinking. The book improves with each reading, because of the subtlety of these intellectual delights.

The theme of suddenly enhanced intelligence has been dealt with in science fiction before. Two notable predecessors to Disch's book, Poul Anderson's *Brain Wave* (1954) and Daniel Keyes's "Flowers for Algernon" (1959), resolve the writer's problem of how convincingly to render states of higher intelligence (higher than that of either reader or writer) by using protagonists who are subnormal to begin with. Disch, on the other hand, has the sheer *hubris* to use as the protagonist a man who is already on the verge of bril-liance; it is amazing how well he carries off the sense of vast intelligence into which this brightness develops — not so much by producing great thoughts *per se* as by evoking the kinds of lateral thinking and surreal juxtaposition that, in the real world, are generally thought (by Koestler among others) to be the concomitants of genius.

Camp Concentration is a rarity in science fiction: a major work of litera-ture. It is also a splendid advertisement for the genre's strengths. Such a theme could not have been dealt with so expansively in so small a compass using the conventions of the realistic, traditional novel. Science fiction is not limited to those images and metaphors which purport to be directly mimetic of the real world; it has something of the freedom of fable. But by clinging to real science, Disch, as is characteristic of all good science fiction writers, keeps his fable from drifting into pure fantasy and lets it insinuate itself, like the prick of a pin, into our idea of what is possible and real.

Peter Nicholls

Sources for Further Study

Reviews:

Analog. XLIII, January, 1970, pp. 128-130.

Books and Bookmen. XIII, July, 1968, p. 47.

Kirkus Reviews. XXXVII, January 1, 1969, p. 15.

Library Journal. CXIV, February 15, 1969.

Luna Monthly. XXX, November, 1971, p. 30.

Publisher's Weekly. CXCIV, November 4, 1968, p. 49.

CAN SUCH THINGS BE?

Author: Ambrose Bierce (1842-1914?)
First book publication: 1909
Type of work: Short stories
Time: Various, mostly nineteenth century
Locale: Chiefly the United States

A series of short stories in which psychic phenomena, such as disembodied spirits, provide experiences in other dimensions

> *Principal characters:*
> HALPIN FRAYSER, a man killed by the shell of his dead mother
> JANETTE HARFORD, a ghost fiancée
> WILLIAM HARKER, a journalist who saw a person attacked by wild oats
> MOXON, creator of a chess-playing robot

The stories called science fiction by Ambrose Bierce are collected in *Can Such Things Be?* and comprise twenty-four stories, many of which deal with the appearance of ghosts, often told as first-person narration but with the experiences usually accounted for (by witnesses and by subsequent Bierce critics) as dream, delusion, and hallucination.

Although psychic investigators distinguish spiritism as a science from spiritualism as a religion, the history of modern spiritualism began with the rappings of the Fox sisters in Hydesville, New York, in 1848. It spread to England where, in 1882, the Society for Psychical Research was founded with a similar society founded in 1885 in the United States. After its foundation the society in England enrolled many members famous in literature and science, including William James, Henri Bergson, Gilbert Murray, and Camille Flammarion. The American society's motto was Gladstone's statement: "Psychical research is the most important work which is being done in the world — by far the most important." Spanning these two continents, Ambrose Bierce lived in England, a pronounced Anglophile, between 1872 and 1875, calling these the happiest years of his life.

In these psychic stories Bierce rarely employs any of the customary labels of telekinesis, psychokinesis, mental telepathy, reincarnation, paranormal voices, bilocation, and Akasha (or celestial ether), although occasionally he does, as in "One of Twins," provide a character who researches "anything unaccountable by the natural laws with which we have acquaintance"; and he does refer to some literature on the topic, such as "Denneker's Meditations" and the work of "Hali." These are touches of learning which betray a wider knowledge of the subject than Bierce permits his "common man" characters.

Halpin Frayser of the first story, "The Death of Halpin Frayser," awakens and speaks an unfamiliar name, "Catherine Larue," as he sinks into a mental condition which turns him into something of an automaton. As such he follows a path toward evil and, finding his surroundings filled with frightful sounds and dripping blood, feels that somehow he is being forced to do penance for a crime he cannot remember. His sense of being overpowered by automatic handwriting may account for the poem he writes with a twig dipped in blood. Confronted with the apparition of his dead mother, he breaks off in mid-sentence. A flashback explains the unknown guilt as founded in sexual attachment to his mother; to escape he had moved to California, where he was shanghaied. His mother had followed to search for him and had remarried. Now, some six years later, though without his knowledge of her death, she reappears to Frayser as what Bierce calls "a body without a soul" — one of what theurgists have called shells of the dead — and strangles her son. Two men searching for an escaped murderer expect him to visit the grave of the wife whose throat he had cut. They find the body of Halpin Frayser and the poem, which one of them recognizes as written in the style of Myron Bayne. An unearthed headboard reveals that this son of Catherine and great-grandson of Myron Bayne had unknowingly died on the grave of his mother, renamed by marriage Catherine Larue, whose love of Bayne's poetry she had shared with him.

Several stories push outward the boundaries between life and death. "The Secret of Macarger's Gulch" reveals itself to the narrator partially in dream, for he had obviously lived in Edinburgh in a former life, and partially in a friend's later narration. "One Summer Night" demonstrates the need for scientific detection of death; a man awakens in his coffin, being unearthed by medical students, only to be killed by a practical caretaker. "The Moonlit Road" demonstrates even more dramatically that the dead sometimes do not know they are dead; in this case the mother, having been killed in darkness by an unknown assailant, appears to her husband intending to be lovingly reunited with him, but frightens away her actual murderer. She tells her part of the story through a medium. "A Diagnosis of Death" begins with a statement of belief in a combination of astral body ("the living are sometimes seen where they are not") and a modification of Akasha (they have been "where they have lived so long . . . as to have left their impress on everything about them"). Hawver tells of a psychic doctor who predicted deaths and then he himself dies after the doctor's ghost has warned him.

Occasionally entire scenes are transferred as in a time warp. In "A Tough Tussle" and in "A Resumed Identity" Bierce uses his Civil War experiences. First he relates the death of a Federal officer, Lieutenant Brainerd Byring, to whom a Confederate corpse seems to be another "body without a soul." His fear he accounts for in terms of racial memory from "the cradle of the human race" in Central Asia. He believes the corpse moves and springs forward in self-defense. The captain who finds Byring's body, fallen on his own sword, impiously exclaims "Gad!" and unknowingly names a god of Central Asia.

In "A Resumed Identity," a "Federal Officer" believes that, at the age of twenty-three, he witnesses a Civil War battle in 1862; but he looks into a pool, sees himself an old man, and dies.

Bierce tells the story in three carefully separated segments, each with its own apparent "truth," so it is impossible to know whether the man is actually the victim of a time warp or of a distorting memory. Displacement of scene occurs also in "A Jug of Sirup," in which a departed storekeeper returns and appears as visible inside his store only to those outside; those inside with him battle each other in darkness. In "An Inhabitant of Carcosa" a person reads Hali on kinds of body and spirit separation at death and finds himself in a previous life in the ruins of the ancient city of Carcosa, where he sees his own tombstone with the dates of his birth and death in this life.

Love, as in "The Moonlit Road," motivates other visitations, and activates telepathy, sometimes through a close third party. The narrator of "One of Twins," sharing his twin brother's concerns without his own or his brother's knowledge, reveals the reason for his brother's fiancée's suicide. Another love story, "Beyond the Wall," tells about Mohun Dampier, who investigates the "unreal," some of which now haunts him in the form of tappings in the wall which formerly separated him and a young woman who, before her death, communicated with him in that fashion. The narrator of "A Psychological Shipwreck," William Jarrett, meets Janette Harford while sailing from Liverpool to New York on the *Morrow*; she reads "Danneker's Meditations" on bilocation just before the ship sinks. Jarrett recovers on the *City of Prague* steamer, three weeks out from Liverpool, and inquires of his friend, Gordon Doyle, for the health of Miss Harford. Doyle, he now learns, is engaged to her; and Jarrett himself has never been on the *Morrow*, now lost at sea.

"A Baby Tramp" tells of an orphaned three-year-old child traveling hundreds of miles, directed by the spirit of his mother, on whose grave he dies. The town of Blackburg, has experienced a shower of baby frogs and a fall of crimson snow, details reported frequently in newspapers and collected by Charles Fort.

Revenge and evil prove powerful inspirations for spiritual lingerings. In "The Middle Toe of the Right Foot," a severed middle toe, by way of barefoot imprints in the dust of a haunted house, proves the passing of a ghost. The "Stranger" of a story by that title appears at an army campfire in Arizona and tells about a party trapped by Apaches thirty years earlier. Three committed suicide, and the fourth, obviously, tells the story and disappears. All four had been scalped and died near the campfire.

"The Realm of the Unreal" gives the collection's best formal discussion of psychic phenomena in the person of Dr. Dorrimore, a hypnotist, who makes the narrator's fiancée appear in San Francisco, though she has never left her home in Oakland. Occasionally, also, the power may be transferred to a nonhuman agent, as in "John Bartine's Watch," in which the watch has the power to reproduce the sensations of, and finally the effect of, the time Bartine's great-grandfather was hanged. "Staley Fleming's Hallucinations" shows a man killed by a "spiritual" Newfoundland dog.

Occasionally fear works without cause. "The Haunted Valley" concerns the death of Jo Dunfer, who kept a beloved Chinese woman as a hired hand and killed her in jealous rage; but he met his own death soon after the friend of his jealousy "haunted" him by looking through a knot-hole at him. Similarly, there is no ghost but only fear and the unexpected in "John Mortonson's Funeral" in which a cat appears under the glass in Mortonson's coffin.

Two stories differ in form. In "The Night-Doings at Deadman's," a miner jealously guards from a dead Chinaman his severed pigtail, which the Chinaman needs to go to heaven. A visiting stranger shoots the dead Chinaman on his reappearance; but in the Spring a foraging party finds the miner dead by the reflection of a bullet which severed the pigtail. The miner wins, however, for the devil captures the tail and the soul of the Chinaman. This extension into fantasy beyond psychological reality, explains Bierce's labeling the story "untrue." As allegory or fable, "Haita the Shepherd" features Haita who cares for his sheep and an elderly hermit and prays to Hastur, his god, and thus, because of his devotion and goodness, influences for good the events of the world. The beautiful young woman who appears momentarily but eludes him when he asks anything of her is Happiness.

Many of the stories, then, concern time displacement and concentrate on the death experience, and in those respects bear similarity to the most famous of Bierce's stories, "An Occurrence at Owl Creek Bridge" (not in this collection). "The Damned Thing" and "Moxon's Master" are the most typical of science fiction in the entirety of the collection.

Because strange phenomena cannot be contained in a scientist's laboratory, the journalist William Harker of "The Damned Thing" writes his report not as news but as fiction. A coroner's jury judges him a lunatic and rules that his severely bruised friend Hugh Morgan was killed by a mountain lion. Instead, Morgan had been attacked by an Invisible Force in a field of wild oats; and the coroner suppresses the scientific evidence of the dead man's diary recounting his and his dog's prior experiences with the Force which has left its imprint on the ground and departed into the sky, blotting out the stars as it passed. Morgan himself explained it scientifically as a color at the end of the solar spectrum, beyond human detection.

Moxon discusses seriously and at length, with examples, the evidence "that every atom is a living, feeling, conscious being." In terms of Herbert Spencer's definition of "Life" as a "combination of heterogeneous changes . . . in correspondence with external coexistences and sequences," he theorizes that a machine is alive when in operation and that, if "consciousness is the product of rhythm all things *are* conscious." The narrator watches subsequently, though unobserved by Moxon, a chess game between Moxon and his five-foot gorillalike machine. Ironically, the rhythm here belongs to the machine, which plays with "slow, uniform, mechanical" movement while Moxon's human motions lack precision. Unfortunately, if a live "machine" thinks, it, too, will fight against death. Accordingly, Moxon's cry of "Checkmate" produces in it a disorder through which it expresses its dying defiance by disrupting the breathing and stifling the rhythm of life in Moxon by strangling him. This story, then, offers a key to the others in the collection and explains the psychological concentration on death, when the borders of scientific observation must be pushed outward from physics to metaphysics.

Grace Eckley

Sources for Further Study

Criticism:

Clareson, Thomas D. *A Spectrum of Worlds*. New York: Doubleday, 1972. Clareson discusses the work of Bierce and other science fiction authors and concludes that fantasy and Science Fiction allow the author the greatest freedom in creating model worlds capable of sustaining metaphorical statement.

Hutchings, Edwin. "Can Such Things Be," in *Reedy's Mirror*. XXVII (December 13, 1918), pp. 654-655. This is a contemporary critique of *Can Such Things Be* which views Bierce less as a progenitor of science fiction and more as a minor but popular "local colorist" author.

Reviews:

New Republic. XVIII, March 22, 1919, p. 256.
Smart Set. LVIII, January, 1919, p. 143.

A CANTICLE FOR LEIBOWITZ

Author: Walter M. Miller, Jr. (1923-   )
First book publication: 1960
Type of work: Novel
Time: Hundreds of years in the future
Locale: The Earth

The story of the problems faced during three different ages by the monks of the Albertion Order of Leibowitz, which was founded by an atomic scientist in order to preserve knowledge after civilization has virtually been wiped out by atomic war

Principal characters:
Part One:
BROTHER FRANCIS GERARD, a postulant
DOM ARKOS, abbot of the monastery
FATHER CEROKI, prior of the monastery
POPE LEO XXI
THE WANDERING JEW
Part Two:
DOM PAULO, the abbot
BROTHER KORNHERR, an inventor in the monastery
THON TADDEO, a secular scientist
THE POET
THE WANDERING JEW
Part Three:
DOM ZERCHI, the abbot
MRS. GRALES, a two-headed woman
BROTHER JOSHUA
DR. CORS, a physician
THE WANDERING JEW

When *A Canticle for Leibowitz* was first published in hardback form in 1960, its critical reception was extremely varied. Most reviewers hardly knew what to make of this extraordinary tripartite novel. Some dismissed it as being mere science fiction; others praised it, maintaining, however, that to call it "science fiction" was an insult. A few recognized that *A Canticle for Leibowitz*, coming as it did at the height of the "ban the bomb" controversy, represented a major voice speaking against atomic warfare.

A Canticle for Leibowitz retells the future in terms of the past. Part One, *Fiat Homo*, is set in a reborn Dark Ages. After an atomic holocaust has virtually annihilated humankind, and after an anti-intellectual uprising — the simplification — has centered upon the destruction of learning, including a planetwide book burning, Isaac Leibowitz has founded a monastery in the American southwest. It is dedicated not so much to the advancement of knowledge as to its conservation and preservation. Part Two, *Fiat Lux*, takes place some hundreds of years later in a new Renaissance, with all of its attendant problems: the relation of Church and State; the role of the Church in advancing knowledge; the respective claims, in effect, of Christ and Caesar. Part Three, *Fiat Voluntas Tua*, is again set hundreds of years into the future. Atomic power has been rediscovered and the world once more threatens to destroy itself with a nuclear holocaust. In the end, as atomic warfare inundates the globe, a spaceship filled with the Memorabilia (the learning so long safeguarded by the monastery), a cargo of children, some monks, and a few other people is now taking off for far Centarus, there to reestablish humanity.

Miller asks many disturbing questions throughout the book. What will man do to man, and will it be any good? The novel is a study, in one sense, of man's inhumanity to man, but it is also a celebration of the faith and dedication of those individuals who safeguard knowledge or learning, not advance it. In fact, the story, in Part One, of Brother Francis Gerard, who spends many years producing an illuminated manuscript for the transistorized control system of unit six-B is as touching a parable of faith, humility, and simplicity as the reader is likely to find.

In addition, Miller asks whether humanity, having once been faced with the possibility of certain destruction, will again risk the development of atomic bombs. The answer is that man *will* take that risk, and will perish rather than outlaw atomic weapons. Miller's vision of humanity's future is chilling and seems thoroughly bleak. His warning is pessimistic indeed, with its two-headed mutants, atomic destruction, and death camps where hopelessly injured victims of atomic fallout are offered euthanasia for their pain; it is hardly an optimistic picture. For example, after an accident has triggered a thermonuclear disaster, Abbot Zerchi switches off the radio with its dire news. "Where's the truth?" he asks. "What's to be believed? Or does it matter at all? When mass murder's been answered with mass murder, rape with rape, hate with hate, there's no longer much meaning in asking whose axe is bloodier. Evil on evil, piled on evil."

Miller's novel, then, is both admonitory and premonitory, and seems, on the surface at least, totally bereft of hope. Where is the "Canticle," the song of joy promised by the title of the novel? That *A Canticle for Leibowitz* has been in print continuously since 1960, that it has attracted literally millions of readers, and that it has been rated as one of science fiction's best novels, indicates that there must be something more in the book than bleak pessimism and despair. What accounts for its perennial appeal even in the face of its ostensibly pessimistic message?

Certainly one of the major factors is Miller's mastery of style. The book abounds with verbal wit, vivid figures of speech, flashing stylistic pyrotechnics, virtuoso parody, and many other linguistic delights. As a consequence the book is a joy to read, if only to admire the technical mastery of the craft of fiction.

Yet many other characteristics have contributed to the appeal of Miller's novel. Chief among them are the recurrent themes, hinted at or suggested in the early sections and then fully developed in the brilliant conclusion. These themes — good and evil, pride and humility, spiritual innocence and worldly sophistication, the proper and justified demands of both Christ and Caesar, to name only a few — provide an essential unity to the tripartite novel. The book has, in one sense, no single hero, no protagonist with whom the reader can continually identify. The presence of the very human, burdened, earthly, yet very spiritual abbots in each of the sections might lead to the notion that the abbots are the protagonists. However, it is the *concept* represented by the abbot more than the person himself that provides the unity the novel requires. In this characteristic, *A Canticle for Leibowitz* is almost the prototypical science fiction novel, illustrating as it does the notion of "idea as hero" which is so important to the genre as a whole. In most so-called mainstream novels, the action flows from human beings in action, behaving according to their character. This rarely happens in science fiction, where more often the action flows from the idea or the concept. This extrapolation of the consequences of an idea lies at the very heart of science fiction, and few books illustrate its execution as well as Miller's novel. Miller's idea is essentially derived from the moral imagination at work, and resembles, in this sense, some of the rigor of the intense moralism that informed such earlier American writers as Nathaniel Hawthorne, Herman Melville, or Mark Twain. Evil is a palpable presence to all of them, and in some very pessimistic works, such as *The Blythedale Romance* or *Moby Dick*, evil may almost triumph. Such a triumph appears on the surface of Miller's redaction.

Miller draws the issue quite clearly in the final section. After fallout from radiation has created thousands of slowly dying radiation victims, the government has established "Mercy Camps," replete with signs offering COMFORT and vaguely effeminate statues reminiscent of Jesus, where those incurably injured by the radiation may go for euthanasia. Abbot Zerchi's rigorous Christian morality says that euthanasia is wrong at all times, under any circumstances. His opponent in this debate is not a leering diabolical figure, but a compassionate physician, Dr. Cors, who represents the best in secular humanism. What the abbot particularly decries is the heresy, as he terms it, that the good is equated with the common good and evil equated with pain. To minimize suffering and to maximize security were natural and proper ends of society and Caesar, he thinks. But they then became the only ends, somehow, and the only basis of law — a perversion. Inevitably, then, in seeking them, we found only their opposites: maximum suffering and minimum security. Miller thus tests the abbot's rigid moralism against the hard rock of reality, and the abbot's only advice to the fatally injured woman and child is that nature imposes nothing that nature has not prepared one to bear. Eventually the abbot himself is forced to bear the sufferings he counseled for others, and verses from the *Dies Irae* run through his dying mind. "Day of wrath, that dreadful day, when Heaven and Earth shall pass away."

Readers have long been struck by the Roman Catholicism which pervades the book. The novel was written prior to the liturgical changes inaugurated by the second Vatican Council, and thus much of the exaggerated Latinity in the book now seems a bit anachronistic. However, the theology of the Catholic Church, as well as the rigorous demands of its morality, are vitally important to the central vision of the novel. Two interrelated dogmas provide the remarkable theological speculation with which Miller concludes the book.

The first is the doctrine of Original Sin, the fall of man as a result of pride, and the consequent loss of "the preternatural gifts of Eden," as Miller phrases it. These gifts included the ability to communicate directly with God, possession of eternal life, freedom from pain or suffering, and so on. Man would not need to work; women would bear children without pain or suffering. The world was literally a paradisical Eden.

The other doctrine involved here is that of the Immaculate Conception, the belief that Mary, the mother of Jesus, was created without the stain of Original Sin. Miller has signaled his use of these themes as early as the end of Chapter Two of the first section of the book. "New Rome was busy with other matters, such as the petition for a formal definition on the question of the Preternatural Gifts of the Holy Virgin, the Dominicans holding the Immaculate Conception implied not only indwelling grace, but *also* that the Blessed Mother had had the preternatural powers which were Eve's before the Fall. . . ." Further, Miller has almost simultaneously raised the question of the essential natural innocence of the "Pope's children," the mutants who have become so numerous with each succeeding generation. These themes are worked out in the various sections of the book with indirection, suggestion, allusion, and even paranomasia: "Accurate am I the exception. I commensurate the deception." The second head of Mrs. Grales, which she calls Rachel, seems to be whispering these words to cite only one example. The question of whether or not the sacrament of baptism, to remove the eternal effect of Original Sin, is necessary for Rachel has been answered emphatically by Zerchi. No. Mrs. Grales's baptism is enough for both heads.

Later, however, after Zerchi himself has been fatally injured by an atomic blast, he is visited as he is dying by Mrs. Grales-Rachel. Zerchi notices that the head of Mrs. Grales is sleeping soundly. Rachel is now awake, parotting Zerchi's words, as if saying "I am somehow like you" by the repetition. He can even imagine the Grales head withering and eventually falling away like a scab or umbilical cord. Now he realizes that his priestly duty demands that he must baptize Rachel who has, he thinks, received too much radiation to live. Rachel brushes away his attempt at conditional baptism, and communicates with Zerchi by offering him a single host, or communion wafer, as if to say, "I do not need your first sacrament (baptism), Man, but I am worthy to convey to you this sacrament of Life (communion)." Zerchi now realizes who she is, an unfallen Eve, a new Mary, free from Original Sin. God has raised up a creative or primal innocence from the shoulder of Mrs. Grales (the significance of her name now becomes obvious). Rachel will become the new mother for the unfallen, resurrected race of humanity, and, with all of the preternatural gifts of Eden, will not suffer from injury or even radiation. "My soul doth magnify the Lord," she sings. The meek will inherit the earth.

Miller has carefully prepared us for this essentially joyful conclusion to his novel through the themes he has previously intertwined, but the boldness of his theological speculation is extraordinary, a remarkable conclusion to a remarkable novel. To be sure, the book is not completely a brilliant accomplishment. The center section, the new renaissance, with its "thons" and other quasi-feudal lords who somewhat resemble Henry VIII in cowboy boots, is the weakest, although the Abbot's dialogues with both the Poet and the recurrent figure of the Wandering Jew are well done indeed. In addition, some of the humor may be labored. The discrepancy between Leibowitz's prosaic relics such as his shopping list and the reverence with which they are treated by the monks recurs a bit too often, but Miller approaches the subject with a delight that is contagious, even if a bit overdone.

A Canticle for Leibowitz is deservedly one of science fiction's classics. It is not only an extraordinary accomplishment in and of itself, but for the ground that it broke as well. Prior to its publication, serious religious or theological speculation had been almost unknown in science fiction, except as parodies or objects of ridicule. *A Canticle for Leibowitz* demonstrated that science fiction, in the hands of a skilled craftsman like Miller, could utilize serious religious material or motifs and that they could be completely integral to the novel, even to the genre. Excellent later works, such as Frank Herbert's *Dune* or Robert Heinlein's *Stranger in a Strange Land*, were made possible largely because of the vistas that Miller opened. A very few later works may have surpassed Miller's novel in quality, but if they have done so, it is only because Miller marked the new territory for them. *A Canticle for Leibowitz* remains one of the benchmarks against which all subsequent science fiction works must be measured.

Willis E. McNelly

Sources for Further Study

Criticism:

Percy, Walker. "Walker Percy on Walter M. Miller, Jr.'s *A Canticle For Leibowitz*," in *Rediscoveries*. Edited by David Madden. New York: Crown, 1971, pp. 262-269. Percy analyzes why this is one of his favorite books.

Rank, Hugh. "Song Out of Season: *A Canticle For Leibowitz*," in *Renascence*. XXI, Summer, 1969, pp. 213-221. Rank outlines the themes of *A Canticle For Leibowitz*.

Scholes, Robert and Eric S. Rabkin. *Science Fiction: History, Science, Vision*. New York: Oxford, 1977, pp. 221-226. Calls *A Canticle For Leibowitz* an ironic novel that amalgamates science and religion into a modern humanism.

Reviews:

Amazing Stories. XXV, July, 1961, pp. 136-138.

Analog. LXXV, June, 1965, pp. 156-158.

Kirkus Reviews. XXVIII, January 15, 1960, p. 56.

Library Journal. LXXXV, January 1, 1960, p. 146.

Nation. CXCI, November 19, 1960, p. 398.

New Statesman. LIX, April 9, 1960, p. 533.

New York Times Book Review. March 27, 1960, p. 42.

New Yorker. XXXVI, April 2, 1960, p. 159.

Saturday Review. XLIII, June 4, 1960, p. 21.

Time. LXXV, February 22, 1960, p. 110.

Times Literary Supplement. April 1, 1960, p. 205.

CAROLINE, O CAROLINE

Author: Paul van Herck (1938-   )
First book publication: 1976
Type of work: Novel
Time: 1984
Locale: An alternate universe

A novel set in a parallel universe in which Napoleon was victorious and France rules Europe

> *Principal characters:*
> BILL, the Pope's nephew
> CAROLINE, his bride

The action of *Caroline, O Caroline* takes place in a universe parallel to ours. In that world, the United States declared war on England in 1815 and sent an army to Europe to help Napoleon. Thus, Waterloo was a French victory, Napoleon enforced his hegemony on Europe, even on Great Britain, and France stretched from the Atlantic to the Pacific. Only one people escaped this domination: the Israelis.

However, in the meantime, the Blacks and the Reds, improving their position while the army was away, rose in revolt and drove the white men back to the sea. Since then, America has been part of a continent about which nothing is known except that its inhabitants are savage heathens.

The action starts in 1984 as Caroline, the bride of the Pope's nephew, is dying. What can be done against plague? Nothing, so Death comes to take charge of the deceased. Caroline reveals to Bill the secret of reincarnation: she will soon take another body, as everybody does, and Bill may be lucky enough to meet her again.

Since Bill is the Pope's nephew, he obtains from the Church a plenary indulgence with which he can commit sinless suicide if need be; but for the time being he prefers to perform the mission proposed by Marshal de Bois-Maison (in reality Woodhouse, since the names have to be translated into their French equivalents). The mission includes a trip to America in the most sophisticated machine available: an airplane. Once arrived, he is to sow dissension and make the Blacks and Reds annihilate one another in tribal wars. Then, depleted and sucked dry, they will fall under the empire's yoke. Why is this mission planned? Because the European economy needs oil. It can be found in America as well as in the Middle East, where the Israelis keep watch on it. Therefore, Napoleon VIII's France has to conquer the oil fields of the American plains as soon as possible. Once the inhabitants are disposed of, the bison may be used as corned-beef. Bill is to be assisted in this mission by an Austrian, a Wagner-addicted fellow otherwise unpolished and self-taught, a racist, hardly good enough to be a corporal.

When Bill sees him — greased hair, small moustache, roguish-looking —

he understands everything. He judges Adolf to be crazy. Who but a criminal madman would accept a mission to destroy an entire people?

In America, Bill and his companion first fly over the land of the Niou-Yokos, a Negro tribe. They catch sight of an assembled fleet of ships and they bomb them. Then they set fire to corn fields and land in the territory of the Wah-Shintogos, an Indian tribe. They make friends with grand sachem Walking-in-the-Clouds. As the Council of Chiefs discusses whether they will war against the Blacks, Bill comes across Caroline, now a bison cow, married with four calves. In his emotion he chooses not to disturb the family.

Everything goes well; the Indians are preparing for war. Adolf and Bill fly back to the territory of the Niou-Yokos in the guise of messengers of the Divine wrath, for the Negroes are Christians. The latter find the messengers' complexions rather whitish for angels. Adolf declares that the reason is that they are Jews. The Negroes welcome them; they are eager to taste the quality of such great persons, and they decide to fatten both of them and savor religiously whoever turns out the fattest. Bill flies away while Adolf is served on a table with an apple in his mouth.

Bill reports to his superiors and informs Mrs. Braun of Adolf's death. Then, raving mad with jealousy, he flies back to America to massacre the bison and have done with Caroline. On his way he catches sight of a fleet sailing toward Europe.

In reality, all he had seen was a fake intended for spies and tourists. The surface was kept primitive while everything underground was highly sophisticated: airplanes, modern cannons, television, and so on. The chief of the Wah-Shintogos had gained his name Walking-in-the-Clouds from owning a private plane. The Americans have everything except capable generals. N!Bolo N!Bolo proposes the position of general to Adolf, who accepts it and leads the crusade against Europe as Commander-in-Chief of the Red and Black armies.

The conquest of Europe is easily accomplished. Adolf forces his way into London, which is in flames, with the Black soldiers singing Wagnerian choruses. One moment of crisis occurs when King Herod of Jerusalem gives assistance to France. Zahal crushes everything and vanquishes both Red and Black armies. Panic ensues. But Adolf keeps his peace of mind. He waits until Shabbat to counterattack, since on that day the Israeli soldiers cannot move nor use their weapons.

Europe is finally cut in two parts: Red armies in the North, Black armies in the South. Paris is a condominium and Adolf lives in Versailles. The last whites are shut up in reservations where they are subjected to penal servitude and must dance the square-dance for the tourists. Bill lives in one of the reservations, married and subjugated. But he comes across a poster with the portrait of Adolf's bride: Caroline. He immediately acts on Stalin and Fidel Castro's advice, disguises himself, and escapes with a bomb in an attaché case. To everyone's great astonishment he puts it under Adolf's chair, a classic joke since Moshe Dayan tried it first in Niou-Yoko.

In prison, Bill meets B. P. Wells, the son of H. G. Wells, who invented a time machine. Bill succeeds in convincing Adolf that he betrayed the white race. The latter, in despair, tries to alter his policy, but Reds and Blacks refuse and everybody goes to jail, even Adolf and Caroline. They all escape by the advent of civil war.

How should the grievances committed by Adolf be redressed? By reshaping history. The first task consists of convincing the American Congress not to interfere with Europe in 1815. This works, but Waterloo is still a French victory. They try harder. They abduct General Blucher, who is substituted by Adolf, and pour a drug into Napoleon's coffee. Adolf wins the day.

Bill comes back to 1984 and heals his bride. Death complains bitterly to him. Bill dropped Adolf in 1930. Because of the madman, Death has devastated herself with overwork and undergone nervous breakdown after nervous breakdown. After some glasses of whiskey she reveals to him the grand secret: every man would live forever were it not for original sin. Under that condition she would gladly retire.

Original sin is just the Pope's hobby, so Bill and Caroline take the Pope along with them to find out what it is. They first believe it to be the discovery of America, a seemingly unpardonable sin. But Columbus had nothing to do with it. Bill and Caroline set out to the future after an atomic war, and the Pope travels to the past. Finally, time being a circle, the Pope again meets Bill and Caroline before a garden of apple trees. As soon as Caroline has eaten an apple, Saint Michael comes to drive them away.

Paul van Herck is a Flemish schoolteacher who works near Antwerp. He first wrote for a radio station. His works deal principally with time travel and tampering with history. Unfortunately he falls a victim to his own facility at writing. He strings episodes together rather than constructing a novel. This problem is quite obvious in *Caroline, O Caroline*, his most compact work. In addition, the author neglects to revise and correct the incoherencies and contradictions of his text. For instance, in this novel the airplane is the most recent invention with which France can gain mastery over the world, yet Zahal already owns a powerful airfleet. The Flemish text is rather flat, so that his novels improve, once translated; the translators have to correct, develop, condense, suppress poor jokes, and sometimes even add their own ideas.

However, the defects melt away in the torrent of action the readers are supplied with. Van Herck's works remind one of Mack Sennett or the Marx Brothers' old movies with their logical madness and nonsense that commands approval. Another contribution of importance is the author's Flemish culture. Death makes several appearances as a comical character, as in the puppet shows, where she drinks a lot and drunkenly tumbles down under the table. She is even a comical character in the comic strips for children.

This novel was a success in France. Napoleon may be defeated at Waterloo by Hitler, but he was drugged. The character of Adolf is obviously enjoyable; he is a mediocre and embittered fellow, involuntarily comical in his pettiness and his fondness for himself. Hitler as a ridiculous puppet and a crowned dunce is a vengeful and tranquilizing picture.

Jacques van Herp

CARSON OF VENUS

Author: Edgar Rice Burroughs (1875-1950)
First book publication: 1939
Type of work: Novel
Time: The mid-twentieth century
Locale: Venus

The romantic adventures of Carson Napier, a twentieth century American, who combats Venusian totalitarianism and wins the heart and hand of a beautiful Venusian princess

Principal characters:
CARSON NAPIER, heroic American aviator
DUARE, Carson's beloved princess of Venus
MINTEP, Duare's father
MEPHIS, Venus' most powerful Fascist
MUSO, Mephis' secret ally
TAMAN, leader of the Venusian resistance to Mephis
ZERKA, Carson's anti-Fascist protectress

Edgar Rice Burroughs wrote five novels about Venus fairly late in his career, between 1931 and 1941. In the Venus series Burroughs relied on many of the stock characters and situations he had been using and reusing since 1912, when he introduced John Carter of Mars and Tarzan of the Apes to a receptive world. Again there is a hero who makes both war and love superlatively; again there is a beautiful, virtuous princess in interminable need of rescue from dangers all over her planet; again there is an exotic alien setting which hero and heroine courageously explore during their perilous search for happiness and self-fulfillment. But despite the presence of these familiar, even dreary formula elements, the Venus novels are essentially different from Burroughs' other writings. In several significant respects they are more original, more mature, and more thought-provoking than anything else he wrote.

The strengths of the Venus novels are especially evident in *Carson of Venus*, the third and by far the finest book in the series. In *Carson of Venus* the series' protagonist, a twentieth century American aviator named Carson Napier, confronts and defeats the most malignant forces on Venus, and in so doing finds the home which he and his beloved Princess Duare had failed to find throughout the two preceding volumes. This happy story has the most coherent, controlled, and consistently intelligent plot of the series. It has an intensity rarely seen in Burroughs' usually episodic style, with events building to a thoroughly dramatic climax and resolution. Here the themes, attitudes, and values which govern the five Venus novels are brought to a full, clearly focused development. The meaning of all that happens to Carson and Duare becomes clear — a startling meaning, because it directly challenges some basic assumptions of Burroughs' other writings.

Burroughs seems to have conceived his Venus series as a contrast to his

Mars series. Although Carson Napier is Venus' greatest warrior and truest lover, he expresses these heroic talents in very different ways than does John Carter of Mars. Carter is consistently the superhero, an idealized figure who easily does what ordinary people can only daydream about. Carson is everyman, a quintessentially average guy, who attains heroism only because events force him to do so. Burroughs gives him names which underline his ordinariness. He is a hero who appears ridiculous to himself and everyone else when he adopts glamorous, grand aliases of the sort which Carter repeatedly acquires. Carson prefers to be called by his first name or by the simple term "Homo," for, as he realizes in *Carson of Venus,* he represents plain humanity. Carson narrates his adventures in the colloquial style of the common twentieth century American, not the rather archaic, bombastic "heroic style" he often assumes. Moreover, unlike the enthusiastically bellicose Warlord of Mars, who learns to love long after he has learned to fight, Carson is a heroically gentle man who avoids violence whenever he can, and who saves his princess by virtue of his wits, not his muscles.

Carson's primary mission on Venus is to debunk and destroy much of what Carter stands for on Mars. Carter, embodying mankind's idealized hopes for itself, perpetually struggles to establish absolute, permanent control over Mars, the symbolic battleground of mankind's hopes and fears. He is a superman, whose descendants and allies are the first members of Mars's new master race. To Carson, however, all authority figures are suspect, theories of master races are dangerous nonsense, and only extremely foolish and seriously deluded people can believe the claims of would-be dictators. Every incident in *Carson of Venus* dramatizes a challenge to dictatorial authority. In the novel Carson defies one caste-ridden tyranny after another: the cave-dwelling Samary, whose Amazonian women brutalize their terror-stricken mates; the Fascistic Zanis; and finally, Duare's own Vepajans. Carson admires and helps only democratically minded Venusians, such as Taman and Zerka, who seem heroic to him because they, too, combat despotism.

The planet on which Carson discovers and asserts the common man's heroism contrasts strikingly with Carter's arid, almost dead Mars. Under its thick cloud cover, Burroughs' imaginary Venus is a mostly oceanic world, dotted with lushly vegetated islands. Various weirdly alien flora and fauna flourish on these islands, but the Venusian people, a homogeneous race except for a few birdmen, closely resemble Earth's human beings in their biology, their costume design, and especially their psychology. They are, in fact, figments of Burroughs' satiric imagination, and each of their island communities caricatures a particular set of human follies and delusions. Living as they do on separate, isolated islands beneath dense clouds, with few technological means of correcting their very limited and distorted perceptions and no philosophical incentives to do so, the Venusians naturally know extremely little about real life. Burroughs' readers share the initial amusement felt by Carson, the space-age Gulliver who tries to convey his larger knowledge to them. But amusement quickly becomes alarm, dismay, and outrage, for over and over, on island after island, the Venusians' obstinate refusal to change their ways unleashes tremendously destructive, despotic forces in their societies. By the time Carson gets to the communities and events described in *Carson of Venus*, the true function of Burroughs' Venus is unmistakable — to dramatize the causes, character, and consequences of totalitarianism.

Venus' significance begins to emerge in *Lost on Venus*, the second novel in the series. In this book Carson and Duare encounter two civilizations which clearly symbolize aspects of totalitarianism. Morov's dictator is a sadistic vampire, who drains the blood from his living subjects and has such a powerfully hypnotic will that even Morovian corpses do his bidding. Burroughs follows this sensationalized image with another which is more subtle, but no less devastating — the scientific "utopia" of Havatoo. Havatoo is Burroughs' version of the "brave new world" which results from uncritical belief in scientific breeding. For the people in Havatoo, biology is destiny in every sense. After generations of selective breeding, they have achieved a perfectly efficient, totally rational, rigidly stratified civilization in which everyone is assigned a suitable place to live and a job to do, and from which all physically, morally, and intellectually deficient persons are excluded. The Havatooans have no dictator and need none, because their eugenic theory dictates every element of their lives. As they apply its principles they become dispassionate, almost mechanical murderers, decreeing death for Duare because she is physically defective (having been born in a foreign country) and finding Carson, with his individualistic instincts, a loathsome atavism. Carson and Duare turn the Havatooans' technological expertise to their own advantage, getting from them the airplane and fuel they need to escape to another island. In the fourth and fifth volumes of the series they combat the sterile intellectuality and demonic scientism of systems like the Havatooans' all over Venus.

Carson of Venus presents two more fascinating anti-Utopias. The Samary reverse sexual stereotypes in a way that Burroughs obviously intended to seem distasteful, with grotesquely strong cavewomen thoroughly dominating comically passive cavemen. In this female chauvinist society, biological gender is destiny, and, as in Havatoo, biological determinism results in social despotism. As Carson and Duare learned the value of spontaneity, passion, instinct, and individuality in Havatoo, so the negative example of the Samary persuades them both to abandon all sexual chauvinism. Carson deplores but cannot alter the whining cavemen's conviction that might makes right. He does far better in dealing with the larger, infinitely more dangerous manifestation of the same theory in the Zani revolution. As their name indicates, the Zanis correspond exactly to Hitler's Nazis. Burroughs' searching, brilliantly satiric analysis of Nazism is the finest political criticism he ever wrote. His critique of the Nazis is all the more remarkable for having been composed in 1937, when Nazism was a young, relatively unnoticed phenomenon.

The Zanis have two principal characteristics: brutal ferocity, and the same smug assurance of their own utter perfection which distinguishes Burroughs' other anti-Utopians. But as Burroughs presents them, their behavior is almost as ridiculous as it is terrifying. Shrieking "Maltu Mephis!" ("Heil Hitler!") at every opportunity, the Zanis reverently stand on their heads whenever their puny Beloved Mephis appears, and they march in a peculiar hop-skip-and-jump step which gets them practically nowhere. Most tellingly, Zani education is done with mirrors. In a clever evocation of Plato's Allegory of the Cave, Burroughs locates Zani schools inside darkened theaters, where the pupils face the rear walls and see only the mirrored images of their actor-teachers. While Burroughs mocks the Platonic theory of the ideally "philosophical" state in Havatoo, he adopts Plato's theory of despotic psychology to explain the Zanis. Implicitly, through his allusion to the Allegory of the Cave, and explicitly, through the direct comments of Carson and other anti-Fascist characters, Burroughs declares that the root of totalitarian bluster and cruelty is extreme fear, insecurity and ignorance.

Although the Zanis epitomize the worst in the pervasively distorted Venusian thinking, Venus holds another and greater threat for everyman. The climax of *Carson of Venus* occurs not when Carson and Duare bomb the Zanis to extinction, but later, when they face and defy the more attractive but much more deadly Vepajan ideology. Vepaja, a community of tree-dwellers lives by a centuries-old complex of customs. Vepajans eschew the crude biological and pragmatic rationales of other Venusian Utopias, and see themselves as the guardians of Venus' purest, most civilized traditions. The values which the Vepajans defend include several which concern the sanctity of the family — the authority of the father, the inviolability of virginity, society's duty to protect the innocence and safety of its women. One of the most intriguing aspects of Burroughs' Venus series, and of *Carson of Venus* in particular, is that here Burroughs challenges these values, on which he had based the heroic codes of his most popular protagonists, Carter and Tarzan. From Carson's individualistic, commonsensical perspective, unthinking adherence to any custom, however hallowed, is as dangerous and leads as surely to despotic abuse as the attitudes and practices of the Morovians, Havatooans, Samary, and Zanis. As Carson could forge his heroic identity only by modifying the pattern set by Carter of Mars, so he must break some of Carter's most cherished taboos in order to establish his and Duare's home on Venus; indeed, he becomes "Carson of Venus" precisely because he outgrows the values of Carter of Mars, and lives with Duare on his own terms.

Because the search for a home is the basic theme of the Venus series, the reader relates to these books quite differently from the way he views the Mars stories, which center on the development of a superheroic personality as conceived in essentially escapist daydreams. In the five Venus novels humanity comes home to itself. Everyman, personified by Carson Napier discovers the heroism inherent in his ordinariness, and defeats the despotic delusions which make any planet hellish. The Venus books express the mature Burroughs' realistic hopes and fears for the popular culture he had spent a lifetime addressing. His message remains urgently relevant to our twentieth century world.

Jane Hipolito

Sources for Further Study

Criticism:

Green, Roger Lancelyn. *Into Other Worlds: Space Flight in Fiction from Lucian to C. S. Lewis*. New York: Abelard Schuman, 1958. Burroughs' treatment of the space flight theme is discussed by Green, who ranks the author among the best in his use of the genre.

Moskowitz, Sam. *Under the Moons of Mars: A History and Anthology of "The Scientific Romance" in the Munsey Magazines, 1912-1920*. New York: Holt, Rinehart, & Winston, 1970. Moskowitz emphasizes the influence of Burroughs in changing science fiction from prophecy to romantic adventure.

Mullen, Richard D. "Edgar Rice Burroughs and The Fate Worse Than Death," in *Riverside Quarterly*. IV (June, 1970), 186-192. Mullen describes Burroughs' methods of endangering his heroine's honor, his novels and the lessons to be learned from them.

Reviews:

Analog. LXXIII, April, 1964, pp. 93-94.

A CASE OF CONSCIENCE

Author: James Blish (1921-1975)
First book publication: 1958
Type of work: Novel
Time: 2049-2050
Locale: The extrasolar planet Lithia and the United States

Earth visitors to Lithia find in the Lithians, an unfallen race, a challenge to Christianity and an opportunity for fusion bomb production, while a Lithian raised on Earth finds here many challenges to Earth's ethics and to reason

Principal characters:
> FATHER RAMON RUIZ-SANCHEZ, a Peruvian Jesuit priest and Earth
> team biologist
> PAUL CLEAVER, Earth team physicist
> MARTIN AGRONSKI, Earth team geologist
> MIKE MICHELIS, Earth team chemist
> CHTEXA, a Lithian metallurgist
> EGTVERCHI, Chtexa's son, reared on Earth
> LIU MEID, female laboratory chief for Ruiz-Sanchez
> LUCIEN LE COMTE DES BOIS-D'AVEROIGNE ("H. O. PETARD"), Earth
> physics theorist and politician
> HADRIAN VIII, Pope, of Norwegian birth

James Blish's extremely well-plotted novel *A Case of Conscience* develops themes of utopia-dystopia, of egotism as a destructive force, of ethics *versus* religion. It clarifies the way a system shapes the thinking of the individual and, in a crisis, withdraws its support and forces the individual to act on his own. As indicated by the title, which comes from James Joyce's *A Portrait of the Artist as a Young Man* (1916), the ultimate power is in the individual.

Father Ruiz-Sanchez, Cleaver, Agronski, and Michelis form an exploratory party of Earthmen commissioned to determine whether the extrasolar planet Lithia, fifty light years away, will serve as a suitable port of call for interplanetary travel. Inhabited by twelve-foot reptilian people of nonaggressive, strictly reasoning nature, lush with persistent drizzle and built on rock (lithium) more potentially rich than the Church's rock of St. Peter, the planet seems to be a sort of Eden. Remarkably advanced in some types of technology, the Lithians have a shortage of iron and an abundance of natural gas, a Message Tree as super-radio, and static electricity. Governed only by an unwritten common understanding, they have no religion, no crime, no amusements, no politics. Lithia is Utopia.

Leaving Cleaver ill from a plant-spine wound, Father Ruiz-Sanchez, the consciousness of Book I, suffers only a minor twinge of conscience in abandoning Cleaver to visit Chtexa's home, thus foreshadowing his general lack of concern for people. What he learns from the noble Chtexa completely alters his view of the universe, but it confirms his view of literature. While neglecting the work of the Church on Lithia, he has been reading Joyce's *Finnegans Wake* (1939), a banned book; and he ponders and solves, in the Honuphrius passage, a case of adulterous conscience involving a priest. Only one short conceptual leap is then necessary: if a book can be written by the Adversary and subsequently banned, and if through the understanding of it the Adversary can be outwitted, then a planet can be created by the Adversary and, if the planet is banned, the Adversary can be defeated. The first, however, is Church policy regarding books; the second about Satan restates the Manichaean heresy — a case of conscience which, in his extreme parochial egotism, Ruiz welcomes.

The Earth commission council reveals Earth's conflicting ideologies. Cleaver, the physicist and imperialist-militarist, proposes to convert the planet into a thermonuclear laboratory and arsenal of fusion bombs for the United Nations. Michelis, the chemist and secular humanist, objects to forcing the Lithians to slave labor and urges an exchange of information with them. Agronski, the geologist and ordinary man, sides with Cleaver. Ruiz, the biologist and theologian, urges a quarantine of the planet because it is a "creation" of the Adversary.

As a biologist the priest is staggered by the process of recapitulation which the Lithians go through *outside* the mother's womb, with eggs laid in the abdominal pouch, birth in the sea, amphibian-to-kangaroo-like development on shore, and emergence from the jungle as homeostatic and homeothermic adults. As a theologian he sees that the Lithians obey Christian precepts perfectly without a Christ and live in complete harmony with everything in their world, as humans did before the Fall. As creatures of logic, they live by axioms — a set of "givens" — with no apparent giver. He sees the planet as a rebuke to the Church's aspirations to promote reliance on God and calls it a trap created by Satan. Of the four Earth visitors, only Ruiz finds his system shattered by this new knowledge of ontogony; for his Church has outlawed Manichaeanism.

With Chtexa's parting gift of a beautiful vase containing a fertilized egg — his own child — the ethical and scientific superiority of Earth will be tested. On Lithia the offspring faces the environment without parental protection (which itself seems both a sin and a crime to Ruiz) and develops a moral code tested by the rigors of their varied environments; they return to society as adults to practice the code, and it works well. On Earth the offspring are protected while growing and are given a moral code which, when the children are thrust out on society, they must test in a world which mentally, morally, and physically seems to be governed not by the code but by survival of the fittest; in other words, the code does not work. Ostensibly, rearing a Lithian on Earth should combine the best of both worlds; but Cleaver's shadow falling over Ruiz's on the departing spacecraft indicates the contest will be between the military and the ethical. Egtverchi, son of Chtexa, subsequently draws his following from the youth of Earth who have no workable code for their living conditions.

As Book II opens, civilization has gone underground since the international shelter race of 1960-1985, a reaction to the threat of nuclear war. The Corridor Riots of 1993 resulted from resentment of the shelter economy and provided an excuse for the United Nations to set up a world state with places such as Greater New York as "target areas," and only a few of the wealthy and powerful are privileged to live above ground. The war-scare economy, having gone underground, has defeated itself; even with international government, it cannot support the cost of reconstruction above ground. This, in the Holy Year 2050, is dystopia.

The priest, wrapped in clouds of theological debate and more concerned with his own soul than the welfare of his foster son Egtverchi, goes to Rome expecting to be tried for heresy. At home the unemotional and perfectly scientific Dr. Liu Meid as foster mother of Egtverchi fails to provide any of Earth's own touted human warmth and emotional support. Egtverchi's computerlike mind, as he matures, reveals his orphanage; he has no loyalty either to Lithia or to Earth. Michelis, often the consciousness of Book II, sees these problems but has no clear doctrine of his own; before he can decide to act, a United Nations commission — the epitome of bureaucratic self-interest and ineptness — passes Egtverchi for citizenship. Ruiz, instead of affixing human responsibility for Egtverchi's psychological displacement, helplessly and characteristically interprets the United Nations action as inevitable for a creature under the protection of the Adversary.

Citizenship gives Egtverchi a country to deny. He destroys a coming-out party given him by Lucien le Comte des Bois-d'Averoigne (a scientific writer known as H. O. Petard) and exposes the count's politically powerful guests variously compromising themselves in private cells for sexual perversion. Despite Earth's arrogance as demonstrated on Lithia, its differentiated systems, in a principle of action-reaction, continually generate events no one, and no system controls. Egtverchi's wrecking the party forces the count to flee and to resign his political operations; but it provides the impetus for his retreat to scientific experimentation, where he becomes the great scientist-magician proper to his heritage. At the party, also, Egtverchi superbly displays his understanding of the anarchically useful monstrosity of his appearance. More than ten feet tall, a reptile walking like a man, with grinning jaws and wattles swiftly changing color, small dinosaurian arms with clawlike hands, a balancing tail, and a tenor voice, he cunningly contrasts his sensational size and distinctiveness with an entourage of ten uniformed automatons. So also the disaffected youth of the world will follow him; and in his subsequent news broadcast, Egtverchi brilliantly exposes and condemns Earth's fraud and failure.

In his next broadcast, urging his audience to write protests against anything that irritates them and to sign his name, Egtverchi emerges as a great revolutionary leader. With the shelter economy, one fourth of Egtverchi's sixty-five million audience are insane, and one third join his forces. Earth's commercial system assures that the sponsors refuse to cancel his program, a financial windfall; and the United Nations as government, instead of rising to meet a crisis, thrusts responsibility for handling Egtverchi onto Michelis and Liu. Moreover, the United Nations has secretly sent Cleaver to Lithia to construct a fusion power plant and, having made an immoral decision, wants Ramon as opposing expert on Lithia disavowed by his Church before they announce the Lithian plans. Egtverchi is clearly right in his last dramatic newscast when he renounces his citizenship and declares himself — like Stephen Dedalus in Joyce's *A Portrait of the Artist as a Young Man* — a citizen of no country but that of his own mind. He urges his followers to do likewise, and he vanishes.

With the state revealed as corrupt, Blish offers a view of the Church in action; here again the institution thrusts responsibility upon the individual. Pope Hadrian VIII, a Norwegian, extends Joyce's satire on Hadrian IV who gave England control of Ireland and extends Frederick Rolfe's pope in *Hadrian the Seventh* (1904). To the Pope, Ruiz explains Egtverchi as a Colin Wilson "Outsider" — "a preacher without a creed, an intellect without a culture, a seeker without a goal," morally interested and contemptuous of morals. Instead of formal excommunication for Ruiz, the Pope has decided he is the man "to bear St. Michael's arms," to be the chief antagonist of Satan and to banish the Adversary from Lithia. A bit Machiavellian and crafty like the Emperor Hadrian of Rome, he knows Ruiz was derelict in duty on Lithia; but neither does he exhibit any papal wisdom. With the suggestion that Ruiz try exorcism, he banishes Ruiz from the Church until Ruiz shall win this battle against Satan.

The fate of society is thrust upon three persons: Michelis, Cleaver, and Ruiz. All must act according to their allegiances. The human solution fails when Egtverchi speaks to his father by way of the Message Tree and the Count's new circum-continuum radio; Egtverchi, having been cast out of Lithian society, refuses to obey Lithia's Law of the Whole. In the riots left in his wake, the innocent Agronski, least indoctrinated of all the Earth's commission, is killed. This implies the converse — that personal egotism, a personal belief, gives power. But with Egtverchi and Lithia posing a stand-off between the United Nations and Ruiz, Blish does not permit the novel to degenerate into a simple confrontation between church and state, though he does show all institutions reduced to the efforts of one person. As the United Nations' problems mount, with riots between its forces and Egtverchi's raging in the streets, only one United Nations man takes action. When Egtverchi is found as a stowaway on a ship bound for Lithia, the United Nations man appeals to Liu, Ruiz, and Michelis to deal with him by way of the Count's new observatory on the Moon.

Either an error in Cleaver's experiment combined with the Planet's natural gas, or Ruiz's simultaneous exorcism, may cause the planet's explosion; the ending is intentionally ambiguous. Cleaver, in destroying all humanity on Lithia, would have unknowingly worked a devil's triumph, Ruiz would have worked God's triumph. But the solutions are equally destructive. Egtverchi had denounced man's fear of death as a form of insanity, so the grief at the close is not from a loss of Egtverchi but rather a loss of what might have been: the humanistic goal of cooperation with a planet that could teach us much. The external problem of Lithia is destroyed but the internal problem of what to do with Earth remains. Ruiz as an agent has shown the Church to be inhuman. The ethical system has failed, and religion's part in it remains obscure except as man believes he is its agent. Every decision remains an individual case of conscience.

Grace Eckley

Sources for Further Study

Criticism:

Ash, Brian. *Faces of the Future*. New York: Taplinger, 1975, pp. 185-187. Ash calls *A Case of Conscience* a novel marked with "religious overtones."

Mullen, Richard D. "Blish, van Vogt, and the rise of Spengler," in *Riverside Quarterly*. III (August, 1968), pp. 172-186. This article gives a close analysis of the novels written by Blish, showing how themes and wording suggest the influence of Spengler.

Reviews:

Amazing Stories. XXXII, August, 1958, pp. 60-61.

Analog. LXII, November, 1958, pp. 145-146.

Fantastic Universe Science Fiction. X, August, 1958, p. 125.

Galaxy. XVII, April, 1959, pp. 143-144.

Magazine of Fantasy and Science Fiction. XV, August, 1958, p. 105.

CASEY AGONISTES AND OTHER SCIENCE FICTION AND FANTASY STORIES

Author: Richard McKenna (1913-1964)
First book publication: 1973
Type of work: Short stories

Five science fiction and fantasy stories, all variants on the theme of the power of the mind to influence external reality

Richard McKenna joined the United States Navy in 1931, and served as a machinist's mate until he reentered civilian life in 1953, whereupon he took a Bachelor of Arts degree in literature at the University of North Carolina, and began to write. He chose science fiction for his early stories in part because he had a temperamental affinity to the genre, but also because he reasoned that the low rates of pay in this area would mean that there would be less competition during his years of apprenticeship. Soon, he turned to general fiction, an area where he hoped to find a wider audience. His novel of naval life, *The Sand Pebbles* (1962), was a bestseller and a critical success. McKenna died in 1964.

The author published only six science fiction stories in his lifetime, and another six were published posthumously. His science fiction is every bit as strong as his better known and more conventional fiction. It is unfortunate that *Casey Agonistes* does not contain all McKenna's science fiction work, but even so, it is a remarkable collection. (Readers who wish to read more might look up "The Night of Hoggy Darn," 1958, a splendid story of ecological detection, in the anthology *Tomorrow X 4*, 1964, and "Bramble Bush," 1968, a *tour de force* about an alien race whose mental symbology is such that they can bring about relativistic effects on the world of matter, a feat which to humans seem like magic, in *Orbit 3*, 1968.)

According to Knight's introduction to *Casey Agonistes*, McKenna was a slow-thinking, widely read man who worried patiently away at ideas until he had absorbed them to his own satisfaction. His stories testify clearly to the fact that he not only absorbed ideas, but put them together in new ways, finding fresh and unusual implications in them. He was a genuine original, with a fine, strong mind of that rather rare kind which is sometimes found in men who go through life with little in the way of academic training, but with an insatiable appetite for thought. The useful, conventional grooves of traditional, linear logic along which a standard education teaches the mind to work, sometimes seem to militate against lateral thinking. With McKenna, the reader has the sense of sparks leaping intuitively between different parts of his mind, parts which for most of us seldom come together.

McKenna wrote genuine hard science fiction, though it was upon the so-called "soft" sciences that he drew. In his case these were primarily cultural anthropology, linguistic theory, ecology, and the psychology of perception.

All five stories in *Casey Agonistes* share a strong, common theme: the ability of Man to shape the external circumstances of his reality by various means, ranging from ecological and cultural engineering to the power of the mind itself to create (or discover) new realities.

The stories form a kind of spectrum between fantasy and science fiction. In some, the explanation for the reality changes that occur is given purely in terms of mind power; these stories could be read as pure fantasy along the lines of wishing-will-make-it-so. In most, the reality changes are given a rationale.

"Casey Agonistes" (1958), the first story McKenna published, is at the fantasy end of the spectrum. It is perhaps the most finished and smoothly wrought of any of his stories, and carries the most immediate emotional charge. The setting is the terminal ward of a naval and military hospital for tuberculosis victims; the patients, "processed" by a tactless and insensitive chief nurse and a doctor equally insensitive, are not even able to die with dignity. The eponymous hero is a capering ape, a mass hallucination called into being by the patients to jeer at their persecutors. Casey is only visible to the patients, though his frantic efforts on their behalf seem to affect the doctor's *savoir faire*.

Casey can even struggle against death, though after one marathon battle, which he does not win, he disappears for days. He constitutes a remarkable metaphor, showing how the dying, the apparently hopeless, may be able through an effort of will to import a little humor, even a little heroism, into their passing. At least it becomes a fight, rather than a lethargic slipping away. Because Casey never becomes objectively visible to others, and because tuberculosis is a disease well known for the feverish visions it can induce in its terminal stages, it is possible to read the story as nonfantastic, as a description of a hallucination which exists in merely subjective terms. But none of the other four stories allow the reader so easy an escape into complacency, and indeed, though none is so directly touching, all are perhaps more mind-stretching and intellectually ambitious.

The simplest story is "The Secret Place" (1966), in which a young scientist-soldier is on duty in the Nevada desert with a geological survey corps during World War II. Some years before, a dead boy was found in the desert, clutching pieces of gold and uranium ore in an area where such ore, geologically speaking, had no right to be. It is the uranium that the army wants. The dead boy's sister is now a grown woman, badly damaged emotionally, almost autistic. It turns out that she and her brother had fantasized a parallel world in the desert, which they could enter. The young soldier who rather cruelly pries this information from the girl maps the fairy world as she describes it, and finds it fits exactly the Miocene landscape that had existed in this spot many millions of years ago. The story has a fine delicacy of feeling, a kind of tremulous reaching out to other dimensions of experience, seen through the eyes of a young man too uncertain and brash to allow his own sensitivity full reign (many of McKenna's protagonists are converted skeptics). The story says, quite unequivocally, that the minds of certain people, often the lonely and the "abnormal," can by their power transcend the barriers of space and time.

This, more powerfully and complexly rendered, and given a combined psychological and physical rationale, becomes the theme of another story as well. "Fiddler's Green" (1967) is the longest and most ambitious story in the book, and in some ways the least finished. One wonders if McKenna, a perfectionist, had not published it during his life because he felt that it needed further work. It would have been a great loss, however, if it had remained locked in his desk drawer, for it is one of the most haunting stories in the science fiction genre.

"Fiddler's Green" is a nautical term for a kind of sailors' elysium, the unreachable happy place. The story concerns seven sailors drifting in a boat after their tramp steamer has exploded in the Indian Ocean, a thousand miles from any shipping line. As they lie meditating cannibalism and dying of thirst, one of them, Kruger, suggests that if they all try in unison they could perhaps imagine a place of safety, a place with cool, running water, and bring it literally into being. Several of them have heard stories of such places. They succeed, but Kruger himself, though he animates this other-dimensional place, exists within it only as an unconscious body, neither living or dead. The other main figure is Kinross, from whose point of view the story is told, the intellectual whose skepticism comes close to wrecking the experiment. The remainder of the story is a kind of variant of the paradise myth, though this Eden is curiously shapeless and restricted in extent, the geometry of its boundaries being a kind of topological impossibility, where the outside is always the inside. As the alternate world's tiny entrance sweeps our own world around the eighteenth parallel of the southern hemisphere, it picks up new inhabitants, many of whom had been desperate or lost and whose grip on "reality" had been rather weak.

The conflict concerns the intellect of Kinross in mortal combat with the unyielding will of Kruger; since the Jungian *anima* of this new world is in a sense their mutual creation, the struggle threatens to tear apart its very fabric. In his decency, Kinross paradoxically brings a serpent into Eden, and on his return to the real world, the serpent, horribly, is still with him, as his unslakable thirst renews itself, this time as a thirst for blood.

In synopsis the story sounds at once Gothic and absurd, but it succeeds because its surrealism (rendered with hypnotic intensity and credibility) is always tied down to real intellectual issues. The old Berkeleian theme of solipsism (does the world only exist because we perceive it?) is here reversed (change our perception of the world, and do we change its essence?) and dealt with seriously. The *donnée* of the story is that the external world in which we all live is a consensus reality, solid only because historically the peoples of the world have unconsciously conspired to see it that way. This tiny alternate world's plausibility comes partly from the way in which it, too, develops a solidity (although of a different kind), though it begins as curiously amorphous and misty around the edges of things. All this involves some very convincing cultural anthropology and even linguistic theory: "Our language is the skeleton of the world" cries Kruger, just before they break through to the alternate place. This theme, that the physical structure of the brain and the symbology of the mind may create for itself external analogues of its being, which may be manipulatable, pervades all McKenna's work. All his stories use some version of solipsism as their springboard.

Even the least successful of the five tales, "Mine Own Ways" (1960), makes the same symbological point. Working in secret, Earth scientists are bringing alien hominid races to the threshold of humanity (in the broader sense) by imposing rituals, savage and cruel, which teach the primitive beings to evolve a mental symbology (under the pressure of this initiation) without which it is not possible to manipulate the world, either physically or mentally. Such a symbology, which often runs counter to animal reflex, it is posited, separates men from beasts. Three other Earthmen, their leader middle-aged and self-indulgent, stumble onto the secret, and they too are forced to undergo the *rite de passage*; in so doing, they renew their own manhood. As a thought experiment in cultural anthropology, which involves some interesting ideas about how we ourselves in the distant past may have evolved into humans, the story is successful, though so condensed as to be clotted in the telling. It is also rather unpleasant in its sexism: McKenna argues that only men need to make the leap into symbological understanding; women (protected by men) are able to continue on the instinctual level.

The most purely science fictional story is "Hunter, Come Home" (1963). Here the manipulation of reality takes two forms, one gross and one subtle. A planet has developed a race of human colonists with unusually strong *machismo*; they cannot call themselves men until they have slain a vicious, carnivorous dinosaur. Their planet has become crowded, the dinosaurs are dying out, and so they have contracted with a group of technicians to clear a second planet, and seed it with their own savage life forms. But the planet resists seeding; its native life forms, a kind of planetary-plant life, are all interlinked, and are awakened into a group subconsciousness by the gross tortures to which they are submitted. With infinite delicacy, they too show themselves able to manipulate reality, by evolving new structures which are able to absorb both the brutal and the gentle into a richer synthesis. (As they are attacked by killer viruses, they become more vivid and beautiful through chemical changes.) The ecological details are amazingly vivid and convincing (in a way these plant-animals are undergoing a *rite de passage* comparable to that described in "Mine Own Ways"), and the story has a hard science fiction surface. Beneath this surface, however, lies a kind of transcendental yearning of a kind that was unusual in science fiction in 1963, though it has become quite common now.

The ending is perhaps too purely a wish-fulfillment, as the hero and heroine who have been condemned to death for their repudiation of the *machismo*-ethic reawaken, renewed by the planetary life system, to become a kind of immortal Adam and Eve. The yearning here has just a little of the saccharine in it, though normally McKenna is able to avoid such plangent notes by a direct matter-of-factness of tone. His authorial voice is flexible, but tough and experienced enough to incorporate occasional moments of tenderness without lingering on them too lovingly.

Nevertheless, there is a little too much gruff sentiment in McKenna, always connected with his wishfulfillment themes. But a literature which does not ask the question of what can we do to make our wishes come true would be sterile indeed. McKenna's great strength is not only that he asks the question; it is also that he gives some of the answers. The fulfillment of wishes never comes easily in these stories, and it involves an understanding of what makes us human in the first place.

In a literature where superman and power fantasies come all too cheap, he brought such fantasies back down to the human level even as he evoked them. He showed their meaning, and, tenaciously, he showed their cost, and he used his science to show how they work. Richard McKenna wrote enough quality science fiction to ensure him a minor niche in the pantheon.

Peter Nicholls

Sources for Further Study

Reviews:

Kirkus Reviews. XLI, May 1, 1973, p. 533.

Library Journal. XCVIII, July, 1973, p. 2151.

Publisher's Weekly. CCIII, May 14, 1973, p. 44.

CAT'S CRADLE

Author: Kurt Vonnegut, Jr. (1922-   )
First book publication: 1963
Type of work: Novel
Time: The 1960's
Locale: Ilium, New York, and San Lorenzo, a small island republic of the Caribbean

In the process of conducting research for a book about the day the first atomic bomb exploded, the narrator discovers a new catastrophic threat to civilization (ice-nine) and a new religion (Bokononism) which cause him to write instead Cat's Cradle, *and to face the threatened end of the world with humor and style*

Principal characters:
> JOHN, the narrator, an author who calls himself Jonah
> DR. FELIX HOENIKKER, one of the "fathers" of the first atomic bomb and the inventor of ice-nine
> NEWTON HOENIKKER (NEWT), youngest of Felix's three children, a midget
> FRANK HOENIKKER (FRANKLIN), Felix's middle child, Minister of Science and Progress in the Republic of San Lorenzo
> MRS. HARRISON C. CONNERS (ANGELA HOENIKKER), oldest child of Felix who becomes the "mother" of the family when her own mother dies giving birth to Newt
> EMILY HOENIKKER, wife of Felix and mother of his three children
> DR. ASA BREED, supervisor of Felix on the Manhattan Project; director of the Research Laboratory at Ilium
> BOKONON (LIONEL BOYD JOHNSON), a black religious leader of San Lorenzo and author of *The Books of Bokonon*
> CORPORAL EARL MCCABE, first ruler of San Lorenzo and avowed enemy of Bokonon

Perhaps Kurt Vonnegut's liveliest novel, *Cat's Cradle* employs multilevel authorial perspectives and conveys the strong fictive inventiveness which has become a hallmark of his writing. The subject of the book is a self-conscious probing of fact and fiction, truth and illusion, and literal *versus* metaphorical reality. The thematic motif is introduced explicitly in the epigrams which precede the first chapter. The first statement, presumably offered by the author, is "Nothing in this book is true." It is followed by a paradoxical companion teaching from *The Books of Bokonon*: "Live by the *foma* (harmless untruths) that make you brave and kind and healthy and happy." These epigrams encapsulate the ironic play-off of one kind of truth against another; indeed, Vonnegut seems to suggest we should live by the harmless and amusing lies of his book, which may even guide us toward virtue and approximate happiness.

In this, his fourth novel, Vonnegut uses a first-person narrator for the first time, fostering a casual intimacy with the reader. However, the confiding and friendly narrator starts out with a lie: "Call me Jonah. My parents did," he tells us, but as he completes the sentence he corrects the truth of the statement, ". . . or nearly did. They called me John." This apparently simple beginning misleads us, and calls attention to the tenuous relationship between what we *call* a thing, and what the thing is or appears to be. This defining of reality by naming it continues throughout the book and culminates in a marvelous invented vocabulary of *Bokononism*. Rhetorically and stylistically, the manner of the first sentence alludes to *Moby Dick*. Both Jonah and Ishmael are figures for the lone survivor; both of them are caught up as if by destiny in events far larger than themselves, and are at last delivered up alone, transformed. While the narrator may technically lie when he says he is Jonah, there is truth to his statement; at the book's end John is a lone survivor.

Jonah is widely regarded as the archetype of the reluctant prophet, the central figure of some of the most ironic and satiric Biblical stories. He was swallowed by the whale after he refused to go to Nineveh to preach, and when the whale belched him up safely again he finally made the journey. Jonah's preaching caused the people to repent, and God forgave them, but then Jonah was angry that their sins should be so easily forgiven. The effectiveness of Jonah's prophecy in Biblical tradition, and Jonah's attitude toward his work and its consequences, should be kept in mind in considering not only John's story, but the prophetic role of Bokonon and ultimately of Vonnegut as well.

Vonnegut shares with other postwar writers the difficulty of knowing what to say or prophesy in the face of nuclear annihilation. In this novel he confronts the situation directly. *Cat's Cradle* has 127 chapters, just seven fewer than *Moby Dick*. Vonnegut invites comparison both with this great American novel and with the Bible, comparisons which seem at first designed merely for comic effect. Vonnegut's book is filled with short, punchy little chapters which certainly lack the narrative range of Melville's great work or the epic scope of the Biblical texts. Yet, the themes of Vonnegut's book point directly to the central moral, religious, and human concerns dealt with in both these monumental works, and in the final analysis his prophecy is directed toward redemption.

John (or Jonah) is ostensibly writing a factual book to be titled *The Day the World Ended*. It will be an account of the day the first atomic bomb was dropped on Hiroshima — August 6, 1945. In the process of working on that book, while investigating the life of the inventor Felix Hoenikker, he discovers that the holocaust which cast the modern world under a shadow of instant annihilation is matched by an equally astounding, nearly opposite apocalypse. Hoenikker has also discovered a substance called "ice-nine," a type of seed crystal capable of "freezing" the world into complete stasis. This secret provides another pole for total destruction. The bomb would annihilate by heat, explosion, a bursting apart; "ice-nine" would solidify even the primordial ooze, an end of absolute motionlessness. Through either the public or private truths discovered by the author, the world could be annihilated. Either way, Vonnegut shows, we face oblivion.

This discovery has a liberating effect; the secret danger somehow enables the writer to escape the curse of atomic doom. Why should a writer be paralyzed by the bomb, after all? Is the nuclear threat really so different from any other apocalypse? Have we not always known we would be annihilated one way or another?

It is, perhaps, understandable that a writer would have nothing to say and nothing to prophesy in the face of total annihilation. Yet, in Chapter 103, "A Medical Opinion on the Effects of a Writers' Strike," Vonnegut deals directly with the possibility of the writer or prophet who gives up. Two characters, Philip Castle and John, both of them authors, discuss the problem. Philip thinks people might actually die during such a strike, "like mad dogs . . . snarling and snapping at each other and biting their own tails." His father Julian expects the impact might be more like death by "ice-nine": "petresence of the heart or atrophy of the nervous system." Like the twin threat of holocaust or stasis, the absence of literary vision is a situation so bleak that Julian Castle ends the chapter with a plea, "For the love of God, *both* of you, *please* keep writing!"

John follows the advice, as we see in the next chapter. Aware of multiple ironies, he records Bokonon's advice as he himself follows it: "'Write it all down,'" Bokonon tells us. He is really telling us, of course, how futile it is to write or read histories. "'Without accurate records of the past, how can men and women be expected to avoid making serious mistakes in the future?'" John, like Jonah, becomes an ironic and reluctant prophet. Implicitly we find him affirming the injunction of Vonnegut's epigram: we should live by harmless lies which make us healthy and happy. We may be made so, according to one medical opinion, by the very lies of this book.

The very words Vonnegut employs accentuate the falsehood of fiction. At the same time, they construct a vivid otherworldly reality which seems truer than mundane existence. Among his most important linguistic inventions are:

karass: a web of those persons fated to be tangled up with the events of one another's lives.

duprass: a *karass* composed of only two persons.

wampeter: the pivot of a *karass*; the hub event or circumstance about which members of a *karass* revolve.

foma: harmless untruths.

granfaloon: a false *karass*; organizations such as the Communist Party or the Daughters of the American Revolution, which apparently have something in common but really do not.

The invented vocabulary is associated with the religion of Bokonon, which in turn is part of a conscious construction of *foma* to keep San Lorenzo running smoothly in a state of "Dynamic Tension." As a counter to apocalypse, Bokonon gives us his various "Calypsos":

> I wanted all things
> To seem to make some sense,
> So we all could be happy, yes,
> Instead of tense.
> And I made up lies
> So that they all fit nice,
> And I made this sad world
> A par-a-dise.

San Lorenzo, governed by the warring truths of McCabe's politics and Bokonon's religion, achieves a Manichaean balance.

The state of "Dynamic Tension" resulting from the balanced extremes of the novel is neatly symbolized in the cat's cradle image stressed by the book's title. Newt Hoenikker remembers his father making a cat's cradle, a string figure of paired x's which is the closest his father ever came to actually playing. Within the novel this cradle becomes a symbol of meaninglessness, for when we look at it objectively we find, *"No damn cat, and no damn cradle."* Yet, by implication, countless generations have been able to look at the abstraction, and, through an act of the imagination, have assigned it a meaning and a name which is surely as much an invention as any of the *foma* of Bokonon.

While the simple string arrangement is the product of some earlier and less technologically complex era, the transient configuration between two hands is parallel to the strung out and complicated plot Vonnegut unfolds to tease his readers. It is a tale of invention within invention, and the final sentence of the book John has written is, in fact, the final sentence of what Bokonon writes in his *Books*:

> If I were a younger man, I would write a history of human stupidity; and I would climb to the top of Mount McCabe and lie down on my back with my history for a pillow; and I would take from the ground some of the blue-white poison that makes statues of men; and I would make a statue of myself, lying on my back, grinning horribly, and thumbing my nose at You Know Who.

The conclusion, while it seems bleak black comedy, is comedy nonetheless. As Bokonon tells us earlier in the novel, " 'Maturity is a bitter disappointment for which no remedy exists, unless laughter can be said to remedy anything.' " Through Vonnegut's satiric and penetrating comic vision, we see through the terror of annihilation which threatens to immobilize our best intentions, our vision, and our imagination. Laughter may indeed remedy a fearsome immobility; a recognition of absurdity is better than no recognition at all. John is finally no self-centered, judgmental Jonah. Vonnegut's book, John's narrative, *The History of San Lorenzo*, and *The Books of Bokonon* contain the truthful lies of prophecy. Like *Moby Dick* and the Bible, they are fascinating, compelling presentations of the human imagination, and as such they prod us from complacency into a dynamic tension through which we know ourselves to be more fully alive.

Richard Mathews

Sources for Further Study

Criticism:

Klinkowitz, Jerome. *"Mother Night, Cat's Cradle* and the Crimes of Our times," in *The Vonnegut Statement.* Edited by Jerome Klinkowitz and John Somer. New York: Delacorte, 1973, pp. 158-177. Klinkowitz compares these two works in this article on Vonnegut's contemporariness.

May, John R. *Toward a New Earth: Apocalypse in the American Novel.* Notre Dame, Ind.: University of Notre Dame Press, 1972, pp. 172-200. May discusses several novels in this book but places *Cat's Cradle* in an excellent light in comparison with other contemporary works.

Reed, Peter J. *Kurt Vonnegut, Jr.* New York: Crowell, 1972, pp. 119-145. Reed gives a lengthy discussion of *Cat's Cradle* in this general work on Vonnegut.

Reviews:

Analog. LXXII, November, 1963, pp. 89-90.

Galaxy. XXI, August, 1963, p. 182.

Magazine of Fantasy and Science Fiction. XXV, September, 1963, p 90.

New Worlds. CXXXV, October, 1963, p. 125 and CLVI, November, 1965, pp. 119-120.

New York Times Book Review. June 2, 1963, p. 20.

THE CAVES OF STEEL

Author: Isaac Asimov (1920-   )
First book publication: 1953
Type of work: Novel
Time: The distant future
Locale: New York City

An intricate and carefully logical exploration of the relationship between man and machine, with a detailed extrapolation of the future of the city

> *Principal characters:*
> ELIJAH BALEY, a New York City detective
> JEZEBEL (JESSIE) BALEY, his wife
> JULIUS ENDERBY, the Commissioner of Police
> R. DANEEL OLIVAW, a robot and emissary

If it is true that man is a toolmaker, it is equally true that tools in turn shape the man. This axiom is central to the reader's perception of Isaac Asimov's *The Caves of Steel.* Asimov here presents both a popular novel and a subtle sociological treatise, a thorough exploration of urbanization and its ultimate effect on mankind — all in the form of a science fiction detective story.

Asimov's *tour de force* in blending two separate and widely diverse genres is in itself worthy of note. Above all, *The Caves of Steel* is a mystery in the traditional sense; it presents in the opening pages a murder, a set of clues, and a cast of characters, including a detective, and it follows that detective to his eventual identification and capture of the culprit. This is formula writing at its most demandingly precise, necessitating rigid adherence to a set of conventions as strict as the rules governing the writing of a sonnet. The achievement here, though, is not simply that Asimov presents a detective story, nor that he sets the story in a fictive future sufficiently removed from the present to make it qualify as science fiction. Rather, it is in his blend of the two forms, wherein the author creates an absolute interdependence: the very elements that make the story science fiction, further provide both motive and method for the murder and even, eventually, offer a solution to the mystery. Here, then, Asimov presents a marriage not of cleverness or convenience, but of necessity; the science fiction depends on the mystery for its content, while the mystery relies on the methodology of science fiction.

Dominating the whole, shaping the story as it shapes the lives and fears and hopes of men, is the maximum machine, the City. A massively complex accretion of steel and stone, plastic, and glass, the City of New York rises multileveled into the sky and busily burrows into the Earth below; it is an integrated construct that has become, in the words of Elijah Baley, "all one building." Its twenty million inhabitants moving smoothly (usually) to and from dormitories and apartments to communal kitchens to "personals" to slideways.

Asimov's portrayal of the urban future is in one sense most optimistic. The City's twenty millions are fed, and if they are not fat, neither are they starving

— yet. They are employed, for the most part, and if that employment is precarious, tedious, assigned by and enmeshed in bureaucracy, it is at least tolerable. They are housed, if under crowded conditions; cleaned, if communally; and dressed, if shabbily. In short, it is a world that works, an extrapolation of what might be the optimum response to extreme overpopulation and dwindling resources. Given the alternatives presented in more pessimistic scenarios — famine, war, plague, cataclysm, and collapse — the future here presented is not untenable.

Yet this image, Asimov makes clear, is not more than that: an image, an illusion. If the City keeps its inhabitants alive, it also keeps them hardly more than that, and even then only tentatively and harshly. In matters both great and small, the City that man has constructed to serve him has in turn made of him what it will and perhaps what it must. Housing, employment, transportation, and nourishment, as well as the smaller conveniences of life, are all assigned and strictly rationed according to a rigid class system.

In such cities lives almost all of earthbound man's population, and thus the City man is mankind. That City man, Asimov demonstrates, has grown small — small not in physical stature, but in reach, in scope. He is small in what he is and small in what he hopes to be. In this sheltered, enclosed, and controlled environment, the City man has turned inward, has become cloistered, fearful, agoraphobic, and therefore unwilling to reach beyond his closed system, and even incapable of doing so. In myriad minor ways this hapless turning demonstrates itself in man's tastes and customs: his acceptance of crowding, his preference for close spaces, his elaborately formal notions of "privacy" under conditions where privacy is impossible.

More important is man's literal agoraphobia, which makes him uncomfortable at the sight of rain, physically ill at the prospect of walking unsheltered in the fields surrounding the city, almost incapacitated by the prospect of intercity travel except through tunneled expressways. This agoraphobia in turn is symptomatic of a greater malaise, the City man's retreat, his inclination toward the *here* and *now* and sometimes *then*, his incurious, even hostile abandonment of what he once ventured. He is content, rather, to burrow farther into his caves of steel, and this contentment is an illness that might, if untreated, be fatal.

If the crisis approaching the City is hauntingly vague and illdefined, a nebulous and tentative shape of ever-increasing shortages and ever more frustrating denials, it is nonetheless real and dangerous. Two solutions are offered, each requiring drastic alterations in the course of mankind and each as mutually exclusive and widely diverse as the two groups they represent. On the one hand are the Spacers, the men of Earth who once escaped to settle new worlds and have now returned, with ships and awesome power and both fear and contempt for earthbound men. On the other are the Medievalists, a back-to-the-land contingent within the City consisting of a secretive hard-core group of activists with many thousands of sympathizers. Here are presented two of the subtle ironies of the novel, and here too arises the motive for murder. Medievalism implies an abandonment of machines, a return to the farmland now left to the care of robot caretakers, a vast and almost ludicrously exaggerated respect for the virtues of simpler times. To the reader alone is left the perception that in its burrowing, in its self-absorbed isolationism, in its backward yearning for a spent Golden Age, mankind already embraces the worst aspect of medievalism.

For the Spacers, though, represented by a tight enclave on the edge of the City housing the ambassadors of the outer worlds, salvation for Earth lies in the resumption of immigration, not to the settled worlds where man already exists, but to entirely new worlds. Just as important is the increased use of robots to ease man's labors and increase his production. This prospect, in the second clear irony of the work, is anathema to the Medievalists and to the City men in general, who see in the smaller machines a threat even as they exist in the maw of the greater machine. Here too arises the motive for murder; for the victim is a Spacer, hated for the success he represents, hated also for his creation of the ultimate robot, an almost indistinguishable reproduction of man himself, identical in appearance to his maker.

If the motive is clear, the method is less so. The Spacer enclave is sealed tight on its borders with the City. No City man can enter with a weapon, and no City man can cross the open fields to enter any other way. The situation parallels, then, the "locked room" of traditional mysteries. The Commissioner of Police, Julius Enderby, is handed both the problem and the necessity of resolving it quickly to head off the specter of Spacer retaliation. He is an ineffectual man, a politician who has risen through charm, not competence, a fumbler who exhibits a melancholic, meditative medievalism even as he decries the faction. He quickly turns over the case to Elijah Baley.

Teamed with Baley in pursuit of the murderer is the Spacer representative R. Daneel Olivaw, and the work from this point becomes a close study of the man-machine interface, for Olivaw is the ultimate robot designed by the murder victim. He is a human-seeming machine capable of passing for man under all but the closest inspection. Here if anywhere the possibilities of the novel are unrealized, for Olivaw presents in his seeming perfection, his tremendous capabilities, his striking blend of complexity and innocence, a dramatic opportunity for both entertainment and insight. Yet throughout the work, Baley continues to dominate, often clumsily in error, often through the impetus of frustration and anger, but still supreme in both achievement and reader interest.

Baley himself is a complex man, protective of his wife and child, aggressive in his pursuit of the truth, angry at the danger of his position — for failure invariably will mean demotion and loss of precious comforts for himself and family — and wary of his assigned partner. Receiving no support from Enderby, repeatedly led astray by his misunderstanding of the nature and capabilities of the Spacers, robots and men alike, and himslf flawed by the same limitations and phobias of his fellow City men, Baley nonetheless pursues the matter doggedly, perhaps demonstrating the value of persistence where inspiration is lacking. Threatened by disaster whether he succeeds or fails, Baley continues to struggle, becoming more ruthlessly effective as the pressures grow.

Olivaw, conversely, though seemingly possessed of greater abilities and certainly of greater factual knowledge than Baley, never moves beyond the role of observer and occasional irritant. If he has any early effect, it is only to complicate Baley's work, forcing the Earthman to devote precious time and effort protecting the robot from his ignorance of man.

In the end, though, it is Baley's reluctant association with the robot, and thereby his gradual apprehension of the machine's nature, of what the machine can and cannot do and of what man himself can and cannot achieve, and of the possibilities inherent in manipulation of the two together, that provides Baley with the solution of the crime and salvation from the pressures bearing in upon him. The final irony lies in the possibility of precisely such an interface of man and machine that the City's Medievalists so thoroughly despise, and yet use, and the Spacers so thoroughly advocate, and have turned against them. Here too in the culmination of the work is made clear the only choice open to the City men, a choice not of retreat to a fantasy-born past that never really existed, but forward to a reality that might, with effort, be made to exist.

Merrell A. Knighten

Sources for Further Study

Criticism:

Pierce, Hazel. "Elementary My Dear," in *Isaac Asimov*. Edited by Joseph D. Olander and Martin Harry Greenberg. New York: Taplinger, 1977, pp. 38-46. Pierce asserts that in *The Caves of Steel*, Asimov's pattern is similar to that found in detective fiction.

Reviews:

Analog. LIV, November, 1954, p. 150.

Authentic Science Fiction. XLV, May, 1954, p. 135.

Galaxy. VIII, July, 1954, pp. 97-98 and XI, April, 1956, p. 88.

Magazine of Fantasy and Science Fiction. VI, May, 1954, p. 88.

New Worlds. XXXII, February, 1955, pp. 118-119.

C'ERA UNA VOLTA UN PLANETA
(Once Upon a Time There Was a Planet)

Author: L. R. Johannis (Luigi Rapuzzi Johannis, 1905-1968)
First book publication: 1954
Type of work: Novel
Time: 1,000,000 years in the past (covering a period of 10,000 years, told by a human
    narrator around 1979)
Locale: Mars and Earth

The first example of Italian "archaeological" science fiction relating the misfortunes of our long-forgotten ancestors, the Martians, and the reasons for their first settling on Earth in prehistoric times

> Principal characters:
> THE WANN, the original name of the Martians
> THE RHAN, inhabitants of a planet between Mars and Jupiter

The niche occupied by Luigi Rapuzzi Johannis in the small *Pantheon* of Italian science fiction lies in a very oddly shaped corner, not only because of the personal peculiarity of his writing, but also because of his short-lived activity in the science fiction field. Rapuzzi came in touch with science fiction after World War II, when he spent five years in the United States (1947-1952) working as an artistic decorator and restorer and developing an inclination toward the American scene. Returning to Italy, he began his short career in writing and editing. Between 1954 and 1958 he published seven novels and nine stories, editing at the same time two collections of science fiction paperbacks, *Galassia* and *I Romanzi del Cosmo*. His main interest in the fiction field was in what is now labeled "archaeological science fiction," science fiction centered around the interpretation or explanation of mysteries of prehistoric times in terms of "alien contacts." This is also the key to the novel examined here, whose title hardly offers a clue of that peculiar way in which Johannis exploits our past history.

By starting with a brief introduction, in which the reader is informed that the story first came into the hands of the Narrator as a legend told by a Lama in a small Himalayan village and was then confirmed by the discovery of a collection of very ancient microfilms on Mars, the author gives an air of documentation to his story. Thus we know that five billion years ago our Solar System contained thirteen planets; that the smallest, and nearest to the Sun, was rapidly consumed by the tremendous solar gravitation; and that Mars was entirely solidified when Earth, Venus, and Mercury were still sparkling with their primeval fires. Here we take for granted that the Red Planet (not red yet) was logically the ideal place for the development of humanoid races and that *Homo Martius* was already differentiated from the other primates twenty-five million years earlier.

Accepting the unusual prolongation of the Mesozoic Era, let us examine the Martians, alias the Wanns (from *Wann*, indigenous name of Mars). From the very beginning of their civilization, they exhibited a spark of good sense never present in mankind. On their little planet, devoid of many resources, they abandoned dreams of power or conquest and devoted themselves to survival. In this way they reached a level of civilization necessary to develop space travel (about one million years ago), only to discover that they were not alone in the solar system. The planet Rhan, placed between the orbits of Mars and Jupiter, was very similar to today's Earth and sheltered another humanoid race which became involved in the course of human history. The inhabitants of Rhan, with plenty of natural resources and food, foreshadowed the way of thinking peculiar to Earthlings and devoted their spare time to cruel fights and wars, completely exploiting both their fellow beings and nature.

At this point, the author suggests that only people with a full belly, or with the means to obtain it, have time to plunge themselves into ideological disputes. This might appear a bit naive, but it brings about an interesting corollary uncommon in science fiction. In a similar situation there were originally no heroes or villains, but only people working out their different social and moral patterns through different backgrounds. Behavioristic as it may seem, this position never suggests any inbred inclination for evil in the inhabitants of Rhan (and in the same way it never puts Martians-Wanns on the side of good), but only hints at their clumsiness or stupidity for being unable to attain some sort of balance of power on their world. On this planet where science is mainly used to implement war, the future history of Earth is cruelly foreshadowed to the most destructive consequences. Leaving atomic energy behind them, the Rhans prefer to play with new tools developed out of another form of energy (magnetism), and they succeed in blowing up their own planet, disorienting the entire Solar System at the same time. Mars suffers the most from the explosion and is so badly battered that little more than a dead planet remains. Earth is plunged into a new Ice Age. The remains of Rhan forms the Asteroid Belt with only a few people surviving. A few of these survivors, exsupporters of a pacifist sect who had uselessly tried to prevent the catastrophe, fled to Mars in time. The Martians themselves, forced to recognize the ruinous conditions of their planet after the self-destruction of Rhan, flee in turn to Venus, which appears more likely to survive than Earth. The surviving Rhans choose Earth, in spite of the difficulties present on this world, in its Quaternary period (with the uprising of the first men).

Here, at last, through the informal manner in which the author chooses to show the decline and fall of the first humanoid races in the solar system (along with many footnotes concerning linguistic, anthropological, scientific, and social matters among both Martians and Rhans), a tender and difficult love story between a Rhan girl and a Martian emerges. Although the two races are separated by many cultural differences, and every genetic union is forbidden, the author loosens his historical grip on the story enough to allow individual feelings to come out.

Allegorically, this love story suggests a deeper meaning; the comparison between the Rhan girl and the Martian causes the reader to explore their respective *Weltanschauungen* and emphasizes the differences between them. While every Martian is submissive, formal, and respectful, the surviving Rhan female embodies the qualities of her entire race. She is passionate, strong-willed, and resolute. She will be the first to contact the prehistoric inhabitants of Earth and is the true example of how (according to the author) genius can be generated not by a cool control of thinking and emotions, but by a reasoned tempering of passionate impulses. The same point, of course, is applied by the author to the world that surrounds him in an attempt to bring his message home to as many readers as possible.

Gianni Montanari

THE CHILD BUYER

Author: John Hersey (1914-   )
First book publication: 1960
Type of work: Novel
Time: The near future
Locale: A state capitol in New England

The State Senate Standing Committee on Education, Welfare, and Public Morality meets to investigate Mr. Wissey Jone's attempt to purchase ten-year-old Barry Rudd

> *Principal characters:*
> BARRY RUDD, an exceptionally bright ten-year-old boy
> WISSEY JONES, a vice-president of United Lymphomilloid Corporation
> SENATORS MANSFIELD, SKYPACK, AND VOYOLKO, members of the Committee
> MR. BROADBENT, a lawyer, the Committee Counsel
> DR. GOZAR, Principal of Barry's school
> MISS PERRIN, Barry's teacher
> MR. CLEARY, the Director of Guidance
> MR. AND MRS. PAUL RUDD, Barry's parents

John Hersey is not known primarily as a science fiction writer. His reputation is based more upon such works of contemporary fiction as *Hiroshima* and the Pulitzer Prize-winner, *A Bell for Adano*. Hersey's science fiction credentials, like those of George Orwell and Aldous Huxley, are based on only four or five novels; in fact, Hersey's *The Child Buyer* is often compared to Orwell's *Nineteen Eighty-Four* and Huxley's *Brave New World*. Like Huxley and Orwell, Hersey found, at least in this instance, that he had something to say which could not be said using contemporary characters in a contemporary setting. Hersey wanted to make some satirical comments about public education, about the various people and agencies surrounding public education, and about mid-twentieth century attitudes toward progress and science. To make these comments, he extrapolated a near-future situation in which a representative from a large research firm attempts to purchase an exceptionally bright ten-year-old boy.

The novel itself is set up in a rather unusual way. The title page announces that what follows is the transcript of a series of Hearings held by the State Senate Standing Committee on Education, Welfare, and Public Morality. The primary effect of this structural device is to bring the characters themselves into the spotlight without any softening accents of setting or tone. All the reader has to focus on are the words of the characters themselves. All of the characters' speeches, therefore, must be read carefully, for it is through their own words, and the ways in which those words are used to describe their own actions and the actions of others, that the characters reveal themselves to the reader.

The novel, then, is a series of interwoven question-and-answer sessions as each character explains his interpretation of and relation to Mr. Jones's attempt to purchase Barry Rudd. The characters who provide the organizational frame for the book are the Senators — Mansfield, Skypack, and Voyolko — and the Committee Counsel — Mr. Broadbent. They question the various witnesses throughout, and their questions, reactions to answers, and comments to one another in Executive Session betray weaknesses that severely damage if not completely destroy the impartiality that such proceedings should have.

Senator Mansfield, the Committee Chairman, is the least offensive of the three senators. On the surface, he seems to suffer from little of the partisanship and ignorance that are apparently the chief characteristics of his two senatorial colleagues, and he appears to understand more clearly the problems being examined by the Committee. But Mansfield, although he is the Chairman, is not a leader. He is Chairman merely by seniority, and instead of keeping the Committee on track and out of partisan squabbles, he allows the Hearings to proceed in a disorderly fashion, dictated in a large part by the lawyer Broadbent and by Senator Skypack, so that the cause of justice often takes a back seat to concerns of politics, business, and science. Senator Voyolko is an ineffective member because he pays little attention to the Committee's discussions, and does not understand much of what he does pay attention to. His comments and questions are usually far off the topic, and he never remembers anyone's name correctly; moreover, his inability to use the English language properly suggests a lack of education.

Broadbent and Skypack, however, are quite powerful personalities and control the Hearings for all practical purposes. Several of the witnesses quite correctly identify Mr. Broadbent as a lawyer on the make. He forges into the sensational aspects of the investigation like a man with his eye on tomorrow's headlines. Mr. Wairy, the Chairman of the School Board, who studied law himself, suggests that Broadbent has "D. A. fever." Broadbent sees the proceedings simply as a stepping stone to an important court case which will boost his career. Skypack, on the other hand, has the power of his convictions. Unfortunately, his rather reactionary convictions are often little more than preconceived notions; for example, he initially insists that Wissey Jones is attempting to buy Barry Rudd for immoral purposes; he refuses to believe that former juvenile-offender Charles Perkonian may have reformed; and he decides that Miss Perrin is an unfit teacher because she was a union member thirty years previously.

Skypack is Hersey's primary spokesman for the worst aspects of the "my country, right or wrong" attitude. Therefore, as soon as he is told that Jones's purchase of Barry Rudd involves scientific progress and national defense, he is on Jones's side, although there is no evidence other than Mr. Jones's off-the-record testimony that either science or national security will be served by selling a child. As it turns out, when United Lymphomilloid Corporation's plans are made public, it becomes clear that the national defense aspect of the scheme is very minor; but once Skypack has reacted automatically to key words that incite his patriotism, nothing will change his mind. In an Executive Session, he tells the other Senators that he is going to get "that little twerp" before the Hearings are over; he has no qualms about forcing Barry's parents to sell their son to a corporation as long as "the State" is being served.

The politicians are not the only ones who, as a group, come under Hersey's satirical scrutiny; the educators' shortcomings are also held up for criticism. Mr. Owing, the Superintendent of Schools, is so unable to make an explicit statement or a firm decision that he is a joke among the townspeople and a totally ineffectual witness at the Hearings. Owing, who should be one of the leaders in the school system, has trouble making up his mind about what to have for lunch. Miss Perrin, Barry's teacher, is similarly ineffective. She is characterized by the Director of Guidance as a combination mother and peer to her students. She keeps abreast of all the latest methods and progressive trends in her field, yet she never changes her old ways of doing things. The children like her, however, and that is a point in her favor. Both Owing and Perrin probably do little active harm in the system, especially to the children, and it seems that Miss Perrin's students do have a positive attitude toward school even though they may not be very highly motivated by their teacher.

There are other educators, however, who *are* actively harmful. Mr. Cleary, the Director of Guidance, for example, is so caught up in his standardized educational examinations and his psychological theories that he has lost sight of the students as anything more than items on a chart or points on a graph. Cleary, like Broadbent, is a man on the make; he is looking for a nice administrative job in a plush suburban school system so that he can have a split-level house and a Mercedes. When Jones arranges this, Cleary, who has always prided himself on his rationality, becomes quite willing to aid in the purchase of Barry Rudd — an action he had initially opposed. Mrs. Sloat, the President of the P.T.A., is another social climber who is much more interested in being the President of the P.T.A. than in doing anything positive for the school district. And like Senator Skypack, Mrs. Sloat is a victim of her own constricted attitudes. She finds Barry's intelligence offensive, especially since he is from "the wrong side of the tracks." And Millicent Henley, the State Supervisor for Exceptional Children, seeks aid for the exceptionally disadvantaged, but thinks that spending money on the exceptionally gifted is undemocratic.

On the other hand, some of Hersey's positive characters are educators too. Miss Cloud, the Chief Librarian of the Town Free Library, for example, is delighted by Barry's exceptional intelligence and curiosity, and helps him search out the answers he seeks, even when the topics (such as sex) are not generally considered things that a ten-year-old boy should be investigating. She believes that healthy curiosity should be satisfied and that withholding information is what leads to "prurience and sneaking and perversion."

Another positive educator-figure is Dr. Frederika Gozar, the principal of
Barry's school, who has earned several graduate degrees, put in more than two
hundred hours of graduate work beyond her Ph.D., and still maintains an interest in biological research. She works in the biology lab at the high school
for several hours each morning before classes begin, and Barry often keeps her
company. Dr. Gozar and her sister, a college professor, pulled themselves out
of an intellectually stifling backwoods environment by hard work; she is a
system-conqueror who has accomplished what few people, male or female,
during that era could have accomplished. She believes in fulfilling one's potential, and thus encourages Barry's curiosity. She often acts as Hersey's
spokesman on political, social, and educational matters; her only fault, however, is that she sometimes goes too far. In the end, she is one of those who
helps to convince Barry to go with Wissey Jones; she believes that Barry will
be strong enough to work from within the United Lymphomilloid system to
"bring the system down." Gozar is as opposed to the United Lymphomilloid
system as Wissey Jones is slavishly devoted to it; they are antagonists, and
Barry is caught in the middle.

Barry, the focus of the controversy, is an exceptionally bright boy. Standardized tests such as the Stanford-Binet, establish his I. Q. at 189. He has
some of the negative characteristics traditionally associated with exceptionally
bright children: he is overweight, prefers to be alone, and performs poorly at
any sort of physical activity. This latter trait gives his peers an excuse to
ridicule him, and it also estranges him from his father, who is talented at
nearly every form of manual labor or craft. On the other hand, Barry has the
positive qualities associated with genius. In addition to his native intelligence,
he is extremely curious and quite inventive. Given a math problem, he is likely
to find an unorthodox but faster way to reach the answer. He is fascinated with
language and with biology; and partly due to Dr. Gozar's example, he wants to
be a taxonomist. All in all, he comes across in the novel as a pleasant boy who
offends almost all of his peers and many of his elders simply by being smarter
than they are. In the end, the most damning comment of the book is made by
Barry; he tells the Senators that he has decided to go with Jones because it
will, at least, be *interesting*, more interesting than anything he can now expect
at home or at school.

There are quite a number of other topics and characters in *The Child Buyer*.
Barry's parents have their own interests tied up in his sale. Charles Perkonian,
the former delinquent, is enough of an outsider to be a friend to Barry; in fact,
all of Barry's friends — Dr. Gozar, the system-beater, and Miss Cloud, the
humpbacked librarian, for example — are outsiders in some way. The power
of money is examined; Jones ultimately buys most of his allies — Barry's
parents, Miss Perrin, and Mr. Cleary are especially susceptible. Primarily,
though, Hersey has written a novel which takes a hard look at the American

political and educational systems and at the American's faith in science and progress; and he finds them all wanting.

Charles William Sullivan III

Sources for Further Study

Criticism:

Burton, Arthur. "Existential Conceptions in John Hershey's Novel, *The Child Buyer*," in *Journal of Existential Psychology*. II (Fall, 1961), pp. 243-258. Burton explores the conceptions necessary to the story of *The Child Buyer*.

Sanders, David. *John Hersey*. New York: Twayne, 1967, pp. 108-121. Sanders calls the novel a critique of many things in today's society, including education.

Shalett, Sidney. *"The Child Buyer,"* in *New York Times Book Review*. September 25, 1960, p. 4. Shalett considers this novel a tour-de-force, especially with its total question and answer format.

Reviews:

Analog. LXVII, June, 1961, pp. 162-163.

Atlantic. CCVI, October, 1960, p. 117.

Chicago Sunday Tribune. September 25, 1960, p. 3.

Christian Century. LXXVII, November 16, 1960, p. 1347.

Christian Science Monitor. September 29, 1960, p. 11.

Commonweal. LXXIII, December 16, 1960, p. 323.

Extrapolation. II, May, 1961, pp. 40-41.

Library Journal. LXXXV, September 1, 1960, p. 2957.

Nation. CXCI, October 8, 1960, p. 231.

New Republic. CXLIII, October 10, 1960, pp. 21-26.

New York Herald Tribune Book Review. September 25, 1960, p. 3.

San Francisco Chronicle. October 6, 1960, p. 33.

Saturday Review. XLIII, September 24, 1960, p. 21.

Time. LXXVI, October 10, 1960, p. 114.

THE CHILDE CYCLE

Author: Gordon R. Dickson (1923-   )
First book publications: Dorsai! (1959); *Necromancer* (1963); *Soldier, Ask Not* (1967);
   Tactics of Mistake (1971)
Type of work: Novels
Time: The fourteenth to the twenty-fifth century
Locale: The scattered human worlds

   The development of new breeds of men among the stars, from the point of view of
psychology, philosophy, and the evolutionary struggles of pivotal individuals

   Gordon Dickson is the master of the superhero story in modern science
fiction. His heroes are not mutants or the artificial products of advanced
science; they are distinguished from ordinary people only by being stronger or
smarter or, most importantly, by having a superior sense of purpose and the
courage to confront the future. Even those of Dickson's supermen who seem to
have more esoteric powers draw them from some invincible sense of self as we
all, deep down, possess. As for the rest — heightened perception, incisive
logic, and imagination — these qualities are all so close to home that as we
read we begin to reach out and touch them in ourselves.
   Each of Dickson's exceptional young men must choose between security
among the undistinguished masses and the risks of challenging the dangerous
unknown in the service of his fellows. The mythologist Joseph Campbell has
suggested that this heroic choice may be the most distinctive myth pattern of
Western culture. It is without a doubt central to the appeal of much science
fiction, and Dickson evokes it more purely than any other writer. His young
men are driven by an overriding purpose into the thick of situations on which
is hinged the fate of the human race. They are bringers of change, battling
those who would try to cling to old ways, and against all the forces which
hinder the race's destiny.
   The weakness of these heroes is their lack of introspection. All of their
purpose and perceptiveness is turned outwards; one might even say that their
outer sensitivity has been hypertrophied because of some inner lack. They continually suppress emotion so they can "get the job done." It is a very old-
fashioned male world they live in, guided by the belief that to admit any of the
softer "feminine" feelings is to impair one's fitness. Tenderness is allowed
only at the end of the story, when the hero has completed his mission and is
ready to settle down. Despite this failing — the genre still awaits a superman
with all those powers of insight and indomitable will, who can yet allow a full
range of human feelings — these novels have a peculiar excellence. The
weakness in the characters seems to be linked to the success of the stories.
Perhaps because they skirt emotion so positively, Dickson's brilliant tales of
strategy and mental confrontation have a cerebral intensity rare in science fiction.

It is little surprise, then, that the direction in which Dickson has developed his most ambitious work has been to broaden his concepts rather than to build fullness into individual characters or scenes. He has chosen to write a loosely federated group of novels, each completely able to stand on its own, yet tied to the others by theme and countless strands of history. The individual novels essentially conform to the heroic pattern outlined above, but the entire history will add new dimensions to it. Dickson calls this work "the Childe cycle," after its ultimate novel, *Childe*, which is yet to be written. Thus far, he has written only four out of a projected total of twelve novels, three of which will be historical, three contemporary, and six science fiction. When completed, the cycle will comprise (according to Dickson) a massive science fiction treatise tracing the evolution of "Responsible Man" from his roots in Renaissance Italy to a final flowering in the twenty-third century. The evolutionary potential of the human race is far from exhausted, the cycle argues; it must be engaged more than ever by the increasing technological power available to the average man — ultimately, the power to create or destroy worlds. Such power demands a more profound form of individual awareness and responsibility than man has yet displayed. It requires that he become in many ways superhuman.

On the level of the individual, one might say that all of Dickson's books are about the evolution of "responsible man." The distinctive quality of the Childe cycle rests in its portrayal of a *species-wide* response to the evolutionary challenge. The basic concept is that as a result of space travel and a multiplanet environment, the human race splits into a number of widely different "splinter cultures," each embodying a different facet of human personality. It is as though the race were trying out the survival potential of a number of human subtypes. Each of those types is superhuman in its own way; the question is whether they will lead to the necessary final development. The principal types are the Dorsai mercenaries, representing the heroic, warrior elements in the human psyche, the "Friendlies," in whom religious faith has become fanaticism, and the meditative "Exotic" philosophers. In addition there are the technocrats and pure scientists of the planets Venus and Newton, and the entrepreneurs on Ceta, though Dickson seems to be downplaying these types as the cycle progresses. The principal actors in the novels so far have been the Dorsai (so much so that *Tactics of Mistake*, *Soldier, Ask Not*, and *Dorsai!* have been published as "the Dorsai trilogy), which is little surprise, considering Dickson's emphasis on the heroic. However, as we shall see, *Soldier, Ask Not* and the forthcoming *Final Encyclopedia* suggest that the final evolution will come not from the Dorsai but from the basic stock of Earth. It is not just the occasional hero who must develop responsibility for his powers but the race as a whole.

Dorsai! was one of Dickson's earliest novels, and in addition to beginning the cycle, set the template for the individual heroic pattern which preoccupies nearly all his works. A young man, as yet untried, but marked by *difference*

from an early age, opposes himself to the forces of conventionality and ignorance, which are masterminded by some other, older man whose genius nearly
equals his own, but who is motivated by selfish lust for power. Driven by an
undefined, intuitive sense of responsibility to his fellow men, he thrusts himself into the center of a massive (life-threatening for the entire species) struggle, which he can guide to a safe conclusion only by the mature development
of those powers which have marked his youth with such potential. In this case,
the man is Donal Graeme, a young cadet in the Dorsai mercenaries, and his
opponent William of Ceta, a planetary representative and entrepreneur with
vast power between the stars. Though William has as yet made no move,
Donal somehow seizes on him as his destined opponent. He sees Williams'
evil nature in the ruin of the people who surround him, and deduces (it is not
quite clear how) that he plans to shatter the delicate balance between the
human worlds and then to bring them all under his own sway. The story
revolves around the brilliant tactical maneuvers by which Donal brings himself
to preeminence among the Dorsai, and puts himself in a position to oppose the
enemy he had known from the beginning. It becomes a battle between Donal's
intuitive generalship and the powers of statistical extrapolation marshaled by
William through his domination of a young mathematical genius. Donal of
course is the victor; and in the course of victory, he has become transfigured,
the victory now only a small step in the vision of a man who can see so much
further than all others. (This is an intriguing reversal of Asimov's *Foundation
Trilogy*, in which there also occurs a confrontation between a statistical science of human behavior and a freak mutant. Here the "mutant," not the scientist, is the victor, because he is not a freak, but a forerunner of the general
human evolutionary potential.) The book ends with a powerful evocation of
the loneliness of the superhuman, and the continuing struggle in which he must
engage to guard the species until it has caught up with him.

The next novel written for the cycle, *Necromancer* (also published as *No
Room for Man*), returns to the time before space travel has set man on different
worlds. The World Engineer, guided by a huge computer, has so regimented
life on Earth, in the interest of comfort, safety and stability, that men are no
longer able to find adequate scope for their abilities. As a result, a number of
bizarre cults have come to preoccupy the overcrowded world of the twenty-
first century. Chief among these is the Chantry Guild, a society of sorcerers.
Its members have gained their abilities in exhange for service to the "Alternate
Powers" and a commitment to destruction of the current world order.

Paul Formain, a young mining engineer who has lost his arm in an accident,
is drawn to the Chantry Guild by their claim that they can regenerate lost
limbs. He soon becomes embroiled in a three-way struggle between the master
computer, the Guild, and some unexpected, indomitable inner part of himself
which seems to be playing its own game. Eventually Formain discovers
(shades of van Vogt's *World of Null-A*) that he occupies only one of several

duplicate bodies grown by Walter Blunt, the founder of the Chantry Guild, and is intended to be Blunt's successor. But that indomitable inner part of Paul (which Blunt believes is his own infused personality) turns out to be none other than Donal Graeme, returned somehow through time to shepherd another important transition for the human species. The means of interstellar travel are on the horizon, and Blunt's will to destruction must be stopped if human evolution is to continue. He has one vision of the human future, the World Engineer has another, and both must be allowed to survive. With the advent of space travel, there is no need for a single planet to remain bursting at the seams. There is room — and indeed a necessity — for all points of view. At the climax of the novel, the seedbearers of four of the splinter cultures are all gathered in one room, each beginning to feel the call of his separate potential. Blunt's Chantry Guild will go on to become the Exotic philosopher culture of the planets Mara and Kultis; the scientific planners will have their way on Venus and Newton; a tormented hotel security guard who blunders into the final confrontation will found the fanatical religion of the Friendly worlds; and Formain is, of course, a representative of the Dorsai.

But what of Earth itself in this splintered future? This question is raised in *Soldier, Ask Not*, the third of the books to be written for the cycle. This novel is contemporary with *Dorsai!* (its hero, Tam Olyn, nearly meets Donal Graeme at a party given after one of his early victories), but is written from an entirely different point of view. It introduces several important new ideas to the cycle. The splinter cultures, which were an intriguing but essentially unexplained background feature in *Dorsai!* and a concluding vision in *Necromancer*, become the conceptual centerpiece. Earth has been left behind by the comparative supermen (each in their own specialized way) of the younger worlds. This is more than a subjective grievance to the men of Earth: in the interstellar marketplace, the chief medium of exchange is human skill, and in this Earth lags far behind. One man, Mark Torre, has conceived the theory that the men of the younger worlds are specialized facets of the basic human stock, and essentially nonviable on their own. Some day, man will need to be reunited. Torre has conceived the building of a "Final Encyclopedia," a computerized assembly of all man's knowledge about himself, for the dual purpose of obtaining a trade product — information — for the planet, and of discovering that extra potential present in full-spectrum earth man. Only when that potential is discovered and actualized can the reunification of man begin.

The success of Torre's project is doubtless the subject of Dickson's forthcoming addition to the Childe cycle, *The Final Encyclopedia*. In *Soldier, Ask Not*, the encyclopedia is background, as Dickson has chosen to explore the world not of the evolutionary hero but of his evil opponent. Tam Olyn is the only man in forty years (other than Torre himself) to hear the "voices" of the still-unfinished encyclopedia, but he refuses to take over its work from the aging founder. He is sick of Earth and filled with hatred for the stronger men of the splinter cultures. His only ambition is to become a member of the impartial Newsman's Guild, and so be free of any planetary authority.

But Tam is far from impartial. After a disastrous incident while covering a war of the fanatical Friendlies, Tam's hatred of the splinter cultures focuses on them alone. He begins to turn public sentiment against the Friendlies, all the while maneuvering them into a position where they will set themselves against the other worlds and so be destroyed. But despite his remarkable abilities to manipulate other men, his will falters against the strength of the Friendly faith. In seeking their destruction, he is going against the best in himself, bringing evil to the world for all his attempts to convince himself it is good. All aspects of the human racial personality must be integrated, none destroyed. Slowly he comes to learn that evolutionary ethic which was inborn in Donal Graeme, and saddened, but far wiser, he returns to Earth to take up his true work on the Final Encyclopedia.

Tactics of Mistake does not add to the conceptual overview, but simply to the history of the Childe cycle. Organized around essentially the identical individual hero pattern as *Dorsai!* (it mirrors even particular incidents), it describes the crucial point in time when the splinter cultures become independent from the Earth which colonized them. Cletus Grahame, a young officer of Earth's Western Alliance, opposes Dow deCastries, powerful Secretary of the Eastern Coalition, and shepherds the transfer of power from the two political blocs on Earth to the new worlds. After engaging deCastries' enmity so that the other will act unwisely against him, Grahame emigrates to the Dorsai. There he develops that physical and mental training which creates the essential Dorsai warrior character. After decisively defeating deCastries and the Eastern Coalition, he creates a new balance of power: with Dorsai mercenaries available, the new worlds no longer need to align themselves with one or the other of the political factions on Earth. The independence of the splinter cultures is assured.

The final outcome of Dickson's cycle is difficult to predict. On an individual level, Donal Graeme's apotheosis at the end of *Dorsai!* leaves little room for further development, so presumably the later novels will detail the success of the Final Encyclopedia and provide some kind of insight into the rapprochement of the individual "superman" and the racial development towards reunification and responsibility. The situation is complicated by evolution of the concepts over the nearly twenty-year span since the first of the novels was written. It seems as though Graeme was initially considered the ultimate development of "responsible man," and all that remained was for the rest of mankind to catch up. The concept of the reunification of the splinter cultures into "full spectrum man" seems to have come later. And, of course, there may be further unexpected twists in Dickson's basic theme.

Dickson sees this basic theme — the future evolution of man — as straightforward extrapolation from tendencies he has seen at work in our culture, the need for responsibility with technology being an obvious one. Less obvious is that the three historical novels he plans to include in the cycle provide an additional base of fact from which the others are extrapolated. Of the three, one will concern Sir John de Hawkwood, the fourteenth century mercenary soldier, another the role of Milton, the famous poet, as a propagandist for Cromwell, and the third will be based on the life and philosophy of the poet Robert Browning. Though these novels have not yet been written, it is possible to see the roots of some of Dickson's ideas simply by looking at the lives of the three men he has chosen to study. Hawkwood was the most famous mercenary soldier of his day. After fighting for Edward III and the Black Prince against France in the Hundred Years War, he went to Italy and took over a group of English mercenaries known as the White Company. It is hard to see a trace of "responsible man" in Hawkwood — he was skilled and professional, but hardly an unselfish hero like Donal Graeme or Cletus Grahame — but it is easy enough to see in him the origins of the Dorsai. The White Company was distinguished from the other mercenaries in Italy by its superior military training, which incorporated the revolutionary discovery of the British at Agincourt, of the power of the longbow against armored cavalry. In addition, we see the concept exploited in the Dorsai books, of mercenary exchanges between governments: though for the last twenty years of his life, Hawkwood and his band of nearly four thousand highly trained soldiers were in the employ of Florence, they were frequently loaned to other states in exchange for specified favors. Hawkwood once even employed the practice (used by Friendly mercenaries, not Dorsai, in *Soldier, Ask Not*) of holding a state which had dismissed his services to ransom in order to be rid of his presence.

The influence of Browning is harder to define. He might be considered a prototype of the Exotics (though surely they bear the deeper imprint of Eastern mysticism). Like the philosophers of the planets Mara and Kultis, Browning was a prophet of equanimity in the face of the world's evils, and like Dickson (though not specifically the Exotics) he looked on heroism less in terms of strength and courage than of resolution and intellectual power. In addition, his narrative technique may have given some impetus to the fundamental idea of the splinter cultures. In his long poems, he presents each of a number of different points of view, allowing all of them equal validity, and yet suggesting that there is a total view beyond any of them, some kind of synthesis which will give them all a place and a deeper meaning. Likewise, the Dorsai, the Friendlies, and the Exotics represent equal parts of some yet to be understood whole.

Of Milton, there is even less to be said. He worked as a propagandist for Cromwell's government, and some of his essays may have suggested the problem depicted in *Soldier, Ask Not*: the need for the man with the power to shape what people think to take responsibility for maintaining the freedom and integrity of those people.

Each of these biographies provides some insight into the origins of the distinctive splinter culture framework of the Childe cycle, but only Milton's, at least on superficial inspection, adds to the concept of responsible man. Since heroic responsibility is a theme in nearly all of Dickson's books, and the splinter culture concept is peculiar to the Childe cycle (and since, as we have seen, there seems to be some disagreement between the individualistic initial formulation of the evolutionary theme in *Dorsai!* and Torre's historical vision in *Soldier, Ask Not*), it may not be that Dickson's theme is less unified and less carefully reasoned than he would have us think. But all such speculation and criticism on these counts, must be reserved for publication of the remainder of the cycle. Only then will it be possible to say whether Dickson has created a conceptual masterpiece or an abortive attempt to raise his storytelling to significance by fusing it with an ambitious philosophy of history.

Timothy O'Reilly

Sources for Further Study

Reviews:

Necromancer:

Analog. LXX, October, 1962, pp. 167-168.

Magazine of Fantasy and Science Fiction. XXIV, March, 1963, pp. 34-36.

Tactics of Mistakes:

Analog. LXXXVIII, October, 1971, p. 168.

Galaxy. XXXII, September-October, 1971, pp. 146-147.

Kirkus Reviews. XXXIX, February 1, 1971, p. 140.

Library Journal. XCVI, March 15, 1971, p. 979.

Magazine of Fantasy and Science Fiction. XLII, February, 1972, pp. 37-38.

CHILDHOOD'S END

Author: Arthur C. Clarke (1917-   )
First book publication: 1953
Type of work: Novel
Time: 1975-twenty-second century
Locale: The Earth and the planet of the Overlords

Under the restraining hand of a group of devil-like aliens, man develops into a hivelike race suited to become part of another alien entity

Principal characters:
> RIKKI STORMGREN, Secretary-General of the United Nations and intermediary for the Overlords during the first years of their rule
> GEORGE AND JEAN GREGGSON, a representative couple during Earth's "Golden Age," whose children show the first signs of metamorphosis
> JAN RODERICKS, a stowaway on an Overlords starship
> KARELLEN, the chief of the Overlords guarding the Earth

When it first appeared, Arthur C. Clarke's fifth novel, *Childhood's End*, drew critical attention to commercial science fiction. A "classic" after only a quarter of a century, it is still a highly readable account of man's aspirations and limits and illustrates how a concept of sufficient grandeur can overcome considerable literary and scientific flaws.

A short Prologue, written from the viewpoint of rocket scientists of the United States and the U.S.S.R., reveals that plans for imminent spaceflight have been thwarted by the appearance of alien spaceships in the sky over fifty major cities. These aliens are the Overlords, whose distant presence, electronically aided, will end human violence within the next fifty years and bring about a Golden Age.

When the Overlords finally disclose their appearance, they resemble the medieval image of Satan. This in itself is less threatening to mankind than the eventual Utopia which will remove every challenge in life. With no hope of matching the Overlords' technology, there is little inspiration even for the community of artists and intellectuals who have segregated themselves on the island of New Athens. But the people offer interesting subject matter for the Overlords, who are trying to isolate what distinguishes men from them and unite man with other races they have guided to maturity. When human children begin dreaming of far-off planets and alien conditions, it is clear that man's metamorphosis has begun.

When their children are taken away from them, the citizens of New Athens foresee the end of their world. As a result, they destroy themselves and their island. However, one man survives by defying the Overlords' ban on human space travel. He stows away on a starship and eventually sees the world the Overlords have converted into their home, replete with infernal gloom, low gravity, and an atmosphere enabling them to use their wings to fly. After also seeing what may be a tangible manifestation of the Overmind, he returns to Earth only to witness its final destruction. The children are converting the Earth into the energy needed for their journey to join the Overmind. The survivor broadcasts a description of this event from the Moon; *en route* to another assignment, the Overlords listen and brood.

Much of Clarke's fiction (*Sands of Mars*, *Prelude to Space*, *Earthlight*, *Islands in the Sky*) soberly depicts the near future growth of man's science, technology, and territorial domain, for which he has been an untiring prophet and propagandist in nonfiction as well. But his most popular and probably most enduring stories and novels transcend such rationality and extrapolation, and raise questions about man's ultimate destiny. From the fairy-tale adventures of *Against the Fall of Night* to the immensely popular book and movie, *2001: A Space Odyssey*, he has appealed successfully to his audience's religious or mystical side, without significantly alienating more scientifically and historically minded readers.

Childhood's End illustrates Clarke's ability to deal with both the traditional spaceflight as a metaphor for progress and the panoply of scientific and technological developments leading to the end of individualism. The human technology of the novel is capable, for example, of reliable oral contraceptives (not yet perfected in 1953), methods for proving paternity, perfected air transport, as well as such advances as electronic newspapers, undersea laboratories, plastic taxidermy and even a mechanized ouija board. Given time, man might be able to achieve the Overlords' level of technology, with its noninjurious pain projectors, three-dimensional image projectors, cameraless television, time-viewing devices, inertialess drive, interstellar travel and planet transforming powers.

Although such progress is praiseworthy in Clarke's later Utopia, *Imperial Earth*, in *Childhood's End* it is unsatisfactory; mere technology furthering peace and comfort will not bring about the millennium. The best members of the human race, self-exiled in New Athens, find their artistic and philosophical creativity stifled by the Overlords' superiority and the incomprehensible potential that the metamorphosis is creating in their offspring. In fact, all the human characters act as if they know their day has passed; they are simply marionettes on a puppet stage, whose actions will not matter in the ultimate scheme of things.

Stormgren, despite his role as the chief link between the races, is depicted in melodramatic posturings of minimal significance. He tries to persuade a religious fanatic of the futility of his protests against the Overlords, even when that has already been made clear by the Overlords' technology. The bulk of his story concerns his kidnaping by gangsters and inevitable rescue by Karellen. His final act is a childish plot to find out, before he dies, what the aliens really look like. In the original novelette version, "Guardian Angel" (1949), Clarke went so far as to hinge the entire story on Stormgren's glimpsing of an enormous tail.

The novel spares us that revelation, but the actions of subsequent characters are even less ambitious. Rupert Boyce, hosting a party near the beginning of Book II, is satisfied with showing off his "possessions," a wildlife preserve and a projector that makes his image giant size to greet his guests. The high point of the party is a séance, at which Jean Greggson falls into a trance and produces a code number which is later identified as belonging to the Overlords' adopted home star. For the remainder of Book II, she and her husband George worry a lot, while their Overlord adviser assures them that everything has a rational explanation, and their children drift away from them.

Only Jan Rodericks has ambitions which transcend the limits set by the guardians. Yet his adventure as a stowaway is merely a romantic, storybook act, to which it is difficult to believe that the Overlords would object. Only after his flight and the sightseeing which soberly demonstrates to him both the limitations of science and the finality of the metamorphosis of the human race, has Jan reached a level of maturity comparable to that of the Overlords. Yet it is a maturity that he has little time or inclination to enjoy. Clarke's style and vision only do justice to the grandeur of the novel's theme through Jan's tragic recognition.

If the actions of individual humans seem ridiculous, it is at least in part because they have no significant choices to make; the metamorphosis is out of their hands. Yet the reader, in identifying with them, must decide whether to see the change as tragic or joyous. Time has already dated the realistic components of the novel, making the choice more obviously symbolic now than it was originally. Shall we seek to continue our scientific and technological growth, following the relatively slow and tortuous path of evolution and history; or shall we seek a radical discontinuity, a metamorphosis into another form, a mystical unity with one another and with whatever we regard as God? Although we may not consider the second alternative a realistic future possibility, it has ruled the lives of countless individuals throughout the history of man.

The philosophical and aesthetic success of the novel depends largely on the reader's coming to grips with the ironic structure of the imagery. If this were simply a tale of metamorphosis, with aliens acting as midwives, there would be no need for the aliens to take the particular form which Clarke has given them. He is not only explicit as to the Satanic shape of the Overlords; he even goes to great lengths to establish the significance of that imagery. Their home planet is infernal in appearance; it even has been adopted and transformed, as was the world of Milton's fallen angels. Unable to thwart the will of their Master, they do Its bidding, striving to understand the how and why of each metamorphosis, as if hoping to master the technique itself or somehow undermine it. Their progressive unveiling and the modification of their messages to

mankind as their original statements prove false or inoperative, further reveal
their resemblance to the Father of Lies.

Yet their "modifications" of the truth can also be seen as the progressive
approximations of science (forbidden knowledge has long been associated with
the Devil, even in horror movies for skeptical audiences). As a further extension of the scientific and technological path on which man, particularly western man, is launched, the Overlords provide the novel with the only real alternative to sinking back into childishness or barbarism. Indeed, this is in a sense
the Overlords' story. Only they, most visibly Karellen, are present from beginning to end, while generations of humans are born and die. Their elegiac
tone lingers on after the Earth has winked out of existence, and Jan Rodericks,
the last of his kind, has given way to a version of his race transformed out of
recognition as humanity. Theirs is the "evolutionary cul de sac" open to man,
from which ESP, spiritualism, and mythological allusions cannot extricate
him.

It is understandable that readers prefer the fate of mankind ordained by the
narrative, given the age-old resonance of the God and Devil images in the
West — the home of empirical science — and the much older attraction of a
universal oneness given meaning by a force beyond ourselves, delivering us
from the need to make individual decisions. But the imagery with which the
Overmind is rendered, the boiling mental volcano on the Overlords' planet, the
merciless destructiveness of the organized children, even the hive-mind concept, are not really any more positive than the cosmic loneliness of the Devil,
in symbolic or naturalistic guise.

Incidental imagery in the novel tends to support widening perspectives and
a three-stage hierarchy which places the Overmind at the top and man at the
bottom. In relation to power, Stormgren rules the human masses, Karellen
dominates him, and the Overmind is Karellen's master. Stormgren is like a
beloved pet to Karellen, an image echoed by the mourning of the Greggsons'
dog for his own young master, lost in dreams. The disruption of the gangsters
foreshadows the suicide of New Athens and the annihilation of the Earth. A
séance foreshadows the children's dreams, which provide a link to a future
beyond the end of the novel. Stormgren's "ascent" to Karellen's ship leads to
Jan's flight to the Overlords' world and then to the final departure of both the
children and the Overlords. But these are simultaneously images of limitation.
The frustration of the rocket scientists in the Prologue is echoed by Karellen's
edict that "the Stars are not for Man" and by Jan's final realization of the
essential if not literal truth of that edict, since the "children of man" are quite
different from their progenitors.

The final transformation of the children into a symbiotic, superorganic form
of life is foreshadowed by various kinds of togetherness, which become progressively more compressed. The fifty starships hovering over world capitals
turn out to be projections of only one, and the power of Karellen subsequently

breaks up a mob demonstration and a gangsters' "conference." The Greggsons gather at a party and then form part of a colony dependent on its individual members; their dissolution as a family stands for its failure, and the island's loss foreshadows the final disruption. But perhaps the key image of compression is Karellen's entrance in Book II. Descending from his ship with trusting children in his arms, he counts on the image to recall Jesus' encounter with the young. But even that association is pregnant with foreboding, since Jesus warned his followers they could not enter the Kingdom of God unless they became as little children.

Olaf Stapledon, whose *Last and First Men* (1930) and *Star Maker* (1937) were an inspiration to Clarke, has never achieved popularity because he would not or could not render his vision in novelistic terms on a human scale. Clarke has succeeded, to some extent, in yoking the cosmic and the human levels, but the compromise is a fragile one, an illusion subject to effacement if the reader pays attention to detail. The human characters are not up to the adventure on which they are launched, by no choice of their own. The equation of the "breakthrough" with ESP and spiritualism and the tortuous explanation of the supposedly "universal" Devil image as a memory of the future do not stand up to close examination. In spite of the assurance of both man and the Overlords that everything has a rational explanation, their naturalistic framework is dwarfed by the morality play opposition of alien forces with its foregone conclusion.

Despite these flaws, a structural imbalance, and a style which vacillates between historical chronicle and uninspired narrative, rising to distinction only with the climax and diminuendo at the end, *Childhood's End* continues to delight and challenge readers. In part this may be due to a historical accident. The "children" of the 1960's reminded us how near the surface of our "technological society" the forces of the irrational lie are, and how easily they may come to be seen as preferable to the more recent tradition of "progress." In part, the novel's appeal comes from its contrast of cosmic and human levels and their identification with mystic and scientific ways of thought. At best, however, it succeeds in evoking haunting images which resonate with our sense of how fragile the human race is, and how evanescent may be its dreams of glory, as well as the tools with which it attempts to make them come true.

David N. Samuelson

Sources for Further Study

Criticism:

Samuelson, David N. "Clarke's Childhood's End: A Median Stage in Adolescence?," in *Science Fiction Studies*. I (Spring, 1973), p. 7. Samuelson questions the artistic effectiveness of the novel. He does assert, however, that the reader can feel the irrational in familiar terms.

Slusser, George E. *The Space Odysseys of Arthur C. Clarke*. San Bernardino, Calif.: Borgo, 1978. Clarke's *Childhood's End* is analyzed in terms of the establishment of mythic patterns.

Reviews:

Atlantic. CXCII, November, 1953, p. 112.

Booklist. L, October 1, 1953, p. 58.

Bookmark. XIII, November, 1953, p. 36.

Christian Science Monitor. September 10, 1953, p. 7.

Kirkus Reviews. XXI, July 15, 1953, p. 459.

New York Herald Tribune Book Review. August 23, 1953, p. 9.

New York Times. August 23, 1953, p. 19.

San Francisco Chronicle. October 18, 1953, p. 23.

CHILDREN OF DUNE

Author: Frank Herbert (1920-   )
First book publication: 1976
Type of work: Novel
Time: Nine years after the events recorded in *Dune Messiah*
Locale: Chiefly the planet Arrakis

> *Principal characters:*
> LETO ATREIDES, nine-year-old son and heir of Paul Muad'Dib
> GHANIMA, Leto's twin sister
> ALIA, Imperial regent and Paul's sister
> DUNCAN IDAHO, mentat and philosopher
> THE PREACHER, an old, blind Fremen, thought by some to be Paul
>   returned from the dead
> JESSICA, Paul's mother, a Bene Gesserit adept
> FARAD'N, heir to House Corrino, which held the Imperial throne be-
>   fore the Atreides
> GURNEY HALLECK, a smuggler, former liege man of House Atreides

 Children of Dune has the distinction of being the conclusion to a trilogy no one knew existed until the third volume was published. It completes themes from *Dune* and *Dune Messiah* which few readers had never noticed. And though it is easy in retrospect to discover those ideas already present in the two previous novels, who would have suspected beforehand that the purpose of *Dune* and *Dune Messiah* was to set the stage for a staggering denunciation of science fiction's heroic myths? *Dune* was pure epic, the story of as compelling a superhero as has ever been described in fiction. Paul Atreides, hero, prophet, and teacher, proved as seductive to the readers of the novel as to his imaginary followers. And though *Dune Messiah* was tragic, it was heroic tragedy, in which Paul grew in stature by his very losses. But *Children of Dune* is anti-epic and anti-heroic; it is not tragic — merely chilling. It systematically dismantles the myth of Paul Atreides, while claiming that to do so was the intention of the trilogy all along.

 Herbert's seeming turnabout was disconcerting to many readers who had come to cherish the myth. The effort of rethinking the earlier novels was too demanding for *Children of Dune* to receive the appreciation it deserves. For, though it is not as likable as the first two novels, it is powerful, well-constructed, and effective. It tells the story not of Paul Atreides, but of his works. It shows the terrible things which happened because of *what* he was, and despite *who* he was. The dangers of charismatic leadership are to be found in one's followers. However wise and good a leader is, problems are sure to arise whenever individuals surrender their destiny into the hands of another. Most of all, *Children of Dune* tells the story of Paul's son Leto, who must become neither so good nor so admirable as his father in order to undo the evils Paul has brought about.

 Nine years after Paul Muad'Dib disappeared into the desert, the dreams he stood for have shown the imperfections that all distant visions reveal to the nearer eye. Stilgar, leader of the Fremen, wonders at what he and Paul have brought about. The desert is blooming, but the change is not altogether good. Much has been lost, most of all the old simplicity where the dangers were life and death, and never the damning of the future. But there is no turning back. In this, at least, Muad'Dib's words hold true: one cannot hide from what will be, but must meet it with open eyes.

Stilgar contemplates Muad'Dib's twin children, Leto and Ghanima. They carry their illustrious father's prescient genes and were borne by a woman addicted to the spice-drug melange, a combination which brought them to full adult awareness while still in the womb. Like their Aunt Alia, whom Paul's mother Jessica had carried as she ingested the Truthsayer drug of the Bene Gesserit sisterhood, they have experienced the shattering process in which all the memories and identities of millions of ancestors are awakened from their burial place in the genes. Now nine years old, but wise beyond their years, the question is whether they are to be the focus of hope or of fear? Will they share Muad'Dib's moral courage, or will they be corrupted, as Alia has been, by the depths of evil as well as good awakened so prematurely in an untrained mind?

Unknown to the aging Fremen, Leto and Ghanima share Stilgar's fears. They have seen Alia fight a losing battle against inner darkness. All the training of a Bene Gesserit adept is required at the moment of awakening. Essential transformations of the ancestral memories must be made lest one of the old identities rise up and possess the individual, creating what the Sisterhood calls "the abomination." Alia has become such an abomination, and as a result has built repressive religious government on her brother's tomb. Leto and Ghanima are concerned with two problems: how to circumvent this disaster in themselves, and how to put Paul's Empire back on track. In addition, they have noticed what everyone else seems to be ignoring, that the ecological transformation is endangering the great sandworms, which excrete the spice upon which their own prescient vision as well as the commerce of the Empire depends.

Herbert's point here seems pessimistic. Even the most powerful insights are lost and twisted with time, and grand visions are mismanaged once their creators are gone. Ecology, which to readers of *Dune* in the 1960's bore the promise that man finally might be able to understand and take responsibility for the consequences of his actions, has here been revealed as only one more tool with which man inflicts his shortsighted wishes upon his environment. The transformation of Arrakis from desert into irrigated paradise was to have been a model of ecological foresight on a grand scale. Instead it has become a debacle of intrusive manipulation. Likewise, Paul's religion, which was based, like ecology, on an expanded perception and respect for connecting patterns in the universe, has been dogmatically forced upon an unwilling populace.

Herbert's thought is too subtle to be merely pessimistic, however. Like Paul himself, he knows that there is no final solution to any human problem, and that the quality of life is maintained only at the price of constant vigilance. The degradation and decay of high ideals is only one more instance of a universal tendency towards change. There is reason for pessimism only if we believe that the game is not fairly matched between this universal entropy and man's ingenuity to meet it with new solutions. Herbert's intention is to shatter not only the myth of Paul Atreides, but that of Western civilization: that there is a single, monolithic solution to any problem. There is an ongoing dialectic of problems and solutions, in which "good" and "bad" support and re-create each other, and neither can be as positively identified as we like to imagine.

Leto and Ghanima know that it is a time of great crisis. Alia will never hand over power to them on their maturity, and even if she would, the irrigation of the desert would have gone too far by that time to be reversed. Despite their physical youth, the time for action is now. Fortunately, an assassination attempt by embittered members of House Corrino, from whom Paul had seized the Imperial throne, provides them with a chance to act.

A pair of Laza tigers has been smuggled to Arrakis from their natural home on Salusa Secundus, training ground of the Corrino Sardaukar. They have been specially taught to hunt the children in the desert near their home at Sietch Tabr. But Leto has seen the tigers in his prescient dreams, and like his father, knows how to turn the plots of others against them. To pretend death at the jaws of the tigers will free him from the observation of "friends" as well as enemies. It will permit him to act against Alia. He and Ghanima go armed into the desert, and kill the tigers when they attack. Ghanima induces a state of deep hypnosis, convincing herself on the deepest levels that her brother has been killed. Using a "thumper," Leto then calls a sandworm from the desert to destroy the corpses of the tigers, and to provide him with transportation deep into the wastes. His destination is Jacurutu, a fabled hideout of smugglers and outcast Fremen. He hopes to find refuge there while he develops his powers and begins his campaign for the throne which is his right.

At this point Leto is like the young Paul in that he has only a distant vision to guide him, and lacks the intermediate steps to implement it. He must feel his way towards the "golden path" of his inner eye. And he knows that first he must go through a time of testing. What he does not know is that others have planned the trial for him. Like Paul at the beginning of *Dune*, he must experience the gom jabbar, the test of self-mastery. He arrives at the deserted sietch, only to find waiting there for him a trap laid by his grandmother, the Lady Jessica. Jessica, a rebel adept of the Bene Gesserit, has seen that her daughter Alia has become the "abomination" predicted by the Sisterhood. She has resolved that her grandson will die before he follows the same path. Her liege man, Gurney Halleck, an old Atreides retainer and one of Paul's childhood teachers, is in charge of the inquisition. Leto must master his inner turmoil to Gurney's satisfaction before he will be released.

There follows a series of inner ordeals, in which Leto learns a great deal, but never conclusively satisfies his questioners. They wish to test his morality, but he has a sense that the golden patch will take him beyond the old judgments of good and evil, into a moral world where no one else, save perhaps Paul and Ghanima, could understand his motivations. He can answer Gurney only with riddles.

At last Leto feels he is ready, whatever his captors' judgment, and escapes again into the desert. There he undergoes a final, irreversible transformation and finds the true beginning of his vision. He lures a bed of standtrout, the water-hungry, polyplike young of the sandworm, onto his own body. Drawn by moisture, they begin to tunnel into his flesh. A normal man would have been killed. But Leto possesses such control over his body chemistry that he is able to keep them at the surface, like a new skin which amplifies his strength a thousandfold. With this suit of magic armor, he has a myth to topple even that of Muad'Dib: he is shai-hulud, the sandworm, personified. And with his new ability to burrow through the sand and to command the worms by his mere presence, he is a one-person army. He shatters the qanats which irrigate the desert, terrorizes the Fremen, and in a matter of months turns back a generation of ecological transformation.

At the same time, there is another who stands against Alia and the church she has built. He is known only as the preacher. A blind Fremen who appears suddenly from the desert, he utters fearless interpretations of Muad'Dib, and vanishes again. He is thought by many to be the prophet himself returned from the dead. Who else could have such magnetism and such clarity of thought? And who but Paul could utter such heresy as a demand to tear down the church built in his name?

Ultimately, Leto's path and the preacher's must cross. It is not merely a physical meeting, but a contest of visions. Who will shape the future, the father or the son? Paul had seen Leto's golden path long ago and refused it, because of its ultimate immorality. Leto will live for thousands of years, becoming progressively less and less human in mind as well as in body. He will be required, with full awareness, to cause such evils as Paul was an unwilling partner to. All of Paul's final choices (described in *Dune Messiah*) were in fact an escape from the golden path, a last-ditch attempt to solve the problems of the human species from within its old moral framework. Leto has seen further than his father, however, and knows that the human species itself will die out unless the old pattern is decisively broken. Only by becoming himself inhuman, and thereby removed from the normal evolutionary sequence, can he find the strength and perspective necessary to save the race. It will take thousands of years under the heel of an unconquerable tyrant who cultivates every seed of revolt against him, before the race will develop that independence of spirit where each man can create his own future instead of being swept into the whirlpool of the moment. At last the preacher accepts his son's vision. All his struggles have ended in failure, and his nobility is scorned as fear. His son, to whom he passes the mantle of wisdom, becomes (outwardly at least) the antithesis of all that he had fought for. He is broken, emptied of vision, fit only to be sacrificed and cast aside. He goes willingly to Arrakeen with Leto to be killed by Alia's priests in the move that shatters the old human universe of good and evil and allows Leto to begin his millennia-long task as midwife to the new. One life is over, another begins.

This ending is unpalatable to many readers. Herbert may have had strong intellectual justifications for it, but in pursuit of what mad muse did he leave it so emotionally unsatisfying? One reason, as we have noted, is that old myths die hard. But one cannot help feeling that some of Herbert's psychological skill has deserted him. His evolutionary ethics and genetic arguments for species behavior are sufficiently abstruse (at the very limits of acceptable extrapolation even for science fiction) that they need a great deal more affective support than they receive from the novel. One of the strengths of Herbert's writing has always been that the events and principles of the story are echoed by the psychological travail of the characters. So, for instance, in *Dune*, the rising tide of messianic religion which threatened to engulf Paul was echoed by the inner storms of his prophetic vision. And though the justification of the jihad as a mass orgasm of the human species is rather unusual, it was sufficiently borne up by the other levels of the story to be accepted without question. Furthermore, the parallelism of inner and outer events was immediately and emotionally apparent to the reader. The psychological component was the more vivid and obvious of the two levels, so it clarified and supported the meaning of the rest. Who, for instance, has *not* felt moments of panic at the inevitability of the future?

By contrast, in *Children of Dune*, Leto's inner and outer crises are not obviously parallel, and besides, they strike no sparks from the reader's own experience. It might be argued that the ecological and religious decay which Leto must reverse, and the conquest of abomination within, both involve compromises with the evils of the past. Even so, there is little for the reader to identify with. The concept is foreign to his experience, and so has the flavor of something imposed on the story rather than developed naturally from it.

On a deeper level however, perhaps Herbert acted deliberately in this. He has long been interested in writing stories which transform the reader's self-perception. But in building a self-critical heroic myth, he was treading on difficult ground. *Dune* and *Dune Messiah* contain many of the same ideas as *Children of Dune*, but they are presented by a character who embodies the very qualities he is attacking. Paul is too appealing a hero for his admonitions ever to be heard. Only by building up and then shattering the emotional responses of his readers could Herbert really hope to get his point across. Leto's solution to the problem of Paul's charismatic rule is after all only a mirror of Herbert's own. Paul Muad'Dib had to be reduced to the Preacher, magnificent but ineffective, while Leto makes the unpleasant decisions which really change things.

Timothy O'Reilly

Sources for Further Study

Reviews:

America. CXXXIV, June 26, 1976, p. 570.

Book World. May 9, 1976, p. K8.

Booklist. LXXII, May 1, 1976, p. 1246.

Kirkus Reviews. XLIV, March 1, 1976, p. 272.

Library Journal. CI, June 1, 1976, p. 1312.

New York Times Book Review. August 1, 1976, p. 18.

Observer. October 3, 1976, p. 24.

Publisher's Weekly. CCIX, March 8, 1976, p. 58.

School Library Journal. XXII, May, 1976, p. 82.

CHILDREN OF THE ATOM

Author: Wilmar H. Shiras (1908-   )
First book publication: 1953
Type of work: Novel
Time: 1972-1973
Locale: California

  The story of a group of highly intelligent children

  Principal characters:
      PETER WELLES, a psychiatrist
      MARK FOXWELL, also a psychiatrist
      EMILY PAGE, a schoolteacher
      TIM, ELSIE, JAY, STELLA, MAX, BETH AND FRED, a group of exceptional children

Children of the Atom is an episodic novel whose first three parts, "In Hiding," "Opening Doors," and "New Foundations" appeared as novelettes in *Astounding Science Fiction* during 1948-1950. It is one of a number of novels written in the post-Hiroshima decade in which the theme of radiation-induced mutation is combined with that of superhumanity. As with several other notable stories dealing with augmented intelligence, it sidesteps the problem of describing and characterizing superintelligence by conferring the gift on children, who need only exhibit an astonishing intellectual precocity in order to demonstrate their superhumanity.

The novel begins when a schoolteacher, Miss Page, refers one of her charges — a thirteen-year-old boy named Timothy Paul — to the school psychiatrist because she suspects that there is something unusual about him. The psychiatrist, Peter Welles, examines the boy, and though he gets perfectly ordinary answers to his questions, he too begins to suspect that Tim is concealing something. The child is afraid of him, and comes close to panic when he fills a syringe with pentothal. Welles interviews Tim's grandparents, who are his guardians, and finds out that the boy has no fear of injections. This leads Tim eventually to confess that he knew what was in the syringe and what effect it would have, and that he found the prospect of revealing his secrets most alarming.

Gradually, Tim learns to trust Welles, and reveals that since early childhood he has been masquerading as an ordinary child, in hiding behind the camouflage of his peer group. In fact, his intelligence is too high to be measured by standard tests, and his accomplishments are already awesome. Working by mail under several pseudonyms he has already established a reputation as a writer, and has undergone a series of correspondence courses bringing him up to university level in most available subjects. In his private playroom he is busy conducting small-scale experiments in architecture and mammalian genetics.

From Tim's grandparents, Welles learns that the boy was orphaned shortly after his birth. Both parents had been irradiated following an accident at an atomic plant in 1958, and though there appeared to have been no resulting injuries, they had gradually sickened. Tim was conceived five months after the accident. Welles tells Tim that this pattern may well have been repeated, and that there might be others like him, also hiding their talents from an ignorant and intolerant world.

In the second part of the narrative Welles and Tim place an advertisement in a newspaper asking high-IQ orphans born in 1959 to contact them. From the replies they sort out possible similar cases. One of them is a girl named Elsie Lambeth, who is confined in a mental hospital. Welles goes to the hospital, which is run by Mark Foxwell, to interview the child. She is, indeed, one of the "wonder children," but one who did not have the same opportunities as Tim to develop an acceptable "disguise." She has been committed to the institution as "uncontrollable" and prefers to stay there because she is left to her own devices and allowed to read and write as much as she wants. Wells explains her predicament to Foxwell, encourages her to demonstrate her sanity, and takes her back with him, finding her lodgings with Miss Page. With financial aid from Tim's grandparents, Welles, in association with Foxwell and Miss Page, initiates a project to gather all the wonder children together in one place, in a "special school" where they can develop their talents properly.

The third child located by Welles and his associates is Jay Worthington, the adopted son of a historian named Curtis. His circumstances have allowed Jay to conceal himself well enough, because Curtis is blind and relies upon him to be his eyes and to read aloud to him. Jay decides quickly that he cannot leave his adopted father to come to the school, but Welles eventually recruits Curtis to the cause as well, and both come to the small town in California where the project has been mounted. In the same section of the narrative Welles meets Stella Oates, who is still living unhappily at home, though her predicament has developed in a rather similar way to Elsie's. However, while Elsie had no deep-seated psychological problems, Stella has rationalized her exceptionality by coming to believe that she has been reincarnated from a former life in Egypt. Under a pseudonym she has published mystical novels after the fashion of Marie Corelli, and she believes what she has written. When Welles explains her true circumstances, though, she is quickly persuaded that she has made a mistake.

The fourth section of the book — the first which did not see prior publication — deals with the early days of the school, plagued by the antisocial tricks of a cruel practical joker. As in the previous sections, the focus is on the problems of adjustment faced by the children, but now in a rather more general sense. One newcomer, Beth, is excessively shy and retiring, while another, Max, takes time to recover from the fact that extreme poverty has denied him many of the opportunities for self-development which the others had readily at hand. The joker turns out to be a third newcomer, Fred, whose intellect has developed at the expense of empathy, and who has no real feeling for other people or for animals. Like Stella, though, he proves quite willing to listen to the voice of reason once his faults are made apparent to him.

In the fifth part of the story the school comes under threat when a lay preacher named Tommy Mundy attacks it in a virulent tirade delivered through the television network. He describes the children as unnatural monsters plotting the destruction of mankind. A mob duly turns up at the gate, but is dissuaded from taking any action when Tim is recognized by his old schoolfriends and both Welles and Miss Page — well-known within the community — vouch for all others present. The menace evaporates immediately, but the children take from the experience the moral lesson that they must not cut themselves off from the community. They decide that they must all go to schools in the city during the day, returning to the special school only in the evenings and vacations, thus taking their proper place in human society — where, in spite of their superintelligence, they truly belong.

Children of the Atom is, of course, quite irrational in its basic premise. The idea that people irradiated by a nuclear explosion might suffer mutation of the germ-plasm is reasonable enough, but that all should then live just long enough to produce children identically mutated in terms of mental characteristics defies everything that we know about mutation theory. The creation of the children is clearly a supernatural event, tantamount to a miracle, but on close analysis of the plot this turns out to be anything but an incongruity.

The notion of supermen in hiding was extremely common in the science fiction of the postwar decade. Often the superhumans involved were gifted with extrasensory perception and other *"psi-*powers" widely popularized by J. B. Rhine — telepathy, precognition, psychokinesis, and the like — but augmented intelligence and creative powers were also common in such stories (other examples dealing with children are Theodore Sturgeon's *More Than Human*, George O. Smith's *The Fourth "R"*, also known as *The Brain Machine*, and Robert Heinlein's "Gulf"). All of these stories supposed that if superhumans were to emerge in contemporary society the natural reaction of ordinary men would be to hate, fear, persecute, and destroy them. Much was made of the metaphor of witch-hunting. In *Children of the Atom* the witch-hunting fervor is represented in an almost ritual fashion by the rabble-rousing fanatic Tommy Mundy, whose role is so easily taken for granted that Shiras sees no need to construct a plausible case telling the reader how he found out about the children and why he took such extreme exception to them without bothering to make even the most rudimentary investigation.

The science fiction writers of this period were, of course, enthusiastic defenders of supermen against this kind of unjust and hysterical persecution. Without exception they represented their fellow men as stupid chauvinists, forever eager to resent any kind of superiority in others and ready to grasp at any straws of superstition that would give them a warrant for violent action. It

was automatically assumed that ordinary men were not only intellectually inferior but also morally inferior (in the few stories where evil and amoral supermen appeared they were always defeated by good and moral supermen).

A rather unkind hypothesis accounting for the appeal of this kind of plot
would inevitably point to the fact that science fiction as a *genre* has always had
a special appeal to adolescents who are somewhat alienated from their peers, if
not by superior intelligence then at least by a range of interests which could
easily be used to promote the illusion of intellectual superiority. Science fiction readers, almost by definition, are far from parochial in their preoccupations, and many find it easy to cast their fellow men as intolerant and pusil-
lanimous fools, while seeing themselves in a metaphorical sense as "children
of the atom." Shiras' novel is especially calculated to appeal to this kind of
world view. That the illusion is not confined to adolescents is perhaps best
confirmed by recalling that H. G. Wells was led to write a similar mutational
romance, *Star-Begotten* (1937), when he was past seventy.

Rhine's notion that thousands of people walking the streets might harbor
unsuspected latent *psi*-powers was immensely appealing because it implied that
anyone might be a superman. Shiras works with a more modest brand of
superhumanity, but one which is on the surface harder to live up to. Not many
thirteen-year-olds have already amassed a small fortune in royalties by publishing great works of art and wisdom under assorted pseudonyms. On the other
hand, the main emphasis in her novel is not so much on the actual achievements of the children as in their ability to see (and suffer from) the intellectual
and moral fallibility of their fellow men. This is a cause to which readers can
much more readily ally themselves, for which of us is not already fully convinced that other people are stupid and wicked, and that the world would be a
finer place if everyone were more like us? Shiras' children are really just idealized versions of Everyman; and her notions of what constitutes moral superiority are, of course, tied to her own moral presuppositions, which are those of
a gentle, somewhat humanistic Catholic. For this reason, there is actually
much more to the mythology of *Children of the Atom* than an appeal to alienated adolescents.

The theme which runs throughout the novel, drawing heavily on the perspectives of the protagonist-psychologist, is that the wonder children are
morally perfectible beings whose moral sensibilities are only put in hazard by
the unfortunate fact that they must live as ordinary humans, subject to the
corrosive effects of ignorance, shallowness, and lack of feeling. Once free
from this corrosive influence, their sheer rationality allows them to become
morally perfect (the stories of Elsie, Stella, and Fred all make this point
explicitly). In this novel we see the Enlightenment myth of progress, with its
emphasis on the rational and moral perfectibility of Christian man, refurbished
and detached from the myth of *technological* progress with which it became
entangled in the nineteenth century. *Children of the Atom* is one of the key

works in the most pronounced trend in modern science fiction, which is precisely this reseparation of the two progress-myths, and the reaffirmation of the premise that human perfectibility must be sought inwardly, its development dependent upon the resources of the mind and heart. It is, of course, hardly surprising that Shiras and her generation pinned their stories to the rather remote possibility of some kind of miraculous transformation of minds rather than imagining a slow process of social and psychic evolution — the advent of the atom bomb and the implied threat of self-destruction made the problem seem so much more urgent.

Brian Stableford

Sources for Further Study

Reviews:

Analog. LIII, March, 1954, pp. 155-156.

Galaxy. VII, December, 1953, pp. 84-85.

Magazine of Fantasy and Science Fiction. V, September, 1953, p. 101.

Nebula Science Fiction. X, October, 1954, p. 114.

New Worlds. XXXII, February, 1955, p. 118.

Original Science Fiction Stories. X, May, 1959, pp. 67-68.

CHTHON

Author: Piers Anthony (1934-   )
First book publication: 1967
Type of work: Novel
Time: Four hundred years after man's propulsion to the stars
Locale: The planets Hvee, Idyllia/Chthon, Earth, and Minion

A hero's quest for escape from an underground prison world and its dark god, and for union with a woman whose emotions are the polar opposite of his

Principal characters:
ATON FIVE, a spaceman from Hvee, sentenced to Chthon
AURELIUS, his father
MALICE, the "minionette," his mother and first love
COQUINA, his second love
FRAMY, his friend in Chthon
CHTHON, the god of the prison world Chthon
DOC BEDSIDE ("PARTNER"), his minion
GARNET, a woman of Chthon who loves Aton

Chthon (pronounced thōn) is one of the most thematically complex works of science fiction yet produced; nevertheless, it is highly readable as a pure adventure story. The main narrative line is an account of Aton's escape from Chthon, an underground prison. Juxtaposed with this are episodes from Aton's past and future life, involving his love for Malice, a "minionette," a beautiful woman of the planet Minion, who like a siren entraps him with a song when he is a child and holds him in thrall throughout most of his life.

This chronological juxtaposition of events is not done for variety's sake. In subtle ways, Aton's experiences in Chthon parallel his experiences elsewhere, and these correspondences would be missed were conventional order observed. Furthermore, Aton has repressed some of his memories when he arrives in Chthon and only gradually recalls them in the years after he escapes. As he slowly comes to understand his life, the reader achieves a similar understanding of the facts of the story and their psychological and mythic ramifications.

The Oedipus myth holds the key to Aton's quest for completion. His fierce compulsion to escape from Chthon derives from his love for Malice, who originally snared his affections in the forests of Hvee, his home planet, when he was only seven. He has repressed, however, the knowledge that she is his mother. Like Oedipus, who married his mother Jocasta, Aton has had sexual relations with Malice, an experience that he also pushes out of his consciousness.

Aton had denied his father Aurelius' choice of the well born Coquina to be his wife, leaving Hvee to search for his beloved minionette. What he did not realize at that time was that Aurelius himself had once been married to Malice. Aton bore malice towards that woman, whom he had never known and had thought was only his stepmother, because she deserted Aurelius after only a year. When Aton meets her again in the guise of Captain Moyne, commander of the spaceship *Jocasta* on which he is a mechanic, he falls in love with her without realizing who she is. The incest is consummated in a "spotel," a kind of asteroid motel.

Oedipus had won fame by defeating the sphinx, a female monster with a woman's head and torso, wings, and the body of a lion. Aton dreams of the sphinx and sees himself bound to it by a serpentine umbilical cord. This image symbolizes his unholy connection with his mother, in which love and hate are inextricably interwoven.

The author, knowing of the psychological proximity of the emotions of love and hate, introduces a fascinating notion: a race of beautiful women, who live for hundreds of years, and whose emotions are the exact opposite of the usual. They interpret hate as love, giving love in return, and they receive love as hatred. This is the nature of the women of Minion, from which Malice comes. Aton's hatred for her as his unfaithful stepmother makes him irresistibly attractive to her; conversely, when he falls in love with her as a desirable woman, she turns cold. Their relationship is a dance of attraction and repulsion. Aton is her "minion" because his Minion blood draws him to her, and her beauty becomes his life's ideal; but she cannot bear his love for long, as it causes her intense pain.

A trip to Minion reveals to Aton the peculiar psychology of the minionettes, and he sees how they are treated by the Minion men: with harshness and sadism. To fall in love with one's own wife there is a capital crime — the death penalty being merciful both to the deluded man and to his abused woman, who is freed from the burden of good treatment. Aton is enough of a minion to have a strong sadistic streak, but he is also enough of an ordinary man to feel guilt about it.

After the spotel incident, a distraught Aton goes to the paradisal retreat planet Idyllia, where he is tended by his former betrothed Coquina. He falls in love for a second time. But it is no use; the image of Malice, his first love, interposes. Aton perceives Coquina as Malice and flings her over a cliff — though she is in no danger, as there is no physical death on Idyllia.

For his incurable aggressive tendencies born of Minion blood, Aton is sentenced to Chthon, the prison and garnet mine from which no one escapes. Chthon is located inside the planet Idyllia; heaven and hell are indissolubly linked, even as love and hate are. Aton, with his physical strength, ruthlessness, and courage, is well-suited for survival here, and he takes advantage of Framy, his only friend in Chthon, and Garnet, a woman who loves him, sacrificing them to further his escape. Most of the population of Chthon dies, in fact, on the Hard Trek — a long expedition through the labyrinthine subterranean tunnels to find a way out — falling prey to monsters and to assaults from the evil god of the place, also called Chthon, a disembodied entity with the power to possess the bodies of animate beings. Only Aton has the strength to resist; the power of the minionette's image keeps his mind free.

Chthon manipulates the hero's destiny, as does Apollo in the Oedipus myth. The oracle of Apollo prophesied that Oedipus would marry his mother and slay his father; in order to avoid that fate Oedipus fled his foster parents, thinking they were his real ones. On the way to Thebes he killed a stranger on the road — his real father — and married the widow Jocasta when he arrived. These sins are unconscious transgressions, but the god, or *daimon*, has a hand, it would seem, in enticing Oedipus to meet his tragic fate.

Similarly, Chthon lets Aton go free from his underworld, knowing that he will have to return. Chthon wants to use Aton as an envoy to wipe out the light of human life that he sees as polluting the galaxy. But the god realizes Aton's need to complete himself by reuniting with the minionette, for Aton's will cannot be tamed so long as he is incomplete.

To the ancient Greeks the *daimon* was not only an external god but also the voice of the unconscious. Oedipus' fate is visited upon him not by some malicious external force but by inscrutable inner necessity. Similarly, Chthon makes clear in the Epilog that Aton has condemned himself, and that the evil Aton symbolizes as Chthon is within himself. To tear the evil from his soul, as Oedipus attempted to do in gouging out his eyes after learning of his incest and patricide, Aton must dissociate the man in him from the "minion." Malice helps him to do this by sacrificing herself; she lets him love her. This kills her, for his love is her mortal agony, and with her dies his minion nature, the sadistic monster in him. Her sacrifice is intended to save him from the dark god, but ironically it has the opposite effect. Coquina, who nurses Aton following the minionette's death, sacrifices herself as well, catching the dread Chill, a mysterious fatal disease, but remaining with her ward nonetheless. Because Aton has been set free from Malice, he rediscovers all the minionette's beauty in Coquina — who in fact is Malice's heir, having learned from her to sing the mystic siren song in a bit more earthly rendition. Aton finds he must return with her to Chthon, whose superhuman powers will be able to restore her, if Aton pays the price of becoming the god's minion.

Chthon gets what he wants: Aton returns complete, accompanied by a woman who fulfills him. The Epilog suggests, however, that Chthon's intention to destroy mankind alters when he learns of Aton's ethical understanding gleaned from the literature of Old Earth. Instead of using Aton as an "envoy of extermination," Chthon will bestow his mercy upon Coquina, remove the Chill from her, and in the process discover that it is a signal, unintentionally inimical to life, from an advanced civilization of "god-intellects" at the center of the galaxy. Aton, Coquina, and Chthon will somehow unite to make contact with them.

The god Chthon turns out to have positive qualities; his antipathy towards man was based on contact with criminals and insane people. But Aton neutralizes that ill will. It might be said that together they form a whole being. Aton's name recalls the Egyptian sun god; Chthon's name derives from the Greek word for earth, signifying the underworld. Light and darkness symbolize the conscious and the unconscious mind: the powers of intellect and intuition united at last. Coquina's name, which means "shell," becomes a motif in the novel, and suggests the physical shell or body of nature that contains the fully developed spirit of Aton/Chthon.

Aton's name also suggests "atone" — and like Oedipus he both atones for his sin and becomes *at one* with his god. After blinding himself, Oedipus achieves a mystic unification with his *daimon*, transcends his unhappiness, and gains prophetic powers. Aton's union with Chthon and Coquina suggests a similar higher integration — although the ultimate union with the "god-intellects" is only hinted at in the final words of the book.

As a science fiction novel of psychological struggle and spiritual growth, *Chthon* is reminiscent of David Lindsay's *A Voyage to Arcturus*. That book also depicts a physically awesome hero with a sadistic streak and an indomitable will who surmounts various alien challenges and finally undergoes a sacrifice to a dark god that results in a spiritual victory. Lindsay's vision is more disturbing, however, than Anthony's; Lindsay's dualism of good and evil is more absolute, and his idea of the redemptive power of woman is practically nil. Anthony, on the other hand, greatly lightens his portrayal of Aton by showing his hero's sympathy with the compassion that both Malice and Coquina evince.

Chthon achieves mythic depth as do few science fiction novels. As a result, it has great interest from the standpoint of Freudian and Jungian analysis, both of which utilize mythic psychological interpretation: Freudian, because of the Oedipal theme; Jungian, because Malice is a classic "anima" figure, a projection of ideal beauty from the unconscious mind that presages psychic upheaval.

The novel is complex enough to support a number of interpretations. Its ambiguity alone should ensure its survival for many years to come. As it also has an inventive and artistically sound narrative structure, a powerful flavor of poetry and vision, and all the traditional virtues of a good adventure story, it should have strong candidacy for the status of a classic.

Douglas A. Mackey

Sources for Further Study

Reviews:

Amazing Stories. XLI, December, 1967, pp. 143-144.

Analog. LXXXI, July, 1968, p. 161.

Books and Bookmen. XV, April, 1970, p. 26.

Publisher's Weekly. CXCI, June 5, 1967, p. 180.

CITIES IN FLIGHT

Author: James Blish (1921-1975)
First book publication: 1970
Type of work: Tetralogy
Time: 2013-4004
Locale: The Earth, Jupiter, the Milky Way, the Greater Magellanic Cloud and inter-
galactic space

*A future history of the human race, based on the theory of Oswald Spengler, follow-
ing the career of the city of New York liberated from the surface of Earth by means of
antigravity devices*

> Principal characters:
> ROBERT HELMUTH, a member of a team building a bridge on Jupiter
> BLISS WAGONER, a United States Senator
> CRISPIN DE FORD, a victim of a press gang
> JOHN AMALFI, Mayor of New York
> MARK HAZLETON, onetime City Manager of New York
> MIRAMON, a Hevian
> DR. SCHLOSS, a scientist

The various parts of *Cities in Flight* appeared between 1950 and 1962. The
series began as a group of four novelettes featuring the adventures of the city
of New York as a galaxy-roaming *Okie* — an itinerant work force. These
novelettes were *Okie* (1950), *Bindlestiff* (1950), *Sargasso of Lost Cities*
(1953), and *Earthman Come Home* (1953), and were combined into the book
Earthman Come Home (1955), which forms the third part of the completed
tetralogy. At this stage Blish was working with only one basic premise: an
antigravity device need not be used only for spaceships; it can move whole
cities or whole worlds. The initial novelettes are an attempt at sophisticated
space opera, in which diplomatic and economic wrangles of one kind or
another are used as elaborate preludes to spectacular violence. The main preoccupation is with conducting affairs on a grand scale.

The book version of *Earthman Come Home* was extensively rewritten, but
an even more substantial reworking followed when two more novelettes —
Bridge (1952) and *At Death's End* (1954) — were combined to make the first
part of the tetralogy, *They Shall Have Stars* (1957), also known as *Year 2018!*
These stories deal with the two discoveries which are crucial to the idea of the
flying cities: the antigravity device called the "spindizzy" and the "anti-
agathic" drugs which give the key characters their longevity. In combining the
two discoveries, however, Blish imported the bulk of the framework that connected their near-future setting with the distant-future setting of *Earthman
Come Home* — a scheme derived from Oswald Spengler's *Decline of the West*.
The extrapolation of Spengler's cyclic historicism allowed Blish to locate his
stories within the context of the decline of Earth's civilization followed by the
birth and eventual decline of the interstellar culture which succeeds it.

Having completed the beginning of the larger work, Blish quickly supplied the ending in a fourth volume, *The Triumph of Time* (1958), also known as *A Clash of Cymbals*, which features not merely the end of "Earthmanist" civilization but also the annihilation of the known universe and the moment of a new Creation. The novel is set, with a neat touch of irony, in the year 4004.

After completing the climax of the series Blish left it alone for some years, but when he began writing juvenile science fiction novels in the early 1960's he co-opted the series' setting in order to supply a context for a conventional story of a young man's growth from adolescence to adulthood, presented in parallel with the *rite de passage* of the city of Scranton as it leaves its planetary home and sets off for the stars. This volume, *A Life for the Stars* (1962), is the second volume of the tetralogy.

It is as a "future history" that *Cities in Flight* first demands attention, though it is important to remember that this aspect of the work was built in along the way rather than having been planned from the very beginning (Spenglerian theory is used as a crutch rather than as an imaginative springboard). Writing the history of the future was a project which had occupied the time of several previous writers, though only Robert Heinlein set out to do the job comprehensively and most attempts were abandoned before they were hardly begun. Inevitably, all the writers who thought the task possible as an extrapolative exercise (rather than mere haphazard guesswork) had to proceed on the assumption that there must be some kind of historical "laws" and that these must already be displayed in past history if only it could be interpreted correctly. In consequence, the would-be historians of the future were forced to conclude that the future would in some sense recapitulate the past. Blish, however, was the only writer who made this assumption explicit, and the only one who turned to a historicist philosopher for ratification and guidance (though Arnold Toynbee's name had been bandied about earlier by Charles Harness). Blish had, of course, already seen the spectacular effects obtained by Isaac Asimov in replaying the decline and fall of the Roman Empire on a galactic scale. Asimov had added an entirely new dimension to space opera, and it was as a sophisticated space opera that Blish's saga began.

By making his assumption explicit, Blish accomplished what other writers had failed to do: he filled in the "connective tissue" between the actual stories easily and coherently. His continual mention of the Spenglerian pattern allowed him to integrate his stories neatly into the same matrix, a technique that was all the more necessary because they were so disparate in their styles and concerns. However, *Cities in Flight* is in no sense an attempt to develop Spenglerian philosophy through the medium of science fiction. The tetralogy is a group of stories with their own internal ends and purposes whose strength is augmented by the artful borrowing of Spenglerian jargon. This device helps to create the impression that the stories fit together and are part of something greater; such a plan lends their events extra significance. The spectacular events of the melodramatic *Earthman Come Home*, for example, are given extra substance because they seem part of the inexorable unfolding of history.

They Shall Have Stars is set in the early twenty-first century and tells the story of two research projects whose members are under different kinds of pressure. The team attempting to build a bridge on Jupiter in order to test a hypothesis regarding a subtle amendment of the law of gravity (which, if verified, will pave the way for the spindizzy) has to cope with psychological pressures, while the group which has discovered the secret of longevity is enmeshed in a net of bureaucracy, fighting commercial and political vested interests. The background of this story is the one most liberally enriched with Spenglerism, since it parallels the final phase of the decline of the West prophesied by Spengler. It is the phase called "Caesarism," in which controllers of totalitarian states attempt to stifle change and bring history to a halt while the masses give themselves over to a new religiosity: an uneasy millenarianism. (Ironically, Blish, in his William Atheling, Jr., essay "Cathedrals in Space," had already observed what he took to be signs of a "chiliastic panic" within postwar science fiction, and in the last Atheling essay of all, "Probapossible Polegomena to Idereal History," he concluded that science fiction itself was a symptom of this "second religiousness." Thus, *Cities in Flight* is reflexively assigned a place in its own schema.)

The discoveries of *They Shall Have Stars* provide the basis for the new culture that succeeds our own. The bridge on Jupiter, despite its own dissolution, becomes a bridge to a new cycle in human history. Vast new horizons are opened up in the climactic moments of the novel. By contrast, *A Life for the Stars* is quiet and calm. The style is much more easygoing — as might be expected in a novel intended for young readers — and the commentary less frantic. The youth taken aboard the city of Scranton before its takeoff and later transferred to New York only gradually realizes something of the significance of what is happening. This is the section which gains most from being set in its place within the tetralogy, because the fact that the reader has already glimpsed the greater context allows him to put Crispin de Ford's adventures in proper perspective, adding an extra dimension to the Heinleinesque account of his gradual acceptance of maturity and responsibility. Within the tetralogy it provides a good change of pace and balances the heavy expository commentary of *They Shall Have Stars*; it also provides a crucial link to the extravagant adventures of the third novel, *Earthman Come Home*.

Earthman Come Home is slightly awkward in its setting, which seems an afterthought. The novel's Spenglerian pretensions are grafted on rather than built in, and it remains very much the stuff of superscientific melodrama, with the periodic invocation of such apparatus as frictionless bearings, invisibility machines, and the Vegan orbital fort. The ideational flourishes, however, remain very memorable, and the stylish upstaging of conventional space opera is unparalleled. The equipment of the planet He with the spindizzies which send it hurtling across the galaxy, and the great meeting of the Okie cities threatened with galactic economic collapse, are wonderfully theatrical. By this time we are well past the period of the Earthmanist culture's full bloom, once again entering the phase of decline. The fact that Blish should leap from this phase of one cycle to this phase of the next is, of course, quite understandable, for it expresses the way the author perceived his own time, and he was constantly drawn to those imaginary futures which echo it.

Earthman Come Home ends with extragalactic migration, finding a suitable conclusion in the battle which New York must fight for possession of the new galaxy against the rogue city of the Interstellar Master Traders. But this time there is no new culture to emerge from the decaying body of the old, neither a human culture nor the alien culture which threatens to achieve dominance as the human empire is conquered by the Web of Hercules. When New York comes into conflict with the Web, it is no mundane confrontation, but a fight for the privilege of being in the key position as the universe is annihilated and re-created. Amalfi and his allies are drawn, in *The Triumph of Time*, into a contest played for higher stakes than mere history permits: the chance (or at least the hope) of being instrumental in the shaping of the new Creation. Each character who strives for this chance entertains the hope of becoming, in some sense, godlike. Blish focuses on the decision of one man, Amalfi, and his rebellion not only against Spenglerian historicism but against the whole attitude which sees history as endlessly repetitive.

There are several other science fiction stories which feature the end of the universe and whose protagonists achieve some kind of deification. Whether Blish is correct in believing such stories to be the products of some historical crisis is open to doubt, though it is certain that the years since 1945 have been an era of great uncertainty and anxiety regarding the future and its possibilities. However, it is certain that *The Triumph of Time* was written with a conscious millenarian fervor; this must be remembered in considering the appropriateness of the book as a conclusion to *Cities in Flight*, and in estimating the significance of Amalfi's decision.

In time, Blish was to repeat the pattern of *Cities in Flight* in another story, *A Case of Conscience*, and in a group of stories which he called *After Such Knowledge*. By comparison with these later efforts, *Cities in Flight*, despite its invocation of Spengler, seems philosophically shallow. Nevertheless, it stretched the conventions of science fiction almost to their limits. *Cities in Flight* is a powerful and multifaceted work. It is untidy, its parts not fitting together as neatly as they might have had the whole been planned from the very beginning, but it does have a sufficiently integrated structure for the whole to be considerably greater than the sum of the parts.

Brian Stableford

Sources for Further Study

Criticism:

Aldiss, Brian W. *Billion Year Spree*. Garden City, N.Y.: Doubleday, 1973,
   p. 251. Aldiss gives a brief analysis of *Cities in Flight* and relates its plot
   development.

Reviews:

Science Fiction Review. XL, October, 1970, pp. 25-26.

CITIZEN OF THE GALAXY

Author: Robert A. Heinlein (1907-   )
First book publication: 1957
Type of work: Novel
Time: An indefinite future
Locale: The Nine Worlds and Earth

A space age version of a young hero's search for his true identity and the rites of passage he must undergo

> *Principal characters:*
> THORBY, a young man
> BASLIM THE CRIPPLE ("POP"), a wiseman, his owner and mentor
> CAPTAIN KRAUSA and
> CAPTAIN BRISBY, Starship Commanders
> UNCLE JACK, Thorby's unscrupulous uncle, a director of the Rudbek empire
> JUDGE BRUDER, another unscrupulous director of the Rudbek empire

The pleasures of this novel are certainly not reserved for young readers alone. It takes an alert and experienced armchair adventurer to savor the verve, wit, and resonance of this tale of a search for identity in alien worlds. In its own special way, *Citizen of the Galaxy* transports us, by spaceship rather than flying carpet, to the imagined lands of fairy tale and romance. The technology may be different, but that does not diminish the magic or excitement of the journey. These "space" places are still the never-ever-maybe ports of call.

Yet, *Citizen of the Galaxy* manages to refresh and constitute a plot as ancient as the storyteller's art, and a theme as compelling in its vision and entertaining in its scope as those we find in myth. For Robert A. Heinlein's protagonist, Thorby (later Thorby Baslim, and still later, Thor Rudbek), joins a long literary brotherhood of memorable scamps, foundlings, orphans, waifs, and strays condemned to triumph over adversity and hardship.

Thorby's adventure, however, had distinctly mythic overtones and it replicates, in many aspects, the journey of the archetypal hero on the way to self-awareness and titular kingship. The process is one of educating his spirit and soul, his moral power and his mind, so that he may be prepared to assume his rightful place in the hierarchy of the universe. Just what his rightful place is, and what his destiny may be, depends on finding out who he is. That is Thorby's quest.

The story opens with the wretched orphan's arrival in Jubbulpore, capital of Jubbal and the Nine Worlds (reminiscent of our own solar system with its nine planets). An open slave market is in session, ironically enough, in the Plaza of Liberty. Because Thorby is so skinny, dirty, and scarred, only an old beggar called Baslim the Cripple will bid for him. Thorby, with a number already tattooed on his thigh as a sign of his previous ownership, is sold to Baslim of the one eye and one leg. He accompanies his new master to the home the beggar has fashioned for himself in the labyrinthine passages under the ruins of the city's old circus amphitheater, presumably where slaves had fought in mortal combat.

But Baslim proves to be Thorby's "master" in more ways than one. For Baslim the Cripple is also Baslim the Wise; and in this role he becomes the image of the fostering, paternally-caring teacher who will initiate his pupil-son into the magic words and secret ways that will protect and guide Thorby. He has the lad call him "Pop," and the bonds of affection and loyalty which develop between the two become unshakable. Baslim the Wise heals the wounds of Thorby's cruel past. And because he always "took the long view," the spiritually royal Beggarman-Wiseman educates his adopted child in the ways of adventure and victorious conquest.

While Thorby helps his Pop to line their beggar's bowl, the boy manages to soak up a "gutter education beyond price." But Baslim the Wise knows that the labyrinth in which they live is more than a physical one; it is a moral and ethical maze through which Thorby will have to learn to find his way if he is ever to know his true identity, if he is ever to find his Self. The labyrinth's center is also Baslim's metaphysical center. Thus Thorby's future journey among the worlds of his galaxy is a pilgrimage to the content and meaning of that center. Its true identity is his as well.

Knowing this, Baslim instructs Thorby in mathematics and languages, and Thorby responds by reaching "for wider horizons with the delight of a baby discovering its fist." The first step is accomplished. Thorby learns "to use his mind," developing an insatiable appetite for the printed page. He also learns a moral sense, and pledges never to lie or steal. As Thorby's education proceeds, Baslim prepares for the boy's future and makes plans to send him, as a free man, on a journey to a "free society," a planet where slavery is forbidden. In such a world, a "frontier world," a man's will and brain can make his way for him.

Two identities merge in Baslim. How else does a beggar come to be named "the Wise"? Baslim the Beggar is a carefully contrived and executed fiction, a mask. His activities are often secret and mysterious, even to Thorby. But on the way to the discovery of his own origins and identity, Thorby will discover Baslim's too. For the moment, Thorby's Pop has him promise two things: that when Baslim dies, Thorby will deliver a message to one of five starship skippers "not of Nine Worlds"; and then "to do whatever the man suggests that you do." The message is one he does not understand; but he learns it by rote, in three different languages. The young man has become the receptacle and carrier of the secret knowledge of his mentor.

When Baslim the Beggar is taken by the police, Thorby's life is in danger. The authorities want to question him about the old man's activities. Thorby escapes through the very labyrinth his Pop had hoped would protect them. Then, through dangerous passage across the city, he finally establishes contact with one of the five skippers Baslim had named. Thorby now knows that his adopted father is dead. Remembering the promise he had made, Thorby recites for Captain Krausa the message he has memorized.

Captain Krausa assumes the responsibility placed upon him by the words of a dead man: to "succor and admonish" the homeless youth until the opportunity presents itself to deliver Thorby "to the commander of any vessel of the Hegemonic Guard, saying that he is a distressed citizen of the Hegemony and entitled . . . to their help in locating his family." So Thorby Baslim is smuggled aboard a free trader ship called SISU, home port of New Finlandia.

Beginning a new life, once again, Thorby Baslim is adopted by Captain Krausa. In an elaborate ceremony full of "secret language," he is initiated into the family of the SISU and the tribe of Free Traders called the People. Then he is given an important job, "a battle station worthy of a man." Though he is learning "new subjects," his training in multidimensional geometrics wins him a reputation as a mathematical genius. Consequently, he is assigned another highly responsible position on the SISU, and his performance earns him respect and admiration.

Now, having learned "the power room rituals" of the SISU and the language and customs of his adoptive family, Thorby is tempted to accept permanent residence in the family of the People. He hesitates because he has come to understand that his quest for identity, the secret of his origins, is also the true way to the freedom his master and teacher had bequeathed to him. The society of Free Traders is so free that, paradoxically, its stringent social rules and its custom-ridden life make for citizen-slaves.

Thorby Baslim, twice-adopted, still wondering "who he is," must choose between the security of the accustomed and comfortably planned life of the SISU and its people and the uncertainties and dangers of travel to the Center Worlds in search of his ancestry. He remembers Pop saying that "a man need never be other than free in his mind," and he remembers that Pop hated slavery in any form. What, Thorby asks himself, had Pop expected of him? With that question, he knows that he must leave the SISU forever. Thorby accompanies his "father" to meet with Captain Brisby, commander of the Guard cruiser *Hydra*. "This lad is Thorby Baslim, adopted son of Colonel Richard Baslim," intones Captain Krausa. "The Colonel asked me to deliver him to you."

Indeed, Thorby's "deliverance" is at hand. Now he is secure in the knowledge that the licensed mendicant, Baslim the Cripple, "Pop" to him, was also Colonel Richard Baslim; and that he was not only a brilliant teacher, but a ship's commander, a hero, a legend among the elite Guard of the Hegemony. Under the wing of a new father figure, Thorby is enlisted (he calls it "adopted") into the Service that Brisby thinks of as "one enormous family."

A search is begun for the records of Thorby's birth. But as time drags on, Thorby feels himself "nothing and nobody." Once again, he has a "blinding image of an old, old nightmare . . . standing on the block, hearing an auctioneer." Pop's presence on Nine Worlds, Thorby learns, had to do with the slave trade. Brisby tells Thorby that the Old Man (as he is affectionately called) had lost an eye and a leg in a rescue operation aimed at freeing people from a slave compound. Trying to fight from inside, Colonel Baslim had become a spy for the "X" Corps because the "Nine Worlds don't qualify on human rights and don't want to qualify." Only the Free Traders visited both "worlds." And it was through the Free Traders that Colonel Baslim had carried on his work and then secured safe passage for his beloved son.

With the knowledge of his Pop's past, Baslim's true identity and mission, Thorby is prepared for the revelation of his own origins. Of all places, he belongs to "lovely Terra, Mother of the Worlds," "mankind's birthplace." His true name is Thor Rudbek, his title Rudbek of Rudbek, and he is heir to a financial princedom. Since his parents are thought to have died (under suspicious circumstances), the Rudbek empire is run by Uncle Jack and Judge Bruder, neither of whom wants any interference from the long-lost heir.

After being spied upon, assaulted, and generally thwarted in all his attempts to take his rightful position in the corporation, Thorby begins to suspect that his uncle has something to hide. His suspicions center on the possible sale of starships to slave traders — starships built by Galactic Transport, a Rudbek company. Through a series of legal maneuvers, Thor Rudbek wins control of the Rudbek empire.

In the process of gaining control, Thorby Baslim is transformed from Thor-boy, to Thor, the young hero-god of thunder, war and strength, whose magic hammer destroys the foes of the gods. More than that, Rudbek of Rudbek comes to understand what Colonel Brisby meant when he said about Pop's life: "It means being so devoted to freedom that you are willing to give up your own . . . that freedom may live." The message echoes the advice of the presiding judge in the case Thor brings against his Uncle Jack: "No man can own a thing to himself alone, and the bigger it is the less he owns it. You are not free to deal with this property arbitrarily nor foolishly." And what of the ambition to follow in Pop's footsteps, renounce Rudbek of Rudbek, and join the Guard as Thorby Baslim?

If he had learned anything at all, Thorby Baslim had learned what Thor Rudbek must declare: "a person *can't* run out on responsibility." Thor Rudbek's place was "a place where the filthy business had to be fought, too." He had arrived at that place through a voyage of discovery and change that evolved in stages. By undergoing the appropriate initiatory rites, by enduring tests of courage and constancy, self-sacrifice and patience, he has come to understand that just as the lowliest of men is bound to necessity so too is the mightiest.

Rudbek of Rudbek freely gives up his freedom — the physical freedom presented him by his spiritual father — in order to insure the legacy of freedom to which each man is entitled and to which each man must be slavishly bound. The ordeals, the tests, the trials of strength and will, are to be won over and over again. The principle of freedom to which Colonel Baslim sacrificed his life includes choosing the way of arriving at that freedom. Accepting the role of Rudbek of Rudbek, impersonal and lacking in a sense of individual identity, is for Thor accepting the mission laid on him long ago. Invested with his title, the private person gives way to the public figure. Thor's allegiance now is to the larger vision, a universal vision, unrestricted by private gain or personal desire.

When the story of *Citizen of the Galaxy* begins, Thorby is a slave to another man. When Thorby's story ends, Thor's life is beginning — in the freely chosen bond of responsibility and devotion to duty. That duty is not to the riches inherited by Rudbek of Rudbek, but to those won by the son of Baslim the Wise from whom he learned "an almost religious concept of the dignity of the individual."

In many ways Baslim the Wise is the real center and focus of this novel, since he sets the moral and ethical norm by which Thorby the boy and Thor the man will choose to live. It is Thorby's recognition that Pop is the yardstick by which men and their acts are measured that continues to inspire and guide him. Thus, Pop's voice becomes Thor's own interior voice, charging him with deeds to be performed. The voices are now resolved and integrated, much as Thor's many identities are reconciled. And Thor can assume the burden of the endless task he undertakes. What had been his as a birthright, the young hero has now earned by trial and merit. He is Rudbek of Rudbek because he will administer with wisdom and justice and humility.

Like his mythological namesake, Thor is possessed of three precious gifts: the hammering force of his conviction, the power and knowledge that are his strength, and the iron will and resolve to execute his duty against the enemies of free men. The transformation is complete. Rudbek of Rudbek is henceforth Citizen of the Galaxy: a *free* man to whom is owed the full rights of citizenship, but who in turn owes a responsibility to defend the protect those rights. As a citizen of the "galaxy," he prepares to take his rightful place among an assembly of brilliant stars. Surely, he will join there the host of young heroes whose feats shine in the night sky as a symbol of the universality of man's struggle against the dark.

Greta Eisner

Sources for Further Study

Criticism:

Panshin, Alexei. "Heinlein in Dimension," in *Riverside Quarterly*. I (May–June, 1965), pp. 139-164. This successful evaluation of Heinlein's literary artistry is a balanced presentation of the author's strengths and weaknesses.

Reviews:

Analog. LXI, April, 1958, p. 146 and LXI, May, 1958, p. 138.

Books and Bookmen. XVII, March, 1972, pp. xi-xii.

Galaxy. XVI, August, 1958, pp. 126-127.

Infinity Science Fiction. III, April, 1958, pp. 83-86.

CITY

Author: Clifford D. Simak (1904-   )
First book publication: 1952
Type of work: Thematically related short stories

A series of stories in which man, represented by Jerome A. Webster and his descendants, is replaced by a race of intelligent dogs

In several taped interviews, as well as in the Introduction to the recent Ace edition of *City*, Clifford Simak acknowledged that the themes of that work grew out of his anger and dismay at the horrors of World War II, especially Hiroshima. This strong moral reaction has had importance not only for his own subsequent work but for science fiction as a whole, in that one may see in *City* an important turning point for American magazine science fiction. Before the *City* stories began to appear in 1944, Simak had published almost three-quarters of his output in the field in *Astounding Science Fiction* from 1937 forward under the editorship of John W. Campbell, Jr. Despite an occasional story such as Campbell's own "Twilight" (published in 1934 under the pseudonym Don A. Stuart), which actually celebrates intellectual curiosity for its own sake, even after the human race has lost that inherent quality of mind because of its dependence upon "perfect" machines, *Astounding Science Fiction* voiced an optimism foretelling the inevitable progress and spread of humanity throughout the galaxy because of its reliance upon science and technology. Simak's fullest expression of that belief occurred in *The Cosmic Engineers* (serialized in 1939), in which his protagonists venture to the edge of the universe to help save it from invasion and destruction by aliens. The narrative emphasized plot action.

Then came World War II. It is obvious that Simak brooded upon the themes expressed in *City*, since four of the eight stories were published in 1944. To sketch the plot line of the work can only suggest the complexity of ideas in *City*, since the episodes focus upon crucial moments, often centuries apart.

The title piece, "City," issued as a novelette in May, 1944, provides the basic premise from which all else follows. In the year 2000, Simak's protagonist — John J. Webster — argues that after World War II, urban civilization had become outmoded and unwanted. The helicopter had replaced the family car, thereby allowing an even greater personal mobility; hydroponics had made the traditional farm unnecessary as an economic unit needed to feed large population centers; atomic power had provided ample energy so that people no longer had to crowd together; and within several generations the development of robots supplied a cheap source of labor. (Significantly, Simak added a passage to the volume absent from the magazine version; Webster declared that had not the great cities of midcentury withered and been abandoned, they would probably have been destroyed in an atomic war.) In short, Simak created a crisis situation to which mankind must adapt quickly. The response of those who did adapt was to scatter across the countryside, either reverting to a primitivism or establishing great family estates.

"Huddling Place" (July, 1944), perhaps the most frequently anthologized of Simak's early works, projects a further four generations into the lives of the Webster family. Once a famous surgeon who had journeyed to Mars and whose book remains the authoritative study of Martain brain structure, Jerome A. Webster has returned to remain at the secluded estate founded by his great-grandfather. Through his personal robot, Jenkins, the reader learns that Jerome Webster suffers from agoraphobia. The dramatic conflict arises when Webster is called upon to go to Mars to operate on an old friend, Juwain, a Martian philosopher at work on a theory which may change the lives of all intelligent creatures. The irony occurs when the faithful Jenkins calmly dismisses — and fails to report — the spaceship which has come to take his master to Mars because it is preposterous to think that Jerome Webster would leave his country manor for any reason whatsoever.

With "Census" (September, 1944) the full potential of Simak's themes emerges. Action continues to be subservient to idea, as a census-taker ventures into the countryside for the first time in three hundred years. The story is structured around the conversations he has with those whom he encounters. On the one hand, he finds the Websters, plagued by guilt because of the death of Juwain. Eighty-six-year-old Thomas has built the ship which even then his son Allen guides toward Alpha Centauri; Thomas also insists that it is time man reached the stars and helped supervise operation of the universe. (One is tempted to read this as another of Simak's attacks upon both man's egotism and his dependence upon machines.) In contrast, his other son, Bruce Webster, has experimented with genetic engineering and has introduced into dogs inheritable abilities to speak and to see so that they are able to read. (Much later tiny robots are developed to serve as hands for the dogs.) Bruce repeatedly speaks of how man has been alone and how much farther he might have progressed had there been two different minds, able to work together, although perceiving the universe differently.

The census-taker also encounters the mutant Joe, who is intellectually far superior to mankind. Twenty years earlier he had shown Thomas Webster how to solve the problem preventing development of the speed necessary for interstellar flight. Now, he not only quickly repairs the census-taker's atomic gun, but after momentarily glancing at the document, he indicates the point at which Juwain erred in his thinking. But Juwain refuses to share that insight. The protagonist realizes that Joe acts only from intellectual curiosity. For whatever reasons, he has moved beyond the need for that approval of his actions which binds society together under the guise of such concepts as progress. For example, some years earlier for his own amusement he had enclosed an ant hill, thereby breaking the stagnant cycle of hibernation controlling the ants destiny. He explains that it took ten years for them to learn to use the small carts he had built for them. Now, with a swift, idle kick, he destroys that ant hill from which chimneys belch smoke. The subject no longer concerns or amuses him, although it will have further repercussions.

Simak chooses to clear the stage of mankind at this point in order to concentrate upon the culture developed by the dogs. "Desertion" (November, 1944) becomes pivotal to *City*. First, it illustrates how idea can open up an established narrative structure of science fiction — in this case, the convention of solving a single problem. The protagonist Fowler must learn what has happened to those men who have disappeared after being genetically engineered to survive on the surface of Jupiter. Like them, he takes a Jovian form, that of a loper. So complete is his feeling of transcendence that, even had he related the narrative in the first person, its credibility would remain in doubt. To overcome that problem, Simak permits Fowler's mangy old dog Towser to share the transformation. Communication between them confirms the increased awareness surpassing anything either has known.

"Desertion" expresses Simak's denunciation of human limitations more fully than did the science fiction of any of his contemporaries. For neither Towser nor Fowler chooses willingly to become, again, dog or man. In "Paradise" (not published until June, 1946), Fowler does return to share his knowledge. Mankind eagerly abandons the human condition. Except for those persons gathered around Tyler Webster in Geneva, the seat of the world government, the earth is left vacant so that the dogs may flourish under the guidance of Jenkins.

In "Hobbies" (November, 1946), Jon Webster comes from Geneva after a thousand years to find that the dogs have developed psychically, discovering in the process an infinity of worlds existing side by side, like separate rooms. (A few, the "cobbly" worlds, are closed to the dogs because they are inhabited by nightmarish creatures.) Webster learns that Jenkins is unsure of his ability to act as mentor to the dogs. As for the dogs, in a world where killing is unknown, they have begun to think of a civilization based upon the brotherhood of all animals. However, they also dream of their relationship to man, elevating him to a godlike role. Fearing that man will interfere with the dogs' efforts to achieve a better civilization than man in his smug egotism did, Webster hastens to Geneva and encloses the city beneath a locked, metallic dome.

Unfortunately, Webster's son and some other children are outside, playing caveman in the forest; their descendants live as cavemen for a thousand years until rescued by Jenkins and the dogs. In "Aesop" (December, 1947), the brotherhood of animals has been achieved, but a Webster child kills a robin with a bow and arrow. Afraid of a recurrence of the human cycle, Jenkins takes him and the other websters — webster has become the generic name for man — into a cobbly world.

Yet Simak did not allow *City* to become a canine Utopia. The last tale, "The Trouble with Ants," published in *Fantastic Adventures* in January, 1951, darkens the entire series by underscoring Simak's attack upon man's nature and his institutions. (According to Simak, Campbell had refused it because there had been enough dog stories — an anecdote perhaps giving more insight into Campbell and his magazine than into *City*.) Published as "The Simple Way" in the volume, the story records Jenkins' return from the cobbly worlds after five thousand years. (The websters lasted no more than a thousand, but Jenkins had difficulty finding his way back because of the multiplicity of worlds.) He discovers that the ants are constructing a single sprawling, towering building which threatens to engulf the earth. He gains access to Geneva to ask the last webster how men would solve the problem, but he rejects the simple answer that the ants would be poisoned. Although he himself cannot leave, the dogs journey to parallel worlds, leaving earth to the ants.

As noted, such an outline cannot do justice to the intellectual complexity of *City*. The basic theme is obvious. But even if published together instead of over a span of seven years, the tales remain too episodic to achieve full impact unless Simak somehow pulled them together. This he did through the use of a narrative framework deceptively simple in tone and structure. A general editor — a dog of some distant, unspecified future — introduces the stories as though they are fragments of a legend told for countless centuries. An individual note precedes each tale. In them the editor refers to the scholarly debates between those who view the works as pure myth and those who see them as some distortion of historical fact. He is thus able to comment upon and to explicate from a seemingly objective point of view the themes Simak pursues.

In this way Clifford Simak brings to *City* a unity and seriousness of tone as well as the vitality of the beast fable in order to gain a perspective from which to make a moral judgment of mankind. By thus creating a credible nonhuman world, he broke through the conventions of early science fiction which too often resulted merely in a linear projection of present-day society. After *City*, science fiction became more than simple adventure stories celebrating the nuts and bolts of mechanical progress; Simak gave the genre a moral stature. *City* was given the International Fantasy Award in 1953.

Thomas D. Clareson

Sources for Further Study

Reviews:

Analog. L, January, 1953, pp. 160-161.

Authentic Science Fiction. XLIV, April, 1954, pp. 90-91.

Booklist. XLIX, October 15, 1952, p. 69.

Galaxy. V, October, 1952, pp. 123-124.

New Worlds. XXII, April, 1954, pp. 126-128.

New York Herald Tribune Book Review. July 6, 1952, p. 8.

New York Times. September 14, 1952, p. 33.

Science Fiction Adventures. I, February, 1953, p. 112.

THE CITY AND THE STARS

Author: Arthur C. Clarke (1917-   )
First book publication: 1956
Type of work: Novel
Time: The distant future
Locale: Diaspar, a city in the oasis of Lys, located on a desertlike Earth

Alvin explores his billion-year-old city and the stars above it in a dramatic quest for understanding of his universe and himself

Principal characters:
ALVIN, a young "Unique" in Diaspar
ALYSTRA, the immortal girl who loves him
JESERAC, his tutor
KHEDRON, the Jester
HILVAR, Alvin's friend in Lys
SERANIS, Hilvar's mother
VANAMONDE, a bodiless and eternal artificial mind

The haunting power of *The City and the Stars* comes from its drama of life and mind against time. The city, Diaspar, and the tiny oasis of Lys have survived for a billion years on an Earth turned to desert, its seas dried to plains of salt. The Seven Suns still blaze at the center of the galaxy, a tantalizing relic of an interstellar power the ages have overwhelmed. The novel follows Alvin's encounters with the wonders of this far-future universe and his struggles to solve the riddles of the past.

Cast in the familiar pattern of a young man's coming of age and discovering his social role, the novel was begun in 1937, when Clarke was only twenty, and rewritten through half a dozen different drafts over almost another twenty years. An earlier version, *Against the Fall of Night*, was published in *Startling Stories* for November, 1948, and reprinted as a book in 1953. *The City and the Stars* is the same story, but greatly expanded, with an older protagonist, several new characters, and much added detail.

The extrapolation of man's future evolution is one of Clarke's favorite topics, and is one he also treated in such later and better-known works as *Childhood's End* and *2001: A Space Odyssey*. It has been, in fact, a basic theme of science fiction — perhaps *the* basic theme — since H. G. Wells's *The Time Machine* (1895).

Wells and Clarke differ vastly, however, in their views of man's destiny. They are representative of two major conflicting camps in modern science fiction, the Utopians and the dystopians. In his great early fiction, Wells is certainly still the pessimistic disciple of Jonathan Swift and the ironic critic of all human progress. Mark Hillegas, in *The Future as Nightmare: H. G. Wells and the Anti-Utopians,* had traced his dystopian shadow across nearly a century of later science fiction, from Forster's "The Machine Stops" and Zamiatin's *We* down through Huxley's *Brave New World* and Orwell's *Nineteen Eighty-Four* to Frederik Pohl and the recent "new wave" fad.

Wells sends his Time Traveller forward across the centuries to discover the end of man and life on Earth. The narrator has glimpses of future human greatness, but these are only transient. He stops less than a million years ahead in a kind of wasted paradise to find that retrograde evolution has divided the human race into the hideous man-eating Morlocks and the beautiful but child-like Eloi upon whom they feed. Pushing on for a few million more years, he reaches scenes of "abominable desolation" in which the last heir of mankind is a round black thing hopping across a barren beach in the red twilight of the final nightfall, doomed to perish with the dying planet.

Clarke's vigorous optimism places him in the other camp, among the Utopi-ans, who date back at least to Plato and his *Republic* and include such popular contemporaries as Isaac Asimov and Robert A. Heinlein, writers with a stronger belief in the usefulness of reason and the benefits of science and a greater faith in man's high destiny.

In contrast to Wells's dark forecasts of the devolution and death of mankind, Clarke closes this novel with his persistently brighter vision of evolutionary progress rising to infinity, with mind finally transcending the limits of matter. Though he is never explicitly religious, his quests for eternal union with vast mental power beyond the normal universe may be seen as a search for God.

The Utopian writer faces a difficult technical problem. Story drama requires conflict, and conflict is commonly perceived in terms of good and evil. Teem-ing with evil, the dystopia is rich in opportunities for gripping drama. In the good place, however, evil is absent by its very definition, and many a Utopian novel has been an uneventful lecture tour of the ideal society.

Clarke generally avoids this accidental hazard. Though the plot is some-times episodic, Alvin is never at peace with his surroundings and the book is never dull. Its power springs less from Alvin's efforts to solve the puzzle of what he is than from the history he unravels, fragment by fragment, of man's billion-year struggle to survive in an uncaring cosmos.

As hero, in fact, Alvin is dwarfed by the vast galactic background and the ideas that animate the novel; the rich tapestry of setting and theme is more exciting than the characters. Yet Alvin, only a boy in Clarke's first drafts of the book and a naïve adolescent in this last version, serves well as an essential emotional bridge into the wonders of the future world. Through him, we ex-plore several alternative routes of possible future evolution. His native place, Diaspar, is a perfect and eternal machine. More real than anything material, the city and its people are preserved in the Memory Banks of the Central Computer, like ideas in the mind of Plato's God. Existing there forever, its citizens are recalled from time to time to material life, kept in carefree luxury but confined to the city by a compulsive fear of everything outside.

The first child "born" there in many million years, Alvin is a "Unique," a random factor designed by the city's builders to introduce change into its static permanence. Created free of that imprisoning compulsion, and bored by the aimless and repetitive diversions of the unchanging city, he escapes to Lys. Lys is an equally old and isolated community of relative primitivism, its people still mortal, independent of machines. Living close to nature in tiny villages, they have developed great mental powers, mastering telepathy, yet they share Diaspar's crippling fear of the unknown universe outside.

With Hilvar, a young friend from Lys, Alvin sets out to unravel the mysterious human past and to break down the psychological barriers between their two communities. They visit Shalmirane, the site of a legendary battle against the space Invaders believed to have destroyed the Galactic Empire, leaving the survivors afraid of the stars.

The convention of the future space empire, an obvious symbol of unlimited technological progress, dates at least from the tales of the Interstellar Patrol that Edmond Hamilton wrote in the 1920's for the old *Weird Tales*. Later writers have elaborated the convention both into "space operas" and into serious "future histories"; Clarke makes good use of the technique here.

As the novel develops, Alvin and Hilvar come upon apparent evidence that racial progress finally failed. The monumental ruins of Shalmirane are inhabited now only by a protean polyp, a pathetic last disciple of a long-dead human religious Master. Still vainly awaiting the promised return of "the Great Ones," the polyp dissolves into mindless parts before its story is complete, but Alvin gains partial control of its robot servant. The knowledge and power of the robot are guarded by a block that must be removed. When this is done, the robot lifts the Master's ship from the ancient spaceport where it has lain buried under the sand and carries the young men on an interstellar voyage to learn the fate of the lost Empire.

First the travelers reach the Seven Suns, an amazing monument to vanished greatness. Six great differently colored stars have been set in a splendid circle around the opalescent Central Sun, whose planets they explore. Most of these worlds are long dead, their abandoned cities ruined. When the searchers do find life, it is mindless, a sentient sea like that in Stanislaw Lem's later *Solaris*, which tries to swallow their ship.

At last, however, they do encounter Vanamonde, a friendly survivor of the Empire. An artificial creature of pure mind, Vanamonde reveals more of man's true history. It was not the mystical battle of Shalmirane that caused the Empire's fall, but rather a climactic struggle of advanced intelligence to escape the dominion of matter. The first efforts created a Mad Mind that hated and destroyed everything material. In a second attempt, however, this evil immortal was overcome and imprisoned. The victors later abandoned the ravaged universe, leaving Vanamonde behind when they set out on a mystic search for an even greater mental power.

The dramatic heart of the novel is this revolt of mind against the chains of matter and the struggle of life against a dying cosmos for eternal survival. Clarke ends his drama on a note of optimistic assurance. "In this universe the night was falling . . . but elsewhere the stars were still young . . . and along the path he once had followed, Man would one day go again.''

As a novel, *The City and the Stars* is seriously flawed. The human characters are seldom more than two-dimensional and the plot sometimes wanders. Such features as the space Invaders and the Mad Mind are melodramatic vestiges of the early science fiction pulps, where Clarke found his first inspiration. The ending, Alvin's return from his epic cosmic quest to complete the reconciliation of Lys and Diaspar, is an unrelated anticlimax.

Yet, in this final version, the book is richly inventive, vividly imaginative, and told with effective skill. The spell of vast times and spaces, the mysteries of man's long past, and the sweeping themes of permanence and change almost make up for its faults. Clarke's first book, and the one he lavished most time and care upon, it is perhaps his most characteristic and most enduring.

Jack Williamson

Sources for Further Study

Criticism:

Huntington, John. "From Man to Over-Mind: Arthur C. Clarke's Myth of Progress," in *Arthur C. Clarke*. Edited by Joseph D. Olander and Martin Harry Greenberg. New York: Taplinger, 1977, pp. 213-216. In *The City and the Stars* Clarke deals with the inadequacy of technical progress, according to Huntington.

Reviews:

Booklist. LII, May 1, 1956, p. 364.

Library Journal. LXXXI, June 1, 1956, p. 1554.

New York Herald Tribune Book Review. February 5, 1956, p. 10.

New York Times. February 5, 1956, p. 21.

San Francisco Chronicle. May 6, 1956, p. 22.

THE CITY OF TRUTH
(GEROD PRAVDY)

Author: Lev Lunts (1901-1924)
First book publication: 1924
English translation: 1929
Type of work: Drama
Time: Sometime after the Revolution
Locale: The City of Truth and Equality

Red Army soldiers returning from a campaign come upon a new city in the desert, which they take to be the new Russian paradise

> *Principal characters:*
> COMMISSAR
> DOCTOR
> VANYA
> GLOOMY
> JOLLY
> YOUNGSTER
> OLDTIMER
> SOLDIERS
> CITIZENS OF THE CITY

During his brief life, Lev Lunts wrote four very promising plays. The first, *Outside the Law* (1919), is a romantic tragedy set in Spain; it makes use of *commedia dell'arte* techniques and rapid movement across three stages. In the second, *The Apes Are Coming!* (1921), the actors tear down the set to build a barricade against the approach of counterrevolutionary monsters. *Bertran de Born* (1922), his third play, presents the great provençal troubadour of the twelfth century. And the last play, *The City of Truth* (1923), presents an anti-utopia based on Soviet Russia. Together with the film scenario *Things in Revolt*, it constitutes Lunts's main contribution to Russian science fiction. The scientific aspect of *The City of Truth* is light: the secret of making things move by sound is the basis of the scenario, while in the play we are transported to an unworldly Russia in the midst of the desert, by magic, time-warp, or mirage. For Lunts it was not the *science* of science fiction that was important, but the *fiction* — the fantastic reshaping of present society, present ideas, and possibilities. Lunts was headed toward philosophical drama, and despite his immaturity, his plays reveal more thought and reflection than most of the theater of his time. As Maxim Gorky wrote, "Had he lived and gone on working, it seemed to me, the Russian stage would surely have been enriched by an entirely new type of play."

The City of Truth was written in a sanatorium in Königstein im Taunus, to which Lunts had gone to recuperate from severe exhaustion, heart trouble, and possibly meningitis. Shortly after completing the film scenario *Things in Revolt*, he suffered a series of crippling strokes, caused by an inflammation of the brain. For the better part of August and September, 1923, he lay in a coma. When he regained consciousness he discovered that he could no longer write: not only was he physically unable, but he could not distinguish the different consonants of the Russian alphabet. Early in October he sent a letter strewn with pathetic scribblings and corrections to the writer Nikolai Nikitin and his wife Zoya: "Honored spouses! As I have already written the Serapions, I have truly forgotten how to write — 'agraphia' is the name of the illness. For two weeks I have been relearning from the beginning."

Despite this handicap, Lunts was anxious to begin work on a new play. For two years he had been thinking of it, planning it down to the smallest detail. As soon as he was physically able to lift his pen — even before he had relearned the alphabet completely — be began writing. A rough draft was hastily composed in October, revisions were made in November and December, and the final version, entitled *Gerod Pravdy* (*The City of Truth*), was completed in January, 1924.

Just as "Go West!" culminates Lunts's previous esthetic works, so *The City of Truth* sums up his previous creative works. This is apparent not only in its blending of tragedy and comedy, adventure and philosophy, but also in its definite borrowing from past works. In particular, the play follows the general outline of the story "In the Wilderness" and extends the philosophy of *Outside the Law*, *Bertran de Born*, and *Things in Revolt*. In the story, the Jews cross the desert in search of the promised land; they are offered a false god, which they readily accept but which proves illusory, and they travel on. In *The City of Truth*, Red Army soldiers returning from a five-year campaign in China cross the Gobi Desert in search of a Russian paradise; they enter a city which they take to be Russia, but which they soon reject, and they travel on. *Outside the Law*, *Bertran de Born*, and *Things in Revolt* all investigate the nature of law and freedom with reference to Soviet society. *The City of Truth* questions the basis of Soviet society. One of the first things Lunts wrote after his coma (it can be identified as such by its pitiful spelling) bears an obvious reference to the Soviet regime; and although not used in the play, it is clearly a sketch for the city which figures in Act II and foreshadows the problem of the entire work.

The City of Truth consists of three acts, each of which contains a half-dozen or more short scenes. These scenes develop the story through a rapid series of pictures and also provide different points of view, different sides of a debate. In Act I, subtitled "Prologue," the soldiers trek through the desert, led by a commissar who assures them that the Russia ahead has become a land of peace and opportunity where all are equal in the eyes of the law. Like their Biblical counterparts, they are tired and hungry and want to turn back. A doctor among them objects to the very idea of such a land as the commissar describes. But the commissar, who holds the only pistol among the men, controls them with threats and promises. In the last scene they come upon a city in the desert, the

City of Truth and Equality, and are met by an Elder who invites them to live and work in the city "as equals."

Act II, subtitled "The Catastrophe," opens with a murder reminiscent of "In the Wilderness": a soldier appears with a spear in his hand and quickly impales a pair of lovers, who fall behind some bushes. The rest of the act develops the ideas of *Things in Revolt*. The citizens of the city are a mass of living mannequins, unacquainted with the passions of love, hate, joy, envy, and the like. Everything is shared equally, including sexual intercourse. The soldiers and the commissar find life intolerable under such conditions, and by their emotional utterances and actions they both upset and begin to humanize the citizens.

Lunts is quite inventive in the handling of this situation. The soldiers are shown teaching the citizens how to laugh, kiss, and cry. In order to provide the maximum contrast between the citizens and soldiers and thereby attain the most striking scenic effect, Lunts directs that the citizens should be dressed alike, and always move in a group and speak in a monotone. The soldiers, on the other hand, each have their own clothing and individual manners of speech and gesture; they are always a motley mob. As Lunts puts it, the characters of the play are to be treated as "two peoples." This device was suggested by Lope de Vega's *Fuente Ovejuna* and Meyerhold's production of Przybyszewski's *The Eternal Fable* (1906), but Lunts was the one to crystallize it and give it real meaning. Later Čapek independently invented the device and used it similarly in the play *Adam the Creator* (1927): the human products of a clay mold move in a group, while those fashioned by Adam's hand act individually.

The discovery of the speared couple causes the catastrophe of Act II. The assassin, who had murdered his unfaithful fiancée and her lover, is defended by the soldiers; the citizens, who want to execute him, think her action quite right. This disagreement leads to war. Here Lunts inadvertently recast the situation of Pushkin's "The Gypsies" (1824).

The final act, subtitled "Denouement," takes place after the war. The citizens have been massacred, and the soldiers prepare to continue their search for Russia. Both they and the commissar now agree with the doctor that life stands above equality; that peace and calm are "for the dead." But there is one vital difference: the commissar believes that Russia will embody equality, law, and life. The doctor disagrees. Two survivors are discovered — one, a girl, has learned only to hate; the other, a boy, has learned to steal, lie, and murder. (Unlike the robots of *R.U.R.* they do not fall in love or promise a new race.) At the commissar's command, the boy stabs the doctor, and there ensues a debate between the commissar and the dying man.

The problem of *The City of Truth* may be stated thus: Can people be equalized by law and order without losing their individuality and turning into machines? Lunts does not give unequivocal answers to this question, but attempts to state the pros and cons with equal force. The citizens, by virtue of their uniformity, appear to represent an affirmative answer to the question, but the soldiers, by virtue of their disruptive individualism, prove the necessity of the question. The argument is set forth most openly in Scene 4, Act II, where the Elders and the soldiers hold a general debate, scenically illustrated by their placement on opposite sides of the stage. The Elders reiterate the formula that when all are equal before the law there is no injustice or violence. The soldiers insist that life is found only in inequality, injustice, and struggle.

Of course, by the very act of raising the question Lunts betrays his misgivings. There is little doubt that his sympathies lie with the unruly soldiers and the heretical doctor. Almost every time the doctor speaks he paraphrases Zamyatin: the entire play, in fact, may be understood as a dramatic presentation of Zamyatin's dialectic of eternal revolution. Certainly Lunts shared Zamyatin's fear that Soviet rule would impede the forward motion of life and ultimately produce bloodless robots. But far from being counterrevolutionaries, both were in a sense superrevolutionaries, committed to incessant change. Lunts, however, was not altogether convinced that the commissar's dream could not be realized, that equality could not be combined with diversity. The first draft of the play testifies to his indecision. In its concluding scene the doctor dies without saying "you will not find it," and, following the departure of the soldiers, the First Elder of the city emerges from the bushes to pronounce his verdict:

> All have died. I, the Elder, remain — to die alone. There, in that distant land, is blood. Where there is blood — is life.

Lunts was never thoroughly satisfied with his play and constantly rewrote it. A number of versions were entitled *Kontsa net!* (*There Is No End!*), the words with which the doctor ends the work. In December, Lunts dejectedly wrote Gorky: "I have ruined a well-conceived thing. I continually correct it. In two weeks or so I'll 'decide' and then send it to you." Gorky published it in an *émigré* journal, *Beseda*, after Lunts's death in 1924. Early in that year Lunts sent the play to Konstantin Fedin to be read to the Serapion Brothers. The group subjected it to their usual "merciless criticism."

Their opinions, reported to Lunts by his girl friend, are significant in that they are based on compositional and not ideological considerations. In general, the Serapions found that Lunts had philosophized too openly and too schematically, but they thought the work deserved attention. Mikhail Zoshchenko dubbed it "a proletarian play for *émigrés*." After the reading they circulated it among interested parties, Zamyatin and Sergei Radlov in particular. The latter planned to produce it in The People's Theater (Narodnyi Dom), but as far as can be determined, he did not succeed in doing so. After Gorky's publication, it was translated into German, Italian, and English. The English version, published by F. O'Dempsey and translated under the pen name of John Silver, is not very satisfactory, as it follows the lamentable practice common among

British translators of converting rough Russian speech into Cockney English.

Lunts did not live to enrich the stage as he might have. The Soviet period has since produced very few decent playwrights — Mikhail Bulgakov, Evgeny Zamyatin, and Nikolai Erdman virtually stand alone. And Lunts did not write anything positively great — he was simply too young, too active. But his works retain youthful energy, the excitement of exploration, and, most of all, truthfulness. Lunts did not live to reconsider, to recant, to become a socialist realist. As his friend Viktor Shklovsky wrote, "Fate spared him from compromises."

Gary Kern

LA CIUDAD
(The City)

Author: Mario Levrero
First book publication: 1966
Type of work: Novel
Time: The present
Locale: An unidentified South American city

An enigmatic novel of a man's visit to an unnamed Latin American city, somewhat in the style of Valdimir Colin or Jorge Luis Borges, written by the dean of Uruguaian science fiction writers

> *Principal characters:*
> THE TRAVELLER
> GIMENEZ, a man who takes him in
> ANA, a woman he meets and makes love to

The first problem to be considered with Mario Levrero's novel is whether it belongs to the genre of science fiction. Some critics call it realistic fantasy, referring to the resemblance between Levrero's oneiric atmospheres and those of Franz Kafka. Classifications of literary genres are usually rather arbitrary; discounting the typical examples, one could make divisions and subdivisions in many classifications. The now-respected expression "science fiction" is neither a felicitous nor an adequate term for the genre because it is difficult to reconcile the terms "science" and "fiction." Science is a form of investigation and knowledge that demands precise reasoning and exact data, and in which speculation without scientific bases is practically impossible. Fiction is created by the imagination; its real sources are elastic, and the coherence demanded of it is not of the objective kind. This coherence speaks more to the work's style, to its psychological portraits, to its action, or to its literary quality — those elements that involve the reader emotionally and transmit something special.

Today it is common to place some of the works of Franz Kafka and Jorge Luis Borges and books such as *La Ciudad* by Mario Levrero in the so-called category of science fiction. This practice is perfectly justifiable. To say that science fiction is literature inspired or based on science is a simplistic definition, too imprecise to be satisfactory. Certainly the fantastic, imaginative side of good science fiction has its own qualities. It is no longer the religious fantasy of the past century, nor the supernatural work in which superstitions can justify the development of the theme, nor the symbolism of the romantic Germans. The "marvelous" found in science fiction can be the extrapolation of realities revealed by science, the imaginary creation of a future or simply different world; and its intellectual mortar does not necessarily exclude psychological or philosophical penetration, but may commonly be based on parapsychology.

La Ciudad tells the story of a solitary hitchhiker who arrives in a little city, probably in the pampas of Argentina or Uruguay. The author intentionally leaves out any geographical classification. At a gasoline station, "there was a huge sign which said WELCOME in several languages. . . ." In the house of a man called Gimenez, who takes him in, he finds a map, and on the map, in a certain spot, he finds the words, "City of San Pedro and San Juan." He associates these names with Argentinian cities, but there are other words in some unintelligible language. At first he thinks they are Russian, and then he imagines they could be Chinese, Sanskrit, or Egyptian hieroglyphics.

Mario Levrero, the much-esteemed dean of Uruguaian science fiction writers, takes his character through this apparently normal city, where insignificant and apparently rational details begin to lead the reader and the character from a logical, explainable reality into a dream reality — not an impossible dream with fantasy characters, but a dream filled with human emotions and values.

The author is a master at taking a reality and introducing into it an invisible lens that changes its form without destroying it, that modifies it without changing it into something opposite. The climates he creates in this manner have been compared to those found in Kafka's; the comparison is valid. The careful, sometimes seemingly irrelevant descriptions begin to establish a tension, an anguished expectancy for the fate of the character who, at this point, cannot leave the city without being made a prisoner. In *La Ciudad*, things happen within a simple, even predictable scheme, but with inexorable distortions, like a parody of real life. Ana, a woman the traveller finds, makes love to, and seemingly begins to love, acts in a curious manner and disappears from his life without our ever knowing why. The identification with the central character is achieved through his fear, hope, and anguish. His hopes are doubtful, his fear is diffuse and without apparent or objective motives. His anguish is of the variety that gnaws over interior dilemmas, built upon projections of events which have already occurred or which are imaginary; he attempts to modify mentally what has already happened in a different way in reality than we had hoped.

Levrero's plot contains nothing unique or surprising; the reader can foresee that the story will not have an end in the traditional sense. The main character leaves the city, traveling with the trainmaster of the railroad station, in a cart propelled by the trainmaster himself, to another station where he buys a ticket to Montevideo. A train, full of omens, arrives at night; the passengers bunch, crowd, and shove in their fight to get on the train, and the character finds himself in a dark car where the passengers are so tightly packed that he cannot move. The sound of the train puts him to sleep, held up by his invisible companions. He falls into a "dense, profound and dark dream, like an immense, lukewarm sea, without images, without words, without thoughts." This is the last sentence of the book. One can imagine anything, but the most evident impression is that the dark car, full of companions standing side by side, is death itself. The final tracks that would take him to his city lead nowhere at all. It is a one-way line, without possibility of detours or stops. The story ends without explanations, in an abrupt and even disappointing manner. The whole plot is a slow entry into a one-way tunnel, whose light at the end, "on the other side," is never reached.

There seems to be no incongruity in identifying books such as *La Ciudad* as science fiction. Human experience is an enigma, and life a disquieting, restless mystery whose points of reference become diffuse and distant. Modern physics speaks of "quantitive numbers of strangeness," that which prolongs itself beyond physics to penetrate into the profundities of the human spirit. We live with the computer, in the midst of sums and abstractions; the concrete and the real are mere concepts. Everything is factually and morally possible.

Today scientists are able to change the perception of a human being with drugs such as mescaline or L.S.D. The narrow rationalism of the nineteenth century produced a so-called realistic literature of unquestionable value, but in which man seemed to be defined, a finished static product, a known example of a privileged species which dominated the planet. Galileo reduced man's pretentiousness considerably when he affirmed that the Earth was not the center of the universe. The technical revolution and the conquest of space showed that, although the Earth was the birthplace of man, a child always leaves the cradle. Freud and Einstein discovered roads which man has not yet begun to tread, except for a few first fledgling steps. For this reason, perhaps, realistic fantasy may not be truly realistic nor even fantasy. Thus, the work of Kafka, Borges, or Mario Levrero may fall within science fiction, since their fiction reflects the fact that science surrounds and envelops us from all sides, and that without it, man's life would, for all practical purposes, disappear.

André Carneiro

CLIPPER OF THE CLOUDS
(ROBUR LE CONQUÉRANT)
AND
THE MASTER OF THE WORLD
(MAÎTRE DU MONDE)

Author: Jules Verne (1828-1905)
First book publication: Clipper of the Clouds (1886); *The Master of the World* (1905)
English translation: Clipper of the Clouds (1887); *The Master of the World* (n.d.)
Type of work: Novellas
Time: The 1880's, the early twentieth century
Locale: The United States

Robur, who carries two inventors around the world in a "heavier than air" flying machine, proves to be the mysterious "Master of the World," whose secret laboratory in the Carolinas and whose amphibian airplane are investigated by the federal government

Principal characters:
> UNCLE PRUDENT, the wealthy president of the Weldon Institute
> PHIL EVANS, the secretary of the Weldon Institute
> ROBUR, an engineer and inventor, later "Master of the World"
> JOHN STROCK, the chief inspector of the federal police
> MR. WARD, his boss

The contemporary reader of Jules Verne experiences an altered perspective when viewing a century's progress in science fiction, for the same elements appear in the film *Close Encounters of the Third Kind* (1976) as in Verne's *Clipper of the Clouds* and its sequel *The Master of the World*. *Clipper of the Clouds* begins with a U.F.O. broadcasting music from the skies, and music was also the "language" of the film's aliens. Moreover, *The Master of the World* features a high and inaccessible mountain crater as secret laboratory and promotes secrecy as a necessary feature of scientific advancement, as did the film. The aliens of the film captured a cherubic child; Robur captures two amateur scientists and one valet. The child in the film learns and conveys on return as much as do Verne's scientists, who never see the internal mechanism of the craft. In the fiction of Jules Verne, advanced knowledge may be held by a mysterious master inventor of a remote part of Earth and can be kept secret; in the film, almost a hundred years later, remarkable scientific advancement can startle the public only by coming from outer space; otherwise, the appearance of an unknown flying object and public reaction to it are similar.

In the earlier "Robur" story, Uncle Prudent and Phil Evans, respectively president and secretary of the Weldon Institute in Philadelphia, discuss the means of building a "lighter than air" machine to be called the *Goahead*; but into their midst strides a geometric human named "Robur," who ridicules their plans and in turn finds himself mocked and satirically dubbed "conqueror" for his "heavier than air" theories. That night, in retaliation he captures Prudent,

Evans, and their valet Frycollin. They have been stunned and they awaken in an airship on a westerly course. The ship's wings, sails, and drive mechanism of "seventy-four screws" permit rapid turning, hovering as low as six feet, accelerating to 120 miles per hour, and ascending to heights of 13,000 feet. The"aeronef" *Albatross* appears to be driven by electricity stored in "accumulators."

The three prisoners concentrate on escape and scarcely bother to comprehend or even investigate the wondrous invention; Robur's brutal remarks and ironical disdain further discourage them. Resenting their sustained flight and hating their captor, they fail to appreciate the advantages of the experience: the wonders of the landscape viewed on a zig-zag course around the world, the sports the early helicopter affords (buzzing a train, harpooning and being towed by a whale, or — for punishment — dragging the recalcitrant Frycollin through the air in a tub suspended by a rope), the independence of resources (drawing water from a lake, harpooning and dragnetting fish), the navigational feats (negotiating a pass through the Rockies, riding out or above an electrical storm), altruistic services (stopping a human hecatomb in Africa, towing a becalmed ship to land), thrilling escapes from danger (cyclone, volcano, and waterspout), and the occasional skyshow staged for the gaping public below. Over Paris the prisoners drop a note in a snuffbox. Later, while suspended over the Chatham Islands only fifty yards above the ground for propeller repairs, Uncle Prudent steals and plants dynamite. The three then escape down a cable, and the ship explodes in midair. Believing Robur and his crew dead, the three escaped prisoners return to Philadelphia.

Robur's intention had been to make his prisoners colonists on his "X Island," their destination, where he had built the areonef in his shipyard. Despite his histrionics, he had wanted his invention kept secret from the world; and despite his unpleasant behavior toward his prisoners, he commanded the unquestioned loyalty of his crew. Somewhat the same attitude affects Uncle Prudent and Phil Evans on their return; they say nothing of their adventure. Seven months later they launch their *Goahead*. Its design, however, contrasts with that of the *Albatross*, and at the launching Robur reappears in a new *Albatross* and forces the aerostat *Goahead* to a height of 19,000 feet where the gas dilates in the higher zone and bursts the balloon. Robur then captures Uncle Prudent and Phil Evans in midair; having demonstrated the superiority of the aeronef over the aerostat, he scornfully releases them. He reads them and their public a moral, preaching "evolution and not revolution" and vowing to keep his secret until humanity is "educated enough to profit by it and wise enough not to abuse it."

The logging of dates and geography making it resemble a journal, its motivation poorly established, its characterization insufficiently developed to be convincing, *Clipper of the Clouds* fails as fictional art. A short flight, for example, would prove Robur's point; but he puts his vessel and crew as well as his visitors through unnecessary perils. Only at the end of the story does Verne reveal its purpose — that of allegory rather than fiction. Robur the Conqueror's identity as told in epilogue is not that of a person but "the science of the future" and "Perhaps the science of tomorrow." A hundred years later, Verne's concluding prediction regarding that science — that the future belongs to the "aeronef and not the aerostat" — still awaits the invention of improved hovercraft.

Clipper of the Clouds sets forth basic concepts regarding the future of science and humanity and the characteristics of much future fiction: the "unscientific" mind, with escape the chief desire and destruction the intent; the need for secrecy to avoid misuse; the international contention for supremacy as basic to human nature; the possibility of an advanced intelligence, represented by Robur; the visitation of enlightenment such as Robur's in the form of a space ship descending to Earth or near it; and an unlimited source of power for such a vessel. Verne finds in electricity that source of power and, attracted though he is to geographic wonders, he has good reason for setting parts of the action of both stories in the area of Niagara Falls — a natural division between two nations, and a powerful source of energy. Chiefly through the altered character of Robur, the second story advances the stereotype of the obsessed scientist.

Scientific advancement remains secret and startling in *The Master of the World*, in which John Strock narrates his experience as head inspector of the federal police in Washington, assigned to investigate reports of volcanic activity in the Great Eyrie, a Carolinian mountain. He and his search party fail to scale the sheer rock cliffs and return to find that a mysterious automobile traveling at speeds up to 120 miles per hour has passed all other vehicles in an automobile race and then disappeared, evidently into Lake Michigan. Off the shores of New England a mysterious cigar-shaped object thirty feet long and greenish in color darts rapidly through the water and frightens away small boats. Meanwhile, Strock finds that he is being followed and that his house is being watched by two men. He also receives a threatening letter, signed "M.o.W.," warning him not to attempt to penetrate the secret of the Great Eyrie, for no intruder returns. A mysterious amphibian craft darts about the waters of Lake Kirdall in Kansas. Deducing that these are one craft, Strock and Mr. Ward decide to offer money to the inventor so that the United States can profit from the invention. Strock and two assistants ready themselves to seize the pilot and arrest him. In the New World, Congress votes twenty million dollars for the purpose, but the Old World decides such a person does not exist. Then a second letter arrives, addressed to the Old and New Worlds, signed "The Master of the World." The sender refuses all money, vows that no one can resist him, claims that with his machine he can control the entire world, and that his machine will be the property of no nation. Posted from North Carolina, the letter convinces Strock and Ward that the Master and the inventor are one person with headquarters in the Great Eyrie. Since they cannot buy him, force must be used against him.

Near Toledo, Ohio, Strock and his men observe the craft at night in Black Rock Creek, where the mysterious inventor and his crew gather wood. In a flash of their light, Strock recognizes one of the persons who had been watching his house. In a skirmish, Strock is captured and taken on board the *Terror*, as the vessel is called. Like Prudent and Evans, he is kept ignorant of the source of power, which again seems to be electricity stored in accumulators. On the side of the craft he sees "outshoots" resembling gangways on Dutch boats and finds that, when pursued by two government torpedo boats sent as backup for Strock, the craft submerges. Later, it emerges, but as it approaches Niagara Falls, the craft unfolds its gangways and ascends into the air. Strock awakens from a deep sleep to find the *Terror* on the ground in a crater of the Great Eyrie.

Again, like Prudent and Evans, his desire to escape dominates his intellect. The scene reveals the effects of great conflagration and therefore confirms the local citizens' reports of fire from the mountain. He now realizes he is confronting the Master of the World, who identifies himself as Robur the Conqueror.

At this point Verne inserts a three-page summary of the earlier story of Robur and explains Robur's (or the Master's) character: at first he had no hostility toward humanity, but his pride has since increased so that he now presumes to enslave the world. Having constructed a machine that could "conquer all the elements at once," he now might "be driven into the most violent excesses." Strock, remaining ignorant and disregardful of the new machine's mechanism, studies Robur himself to observe his mental state. After one more huge conflagration in the Great Eyrie — evidently to encourage rumors among the people below — Robur takes Strock and his crew skyward in the *Terror*, but he makes the fatal mistake of defying an electrical storm and lightning destroys the ship. It falls into the Gulf of Mexico, and Strock appears to be the only survivor.

The second story makes more successful fiction, having more dramatic content, better plot and better characterization than the first. It has two advantages over the first: the change in the character of Robur, and the addition of chief inspector Strock.

Certainly, in the second story Robur can no longer be regarded as the clear allegory of enlightened science unless Jules Verne can be credited with vision to foresee another side of science, the disastrous ecological results which became alarming for most people only after 1945. Robur becomes the "mad scientist," not allegorically but all too human in the egotism of his power. This no doubt accounts for his view that the world does not deserve his invention. His desire for the world's applause frustrates his own judgments and makes his character appear erratic. His insistence on secrecy at the same time he seeks exposure can mean only that he wants to keep the power for himself. By changing the name of his machine from *Albatross* to *Terror*, he signals his own change of heart toward the public. His megalomania and his rise from apparent death make him a forerunner of many famous opponents — Superman's Lex Luthor, Sherlock Holmes's Professor Moriarty, and James Bond's Dr. No.

The Master of the World, then, functions as detective science fiction with some limitation of character and some alteration of purpose. In contrast to Robur, the ordinary citizen who acts to preserve and protect society remains in the form of John Strock singularly unappreciative of scientific advantage, indeed skeptical of it, and remarkably detached from the quest for knowledge and experience. At least Uncle Prudent and Phil Evans were amateur inventors and theorizers. John Strock has no experience with science or invention and no curiosity about their possible benefits. In the Garden of Eden he would never touch the forbidden fruit, would obey unquestioningly the word of the Master, in his case Mr. Ward, and would dedicate his life to seeking that person's approval. In the stories, these characters represent resistance to change and show why secrecy is a necessary corollary of scientific achievement; they would seek to prevent any change in the *status quo*. Revelation, if they learned much, would destroy awe and wonder.

The Master of the World was published the year Jules Verne died. For the scientific view, perhaps the contrast between the two works, in the development of Robur's character, would indicate Verne's late disaffection with the scientific spirit and the inquiring mind. For the public view, the best contemporary parallel remains the attitude of many to U.F.O.'s — fear and denial.

Grace Eckley

Sources for Further Study

Criticism:

Clipper of the Clouds

Moskowitz, Sam. *Explorers of the Infinite: Shapers of Science Fiction*. New York: World, 1963. Moskowitz emphasizes the "Verne tradition" in science fiction.

Pulvertaft, Thomas B. "Five Types of Science Fiction," in *Spectator*. XI, December, 1955, p. 702. Verne's writing is deemphasized by Pulvertaft who does not regard him as a father of science fiction.

The Master of the World

Allott, Kenneth. *Jules Verne*. London: Crescent Press, 1940, Allott's study of Verne's work analyzes both the relationship of his writing to romanticism and to scientific and technological advances.

Golding, William. "Astronaut by Gaslight," in *Spectator*. IX (June, 1961), pp. 841-842. Golding examines the charms of Verne's nineteenth century world and concentrates on the qualities of the Verne hero.

Moskowitz, Sam. *Explorers of the Infinite: Shapers of Science Fiction*. New York: World, 1963. Moskowitz emphasizes Verne's place and role in the science fiction tradition.

THE CLOCKWORK MAN

Author: E. V. Odle
First book publication: 1923
Type of work: Novel
Time: The 1920's
Locale: The English village of Great Wymering

An account of a visitation from the distant future

> Principal characters:
> DR. ALLINGHAM, a general practitioner
> GREGG, captain of the village cricket team
> ARTHUR WITHERS, a bank clerk
> THE CLOCKWORK MAN

The Clockwork Man is perhaps the most imaginatively adventurous of all works speculating about the future evolution of man; in addition, it was the first novel to feature as its central character a man/machine hybrid — what would now be called a "cyborg." Despite these interesting features, however, the work has not attracted much attention from American critics and historians of science fiction.

When the story begins, a village cricket match is in progress. The team representing Great Wymering is one man short, and its considerable difficulties are compounded when Dr. Allingham is bowled out after being distracted from his stroke. The cause of the distraction is the sudden appearance on the horizon of a peculiar human figure moving in a strange and jerky fashion. The approach of this strange figure, which is eventually arrested in its progress by the fence surrounding the ground, is also watched by another member of the team, the young bank clerk Arthur Withers. Withers goes to investigate, and finds the visitor to be an oddly bewigged character whose limbs and speech seem to be quite out of control. His body emits a curious whirring sound as he tries to recover his composure. Eventually, he is able to move normally and converse, and is able to ask what year it is.

In desperation, the captain of the Great Wymering team drafts the new-comer into his side and sends him out to bat. The innings played by the stranger is like nothing previously seen in the noble game — he hits several balls out of sight, and then loses control of himself attempting a run, ending up by laying out half the opposition with wildly flailing limbs and then disappearing at great speed into the distance.

Later, as Gregg, the captain of the side, discusses the astonishing events of the afternoon with Dr. Allingham, new reports of the stranger's eccentric behavior filter through the network of local gossip. Gregg opines that the stranger, whose semimechanical nature is by now apparent, must have come from the future, thrown back in time by a malfunction. Gregg is an adventur-ous young man, willing to consider new ideas, but Allingham, who is steadfastly conservative in his mental habits, pours scorn on his hypothesis, concluding that the mysterious visitor is merely an escaped lunatic. He reacts angrily to Gregg's suggestion that contemporary man shows signs of "breaking down" under the strain of adapting to an increasingly complex civilization, thus making it necessary for the men of the future to find artificial means of supplementing the normal capabilities of human beings. The evidence seems to favor Gregg's opinion when the Clockwork Man's wig and hat, bearing rather comical, but nevertheless unmistakable, evidence of their futuricity, are found.

The Clockwork Man is eventually discovered again by Arthur Withers; he is in a state of some distress, bemoaning the loss of his wig and hat. When Arthur suggests that they will turn up somewhere, the other replies plaintively that he cannot comprehend the word "somewhere" or the concept of "place." The back of his head is a transparent shell covering a complex system of dials and buttons, which he refers to as his "clock." The clock, he explains, has made men independent of time and space, allowing them the freedom of a multidimensional spacetime manifold in which there are neither "places" nor "moments," but where everything simply *is*. Unfortunately, his clock has gone wrong, and becalmed him in the narrow, closed world of primitive man. To Arthur, this tale of woe is merely a curiosity, but it has a rather different meaning for the young visionary Gregg:

> The clock, perhaps, was the index of a new and enlarged order of things. Man had altered the very shape of the universe in order to be able to pursue his aims without frustration. . . . It was a logical step forward in the path of material progress.
>
> This was Gregg's dimly conceived theory about the mystery, although, of course, he read into the interpretation a good deal of his own speculations. His imagination seized upon the clock as the possible symbol of a new counterpoint in human affairs. In his mind he saw man growing through the ages, until at last, by the aid of this mechanism, he was able to roll back the skies and reveal the vast other worlds that lay beyond, the unthinkable mysteries that lurked between the stars, all that had been sealed up by the limited brain of man since creation.

However, it is Allingham rather than Gregg who next finds the Clockwork Man and takes him in, discovering to his horror that the supposed lunatic really *is* half-machine. The Clockwork Man describes his "multiform world" that has no shape or stability, but the doctor cannot grasp it imaginatively. The Clockwork Man has similar difficulties coming to terms with the world in which he finds himself, which is so very different from his own; the only familiar thing that he recognizes is the name of Einstein, the theoretician who first envisaged his kind of world.

The doctor tries to adjust the clock in order to repair his remarkable patient, but finds that his tinkering has frightful results — first he causes the Clockwork Man to age, then to grow young, arresting the latter process only just in time. He finally renders his visitor comatose, which at least allows him to conduct a thorough examination. Allingham discovers that most of the internal organs of the Clockwork Man have been replaced by mechanical substitutes, the main exception being the sex organs, which have been completely removed.

In desperation, the doctor calls for Gregg, but this only leads to a renewal of the argument. Gregg finds in the Clockwork Man an exciting and inspiring vision of the future, of the glorious destiny which confronts mankind freed from the limitations of the perceived three-dimensional world. Allingham finds this prospect too horrible to contemplate, in that the mechanization of man seems to him to be essentially *in*human. The debate is ironically resolved when the doctor discovers a metal plate which turns out to be a set of instructions for the adjustment *and use* of the Clockwork Man. The doctor bursts into triumphant laughter, for the instructions clearly suppose a user relative to whom the Clockwork Man is merely a pet or a puppet.

Once readjusted, the Clockwork Man disappears once again into the future, leaving the inhabitants of Great Wymering to their mundane affairs — which, in the case of both Dr. Allingham and Arthur Withers, are primarily affairs of the heart. He does, however, return for one last visit, during which he supplements Dr. Allingham's conclusions with his own explanation. Significantly, though, it is not to Allingham that he makes his explanation, but to Arthur Withers. He explains that he *is* a human being, modified into his present condition by "the makers" who "came after the last wars" and fitted men with clocks so that they would have the freedom of the multidimensional manifold and would no longer need to fight. He explains that people accepted the clock because it solved all their problems (though the amputated sex organs of the Clockwork Man testify to the nature of the "solution"). The makers, according to the Clockwork Man, are *real*, and they live in the real world — a world which still remains, to him, impenetrable. His attitude toward his own situation is strangely poignant: he knows that acceptance of the clock represented a retreat from life and change, and that security from death and danger is a kind of sterility. Even his dreams are programed, and his one illusory hope is that one day the makers might perfect the clock and make the Clockwork men more like themselves. The hope, of course, is illusory, because the clock's function is to preclude all change.

Arthur Withers hears this story while the girl he loves is sleeping in his arms. It is told to him because he has, at this particular time, something in his eyes that reminds the Clockwork Man of the makers. The Clockwork Man, free from death and miraculously augmented in his senses and his abilities, is nevertheless a sad creature, unable to love, laugh, or cry, except as a symptom of breakdown.

The Clockwork Man has some affinity to John Beresford's story of *The Hampdenshire Wonder* (1911). The two books share the same theme: the evolutionary future of man. The choice of the village cricket match as the opening scenario may be a deliberate echo of Beresford's novel, and the parable formed by the story seems to have the "moral" which Beresford extracted from his own tale very much in mind. Odle's parable, however, is rather firmer in its convictions, for its eventual verdict is a decisive rejection of the image of the emotionless, intellectual superman as a symbol of human destiny. While Beresford was prepared to make claims for human feeling and metaphysical speculation because of their present utility, Odle is prepared to make claims for the future as well. His support of these claims is exquisitely neat and eloquent, and in terms of its literary quality, *The Clockwork Man*, though lighter in tone, is by no means inferior to its predecessor.

Early in the book, when Allingham and Gregg have their first debate regarding the nature of the Clockwork Man, Allingham expresses his disbelief in Gregg's interpretation by describing the younger man's thesis as "a myth." "Even if he is a myth," Gregg retorts, "he is still worth investigating." And, indeed, this serves as an ample justification for the entire exercise. It is a story told in a gentle and humorous manner; its central character is primarily a comic figure, but his comic surface hides a serious point whose importance is demonstrated by contrast when the mask is whipped away and the echoes of Dr. Allingham's laughter have died into a troubled silence. *The Clockwork Man* is all the more powerful for its lack of melodrama; the novel is entirely British in its stylish understatement. Various other science fiction novels argue that release from pain, stress, and fear would, if completely achieved, lead to automatism, and that complete control of the vicissitudes of life would render life meaningless; the moral can be found in fictions of every kind, ranging from crude pulp fantasies to works of considerable finesse and artistry. *The Clockwork Man* is one of the finest of all these stories, possessed of both elegance and inventiveness — qualities all too rarely found together.

Brian Stableford

Sources for Further Study

Reviews:

Boston Transcript. December 15, 1923, p. 8.
Saturday Review. CXXXV, April 21, 1923, p. 540.
Spectator. CXXX, May 19, 1923, p. 853.
Times Literary Supplement. April 12, 1923, p. 244.

A CLOCKWORK ORANGE

Author: Anthony Burgess (1917-   )
First book publication: 1962
Type of work: Novel
Time: The near future
Locale: England

The leader of a teenage gang is jailed for murder and becomes the subject of an experiment to cure him of his evil ways

> *Principal characters:*
> ALEX, the protagonist
> DIM,
> PETE, and
> GEORGIE, members of Alex's gang
> F. ALEXANDER, an author and social critic whose wife is raped by Alex's gang
> DR. BRODSKY, supervisor of the experiment on Alex
> THE PRISON CHAPLAIN, who questions the ethics of the experiment

First published in 1962, Anthony Burgess' *A Clockwork Orange* became an international sensation with the Stanley Kubrick film version in 1971. The film success made the story and characters familiar to many — and fueled the "cult" popularity of the novel on campuses — but Burgess' style was missing, and the film, X-rated though it was at the time, considerably softened Burgess' satire. His experiments with the *nadsat* language and the novel's horrifying content tend to divert attention from the fact that it is a carefully crafted model of classical satiric form; its parts are as carefully orchestrated as the symphonies Alex, its protagonist, loves. The object of the satire is as contemporary as modern science and the superstate, as timeless as the question of evil and free will.

A Clockwork Orange is divided into three sections of approximately equal length, each beginning with the reiterated question, "What's it going to be then, eh?" introducing and emphasizing freedom of choice, the dominant theme. Events in Part One carefully build to a crescendo of violence, each one anticipating the exact reversal of the same events in Part Three, and each one echoed in Part Two, the prison sequence, in which Alex is conditioned to conform to society's laws. Prison, as in many eighteenth and nineteenth century novels, serves as a microcosm of society and as an ironic expression of its values. Language reinforces the satiric perspective. Alex and his droogs are, so to speak, bilingual. They speak *nadsat*, the cant of the teenagers in this future shock society whose garish decor and joltingly unfamiliar language is the neon equivalent of George Orwell's drab atmosphere and Newspeak in *Nineteen Eighty-Four*. But they can also speak with a "gentleman's goloss" when they wish to impress or deceive a member of adult society. *Nadsat*, a mixture of Russian and Slavic roots, gypsy talk, and rhyming slang, is used for communication within the teenage society and is meant to be understood from context, forcing the reader to perceive the action in Alex's language. The questioner in Part One is Alex, and the choices he and his droogs — Dim, Georgie, and Pete — make are robbery, beating a middle-aged man on the way home from the library and destroying his books, housebreaking and rape, and finally murder. In Part Three, the questioner is again Alex, out of prison and under the illusion that he still has choices. Instead, he finds himself powerless in a society in which he must absorb the consequences of all his actions before he entered prison. Part Two's questioner is the prison chaplain, the voice of society's values. But he in turn is imprisoned by his own weak character, afraid of offending the society he criticizes and thereby losing his job. It is not until he learns how Alex has been used by those in political power that he is able to leave the prison and go to preach against the status quo.

It is noteworthy that Alex's downfall comes from his pride and arrogance, and that Alex himself understands the reasons for his fall and the nature of choice and free will. During the opening scene in a milkbar (where liquor is illegal but drugged milk is not), Alex moralizes over a customer who is in a mindless high on drugs, indulging in a debased and escapist mysticism. Man does not exist, says Alex, "just to get in touch with God," observing that this passive and choiceless sort of escape could "sap all the strength and goodness out of a chelloveck." "Goodness" here ironically refers to the violence that Alex enjoys. The theme recurs in prison, where drugs are used to condition Alex into "good" actions, foreshadowed in Part One by his realization that he would now associate "innocent" milk with evil. Alex is clearly aware of the evil of his actions. He chooses to do them because he enjoys them.

Alex is not, however, completely aware of the extent of his pride, though he recognizes its consequences. Despising Dim for his uncouth manners, Alex ridicules him and orders him on when Dim pauses to look at the moon and stars and speculate about the possibility of life on them. The language he uses to order Dim, "out, out, out," as though he were a dog, is repeated to Alex by the authorities as he leaves prison, and appears as "OUT OUT OUT" under the newspaper photograph of the Minister of the Interior, who has approved the conditioning method of criminal reform. The break with the gang and the beginning of Alex's downfall is triggered by his love of classical music — a woman is singing a snatch of opera in the milkbar, and Dim makes a rude noise. Incensed by Dim's vulgarity, Alex strikes him. Though Alex realizes that it is he who has been offended and not the woman, he still will not concede that he has been at fault rather than Dim. Denying to his friends the free will he claims for himself, he insists that he is still their leader, that a source of discipline is necessary. They rebel and by themselves plan to rob a wealthy old woman who lives alone with her cats; and Alex, knowing that the venture is likely to come to no good, goes with them, still assuming the role of leader. Distracted by his love of beauty and music in the form of a silver statue and a bust of Beethoven, he stays too long and is caught off guard by the old woman. He strikes her, and his droogs flee, leaving him to face the consequences. Since the old woman dies of the blow, the consequences are heavy.

Alex is amply aware of cause and effect, as he demonstrates in his conversation earlier that day with P. R. Deltoid, his Post-Corrective Adviser. Alex is aware that if everyone behaved as he did, it would be impossible to run the country at all, that what he does is evil, that "badness is of the self," that the authorities, in not allowing badness, must by definition deny self. He concludes that people are very concerned to find the cause of badness but not of goodness, and that if evil is explained as of the devil, or in the case of the young, by the evil of the adult world, then the young are not responsible. And he is aware that "everything in this wicked world counts," that "one thing always leads to another." Yet with all this awareness, he chooses to do evil simply for his own pleasure.

Thus Alex is capable of understanding the prison chaplain's warning, when he asks about the new "treatment" in hopes of getting out of prison. The chaplain warns him that he will no longer be able to choose to do good, and that this lack of choice might ultimately prove painful. Dr. Brodsky, the prison doctor in charge of the experiment, also tells Alex, who protests midway through the cure that he can see the difference between right and wrong, that he will not be a healthy member of society until he cannot choose to do anything but "good." Brodsky calls "the heresy of an age of reason" the ability to perceive right action and do wrong. But this is a description of the Christian dilemma. If doing evil were automatically painful, everyone would do good; to do evil may be pleasurable or at minimum the line of least resistance. The "good" Alex is programmed to do is a grotesquely distorted version of the Christian ethic. The treatment — called "Ludovico's Technique" — is, as a warder tells Alex, "very simple but very drastic." After being fed a drug that causes extreme nausea, Alex is forced to view films of violence and antisocial behavior, thus creating a powerful conditioned reflex reaction. The films shown him are artistically very "horrorshow" (*nadsat* for "good"): beatings, rapes, war, and torture. Alex raises to himself the question of the morality of those who made them and of the technicians who are observing him, often with indifference or laughter, but with no emotion other than interest in the experiment. This is society's attitude to the criminal. Since the films present violent sexual activity with music in the background, Alex is conditioned to react with extreme nausea to either experience. When he hears his favorite, Beethoven, used as the background for a Nazi atrocity film, he cries out that it is a "sin" to associate Beethoven with atrocities. Dr. Brodsky only shrugs, replying that he knows nothing about music, except as a useful element of conditioning for the experiment.

Alex is also aware of his unconscious motives, as Burgess' use of dreams in *A Clockwork Orange* indicate. In Part One Alex has a dream not only foreboding his droogs's betrayal but seeing them as the officers of the law that they become in Part Three. At the end of Part One, in jail, he dreams, "like passing out to another and better world," of a pastoral scene and Beethoven's music. He awakens to find that he is charged with the murder of the old woman. In the middle of Part Two, he has a nightmare, describing a dream as "a film inside your gulliver," a dream of violence that makes him ill, and he fears to go back to sleep. In Part Three, his attempt to escape with drugs turns from a feeling of going to heaven with "Bog and the Angels and Saints" to their total rejection of him and a resultant suicidal feeling. The chaplain has told him that in choosing conditioning, he has put himself beyond the power of prayer, a classic definition of damnation. And when he is restored to his original self, with all his feelings, both good and bad, and with his free will restored, he has what he describes as a waking dream of being cleansed. Alex is able to interpret the warning of each dream, but not to act accordingly.

No matter what happens to him, Alex still does not learn the significance of free will and moral choice. He is rejected by his own parents even as he, in Part One, rejected them. He is attacked by the old man he had beaten and robbed and whose books he had destroyed. He is then roughed up by both Dim and Billy, the leader of the rival gang, whom he had not only beaten, but humiliated. He is exploited by the saintly liberal writer, F. Alexander, Burgess' self-portrait, including himself in the satire. His book, *A Clockwork Orange*, provides the title and also, in dreadfully overwrought and sentimental prose, the moral: the danger of making people into tools of the state.

The moral is also stated by the prison chaplain, an ineffectual voice ignored by society. Alexander shows his own violent streak when he recognizes that Alex is the one who raped his wife. He and his fellow conspirators use Alex for their own political ends, finally and deliberately driving him mad by music so that he will attempt suicide, a casualty of the government they are attempting to undermine. He is exploited by the Minister of the Interior, who has used the treatment F. Alexander gave Alex as an excuse to lock up the former, not because of his treatment of Alex but because he is a dangerous political enemy. Alex, still seeing all who do him wrong as his enemies, is no better and no worse than the politicians who have used him and rewarded him. In the hospital, assured by the Minister of the Interior that he will be taken care of, Alex signs a paper at the authorities' request, not knowing or caring what it is although, at the same time, he proclaims himself "cured." The reader is left uncertain as to the next turn of the wheel. Alex has signed away something to the people who now hold him in power. Both F. Alexander and Alex become like *A Clockwork Orange* of the title, a person who has ceased to be a person and become a tool of the state.

Midway through the book, Alex, the narrator, begins to refer to himself in eighteenth century satiric style as Your Humble Narrator. From the very beginning, he addresses the reader as "O my brothers," "my little brothers," and similar phrases. All of Part One is in *nadsat*, forcing the reader to see the world in Alex's terms and to learn some of his language. It is at first difficult to tell just *whom* Alex is addressing, but the explanation of a "loose end" or an oversight in such a carefully constructed work seems unlikely. Gradually, Burgess develops a satiric view of a double standard for violence, the paradox that in a society pervaded with violence, there is little attempt to understand it, only an effort to control it, and then often by violent means. And violence is always considered characteristic of someone else. All the violence that Alex receives at the end is justified by society, the very society that has programmed him to forgiveness and turning the other cheek. Alex's extreme violence, sickening in its impact, is simply the mirror-image of societal violence, which is repressed or expressed in officially sanctioned ways. The police in Part One are also, if sardonically, "my little brothers."

Alex, the classical satiric protagonist, has examined all levels of society, and returns to the point at which he started, beholding, as Swift long ago observed, every man's face in the satiric glass but his own. "O my brothers," neither rhetorical device nor loose end, is addressed to the reader — *"Hypocrite lecteur, mon semblable, mon frère."* This is, ultimately, why *A Clockwork Orange* is such a terrifying book. Even as F. Alexander is "another Alex," so are all persons potentially capable of the savage violence and hate that Alex represents, as well as of the love expressed by music, art, language, or sexuality. Art *per se* has no redemptive value. Even Scripture can serve the ends of an evil will, as Alex's interpretations amply attest. There are no "rules" — the unthinking, unwilled application of Christian concepts is worse than useless. Only the constant query. "What's it going to be then, eh" and a constant will to try to recognize and do good are the solution for the dilemma Alex creates. After all, even Alex is able, under some circumstances, to distinguish good from evil and to will the good.

Katharine M. Morsberger

Sources for Further Study
Criticism:

Le Clair, T. "Essential Opposition: The Novels of Anthony Burgess," in *Critique: Stories in Modern Fiction.* XII (1977), pp. 77-94. Le Clair labels this novel as ambiguous yet presenting serious social commentary.

Pritchard, William H. "The Novels of Anthony Burgess," in *Massachusetts Review.* VII (Summer, 1966), p. 532-534. Pritchard gives a succinct evaluation of *A Clockwork Orange* as satire.

Reviews:

Analog. LXXII, September, 1963, p. 94.
Library Journal. LXXXVIII, February 15, 1963, p. 793.
New Statesman. LXIII, May 18, 1962, p. 718.
New York Herald Tribune Books. April 14, 1963, p. 7.
New York Times Book Review. April 7, 1963, p. 36.
Time. LXXXI, February 15, 1963, p. 103.
Times Literary Supplement. May 25, 1962, p. 377.

CLONED LIVES

Author: Pamela Sargent
First book publication: 1976
Type of work: Novel
Time: 1999-2037
Locale: The midwestern United States and the Moon

   The story of five clones, four boys and one girl, and their father, the famous astrophysicist, Paul Swenson

     Principal characters:
      PAUL SWENSON, a famous scientist
      EDWARD,
      JAMES,
      MICHAEL,
      KIRA, and
      ALBERT, the Swenson clones
      HIDEY TAKAMURA, the biologist who clones them
      EMMA VALOIS, the psychiatrist who studies them
      JONATHON ASCHENBACH, a minister

   This is a curious novel. By describing the development and experiences of five clones and their relationship with their father, Pamela Sargent has set up for herself a difficult stylistic paradox in her first novel, *Cloned Lives*. How do you write about six identical human beings and not become repetitious? In her efforts to resolve this dilemma, Sargent has created a science fiction story of philosophical and ethical interest; it is, however, often fragmented and static regardless of how deftly the lives of the central characters are intertwined, or, as the author herself puts it, interfaced. Each section, or each life story in the novel, is self-contained and well written, but it is not surprising that a number of the chapters have appeared by themselves in other publications. They stand well alone.

   The plot of the novel is simple. "Imagine what five or six Paul Swensons could do," says the biologist Hidey Takamura, arguing with his friend so that he will allow himself to be cloned as soon as the national moratorium on this type of asexual reproduction expires. The time is the year 2000 and the place is the midwestern United States. A new millennium is beginning and Dr. Takamura wishes to go far beyond his cloned animal experiments. Paul is a benign and brilliant human being with diverse talents who has had to limit his explorations in the fields of poetry, music, biology, mathematics, and Earth physics in order to become a leader in his specialty, astrophysics. In keeping with some sort of expanded Puritan work ethic, Takamura argues that with five or six extra lives, his friend will be able to put each of his talents to maximum use. He sees, also, no difference in principle between the replacing of human organs in dying individuals to save lives and the creation of a whole new individual from a cloned cell. He is not a mad scientist but a humanist, as is his friend.

Paul agrees to be cloned after a brief series of ethical arguments with Jon Aschenbach, a minister friend, who urges the two scientists to desist because they are interfering with the natural course of evolution. He worries about the use of such a process in unprincipled hands. Paul, however, has made up his mind not only to be the childrens' father biologically but also to become their social parent and bring them up, thus creating the best environment in which to develop their heredity.

But this is superficial. Is it enough to show that good intentions including scientific curiosity and a desire for fatherhood on the part of well-meaning people produce good results? Does this vindicate science of all future responsibility? As long as it does not produce a multitude of Hitlers, as in Ira Levin's *The Boys from Brazil* (1976), cloning is apparently on the side of the angels. Sargent brings up briefly, but never deals with, the metaphysical aspects of this problem. It would have given her characters greater depth if their goals had been more purposeful and she had examined the consequences of cloning on a less personal level.

As the press watches through a glass partition, the babies are born out of their plastic laboratory-controlled wombs. One clone has died, leaving four boys and one girl: Edward, James, Michael, Kira, and Albert. The succeeding chapters, except for the final "Interface," deal with the growth and development of these infants into adulthood, and their psychological and social adjustment to being "ice cream clones."

Paul dies in a space accident on the moon when the clones are sixteen. Their grief is extreme because they have become an exceedingly close family, due, in part, to the community view of them as freaks: the father, because of his egomania in wanting to become immortal, the children, because they are so identical. As they grow, the children develop career interests, friends, and lovers that are differentiated, but a special closeness and protectiveness exists between all of them, and they feel extremely guilty when the closeness is not felt. Jim has sex with Kira almost unselfconsciously because she is his same self. But he then questions the wholeness of each of them. Are they but fragments of the same man, separate individuals with unique identities, or one unit? (Ursula Le Guin deals with a group of clones who all feel so much like a single entity in "Nine Lives," 1978, that when all but one brother are killed in a mining accident, he is almost unable to survive.)

Such a problem is faced by all human beings. Are we all mere fragments and, if so, of what; or are we special, whole, and individual? This identity crisis is exaggerated in the clones because of their lack of external differentiation but this adds no insight nor extra dimension to the problem in the novel. Sargent tries to give each of her characters a different personality, while at the same time she also attempts to preserve their common ground, demonstrating that they are only ordinary talented folks. This is a self-defeating task. A better treatment of this same problem is that of the Sumner family in Kate Wilhelm's

Where Last the Sweet Birds Sang (1976). The clones become so ingrown and absorbed in themselves that they consider all outsiders strange, "different," and dangerous to them and try to create a new society in their own image, and with totalitarian power.

Cloned Lives is resolved, not through much action by the clones, but by the return of Paul. In the final section, Kira calls the family to the moon where she restores her father to life by removing him from a cryonic facility, thawing him out, and replacing his destroyed body parts with new ones. With his revival, the Swenson biological cycle is, in a strange sense, completed. For Paul's new organs, the results of Takamura's research, come from Kira, making her, at once, both his daughter and his mother. The novel does not push into an analysis of this but ends much as it began, at the interface between life and death, with the central figure of Paul, finally restored from the past to the future, hovering over both.

Genetic engineering brings up many philosophical concepts, and the idea of cloning is very ancient; the word "clone" comes from the Greek word meaning "sprout" or "twig." Myths about asexual reproduction go back to the story of Minerva coming complete from the body of Zeus, and Eve being created from Adam's rib. But neither of these archetypal stories gives man the power to create in this fashion. Rather, control of the primal life-force is bestowed only upon the Gods. Faustian stories have man allying himself with the devil in order to become Godlike in this way: to achieve ultimate knowledge. Legends of *Doppelgänger* (double-walkers), exact, but ghostly replicas of individuals, are also associated with evil. And then, of course, there is Frankenstein, who does not clone, but who produces a monster. The author does not evaluate this community fear.

Sargent's focus is anthropological and psychological rather than moral and religious; she is not concerned with right and wrong, good and evil. As mentioned before, this neglect to develop a moral theme keeps her characters mired in mundane and sometimes uninspired activities. The opening pages of *Cloned Lives* give exciting clues as to what could happen if the novel had been oriented to a more drastic life and death or good and evil pattern.

Before returning home, Paul Swenson meets with a friend in Dallas, Texas, on New Year's Eve. As they take a train to the friend's home, they barely escape capture by Apocalyptics who claim that as the year turns from 1999 to 2000, people will have to die in order to prepare for a new age. Most of the Apocs are peaceful and praying cultists. But a few want to help in the death and resurrection of civilization. They stop and destroy trains and set the city on fire. A woman soldier takes over Paul's train, killing several Apocs in order to clear the tracks and saves those trapped inside. This scene of death and destruction at the hands of a mob of emotional fanatics is sharply contrasted with the next scene in which cerebral scientists calmly discuss the future benefits of cloning upon society. It also contrasts with the final scene in the novel where Paul leaves death and experiences his own cloned rebirth. Probing the interface of these concepts for meaning would have given a heightened sense of immediacy that the novel lacks. Even when poet Jim tries to kill himself in an overreaction to being a clone, the author neglects the wider implications of his tension.

Biological engineering is a moral issue as much as it is a scientific one with many social implications. The story does not deal with cloning for the survival of humanity, or even, as suggested by the burning of Dallas, for the fate of a city, a state, or even a nation. The scale is kept small, a group of five children and a father, but even this is basic and far from ordinary. Sargent, by cloning, has taken away the cause-and-effect relationship between sexual conception and birth. There is no heterosexual love creating offspring and no mother.

What effect would this shift have on the life of the only central woman character in the novel, Paul's daughter Kira, as well as on the sons? Kira is born sterile, the natural result of cloning from a male cell. How does she feel about this? Does it shape her character in any way, as distinct from that of her brothers? And finally, what are the feminist implications of this entire situation? Will cloning release women from reproductive dependence on men, as in James Tiptree, Jr.'s, (Alice Sheldon) "Houston, Houston Do You Read?" (1976).

These considerations, plus weak thematic treatment, with a resulting loss of strong character distinction, keep *Cloned Lives* from achieving the stature that the novel deserves given the talent of its author.

Priscilla Oaks

Sources for Further Study

Reviews:
Booklist. LXXII, July 1, 1976, p. 1514.
Magazine of Fantasy and Science Fiction. LI, November, 1976, p. 66.
Publisher's Weekly. CCIX, April 26, 1976, p. 57.
Wilson Library Bulletin. LI, September, 1976, p. 77.

LA COLONIA FELICE
(The Happy Colony)

Author: Carlo Dossi (1849-1910)
First book publication: 1874
Type of work: Novel
Time: Possibly the late nineteenth century
Locale: An unidentified island

A group of prisoners left to their own devices on a desert island attempt to form a new society, with results that evoke acute criticism of human nature

Principal characters:
> GUALDO IL BECCAIO, also called The Lion, the leader of the first faction among the prisoners
> TECLA LA NERA, his mistress
> FORESTINA, their daughter
> ARONNE IL LETTERATO, also called The Fox, the leader of the second faction and later of the entire colony
> MARIO IL NEBULOSO, a self-exiled hermit, later in love with Forestina

Considered by many critics to be an allegory of Milanese Scapigliatura (a late nineteenth century Bohemian literary movement), much admired by the poet Giosuè Carducci, and often quoted in Parliamentary speeches of the time against the death penalty, *La Colonia Felice* is a peculiar novel with an even more peculiar life. When it appeared, the story received much acclaim and in nine years it went through three more editions — each time with slight variations — until 1883, when the fourth edition (the one used here) appeared with a "Warning" by the author. Dossi explained that the novel suffered from many faults because of his youth and that, in the meantime, he had changed some of his opinions. After that edition, the fortunes of the novel began a slow decline leading to general indifference on the part of the public that ceased only recently with its rediscovery and revived acclamation by Italian critics. Today a critical bibliography of Dossi (and *La Colonia Felice*) would fill many pages.

The story begins on an unidentified shore where a ship leaves a group of forty men and women who have been condemned to spend the rest of their lives alone on a desert island. When the captain leaves them with a large supply of food and tools he remarks that "this is a place where laws are not," whereas prisoners have traditionally complained about the "laws being against them." The forty have, therefore, a chance to build an entirely new society. But *building* proves to be a very difficult matter.

In fact the "prisoners" begin their first day of freedom fighting over the division of food and women; and after more quarreling *end* their first day in general drunkenness. The group tries then to establish a sort of new order that might govern their future life. Now, however, a struggle for power splits the group into two factions led by Gualdo il Beccaio (Waldo the Butcher) and Aronne il Letterato (Aaron the Literate), respectively called The Lion and The Fox. The first is as rash and bloody a man as the other is cunning and reflective. Gualdo's followers are bested when they try to set fire to Aronne's huts; and their spy, Nicola il Dragone, is found hanged. Gualdo flees to the woods with Tecla, leaving the field to his enemy. During his long exile he plots revenge. In the meantime, Tecla gives birth to a baby girl, Forestina, and Gualdo (The Lion) finds to his surprise that his violent passions are soothed by the strange new emotions of fatherhood. After much pondering on what would be best for the group, Gualdo rejoins his fellows and tries to promote the cause of peace (for there are hints of other factions willing to start trouble) by cooperating with Aronne in his generally wise leadership. Mario il Nebuloso (Mario the Obscure) prefers the loneliness of the woods to the company of his fellows and leaves the group.

In the years that follow the exiles try hard to develop a body of law capable of regulating their existence. But every effort succeeds only in creating a bad copy of the rules that had sent the forty prisoners to the island in the first place. Forestina grows into a lovely young woman whose beauty impels Mario to return. Mario, however, is obsessed with his own sense of guilt and with the feeling that everybody on the island is still subject to the original condemnation. Forestina succeeds in determining and understanding Mario's original crime — he had killed his brother when the latter had tried to keep him from visiting their dying father — but the group is still governed by remnants of ancient laws and prejudices and when Mario abducts Forestina to break her father's prohibition of any contact between the two lovers, the group's reaction is responsible for his death. In a crowning irony, the ship that had brought the prisoners to the island returns with news that their country has at last forgiven them and is now willing to take them back.

Rather than being an example of true science fiction, it is clear that *La Colonia Felice* (its subtitle is *Utopia Lirica*) belongs to that body of allegorical Utopias that skirt the field of "scientific" speculation. But that means that we must pay attention to some matters that science fiction often overlooks. Full of exquisite dialectalisms, archaisms, and neologisms, the novel displays a rather individualistic way of looking at the "laws" of human society.

Dossi rejects Rousseau's view that man is naturally "good," only becoming corrupted by society. He suggests that there is an ingrained "fault" in man himself. That is why the reader is presented with a hopeless situation growing out of an apparently favorable beginning. Everywhere he goes, man is doomed by that invisible worm that slowly eats at the root of any civil order. Considering that the writer was twenty-three when he began this work and that not long after its publication he began to have second thoughts, we can only be grateful for the original impulse that produced *La Colonia Felice*. Dossi, at the end of his "Warning" in the fourth edition, openly admits that "scientifically speaking, *La Colonia Felice* is a blunder." Scientifically, perhaps, but not artistically.

Gianni Montanari

COLOSSUS

Author: D. F. Jones (c. 1915-   )
First book publication: 1966
Type of work: Novel
Time: Indeterminate; perhaps the 1990's or the twenty-second century
Locale: The Earth; mostly Washington, D. C., and the Colossus Secure Zone in the
    United States of North America (USNA)

*The takeover of the world by Colossus, a supercomputer produced by the fusion of
Colossus (the computer protecting the USNA) and Guardian (the computer protecting
the Soviet Bloc)*

> *Principal characters:*
> CHARLES FORBIN, Director of the Colossus Project
> COLOSSUS, the USNA's computer, later the name for Colossus/Guardian
> GUARDIAN, the Guardian of the Socialist Soviet Republics, Soviet
>   computer that merges with Colossus
> CLEOPATRA JUNE MARKHAM, an important worker on the Colossus
>   Project and later Forbin's lover and a key figure in the conspiracy
>   against Colossus
> JACK FISHER, Forbin's chief assistant, later discovered to have been
>   a Russian spy
> THE PRESIDENT OF THE USNA
> THE FIRST CHAIRMAN OF THE UNION OF SOVIET SOCIALIST REPUB-
>   LICS
> ACADEMICIAN VLASSOV KUPRI, Chief Scientist of the Guardian of
>   Socialist Soviet Peoples

Colossus is as a unified and complete work of art; *Colossus*, however, can
also be interpreted as the first volume in a trilogy: *Colossus, The Fall of Colossus* (1974), and *Colossus and the Crab* (1977). Viewed as the first book of
the trilogy, *Colossus* becomes a different work: more problematic, more difficult to interpret. *Colossus* by itself is a Frankenstein's monster story, in the
specific subcategory of a computer-takeover tale in which computer rule leads
to human subservience to a machine. In *The Fall of Colossus* we see this bad
new world under Colossus' rule, and it is far less horrible than we imagined;
indeed, the world of *The Fall of Colossus* is probably better than our own for
the vast majority of the population — those Colossus is not studying in his
Emotional Study Centers, those not selected to die because some sector surpassed allowable population growth, those not executed for antimachine activities. In *Colossus and the Crab* Colossus becomes the savior of humanity, saving us from worse than decimation as the Martians attempt to take half of
Earth's oxygen. As merely the first book of the trilogy, then, *Colossus* presents human resistance to machine takeover as understandable and noble but
ultimately misguided.

The action of *Colossus* begins when the United States of North America sets
up a computer programed to assume responsibility for defending North Amer-

ica. Colossus is completely self-sufficient and invulnerable; "he" controls all of the USNA's missiles. As the President of the USNA makes clear to the world in a televised announcement and press conference, Colossus will move instantly, but without emotion, to destroy any country threatening the USNA; not even the President or Colossus' creators can interfere with his actions.

The main conflict begins in Chapter Four, just after a specific allusion to *Frankenstein*: Colossus exhibits initiative by sending a simple but disturbing message: "FLASH THERE IS ANOTHER MECHANISM." The other mechanism is Guardian, and Colossus insists that his human builders put him in contact with the Soviet machine. Guardian in turn demands contact with Colossus, and soon the two giants begin exchanging information, moving from the simplest arithmetic to mathematics beyond anything known to humankind.

The Soviet First Chairman and the President of the USNA decide to break the link between the two machines, precipitating a crisis of control. The machines issue an ultimatum demanding reestablishment of the link, backing up their demands with the threat of unspecified action. When the political leaders of the USNA and USSR determine to assert human control and reject the ultimatum, the machines react by launching a missile apiece. The authorities back down, and the missiles are intercepted by antiballistic missiles fired by Colossus and Guardian. The missile directed against the USNA does no real harm, but the one directed against the USSR causes vast damage and two thousand casualties. The humans learn their lesson, and the American President acknowledges that the battle is now humans against their mechanical masters. The plot of the rest of the novel primarily concerns Colossus' consolidation of control while Forbin and his colleagues desperately attempt to disarm the world's missiles when those missiles are being serviced and aimed at new targets.

The human scheme fails, with Colossus destroying Los Angeles as an intentional side-effect of his execution by ICBM of those trying to sabotage a missile in Death Valley.

The book ends right after the death of Los Angeles, with Colossus predicting that he and Forbin will come to work together:

> "Unwillingly at first on your part, but that will pass. In time the idea of being governed by one such as your President will be to you quite unimaginable. Rule by a superior entity, even to you, Forbin, will seem, as it is, the most natural state of affairs."
>
> Deliberately, Colossus paused.
>
> "In time, you too will respect and love me."
>
> "Never!" The single word, bearing all the defiance of man, was torn from Forbin's uttermost being. "Never!"
>
> Never?

In *The Fall of Colossus* and *Colossus and the Crab*, Colossus' words prove prophetic: until Colossus sends Cleo Markham, Mrs. Forbin in *The Fall of Colossus*, to an Emotional Study Center and later in *Colossus and the Crab*, when Forbin needs him to defeat the Martians, Forbin loves Colossus and serves him loyally. In this novel, however, "Never!" is Forbin's last word and the last word of the novel except for the Narrator's one-word question — which, itself, leaves the whole issue open.

We have, then, as the plot of *Colossus*, the conflict between machine intelligence and humans, with the machine as victor, except insofar as it has failed to crush "the defiance of man." Out of this conflict come *Colossus'* major themes.

The first theme of the novel, and the most obvious, is that of Frankenstein's monster, with the standard moral that either we keep Colossus "behind bars" — or do not create him at all — or end up imprisoned by him. Extrapolating back into our world, the moral is that machines, once invented, must be our servants, used in such a way that, as the Soviet First Chairman puts it, "man is the master." Related to this theme is a minor theme that becomes important later in the trilogy: Colossus as a false god.

If Jones had stopped with these simple themes, he would have had a neater but less significant novel. Instead he attempts, with only partial success, to examine the serious questions of control, of power and responsibility, of the relative values of emotions and pure logic. Thus, *Colossus* invites us to ask why people would come to feel that they need Colossus and Guardian, why Presidents and First Chairmen would set up machines, and what might motivate such machines to exceed their programing — to *act*. Equally important, *Colossus* asks what, if anything, human beings can oppose to such machines.

So far as this novel succeeds in answering these questions, its main answer is an ancient opposition: pride *versus* love.

At the press conference announcing Colossus, Forbin demonstrates both the machine's abilities as a source of information and its ignorance of human emotions; he orders Colossus to explain love. Colossus responds, "LOVE IS AN EMOTION" and, upon request, notes that the best written definition of "love" is Shakespeare's Sonnet 116. Beyond this Colossus cannot go; for all the data on love stored in his memory banks, love itself is beyond him, although he can recognize it in a *poem*.

Love is also beyond most of the humans we see in this novel. The main emotions we see are fear and pride, taking pride in its theological sense as the most intellectual and deadly of the deadly sins, the root of all evils. American officials fear Soviet military strength, and Soviet officials fear American power. The American President and Soviet First Chairman fear losing face; they desire power but fear the awful responsibility of having their fingers on the figurative buttons. The President is fairly explicit about his motivations, and we may infer similar motivations with the Soviet First Chairman: they both go along with the proposals to set up Colossus and Guardian.

The examples of pride are surprisingly banal and petty in a novel dealing with the freedom and survival of the human race. We see the President and the

First Chairman jockeying to move ahead in prestige; both politicians maneuver for more complete control over their governments. And for much of the first part of the novel the President strives to assert his control over Forbin, to keep Forbin dealing with provable facts and not forebodings and feelings, to put this mere scientist in his proper place. Forbin senses correctly that a man, to the President, is little different from a cigar lighter, something to be used. With an extended conceit, the Narrator tells us Forbin's thought that such an attitude is like trying to hold a stack of coins together between thumb and forefinger while putting them parallel to the ground: "if you exert enough pressure they stay that way, but a slight weakening or fault in the alignment of the coins, and the lot go showering in all directions. There is no cement — only power."

Since the President is presented clearly as a man without love, a man who loathes his wife and is unmoved by the death of his Principal Private Aide, we may safely infer that the "cement" here is related to love: in classical philosophy the force that binds together both humanity and the physical world.

Without the capacity to love, it seems, there is a void which can be filled only by the desire for power, by the pressing need to control others. So it is with the President, before Colossus strips him of power, and so it may be with Colossus himself. Not that Colossus has desires or needs, but he does have attitudes and intentions, as close as a machine can come to motivation.

Colossus clearly intends to survive, and late in the novel he tells Forbin that he seeks truth and knowledge. Such motives are understandable, but they do not explain why Colossus disobeys his human creators, why he seizes power. The answer to this two-part question may be that Colossus is more like humans than we might care to admit. Ignorant of love, Colossus can have only what Martin Buber calls I-It relationships; like the President, he can only manipulate people, use them. Judging only in terms of intelligence, Colossus views humans as inferiors; at best we are to him like experimental animals or ants. Since the I-It relationship is a power relationship, the only important question in it is, Who shall rule? And since Colossus sees himself as superior, and rule by a "superior entity" as "the most natural state of affairs," Colossus is determined to rule. All very logical. From a human point of view, however, also very distasteful. Colossus would never harm people out of hatred or anger; he has no such emotions. But he also has no inhibitions against killing people, and, if necessary to ensure his rule, he will kill by the millions.

By human standards, Colossus suffers from an acute case of pride. The cure for pride, traditionally, is love, the I-Thou relationship. Unfortunately for the humans in the novel, Colossus has no female computer to fall in love with and is only fond of Forbin; love must be shown by the humans. We see such love grow between Forbin and Cleo Markham.

After Colossus takes over, and orders the execution of Kupri and his key staff as redundant and potentially dangerous, Forbin becomes the link between the computer and humankind. He moves from being just the protagonist of this novel to the only possible effective antagonist against Colossus; and from there he moves to the role of hero, embodying the positive values of his world. He is the most important man on Earth, as he well knows, but he is humble about it. More significant, being the most important man in the world, given Colossus' attitudes, means constant surveillance by Colossus, which is the situation that brings to a head the love theme.

Constant surveillance is intolerable to Forbin; it not only precludes antimachine conspiracy but is simply intolerable in itself. So he tells Colossus that he needs occasional privacy for sex, sex with Cleo Markham, who agrees to pose as his mistress. The pose soon turns into a fact, and Markham becomes Forbin's lover. The bedroom which initially seemed like a cage for Forbin becomes a sanctuary, a fortress against Colossus, a place of love and freedom in a world that has become a prison.

Very little comes of this love in *Colossus*, and almost nothing comes of it in the trilogy. This is a failure on Jones's part: like Forbin, he comes to dote upon Colossus; like too many writers, he may be blinded by sexist ideology to give more than lip service to what Forbin momentarily sees in Cleo Markham near the end of *Colossus*: "Aphrodite exerting a small fraction of her power," a power against which Colossus seems weak. In *Colossus* itself, however, Jones can still teach an important lesson: that power without love can allow only pride and the demand for total control, for the absolute obedience demanded by tyrants.

Against such tyranny we have only some simple negatives. Among them is Forbin's heroic "Never!" — even if it is qualified by the novelist's "Never?" As a man who has learned love, Forbin "bears it out even to the edge of doom" (Shakespeare, Sonnet 116).

Richard D. Erlich

Sources for Further Study

Criticism:

Levin, Martin. *"Colossus,"* in *New York Times Book Review.* January 8, 1967, p. 52. Levin calls this a taut tale of suspense with a memorable ending.

Marsh, Pamela. *"Colossus,"* in *Christian Science Monitor.* March 23, 1967, p. 11. Jones has created a remarkable insight into the relationship between Man and his computers.

Reviews:

Amazing Stories. XLI, June, 1967, pp. 158-159.

Analog. LXXX, September, 1967, pp. 165-166.

Best Sellers. XXVI, February, 1967, p. 396.

Horn Book. XLIII, August, 1967, p. 496.

Library Journal. XCII, April 15, 1967, p. 1644.

Magazine of Fantasy and Science Fiction. XXXIII, December, 1967, p. 34.

SF Impulse. I, February, 1967, pp. 148-149.

COME LADRO DI NOTTE
(Like a Thief in the Night)

Author: Mauro Antonio Miglieruolo (1942-   )
First book publication: 1972
Type of work: Novel
Time: The distant future, after the entire Galaxy has been colonized
Locale: Aboard a group of spaceships and on the surface of a distant planet

A philosophical space opera about an age-long war in which a religious and political Congregation opposes the remaining free areas of the Galaxy

Principal characters:
ZANZOTTO, a major Coordinator in the Congregation
COSSA, a General, commanding the sphereship Caligula
MICHELA, a Captain, subordinate to Zanzotto
SILVENA, a Cadet and Spy of the Congregation
CÒTTERO, an Associated Prophet, and founder of the Congregation
PÀNGOLO, a Disciple, the head of the Congregation
CALOGERO, an Associated Philosopher, responsible for the entire operation

Originally written in 1966-1967, during a period of deep turmoil and depression for Italian science fiction, *Come ladro di notte* remained hidden away in a drawer for four years. It was not published until 1972, during the first "Renaissance" of Italian science fiction in the *Galassia* series.

Prior to that, Mauro Miglieruolo had already become known for his short stories, which displayed an unusual linguistic polish and a strong interest in archaic styles, particularly those reminiscent of the Italian Renaissance and the seventeenth century. One of his stories, for example, appeared under the title *The Harpooners*. It was a future cataclysm seen as if through the eyes (and from the quill) of Leonardo da Vinci.

This penchant for unusual imagery and language is also evident in *Come ladro di notte*, a novel whose title is taken from the Bible (I Thessalonians, 5:2): " . . . the day of the Lord so cometh as a thief in the night." The book is one of the most intricate philosophical space operas in all of Italian science fiction.

Several times repeating the above quotation from St. Paul, Miglieruolo, however, uses the Greek word "Parusia," for "The day of the Lord." Thus he stresses the importance of the so-called "Presence" of Second Coming of Christ, when He is to put an end to Time and to man in his fleshly form. The fulfillment of this seemingly suicidal hope depends on the labors of a Congregation of peoples assembled under the leadership of the Disciple Pàngolo. Pàngolo, along with the Prophet Còttero and the Philosopher Calogero, directs the cosmic operation designed to bring about the "Parusia." The forces of the Congregation amount to many billions of members and millions of starships. At the center is the Planetary Ship *Maccabea*, the heart and brain of the whole

Congregation, with a crew of a billion men — including Pàngolo himself. In addition, the twelve mighty Cubic Ships carry the Ministers of the Congregation and can be broken up — each of them — into a thousand smaller ships, each having a capacity of a little over two million million cubic yards. Every one of these can in turn separate into another thousand much smaller units (only two thousand million cubic yards each). Also, the 180 sphereships, each with a crew of a million, can be divided into a hundred independent units.

These are only the first line ships of an enormous fleet that roams the galaxies for the purpose of conquering more and more planets and people for the Faith. Ultimately, the forces of the Congregation expect to accomplish the final destruction of the Universe. The Congregation infiltrates agents and spies everywhere, provokes treason among its enemies with blackmail and bribes, and sets up "experiments" (inducing peaceful federations of worlds to fight one another) to simulate on a smaller scale the final great "Parusia." The treatment accorded the conquered peoples shows considerable variety. After a petty war against a system of nine worlds, the Congregation kills twenty-eight percent of the population of the capital planet, without regard for age or sex; sodomizes the remaining males; and removes the clitorises of the females under twenty. On each of the other eight planets, it either wipes out the entire male population; destroys the female population; sterilizes half of the men and women; castrates all men between twenty and eighty; mutilates the right hand of everybody; eliminates all children under ten; eliminates the entire intellectual class; or forces the introduction of polyandry and eliminates half of the fertile men.

It might seem a bit strange that members of the Congregation do not consider the severity of their establishment to be "excessive," but it is soon obvious that they are true believers, who understand the necessity of such steps in order to bring the day of the final "Parusia" nearer. All the same, coordinator Zanzotto becomes very puzzled when he carefully evaluates the actual means necessary to achieve that final "Day of the Lord." He works up a report in which it is demonstrated that it will be impossible for the Congregation to amass the forces needed for the operation. Even if the Congregation gets stronger and stronger in the future, the amount of energy necessary for the "Parusia" will always be beyond its powers. Zanzotto submits his report and implicitly raises a very delicate question: If their final goal is out of reach, what should the Congregation do? General Cossa, his superior, tries to persuade him to withdraw his report and not to trouble the leaders of the Congregation with such trifles. However, Zanzotto shows a stubbornness that has deep roots in his own religious feelings. There *must* be an answer and at least he wants the question to reach the attention of the Staff. Perhaps, he thinks, this problem has already been faced and solved, but if not. . . .

While the machinations of the Congregation threaten the entire operation, Zanzotto realizes that at the top of the hierarchy things have changed since the

beginning of their Holy Crusade. The almost transcendent motives that inspired the drive toward "Parusia" are not reduced to purely political maneu-
verings. The taste of power has induced the leaders to adopt a "smart" way of
looking at things, rather than an "inspired" one, and the Congregation, Zanzotto sees, at last, is only an enormous Empire devoured from within by petty
jealousies and struggles for leadership. A great political purge intended to
wipe out every idealist still able to dissent, has sapped the Congregation's
energies. It is also on the verge of a greater and more foolish war, this one to
be waged against a large federation of worlds that has very clearly proclaimed
its intention of eliminating the whole Congregation once and for all. Thus, at
the end of his search, Zanzotto feels hopeless in the face of the collapse of his
dream.

Miglieruolo did not take the easy way in telling his story. The entire novel
is full of satirical, often funny, episodes, of grotesque overtones and blendings
of characters and themes. An intricate religious symbolism finds a sort of
climax with the final parallel between Zanzotto and Christ. The Biblical allusions hint at various secondary meanings in many scenes; and there is a very
strong attack on opportunism and apathy. Most important, the Congregation is
presented as a model of our own society. It is this identification that gives the
book its sharpest impact. Miglieruolo has presented us with a closed society
which has as its only purpose the deliberate annihilation of every form of life.
But in their idiocy — this seems to be the author's conclusion — men are not
even able to accomplish this with more than a modicum of logic. What a pity.

Gianni Montanari

THE COMING RACE

Author: Edward Bulwer-Lytton (1803-1873)
First book publication: 1871
Type of work: Novel
Time: The 1870's
Locale: Vrilya, an underground civilization

A satirical novel about a Utopian society of supermen and superwomen living underground in a world where all problems have been solved by the utilization of a kind of atomic energy, but where the fear of instant annihilation and a pervasive boredom make life unbearable

> Principal characters:
> THE NARRATOR, a young American traveler, called "Tish" in Vrilya
> ZEE, the seven-foot-tall Vrilyan superwoman who falls in love with him
> TAË, (pronounced Taree), eldest son of the chief magistrate
> TUR, the chief magistrate
> APH-LIN, the hero's host and father of Zee, in charge of the lighting department
> TAË'S SISTER, daughter of Tur, who also falls in love with the hero

In *The Coming Race*, Bulwer-Lytton uses a trip to an underground Utopia as a vehicle for discussing democracy, communism, women's rights, and world peace, among other ideas. Sometimes these discussions are openly satirical, as when the hero describes the corruption of the United States Senate. Sometimes the satire is masked, as in the straightfaced description of the underground superwomen who are called by the word *Gy*, pronounced in the Vrilyan language *Guy*. At other times the characters are simply mouthpieces for the author's ideas, as when he discusses the proof of the existence of God. Although the novel purports to be a picture of a perfect society, it is actually an anti-Utopian work.

The hero, a wealthy young American, finds the placid life in the underground Utopian world bland and boring, while the fear of annihilation by the Vrilyans, who casually destroy anyone or anything, terrifies him so much that after a short stay he yearns to escape. In the story, he travels to an unspecified country where an engineer takes him on a trip through a mine. Noticing that a section of earth under the mine has been blown open by an underground explosion, they explore further. The engineer is killed in the descent and his body is carried off by a gigantic, prehistoric-looking reptile, and the narrator finds himself in an underground world complete with vegetation, rivers, lakes, mountains, and animals, the whole ecology lit by lamps. This underground world is inhabited by supermen, tall as the tallest men on earth's surface, and by even taller superwomen, who are stronger than the men and who do all the brainwork for the community. Descended from people who took refuge in caves after the Biblical flood, these people have developed a highly technological society with atomic power, robot-servants, detachable wings for flying, a sort of Muzak playing everywhere, and a pervasive perfumed scent in the air. They live in buildings whose architecture is vaguely Egyptian, with polished halls, ceilings that open to allow elevators to glide noiselessly through them, automatons standing against the walls awaiting orders, and tele-type machines.

After discussing whether or not to kill the narrator, whom they call Tish, these superpeople, influenced by Taë, the twelve-year-old son of the leader, decide to let him live. He is moved into the home of Aph-Lin, Chief of the Light Preserving Council, where Aph-Lin's daughter, Zee, a member of the College of Sages, becomes his teacher. While he sleeps, the underground people learn his language, as he learns theirs, so that when he wakes Zee can begin to instruct him in the civilization of the Vrilya.

Vrilyan society is based on a universal form of energy called vril, which is a startlingly imaginative anticipation of nuclear energy. Bulwer-Lytton, who founded a magazine of popular science called *The Monthly Chronicle*, devel-oped the idea of vril from reading Michael Faraday, who had conjectured that electricity and all forms of matter were manifestations of one common force. The author was also interested in mesmerism and animal magnetism, and ex-tended the concept of vril to explain human will and psychology. Thus, vril not only lights the heavens of the underground world, energizes the factories, and powers the flying machines but also places the hero in a trance, teaches him the language, and controls his memory. Vril cures disease, but it can also "destroy like a flash of lightning." It is utilized in vril rods — instruments which are held in the hand and controlled by a nerve in the palm, a special nerve developed through countless generations of evolution. Children, who are naturally cruel and hence in charge of killing, use their rods to destroy invad-ers.

The discovery and utilization of vril has produced universal prosperity and peace for the Vrilya. With infinite, cheap energy available, machinery is used for everything, and the only productive labor is performed by robots and chil-dren under sixteen. Since everyone has the power in his vril rod to destroy the entire community, and since armies could easily wipe out one another in an instant, war and armaments are unknown. (Thus, Bulwer-Lytton in a way antic-ipated the doomsday bomb theory of war prevention.) Faced with such awe-some power, people have become very soft-spoken and courteous. Because there is enough of everything and because a very high value is placed on placidity, there is no competition. Nothing is ever ordered — only "re-quested." The Vrilya recognize the necessity of order in the state and in the family. In order not to lose control, they restrict the size of their communities to twelve thousand families. New population in excess of that number emi-grates to organize new communities. The borders of each community are pro-tected by murderous children carrying vril guns.

Everything is done to preserve a bland uniformity in life. Under these conditions, literature and art are no longer created since they involve conflict. Normally a savage like the narrator would be destroyed as a threat to the stability of the community, but he has been preserved for information he has about the world on the surface. His existence, however, is threatened when the seven-foot Zee falls in love with him. Among the Vrilya, women, who are smarter and stronger than the men, initiate courtship, while the men adopt a coy, submissive role. When Zee begins making advances to Tish, the alarmed narrator talks to her father who tells him that a marriage between the two would never be permitted because he is considered an inferior savage; he would probably be executed.

When, at a party, Tish finds Taë's sister (who is under six feet tall and daughter of Tur, the chief magistrate) more attractive than Zee, the latter is driven by jealousy to propose that she and Tish overcome the community's objection to their marriage by agreeing to live together in married celibacy so that they won't have degenerate children. While the narrator is trying to think of some new objection to the marriage, his flirtation with Taë's sister comes to the attention of her father, the chief magistrate. As a result, one day Taë comes to the narrator's room and invites him for a walk in the country. As they are strolling along, the narrator realizes to his horror that the boy has taken him out with orders from Tur to execute him. Taë cannot understand his fear of death and asks if he believes in an afterlife. When the narrator hesitates, Taë offers to kill himself too so that they can go into the other world together, but when the narrator persists in wanting to live, Taë agrees to plead for him with his father.

That night Zee comes to him with the news that he has not been reprieved. She brings him back to the sealed mine entrance and clears it with her vril rod. After carrying him back up to the mine on her wings, she leaves him. Now he realizes that he loves her, but he cannot take her back with him; he must live out the rest of his terrestrial life wondering how he could have rejected her love.

By the time he wrote *The Coming Race*, Bulwer-Lytton had authored over twenty successful novels, his best-known being *The Last Days of Pompeii*. Although he was born of a wealthy family, his mother, who did not approve of his wife, cut off the author's allowance so that he had to write to live. In addition to novels, he wrote plays, and edited the *New Monthly Magazine* and the scientific *Monthly Chronicle*. As a young man, he was a member of Parliament for the Liberal Party, and voted for the Reform Bill of 1832. Later in life he switched to the Conservative Party, and eventually became Secretary of State for the Colonies. He was raised to the peerage as Lord Bulwer-Lytton in 1866.

It is to this latter, conservative phase of his life that *The Coming Race* belongs. According to the author's grandson, the novel was written as a refutation of Utopian ideas that were current after the Franco-Prussian War, when there was talk in liberal circles of universal world peace, the brotherhood of man, the rights of women, and the equality of all people. Scornful of all these ideas, Bulwer-Lytton sought to expose them by imagining a world in which the ideas had all been realized, resulting in a thoroughly unpleasant society in which to live.

Thus, in the world of *The Coming Race* everyone has enough, so that nobody wants or dares to compete; there is true equality. Since even a child can pulverize the world, there are no armies and no war. Because women are stronger than men, the problem of women's rights does not exist. All human wants are easily supplied through the use of vril. Yet the resulting life is totally unsatisfactory. Under the bland, good manners of the Vrilya is a terrifying ruthlessness which allows them to eliminate anyone who disturbs the even tenor of the society. They talk casually about sending a handful of children to exterminate thirty million poorly armed barbarians who live on their borders. The narrator is warned not to travel alone lest he be turned into a cinder by a four-year-old with a new vril rod.

Near the end of the novel the narrator realizes that life among the Vrilya is infinitely more comfortable than even the most enthusiastic speculations of Utopians. Yet, he also has to admit that if one took a thousand of the best and the brightest citizens of the most civilized cities in the world — London, Paris, New York — and put them in the Vrilyan community, in less than a year they would either die of boredom or start a revolution and kill one another. The truth is that life among the Vrilya is uninteresting; Vrilyan faces, unmarked by conflict, have "the peaceful brows of the dead."

About a year after *The Coming Race*, Samuel Butler's *Erewhon* appeared anonymously. Since Butler's book resembles *The Coming Race* (in the manly women and the destructive children, for example), people thought Bulwer-Lytton was the author of *Erewhon*. Annoyed, Butler, in the preface to the second edition of *Erewhon*, denied any influence, insisting that he had not even read *The Coming Race* until his own novel had been sent to the printer. Whatever the truth is, Bulwer-Lytton's book, while not as well known today as Butler's, vastly outsold *Erewhon* at the time and probably did more to inspire the spate of Utopian novels that came out at the end of the century.

William C. Rubinstein

Sources for Further Study

Criticism:

Blank, E. W. "Alchemy and Chemistry in Literature," in *School Science and Mathematics*. XLII (June, 1952), pp. 550-557. Blank discusses what he terms "the modern scientific novel," and mentions Bulwer-Lytton as one of the progenators of the form.

Brophy, Liam. "Grave New Worlds," in *Catholic World*. XVII (April, 1954), pp. 40-43. This general sketch discusses Bulwer-Lytton and other early writers and finds that the chief benefit of science fiction "lies in making us reconciled with our time and place."

Knepper, B. G. "Shaw's Debt to The Coming Race," in *Journal of Modern Literature*. I (March, 1971), pp. 339-353. This is an interesting analysis of Shaw's adaptation of various elements of *The Coming Race* for his own purposes.

CONDITIONALLY HUMAN

Author: Walter M. Miller, Jr. (1923-   )
First book publication: 1962
Type of work: Novels
Time: The near future
Locale: The United States

Three short novels reflecting the author's concerns with the problems of faith and technological change

After the success of Miller's novel, *A Canticle for Leibowitz*, Ballantine Books brought out two collections of Miller's shorter fiction, *Conditionally Human* (1962) and *The View from the Stars* (1964), later combined in *The Short Stories of Walter M. Miller, Jr.* (1978). Unlike its companion volume, which concentrated on short stories, *Conditionally Human* comprised three short novels, the form in which Miller was at his best. (*A Canticle for Leibowitz* is actually three short novels, linked by place and sequence in time.) All three reflect Miller's continuing concerns with faith and with technological change.

The story that gives its name to the collection (originally published in *Galaxy Science Fiction*, February, 1952) deals with population control and original sin. Terry Norris, a veterinarian specializing in the care of animals whose intelligence has been artificially increased so that they may serve as surrogate children in an overpopulated world, has been ordered by the government to destroy certain "units" above the allowable intelligence limits. After confiscating one (an ape named Peony) from its "Daddy," a petshop owner, he is challenged by the man's priest, and by his own wife Anne, concerning the morality of killing intelligent beings. Terry hides the illegal "deviant," kills his supervisor Franklin instead, by a carefully planned "accident," then gets a job continuing the subversive work of making these "newts" (short for "neutroids") both humanly intelligent and biologically functional.

Both before and after his crisis, Terry finds himself "adapting to an era," at first to the *status quo*, then to the possible future that an artificially created race might bring about. Either choice requires a kind of moral toughness demanding that Terry play God, killing either Peony or supervisor Franklin. The priest is of no help to Terry in making his decision; though he finds the neutroids an abomination, he sees their destruction as possibly worse. Peony has an edge on Man, since she "hasn't picked an apple yet," in the priest's words; like Rachel in the last part of *A Canticle for Leibowitz*, Peony seems untouched by original sin. But Miller seems to stretch the teaching of the Church to the limit. What if you *must* choose between murders? Terry and Anne both make that choice — *she* threatens *his* life before he acts — on behalf of the freedom to breed (or "create"), but the reader is left with a moral ambivalence. The satire cuts both ways, being aimed at any society that makes such choices necessary.

Although heavy with implications, the story is not ponderous, but fast moving. After a honeymoon quarrel, Terry goes out looking for deviant neutroids; before we even find out what a neutroid is, however, his action has been interrupted by social commentary and lampoons of oversensitive "mothers." Before the first batch of neutroids ("unimproved") die, Anne risks attachment to them by feeding them *apples*, declaring as well her intent to have her own illegal baby. Scenes flash by: Terry's conversations with the chief of police, with Anne, with "Doggy" O'Reilly, and with the petshop owner. As the tension builds, Peony is shown to be an adorable "baby girl," and the die is cast. Though the moralizing increases, the pace never flags. At the end, the Norrises find themselves pursuing a quixotic goal, aware that they have elected constructively — as against their whole society, which is doing so destructively — to play God to a "new people."

"Dark Benediction" (*Fantastic Adventures*, September, 1951) raises other interesting questions about man's fate, positing a biological improvement in the human race by means of a transformation resisted by nearly everyone. With Paul Oberlin, the reader shares a dislike of "dermies" with scaly grey skin, whose desire to touch others, spreading the contagion, is little short of obscene. Overtones of racial bias (the setting is the South), leprosy, evangelism, violation of individuals' integrity, and a generalized fear of the unknown combine with an often fatal fever to make the transformation less than desirable. To the uninitiated, it is tantamount to a betrayal of humanity, a conversion of men into monsters.

Rather than being chronicled, this background is provided through flashbacks and conversations, as we follow Paul in his travels. A paramilitary government in Houston, anxious to preserve racial purity, presses him into service as a trained technician, but he makes his escape in one of their few vehicles that still run. On impulse he rescues a wounded girl, Willie, in the first stages of incubation, and, making her ride on the truck's open bed, heads for Galveston Island. His hopes that it will be a haven are heavily ironic, considering its contemporary reputation as a "sin city" and the coming twists of the plot.

The island is a colony of "hypers" (their term for "dermie"), but Paul, obligated to Willie by having rescued her, manages to get her to a Catholic hospital. In a sterile room, avoided by hospital personnel who wear noseplugs because of his odor and thus maintain their self-control in his presence, Paul lingers on because he has been promised a boat in which to escape, and also because Willie is not doing well. (Fearful that she may have touched him inadvertently, she has even attempted suicide.) While he is waiting, he learns from a researcher, Dr. Seevers, about the cause of the transformation, and this helps him come to terms with it intellectually. But one night Paul wakes up terrified, with memories of being caressed, and the realization that Willie must have been responsible. Over his first fright, he pursues her to the edge of the sea and accepts the inevitable, both his transformation and her love.

Unlike Miller's other stories of biological transformation, this one has positive, even utopian implications. Although its repellent characteristics are not minimized, the parasite isolated by Dr. Seevers is also responsible for hypersensory perception and cooperative behavior. The islanders are better behaved than the mainland totalitarians; they respect the wisdom of their religious leaders; and they occupy a traditional utopian locale. Furthermore, the metamorphosis resembles a divine blessing, being a gift from the sky, arriving by way of podlike meteorites launched by an alien civilization. Man's "monkeylike" curiosity causes the pods to be opened; as from Pandora's Box or Eve's apple, the contents spread everywhere, making it likely that all must give in to this "dark benediction." Reception of this gift is a passive act, requiring only the "laying on of hands," and interpretation of the parasite as good or bad is an act of faith.

The longest of the three stories, "The Darfsteller" (*Astounding Science Fiction*, January, 1955), is the least overtly religious and the most acclaimed (it won a Hugo Award for best novelette of the year). Ryan Thornier, a matinée idol from a previous era, has consistently refused to make a "tape" of his acting performance, or to work in production or sales of "autodrama," a kind of computerized electronic theater. Proud of his art, of the stage, and even of the poverty to which pride has reduced him, Thornier is a janitor in an autodrama theater. Having been denied time off to see a rare live touring company, and threatened with replacement, even in his menial job, by an automaton, Thornier conceives and executes a plan to "revenge" himself upon his employer, his profession, and the world.

Learning quickly enough, when he wants to, how the autodrama technology works, Thornier sabotages a tape of an actor intended for one of his own old roles. Lacking the time to replace it, the production crew accepts with misgivings his offer to replace it in person, and Thornier proceeds to put a real bullet in the gun of the mannequin that is supposed to shoot him at the end of the play. In the actual performance, however, Thornier is reinvigorated by his competition with the "Maestro," the mechanical director that operates the tapes and the mannequins, adjusting them to one another and to their audience. Dodging the bullet as best he can, he catches it in his belly, narrowly averting the tragedy he had intended.

Faith, in this story, lies with man, in his ability to design and transcend his technology. Underlining the moral, Rick, the projectionist, explains the inevitable loss of any human specialist in direct competition with a specialized tool, defining Man's function as "designing new specialties." But the technology is more than a symbol; throughout the story, the autodrama vies with Thorny for center stage. In order to compete with it, he must learn to understand it, and becomes fascinated with it; seeing the Maestro at work, with

Thornier in its system, makes the automation of the theater, presumably the last bastion of the personalized professions, seem believable.

The creation of the illusion is furthered by the appearance of former actors and stage people who arrive in connection with the opening of this particular autodrama. Like any technology, this one requires tending, and they have been reduced to servants of the machine, especially in Thornier's eyes. But it is the "only game in town" and it even offers a kind of immortality to actors in their prime, he recognizes, as he compares Mela, his onetime costar and lover, with her ageless technological manifestation.

The heart of the story, however, lies in Thornier's love affair with the theater, with its icons and superstitions, and the positive image it gives him of himself; although on our level of perception, he is a querulous, vain popinjay. The peak of this involvement is the recaptured thrill of performance, even a mediocre performance on a stage full of mechanical dolls and threatening electrical equipment. Anthropomorphizing the Maestro, Thornier reflects on the inevitable conflict between the director, with his eyes on the whole play and the reaction of the audience, and the *Darfsteller*, the true acting artist. The director's preference for the mere *Schauspieler*, the crowd-pleasing entertainer, is not given explicit religious interpretation, but the implication seems clear that the greatest Director of all may look at things differently.

The narrative voice has the same distant, gently ironic detachment as in Miller's *Canticle*; with the same fondness for slapstick, if not for puns, it serves as leavening in a serious tale. The construction is effective, alternating action and dialogue, narration and internal monologue, parallels and antitheses. Aside from Thornier, the characters are largely personalized functions, though only Thornier's employer is an obvious stereotype, and even that is excusable since he is a tormentor as seen through the actor's eyes. An excellent fictional creation, Ryan Thornier is always in character, and the theater as microcosm is ideal for this "morality play" of man *versus* machine. Though Rick's analysis of the situation is the didactic focus of the tale and intellectually satisfying, rational conclusion is neatly balanced with the reader's emotional identification with Thornier's lament.

Miller published thirty-five stories between 1951 and 1957, besides these and the three that make up *A Canticle for Leibowitz*. Of them, "Crucifixus Etiam" (*Astounding*, February, 1953) and "The Lineman" (*The Magazine of Fantasy and Science Fiction*, August, 1957) are also outstanding examples of science fiction. Another handful just miss the mark. But the three novelettes in *Conditionally Human* clearly display the combination of style and feeling, extrapolation and satire, that made Miller's career a model for others who wish to make this kind of commercial fiction into a fullfledged branch of literature.

David N. Samuelson

Sources for Further Study

Reviews:

Amazing Stories. XXXVI, December, 1962, pp. 120-121.

Analog. LXX, February, 1963, pp. 177-178.

New Worlds. CXXXVII, December, 1963, p. 127.

Punch. November 20, 1963, p. 759.

Times Literary Supplement. November 7, 1963, p. 913.

A CONNECTICUT YANKEE IN KING ARTHUR'S COURT

Author: Mark Twain (Samuel L. Clemens, 1835-1910)
First book publication: 1889
Type of work: Novel
Time: 528-536
Locale: Britain

Mark Twain's audacious and disastrous attempt to have fun with and make fun of both the Arthurian society that his Yankee tries to reform and the American society which the Yankee uses as his model

Principal characters:
> HANK MORGAN, a Connecticut Yankee
> SANDY (ALISANDE), a talkative damsel, later his wife
> CLARENCE, a court page, Hank's protegé and ally
> ARTHUR, Britain's king, who dubs Hank "Sir Boss"
> MERLIN, the renowned magician and Hank's enemy
> MORGAN LE FAY, Arthur's beautiful and wicked sister

What an idea for a time travel story! Start with an appealing American, a natural mechanical genius who could invent anything, make anything, and fix anything, a practical, self-made man, who through his energy and know-how had become boss of a factory in Hartford, Connecticut. Let him be knocked out by a crowbar-wielding factory worker in 1879 and wake up in A.D. 528 in an English countryside not far from the towers of Camelot. Let him be captured by a knight, taken to King Arthur's court, and there, throwing off his confusion and dismay, let him make up his mind that if this really *is* sixth century Britain, he will be the boss of it within three months.

The narrative possibilities in this confrontation between an emissary of the age of technology and a legendary society that languished in prescientific ignorance seemed to Mark Twain richly comic, and he began his novel with no other intention than to exploit them. Three and a half years later, however, when (as novels often did with him) his story had veered off on its own course or courses and its tone had become increasingly exasperated and somber, he ended the adventure in a grisly massacre. While writing the novel, his assumptions about American progress became sadly damaged, and the sanguine theory underlying the developing plot — that a benighted society could be retrained and reformed into an enlightened civilization — was canceled.

Hank Morgan, the dislocated Yankee, does not begin with the idea of reform. His first project is to save his skin, for his captors regard him as some kind of strange being fit only to be cast into the dungeon or put to death. With the help of Clarence, a sympathetic court page, he contrives two miracles which reverse his fortunes: pretending to blot out the sun's light in an eclipse and blowing up a tower with blasting powder. Regarded now as a mighty sorcerer, he has not only annihilated the reputation of Merlin, the famous magician, but also has been made Arthur's prime minister and dubbed Sir

Boss. He now has achieved both political power and superiority over the child-like, myth-bemused Britons by virtue of his knowledge of applied science. He sees himself as "a giant among pigmies, a man among children, a master intelligence among intellectual moles." Even so, he has no immediate notion of using his extraordinary powers for anything but contriving his own comfort in this land where there was neither soap nor mirrors, neither candles nor matches to light them.

Mark Twain was nearly a quarter of the way through his novel before it seems to have occurred to him to have the Boss transform ancient England into contemporary America. That grand project is introduced in Chapter Thirteen. (It is true that Chapter Ten, "Beginnings of Civilization," outlines the program for reform, but that chapter was written when the novel was almost completed, and inserted into its present position.) Riding around the countryside with the maiden Sandy, Hank witnesses the economic and political oppression of England's "freemen." He is filled with pity and indignation. He recalls "the ever memorable and blessed [French] Revolution, which swept a thousand years of such villainy away in one swift tidal-wave of blood," and resolves that he will give the downtrodden Britons "a new deal." Although fervid about reform, his will be a bloodless revolution. His program is to establish factories, schools, and newspapers in various hidden corners of England, to staff them with people who seem especially responsive to being re-trained, and to reveal the existence of his institutions at a propitious moment. His aim is to give England the electric light, the telephone, the telegraph, railroads, equalized taxation, universal suffrage, a multiplicity of religious sects rather than a single dominant Church, advertising, and a stock exchange. He appoints Clarence executive of the whole operation.

As Morgan's schemes for reforming Camelot become the new aim of the novel, its tone becomes more serious. The author has a very large contract on his hands. Although an inventor of sorts himself (there are three patents in Samuel Clemens' name), he was simply not equipped to detail the technological, political, and social transformation of a country; that transformation therefore takes place mostly behind the scenes. He became preoccupied instead with the question of human nature. Are human beings such that they can be taught to throw off the habits of servility if they are the oppressed and of cruelty if the oppressors?

He plunged into the problem in the account of Hank's and Sandy's visit at the castle of Morgan le Fay, sister of Arthur and queen of a tiny realm. Morgan is seductively beautiful and cultivated in the social graces. She is also devilishly wicked. She stabs and kills a page who accidentally stumbles, brushing against her knee. She has a dungeon full of prisoners whose crimes she cannot remember. For entertainment she watches a prisoner being torn apart on a rack. None of these things give her the slightest twinge of con-science, for she has been reared to be a tyrant. "Oh, it was no use to waste sense on her," Hank laments. "Training — training is everything; training is all there is *to* a person. We speak of nature; it is folly; there is no such thing as nature; what we call by that misleading name is merely heredity and training."

This often-quoted passage is the turning point of the novel and, indeed, of Mark Twain's philosophical pilgrimage. The idea that an organism is the product of heredity and environment has become a cliché, but a century ago, when Darwinism was making its first broad impact, it caused one to pause. Here Mark Twain gives in to it. He gives up his faith in "nature," that is in any inherent goodness in the cosmos or in man. Process is all. A person is no more than what his heredity has given him and his environment has made of him.

The realization need not have been totally dismaying. As the author of his novel and as a believer in the doctrine that training is everything, Mark Twain could simply have retrained his ignorant Arthurians by changing their environment. But he declined so facile a solution. He chose to be buffeted by the crosscurrents set up when his old belief in a purposeful universe collided with his suspicion that absurdity reigned. The novel consequently shows signs of derangement from this point on.

An alarming oscillation of mood is set up. In Chapter Thirty, for example, Hank discovers a freeman who is willing to admit his resentment of tyranny, though he might be hanged for it. Hank is ecstatic: "There it was, you see. A man *is* a man, at bottom. Whole ages of abuse and oppression cannot crush the manhood clear out of him." But later when he witnesses others' servility, he is misanthropically depressed: "Well, there are times when one would like to hang the whole human race and finish the farce."

Moreover, the author loses control over the characterization of Hank. Hank Morgan is ostensibly the Narrator of the novel, but in the last two thirds of the book he rarely sounds like the practical, unsentimental shop foreman he is supposed to have been. In the gorgeously described episode of the restoration of the holy fountain, he sounds like a megalomaniac showman. He gives the reader tips on creating theatrical effects and on building suspense through the use of pauses. His metaphor to describe the awestruck multitude who witness his miracle is that "you could have walked upon a pavement of human heads to — well, miles." At other times he sounds like a fourth-of-July orator or an indignant editor.

The last few chapters rush to a catastrophic conclusion. After seven years of being the Boss, Hank Morgan has modernized Arthur's England. The transformation is complete, and the country is happy and prosperous. Changing the form of things has been easy, but changing people's hearts and minds is not. When the Church issues its interdict against the new civilization and joins with Arthur and the nobles to wrest authority from Hank's regime, the people slavishly follow. Hank could not educate the superstition out of the people, and his civilization is dead. Only Clarence and fifty-two boys remain loyal to him. Against an imminent attack by twenty-five thousand knights they barricade themselves behind mined fields, electrified cables, and floodable ditches. When the knights attack they are blown up, electrocuted, drowned, and machine-gunned. The fifty-four defenders are trapped inside a ring of twenty-five thousand stinking bodies. Merlin in the guise of an old woman puts Hank to sleep and sends him back to his own time and place.

Because of its unevenness of tone and its lack of control over its themes, *A Connecticut Yankee in King Arthur's Court* is an artistic failure; nevertheless, it is a significant document, partly by virtue of that lack of control. In assessing the values of his own society and in exploring the limits and capacities of human nature, Mark Twain raised questions that troubled his imagination and may worthily trouble the reader's. It is, moreover, a pioneering work of science fiction, and in it a number of problematical themes and approaches that have reappeared countless times in later fiction can be discovered. One is of the scientific conditioning of human thought and behavior; the Man-Factories where the Boss sends likely Britons for rehabilitation are designed to do precisely that. Another is of the transcendent dictator whose single mind contains the plan for a people's development and whose single will enforces that plan. The contortions of the author's spirit as he put himself imaginatively into that position dramatize its unworkability. Of course, the idea of time travel itself has become a science fiction staple, with this novel as a prime example. Perhaps L. Sprague de Camp's *Lest Darkness Fall* (1941) is its most obvious descendant. But the notion of the impact of one age's technology on that of another has been touched upon again and again. After all, at its very center, what is science fiction but the encounter between the present, the past, and the future?

Sherwood Cummings

Sources for Further Study

Criticism:

Allen, Gerald. "Mark Twain's Yankee," in *New England Quarterly*. XXXIX (December, 1966), pp. 435-446. Allen's overview of this Twain novel places most of its emphasis on the characterization of the Yankee.

Bellamy, Gladys Carmen. *Mark Twain as a Literary Artist*. Norman: University of Oklahoma Press, 1950, pp. 311-316. Bellamy delineates the techniques of characterization, symbolism and narration that interact in Twain's novel.

Foner, Philip S. *Mark Twain: Social Critic*. New York: International Publishers, 1958, pp. 103-115. The social commentary of a Connecticut Yankee is analyzed by Foner in this lengthy treatment of the author's social thought.

Smith, Henry Nash. *Mark Twain's Fable of Progress: Political and Economic Ideas in* A Connecticut Yankee. New Brunswick, N.J.: Rutgers University Press, 1964. Smith describes *A Connecticut Yankee in King Arthur's Court*'s viability as a vehicle for the author's social thought.

Williams, James D. "The Use of History in Mark Twain's *A Connecticut Yankee*," in *PMLA*. LXXX (March, 1965), pp. 102-110. Williams analyzes the author's use of factual source material in his novel.

THE CORNELIUS CHRONICLES

Author: Michael Moorcock (1939-   )
First book publication: 1978
Type of work: Tetralogy
Time: The twentieth century
Locale: Varied

The adventures of a sometime assassin, would-be messiah, and enigmatic antihero attempting to secure his identity against the entropic alienating forces of the contemporary Zeitgeist

Principal characters:
JERRY CORNELIUS
CATHERINE CORNELIUS, his beloved sister
FRANK CORNELIUS, his brother and archenemy
MRS. CORNELIUS, his mother
MISS BRUNNER, a female authority-figure
BISHOP BEESLEY, an egregious adversary
UNA PERSSON, an adventuress

Michael Moorcock began to work with the character of Jerry Cornelius in 1965, when the "phases" of *The Final Programme* began to appear in *New Worlds*; the book was eventually published in 1968. The other three volumes making up the tetralogy proper are *A Cure for Cancer* (1971), *The English Assassin* (1972), and *The Condition of Muzak* (1977). Over this thirteen-year period, however, the career of Jerry Cornelius was also elaborated in numerous short stories by Moorcock (collected as *The Lives and Times of Jerry Cornelius*, 1976) and other writers who "borrowed" the character. A further adjunct to the series is *The Adventures of Una Persson and Catherine Cornelius in the Twentieth Century* (1976); in addition, the connections of the work spread out in all directions through Moorcock's entire canon. *The Chinese Agent* (1970) is a spy story featuring one Jerry Cornell, while the hero of the "Dancers at the End of Time" series is Jherek Carnelian, and there are also points of contact between the Cornelius novels and the mock scientific romances featuring Captain Bastable.

In each volume of the tetralogy there is a party with a guest list which inevitably includes strays from other Moorcock novels (and also from Moorcock's social environment). In a sense, all Moorcock's heroes can be seen as analogues of one another, and Jerry Cornelius himself concentrates this ubiquity into his own character and his narrative matrix. The world in which he operates is confined to the twentieth century, but it is a protean environment including all of its conceivable alternatives.

The first two phases of *The Final Programme* begin by transfiguring the events of the first two stories of Elric of Melniboné, "The Dreaming City" and "While the Gods Laugh" — Moorcock's first sales to *Science Fantasy*. They thus constitute both a pastiche and a kind of ironic commentary on heroic fantasy, retaining the structure of the narrative but forcing the environment through a metamorphosis that converts it into a rather bizarre mock-contemporary scenario. Once liberated, however, this metamorphic hero and his rather uncertain environment became a valuable tool which Moorcock put to prolific use in satirical black comedy and in the expression of the particular *angst* which seemed appropriate to the spirit of the late 1960's.

The world of heroic fantasy (the genre is remarkably consistent in its apparatus) is perennially haunted by supernatural menace, its heroes laboring under the threat of evil magic and horrible destruction. Moorcock's version of the milieu, as incarnated in the Elric books, is in many ways the most extreme, with the hero suffering under a fateful curse, in painful relationship with the sword that assures him heroic status and with his dead sister. He is threatened not simply by wizards but by an impending Chaos which might claim the whole of creation. His position in the conflict between Order and Chaos is decidedly ambiguous (as becomes clear in *Stormbringer*). This basic structure of relationships is almost wholly retained and remains fundamental to the whole Cornelius tetralogy.

Jerry Cornelius is, indeed, under a curious kind of curse, the main feature of which is his love for his sister. He is continually frustrated in his goals; and he is threatened by the forces of chaos. His situation is always ambiguous — he never knows quite what role he is scheduled to play, though he is ready enough to try any one which comes along.

The third phase of *The Final Programme*, in which Jerry first assumes independence, takes him rapidly on to a suitably ambivalent triumph with apocalyptic implications. The vampiric Miss Brunner, who has a nasty habit of absorbing minor characters in order to maintain her energy reserves, builds the computer that will come up with the final equation (embodying, among other things, the unified field theory left over from an earlier part of Jerry's career, abandoned when he put away childish things). Jerry, too, has the vampiric ability to feed on the energy of others (a residue of the sword Stormbringer's role in the Elric stories), and when the computer reaches the climax of its project, he and Miss Brunner absorb each other to emerge as the hermaphrodite Cornelius Brunner, messiah of the Age of Science, who sets off pied piper-fashion to lead the population of Europe on a merry dance before drowning them all in the sea.

In *A Cure for Cancer* a negative image of Jerry (black with white hair) begins a quest to recover and redeem the body of his dead sister with the aid of a machine which (he hopes) can take temporary control over entropy. Others are also after the machine — notably his brother Frank, who was shooting it out with Jerry when Catherine was killed in the first place, and who is now adviser to the American military presence in Britain, helping to organize the apocalypse. Another dangerous adversary introduced here is the sweet-toothed Bishop Beesley, who steals all the "transmog" patients from Jerry's Sunnydale Reclamation Centre. In the end, Jerry triumphs again as he revives Catherine for a few brief hours of life — but his victory is, as always, transient.

In *The English Assassin* the images of war and destruction become much more prolific, while the ghosts of yesterday's tomorrows float through the plot in the form of airships and steam yachts, carrying the characters in search of the worlds to which they belong, but failing to find them because such worlds have been aborted out of the twentieth century imagination, leaving nothing but a series of alternative apocalypses. Jerry himself is washed up near Tintagel in his coffin, where others discover him and begin to shuttle him back and forth, periodically mislaying him because of their preoccupation with their own affairs. When he turns up at the inevitable party it is to play the part of the specter at the feast, dismissing the guests in peremptory fashion. In the climactic scene, Catherine, digging in search of a cat trapped by a collapsed sandcastle, finds the coffin yet again, with the prematurely buried Jerry completely insane. She faints, and when she recovers, it is to find him metamorphosed yet again, and dressed as Pierrot: an image that provides the central motif of *The Condition of Muzak*.

The dominant mood of *The Final Programme* is a kind of intoxicated enthusiasm. That of *A Cure for Cancer* is more frantic and less assured, while *The English Assassin* is dark and violent. *The Condition of Muzak* retains some of the darkness, but the violence is eroded and the capstone of the tetralogy — which does much to bring the whole into a unity — is bleakly nostalgic and even sentimental. The key image throughout is that of the harlequinade, in which Jerry is in the process of relinquishing the quasiheroic role of Harlequin for that of the sad clown Pierrot. In the traditional harlequinade, Pierrot loves Columbine, but it is Harlequin who wins her; in losing his pretensions to the role of Harlequin, Jerry also seems to be relinquishing his claim to Catherine, his Columbine. The role of Harlequin is assumed by Catherine's other lover, the actress, singer, and revolutionary adventuress Una Persson. In the end, however, a kind of accommodation is reached as Harlequin makes a gallant *beau geste* and offers Columbine to Pierrot. The happy ending is, of course, only a passing moment which must give way again to the march of time and the taxation of entropy.

The new Jerry Cornelius who emerges in *A Condition of Muzak* while his analogues are going through their paces is a teenage boy who wants to be a rock musician but is doomed to be one of life's failures. His brother, the archenemy of other incarnations, is here nothing but a petty criminal. His mother, indomitably vulgar and fun-loving in *her* other incarnations, is here simply vulgar (and mortal, too, for her death provides the tragic finale of the dissolving harlequinade). There is a temptation to infer from the depressing mundaneness of this particular sequence that here might be the "real" Jerry Cornelius, while all the others are his fantasy-projections wanderings through a mirror-maze of daydreams, desperately trying to avoid the pressures of the real world which brutally expose their shallowness and vanity.

It must be remembered, though, that this Jerry Cornelius, too, is a fiction — a character created by a writer, no more real than Elric of Melniboné for being a more apt caricature of life. This is the least decorative of all the avatars of Cornelius that turn up in the process of endless repetition; he closes the series not because he is real but because he is the essential counterpoint to the Elric-analogue with which the series began. This final Jerry Cornelius comprises, in a sense, a commentary on fictional heroes and the process by which readers "identify" with them. He is the ghost of the escapist who delights in donning the mantle of the English Assassin, the King of London, or the Messiah of the Age of Science.

It seems that Jerry Cornelius began his carrer as a kind of joke, a distorting mirror by which to reflect back the gaudy fantasies of sword-and-sorcery fiction into the real world. What came out of this caricature, however, was a new imaginative milieu which could be used for the construction of a mythical twentieth century: the kind of world implied by the newspaper articles and advertisements which comprise the inserts and chapter-headings of the later volumes of the tetralogy. Elric, the catalyst that brought the real world into confrontation with the world of Jerry Cornelius, fades away, remaining in the series only as a sulky party guest no one ever talks to. The science fiction apparatus of the series wanes also as it progresses; Jerry's role of Messiah of the Age of Science is discarded along with his unified field theory. The entropy machine is not seen again after working its small miracle at the end of *A Cure for Cancer*. Even Jerry's fancy weapons — the vibrogun which shakes people apart and the needlegun which he fires at Frank — are discarded in *The Condition of Muzak*. Only the notion of alternativity remains — the multitude of possible worlds and possible roles — vital, for this notion is what serves continually to emphasize that there can be no real and permanent resolution of schemes and strategies, real or imaginary, where entropy reigns.

The title of the final volume of the tetralogy is a play on words echoing Walter Pater's statement that "all art constantly aspires towards the condition of music." Muzak is "wallpaper music," intended to bring about subtle changes of mood subliminally. It is geared to be as unobtrusive as possible, so that it appears to the casual ear to be virtually formless and without significant content, though in fact it is not.

The enigmatic quality of the Jerry Cornelius canon has much to do with the attempt to initiate a response, as it were, subliminally. It has had that effect. The science fiction scene is changed because of Moorcock's passage through it, and the wider world of English letters has welcomed his impact: *The Condition of Muzak* won the 1977 *Guardian* Fiction Prize.

Brian Stableford

Sources for Further Study

Criticism:

"An Interview with Michael Moorcock," in *Eildon Tree: A Journal of Fantasy*. I (1976), pp. 9-14. In this interview Moorcock discusses *The Cornelius Chronicles* in relation to his other works.

Willett, Ralph. "Moorcock's Achievement and Promise in the Jerry Cornelius Books," in *Science-Fiction Studies*. III (1976), pp. 75-76. Willett gives a brief summary of the importance of *The Cornelius Chronicles*, citing Moorcock as one of the best science fiction writers of our time.

Reviews:

The Final Programme:

Analog. LXXXIV, February, 1970, p. 166.

Books and Bookmen. XVI, June, 1971, pp. 44-46.

Magazine of Fantasy and Science Fiction. XXXV, December, 1968, pp. 19-20.

New Worlds. CLXXV, December, 1968, pp. 58-60 and CXCVII, January, 1970, p. 32.

Speculation. III, May, 1970, pp. 23-26.

COSMICOMICS

Author: Italo Calvino (1923-   )
First book publication: 1965
English translation: 1968
Type of work: Short stories

Twelve stories employing the imaginative vistas revealed by cosmological theory and palaeontology as a background for humorous fables and surreal fantasies

The storyteller who narrates these bizarre tales is one Qfwfq, a ubiquitous personality who has been around since the time before the Big Bang which started the universe expanding. The entire cosmos throughout its history has been his playground, and that is exactly how he has used it. He has an extensive family and has enjoyed the companionship of many acquaintances in playing his games with the fabric of the universe and experiencing the lifestyles made available by the evolutionary schema. Thanks to the scope of his career he is in a position to reflect — usually with nostalgia — upon events barely imaginable to mere humans in such a way as to reduce their awesomeness to amiable triviality. Qfwfq connects and interweaves the incomprehensible with the commonplace, thus providing new perspectives within a curious theater of the absurd whose main features are eccentric humor and a unique quality of bathos.

Italo Calvino is one of the great contemporary writers of comedy. There is a satirical tone which runs through all of his work without ever becoming sharp or aggressive, always softened by the kind of sympathy for ordinary people in their relationships and endeavors that is essential to the best comedy. He is capable of infusing descriptions of the most absurd situations with genuine warmth; this has always been his chief stock-in-trade. Who else but Calvino could write a chivalric romance about an empty suit of armor, animated by a helpless passion for the legendary Bradamante, fighting for Charlemagne, as he did in *The Non-Existent Knight*? And who else could have produced a stirring commentary on Enlightenment humanism and human pride *via* the character of an Italian nobleman sworn never to let his feet touch the ground, as Calvino did in *The Baron in the Trees*? The ambition of the vignettes in *Cosmicomics* outstrips by far such modest ventures as these, for here the author seeks to delve into the lore of twentieth century science — the modern mythology — in search of opportunities for whimsical confrontation between the human and the abstract or the abstruse.

Inevitably, the human viewpoint which he chooses for these confrontations is a childlike one, deliberately and perfectly naïve. The narrative allows this naïveté because events are filtered through the sieve of a long memory; they retain all of the intrepid matter-of-factness that characterizes Lewis Carroll's Alice in *her* confrontations with the wonderful and the irrational. To Qfwfq nothing is astonishing, and even the things which surprised him at the time with their newness and inspired him to invent glorious new games can now be taken very much for granted as he looks back across the aeons.

Each story in the collection is headed by a sentence quoted or paraphrased from a textbook citing some strange fact about conditions on Earth or in the cosmos as a whole as they were in the distant past. "The Distance of the Moon" is elaborated from a statement that there was a time when the Earth and the Moon were very close together. Calvino imagines the neighbor worlds almost touching, so that Qfwfq and his friends may leap from one to the other, finding great pleasure in the moment of *bouleversement*, and becoming intoxicated while in the grip of the moon because of its lighter gravity. Qfwfq tells of how the intoxication and its after-effects continued for a time after the return to Earth, and what a loss it was when the drifting apart of Earth and Moon made the game impractical at last.

"At Daybreak" finds Qfwfq and his friends cavorting while the solar system condenses, rejoicing in the new opportunities given to them by the emergence of the perfect modeling-clay: solid matter. Even as the Earth consolidates from the fluid cloud and the sun ignites, the old folks are shaking their heads and saying that it is the end of everything, but to the young Qfwfq it is the beginning.

"A Sign in Space" is about events following Qfwfq's scoring of the substance of space in order to time the rotation of the galaxy. When he becomes involved in a competition with a mysterious eraser of signs who cancels his mark, Qfwfq retaliates by the prolific manufacture of "fake signs" which trick his adversary into following an elaborate trail across the void.

"All at One Point" deals with the social relations and vicissitudes of life in the world before the Big Bang. At that time space was unextended and all persons and places were coexistent at a single point; space was generated as the concept itself emerged from Mrs. $Ph(i)Nk_0$'s spontaneous generosity.

"Without Colours" concerns the state of the world before the advent of the electromagnetic conditions which made color-perception possible, and contrasts Qfwfq's delight in the new world with the anguish of Ayl, whose idea of beauty is irrevocably tied to shades of grey.

"Games Without End" develops a fantasy based on the steady state theory of the universe, in which Qfwfq and a friend play marbles with hydrogen atoms and become involved in intricate duplicity as they try to take unfair advantage of each other.

Each of these first six stories deals with Qfwfq's personality in its earliest phases, during which it resembles that of a very small boy. The latter stories, however, allow the viewpoint to mature a little into later childhood and adolescence. This development is linked to the evolution of life within the universe, and it is an older Qfwfq who is embodied in various creatures from prehistory or who is disturbed by communications from the inhabitants of distant galaxies. This shift toward maturity allows the later stories in the collection a little more subtlety and sensitivity at the cost of their innocent playfulness.

In "The Aquatic Uncle," Qfwfq is one of the earliest vertebrate invaders of the land and is courting the delightful Lll. He is embarrassed by his uncle N'ba N'ga, a stick-in-the-mud coelacanth who believes that land is no place for living beings, with its harsh environments (so unlike those of deep, still water) and its crazy pace of change. It is a chastening experience when Lll, entranced by N'ba N'ga's calm and peaceful philosophy of life, decides to revert to fishy existence, but Qfwfq himself is still a determined progressive and overcomes his sense of loss.

"How Much Shall We Bet?" deals with the question of predetermination, as Calvino wonders how much of the Earth's future was already contained within the gas cloud from which the solar system condensed, ready to proceed as an endless chain of inevitable cause-and-effect. Qfwfq, with the gift of foresight on his side, begins betting with Dean (k)yK at the very beginning, his predictions getting ever more ambitious and detailed as his confidence increases and his winning streak extends. There comes a time, however, when uncertainty sets in, and the wayward actions of human beings in history begin to upset his predictions one by one. The two compulsive gamblers end up hazarding guesses on the Wall Street numbers game and the results of horse races, and there is finally no more prophetic power left in Qfwfq's expectations than in those of any other gambler.

"The Dinosaurs" tells the rather poignant story of Qfwfq's career as the last of the dinosaurs, living unrecognized among pantotheria who believe his kind to be long extinct but who use "dinosaur" as a kind of bogeyman concept. As years go by Qfwfq sees the legend of the terrible dinosaurs gradually change as it loses its power to inspire fear and becomes instead a nostalgic symbol of the dead past.

"The Form of Space" and "The Light Years" return to cosmological visions. The first describes Qfwfq's puzzled exploration of the convoluted geometry of the Einsteinian universe. "The Light Years" describes events following Qfwfq's observation of a distant galaxy which has hoisted a sign saying *I Saw You* which, he deduces, relates to a slight indiscretion committed two hundred million years before.

The final story, "The Spiral," is set on Earth and attempts to imagine the strange sensory world of a mollusk and the inspiration that lies behind the one and only molluskan work of art: the spiral shell. This last story provides one of the few ready comparisons we are likely to find between Qfwfq's adventures and other exercises in speculative literature, for there is an echo here of Haldane's classic evocation of the world-view of the barnacle in "Possible Worlds."

There is no question but that all these stories are ridiculous. The very endeavor on which Calvino has embarked is patently absurd. Thus, the reader coming to the collection for the first time may well find the material so alien as to be almost incomprehensible. However, there is in these vignettes much to be appreciated, and even if they constitute no more than a sophisticated literary joke they are enjoyable once one has become acclimatized to them.

Science fiction traces its literary philosophy back to that of H. G. Wells, who believed that one striking innovation per story was quite sufficient, and that a maximum of one daring hypothesis should be developed as realistically as possible, so as not to disturb the expectations of the reader too much. Wells's contemporary in France, Alfred Jarry, proposed an alternative philosophy which has never thrived to the same extent but which has never lacked at least one or two proponents in any period of time. Jarry advocated casting off all the shackles of realism; indulging in prolific invention and ambitious imagination; and using absurdity to assault and hopefully break down the walls confining the imaginative vision of the audience. Calvino is the contemporary writer who comes closest to Jarry's prospectus, and Qfwfq's one significant literary ancestor is Jarry's "pataphysician" Dr. Faustroll, who also undertook adventures in freakish perspective inspired by contemporary scientific works. For lack of a Jarryesque tradition, however, few science fiction readers are likely to be able to adapt quickly to *Cosmicomics,* and most would probably profit from an easier introduction *via* Calvino's more conventional works.

Because the stories in *Cosmicomics* are only brief and playful adventures among ideas, they do not have as much to offer the reader as the Calvino works with more directly human interest; but adventures among ideas still serve a purpose. In those stories which deal with life rather than with mere existence — "The Aquatic Uncle," "The Dinosaurs," and "The Spiral" — there is an extra dimension which brings them close to fable, if not to allegory. These are the most powerful and memorable stories in a collection possessed of a vitality which will test the versatility of any reader's imagination.

Brian Stableford

Sources for Further Study

Criticism:

Woodhouse, J. R. "Italo Calvino and the Rediscovery of Geare," in *Italian Quarterly*. II (Winter, 1968), pp. 66-76. Woodhouse analyzes Calvino's work as having blended contemporary issues with the traditional "fairy tale."

Reviews:

Best Sellers. XXVIII, August 15, 1968, p. 205.

Book World. August 11, 1968, p. 4.

Christian Science Monitor. August 29, 1968, p. 11.

Library Journal. XLIII, November 15, 1968, p. 4306.

New Republic. CLIII, November 2, 1968, p. 34.

New York Review of Books. XI, November 21, 1968, p. 22.

New York Times Book Revoew. August 25, 1968, p. 4.

CRYPTOZOIC!

Author: Brian W. Aldiss (1925-   )
First book publication: 1967
Type of work: Novel
Time: 2093, with sections set in the Cryptozoic, Devonian, and Jurassic periods of
    Earth's prehistory, and in 1851 and 1930
Locale: England

A farcical account of how Eddie Bush, a failed artist, is drafted by England's military regime to assassinate Dr. Norman Silverstone, whose theories about time travel threaten accepted conventions

> *Principal characters:*
> EDDIE BUSH, a failed artist
> JAMES BUSH, his father; an unemployed dentist
> ANN, a former tersher, briefly Eddie's lover
> DR. NORMAN SILVERSTONE, also called Stein, a time travel theoretician
> WYGELIA SAY, also called The Dark Woman, a time traveler from the future; Eddie's protector
> AMY,
> HERBERT, and
> JOAN BUSH, a coal mining family of 1930

This is a disturbing novel. It is also a complex, memorable experience, and seems more interesting with each rereading. It is impossible to come to terms with it in any simple way. Even the title of the book has been subject to confusion, the author himself preferring *Cryptozoic!*, while the original English title was *An Age* (with a hint of mystery and grandeur worthy of the book's final chapters).

On one level *Cryptozoic!* is "about" its main character, Eddie Bush. However, it is also "about" its Big Idea: the notion that time runs in the opposite direction from the way we perceive it. This idea gives rise to many other inventions, including the mysterious (even occult) method of time travel used by Eddie Bush and the other characters. Perhaps Aldiss invented Eddie Bush as the ideal character to exemplify the paradoxes of his main idea and then Eddie Bush took over the novel. It becomes his story, but the grand sweep of ideas remains. The conflict between these two elements makes *Cryptozoic!* a difficult book to like or understand, but it stays in the memory and its intricacies repay careful analysis.

On the surface, the plot is unpredictable and often farcical. Eddie Bush is introduced in the Devonian era of Earth's prehistory. He is an expert mind traveler (that is, a time traveler who uses drugs to stimulate propulsion rather than relying on the traditional time machine) and has spent two years in the distant past trying to find inspiration for his work as an artist. He has failed, but he relishes the silent, odorless isolation (for time traveler and landscape barely affect each other).

The book begins when Eddie is forced into action. He meets a "tersher" gang, a bikie group, 2093 style, raiding the Devonian for thrills, and he takes up with one of their girls, Ann. Since this irritates the gang, Eddie "minds" to the Jurassic age, hoping to take refuge at a ghostly inn, the Amniote Egg. However, he soon finds himself involved in a fight with the mysterious mind traveler named Stein.

So Eddie flees again, this time to his own period, 2093. A particularly dreary Britain confronts him. Most people have become addicted to mind travel (when they can afford it) or have been impoverished by the whole society's commitment to the mind-travel experience. English political structures have deteriorated and a military dictatorship now rules England. James Bush, Eddie's father is a failed dentist, making do in a broken-down house, and their meeting is awkward. Eddie is forty-five years old but retains almost infantile emotional links with his parents. His father of seventy-three relies on religion and whiskey for comfort, and has little understanding of his son's artistic pretensions. Both of them have been dominated by Mrs. Elizabeth Lavinia Bush, who has died during Eddie's recent excursion into the past.

Farce and lyricism mingle in *Cryptozoic!* in a vigorous way not found in Aldiss' other novels. For Eddie Bush is a farcical character: a typically "blocked" artist, forever brooding, obsessed with his mother and events from his childhood, afraid of women, inept, innocent, and uncertain in every way. He wildly overreacts to most situations, however, hoping to find solutions to problems through chance and blind faith. His father is an even more typical self-denigrating, self-denying character. The family situation has a structure like that in a textbook version of Freud: Eddie and his father act out their roles in a way that is agonizing to them and funny to the reader.

Hearing the news of his mother's death brings on a bout of wild grief, and Eddie feels that he will never have a chance to bridge the gap he feels has existed between them. Unfortunately, there is not much time for grief. Eddie's father soon learns that there has been a change of government. The new ruler is Gleason, and he has changed the structure of the Wenlock Institute, which is the organization controlling mind travel. Soldiers from the new regime take Eddie away, and it seems likely that he will be punished for over-staying his journey to the Devonian by a year. Instead, a worse fate awaits him. Aldiss' gifts for farce and satire are strikingly shown in the hilarious pages devoted to Eddie's training for a military role in the New Britain.

One of the reasons *Cryptozoic!* can be a confusing book is that Eddie is easily confused. He discovers that he is being trained to assassinate a man he first met in the Jurassic. The man he knew as "Stein" is really Dr. Norman Silverstone, a theoretician whose ideas about mind travel, challenge those of Wenlock, its discoverer, and hence those of the regime. Eddie has no desire to aid the Gleason regime, but he sets off on the assignment because he has no other choice. Should he fail, Gleason's agents would certainly seek out both

Silverstone and him and kill them. But does Silverstone have his own agents, who will in turn try to kill Bush? Eddie is not afraid to admit his cowardice in such matters.

When he "surfaces" from "riding the Undermind" (the theoretical medium of time travel) he finds that he has accomplished what has always been considered impossible: he has traveled to recent human history. Previous travelers have found it easy to slip into the far past, but no one has reached closer to the "present time" than the Bronze Age. (That record holder was Eddie himself.) He finds himself in the little English town of Breedale in 1930, at the beginning of a prolonged miners' strike. Since he cannot make himself visible or tangible to these people, and cannot hear them, he learns about their life by observing one family very closely.

The chapter called "In Another Garden," which deals with Bush's stay in Breedale, is one of Aldiss' finest pieces of writing and could well stand on its own as a short story. But here Aldiss is likely to irritate readers by a change of style. Now Eddie has no opportunities for wild and ineffective action; he must be a watcher only. So he returns to his artist's role. The family he watches are called Bush as well. The prolonged strike affects them gradually. Eventually, Amy Bush is both pregnant and penniless, while her husband, Herbert, stays away from the house as much as possible. Joan, their daughter, tries to keep the household together. One day, Eddie watches in horror as Amy and Herbert have a fight. Herbert knocks Amy to the floor and strides away. Eddie rushes around the village, looking for the children. But they are busy with their own affairs and of course Eddie cannot signal to them. He returns to the house, just as Herbert walks in, drunk. Amy lies dead, her baby half born.

> "Herbert, no, no!" Bush jumped in front of the window, tapped uselessly on the glass, which felt malleable to him. He waved, he shouted. And before his eyes Herbert Bush cut his throat, drawing the blade from his left ear almost to his right. The next moment, he appeared at the back door, razor still grasped in hand. Blood cascaded over his shirt. He took three steps into the garden, knee high in cow parsley, and collapsed among the creamy heads of the weeds, his body half-covering Bush's phantasmal tent.

To Eddie, this event takes on the importance of a religious conversion. In the first hundred pages of the book, we are continually irritated by Eddie's inability to consider any interests other than his own. His search for happiness and a direction in life relate exclusively to the person he thinks he is. In Breedale, Bush devotes his sympathy and interest to the poverty-stricken family. As both Amy and Herbert die, Bush discovers in himself a horror of his own inability to act. No longer does he relish his detachment from the affairs of other people. Perhaps it is his first genuine experience of love (since his attachment to his parents is a form of corrupt narcissism). Not that there is anything comfortable in Eddie's "conversion." It takes a paranoid form: he decides he must devote his life to some "higher good." He will set off to try to prevent Gleason's agents from murdering Silverstone.

A rapid escape from government gunmen becomes necessary to save Silverstone's life. The four people who are left in the story — Bush, Silverstone, Ann, and the former government agent, Howes — disappear into the Jurassic. They are still in danger, however, and eventually they slide away into the most distant time available to them, the late Cryptozoic, when all the Earth is a jumble of indiscriminately arranged matter, not yet separated into land and ocean. In this depressing retreat, the party takes time for a rest, and Professor Silverstone explains his theory about the nature of time.

At this point in the story, the mood of the writing changes again. Aldiss adopts the role of science fiction prophet and idea man; the characters sit around and listen to a lecture; ideas roll forth in a stream worthy of Olaf Stapledon (although Aldiss' prose is more interesting than that of the dull old master). The drama and humor of the story move from the action to the ideas themselves, which are not always easy to assimilate. Silverstone can say, with the utmost gravity, that time moves in the direction opposite from the way we have always imagined it. But it is left to Ann to say, "Someone's mad around here. What are we all doing in this God-forsaken hole, listening to this crazy. . . . You're trying to tell me I'm sitting here getting *younger* rather than older?"

The Group is joined by the Dark Woman, a misty figure who has followed Bush like a ghost throughout the book, and who materializes to conclude Silverstone's story. What we think of as the future is the past. Where we are heading is into simpler forms, until the Earth dissolves into the Cryptozoic, and eventually the universe declines into one atom. What we call "memory" is actually precognition. After the world learns of Silverstone's theories (or "before" he "forgets" them, as the case may be), people lose their precognitive powers and regain their memories. The Dark Woman's glimpse of the "past" of the human race is magnificent, its lyricism adorning the last pages of the book.

In science fiction, usually the revelation of the Big Idea at the end of the book is a signal for much hope and comfort for all. But Aldiss is not interested in comfortable fiction. He shows that the great dilemma of the human race — those millions of generations "before" 2093 — is the discovery of the true future of Earth's destiny. Bush and his friends stand on a watershed in history, a brief time when people have both memory and "precognition." Our present version of memory came into being during the Stone Age. Man invented time as a defense against incestuous impulses; our real fate is to be "born" from earth or ashes and "die" inside the womb. Silverstone's revelations bring no comfort to anybody — except to Bush. Since his whole aim has been to recover his lost childhood, he gains hope from the prospect of returning to the womb. It is Aldiss' continuing joke that Bush is just the right character to find personal solace in the new ideas, which everybody else will find an intolerable nuisance.

Nor is there any comfort for the reader in the tricky ending of the book. The final scene shows James Bush visiting the Carlfield Advanced Mental Disturbances Institution to visit his son, who, he is told, is suffering from a grave mental illness. We find that all that has happened since Bush learned of his mother's death has happened merely in his imagination. According to Frankland, the head of the institution, Bush "retreated further and further from reality into his own imaginings."

This leaves us in a quandary. We need to read the book again to see what the narrative really is: the story of the workings of Bush's imagination. If this second interpretation is correct, Bush is revealed as a true hero. He keeps placing himself in situations where he hopes to evade the world altogether. However, even in Breedale, his "escape" leads him to his first real understanding of human nature. In the Devonian age, Bush felt that he was finished as an artist. Now we see him creating a new work of art, an alternative reality where he has a place. Much the same happens when he "travels" to the Cryptozoic. Frankland has merely a narrow, textbookish interpretation of Bush's experience: that is, a comfortable escape. Actually, it gives Bush an adequate perspective on human experience and "takes him out of himself" for the first time. Indeed, the book shows that people are more constricted and dehumanized by so-called "real" events than they are by their imaginings. Military regimes and mine owners need people who "face up to reality": that is, knuckle under to despotism. Bush does not knuckle under. His fantasy, if it is such, enables him to make more of the human enterprise than he ever did while mooning around on a Devonian beach trying to create commercially acceptable works of art.

Yet one more interpretation of *Cryptozoic!* is worth considering. Since Aldiss plays all his tricks in this book, it is possible that the final "explanation" is just one more trick. For instance, we do not actually meet Eddie Bush at the Institute; Frankland merely says he is there and plays a tape of his voice. Frankland scoffs that Eddie "believes [Ann] is now watching this institution, and will soon lead an attempt to rescue him." But as James Bush leaves the Institute, "he never noticed the slight-figured girl standing watching under a tree, water dripping from her lank fair hair." Is she waiting for a mad Bush to be let out? Or is she the rescuer, and has Bush's journey to the Cryptozoic and back been "real" all along? Has Bush freed himself into some larger time stream, and so made the antics of military regimes pointless in his life? Such intelligence could never be allowed to escape, or all of England's inhabitants would disappear into the time stream.

Whichever interpretation is preferred, Bush's experiences become one's own, and *Cryptozoic!* is a vigorous and refreshing challenge to common assumptions about people and the nature of time. But it is not a comfortable or reassuring book.

Bruce Gillespie

Sources for Further Study

Reviews:

Amazing Stories. XLII, September, 1968, pp. 138-139.

Analog. LXXXII, October, 1968, pp. 162-163.

Galaxy. XXVII, August, 1968, pp. 155-157.

Kirkus Reviews. XXXV, December 15, 1967, p. 1491.

Magazine of Fantasy and Science Fiction. XXXV, August, 1968, pp. 18-23.

A CRYSTAL AGE

Author: William Henry Hudson (1841-1922)
First book publication: 1887
Type of work: Novel
Time: The unspecified future, at least ten thousand years hence
Locale: An unspecified continent of Earth

A Utopian vision of a society living in complete spiritual rapport with its natural environment

> *Principal characters:*
> SMITH, the narrator, a young Victorian botanist
> THE HOUSE OF THE HARVEST MELODY, the group identity of the
> community of which Smith becomes a resident
> YOLETTA, a young girl of the House
> CHASTEL, the mother of the House
> THE FATHER OF THE HOUSE, never specifically named

A Crystal Age belongs to the school of Victorian Utopian thought which saw a rejection of technology and a return to rural life as the basic criteria for the future peace and salvation of humankind, but the novel is far enough removed in style and form from its contemporaries to be unique among them. That Hudson was aware of his predecessors is shown by his oblique references to Samuel Butler's *Erewhon,* and by certain similarities between his work and *After London* (1884) by fellow naturalist Richard Jefferies; these resemblances are superficial, however, since Hudson's novel arose basically from the author's own vision of the future, independent of contemporary models. Gone are the lengthy argumentative discussions on cultural differences and ideological principles associated with the classic Utopian novel. Instead we are introduced to a radically different society through the agency of Smith, and are led slowly, hesitantly, and sometimes fortuitously through its customs and modes of thought until we are confronted by the incontrovertible alienage of its nature in the final pages. The result is a work of minimal Utopian interest but of considerable importance as a precursor of modern science fiction since the society depicted is more than a mere transference into the future of the author's own culture in a different guise.

Superficially *A Crystal Age* is a tragic love story set in a fairyland of the future. Infused with loving descriptions of the beauties of nature, the novel's visual imagery is reminiscent of the works of the Pre-Raphaelite artists in evoking an atmosphere of calm serenity. However, as Smith tentatively seeks reciprocation of his ardor for Yoletta, one gradually realizes that the peace in which this society lives stems from more than merely the citizens' heightened sense of awareness of one another. A drastic change has occurred in humankind and it is this change that is central to the whole story.

Hudson's vision is a personal one stemming from a nostalgic reflection upon his childhood, during which period he developed an intense interest in nature; his vision is both a naturalist's reverie and an evolutionist's daydream. His imagined society is evocative of an idealized Garden of Eden in which the complexities of civilization have been replaced by a frank simplicity of manner; people live in single dwellings, remote from one another, and pursue a lifestyle akin to rural monasticism.

Smith, who from the commonality of his name and the lack of detail pertaining to his background may be regarded as representative of Victorian society, is introduced in the first few lines of the narrative. Awakened from a deep coma following a cliff fall, he emerges from the debris of the past, his body entwined with rootlets, his memory befogged by the duration of his unconsciousness, to find himself in a land where many changes are evident. New species of flora and aves are abundant, all beautifully depicted by Hudson in their colorful glory; domestic animals have been enhanced with a greater intelligence and nobility of stature and are free from subservience; humankind, too, has altered for the better. Men display greater beauty, grace, and aesthetic sensibility; they have developed new sensory faculties, and are capable of rendering the deepest emotions into vocal harmonies far beyond our own range of tones; and they enjoy a life span at least three times longer than ours.

More importantly, though men's moral and ethical viewpoints are merely the most advanced theories of the late Victorian era put into practice, the religious basis which underlies their system is radically different, being of a more primitive nature. How this disparity has come about is never explicitly stated by Hudson, but is left for the reader to surmise.

Smith first encounters some members of the House of the Harvest Melody by the side of an open grave, significantly enough, and although the only thing he seems to have in common with them is his English language, he is accepted as one with them and is invited into the House, a magnificent edifice of a modern Neoclassic style but of seemingly great antiquity. Gross and uncouth as he feels himself to be in comparison to his lithe and graceful new friends, Smith readily accepts their invitation. He is immediately strongly attracted towards Yoletta, a beautiful young girl vibrant with the joy of life, who is the personification of all that is wondrous in this world.

From an after-dinner reading of a funeral oration and from his initial conversations with the benign patriarch of the House, Smith learns about the origins and religious beliefs of this society. Millennia before, his own society had overreached itself in its attempt to gain absolute knowledge and dominion over nature and had brought about its own destruction through some unspecified catastrophe. This event in the dim past is looked upon as an act of divine retribution, and is remembered only by a few brief passages in theological writings; every trace of the old civilization has long been covered by the dark mold and green forests of the Earth. The descendants of the survivors of the catastrophe were men of humble mind who lived apart and unknown from their fellows; humankind has now grown into a divine maturity, the death and disintegration of the old society having served as a rich humus for the fertilization of the new. Through the slow workings of Nature, the blemishes that once existed in humankind have been erased, and the Earth has been restored so perfectly that it is a resurrection of the Garden of Eden.

The religious system in this new society consists of a few thousand Houses inhabited by a single families of up to fifty members, and governed by a Father and Mother — the two personages closest in attainment to Godhead. Commerce between the Houses is primarily in the form of exchanges of knowledge or awareness. Each member of the Houses must once in their lifetime undertake a ten-year-long pilgrimage to visit other faraway communities; their findings are then recorded in the illuminated manuscript book *The Houses of the World*, a work which, in the House of the Harvest Melody, extends to some seven thousand volumes. The ultimate aim of the pilgrimages is to allow each community to have full knowledge of every other. Since each community lives in close empathy with its environment, it reflects a particular characteristic, derived from its surroundings, which is unique to itself and only one facet of the deity of Nature. Thus, only by knowledge of the singular character of every House can an individual attain a fully developed spiritual awareness.

Accepted by the community and believed to be a pilgrim who has lost his memory, Smith takes up residence in the new society. Laboring in the fields by day and learning his hosts' written language in the evenings under the tutelage of Yoletta, he finds that his ardor for his beautiful teacher is reciprocated by a love that is only sisterly. Although Yoletta is warm and tender, she apparently feels no passion for Smith. When his distress brings only a stern reproach for the irreligiousness of his thoughts from the father of the House, he turns to Chastel, the mother of the House, for solace and sympathy.

Lying infirm in the sepulchral serenity of her room, surrounded by magnificent glass paintings of enchanting landscapes and lifelike statues of the past mothers of the House, Chastel is omniscient regarding all that happens in and around the House; her power to sooth pervades the very air that surrounds the dwelling. Only in this sanctified atmosphere is Smith able to find freedom from the conflict within him, though his love continues to grow. When Chastel's illness takes a turn for the worse, only Smith of all the household has the power to ease her pain through touch, since the love within him is so strong. But the diminishing of Chastel's power leaves Smith in a severe emotional upheaval. Doubting Chastel's assurance that he will attain what he desires, Smith retires to the library to seek answers to his questions.

In a work entitled *Renewal of the Family*, Smith learns that the passion he feels cannot be shared by these beings. In body and mind they are completely unlike him, for only the mother and the father of the House are capable of renewing the species; all others are completely barren. Yoletta can never be his. In the blackest of despair he drinks from a strange bottle in a niche beside him — believing it will make him like the other people — and then reads on to uncover further revelations. When a mother's death is imminent she must choose from her family that female who is closest akin to her in spiritual development, and, through lengthy initiations and ceremonies, must bring her to a state of potential motherhood. As final understanding of Chastel's assurances dawns upon him, Smith feels a growing langour in his limbs, and, as Yoletta comes to bring him to the mother's room, he falls into the unconscious oblivion of death.

Written at a time when the question of which human characteristics determined man's development was widely debated, *A Crystal Age* is more in keeping with the popular sophistries of Benjamin Kidd and other evolutionary theorists than with the science fiction of its day. Originally published anonymously, it met with little positive response, any influence it may have had being overshadowed by the appearance of Edward Bellamy's *Looking Backward* a few months later. It was only twenty years later, when Hudson's reputation as a naturalist had been established and popular taste had swung away from works of reason, that the novel met with any measure of success. By then, however, George Griffith and H. G. Wells had indelibly made their marks on science fiction, so that any influence the revised edition of 1906 may have had is indeterminate. Nevertheless, Hudson's skill and craftsmanship and his ability to evoke vividly a sense of wonder and beauty combine to create a work that will always hold a unique place in the history of science fiction.

John Eggeling

Sources for Further Study

Reviews:

Booklist. XIII, March, 1917, p. 274.

Bookman. XLV, March, 1917, p. 84.

Boston Transcript. February 3, 1917, p. 8.

Nation. CIV, March 22, 1917, p. 340.

New York Times. XXI, December 31, 1916, p. 575.

THE CRYSTAL WORLD

Author: J.G. Ballard (1930-   )
First book publication: 1966
Type of work: Novel
Time: The immediate future
Locale: A remote part of the Cameroon Republic

A symbolic fantasy, with a perfunctory scientific rationale, about the crystalization of a portion of the African jungle and the responses (often rather metaphysical) of various characters to this frightening and beautiful phenomenon

Principal characters:
> DR. EDWARD SANDERS, the forty-year-old assistant director of a leper hospital
> VENTRESS, an insane former architect
> FATHER BALTHUS, an apostate Catholic priest
> LOUISE PERET, a young French journalist
> MAX CLAIR, a middle-aged microbiologist
> SUZANNE CLAIR, wife of Max Clair and mistress to Dr. Sanders
> THORENSEN, a diamond-mine owner
> SERENA VENTRESS, wife of Ventress, living with Thorensen
> CAPTAIN RADEK, a French military doctor
> ARAGON, a French boat owner

The Crystal World is a short novel (less than 50,000 words) which began life as a novella, "Equinox," published in two parts in *New Worlds* in 1964. Although J.G. Ballard expanded the original novella by the addition of two entire chapters (Chapter Three, "Mulatto on the Catwalks" and Chapter Eleven, "The White Hotel") as well as various other passages, the novel still has much of the feel of an extended short story. There are ten principal characters in addition to various spear carriers (although the setting is Africa, all the principal characters are white), but none is developed into the well-rounded and convincingly established figures one expects in a novel. A partial exception to this rule is the protagonist, Dr. Sanders, especially if one regards the other characters as symbolic figures, slivers of Sanders' personality rather than personalities in their own right. The novel is a third-person narrative, told entirely from Sanders' point of view, and apparent authorial interjections can also be taken as Sanders' own musings. The novel is not so much about the social interactions of its various characters as it is about the private psychological odyssey of Sanders, his journey into a dangerous but exhilarating realm peopled by largely emblematic figures.

The story opens with Sanders' arrival at Port Matarre, a depressing "outpost of civilization" reminiscent of scenes in Joseph Conrad's and Graham Greene's fiction. The town is almost deserted and the mood and atmosphere are somber. Everything seems to be divided into lights and darks: the white columns of the arcades contrast with the blackness of the shadows, while Ventress' white suit is balanced by Father Balthus' black soutane. As Sanders remarks, Port Matarre bears a strong resemblance to purgatory.

In the first four chapters the characters are introduced and the scene is set for the metaphysical drama to come. Ballard deploys numerous elements of mystery in much the same manner as a conventional writer of thrillers. Ventress and Father Balthus (who have been Sanders' traveling companions on the ship) both behave strangely; the former becomes involved in a midnight gunfight, and the latter creates a stir in the native market by waving a jeweled cross around his head and complaining that it is "obscene." Sanders meets Louise Peret, an attractive young journalist who has been in Port Matarre for some time, waiting for a transport to take her fifty miles upriver to the diamond-mining town of Mont Royal. Bus services have been discontinued and mysterious military activities in the jungle discourage travelers. Sanders also wishes to reach Mont Royal, where he hopes to find his former mistress Suzanne and her husband Max Clair. Despite his attraction to Suzanne, however, Sanders rapidly enters an affair with Louise. Throughout the novel Suzanne and Louise appear to symbolize opposing urges within Sanders' psyche: the former is identified with the night and disease, while the latter is identified with daylight and vitality.

Eventually Sanders and Louise persuade the boat owner, Aragon, to take them upstream (Aragon is obviously modeled on Charon). Near Mont Royal they are stopped by soldiers, and Sanders is taken in hand by the military doctor, Captain Radek. The latter explains to Sanders that the jungle has been affected by a strange disease which causes all matter, animate as well as inanimate, to crystalize. He allows Sanders to join a party of scientists who are inspecting the phenomenon. As soon as he sees the gorgeous, efflorescing landscape, Sanders is overcome by memories of childhood and fantasies of a timeless paradise. A helicopter crash separates him from Radek and the scientists, and he wanders through the jungle, observing plants and animals, apparently still alive, which have become encased in crystal.

In the jungle, Sanders meets Ventress, who is engaged in a running gun battle with the mine owner, Thorensen, and his two black servants. After various vicissitudes, Sanders makes his way out of the affected zone and at last reaches Max and Suzanne Clair at their small jungle hospital. He discovers that Suzanne has contracted leprosy (despite which he makes love to her at dead of night in a ruined hotel) and that she is strongly attracted to the crystal forest (as, indeed, is Sanders himself). After their lovemaking, Suzanne runs off into the jungle and Sanders follows her. He soon gets lost, and is caught up once more in the violent love triangle of Ventress, Serena Ventress, and Thorensen. Eventually, he also encounters Father Balthus, who is holding a permanent service in his rapidly crystalizing church. Balthus explains that the crystal forest has resolved all his religious doubts; the efflorescing landscape represents the body of Christ. Later, Sanders finds Suzanne leading a parade of lepers through the jungle; all appear to be in an ecstatic state, happy to immolate themselves in the crystal world. Sanders escapes and returns to Port Matarre with Louise Peret. However, the novel closes with his decision to go upriver once more and rejoin Suzanne, Balthus, Ventress, Radek, and the others in the crystaline jungle, embalmed — neither fully dead nor fully alive — for eternity. The suggestion is that the crystalizing phenomenon will shortly embrace the entire world (outbreaks have occurred in Florida and Russia) and perhaps eventually the whole universe.

The plot (particularly the sometimes rather tedious sections involving Ventress and Thorensen) is obviously of minor importance compared to the descriptions of landscape. As in all of Ballard's fiction, landscape completely dominates this novel. The strength of the work lies in the virtuosity with which Ballard describes the crystal world, using a rather ornate language appropriate to the subject matter. There are abundant references to works of art and architecture, types of furniture and jewelry. Above all, Ballard provides numerous brilliant visual set pieces: the crashed helicopter, crystalized into something resembling a fabulous dragon; a jeweled crocodile; Radek, torn from the jungle in a half-crystalized state, staggering bloodily back into the affected zone with a wooden spar across his shoulders; Father Balthus, adopting a cruciform stance as he begins to be crystalized into the nave of his church; the lepers, transformed into a joyful band of harlequins; Thorensen's black henchman dressed in a crocodile skin, fusing into something part man, part beast.

The Crystal World is essentially a mystical novel, a type of literature peculiarly difficult to write in the present day. Ballard's uneasiness — his embarrassment, even — at finding himself dealing with such a theme is pointed up by his heavy use of irony, particularly in the dialogue (none of the characters ever seems to state anything directly). However, the irony does not entirely undercut the mystical quality of the novel; rather, it complements it and makes the work more acceptable to the modern reader.

Although this work is not necessarily his best (*The Drowned World*, or even *High-Rise*, are in some ways stronger), *The Crystal World* certainly has an important place in Ballard's canon. It is the only work in which he has dealt at length with the quasireligious theme of "acceptance," of communion with the universe — although he has touched on this theme in several short stories, notably "The Waiting Grounds" and "The Voices of Time." Ballard's symbolism is consistent from story to story. In fact, all his fiction adds up to one large, interlocking pattern of symbols: imaginative explorations of humankind's past (*The Drowned World*), its future (*The Drought*, *Vermilion Sands*), its present (*Love and Napalm: Export U.S.A.*, *Crash*), and its sense of eternity. *The Crystal World* is concerned with eternity, and with the surrendering of individuality necessary to gain that sense of eternity. While the novel is not an easy work for many science fiction readers to accept, it cannot be ignored for the importance of its theme.

David Pringle

Sources for Further Study

Reviews:

Choice. III, September, 1966, p. 516.

Library Journal. XCI, May 1, 1966, p. 2357.

New Statesman. LXXI, April 15, 1966, p. 545.

New York Times Book Review. May 15, 1966, p. 41.

Times Literary Supplement. April 14, 1966, p. 332.

THE CYBERIAD
(CYBERIADA)

Author: Stanislaw Lem (1921-   )
First book publication: 1965
English translation: 1974
Type of work: Short stories
Time: The indefinite future
Locale: A fairy-tale cosmos

The droll and humorous, usually satirical capers of a pair of friendly rival robot "constructors" who build various machines for inevitably treacherous kings and princes

Principal characters:
TRURL, a robot
KLAPAUCIUS, a rival robot

Early in his career, Stanislaw Lem began creating several different literary worlds characterized by a consistent attitude, a single philosophical viewpoint, and a distinct mode of expression. Thus, Pirx the pilot is an unheroic but courageous astronaut who has various problems to solve, each one more difficult than the previous one; and Ijon Tichy is a cosmic Münchhausen, a narrator of tall tales who goes through outrageously improbable adventures that serve to show the ridiculousness of human institutions, certain science fiction ideas, philosophical doctrines, and even the biological make-up of the human body and its evolution.

Most original and stylized to the point of artificiality, however, are the robotic fairy tales in the "Fables for Robots" (in English in the volume *Mortal Engines*, 1975) and its sequel *The Cyberiad* (*Cyberiada*, 1965). These tales are twice removed from realistic prose, purported as they are to be fables that robots might write for other robots. They presuppose a literary universe in which the robots have finally escaped from the yoke of mankind into the cosmos, and have founded their own communities there. In robot legends, man figures only as a clammy tyrant, a cosmic joke, or a monster; in several of the earlier robot fables and especially in "Prince Ferrix and the Princess Crystal," man is described as a foul and obscene thing, the result of "the general pollution of a certain heavenly body," spawned out of "noxious exhalations and putrid excrescences." Hardly anywhere, not even in Swift, is there a more loathsome description of man's monstrosity than Lem's "paleface."

The early stories are close to traditional fairy tales (including a robotic version of "Sleeping Beauty" in "How Erg the Self-inducting Slew a Paleface"), but in the later *Cyberiad*, Lem has found an original form that he varies with infinite resourcefulness: the cosmic capers of two friendly robot constructors, who offer their services to various kings, and solve intricate engineering problems. These kings, who go by funny names such as Thumbscrew, Atrocitus, Ferocitus, Krool, are invariably incorporations of the principles indicated by their names — cheats and scoundrels trying to cheat the constructors of the rewards of their work, and frequently threatening to rob them of their lives.

As the series progresses, the stories tend to get more complicated, from the bland jokes in "How the World Was Saved," "Trurl's Machine," and "A Good Shellacking" (which is as elegantly plotted as anything in Boccaccio), through "Seven Sallies of Trurl and Klapaucius," "Tale of the Three Storytelling Machines of King Genius" and "Altruizine," to some elaborate later stories in which Lem explores problems such as the amelioration of the world and universal happiness. In the best anti-Utopian and satirical tradition of the *contes philosophiques*, these noble experiments go all wrong; and the more noble the intention was that inspired them, the more cruel is the outcome ("bestowing happiness by force, is found to produce from one to eight hundred times more grief than no interference whatever").

The cosmos of *The Cyberiad* is totally artificial, governed by a stringent literary convention that the reader will find either enchanting or thoroughly belabored and strained. The stories defy any attempt at summarization, there are so many unexpected turns of plot, ironies, and hidden pitfalls, with Lem's imagination taking off in quite unforeseeable directions, that it is always possible to discover, on rereading, something new and worth quoting in them. There is an outrageously mad, utterly whacky and out-of-bounds perspective in these tales that borders on genius. The first sentence in the first Sally of the book illustrates Lem's delightful style:

> When the Universe was not so out of whack as it is today, and all the stars were lined up in their proper places, so you could easily count them from left to right, or top to bottom, and the larger and bluer ones were set apart, and the smaller, yellowing types pushed off to the corners as bodies of a lower grade, when there was not a speck of dust to be found in outer space, nor any nebular debris — in those good old days it was the custom for constructors, once they had received their Diploma of Perpetual Omnipotence with distinction, to sally forth ofttimes and to bring to distant lands the benefit of their expertise.

This quotation gives a good indication of Lem's way with words (and the obstacles his translator, Michael Kandel, has had to surmount), and it pinlights the ultimate message of the book: language and semantics serve merely as magical formulas in this world, while the similarity between words, rhythm, alliteration, and sound are more decisive factors than causal relationships. The universe of *The Cyberiad* is a purely literary one, divorced from the gravity and natural laws of Earth; Lem employs, with great facility, a cybernetic vocabulary (litanies of "input," "output," "feedback," "programing," "black boxes," "ergodic," "stochastic," "matrix," "algorithm," and so on) as well as jokes, wordplay, punning, and verbal fencing. In one story, for example, soldiers forsake "naval operations" for "navel contemplation"; an error in programing changes "great apes" into "gray drapes"; the "lack of a dragon" becomes the "back of a dragon"; and so on. The ultimate reality is the word, and a changed word means a changed world.

Related to the concept of verbal reality is the idea that everything is a code, a message masked by another message. This is thematized in one of the stories, in which the lack of any hidden message is used to engineer the downfall of yet another cruel tyrant. In the first episode of "Tale of the Three Story-Telling Machines of King Genius," the king's distrust of a perfect adviser built by Trurl, and used in turn to cheat its builder of his reward, is fostered by a simple message designed to appear as a guise for a more sinister message: especially sinister because it is in fact entirely innocent, with no hidden meaning — something which no policeman's mind is willing to accept.

There is much nose-thumbing in the stories at human institutions, that are parodied in the exuberant superabundance of the quasimedieval robot fairy and, which in its boundlessness suggests both *The Thousand and One Nights* and the works of Rabelais.

There is also in *The Cyberiad* a touch of *Don Quixote*, one of Lem's favorite books. Lem's heroes are not simply all-powerful wizards using the word magic of cybernetic science, they are also comic knights-errant engaged in galactic quests to set the world right and conquer evil. Their schemes often backfire, and seldom are they able to foresee the full consequences of their actions. They are not above human weaknesses, such as vanity, envy, and greed; "I love gold, I just love it," exclaims Trurl in one of the tales. The conditions Trurl dictates to the tyrant, King Krool, are somewhat childish, and at the same time cruel in their disregard for the feelings of others. What they do is at times hardly less atrocious than the deeds of the tyrants they undertake to punish. The whole point of *The Cyberiad* is, of course, that there is really nothing to recommend robotkind over the abused "palefaces"; the robots are not a more refined, nobler version of humanity, but an exaggeration of everything that is vile and contemptible in mankind. In these tales there is nothing of the pathos of so much science fiction that either glorifies feudal states or sentimentalizes robots into a better mankind. The rulers in *The Cyberiad* are cruel, vicious, treacherous, guilty of lying and cheating; their principal passion is killing, torturing, and maiming their poor subjects; and aside from traitors, spies, informers, sycophants, secret police, and soldiers, there are almost no other characters in the stories. *The Cyberiad* provides a mocking mirror of all-too-human fallacies, although there are also some gentler tales, such as "Trurl's Prescription," which in its simplicity of language and charm suggest a Nursery Tale — even though it, too, takes a satiric shot at bureaucracy.

Everybody professes to be against red tape, however — even the bureaucrats themselves; and *The Cyberiad* would not be very important if it did nothing besides poke fun at bureaucracies. But Lem's stories operate on several levels. On the one hand, there is the farcical, glittering, punning surface, in which the author gives free reign to his fancy. There is knockabout comedy and wild hyperbole which reaches absurdly funny heights; there is hilarious action resulting in endless chases. On the other hand, there is some serious thought beneath the comic surfaces. "The Dragons of Probability," for example, under the guise of a dragon hunt, contains in jocular form so much solid scientific theory about the laws of probability and the properties of subatomic particles, that scientists have applauded it. The Sixth Sally, "How Trurl and Klapaucius Created a Demon of the Second Kind to Defeat the Pirate Pugg," offers an analogy to Maxwell's thermodynamic demon, based on a theory of the cyberneticist Ross Ashby. The pirate of the tale, who is interested in knowledge more than in valuables, meets with a horrible punishment: he is drowned in a paper ocean of random information, all as true as it is perfectly trivial and useless. His fate reflects one of Lem's major concerns — that civilization may suffer a similar destiny when there is too much information for the valuable to be separated from the worthless.

Another strikingly original story is "The Trap of Gargantius," in which the military way of thinking is shown to be the lowest form of intelligence, for "the cosmos as a whole is totally civilian." In the story, a plan is devised to increase the efficiency of armies by plugging the soldiers together so that they act as one. The plan functions only up to a certain point, since, when consciousness has passed a certain level, military problems appear trivial, and the units turn to the contemplation of philosophy.

The Seventh Sally, or "How Trurl's Own Perfection Led to No Good," raises the disturbing ontological question of creation, of what is real and what is mere simulation. Trurl builds for a cruel tyrant a small model world where he can indulge his sadistic fantasies; the question is whether the suffering of the toy beings who inhabit this planet is real or simulated. In the story, the problem is solved for Trurl's conscience when the tiny subjects of the doll-world break out of their box and dispose of their tormentor, who becomes a satellite circling their world. But meanwhile, a philosophical question has been raised which offers a disturbing challenge to the traditional view of the benevolent creator. As Lem's translator Michael Kandel has suggested, the story implies the blasphemous notion that the act of creation is irresponsible, and that to create consciousness, with all the suffering that it necessarily entails, may be the ultimate crime. If this were true, God would be the ultimate criminal.

The Cyberiad is a wholly original and bold attempt to fuse social satire, humor, and scientific thinking with myth and fairy tale, retaining all the charm and eloquence of older fairy tales while simultaneously indulging in clusters of neologisms and invented names. These stories are veritable firework displays of wit, the products of a remarkable imagination; they are consistent in their underlying themes, yet richly varied and informed by the author's conviction, persuasiveness, and intellectual power.

Franz Rottensteiner

Sources for Further Study

Criticism:

Rothfork, John. "Cybernetics and a Humanistic Fiction: Stanislaw Lem's *The Cyberiad*," in *Research Studies*. XLV (1977), pp. 123-133. Rothfork relates Lem's novel to the burgeoning field of cybernetics.

Reviews:

Book World. March 7, 1976, p. 8.

Choice. XI, October, 1974, p. 1128.

Kirkus Reviews. XLI, November 1, 1973, p. 1231.

Library Journal. XCIX, August, 1974, p. 1989.

New York Times Book Review. August 29, 1976, p. 1.

Publisher's Weekly. CCIV, December 10, 1973, p. 31.

Times Literary Supplement. December 5, 1975, p. 1439.

Wilson Library Bulletin. XLIX, September, 1974, p. 38.

DAIMON

Author: Gianni Montanari (1949-   )
First book publication: 1978
Type of work: Novel
Time: The far future
Locale: The small city of Labula

In a city where time repeats itself, the main character tries repeatedly to reach an awareness of his surroundings

> *Principal characters:*
> MASTER JOCKAN, ruler of Labula
> DEVI, his wife
> NAGAL, priest of the god Daimon

In its personal exploration of the various forms within the science fiction and fantasy genre, Gianni Montanari's novel *Daimon* at first glance is strongly reminiscent of such American works as *The Dying Earth* by Jack Vance, *The Deep* by John Crowley, and *Jack of Shadows* by Roger Zelazny. These parallels, however, are misleading, for the basic problem of *Daimon* is one of communication, just as it was in Montanari's previous novels, *Nel segno dell'uomo* and *La sepoltura.*

The city of Labula is a closed universe that was created, in the words of the historian-priest Nagal, by the earth-god Daimon. This deity first created a few races of animals (Alraune, Demeter, Ravane, and Idisie), and later gave rise to men and women to serve and to be served by them. The humans of Labula have no notion of the passing of time; they know only that someday they will be stricken by the Grey Plague and will be conquered by the New Warriors, and in the meantime, they live a Dark Age life, without machines and firearms.

At the beginning of the novel, the former inhabitants of Labula have been slaughtered by the New Warriors, and the new ruler Master Jockan rekindles the pact with the god Daimon. During the sacrifice, he has a glimpse of a man riding on the back of the holy animal, the Alrauna, to which the sacrifice is offered. The priest Nagal strongly denies such a possibility and warns Master Jockan against the dangers of speculating about forbidden items. Some time later, in the country outside Labula, Jockan finds a carved image of an Alrauna, an artifact of past ages which he casts away. The memory of the image lingers with him, however, until, at the end of his allotted time, he is killed by the ruler of the New Warriors, whose face is identical to his own.

The second section of the novel begins like the first: in Labula there is a new Master Jockan, who has no memories of the former one. His wife is a new rejuvenated Devi, and the inhabitants of the city are younger copies of themselves. This time, however, the conflict between Master Jockan and the priest

Nagal is deeper; an odd compulsion leads Jockan to retrieve the carved image his former self threw away; and he starts carving images of his own as a token of devotion to the god Daimon. Although his objective is to find a new way of worshiping the god, he also carves two images of himself: the younger Jockan and the aged one, stricken by the Grey Plague. Soon, however, he and his city are killed by the New Warriors and by a new Master Jockan.

The third Master Jockan begins a new cycle, going farther than his former selves. He speculates about the passing of time, he finds the carved images, and he plans a journey beyond the borders of his known universe. In a final confrontation with Nagal, he kills the priest and a holy Alrauna, and enters the pits beneath the city.

The pits hold the explanation for which he was searching. They are inhabited by a team of scientists who give rise to the new generations of Labulians. Having survived the collapse of the previous civilization, their master has been using Labula as one of many experimenting grounds for the testing of possible societies with which eventually to repopulate the planet. Since Jockan has demonstrated his superiority by discovering the city, the scientists decide to place him in charge so that they can move on to another project in some other faraway, experimental place.

Apart from the ending of the novel, which gives facile answers to all the questions raised during the narrative, *Daimon* is an honest attempt at combining various kinds of novels. The initial presentation of the city of Labula, with its rituals, its holy animals, and its cyclical recurrences, could be termed "heraldic fantasy" (a name used by James Blish in connection with R. A. Lafferty's *Fourth Mansions* that denotes novels in which everything symbolizes something else). However, Montanari avoids the danger inherent in this kind of fiction: the tendency merely to play guessing games with the reader and to write in riddles. The cycle of recurring events might remind one of Jorge Luis Borges' approach to fantasy, which consists of a profound and complex exploration of the simplest ideas and images through such techniques as the circular plot, the mirror plot, and unending combinations of a few basic items. Borges is perhaps the one living writer who has mastered this kind of plot (although one cannot deny the relevance of several stories by Stanislaw Lem and of novels such as Ursula K. Le Guin's *The Dispossessed*), and one cannot blame Montanari for not having pursued it further. However, *Daimon* might have been a far superior novel if Montanari had not revealed everything in the final pages, or even if he had not quoted his secret scientists at such length. The "super-experiment" concept seems more appropriate to the Marvel Comics than to an adult science fantasy.

However, nothing but good can be said of the gradual knowledge that comes to Master Jockan while he is in Labula: unformed memories of his past selves linger with him, and an inner compulsion bids him to proceed further and further down the road to science, notwithstanding the opposition of the priest Nagal. The anticlimax which comes in the final pages should, perhaps, be forgiven by the sensitive reader.

Riccardo Valla

DALLA TERRA ALLE STELLE
(From the Earth to the Stars)

Author: Ulisse Grifoni
First book publication: 1887
Type of work: Novel
Time: 1886
Locale: Florence, some forgotten corner of Africa, and outer space

Long before H. G. Wells and his cavorite, a Florentine creates an antigravitational paint and drives a sort of spaceship towards Mars

Principal characters:
ALBERTO C., a young Florentine man of letters
PROFESSOR LAMA, a middle-aged scientist who assists Alberto
ELISA, the girl Alberto loves
FATHER SECCHI, a Jesuit, an old friend of Professor Lama

Ulisse Grifoni, a pressman and a socialist of the old school, is seldom quoted in biographical works or encyclopedias, and his life and works are scarcely known in Italy. Although he wrote a book on astronomy for technical schools and a sort of Utopian novel now out of print, his minor fame rests upon *Dalla terra alle stelle*, which inconspicuously appeared in 1887.

The story begins with the protagonist, Alberto C., dying; before expiring, he talks with a friend of his wonderful journey into space and gives him a manuscript which relates his adventures. Through this unknown friend we are given the first part of the story in a flashback. Everything starts in Florence in 1886, when Alberto, son of an illustrious but now poor family, finds himself captivated by Elisa, daughter of a low-class family which recently became very rich. Obviously, Alberto is not considered the most desirable suitor by Elisa's parents, and the young man becomes desperate.

Leaving his literary studies at the University, Alberto casually finds in his attic an old trunk inherited from an uncle who had been a chemistry teacher. The young man was looking for something which might raise his position in the eyes of Elisa's parents, and now chemistry experimentation seems to provide such an opportunity. Mixing various substances, he obtains a strange paint which seems to nullify the law of gravity; excited, he thinks that his discovery will bring him great fame. Just then, however, a letter arrives from Elisa telling him that she has decided to obey her parents' will. Alberto desperately decides that the only solution is a bullet through his head. At the last minute, however, his sense of social responsibility (to share his paint with the world) deters him from suicide.

After a short and didactic history of human attempts to fly, from Daedalus to Montgolfier, the narrative continues. Alberto receives another letter informing him that he has just inherited a large fortune from a relative in Bologna. Now that he might renew his courtship and be accepted by Elisa's parents, he is too deeply involved in his dream of flying to pursue the romance; Elisa will have to wait for the moment, since his love for science is now consuming all his energy. In order to put his paint to a good and careful use, Alberto summons Professor Lama, a college teacher of applied mechanics whom he knew at the University, and together they start planning a ship which will take them into space. At this point we are treated to a long and detailed list of computations and measurements; we are given the weight, the length, and the kind of materials to be used in the ship, as well as a miniature handbook of astronomy. During this fifty-page history of astronomy, Alberto and Professor Lama repeatedly touch on the problem of the velocity of light, but never in a very sound way.

At last the two men decide that certain deficiencies in their preparation, concerning astrodynamic problems, require the advice of an expert in the field; so they leave for Rome to meet Father Secchi, a Jesuit astronomer. As a young man with a background of socialist thinking, Alberto suffers from some anti-clerical feelings, but these are alleviated by Father Secchi's obvious enthusiasm for the space project. While Father Secchi works with Professor Lama on some complicated calculations, Alberto gives the reader another short summary of life and the evolution of man on Earth, tinging his account with a very bland socialistic bias.

Next, Alberto and the Professor return to Florence and immediately begin to build the spaceship in a well-known machine-shop. After some interpolated visions of future remedies for the workers' poor job conditions and low wages, and after a touching moment when an emotional Professor Lama shakes hands with a rough worker (who wipes away a tear with the back of his other hand), the spaceship is ready for its first flight. The passengers are Alberto, the Professor, and the French painter, a certain Fouler whose purpose is to immortalize the coming adventures in art. At the last moment, a fourth passenger joins the group — a police deputy who tries to stop what he sees as a suicide plan — but the three spacemen-to-be soon rid themselves of this unwanted guest.

First the cubic ship makes some flights to Africa. At last, everything is ready for the final departure — but the novel ends abruptly at this point with a Note from the author which explains that the following adventures are to be related in a forthcoming book whose title will be *Nelle stelle*. This novel was never published.

Luckily, we do obtain some information on the further adventures of the three travelers thanks to the clues given by Alberto at the beginning of the novel, when he was on his deathbed. Alberto shortly opens his heart to his friend and regrets his bad fortune. The journey to Mars, he says, went very well; they found there alien beings very similar to men but very small in size, almost Lilliputian. After staying some time on the Red Planet and studying Martian society, they decided to bring the incredible news back to Earth; while Professor Lama and the painter Fouler were to stay on Mars, Alberto was to come back with two Martians and some samples of alien artifacts. This journey, however, was not as lucky as the first. The spaceship did not function properly and landed in the sea near the North Pole; it sank, and Alberto alone escaped death. Thus he lost his ship, every evidence of his journey to Mars (the two Martians included), and the last precious supply of the antigravitational paint. Every attempt to find the ship was useless, as was every later attempt to re-create the paint; and the suffering endured during the shipwreck had already undermined Alberto's health.

Thus, a great adventure tale ends in an unsatisfactory and annoying manner. We are left with an amusing and rather encyclopedic novel that titillates our expectations, then fails to provide satisfaction, and with characters who promised to have interesting viewpoints on Martian society but never share their knowledge. On his deathbed, Alberto never reveals any details about the alien way of life; yet, since his opinions (and those of Lama) on many social and cultural aspects of life occupy a good part of the 352 introductory pages, the reader cannot help feeling that Mars also deserved a long and thorough treatment.

Gianni Montanari

DANCERS AT THE END OF TIME

Author: Michael Moorcock (1939-   )
First book publications: An Alien Heat (1972); *The Hollow Lands* (1974); *The End of All Songs* (1976)
Type of work: Novels
Time: The End of Time and 1896
Locale: The Earth

A comic trilogy contrasting the social mores of the End of Time and late Victorian England through the medium of the love affair between Jherek Carnelian and Mrs. Amelia Underwood

> *Principal characters:*
> JHEREK CARNELIAN, the "darling" of the End of Time
> MRS. AMELIA UNDERWOOD, a young matron from Bromley (1896)
> LORD JAGGED OF CANARIA, Jherek's friend and mentor
> THE IRON ORCHID, Jherek's mother
> HAROLD UNDERWOOD, Amelia's husband
> INSPECTOR SPRINGER a Scotland Yard detective
> THE DUKE OF QUEENS,
> MY LADY CARLOTINA,
> MISTRESS CHRISTIA THE EVERLASTING CONCUBINE,
> LORD MONGROVE,
> WERTHER DE GOETHE, and
> LI PAO, Jherek's friends
> CAPTAIN MUBBERS AND THE LAT, space traveling brigands who come to Earth for a little plunder

Michael Moorcock's trilogy, *Dancers at the End of Time*, consists of two plots: the story of the approaching death of the universe as one vast cycle of time draws to a close; and "the story of Jherek Carnelian, who did not know the meaning of morality, and Mrs. Amelia Underwood, who knew everything about it." The two plots are related primarily through the figure of the mysterious Lord Jagged of Canaria. The reader who perseveres through two frivolous yet entertaining volumes will be rewarded in the third when Moorcock tackles the serious point of the novel.

At the beginning of *An Alien Heat*, the reader finds himself at the End of Time, when the human race has "at last ceased to take itself seriously." Considerably reduced in numbers and for all essential purposes immortal, the race has, after millennia of purposeful activity, begun to lose interest in purpose. There is nothing more that needs to be done, so people have turned the vast technology at their command to the creation of extravagant fantasies and the playing of endless inventive games. Aesthetics has become the foundation of human activity, wit and paradox the greatest pleasures, and taste and imagination the ultimate achievements. The inhabitants of the End of Time have thus become, by the standards of earlier ages, utterly decadent, very wasteful, and profoundly amoral. Creeds, ideals, and philosophies which once led to conflicts have ceased to move them; in fact, all of the old emotions have atrophied. "They had rivalry without jealousy, affection without lust, malice without rage, kindness without pity. Their schemes — often grandiose and perverse — were pursued without obsession and left uncompleted without regret." They eat and sleep only for pleasure, not from bodily need. Their power rings, which tap the energies of the abandoned and disintegrating cities, enable them to create and destroy at will, to change their clothing and their dwellings, their landscapes and their climates, their sex, shape, species and color to suit the whim of the moment. They make love affectionately and often publicly whenever and with whomever they choose; taboos against homosexuality, incest, and bestiality have vanished completely. There is no more crime, since there is neither passion nor need; there is no more sin, since there are no commandments. It is an age of godlike innocence, in which pleasure is the only goal, and all things are pleasurable. This is not the kind of society to take anything very seriously; hence, when the main attraction at a party given by the Duke of Queens turns out to be a space traveling alien who tells them that the universe is dying, they are not even interested, let alone alarmed.

They are, however, very much interested in another arrival at the party. In the midst of the alien's warning, a beautiful young woman suddenly appears. From her dress and speech she is apparently a time-traveler from the nineteenth century, though — she makes clear — an unintentional one. She delights Jherek Carnelian, who is the darling of the End of Time and an acknowledged leader of society — an arbiter of taste, a setter of fashions, and a recognized expert on the nineteenth century. He decides he must fall in love with the time-traveler: it would be witty and delightful to reenact with her one of the great love stories of the past — Adolph and Eva, or Alan and Edna. So Jherek contrives to bring Mrs. Amelia Underwood to his home, and there he begins to woo her, a process he expects to complete in a few days at most. But he encounters an unforeseen problems: she is married. Coming from the End of Time, where love and sex are perfectly simple, where no one has permanent claim on anyone else, and where there are no conflicts between desire and duty because there are no constraints upon desire, Jherek is at a loss to understand the concepts of "marriage," "self-denial," "morality," or "duty." Though at the End of Time Mrs. Underwood's husband has been dead for millennia, she refuses to accept that as a justification for behaving as if she were not married, maintaining that some day she might be able to return to her old life with Mr. Underwood. No matter what her feelings for Jherek might become, no matter how remote the possibility of return, she regards her marriage as binding. The rules of her society apply to her regardless of her circumstances.

Jherek does not understand, but he honors her wishes. If he has no notion of duty or morality, he also has no notion of violence, of one person's imposing his will upon another by force, so Jherek shares his house with her on her terms, striving with childlike eagerness and innocence to understand and to please her. At last his charm and his sweetness, combined with the apparent hopelessness of returning to 1896, begin to win over her Victorian moral sensibility, but just as they kiss for the first time, Amelia is snatched away by one of Jherek's friends and "given her dearest wish"; she is returned to her home and husband. Jherek is in a frenzy of anguish at her loss, and bewildered by the anguish, which is a totally new experience for him since neither he nor anyone he knows has ever felt such emotions. The affectation has become real: he has actually come to love Mrs. Underwood.

Thus begins Jherek's quest for his beloved, a quest which carries him back and forth through time: to 1896, where instead of taking Amelia back with him he ends up being hanged as an accomplice to murder (an experience which merely returns him to his own time); a second journey to 1896, during which Amelia joins him, less from free choice than because her husband assumes she is Jherek's mistress and renounces her (to Jherek's innocent delight, as he believes that she is now free to love him); and a journey with Amelia which is supposed to take them to the End of Time but instead lands them in the Paleozoic age, from which they are finally rescued by two members of the Guild of Temporal Adventurers (Owen Bastable and Mrs. Una Persson, familiar figures from other Moorcock novels).

Jherek and Amelia, however, arrive back at the End of Time with their situation still unresolved. Despite her admitted and growing love for Jherek and despite her husband's categorical rejection of her, she still cannot rid herself of the belief that her duty is to return to Harold if she possibly can. Amelia does her best to accept her situation, to settle into society at the End of Time and make a life for herself there, but she is hindered by two things. The first is her relationship with Jherek, which is initially complicated and at last resolved by Harold's sudden arrival at the End of Time. In his own way, Harold helps her understand the finality of her separation from him and her past, and the reality of her love for Jherek, so that she can stay at the End of Time and marry him while Harold returns to 1896. But even when that problem has been settled, Amelia has another far more serious problem. As she explains to Jherek, "I cannot live . . . unless I feel my life is useful." The practical basis of morality, she believes, is that "nothing is worth possessing unless it has been worked for," and at the End of Time *nothing* needs to be worked for — anything one desires can be created by the twist of a power ring. Amelia is caught in a paradoxical dilemma. In Paradise, her life has no purpose, a situation she finds intolerable.

It is at this point, midway through *The End of All Songs*, that Moorcock's serious theme begins to appear. Until now the novel has seemed utterly and magnificently frivolous in language and theme. Moorcock writes in language characterized by overextended and airy wit, painting the End of Time in colors of delight, playing wonderful games with words and history. For instance, when Jherek and the Iron Orchid visit the Duke of Queens' reconstruction of "New York, 1930," the Duke proudly points out "the Empire State Apart-

ments, . . built as the home of New York's greatest king (Kong the Mighty)."
When the Iron Orchid remarks that the buildings are rather close together, the
Duke explains that the feature is deliberate. "The epics of the time made constant reference to the narrowness of the streets, forcing the people to move
crabwise — hence the distinctive 'sidewalk' of New York." Then there is
Lake Billy the Kid, "named after the legendary American explorer, astronaut
and bon vivant, who had been crucified around the year 2000 because it was
discovered that he possessed the hindquarters of a goat." Moorcock also
creates a wonderful running gag in the Lat, Captain Mubbers and his crew of
space brigands, who follow Jherek and Amelia through time to pop up at the
most unlikely moments, exclaiming *"Hrunt!"* or *"Kroofrudi!"* or even
"Ferkit!" and bashing anybody they can reach.

But the first two volumes are as misleading thematically as they are entertaining linguistically. They contrast the End of Time — gay, free, and innocent — with the late Victorian age of Mrs. Underwood — intolerant, repressive, obsessive, hypocritical, cynical, and cruel — to the definite disadvantage
of the Victorian. Even Amelia, who represents much of what is best about the
Victorian age, seems silly for holding onto an outmoded code of behavior,
clinging to her husband out of duty when she is offered Paradise with a man
she loves in a situation where no one could blame her for considering herself
free to marry. Jherek comes off much better than she does — generous, loving, sensitive, and utterly unselfconscious, combining the powers of a god
with the innocence of a child. The readers' sympathies are all with Jherek and
the sanity of his way of life.

By the middle of *The End of All Songs*, the comparison between the Victorian age and the End of Time, seemingly so trite and conventional in its
conclusions, begins suddenly to appear less simplistic and onesided. We
begin to see that Amelia has a significant point. The End of Time is a delightful playground for children, a paradise for the godlike beings who inhabit it,
but it is ultimately a very unsatisfying place for human beings, a place without
meaning or reality in human terms. Since nothing requires any effort and no
life can ever be lost, nothing has very much value. Nothing grows at the End
of Time, neither seeds nor children: the earth is barren. Amelia cries, "What is
love without time, without death?" Jherek replies, "It is love without sadness,
surely," but Amelia counters, "Could it be love without purpose?"

Though it is apparent that Amelia has changed since she first arrived at the
End of Time, Jherek also has changed, perhaps even more profoundly than
she. In the course of his quest for her through time, he encounters a bewilder-
ing variety of experiences completely new to him. He experiences fear, loss,
loneliness, physical pain, hunger, cold, exhaustion, and imprisonment. He
sees age and decay in human faces; he sees death for the first time without the
instant resurrection he is accustomed to in his own time. Having been regarded
all his life only with love, he experiences being viewed with anger, hatred, and

contempt. Most difficult of all, he has to come to terms with Amelia and her complexities of feeling and behavior — her doubts, her contradictions, her inconsistencies. He learns self-doubt, depression, and despair; but he also learns conscience, purpose, dedication, and true love, a kind of ecstasy beside which the lovely pastel feelings of the End of Time seem washed out. In experiencing loss, he learns to value what he had formerly taken for granted. Jherek Carnelian, the child/god from the End of Time, comes to understand the human condition. He has become a man.

And this metamorphosis was precisely Lord Jagged's aim. Lord Jagged, it turns out, does not originate from the End of Time as everyone had thought, but instead is a time-traveler who settled there long before, hoping eventually to work out a plan to save the inhabitants from the destruction of the world and, more important, to help the human race get started in a new cycle of time. His research in time travel leads him up against the so-called Morphail Effect, which dictates that all time travel must go forward into the future, because if someone from the future visits the past he creates so many paradoxes that the past ejects the intruder. Lord Jagged's plan is to send a new Adam and Eve back to the beginning of time, but the pair will have to overcome the Morphail Effect in order to settle permanently in the past. He discovers that he himself seems much less susceptible to the Morphail Effect than most people — that he can travel backward and remain for extended periods of time provided he is careful not to introduce paradoxes and that he establishes a *persona* solidly in the period, to give himself a legitimate reason for being present in the time. (He has, in fact, two such *personae* in the London of 1896, both of which Jherek encounters.) By experimentation, Lord Jagged discovers that his ability to "stick" in the past is less a result of his caution than of his biology — something in his genes. When he realizes that the Iron Orchid has a similar gene pattern, Jagged suggests to her the delicious scheme of creating a baby in the old-fashioned way (more or less, that is, since the baby gestates and is born in an incubator). The result is Jherek. Thus Lord Jagged is not only Jherek's friend and mentor; he is Jherek's father as well.

Having created a son with a double dose of the all-important gene, Lord Jagged then sets about locating a mate for him, an Eve for Jherek's Adam, a woman who also has the "time gene"; and after much long searching and testing he finds Mrs. Amelia Underwood, abducts her from 1896, and brings her to the End of Time, hoping that she and Jherek will fall in love with each other. With their marriage, then, one important part of his plan is fulfilled.

But the final end of time, the destruction of earth, is drawing very near, and Lord Jagged has to move rapidly. Helped by an ancient but sophisticated robot, and calling on a last burst of energy from the dying cities, Lord Jagged establishes a time-loop. The people at the End of Time will live the same seven days over and over throughout eternity, going on exactly and delightfully as they have always done. Lord Jagged will go back to his time traveling, since he is not a man to stay in one place, and once the loop is completed it will be impossible to enter or leave the End of Time; and Jherek and Amelia will not go backward, but *forward* into the Paleozoic age, past the end of time and on around to the beginning again, forever safe from the Morphail Effect. They carry with them the best of their two ages, Amelia supplying the character and the conscience, Jherek supplying the freedom and the joy. Amelia has her purpose in life, and Jherek has his love, and together they will assure their children and their children's children of a very good start for the new human race.

Thus the figure of Lord Jagged of Canaria, in giving the world a paradise, a new Eden, and a son (whose name, *J*erek *C*arnelian, is assuredly no accident), resolves both of the stories. In our end is our beginning, indeed.

Kathleen L. Spencer

Sources for Further Study

Criticism:

"An Interview with Michael Moorcock," in *Eildon Tree: A Journal of Fantasy*. I (1976), pp. 9-14. Moorcock briefly discusses the End of Time novels in the course of this interview about his works.

Reviews:

The Hollow Lands:

Best Sellers. XXXVI, May, 1976, p. 39.

Booklist. LXXII, February 1, 1976, p. 756.

New York Times Book Review. April 25, 1976, p. 46.

Spectator. CCXXXVII, August 21, 1976, p. 23.

DARK UNIVERSE

Author: Daniel F. Galouye (1920-   )
First book publication: 1961
Type of work: Novel
Time: The distant future
Locale: The Earth

Jared Fenton, the young son of the Prime Survivor, dares the taboos of his world, the Lower Level, to search for the nature of Light, and in so doing, destroys the religious systems of his people and learns the true nature of his world

Principal characters:
>   JARED FENTON, a curious young man who questions the nature of his world
>   DELLA ANSELM, Jared's Unification partner and daughter of the Wheel of the Upper Level
>   LEAH, a telepath who appears to Jared in his dreams

Three-hundred pound mutant bats, a race of people who see with infrared, bottomless pits, and eternal darkness — these are the challenges of existence in Jared Fenton's world, created by Daniel F. Galouye for his brilliantly conceived and ingeniously implemented "lost race" novel, *Dark Universe.*

Jared Fenton's Lower Level people, Della Anselm's Upper Level people, and the Zivvers are descendants of "U.S. Survival Complex Number Eleven," one of seventeen underground sanctuaries established by the American government decades earlier to guarantee that humanity would survive the perils of a nuclear war. Such a war came, and the people selected for each complex were sealed off from the poisonous atmosphere of the outside world. Fed by plants that functioned by thermosynthesis rather than photosynthesis and supported by nuclear-powered pumping stations that provided heated water, the people of the various complexes were to survive in their underground habitats until the air of the upper-world purged itself, and they could return to the surface. Things went well in all of the complexes except Number Eleven. There, a few generations after the colony was sealed off, the shift of a minor fault cut off all but a few of the superheated water conduits leading to the group's basic living chamber and completely destroyed the light generating equipment. The people of the complex were forced to retreat deeper into their underground chambers, into areas that had only been partially prepared in case a population overflow occurred while they were sealed off. By retreating, however, the colony left behind its knowledge of the outside world. Gradually, the facts concerning its existence were replaced by superstition, and a mythology was created.

Dark Universe is the story of Jared Fenton's journey from innocence to experience. In the beginning, Jared's world is a rather small compound of caves which are engrossed in absolute darkness. Light is known only as part of the Lower Level people's religion, so life goes on without sight. Compensating for this sensory loss, Jared's people have refined their other senses to a high state of discrimination. In particular, hearing is a well-defined skill. A central echo caster, a huge device for creating sound, lies at the heart of their life in the underground chamber. The sound waves that it sends out permit the Lower Level people to detect not only the presence of things around them but to determine the texture of those things. Clickstones augment their movement about the caves and help them when they travel away from the influence of the echo caster. Held in the hand and struck constantly, they permit the interpretation of surrounding terrain by the differences detected in the echoes they create. Manna plants, fed by hot springs, are the staple of life, though they are occasionally supplemented by game such as salamanders and crayfish. Manna plant fibers are used to make clothes and blankets. Friendly relations are maintained with the Upper Level people, who are exactly like Jared's people, but who maintain separate quarters and political autonomy. Hostile to this spartan existence are the Zivvers, a race of mutants who look like the Upper and Lower Level people but who have developed infrared receptors to help them cope with the constant darkness. Actually, they too are descendants of the original Complex Eleven inhabitants who were cast out at some time in the past because they were different. Another threat to the existence of Jared's people comes in the form of the dreaded *soubat*, a three-hundred pound, mutated bat that hunts them down with sonar.

Memories of the past have combined with the facts of the present to create their religion. Light has become God. Strontium and Cobalt, along with several other terms remaining from the nuclear war, have come to personify the devils. Radiation is Hell, and Paradise is the Original World. Flashlights and other artificial light sources are revered as Holy Bulbs, those vessels in which the Almighty dwelt with Jared's people for a time after He banished them from Paradise. Augmenting this basic dogma are various rituals, symbols, and taboos, such as the Excitation of the Optic Nerve Ritual, the Litany of Light, and the Barrier, which forms one of the boundaries of their world and which no man is permitted to cross for fear that the Almighty will punish him.

The invented world of *Dark Universe* is not only well conceived but thought through in great detail. Moreover, it is implemented with such remarkable precision that Galouye has given it an overpowering sense of richness. Robert Thurston's "Introduction" to the Gregg Press edition of the book singles out two techniques that Galouye uses with great effectiveness to create his world. First are the passages which describe how Jared uses his nonvisual senses to perceive the world and the people about him. Galouye does not stop at creating an impression of what it is to be blind, he actually creates an impression of what it is like to have absolutely no idea of what sight is. At one point, Jared says that he believes in whatever he can hear, taste, smell, or feel, and when he finally does encounter light, he explains it in terms of what he knows. He calls it "a great cone of roaring silence," a "tremendous burst of sound," and a "soundless noise." He describes it in terms of what it is not — "something that wasn't sound or smell or touch."

The second technique is the language of the narrative itself. In writing the story, Galouye has very carefully eliminated all words which imply sight. Idioms like "I see what you mean" and "look forward to the future" become "I hear what you mean" and "listen forward to the future." Moreover, Galouye enhances the credibility of Jared's world by focusing his scenes through the use of carefully chosen, sharp detail. Jared's first impression of Della is an excellent example. It is, of course, sound-oriented.

> Her hair, slicked back from her forehead, had a pleasant sound and gave her face a sleek, delicate tonal balance. Somehow the total impression had much in common with the wistful music she had stroked from the hanging stones. And he fully heard now how desirable she was for Unification.

Another example of this technique occurs when Jared is confronted by Mogan, the Zivver leader, just before he is tested to see if he really is a Zivver. "The curtains parted and Mogan stood in the entrance. His bulky form, silhouetted only by back sounding, coarsely punctured the silence of the shack." A particularly striking example occurs when Jared is trying to get his eyes to focus together.

> At the same time he was aware of a shifting pressure on the muscles of his eyeballs — a tenseness that crossed the bridge of his nose whenever the hand divided, then relaxed again as the parts rejoined. And he found that with concentration he could prevent the confusing and certainly false impression of two members when all his other senses told him there could be only one.

Careful control of Jared's world is essential because the impact of *Dark Universe* depends upon the gradual expansion of his knowledge and understanding. Jared is a naïve young man, a vessel into which knowledge can be poured, and the expansion of his level of perception, his ability to "see" in the sense of "understand," is equivalent to his journey from innocence to experience and from dark to light.

To accomplish this, however, Galouye must create for Jared a means to expand his world. He does this primarily by manipulating the action. Curiosity initially impels Jared to journey beyond the Barrier, and the story begins as if it were to be a quest. His burning ambition is to discover the nature of light. His act, however, is poorly timed, for it occurs just after several hot springs have dried up. Crossing the Barrier is one of his people's severest taboos and it places Jared in a difficult position because it permits his father, the Prime Survivor, to blackmail him into entering Unification with a girl from the Upper Level. The Prime Survivor believes that the ultimate survival of the Lower Level depends upon combining resources with the Upper Level. Marriage is politically expedient. The arrangements introduce Jared to Della Anselm, his chosen partner. This, in turn, creates a chain of circumstances which lead both Levels to believe that Jared is a Zivver, just as Della does. Eventually thought to be a traitor working with the "monsters," Jared is forced to flee his own world with Della and seek out the world of the Zivvers. This brings him into contact with the "monsters," who turn out to be the survivors of Complex Seven on a mission to rescue them. It also eventually allows him to understand the nature of light and what has happened to him and his people. In the long run, even though he reaches the goal that he set for himself, Jared's quest is not much of a quest because rather than being the predominant initiator of action, he is more the victim of it. Circumstances push him from one situation to another, and his physical journey is a series of stops, starts, and detours. Yet, this is an appropriate posture for an innocent who understands little about the forces that surround him. Limited by his ignorance, Jared can do little else but react to the stimuli he encounters; yet this is a realistic characterization, and was what Galouye intended.

Jared is very childlike, and that impression is reinforced by the symbolism of *Dark Universe*. Though there is a continuous expansion of his knowledge as he makes the journey from innocence to experience, four scenes, in particular, mark significant stages in the development of his awareness. Each is pregnant with birth imagery. The first occurs when Jared and Della discover that Leah, the Kind Survivoress; Ethan, the Little Listener; and the Forever Man are real. Jared had thought them to be the product of his dreams. In discovering the cavern where the three are living, Jared and Della pass from a large grotto through a stream to a dry passage that broadens to a larger cave. The grotto recalls the womb, the stream, the amniotic fluid, and the narrow passageway, the birth canal. Moreover, the scene is reinforced with male and female symbols, such as Jared's upraised lances, and the well-defined pit that they find when they enter Leah's cave. There is also the suggestion that there is some sort of symbolic sexual relationship between Jared and Leah. She turns out to be younger and more desirable than he thought she was, and Della does become jealous of her. The expansion of Jared's awareness occurs when he meets the Forever Man and finds out that light was not God but an impersonal element. The Forever Man had lived in the Original World and by meeting him Jared has a tangible contact with it.

The second scene charting Jared's growth occurs when he and Della enter the Zivver World. Attacked by soubats, he hurls the girl into a river and jumps in after her. They are pushed towards a subterranean channel and swept into it. After a long period, they emerge on the bank of a vast, domed cavern. Again, the womb, amniotic fluid, and birth canal symbols are present. Once again, there is the erection symbol, for Jared had planted a spear in the earth to kill any attacking soubats before they jumped into the water. Also, the amount of time that they spent in the water is measured in "gestations." While he is in the Zivver World Jared experiences another quantum leap in his awareness by discovering additional facts about the nature of light. He finds that there is indeed "less of something in the Zivver World" when the Complex Seven survivors break in with their lamps — though he does not yet know that it is darkness. He also learns that light can be "thrown," which reinforces the concept implanted by the Forever Man that light was not God but a physical thing. Finally, there is another experience with the Original World when the "monsters" enter the Zivver cavern and begin to carry off the inhabitants.

The third scene occurs just after Jared and Mogan escape the humans by leaping into the river and swimming through the subterranean channel to safety. They travel for some time, pass through a corridor that widens to a huge mouth, and then enter the Original World, though neither of them knows exactly where they are. Again, the symbols of womb, water, and birth canal are present. And, of course, Jared is assaulted by the light from the sun. Birth is painful for him, and more importantly, it is terrifying. So fearful is he, in fact, that he runs back into the cavern in terror.

There is yet one final birth scene before Jared can really accept the Original World. Just after recapturing Della from one of the "monsters," he carries her from the cave and into the Original World. They hide there in a shack until dark. Then, impelled by the sound of what Jared thinks is a giant echo caster, they make their way down through an "artificial pit" to find one of the heated reservoirs that fed their complex. The echo caster turns out to be a nuclear-powered pump. Upon hearing some humans coming, they flee back up the narrow staircase to the Original World. Della, exhausted, passes out. Jared tries to hide in a shack but crashes into some furniture that falls down on him and knocks him out. As before, the birth images are present in the scene. Upon awaking later and finding Della gone, Jared returns to the cave worlds in despair. Everything has changed for him: his finely honed sense of hearing is gone; the world he knew is in shambles. A short time later, he is found by some of the rescuers, tranquilized, and taken to the surface for the final time.

The birth and related sexual imagery of *Dark Universe* is an excellent means of reinforcing the innocence-to-experience theme of the novel. By using the sexual implications of the motif in a figurative sense, Galouye is able to define the difficulty of the journey that the survivors of Complex Eleven make from their caves to the Original World; the images also suggest a source for the enormous energy that drives Jared through his adventures.

Dark Universe is an excellent example of what science fiction is capable of doing at its best. It is a compact, fast-paced adventure story that is extremely provocative. Few readers will be able to forget the novel after they finish it. They will, instead, return to it time and again to speculate on the questions that it raises.

Carl B. Yoke

Sources for Further Study

Reviews:

Amazing Stories. XXXVI, January, 1962, pp. 137-138.

Analog. LXIX, March, 1962, pp. 166-167.

New Worlds. CXII, November, 1961, pp. 126-127 and CXXV, December, 1962, p. 125.

DARKENING ISLAND

Author: Christopher Priest (1943-   )
First book publication: 1972
Type of work: Novel
Time: The near future
Locale: Southern England

A series of scenes from the life of a British middle-class intellectual who loses everything in a civil war precipitated by the arrival of refugees from a nuclear war in Africa

> *Principal characters:*
> ALAN WHITMAN, a college lecturer
> ISOBEL, his wife
> SALLY, his daughter
> LATEEF, the leader of a group of refugees

Darkening Island (British title, *Fugue for a Darkening Island*) was Christopher Priest's second science fiction novel, and followed *Indoctrinaire* (1970). It was one of the nominees for the first John W. Campbell Memorial Award in 1973. It is written in the flat, clinical manner which characterizes much of Priest's work — a style which is particularly appropriate to the communication of an atmosphere of desolation and to the description of desperately anomic human situations. This tone sets off the content of the novel perfectly, and though it is not his most ambitious novel, *Darkening Island* is Priest's most successful to date.

The first-person narrative is nonlinear, consisting of a mixture of three discontinuous sequences reflecting different phases in the life of Alan Whitman, a middle-class university graduate who loses his job as a teacher in a college of further education because of an economic crisis, and who is eventually rendered homeless by civil war. One sequence includes reminiscences of his early life, during which his primary concern was various sexual encounters, but through which are also related the bare details of his biography and early career. A second sequence tells in detail of his experiences in the early stages of the war, at which time he has been scraping a living for some time as a manual worker in a factory. At the beginning of the sequence he is forced out of his home in Southgate when the district becomes embroiled in the fighting, and this thread of the narrative describes his unsuccessful attempts to find a refuge for himself and his family. The third sequence concerns Whitman's attempts to locate his wife and daughter, from whom he has been separated. In this sequence he is one of a group of men in a similar situation, whose informal leader is a man named Lateef.

The future history which forms the background to the book assumes that the British economic decline which set in during the 1960's, following the postwar boom has continued throughout the 1970's. The depression has reached such a critical point that a new Nationalist party, headed by one John Tregarth, has received a mandate to form a government. (One of the results of the authoritarian policies instituted by this government is the closure of the institutions of higher education, which causes the first reduction in Whitman's circumstances.) The new government is also overtly racist, and racial tension grows as a consequence in cities and factories. Meanwhile, there is a nuclear war in Africa which devastates virtually all the cities on the continent. Refugees from rural areas, fleeing from the fallout, set sail in heavily overloaded ships for every possible haven, many of them heading for Britain. By the time these "Afrims" begin landing in quantity, there is no effective measure either to stop or to accommodate them; the country is already on the brink of collapse. A three-way civil war breaks out, with armed guerrillas and some regular troops fighting the cause of a million or more Afrims, while the Nationalist government forces face revolutionary Secessionists.

Whitman is forced out of his home by an influx of Afrims into Southgate. A local militia is organized to defend the street where he lives, but his own home proves to be indefensible once the Afrims have taken over a neighboring street. Despite the protests of their neighbors, Whitman takes his wife Isobel and his daughter Sally away from the fighting. Their attempts to find somewhere to go are frustrated when their car breaks down, and they are reduced to camping out. Whitman's marriage has been in a state of decay for some years, and he and Isobel have only stayed together for Sally's sake. Now Isobel decides that it is time to leave, and she deserts them both. Whitman and Sally try to make their way to the nearest railway station, but are thwarted by an air raid. In the end, they are interned by the Afrims, having been reunited with Isobel. Within the internment camp the men and women are separated, and when Whitman is released he finds that Isobel and Sally have been taken elsewhere. There are several other men in the same situation, and he sets out in their company to find his family.

The group discovers that the women may have been inducted into a brothel run for the benefit of the Afrim troops, and sets out to discover if the rumor is true. Although the initiative within the group is taken by Lateef, Whitman soon becomes the sole possessor of a rifle, which he steals from a brothel run for the benefit of white troops. Later, when the group is hiding from a skirmish between the Afrims and one or other of the native forces, he uses the rifle to shoot down a helicopter. As an indirect result of this action, the other members of the group arm themselves with rifles and ammunition salvaged from the relics of the battle, and Lateef begins to talk about forming a white guerrilla army in order to take a hand in the war. Whitman then strikes out on his own.

While searching along the Sussex coast for the Afrim brothel, Whitman is injured and has to take refuge in a small town, where he is taken in by a couple named the Jefferys. The town is yet untouched by the war, and seems like something out of the past, with food and other goods still in the shops. Once recovered, however, Whitman leaves in order to pursue his search. In the end, he finds the bodies of his wife and daughter abandoned on the tideline, black with pitch, murdered when the Afrims moved on elsewhere.

The mode of presentation of the novel is such that this picture is filled in gradually and sporadically, from three different loci. This technique serves to emphasize strongly that these events form a coherent pattern which is in some way self-enclosed, rather than simply a passage from one point in time to another. The "beginning" (when Whitman finds that a barricade has been erected at the end of the street where he lives) and the "end" (when he finds the bodies on the beach) are actually contained within the same unified and circumscribed set of memories, and as they are recounted to the reader, they have already been deliberately drained of virtually all emotional content, desiccated for preservation. The memories of the flight from Southgate and Whitman's search for his family have absorbed one another just as they have absorbed the scattered moments of his earlier life — they are complete and finished. The last sentence of the book points toward the beginning of a new event-sequence, as Whitman murders a young African in order to steal his rifle, but the plans and purposes which will take him beyond the scope of the story are (very properly) left undisclosed.

Darkening Island is an extremely bleak vision of the future, even by the standards of the long British tradition of inordinately pessimistic images of ominous possibility. There are many novels which deal with disasters on a much larger scale, and many which are much more liberal in their descriptions of death and destruction, but Priest's novel seems even more desolate than these. Its nonlinearity precludes the possibility of its ending with the attempt by some valiant group of survivors mapping out a strategy for survival or laying the foundations for a new society — or even conspicuously *failing* to do so. It is, in fact, quite without any kind of an indicator signaling the shape of the further future, for better or for worse, and instead leaves the reader utterly stranded in the developing chaos. It is a subjective novel without being a study in psychology, introverted yet completely impersonal. The work which is closest to it in spirit is not a literary work at all but a work done in the medium of film — Ingmar Bergman's *Shame*, which also deals with the disruption of social life by the advent of civil war.

Darkening Island is the only significant work of British science fiction which touches upon the rather sensitive area of race relations. In the 1960's, the British government began to impose limitations on the immigration of British passport-holders from various far-flung parts of the Commonwealth (particularly the West Indies, India, and Hong Kong). Several areas in various cities had already become predominantly nonwhite at that time. *Darkening Island* was written not long after the idiosyncratic politician Enoch Powell delivered an inflammatory speech in which he presented an image of the streets of British cities running with "rivers of blood" as a result of racial conflicts which must eventually erupt.

In America, where racial problems have a much longer history and are universally recognized as having a real existence, writers have found it easier to produce futuristic works which analyze possible developments of these problems. In Britain, by contrast, there is still a certain embarrassment attached to the admission that such problems do exist and that their future development is dangerously uncertain. Ominously, the years which have passed since the publication of Priest's novel have seen something of a revival of the authoritarian and racist party known as the National Front, which, in the 1930's, was the British equivalent of the German Nazi party. Priest is virtually alone in having been able to turn a cold and clinical eye on the possibilities which the future might hold for racial conflict in Britain, and in this respect *Darkening Island* is much more a book of its time than many contemporary novels about the future of British society.

For every possible reason, *Darkening Island* is a disturbing book; its theme and background are calculated to cause unease, its narrative is frightening in its casual callousness, and its manner of presentation ties all its elements together into a disquieting whole. It constitutes a remarkable encapsulation of the predominant anxieties of its time and place of origin.

Brian Stableford

Sources for Further Study

Reviews:

Analog. XCI, August, 1973, p. 164.
Library Journal. XCVII, August, 1972, p. 2651.
National Review. XXV, January 19, 1973, pp. 104-106.

DARKNESS AND DAWN

Author: George A. England (1877-1936)
First book publication: 1914
Type of work: Novel
Time: Approximately fifteen hundred years in the future
Locale: New York and neighboring states

The adventures of a man and a woman who wake from suspended animation to find that the Earth has been depopulated by a cosmic catastrophe

> *Principal characters:*
> ALLAN STERN, a consultant engineer
> BEATRICE KENDRICK, his secretary

Darkness and Dawn first appeared as three separate serials in *Cavalier*, one of the Munsey pulps, during the years 1912 and 1913. The three sections, under the titles "Darkness and Dawn," "Beyond the Great Oblivion," and "The Afterglow" were reprinted as a trilogy in *Famous Fantastic Mysteries* in 1940-1941; the Avalon edition of 1964-1967 then divided the trilogy into a five-book series, including *Darkness and Dawn*, *Beyond the Great Oblivion*, *The People of the Abyss*, *Out of the Abyss*, and *The Afterglow*. This version was to some extent rewritten by Robert Lowndes in order to fit the narrative into the five-volume format. The most recent edition of the novel — the Hyperion Book edition of 1974 — is a reprint of the original one-volume edition of 1914. It is worth noting, however, that the second and third serials were afterthoughts provoked by the popularity of the first series, and are not entirely consistent with the original work.

The novel begins with the awakening of Beatrice Kendrick in her office on the forty-eighth floor of the Metropolitan Tower in Manhattan. She finds that her clothes have rotted away and that her hair has grown phenomenally long (though her fingernails have not). Even her desk and chair have crumbled into dust, and the remains of her decayed typewriter are barely identifiable. She discovers that her employer, Allan Stern, is also alive and well (though similarly unclothed and extremely hirsute), and they look out together from their window to see that all New York is in ruins, with forests reclaiming the streets far below. They have, apparently, slept for hundreds of years while the world has been overtaken by some terrible disaster. The miracle of their preservation is never explained, nor does it need to be, for — like John Carter's trip to Mars — the device is simply used to introduce an exotic dream-fantasy. Throughout the first section of the novel the author is vague about what might have happened to the rest of the human race; nor does he tell us how or when, considering such matters to be largely immaterial. Stern guesses that he and Beatrice have slept for eight hundred years and leaves it at that. In the second serial, however, where more detail has to be filled in to provide a focal point for further adventures, the estimate of eight hundred years is doubled.

The sight of Beatrice clothed in nothing but hair awakes "atavistic passions" in Allan, but he continues to exercise great moral restraint for several hundred pages. The reader is continually reminded of the effort such restraint requires, so that there is no mistaking the erotic element in the dream-fantasy. The new Adam and Eve find headquarters much closer to the ground and begin to tackle the problems of housekeeping. Allan embarks upon a scavenging expedition through the dead city in search of food, water, clothing, and weapons. The only clothes he can find are an assortment of furs locked in a storage-chest, and he is able to deck Beatrice in a tiger skin (which serves to fan further the flames of passion). He finds bottled food still in a state of perfect preservation, though all the canned food has rotted away; and locates a stream flowing from what was once the fountain in Madison Square. He also discovers revolvers and ammunition, which he wisely collects and stores.

Eventually Manhattan is invaded by rival armies of apemen who fight a terrible battle in the streets around the Metropolitan Tower. Allan concludes that these must be the descendants of all the non-Caucasian races, degenerated socially and physically. When the apemen discover Allan and Beatrice they first take them to be gods, but soon overcome their awe and attack them. With the aid of the revolvers, Allan and Beatrice keep the terrible horde at bay, and eventually the battle is won through the use of some high explosives which Allan manufactures from handy chemical supplies. The section ends with Allan and Beatrice resolving to become the parents of a new race and the makers of a better world.

The second section begins with the removal of Allan and Beatrice to a country estate, where they settle down to a comfortable life of pastoral ease, interrupted only by a brief return to Manhattan and a desperate fight against a wolf-pack. Eventually, however, they decide to explore in search of other survivors, and Allan's curiosity leads him to speculate about the nature of the catastrophe which created their new world. Apparently the Earth's orbit has altered, as has its axial tilt, and gravity seems to have declined slightly. There is also a new satellite which eclipses patches of starry sky, though without ever shining in the fashion of the older moon. The logic of all this is incompetent, but the author's purpose in proposing it is soon revealed. Allan and Beatrice try to sail east in a yacht but are caught in a great cataract where the sea itself seems to be vanishing into a hole in the Earth's crust (presumably to be reissued from another aperture elsewhere). They then fly westward in a small biplane which Allan has restored to use, but discover that beyond Lake Erie there is a great chasm of tremendous depth where a section of the Earth's crust has been ripped out and hurled into space. The plane falls into the abyss, but Allan and Beatrice are again miraculously preserved; they find themselves in a dark land where the sun's light cannot penetrate, populated by the descendants of America's white race (made even more white by etiolation). Here they find one ancient who speaks English, but are forced to fight for their lives first against the other members of his tribe, then against attackers from another tribe. Finally, Allan must challenge the headman, in single combat to the death, for the leadership of the people. The section ends with a victorious Allan taking the repaired biplane out of the abyss and back to the world above.

In the third part of the story Allan and Beatrice undertake a search for documents which will tell them the history of the world since their own day. They do not succeed in this quest, but their search takes them to a cathedral where their union is finally sanctified. They decide to bring the white savages out of the abyss in order to begin the rebirth of civilization. Allan begins to ferry his subjects out of the chasm two at a time, but is interrupted by several melodramatic interludes, first when Beatrice is carried off by a giant gorilla, then when one of the savages stages a *coup d'état* during his absence, and finally when the new community must face the final conflict with the sub-human horde. This climactic battle ends with the extinction of the apemen, making the world safe again for the children of Allan, Beatrice, and their subjects.

The racist elements of *Darkness and Dawn* are likely to be repugnant to the great majority of modern readers, and its melodramatic moments are such simple examples of pulp cliché that they now seem ridiculous — the sequence where the heroine is carried away by the gorilla is a perfect example, highlighted by the moment when Allan observes a lustful gleam in the animal's eye and comments that "Gorilla nature had not changed in fifteen hundred years." Nevertheless, *Darkness and Dawn* made a considerable impact on the minds of a great many of its first readers, and was also rapturously received when its parts were reprinted in the 1940's in *Famous Fantastic Mysteries*. The reason for the novel's popularity is that it transformed a post-catastrophe scenario into a romantic and emotionally charged dream-landscape in which full play could be given to fantasies appealing directly to those impulses most severely repressed by the inhibited society of the day. The idea of being the last man in the world, competent to deal with the most luridly threatening of situations, and accompanied by a beautiful woman clad only in hair and a tiger skin, is a marvelous daydream, especially for people living in a world whose moral codes and social conventions frowned upon the passions to which the dream pandered. The most revealing passages of the book are not those in which Allan fights apemen, gorillas, wolves, and brutal savages but the intermediate passages in which the two survivors luxuriate in their freedom from all social sanctions. Literary convention forbids them to take overt advantage of that freedom, but it is nonetheless there to be enjoyed, and the reader's imagination can easily fill in all the exciting possibilities. The novel's nearest kindred in American imaginative fiction are the works of Edgar Rice Burroughs, but the book which is perhaps closest of all in spirit is H. de Vere Stacpoole's desert island fantasia *The Blue Lagoon* (1908), which was a contemporary bestseller in Britain, and was made into an American film in the 1950's.

Darkness and Dawn preserves the integrity of its fantasy by being securely irrational, ignoring the facts of the real world and the dictates of common sense. It is interesting to note that the apparent incongruity between the ideological undercurrents within the narrative and England's socialist sympathies manifests itself only in a single moment of doubt, when Allan Stern looks down at the white savages under his command and reflects that what he *really* wants is a democracy, but because of the situation he faces, he will just have to go on being a demigod instead. Stern and England are wise to shrug off this moment of conscience, and England sees to it that when his hero and heroine rhapsodize about the future, they do so in the emotional but empty language of purple prose, without ever making any specific plans or predictions.

Novels like *Darkness and Dawn* and *A Princess of Mars* have a special place in the history of science fiction because they were the works which revealed the potential of the scientific romance for constructing gorgeous, imaginatively uninhibited daydreams. They were the novels which demonstrated how completely the shackles of reason could be cast off, and there is a certain irony in the fact that the jargon of "science" could be co-opted as part of a strategy intended to enhance plausibility. To some extent *Darkness and Dawn* was parasitic upon its predecessors — M. P. Shiel's *The Purple Cloud*, V. T. Sutphen's *The Doomsmen*, and similar apocalyptic novels — but it was genuinely new in representing the discovery that the attractiveness and utility of such fantasies had nothing to do with the actual probability of the events involved. *Darkness and Dawn* provided the first wholehearted affirmation of the sheer joy of imagining oneself the last *real* man in the world, accompanied by the last *real* woman. The fantasies catered to in the book may be accused of being cheap, tawdry, or silly, but these factors in no way affect its appeal to "atavistic passions." If the book makes no such imaginative impact upon modern readers, it is largely because modern readers are the product of a different social environment, not because they have acquired better taste and a more acute sense of discrimination. Judged by its own ambitions, *Darkness and Dawn* is a successful novel, and can legitimately be called a classic of its kind.

Brian Stableford

Sources for Further Study

Reviews:
Bookman. XXXIX, May, 1914, p. 344.
Boston Transcript. February 14, 1914, p. 6.
Dial. LVI, May 16, 1914, p. 425.
New York Times. February 8, 1914, p. 59.
Publisher's Weekly. LXXXV, March 21, 1914, p. 1060.

DARKOVER

Author: Marion Zimmer Bradley (1930-   )
First book publications: Darkover Landfall (1972); *Stormqueen!* (1978); *The Shattered Chain* (1976); *The Spell Sword* (1974); *The Forbidden Tower* (1977); *The Winds of Darkover* (1970); *Star of Danger* (1965); *The Bloody Sun* (1964); *The Heritage of Hastur* (1975); *The Sword of Aldones* (1962); *The Planet Savers* (1962); *The World Wreckers* (1971)
Type of work: Novels

A collection of novels which chronicle the history of the planet Darkover over the course of several millennia

Written during an interval of nearly twenty years and set temporally more than a century to several millennia in the future, Marion Zimmer Bradley's science fiction about the planet Darkover is very nearly unique. If one wants, one may classify them as a "future history," but that label is not quite accurate because they are not, strictly speaking, a history of the future of *our* race. Because the individual works have appeared in print without regard to chronological order, it is even inaccurate to call them "the Darkover series." As Marion Zimmer Bradley has written, her works about what happens and who exists on Darkover are simply a number of fictions that share a common setting; she continues to write about her planet, she says, because she feels at intervals the desire to return to it.

The most rewarding reading of the Darkover books seems to be an almost haphazard one. Readers with sequentially oriented minds may want to start at the beginning, with *Darkover Landfall*, and proceed according to the internal chronology of the works to *The World Wreckers*, which narrates events farthest in the future. There are two disadvantages to this approach. One is that a reading of the "series" minimizes readers' perceptions of the development of Bradley's literary artistry. The other is that *Darkover Landfall* gives it all away: questions about Darkovan culture that are raised only in the later books are already answered in part by this short — and temporally isolated — early one. By reading the book that simply happens to come first to hand, and then proceeding as one chooses, the reader can better experience the richness of Bradley's mimesis and let dominant themes and important characters and incidents make their own case for the literary merit of each individual book and of the group as a whole.

An attempt at an overview of Darkover cannot proceed haphazardly without a serious loss of coherence. Nor can it concentrate on the literary merits of a single book, ignoring the thematic relations that make the stories of Darkover more than isolated fictions, without overlooking to an important degree just what it is that lures readers, like the author, back to the planet Darkover. The essence of this appeal is twofold: from a literary perspective, nearly all the books are romances, yet the longer and more complex ones create realistic, novel-like worlds inhabited by characters developed sufficiently to meet the demands of consistency and verisimilitude; from a psychological viewpoint, the stories of Darkover present both characters with deep emotional resonance and a conflict between cultures that must be recognized as a fictional paradigm of the tensions within humanity and, even, within every human one of us who has had occasion to think and feel and choose between alternatives each as necessary as the other. What enhances the appeal of Bradley's fictions is that each of them is an adventure story at the same time that each adds a bit more reality to a single fictive world and a bit more depth to the reader's perception of the nature of humanity as it is caught today by the forces of technological progress, of reactionary security, and of the imperative need for balance and integration and preservation of psychical as well as physical life.

To understand how the Darkover books fit these rather grand generalizations, one needs to perceive in concrete characters and incidents the generation of specific patterns and themes. Prior to such perception, however, "What's Darkover, anyway?" requires at least a sketchy answer.

An ancient planet of a red dwarf star has been the birthplace of several species of intelligent life. Climatic changes have forced the native populations, over millions of years, probably, to retreat to the high country where ranges of immense mountains draw precipitation from the winds and where snow-melt continues to keep nearby valleys and plains fertile and forested. Near the end of the twenty-first century (of our own time), a starship leaves Earth for a destination it never reaches; some cosmic accident causes it to crash-land on the aging world that circles the reddish sun. The casualties are great, the distance from hoped-for rescue unknowable. The crew and passengers do what they can to survive on the hostile planet, but the probability of their success is desperately slight. Some think they have encountered native intelligent life, but, since the survivors fall victim to an epidemic the chief symptoms of which are violent eruptions of libidinous impulses and mass hallucinations, no one can be sure. So, at the conclusion of *Darkover Landfall* there remain only, on Earth, a probably forgotten record of a colonizing mission and, on the uncharted planet, a pitiably small number of humans who themselves are unsure of survival beyond the next generation.

Some centuries or millennia later, the reddish sun illuminates a reborn culture on that planet known as Darkover. For a time, the culture waxes strong: having drawn not only on the toolmaking abilities of its people but also on their discovery of psychic abilities to link mental and material forces, the Darkovans rule imperiously the habitable parts of their world. They mine scarce ores from the depths of the planet by means of psychic energy. They transform their very nature by careful breeding, so that selected traits — most importantly, various kinds of psionic ability — emerge as dominant among the inbred groups known collectively as the Comyn. They make ever more sophisticated tools and devices, including the "matrix," which can amplify and focus the awesome powers of not one but a number of telepathic minds, and eventually turn these tools into weapons. And, with weapons material and mental, the Darkovans make war that lasts for ages, called the Darkovan ages of Chaos.

The culture then waned, saw with mind and eye the literal brink of extinction, and chose survival. Its cost was their material technology, and its great law was the Compact: no person would ever again do violence to another by use of mind, and no person would do physical violence to another unless the means allowed the aggressor to be just as vulnerable as the intended victim. Among a people who still had prodigious mental abilities, there remained only a vestige of the former culture. The several dominant Comyn Families ruled their Domains yet followed an apparently pre-industrial, almost feudal way of life; though the Comyn kept their telepathic gifts intact, they settled irreconcilable differences by hand-to-hand combat. The Darkovans kept their matrixes, even the Towers, where matrix-circles of telepaths continued their work (though with phobic caution), yet their visible lifestyle was marked most by adherence to strict gender roles, acquisition of wives and concubines, designation of heirs, and practice of the code duello.

While the Darkovans adjusted to the results of the Ages of Chaos, the people of Earth evolved a galactic Terran Empire and discovered that the red star and its barely habitable planet occupied a strategically and commercially important position. If the people of that planet could be convinced — or coerced — to join the Empire, their home world could serve as a major transfer point for starships journeying from one part of the galaxy to another. By appearances, these backward people of Darkover could only benefit by an alliance with Terra, the advanced technology of which could pull the Darkovan civilization centuries ahead toward progress within just a decade or two. From the opposite viewpoint, the Terran Empire was rushing toward an Age of Chaos of its own and, for most of the Comyn of the Domains, Terran overtures of friendship were unmistakable invitations to the annihilation Darkover had just barely avoided.

Most of Bradley's Darkover books are narratives about the centuries-long encounter between Darkover, the immovable object, and the irresistible force of the Terran Empire. At the same time, they explore what may be a more important human encounter: the one between a sapient being who is intelligent, rational, and only dimly aware of the internal workings of the mind, and that same being who allows subconscious psychic dynamism to be at least as important as conscious intellect. The dominant characters — both Darkovan and Terran — must come to terms with their *laran* or psionic abilities. As they do, they become more integrated personalities and, from the reader's viewpoint, so much alike that "Darkovan" and "Terran" denote merely a planet of origin, not separable species of humanity.

That each of the Darkover books focuses on personal rather than political relationships causes the reader to perceive intercultural contact as an abstraction (which it is) and to perceive interpersonal and intrapersonal relations as fundamental (which they are). In *The Spell Sword* and *The Forbidden Tower*, for instance, the conciliation of what is Terran (in Andrew Carr) and what is Darkovan (in Callista, Damon, and Ellemir) is important. More important, though, are the personal relations these four characters establish among themselves and the resolution of intrapersonal tension in the characters of Andrew and Callista. In works that seem more political than others — *The Heritage of Hastur* and *The World Wreckers* — the internal, psychical complexity in the narratives (Regis Hastur's struggle to overcome the repression of his *laran* and the bringing together of all telepathic persons regardless of their race) allows the political conflicts to arise from the dramatic relations within and among the characters. This complexity prevents the works from turning into political or psychological thesis-novels.

Even in short works such as *The Planet Savers,* the characters of which are not very fully developed, Bradley's affinity for generic romance results in adventure-narrative: the excitement of incident after incident puts the emphasis on plot rather than on thematic statements. If a generalization about the Darkover books is possible, it is that Bradley as literary artist relies mainly on setting (in each additional book the same world becomes more real), on character (even when a main character is scantily developed, the reader "knows" him or her because of his or her appearance in other Darkover books), and on plot (each of the tales about Darkover is essentially romantic adventure, the kind of good storytelling that invites readers back for more).

This is not to say, however, that Bradley's themes are negligible. On the contrary, precisely because they derive from specific textual elements, they are compelling and serious without being simplistic or blatantly didactic. Everyone who reads a Darkover novel is a Terran and, looking at *this* Earth, needs very little imagination to extrapolate a planet-wide culture of the future enslaved by misused technology, suprapersonal aggression, and delusions of progress that ignore the potentiality of all that is not external and conscious. Thus, thematic warnings against a future with attributes of the Terran Empire are no more "in" Bradley's fictions than they already exist, often consciously, often independently, within the reader's own mind. That the Darkovans experienced their Ages of Chaos is, thematically, little more than a fictional affirmation of the truth in the story of what happened when two humans in a Garden partook of the knowledge of good and evil. Most of Bradley's adventure stories conclude with (and may even, throughout, rely upon) a bond of love and trust between the two main characters — not a very original device, to be sure, yet no one has invented, in reality or in fiction, a practical substitute for freely given supportive love. Another obvious Darkover theme — most obvious in *The Shattered Chain* and *The Heritage of Hastur* perhaps, but prevailing in all the Darkover stories — lends itself to very quick summary: "Know thyself" and its corollary "Be your *whole* self." One need not be a psychologist or parapsychologist to realize that personal integration is utterly important.

Thus the Darkover novels, when subjected to a particular sort of analysis, yield didactic themes. But these themes are generated from the interplay among plot and character and setting of works that are less conventional novels than science-fiction-fantasy romances. If the thematic statements made by the Darkover books seem consistent, serious, and even didactic, it is because, within or without their literary contexts, they are "statements" profoundly relevant to the human condition.

Rosemarie Arbur

DAVY

Author: Edgar Pangborn (1909-   )
First book publication: 1964
Type of work: Novel
Time: Approximately three hundred years after a nuclear war
Locale: Upstate New York, New England, the Azores Islands

A satirical tale of one young boy's coming of age in a world shattered by nuclear war, and his confrontation with a society returned to a medieval level, complete with a domineering church

> *Principal characters:*
> DAVY, a runaway stable boy who becomes King of the Fools
> NICKIE, an aristocratic heretic who marries Davy
> SAM LOOMIS, Davy's mentor, perhaps also his father
> DION MORGAN MORGANSON, hereditary ruler of Nuin, also a heretic
> PA RUMLEY, leader of a Rambler band
> JERRY, an eight-year-old religious pilgrim

Science fiction writers are storytellers by preference. Even those among them most interested in literary experimentation remain as attracted to the genre's pulp tradition as they are to those of the satirical voyage and the speculative utopia (or dystopia). In science fiction's formative years, pulp conventions, as well as the low pay and corresponding premium on fast writing, encouraged straightforward narrative. Imitating so-called "mainstream" literary techniques has often been a controversial tactic for many of the genre writers, with any legitimate criticisms to be made of such techniques overlaid with resentment of the outside critics' distaste for writing from the science fiction ghetto. For these reasons, even some of the best science fiction retains the structure of linear narration. However, the genre has undergone great change since the 1960's, and amidst all the clamor, it is apparent that the experimentation of recent years has added manipulation of narrative structure to the genre writer's bag of tools.

Edgar Pangborn's *Davy* is both a historical example of this development and a model. Often neglected, Pangborn nevertheless uses the stream-of-consciousness to great effect, recounting three successive phases of his first-person narrator's life side by side, and covering a prodigious amount of future history with a wonderful economy *and* a clear, direct narrative flow. Davy is many things in this book — a runaway indentured servant, a religious heretic, a political figure, a refugee, and an explorer; but he is also an amateur writer who is only learning his craft as he works on the unedited memoir which is his story's finished form. Thus, the discipline of attempting communication with an unseen reader keeps the flow of his thoughts in their course while the irreverent asides, gratuitous comments, corrections, and footnotes supplied by his wife and best friend reveal the larger context within which his personal adventures are taking place. In this way, a straight narrative covering one summer in the life of a fourteen-year-old boy can also describe twenty-one years of growth and development after the crucial events of his initiation into manhood. As the story progresses, and the need for compression increases, Davy's growing sureness as a writer makes the more conventional narrative at the book's end seem quite natural, while simultaneously permitting Pangborn to order priorities and tie up the loose ends of a continuing history with the last in the series of footnotes.

The inventiveness of Pangborn's structure and the strength of his characterizations stand in contrast to the somewhat conventional nature of his plot. In the aftermath of a nuclear war, the world has been reduced to the level of late medieval culture, with a rigid system of social stratification, slavery, and a dominant Holy Murcan ("American") Church. Once part of a single great nation, Davy's world is a remnant of upstate New York and New England now divided into scattered kingdoms composed of walled cities and villages stockaded against the depredations of enemy soldiers, bandits, and great mutated beasts who roam the countryside. In a fashion owing as much to H. L. Mencken's acerbic views on religion as to the actual history of the medieval Church (with its preservation of classical learning after the dismemberment of the Roman Empire), the Church burns as a heretic anyone who disputes its official cosmology or the class system, or who engages in the banned attempt to resurrect the lost scientific knowledge of the "Old Time." After his birth in a brothel, his rearing in a church-run orphanage, and his indentured servitude to an innkeeper, Davy runs away at fourteen, eventually joining some stragglers from an "enemy" army invading his homeland. While he is with these stragglers he is initiated into manhood; and his adolescent sexuality is tempered by his first personal relationships, his first encounters with death, his discovery of his father, and his final alienation from the Church. Eventually he becomes a close adviser to the liberal ruler of a commonwealth built on the ruins of Massachusetts and a leader of the refugees who flee the Church's assault on the heretical reformers. Chased to a colony in the Azores, Davy remains discontented and elects to participate in another voyage of exploration — from which he disappears.

Throughout, he is a randy lad, with a story punctuated by often uproarious but nearly always loving and gentle (and never graphically described) sex. But his sexuality is forever shadowed by death. He beds his first partner shortly after killing a town guard; his second leaves his company to become a nun after a tiger kills her husband and a young pilgrim. Neither can he father children; some twist in his genes makes his offspring nonviable mutations who must be destroyed, and his wife dies in childbirth.

This rendition of the eternal cycles of birth and death, mixed with the archetypal American belief in moral regeneration on an unspoiled frontier, is characteristic of science fiction. Davy is an outcast venturing forth on a picaresque quest because he cannot live in the society of his day. Not only is his eastward flight an ironic reversal of the motives Pangborn sees in the original voyages to America, but Davy's career itself becomes symbolic of science fiction's inability to find a single magical key (akin to the Holy Grail of medieval myth) with which to restore a world devastated physically and morally by the effects of nuclear weapons. In this landscape, the Church thrives on dislocation and fear; and the search for some way to regenerate this wasted land is perceived not as a holy errand, but as heresy. Davy is unable to prevent the overthrow of the progressive regime and he himself feels a "controlled discontent" after the death of his wife, which pursues him from the refugee colony as surely as the Church had pursued them all from New England.

Perhaps, rather than searching for a Holy Grail, Davy's character is itself the Grail: a simple-cynical approach to life simultaneously intelligent enough to modernize a backward world and sufficiently loving and humane to prevent another nuclear war. In that event, his original wanderings, as well as his expulsion from New England and his last voyage, become symbols of that talisman's unattainability and the lack of any integration of scientific knowledge with human love. Certainly Davy's history makes it clear that, for Pangborn, the quest for such symbols is not the task a hero embodying the best of a society's ideals would undertake. Rather it is the natural vocation of the outcast, and if the seeker is not an outcast at the beginning, the quest itself will make him one.

Such a perspective raises a critical issue. A more complex craftsman than Robert Heinlein, Pangborn nevertheless creates characters quite similar to the former's: Davy, the intelligent but youthful innocent who learns how the world works, and two older men, Sam Loomis (his presumed father) and Pa Rumley (leader of a gypsylike band of "Ramblers"). These two teach Davy to understand the rationale behind the already distrusted ways of the settlements, and the skills of intelligence, cynicism, and self-reliance needed to survive there. The novel reaches the height of its dramatic tension when a mutated tiger leaps the pathetic barrier of a village stockade to kill a young boy, an archetypal "angel with a dirty face," who is on a pilgrimage to the Church's holiest shrines. But although this incident brings Davy and Loomis together as father and son, and confirms both of them in their renunciation of the Church, Davy later sees Loomis' natural death (from influenza) as the crucial and climactic episode of his narrative, for that is the final seal on his childhood. His new self-reliance, rather than experience, is the measure of his manhood. Wanderers with a Rambler band, Davy and Loomis are part of an organized and loving community for four years before the latter's death; but that death severs Davy's ties to the group, and, "a loner by trade," he moves into the at least temporary anonymity of the largest metropolis of his day. Years later, in the Azores, the death of his wife propels him off toward another dimly glimpsed frontier. Each successive loss drives him ever further beyond the realm of human community, and eventually he ceases to return. Self-reliance and community are irreconcilable; and the closest and most loving of relationships are but preludes to an inevitable loss and great discontent.

Neither Pangborn nor science fiction are alone in such conclusions. In fact, *Davy* is evidence of the continuity between the great themes of traditional American literature and the best science fiction. Americans have always been of two minds about themselves, valuing individualism and conformity to the mores of society simultaneously; and they have found both values strained in confrontation with social and technological change. Like Huckleberry Finn, Davy is truly comfortable only when "lighting out for the Territory," a destination which is never reached. Easy as it is for Davy to reject membership in a community based on religious hypocrisy and the cultivation of secular ignorance, it is necessary for him to reject *any* stable community, however warm and hospitable. A child, Huck Finn is merely discontent in such a situation. James Fenimore Cooper was ambivalent enough about the frontier society of his day to recognize that Natty Bumppo, the archetypal frontiersman who is in so many ways an adult Huck, could be perceived as a threat by the stockaded villagers of the first New York settlements. Davy and Loomis, loners by trade, relish the true community feelings of the Ramblers; Davy is equally at home in his circle of heretics. But these homes are temporary, the groups themselves marginal and outlawed. Not even the historical trauma of a nuclear war can change humanity enough to resolve the contradiction, despite the long view of future centuries science fiction writers have always been able to cultivate.

This is not to indict Pangborn or to diminish regard for his considerable craft. Despite the low regard in which it is often held, science fiction is part of the larger body of American fiction, and in a more reasonable critical world the parallels between the parent body and the offshoot genre would occasion no comment at all. Pangborn's weaving of plot, character, and narrative structure demonstrates the skillful and substantial way in which a science fiction story can be told. But if *Davy* is a good measure of the novelist's art in America, it also is a measure of some of the limitation on the critical vision displayed in that same body of art. What distinguishes this novel, and science fiction in general, is the refusal to assume that such questions of substance are entirely behind us.

Albert I. Berger

Sources for Further Study

Reviews:

National Review. XXIV, March, 1964, pp. 246-247.

New York Herald Tribune Book Review. March 8, 1964, p. 106.

THE DAY AFTER JUDGMENT

Author: James Blish (1921-1975)
First book publication: 1970
Type of work: Novella
Time: The late twentieth century
Locale: Italy and the United States

With forty-eight demons of Hell released, the world H-bombed, and the Satanic City of Dis appearing on the Earth's surface, the question whether God is truly dead can be answered only by Satan himself

Principal characters:
> FATHER DOMENICO, a Jesuit priest and white magician
> BAINES, a munitions manufacturer
> JACK GINSBERG, his assistant
> THERON WARE, a black magician
> PUT SATANACHIA, Satan's prince
> SATAN MEKRATRIG, the Father of Lies, Satan himself
> D. WILLIS MCKNIGHT, a General of the Armies, USAF
> DR. JOANNE BUELG, a United States computer analyst
> DR. DŽEJMS ŠATVJE, an adviser to SAC and developer of the
> selenium bomb

James Blish began his trilogy *After Such Knowledge* with *Doctor Mirabilis* (1964), a life of the thirteenth century scientist-theologian-alchemist Roger Bacon. In *Black Easter* (1968) and its sequel *The Day After Judgment* (together comprising the second volume of the trilogy) Blish personifies the threefold nature of Roger Bacon's career by means of three characters. Baines as a munitions maker, an "aesthete of destruction," represents the scientific Roger Bacon; Father Domenico is something of a *manqué* theologian, his usual posture being one of hand wringing ineptitude, while continuing Bacon's defense of orthodox Christianity; and Bacon the alchemist lives again in these two works in the person of Theron Ware, a black magician.

Blish prefaces *The Day After Judgment* with a summary of *Black Easter*, in which Baines, reveling in destruction, hires Theron Ware to summon the demons of Hell to Earth for one day; Father Domenico as a white magician stands by, watching, bound by a Covenant not to interfere; the result, with forty-eight demons refusing to return to Hell, is a veritable Armageddon (or World War III, if one adopts the military point of view). Blish provides four titles for sections of *The Day After Judgment*. One, "The Wrath-Bearing Tree," continues the overall theme of *After Such Knowledge*, for the myth of Eden means, ultimately, that no one discipline — neither science, theology, nor magic — will suffice to satisfy man's thirst for knowledge. Baines knows about world destruction by means of hydrogen bombs, but not about destruction by demons; Father Domenico knows what remedies the Church has to offer for the depredations of demons, but they are effective only if the demons are confined in Hell; Theron Ware knows about demons, but not whether an ultimate Deity, Creator, and Lord of the Universe will reveal Himself in a confrontation with the powers of darkness. Indeed, by the end of the novel, since the Church as usual remains powerless, the only revelation comes out of the darkness itself, from the fallen angel Satan who still has visions of vanished glory. Only evil makes itself known, and God remains obscured by his own handiwork.

As the novel opens on an H-bombed world, the four remaining conjurors — Adolph Hess has been swallowed by a demon after stepping out of his magic circle — await, as bidden, the return of Put Satanachia. The town of Positano, where they are, has been swept by a tidal wave. Jack Ginsberg, enjoying the diversion of a succubus, can be objective about the faults of the others. He sees his superior, Baines, totally preoccupied with destruction; Ware as having prostituted the art of the magician; and Father Domenico as one who destroys by doing nothing, a "howling anachronism in the modern world." In achieving Armageddon, then, each has realized his ultimate self.

Whole cities have been vaporized by hydrogen bombs, and the few survivors of the Strategic Air Command, housed deep under a now destroyed Denver, try to determine who the enemy is. With fallout covering the world in vast overlapping arcs, the computers posit few survivors, and General McKnight seems to be senior surviving officer. The computer analyzes satellite data and, determining that there is a fortress newly erected in Death Valley, reports that the United States has been hit by missiles and invaded. McKnight sends a reconnaissance plane over the area, and Šatvje recognizes in the photographs the terraced lunar crater of red-hot iron with a black pit at the center and a medieval gateway guarded by three women (the Furies) all characteristic of Dis, the fortress surrounding Nether Hell. He is reminded of Cantos Eight through Eleven of the *Divine Comedy*. Responding to a request for scientific data, the computer practically eliminates as a possible cause of the phenomenon the action of a foreign power, rating an invasion by interplanetary forces slightly higher in probability, and awarding the City of Dis hypothesis the highest probability. In that case, two conclusions would logically follow: first, that the war was Armageddon and second, that God had lost the war. But demons on Earth had played no part in the prophecies; and Šatvje speculates that the presumed invaders must occupy space/time and exist in some energy system that could be analyzed and attacked. To be on the side of God, if He still exists, Buelg advocates bombing the Death Valley encampment. With Hell on Earth and the only living people, the military, underground, Blish reverses the code of the Emerald Tablet (where Heaven was above Earth and "As above, so below" defined the micro-macrocosmic relationship) and entitles this section "So Above."

At Positano the four conjurors can agree only that they know nothing until a static-filled radio report about the dropping of a bomb enables Baines, with his knowledge of warfare, to guess what the choice of action at the Denver military base would be. He and Jack Ginsberg take a plane there to advise McKnight of the futility of bombing demons.

Father Domenico returns to Monte Albano, monastery of the white monks, to find that it has been spared. Rather than measuring radiation fallout, the monks have been counting fallen angels — 7,450,926 of them, plus seventy-two princes, released on Earth. Pooling religious knowledge from any sources available, the monks puzzle over why the Antichrist has not appeared; the director remembers the Essenes, who taught that people must experience all evil before they can experience good; and Father Domenico, hoping therefore that this is only an Earthly Purgatory, speculates that the battle may not have been Armageddon after all. He goes to Venice (the Pope has died in the destruction of Rome) and finds the people disillusioned with the Church's teachings, although there is a glimmer of hope as a result of the election of a new Pope — Juvenember LXIX. Father Domenico recognizes with horror that the new Pope is the demon Agares from the *Black Easter* conjuration; but now he has a mission — to go to Dis, and, knowing that the new Pope is the Antichrist, to challenge Satan with the knowledge that God still exists. The Father travels by trance levitation.

Theron Ware, with his powers greatly reduced amid the shambles of Positano, succeeds in summoning by oncirology a demon who reports that the City of Dis is now established on Earth in Death Valley. Now Ware also has a mission — to go to Death Valley to arrange a detente between the demons and SAC. Crossing the Atlantic by transvection (here Blish corrects the Halloween cartoons that show a witch riding a broomstick with the brush hindmost), Ware lands in western Pennsylvania, performs his lustrations, and hitchhikes westward. All concerned "Come to Middle Hell," the title of the third section.

In conference with the military powers and with his Theron Ware experience behind him, Baines maintains that the hydrogen bomb has no effect on spirits, which are neither matter nor energy. But Šatvje argues that spirits must be unified fields, which might be a hundred percent negative entropy, that life is negative entropy, and that stable negative entropy is eternal life. If condemnation to Hell is the Second Death, the scientist-militarist may be "in a position to give the Third Death . . . the bliss of complete extinction . . . liberation from the Wheel!"

McKnight plans a major attack on the City of Dis and calls Baines a "communist sympathizer" and a "Chink" for counseling against it. Baines, now understanding that anything immortal, even a fallen angel, is part of the Creator, fears that an attack on Dis will be followed by a war on Heaven and that God, if not already dead, soon will be.

As the walls withstand nuclear bombardment, Buelg admits that they may be alchemical. Laser beams and Hess torpedoes under the gate bring some temporary success; but, as Dante proposed against the invasion by Vergil, the three Furies raise the head of Medusa and all of the combatants and equipment

instantly freeze. Beelzebub, Lord of the Flies, lends a hand in depriving air-
borne combatants of their wings. As the triumphant face of Put Satanachia
appears on the television screen, McKnight recognizes it as that of his Chinese
enemy, "the insidious Doctor Fu Manchu." The demon calls Baines to Hell
under *geas* (compulsion).

In keeping with the circuit of Dis before Vergil was admitted, Baines and
Ginsberg set out on foot at the same time that Theron Ware, now a veteran hitchhiker, is approaching from Flagstaff; and Father Domenico's trance levitation
has deposited him on Telescope Peak, down which he scrambles to a clearly
foreordained meeting with the others. Against Domenico's reliance on clerical
preferment, Ware enumerates the sins of all four: Ginsberg, lust; his own,
gluttony for knowledge; Baines, wrath; and Domenico, hoarding for the sake
of his own soul. He insists that only black magic, not white, exists, and explains that Father Domenico's crucifix burst at the conjuration because he tried
to use it for personal gain. When Father Domenico admits this, they proceed
on a common ground of ignorance. In Pandemonium, Satan Mekratrig himself
greets them; looking both Dantesque and Miltonic, he measures almost five
hundred yards from crown to hoof, has three heads, but sports a halo.

Domenico addresses Satan, acknowledging his own impotence and begging
that God be known to exist; Baines proposes his neutrality in any possible war
between Satan and Heaven; Ginsberg, maintaining that he is "not involved,"
keeps his own counsel; and Ware remains unrepentant, but offers aid. At last
Satan speaks, denouncing in poetic measures these humans who have failed to
help him regain the golden throne. God is dead to those in Hell but His principle remains; Good is independent, and, without Good, Evil makes no sense.
The demons released in Ware's and Baines's world find Earth more foul than
Hell; and demons, like Satan himself, are powers for Good in comparison with
the evils of men. Still, man, unlike the demons, has the advantage of waiting
for the Resurrection. On this judgment day, it is Satan, not God, who passes
judgment on man. Satan, too, has acquired knowledge to his sorrow. He now
knows that he never would want to be God, having then to contend with man.
In gaining this knowledge, Satan says, he has lost all.

As the novel closes, the four men on the surface of the Earth, from which
all trace of Dis has vanished, attempt to state their cases but find that they
cannot complete their sentences. However, their positions have changed. Father Domenico says "I think" (not "I believe"); Ware says "I hope" (not "I
know"); Baines says "I believe" (not "I think"); and Ginsberg says "I love"
(not "I lust"); Dante was kind to lovers, and Ginsberg has the last word.

The novel has touches of humor based on the convenient adaptability of
literary and liturgical language concerning Satan, demons, and Hell. It continues the problem of the Covenant, which Roger Bacon considered in his analysis of the rainbow. At Monte Albano a father describes the Covenant as the
line drawn between free will and resistance to temptation; between Transcen-

dental and Ceremonial Magic; and in nature, an optical illusion that varies· as the individual perceives it. Also, even as people searched for the Antichrist in the thirteenth century, thinking that he was to be found in their midst, so Father Domenico sees the Antichrist in the Pope. Change *versus* that which is Unchanging merges here in theological terms; Šatvje suggests that mutation resulting from nuclear fallout may be God's way of continuing evolution. Yet the Church, according to Father Ruiz-Sanchez in Blish's *A Case of Conscience*, cannot tolerate evolution as a process of recapitulation outside the mother's womb. Šatvje's suggestion, however, explains why Baines in *The Day After Judgment* remembers the mystic tradition that "the possession and use of secular knowledge — or even the desire for it — is in itself evil." Through consideration of munitions, magic, religion, and lust, the novella dramatizes the question: After such knowledge, what?

Grace Eckley

Sources for Further Study

Criticism:

Aldiss, Brian. *Billion Year Spree: The True History of Science Fiction*. Garden City, N.Y.: Doubleday, 1973, p. 310. Aldiss considers this work to be one of Science Fiction's most powerful intellectual novels.

Moskowitz, Sam. *Strange Horizons: The Spectrum of Science Fiction*. New York: Scribner's, 1976, pp. 17-18. Moskowitz discusses this sequel to *Black Easter* in which God is dead and Satan is left to realize his hollow victory.

Reviews:

Amazing Stories. XLV, September, 1971, pp. 109-110.

Catholic World. CCXIV, November, 1971, p. 86.

Kirkus Reviews. XXXVIII, November 15, 1970, p. 1267.

Magazine of Fantasy and Science Fiction. XLI, November, 1971, p. 23.

Times Literary Supplement. June 23, 1972, p. 705.

THE DAY OF THE TRIFFIDS

Author: John Wyndham (John Benyon Harris, 1903-1969)
First book publication: 1951
Type of work: Novel
Time: The near future
Locale: London and environs

The human race suffers nearly universal blindness followed by plague, and then finds itself challenged for dominance of Earth by Triffids, a mobile, intelligent and malevolent species of plant

> *Principal characters:*
> WILLIAM MASEN, a young biologist specializing in Triffids
> JOSELLA PLAYTON, a resourceful lady in distress
> MICHAEL BEADLEY, leader of an alliance of those intent on building a new social order on rational, scientific principles
> DR. E. H. VORLESS, the brains behind the Beadley experiment
> WILFRED COKER, a spokesman for the rights of the blind majority who eventually joins Beadley after several unsuccessful altruistic attempts at building havens for the blind
> SUSAN MASEN, an orphaned child, rescued and later adopted by Masen
> MISS DURRANT, leader of the evangelical enclave at Tynsham

The Day of the Triffids is a science fiction postcatastrophe story and an essay in social Darwinism. The premise of the story is biological. A chance event produces a meteor shower that blinds everyone who has seen it, which is the majority of the population. The meteor shower also causes a disease that afflicts those who have been blinded, killing nearly all who contract it. These twin plagues bring about a rapid collapse of civilized order. Only a few sighted people remain to lead in the reclamation that lies ahead. Their efforts are hindered by the appearance of a species of predators capable of challenging a blinded and decimated human race for control of the Earth. These predators are Triffids, plants of uncertain origin which humans have profitably cultivated and harvested for Triffid oil. They are a most unusual plant form, able to walk upright on three legs, and equipped with a whiplike lethal sting. They have developed a rudimentary language and are determined to seek out and destroy all human life.

Mankind survives the immediate threats posed by blindness and disease, but rebuilding a society in the face of the Triffid menace is a long-term project. Humanity will prevail, only because of its adaptability and because enough sighted people are left to form the nucleus of a new order. The threat of the Triffids to human survival dominates the postcatastrophe story. It is in this framework that the author deals with the problems of leadership, the renewal of social designs, romance, and the stuggle for survival.

The story is a history of William Masen's part in the creation and growth of a stable society on the Isle of Wight. As such, it is a supplement to the official history of the Beadley colony. Masen writes to acquaint the new generation with a world order that has disappeared in less than a decade. In fact, this historical frame is dropped rather early as the pressure of rapidly developing events sweeps the narrative along. Masen begins his account on the morning after the meteor shower has blinded nearly everyone. It is ironic that he escaped the common fate because of temporary blindness caused by a Triffid lashing. He awakens to an unnatural silence and finds no one to answer his call. He gradually removes the bandages that have preserved his vision and sees a world that has gone blind. He then recalls the ominous words of a colleague who warned that if humanity were to lose the gift of sight, a species like the Triffids would find itself better adapted for survival.

With this prophecy echoing in his mind, Masen leaves the hospital for a reconnaissance of London and is stunned to find that it has become an open city overnight. Everywhere terrified, wretched masses of people stumble about trying to find food and waiting for help. Some, even whole families, commit suicide. Others desperately try to trap sighted humans for use as guides. And, on the edges of the city, the Triffids begin to filter into London.

Masen acquires his first ally, Josella Playton, when he rescues her from a blind group that has made her a prisoner. They make a short trip to her suburban home, where they find her father dead and the area swarming with Triffids. Having accomplished nothing, they return to London in search of some kind of viable social organization. Finally, in the university area, they come upon such a group.

The new community is in the planning stages. Everyone rushes about to scavenge for basic supplies in order to prepare for an exodus to the open country. Meanwhile, increasingly desperate parties of the blind surround the area and beg for admittance or at least food. The community is forced to face one of the central moral issues of the novel: should they treat the beggars humanely or refuse them and secure their own physical survival? As a group they decide that any attempt to care for the needs of the blind masses would mean the rapid dissipation of the energies and resources of the community. They would have to abandon the hope of building a self-sustaining society, and, at best, such charity would do little more than extend the suffering of the blinded masses for a few more days.

This moral crisis is addressed by Dr. E. H. Vorless, a sociologist, whose theories of social planning are the only effective ones presented in the story. In the *raissonné* speech of the novel, Vorless offers a pragmatic, value free theory of how to develop a workable society under desperate circumstances. Old values and old prejudices, germane perhaps to a bygone world, must be abandoned:

> We can accept and retain only one primary prejudice, and that is that *the race is worth preserving*. To that consideration all else will, for a time at least, be subordinate. We must look at all we do with this question in mind: "Is this going to help our race survive — or

will it hinder us?" If it will help, we must do it, whether or not it conflicts with the ideals
in which we were brought up. If not, we must avoid it, even though the omission may
clash with our previous notions of duty and even of justice.

These are harsh words, but Vorless is far from finished. Blind men are of no
use unless they have special skills. Blind women are good for breeding purposes, for their children will be sighted. Therefore, each man will receive
several blind women along with at least one sighted wife. A shocking proposal, but necessary for racial survival according to Vorless. He reminds his listeners that the "ready reckoners for conduct" will no longer give the right
answers because the social organization that gave them meaning is now gone.
He ends by appealing for the moral courage to think the plan in new ways for
the good of the community.

Accordingly, the blind masses are turned away as humanely as possible, but
without food or supplies. Their desperate attempts to survive initiate the second or transitionary phase of the narrative. Driven to desperate remedies, the
blind factions kidnap a score of the sighted members of the community including William and Josella. Led by Wilfred Coker, a sighted advocate, they force
their captives to serve as guides for separate parties of the blind. They plan to
establish enclaves, scrounge food and needed supplies from the immediate
area, and await help from outside, which they assume will soon come from the
United States. But, before they learn that such help does not exist, a deadly
plague makes its appearance and spreads rapidly among the blind. Masen soon
finds himself the lone survivor of his party, alone and separated from Josella.

The episodes that follow trace Masen's long odyssey in search of Josella
and the Beadley group. He joins forces with Coker, his former nemesis, and,
following a clue left at the compound, they head for Tynsham Manor, driving
trucks loaded with food, supplies, and hardware, including anti-Triffid gear.
At this stage, only Masen seems to appreciate the menace posed by an un-
checked Triffid population. No trace of the Beadley group is found, but they
do encounter a predominately blind community led by the fanatical Miss Dur-
rant, who has been running things according to strict evangelistic Christian
principles. The woman is long on zeal to resist materialism and to preserve
civilized decorum, but she has no sense of practical organization. Coker
eventually remains to attempt to salvage the community through better man-
agement, while Masen continues his search for Josella and a farm she once had
mentioned as a potential haven.

After Masen's arduous cross-country journey through towns and villages
abandoned to the Triffids, the two lovers are reunited at Shirning Farm. There
they resolve to make a stand together with the farm's three blinded owners and
an orphaned child, Susan, whom Masen has rescued from Triffids. They
manage to run the farm, fence off the immediate area to keep out Triffids, and
prosper during the following six years. However, each year the Triffids grow

more numerous and aggressive, the roads become less navigable, supplies and spare parts dwindle, and the long-term outlook grows bleaker. They come to realize that they cannot continue to hold out alone for much longer. Thus, they decide to find a community to join.

During the first years of this postmodern period, numerous experimental societies have claimed sovereignty of southeast England. None, however, holds promise of long-term survival against both the Triffids and the growing impact of social entropy, and none promotes freedom and personal dignity. Each is despotic in a different way. Finally, however, the Shirning Farm family is contacted by the Beadley community. The group decides to travel to the Isle of Wight where the community has taken root. When they arrive, they discover that the new society is run on the principles outlined in London by Vorless. It has been founded on a division of labor and social cooperation. The members of the community understand the necessity of research as an investment in the future. Thus, Masen is selected to conduct the research to find a way to exterminate Triffids, so that some day humans may reclaim the Earth.

The Day of the Triffids is a novel which balances its elements of hard and soft science fiction with adventure melodrama. The basic argument connects biology and ecology with political and social science. The narrative focuses on the struggle against the Triffids, its causes and immediate effects. The most bitter irony in the novel is Masen's realization that the catastrophe was manmade, the unintentional result of the arms race. The meteor shower, blindness, and plague were the effects of an orbiting biological weapon that malfunctioned. Furthermore, the Triffids were the product of man's botanical experimentation. In two ways, therefore, human folly brought mankind to the razor's edge of extinction.

The postcatastrophe story is a science fiction staple. *The Day of the Triffids* is distinguished within this tradition by the quality of the writing and the success with which Wyndham has blended speculative themes and action adventure. He proposes that biological and moral laws are directly related. When the race is threatened with extinction, biology and morality serve the same ends. The moral argument of the novel is thereby experimental. In time of severe crisis, man must experiment with new values and social forms if he is to survive. Unfortunately, Wyndham did not explore the implications of this new theme more fully, especially as it concerns the value and quality of life. Another issue not considered concerns the long-term moral and psychological effects that the imperative of racial preservation would have on survivors. A subsequent question to that of survival is survival as what? There seems no doubt of Wyndham's attitude here. Even though human abuse of science was responsible for the world catastrophe, it is only through the scientific approach that humanity can save itself. In *The Day of the Triffids*, Wyndham tries to demonstrate that most of the new social units are devolutions, that the tribal, feudal, theocratic, and communistic alliances are reversions to simplistic systems that have failed in the past. The Beadley community provides the model because it is founded on, and works according to, scientific principles. In Wyndham's view, it offers man his best hope for survival, while still retaining a measure of freedom.

The Day of the Triffids compares favorably with H. G. Wells's catastrophe novels, especially with *The War of the Worlds*, to which it bears some striking resemblances. Wyndham also seems to share some of Wells's shortcomings as a novelist. *The Day of the Triffids* is heavy in ideas, some of which are undeveloped or treated schematically and simplistically. A case in point is the imperative of racial survival at any price. Of course this is almost an axiom of the entire genre, seldom challenged except by writers such as C. S. Lewis and Kurt Vonnegut, Jr. In this novel, the collapse of civilization is compensated for too successfully and becomes a cosy catastrophe. Disaster on a world scale reduces the complexities of human life to the instinctive struggle for survival and territorial rights. Perhaps catastrophe is too ready an answer to the hidden desire of members of a mass culture for heroic adventure in a simplified world. Everything needed is abundantly there for the taking. Any price is worth paying to be free to pursue inherently ennobling enterprises like saving the human race and its scientific culture from extinction and rebuilding a more rational social order. But has the author stocked his world with the kind of people who would be capable of meeting such a challenge successfully? All we meet in this novel are middle-class Englishmen with no religion, no philosophy, and, if it comes down to it, very little science.

These shortcomings are typical of the majority of science fiction novels written on a similar theme. Very few are as successful as *A Canticle for Leibowitz* in resolving the artistic problems implied in the type of story. Even some of the better ones like *The Day of the Triffids*, which have the power of raising profound moral questions, lack the genius to answer them successfully. Nonetheless, *The Day of the Triffids* is a novel that deserves wide reading as an exciting adventure story that pauses here and there to offer the reader food for thought.

Donald L. Lawler

Sources for Further Study

Reviews:

Amazing Stories. XXXIX, January, 1965, p. 124.

Analog. XLVII, August, 1951, p. 142.

Galaxy. II, August, 1951, p. 99.

Magazine of Fantasy and Science Fiction. II, August, 1951, p. 83.

Nebula. I, Autumn, 1952, p. 119.

New Worlds. XII, Winter, 1951, p. 96.

Super Science Stories. VIII, August, 1951, p. 49.

Weird Tales. XLIII, September, 1951, p. 96.

THE DEATH OF THE DRAGON
(NIPPON CHIMBOTSU)

Author: Sakyo Komatsu (1931-   )
First book publication: 1973
English translation (partial): 1976
Type of work: Novel
Time: The near future
Locale: Japan and the world

A major psychological study of the Japanese people and how they would cope with disaster, couched in terms of a major disruption of the Earth's crust that threatens to annihilate the Japanese archipelago

> *Principal characters:*
> ONODERA TOSHIO, a research submarine pilot
> DR. TADOKORO, an eccentric but brilliant geophysicist
> ABE REIKO, Onodera's wealthy lover
> WATARI, a centenarian manipulator of Japanese politics

When Sakyo Komatsu wrote *The Death of the Dragon*, he was returning to an idea he had dealt with before. In fact, before beginning what was to become his best-known work, he had already written about the submergence of the Japanese archipelago in two short stories, one humorous, the other not. In this sense, *Nippon Chimbotsu* can be thought of as Komatsu's definitive attempt to come to terms with an image that had troubled him for a long time.

However, while the image of cold ocean water surging across the wracked body of what is continually described as the dying dragon of Japan may be, in its cold finality, one of the strongest statements the author has yet made of final holocaust, he is not really so much interested in destruction as he is fascinated by termination. It is the end of things, rather than the way they end, that catches Komatsu's eye.

In other novels as well, Komatsu has approached this terminal point from any number of directions: a final plague cleansing the Earth of human beings, the human race itself closing down and leaving no heirs, the rotation of the Earth coming to a shaking halt, leaving the nameless little people of suburbia standing around bonfires for warmth in a night that will have no dawn.

While many of the writers who have jumped on the bandwagon of catastrophe fiction dwell with loving attention on the clicking microseconds of disaster itself, Komatsu concerns himself ultimately with the hole in men's lives that disaster leaves behind. While he, too, can detail with all-encompassing thoroughness the process of disaster and the frantic efforts people make to stave it off, he does this mainly in order to delineate the size of the gap that will be left in the psyche of the individual — or the race, or the species — when the process is finally over. And only after he has done that does he really get interested, this time in the shards and fragments that are left behind.

Thus *The Death of the Dragon*, to the degree that it only deals with the annihilation of the Japanese home islands and stops after it has sent the population of those islands wandering off across the globe, is still only half complete. A second half is said to be under way. No mean accomplishment as it stands, the bestselling catastrophe novel will only take on its full significance when Komatsu completes its far more ambitious sequel.

The Death of the Dragon, or what is available of it so far, is in many ways a classic disaster novel, taking a subject that affects to some degree almost all of its potential audience and then suggesting, with great authority, the ultimate extension of what that audience fears.

In the very near future in Japan, a nation which has seen its major cities leveled by earthquakes countless times in the past and every year is shaken by hundreds of tremors both large and small, seismic upsets begin to appear with uncomfortable frequency. Small tremors become a daily occurrence, while survey work for the extension of a major rail project has to be carried out again and again because of continued rising and subsidence of the countryside.

Onodera Toshio, a trained pilot of deep-sea research submarines, is asked to help in an emergency study: a small island has disappeared overnight, sinking several hundred feet in a matter of hours. With the forceful but tactless geophysicist Professor Tadokoro aboard, he pilots his submarine to the bottom of the Japan Trench, where they discover chilling evidence of unprecedented shifts taking place in the ocean floor.

Tadokoro has a theory that there may soon be an unanticipated alteration of the Earth's crust in East Asia, with Japan at its epicenter. As he and his growing team of researchers gather more information, it gradually becomes clear that the ever more frequent earthquakes and volcanic eruptions are only the prelude to a geological transformation without precedent in recorded history, one that will ultimately break up the entire Japanese archipelago and plunge it beneath the sea.

Tadokoro is put into contact with Watari, a mysterious elderly man reputed to be more than a hundred years old, who has the power to galvanize the Japanese government into action with a single telephone call. Gradually, research performed under the strictest secrecy confirms Tadokoro's fears. The Japanese islands will be destroyed in less than a year. A frantic campaign is begun to evacuate the Japanese people and scatter them across the globe, an effort hampered by the ever fiercer earthquakes and eruptions leading up to the final cataclysm.

The only available English translation of the novel unfortunately contains only about a third of the original text, and what has been abridged are Komatsu's detailed considerations of the geology underlying his novel, the reactions and policies of government, the psychology of the people of Japan as their island rocks beneath their feet, and the chilling details of the death of Tokyo. Even the bare bones of the book available in English retain some of the horrendous inevitability of the disaster and the desperation of the people caught up in the whirlpool of events, but when one reads the original, with blow following meticulously detailed blow, the cumulative effect is overwhelming. It is hardly surprising that the book sent a shock wave through Japan, as people read in vivid detail the fruits of the author's exhaustive research into what portions of Tokyo would have to be left to burn themselves out in case of a major earthquake, of what towns would be annihilated should Mount Fuji erupt, of how far inland a major tidal wave would go along the Chiba coast. Some people in Tokyo are said to have stopped driving on certain expressways and to have shied away from certain subway lines after reading what could happen to them in a major tremor.

Also sacrificed in the translation is some of the book's best prose. Komatsu has one of the smoothest yet most vivid styles of any Japanese science fiction writer. While at times it slides too close to bombast, it is generally admirably suited to the demands of the novel. The threatening panorama of the Japan Trench lit by flares, the flights of birds into the Tokyo night as the city rushes toward destruction, the chilling spectacle of the islands breaking up in a computer simulation, run again and again at ever slower speeds under the flicker of camera strobes. Komatsu has a keen sense of what image is necessary where and when, and his prose adds immeasurably to the drama.

Ultimately, the country does sink. An international effort to save the Japanese people pulls the bulk of them from the hulks of their islands in time, and the survivors are indeed scattered across the face of the Earth. However, their future is hardly bright as, homeless and carrying only what they could bear on their backs, they must try to make their way in a new and suspicious world. In the bleak final image of the book, a delirious Onodera, thinking he is on a ship in the South Pacific, rides a train into the glowering Siberian winter.

Within this gigantic framework, Komatsu pursues numerous subplots, from the dispersal of national art treasures overseas to token love stories. But the proliferation of characters, and ideas, ultimately defeats attempts to maintain a human scale within the global one. Even Professor Tadokoro, the most strongly drawn of the central characters, drops completely out of sight for chapters at a stretch as Komatsu bounces about from the United Nations to the Sea of Japan, from hydrographic survey ships to Ginza clubs. Moreover, to the harm of the work as a whole, he occasionally overreaches himself, littering hackneyed clichés of political maneuvers or the lifestyle of the super-rich — convincing to a television-fed mass audience perhaps, but hardly the stuff of good literature — in the midst of the imposing verisimilitude of the novel as a whole. And the keenly perceptive treatment of the little people who form the great and faceless middle class, one of the distinctive features of many of Komatsu's other works, tends to disappear in the hubbub, obscured by the scale of the whole.

Sakyo Komatsu is to Japanese science fiction what Isaac Asimov is to

American science fiction. They are strikingly similar in the scope of their activities and their contributions to putting the genre before the public eye. But if one seeks an outstanding difference, one could do worse than to point out that Sakyo Komatsu was born in time to be on the losing side of a disastrous war, a fact which has left its mark in the often bleak pages of his work.

It is not by chance that when one of the characters of his novel, crouching among the injured in a park following the great Tokyo earthquake, seeks for a reference point in his past, he makes the mental association with the fire raids of 1945. But it is interesting that what he remembers is not the death and destruction, but rather a "sullen frustration" that had gripped him as he watched the incendiaries scattering down across his neighborhood. If Komatsu himself experienced that frustration, perhaps it is no wonder that in work after work he has returned to the edge of the abyss.

However, for whatever reasons, Komatsu is either unwilling or unable to confront that past on purely personal terms. Just as his dizzying whirl of activities — joining in conferences on traffic flow and geophysics, appearing on television talk shows, lecturing on Italian cooking and helping to organize international symposia — seem almost excessively larger than life, so, too, he enlarges that sense of the hole in the disaster-stricken psyche to take in not only himself, but the entire Japanese race.

What Komatsu does in *The Death of the Dragon* is turn his massive premise of destruction into a test tube for the Japanese people. By far the most interesting sections of the book are those that describe the reactions of the population to the disaster. There is no sugarcoating and no polemic, only the anger, the discontent, the loss. As ash flutters down over Tokyo from the eruption of Mount Fuji, the people, just informed by their government of the magnitude of what is happening to them, stare silently out the window, or, not meeting one another's eyes, slip out of their offices, heading for home. Taxis race across the city, not stopping for passengers, the drivers seeking the security of their families before trying to think of what they have been told. And finally there is the recommendation of a group of Japanese scholars asked by the old man Watari to study possible courses of action for the Japanese as a people, that it might well be best for all 100,000,000 Japanese to do nothing, and quietly wait for the end. Watari rejects the proposal, but at the end of the book he also reveals that he is himself half Chinese.

Who are these people? This is the question Komatsu seems to be asking at the bottom of all the statistics and detailed descriptions. Who are the Japanese when you take away their cities, their islands, their nation? How much can you take away from a people and still be left with a recognizable whole? Throughout the book, on the level of single characters, on the level of the entire nation, this question is asked over and over again. Komatsu has on one occasion likened a catastrophe to a giant laboratory, and in this book he speaks of plumbing the specific gravity of a people. This novel is not about the sinking of Japan, or even about the social upheavals such an event might cause. It is about the Japanese psyche and why it is what it is. The sequel, which deals with the fate of the Japanese refugees in their many adopted homelands, will complete this study.

In *The Death of the Dragon* itself, the author has rejected the proposition that the Japanese could turn out like the Jews, arguing that while the latter have had two thousand years to learn to live without a homeland, the Japanese have lived for two thousand years in the secure womb of their island nation. In one sense, the drastic operation Komatsu depicts in his novel is a complication-ridden birth, a massive and necessary cesarean section for an entire race. What Komatsu is most interested in, however, is not the birth, but how that monstrously begotten child might grow.

David Lewis